W9-BJD-860

SIEGFRIED GIEDION was born in Switzerland and educated there and in Germany and Italy. At Weimar he was associated with Walter Gropius, with whom he played an important part in the introduction of modern architecture in Switzerland. He taught at the Federal Institute of Technology and also was Mellon Lecturer at the Washington National Gallery and Charles Eliot Norton Lecturer at Harvard University. His other books include *Space, Time and Architecture; The Eternal Present; The Beginning of Art;* and *The Beginnings of Architecture.*

MECHANIZATION TAKES COMMAND

SIEGFRIED GIEDION

MECHANIZATION

TAKES COMMAND

a contribution to anonymous history

The Norton Library
W · W · NORTON & COMPANY · INC ·
NEW YORK

First published in the Norton Library 1969 by
arrangement with Oxford University Press, Inc.

PUBLISHED SIMULTANEOUSLY IN CANADA
BY GEORGE J. MCLEOD LIMITED, TORONTO

SBN 393 00489 9

PRINTED IN THE UNITED STATES OF AMERICA
3 4 5 6 7 8 9 0

FOREWORD

In *Space, Time and Architecture* (1941) I attempted to show the split that exists in our period between thought and feeling. I am trying now to go a step further: to show how this break came about, by investigating one important aspect of our life — mechanization.

At the origin of the inquiry stood the desire to understand the effects of mechanization upon the human being; to discern how far mechanization corresponds with and to what extent it contradicts the unalterable laws of human nature. The question of the limits of mechanization is bound to arise at any moment, as the human aspect, which is fundamental, cannot be disregarded.

The coming period has to reinstate basic human values. It must be a time of reorganization in the broadest sense, a time that must find its way to universalism. The coming period must bring order to our minds, our production, our feeling, our economic and social development. It has to bridge the gap that, since the onset of mechanization, has split our modes of thinking from our modes of feeling.

My first intention was to outline briefly the effects of mechanization, basing the study on specialized research in the particular fields with which we have to deal. I soon realized that this was impossible. Over vast stretches no research was available. I was unable to find any account of such revolutionary events as the development of the production line or the introduction of mechanical comfort and its tools in our intimate environment. I had, therefore, to go back to the sources, as I could not hope to understand the effects of mechanization without knowing, in outline at least, its evolution.

The process leading up to the present role of mechanization can nowhere be observed better than in the United States, where the new methods of production were first applied, and where mechanization is inextricably woven into the pattern of thought and customs.

But an amazing historical blindness has prevented the preservation of important historical documents, of models, manufacturer's records, catalogues, advertising leaflets, and so on. Public opinion in general judges inventions and production exclusively from the point of view of their commercial success. To excuse this attitude the standard answer is: 'We never look backward. We look forward.'

This means the discarding of time, both past and future. Only the present day matters. Later periods will not understand these acts of destruction, this murder of history.

One cannot blame the industrialist who dumped into the river apparently worthless documents. Nor, perhaps, can one blame the Patent Office for ridding itself (in 1926) of the original patent models. The historians who did not succeed in awakening a feeling for the continuity of history are to blame. The precious remnants of bygone periods would never have been collected or taken care of if several generations of historians had not shown us their significance.

The attitude described above had some direct consequences for the research underlying this book. Work for which a considerable staff should have been employed had to be done almost singlehanded. This led unavoidably to incompleteness, yet it had the advantage that, from the outset, the selection of the material was done by one individual. *Mechanization Takes Command* will serve perhaps more to reveal existing gaps than to fill them.

The gaps will show, we hope, how badly research is needed into the *anonymous history* of our period, tracing our mode of life as affected by mechanization — its impact on our dwellings, our food, our furniture. Research is needed into the links existing between industrial methods and methods used outside industry — in art, in visualization.

This is an exacting task for which special training is needed. It is a matter of sifting the historically important from the less important. It demands a power of discrimination, even of vision — a hard task for which carefully prepared scholars are needed. Nothing of the kind is earnestly provided for in the curricula of present-day universities. Chairs of anonymous history ought to be created, with the task not only of showing how facts and figures are to be gathered, but of showing their impact on culture and their meaning for us.

The first condition, of course, and the most difficult one to fulfil, is that the people in general should understand how their work and their invention — whether they know it or not — are continually shaping and reshaping the patterns of life. Once historical consciousness is awakened, self-respect will awaken too, a self-respect that inspires every true culture. This renewed awareness will find means of preserving the key sources to American history.

I mentioned the primitive conditions under which this book had to be done, as an apology for its apparent incompleteness. I wish, however, to express my deep gratitude for all the personal help I received from many sides, and I wish to mention particularly the historian Herbert C. Kellar, Director of the McCormick Historical Society, Chicago; of industrialists like C. F. Frantz, President of the Apex Electrical Mfg. Co., Cleveland; of Mr. A. W. Robertson, Chairman of the Board of the Westinghouse Electric Corporation, Pittsburgh; of Mr. William Eitner, of the General Electric Mfg. Co.; and of many others mentioned in the text.

I am deeply indebted to Mr. Martin James who, with never tiring care, prepared the English version in collaboration with the author, and to Miss Lotte Labus for her constant help and the editing of the index, which will prove a valuable help in interrelating facts and notions. Mr. Herbert Bayer and Mrs. Elisabeth Wolff assisted me with the layout.

Research and manuscript, with the exception of the conclusion, which my friend Mr. J. M. Richards of London kindly corrected, were finished during my second stay in the United States, from December 1941 to December 1945. Last but not least, I had the precious advice of my dear friend, the late L. Moholy-Nagy.

Special tribute is due to the Oxford University Press and its staff, who achieved the production of this book, which proved harder than we had foreseen.

To facilitate the reading, special care was taken in the choice and the layout of illustrations. Captions are provided in such a way as to convey the broad outline independently of and simultaneously with the text.

ZURICH, DOLDERTAL — S. GIEDION

November 1947

CONTENTS

Part I

ANONYMOUS HISTORY

Part II

SPRINGS OF MECHANIZATION

Part III

MEANS OF MECHANIZATION

Part VI

MECHANIZATION ENCOUNTERS THE HOUSEHOLD

Part VII

THE MECHANIZATION OF THE BATH

IN CONCLUSION

PART I ANONYMOUS HISTORY

ANONYMOUS HISTORY

History is a magical mirror. Who peers into it sees his own image in the shape of events and developments. It is never stilled. It is ever in movement, like the generation observing it. Its totality cannot be embraced: History bares itself only in facets, which fluctuate with the vantage point of the observer.

Facts may occasionally be bridled within a date or a name, but not their more complex significance. The meaning of history arises in the uncovering of relationships. That is why the writing of history has less to do with facts as such than with their relations. These relations will vary with the shifting point of view, for, like constellations of stars, they are ceaselessly in change. Every true historical image is based on relationship, appearing in the historian's choice from among the fullness of events, a choice that varies with the century and often with the decade, just as paintings differ in subject, technique, and psychic content. Now great historical panoramas are painted, now fragments of everyday things suffice to carry the feeling of an epoch.

The historian deals with a perishable material, men. He cannot calculate the course of future events like the astronomer. But in common with the astronomer, he may see new constellations and hitherto invisible worlds appearing over the horizon. And like the astronomer, he must be an ever-watchful spectator.

His role is to put in order in its historical setting what we experience piecemeal from day to day, so that in place of sporadic experience, the continuity of events becomes visible. An age that has lost its consciousness of the things that shape its life will know neither where it stands nor, even less, at what it aims. A civilization that has lost its memory and stumbles from day to day, from happening to happening, lives more irresponsibly than the cattle, who at least have their instincts to fall back upon.

History, regarded as insight into the moving process of life, draws closer to biological phenomena. We shall speak little, here, of general lines and great events, and then only when necessary to connect occurrences with the bedrock in which they are rooted.

We shall inquire in the first line into the tools that have molded our present-day living. We would know how this mode of life came about, and something of the process of its growth.

We shall deal here with humble things, things not usually granted earnest consideration, or at least not valued for their historical import. But no more in history than in painting is it the impressiveness of the subject that matters. The sun is mirrored even in a coffee spoon.

In their aggregate, the humble objects of which we shall speak have shaken our mode of living to its very roots. Modest things of daily life, they accumulate into forces acting upon whoever moves within the orbit of our civilization.

The slow shaping of daily life is of equal importance to the explosions of history; for, in the anonymous life, the particles accumulate into an explosive force. Tools and objects are outgrowths of fundamental attitudes to the world. These attitudes set the course followed by thought and action. Every problem, every picture, every invention, is founded on a specific attitude, without which it would never have come into being. The performer is led by outward impulses — money, fame, power — but behind him, unbeknown, is the orientation of the period, is its bent toward this particular problem, that particular form.

For the historian there are no banal things. Like the scientist, the historian does not take anything for granted. He has to see objects not as they appear to the daily user, but as the inventor saw them when they first took shape. He needs the unworn eyes of contemporaries, to whom they appeared marvelous or frightening. At the same time, he has to establish their constellations before and after, and thus establish their meaning.

History writing is ever tied to the fragment. The known facts are often scattered broadcast, like stars across the firmament. It should not be assumed that they form a coherent body in the historical night. Consciously, then, we represent them as fragments, and do not hesitate, when necessary, to spring from one period to another. Pictures and words are but auxiliaries; the decisive step must be taken by the reader. In his mind the fragments of meaning here displayed should become alive in new and manifold relations.

Before we entered upon the present work we tried, at Yale University in the winter of 1941, to suggest in broad outline what brought us to anonymous history. At that time we could not foresee how far the inquiry was to lead. For this very reason a few passages as then spoken may not be out of place:

Any inquiry today into the rise of our modern way of life must remain incomplete. There is no lack of works tracing the broad political, economic, or sociological trends of our time. Specialized researches into the various fields are also available. But few bridges have been thrown between them.

If we seek a more general insight into the rise of our way of life — of our comfort, of our attitudes — we are stopped at every turn by gaps and unanswered questions.

We know furthermore that isolated studies are inadequate to embrace the complex structure of the nineteenth century. More than the bare history of an industry, an invention, an organization, we have to observe what was occurring in various other fields at the same time. Then we see that without conscious forethought phenomena simultaneously arise, bearing striking similarities to one another. They need only be displayed side by side to call into consciousness the tendencies and sometimes the meaning of their period.

Iron filings, these small insignificant particles, by the interference of a magnet become form and design, revealing existing lines of force. So, too, the details of anonymous history can be made to reveal the guiding trends of a period.

Our task is clearly outlined: to inquire how our contemporary life, with its mixture of constituent and chaotic elements, came about. The difficulty lies in sifting and separating those facts that may be called constituent and that are the true pointers of their age. Once this has been done the material does the rest.

Anonymous history is directly connected with the general, guiding ideas of an epoch. But at the same time it must be traced back to the particulars from which it arises.

Anonymous history is many sided, and its different departments flow into one another. Only with difficulty can they be separated. The ideal in anonymous history would be to show simultaneously the various facets as they exist side by side, together with the process of their interpenetration. Nature does this in the eye of the insect — a lens of multiple facets — fusing its distinct images of the outer world into an integrated picture. The individual does not have such power. We must be grateful if this objective is fulfilled only in the fragment.

PROCEDURE

In *Space, Time and Architecture* we attempted to show how our period came to consciousness of itself in a single field, architecture.

Now to broaden the scope, we shall observe the coming about of mechanization, that almost unescapable influence over our way of life, our attitudes, our instincts.

We shall deal with mechanization from the human standpoint. Its results and its implications cannot be simply stated. The prerequisite is that we should understand its tools, even if our interest here is not a technical one. It is not enough for a physician to know that a body is attacked by a disease. Even if he is not a bacteriologist, he must push his research into usually invisible realms, he must have a modest knowledge of bacteriology, he must know when the organism was attacked and how the tuberculosis spread. Likewise, the historian cannot dispense with the microscope. He cannot relent in tracing the theme to its origins. He has to show when an idea first appears; how quickly or slowly it spreads or disappears. He cannot confine himself to mechanization alone any more than the doctor can to bacteria. He must take psychic factors into reckoning, for often they exert a decisive influence. In our case art represents the psychic factor. It will serve as the surest aid to an understanding of certain phenomena.

We begin with the concept of Movement, which underlies all mechanization. There follows the Hand, which is to be supplanted; and Mechanization as a Phenomenon.

Mechanization of the Complicated Craft

The elimination of the complicated handicraft marks the beginning of high mechanization. This transition takes place in America during the second half of the nineteenth century. We shall meet with it in the callings of the farmer, the baker, the butcher, the joiner, and the housewife. But only in one instance shall we follow it closely: in the masterful transformation of the door lock from handicraft to mechanized production.

The Means of Mechanization

The symptom of full mechanization is the assembly line, wherein the entire factory is consolidated into a synchronous organism. From its first appearance in the eighteenth century down to its later and decisive elaboration between the two World Wars, the assembly line is an American institution. What we shall have to say about it is but roughly carved out. So far as we know, no historic account yet covers this most significant factor in America's productive capacity. For this reason, but especially because they closely touch upon human problems, the assembly line and scientific management will be given somewhat closer treatment.

Mechanization Encounters the Organic

What happens when mechanization encounters organic substance? Here we face the great constants running through human development: soil, growth, bread, meat. The questions involved are but narrow sectors of a far broader complex: man's relation today to those organic forces that act upon and within him. The catastrophes that threaten to destroy civilization and existence are but outward signs that our organism has lost its balance. Their causes lie deeply buried in the great anonymous movements of the epoch. Our contact with the organic forces within us and outside of us has been interrupted — a paralyzed, torn, chaotic condition. This contact is increasingly menaced as the tie with basic human values becomes frayed. Here, if anywhere, overturn has become inevitable.

We shall therefore open with the question: What happens when mechanization meets an organic substance? And shall close by inquiring into the attitude of our culture toward our own organism.

MECHANIZATION OF AGRICULTURE

After remaining stationary for a thousand years, the structure of the farmer is revolutionized. At first in literary and tentative ways, in the eighteenth century; experimentally in the first half of the nineteenth century; sweepingly in the second half. England forms the hub of the movement during the eighteenth century, the American Middle West during the latter half of the nineteenth. Here begins what is perhaps a new chapter in the history of man: a changed relation to the soil and the uprooting of the farmer.

Of the instruments of mechanization we shall touch only the reaper, which by its replacement of the hand holds the most important place among the tools of mechanized agriculture.

BREAD

What happens when mechanization comes up against an organic substance, bread, which, like the door lock or the farmer, belongs among the symbols of humanity? How did mechanization alter the structure of bread and the taste of the consumer? When did this mechanization set in? How are popular taste and production related to one another?

MEAT

What are mechanization's limits in dealing with so complex an organism as the animal? And how does the elimination of a complicated craft — such as the butcher's — proceed?

Still of unmeasured significance is mechanization's intervention in the procreation of plants and of animals.

Mechanization Encounters Human Surroundings

What happens to the human setting in the presence of mechanization?

Dangerous tendencies declare themselves before the advent of mechanization (on which the whole blame is thrown) and independently of it. There is no doubt that nineteenth-century mechanization facilitated these trends. But they appear distinctly in the interior before the impact of mechanization is felt.

The Changing Conception of Comfort: Medieval Comfort

We shall look to the late medieval period for a secure starting point. Here lie the roots of our existence and of our continuous development. Since typological researches in this field are unfortunately lacking, the Middle Ages will be included and dealt with from this point of view. What interests us in the first line here is the type of comfort developed in different periods. How did the Middle Ages understand comfort? How does the medieval conception differ from our contemporary view? Where do connecting links exist?

To take a short path, we shall follow the relation between man and space. How does man order his intimate setting in the fifteenth century, the eighteenth, the nineteenth, the twentieth? How, in other words, has his feeling for space changed?

A parallel question is that of *human posture* in the various periods, and of posture's projection into seating.

Comfort in the Eighteenth Century

The creation of modern sitting comfort is to be sought in the Rococo. The Rococo's great power of observation in shaping furniture organically so as to favor relaxation of the body forms a counterpart to that period's exploration of the plant and animal world.

Late eighteenth-century England is primarily concerned with the technical virtuosity of the cabinetmaker, and affords, within the most refined type of handicraft, a foretaste of the mechanized furniture of the nineteenth century.

The Nineteenth Century

The Beginnings of Ruling Taste

More than in the Rococo, in which Louis XV's role was not a very active one, a particular type of man becomes decisive in the Empire: Napoleon. Here phenomena appear, such as the devaluation of symbols, which have been laid at the door of mechanization alone.

The Mechanization of Adornment

The misuse of mechanization to imitate handicraft production and the use of substitute materials comes to the fore in England between 1820 and 1850. The blurring of the instincts is clearly recognized by English Reformers around 1850. Through criticism and encouragement, attempts are made to influence industry directly.

The Reign of the Upholsterer

From the upholsterer's hand comes that cushion furniture of the latter half of the century which seems to have lost all structure. These are transitory products of a surprising longevity. To avoid vague judgments, we have thought it useful to consider them typologically.

What types are found? In what way are they connected with mechanization? How is their form related to the introduction of spiral springs? When do they first come into use?

The Surrealists have given us keys to the psychic unrest that haunted mechanized adornment, cushion furniture, and the whole interior.

The Constituent Furniture of the Nineteenth Century

Over against the ruling taste stands the unexplored complex of 'patent-furniture.' In this case, mechanization is harnessed to the opening of new fields. Here, where unobserved, the creative instinct of the nineteenth century reveals itself, fulfilling needs formerly without solution. This furniture that answers to the posture of the nineteenth century is the work of the engineer. It is based on movability and adjustability to the body. In America, between 1850 and the late 'eighties there grew a facility never known in Europe for solving *motion problems* of this kind, which America lost back to the influence of ruling taste after 1893.

The Constituent Furniture of the Twentieth Century

The initiative now passes into European hands. The new furniture created in this period is bound up with the spatial conceptions of the new architecture.

It is a furniture of *types*, not of individual pieces. It is the work, with few exceptions, of the architects who at the same time became the leaders of contemporary building.

Mechanization of the Household

The mechanizing of the housewife's work is not unlike the mechanizing of the other complex handicrafts. The alleviation of domestic drudgery proceeds along like paths: first, through mechanization of the work process; and again by its organization. Both are best observed in America, in the early 'sixties, and — at their peak — in the period between the two World Wars.

Questions that require an answer are, among others:

Is household rationalization connected with the status of woman in America? Is it rooted in the Quaker or the Puritan outlook?

The organization of the kitchen had its starting point in the new architectural movement in Europe around 1927. It came about in the general reshaping of the house.

We have placed the mechanization of the hearth at the head of the various mechanisms. An ever-growing concentration and automatization of the heat source is observed — from the coal range to electric cooking. This trend seems to be still in progress.

We shall survey the various aids to mechanical comfort in the household, their individual appearance and general acceptance. Central among them are the mechanized cleaning appliances: for washing, for ironing, for dishwashing, for removing dust, etc. The influence of feeling upon the aspect of the appliances cannot be overlooked: streamline style.

Only when the mechanical appliances had already been worked out and were becoming popularized did the interest of American industry turn to the integration of the appliances within the work process. Thus emerging in the mid-'thirties, the streamline kitchen was raised, with its devices, into the idol of the house.

It was in the time of full mechanization that the domestic servant question, recognized around 1860 as irreconcilable with democracy, became an immediate problem: the servantless household. Connected with the servant problem was the attempt to reduce the ever-rising cost of mechanical utilities by a rationally planned mechanical core of the house.

Mechanization of the Bath

The history of its technical equipment affords no standard by which to evaluate the modern bath. Closer insight is immediately gained in registering the uncertainty and wavering throughout the century from the moment a choice between types became necessary.

Just as it left no style untouched, the nineteenth century left none of the historical types untried. But scant progress was made, outside of reformistic propaganda or the development of luxury bathrooms. For the masses of the population, only the cheapest mode of bathing was seriously debated.

The chaos around 1900 appears in the failure of the expert to recommend a single satisfactory bathtub. But even this would have offered no historically acceptable standard, and the question remains: is bathing a simple ablution, or is it part of a broader concept, regeneration of the human organism? Looking backward, we find that in past cultures the bath was embodied in types affording total regeneration. Though shortened to the utmost, a typology of Western regeneration will have to be drawn up. Ancient, Islamic, Late Gothic, Russian regeneration seem to reflect a common archetype, its path traceable to the interior of Asia.

All these types aim not merely at outward ablution, but at a total vivification of the body by differentiated means, which vary with the culture. Our civilization from the waning Middle Ages on has believed that it can do without a systematic type of regeneration to help the organism recoup the damage which each civilization in its own way entails.

Mechanization did no more than give a glittering façade to the most primitive type of bath.

Toward a Typological Approach

A treatment of problems suited to our day will constantly bear interrelations in mind. This leads to a typological approach. The history of styles follows its theme along a horizontal direction; the history of types along a vertical one. Both are necessary if things are to be seen in historical space.

The specialistic approach that grew in strength through the nineteenth century brought stylistic history to the fore. Typological thinking rarely finds a place there, and mainly when unavoidable, as is the case in the encyclopedias of furniture. The French contributions around 1880, in which a vein of universality still runs, are the more satisfactory in this respect. The large *Oxford English Dictionary* too is sometimes a friend in need.

We are interested in following the growth of phenomena, or if one will, in reading their line of fate, over wide spans of time. Vertical sections make it possible to trace the organic changes of a type.

How far a type need be followed back into its history varies with the case. There are no rules or recipes. It is not the historian who guides, but the material. Some of the developments will call for far-reaching retrospect, others only for rapid backward glances. What is essential is the panoramic and simultaneous view. This may lead to discontinuous treatment. For only through simultaneous perception of various periods and of various fields within a period can there be insight into the inner growth.

Conceiving of history as constellations, the historian can claim one more freedom. He assumes the right to observe at close range certain phenomena, certain fragments of meaning, while omitting others from his field of attention. This may lead to unwonted proportions, as in contemporary painting when a hand is made to spread over the picture while the body remains a hint or a fragment. This freedom in handling proportion is no less necessary when one seeks to represent the meaning of historical complexes.

Dates

The historian's objectivity may be voiced in a treatment faithful to the nature of the material as well as to its constellations in time.

Dates are the historian's yardstick. They enable him to measure off historical space. In themselves or when pinned to isolated facts, they are as meaningless as the numbers on a ticket. But conceived in interrelation, that is vertically and horizontally connected within the network of historical objects, they delimit constellations. In such cases dates take on meaning.

Dates marking when and where phenomena first appear or have become commonplace in various spheres form complexes that give objective insight into growth.

PART II SPRINGS OF MECHANIZATION

MOVEMENT

Ever in flux and process, reality cannot be approached directly. Reality is too vast, and direct means fail. Suitable tools are needed, as in the raising of an obelisk.

In technics, as in science and art, we must create the tools with which to dominate reality. These tools may differ. They may be shaped for mechanization, for thought, or for the expression of feeling. But between them are inner bonds, methodological ties. Again and again, we shall recall these ties.

Movement: The Classical and Medieval Attitude

Our thinking and feeling in all their ramifications are fraught with the concept of movement. We owe, in large measure, our understanding of the world to the Greeks. From them we inherited a magnificent foundation: mathematics and geometry, modes of thought and expression. Yet, we have departed a long way from the Greeks. In many respects we have gained; in the main, we have lost. One of the spheres in which we have gone beyond Greece is in the comprehension of movement. The urge to explore movement — that is, the *changing* in all its forms — determined the channels through which flow our scientific thought and ultimately our emotional expression.

If the Greeks did not find an adequate explanation of movement, if they did not reduce it to exact logical terms, it was not because they were incapable, but because of their fundamental view of the cosmos. They lived in a world of eternal ideas, a world of constants. In that world, they were capable of finding the appropriate formulation for thought and feeling. We inherited their geometry and their logic. Aristotle and all antiquity with him thought of the world as something reposing in itself, as something that had been in existence since the beginning of time.

In opposition came the religious idea that the world was created and set in motion by an act of will. In high Gothic times, this conception of the moved world yielded scientific consequences. The Scholastics rehabilitated Aristotle. As is well known, Aristotelian authority became so powerful in the seventeenth century that it almost succeeded in crushing the new idea of a world based on movement (Galileo). At the same time the Scholastics challenged

Aristotle on an important issue. Thomas Aquinas' questioning how the world was created from nothingness, and what principles and first causes underlay God's action, led to a searching into the question of change and, closely related to this, into the nature of movement.

As the Greek temple symbolizes forces in equilibrium, in which neither verticals nor horizontals dominate, the earth in the classical view formed the forever immovable center of the cosmos.

The soaring verticals of the Gothic cathedrals mark no equilibrium of forces. They seem the symbols of everlasting change, of movement. The stillness and contemplation emanating from these churches escapes no one; but, at the same time, the whole architecture, both within and without, is caught up in an unceasing stream of movement.

Parallel in time, the Scholastics become ever more concerned with explaining the nature of movement. The hypothesis of the earth's daily rotation was increasingly discussed, as Pierre Duhem has pointed out, by the circle of Parisian philosophers from the fourteenth century on. Nicolas Oresme, Bishop of Lisieux (1320?–82), gave ample support to this hypothesis,[1] and — says Duhem, the great French physicist, mathematician, and historian — with greater precision than Copernicus later. Oresme propounds the theory in a penetrating commentary to the first translation into the French, made at Charles V's behest, of Aristotle's Treatise on the Heavens (*Du Ciel et du Monde*). He entitles the relevant chapter: 'Several fine arguments . . . to show that the earth moves in daily movement and the sky not.'[2] Here he proposes that the movement of the heavens can equally well be explained by the circling of the earth around the sun; that the earth revolves, not the sky around the earth. To Pierre Duhem's question whether Oresme inspired Copernicus, it has been objected that Copernicus started from the logical and geometrical contradictions of the Ptolemaic system.[3] This in no way lessens Oresme's achievement.

Nicolas Oresme rises from the brilliant circle of Parisian Scholastics, its last great representative after Jean Buridan (1300–*c.*1358) and Albert of Saxony (1316–90). Ever present in their discussions and cogitations is the giant figure of Aristotle. There was no other guide. On him they test their thought; on

[1] Pierre Duhem, 1861–1916, has brought this aspect of Nicolas Oresme to light in 'Un précurseur français de Copernic, Nicole Oresme (1377),' *Revue générale des sciences pures et appliquées*, Paris, 1909, vol. 20, pp.866–73.

[2] *Le livre du Ciel et du Monde*, Oresme's French translation of Aristotle, has recently been printed in *Medieval Studies*, vols. III–V, New York, 1941, with a commentary by Albert D. Menut and A. J. Denomy.

[3] Duhem's third volume of his *Etudes sur Léonard de Vinci, Les précurseurs parisiens de Galilée*, Paris, 1913, demonstrates in monumental fashion that the principles of Galilean mechanics were already formulated in this circle.

him it kindles. He affords the one foothold. They grope in scientific night, cautiously feeling their way into the unknown. Now they argue, against ancient authority, that the earth turns; now, that it does not. We must take care not to read into their theological and Aristotelian conceptions our own mathematical conception, one that has been growing in our consciousness ever since Descartes. Amid their groping they think as boldly as the Gothic master builders; they lay aside the fantastic Aristotelian conception of movement, and put a new one in its place — one that still prevails.

The Fourteenth Century, First to Represent Movement

All that concerns us in this connection is the first *graphical representation of movement*. The treatise in which Nicolas Oresme achieves this, the treatise *On Intensities*,[4] proceeds after the Aristotelian fashion from the general investigation of the qualities and quantities of an object. Oresme seeks insight into the changing intensity of a quality. He determines this by a graphical method. He traces the extension (*extensio*) of the subject or bearer on a base line that corresponds to Descartes' x-axis of the seventeenth century; and he marks the intensity of the bearer in different stages by straight lines drawn vertically from the base line (y-axis). The ratio of the intensities to one another appears in these vertical lines. The changing quality of the bearer is represented in the geometrical figure delimited by the summits of the vertical lines. Oresme's treatise is accompanied by marginal figures in one of which (fig. 1) the intensities rise side by side like organ pipes.[5] The curve they delimit represents variation in the quality.

Oresme carries over this basic method as he investigates the essence of movement, thus gaining insight into the nature of speed (*velocitas*) and of acceleration. By a graphical method he represents movement, time, speed, and acceleration.[6]

What was new in Oresme's graphical system? Oresme was the first to recognize that movement can be represented only by movement, the changing only by the changing. This is done by repeatedly representing the same subject at various times. To portray a subject freely several times in a single picture was not unusual in medieval art. One has only to think of the late Gothic works in which the same figure (for instance Christ in the stations of the Cross) appears

[4] *Tractatus de uniformitate et difformitate intensium.* MS. Bibliothèque Nationale, Paris. Printed in several editions, toward the end of the fifteenth century.

[5] See also H. Wieleitner, 'Ueber den Funktionsbegriff und die graphische Darstellung bei Oresme,' in *Zeitschrift fuer die Geschichte der mathematischen Wissenschaften*, dritte Folge, vol. 14, Leipzig, 1913.

[6] Summarized in Ernst Borchert's doctoral thesis 'Die Lehre von der Bewegung bei Nikolaus Oresme,' in *Beitraege zur Geschichte und Philosophie des Mittelalters*, Band xxxi, 3, Münster, 1934, p.93.

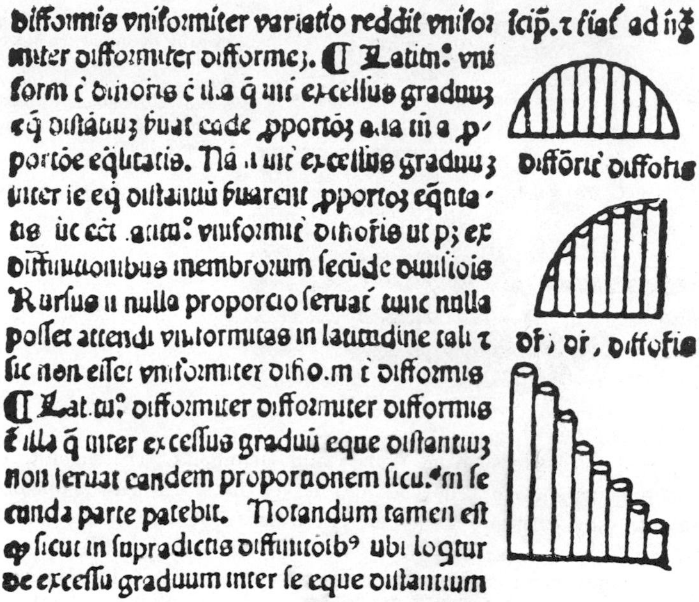

difformis uniformiter variatio reddit unifor lcip.z fiat ad in
miter difformiter difforme;. ¶ Latitu? uni
form i difformis i illa q̄ uni excessus graduū
eq̄ distantiū hunt eade proportōe et si nō p
portōe equalitatis. Nā si uni excellus graduū difformi difformis
inter se eq̄ distantiū huarent proportōe equalita
tis ... uniformiter difformis ut p; ex
diffinitionibus membrorum secūde divisionis
Rursus si nulla proporcio seruat tunc nulla
posset attendi uniformitas in latitudine tali z dif, dif, difformis
sic non esset uniformiter difformis i difformis
¶ Lat.tu? difformiter difformiter difformis
i illa q̄ inter excessus graduū eque distantiū
non seruat eandem proporcionem sicut in se
cunda parte patebit. Notandum tamen est
q sicut in supradictis diffinitionib? ubi loquitur
de excessu graduum inter se eque distantium

1. NICOLAS ORESME: The First Graphic Representation of Movement, *c.*1350. *The changing qualities of a body were graphically interpreted for the first time by Nicolas Oresme, bishop of Lisieux. The variation is shown by verticals erected above a horizontal, the later X-axis.* (Tractatus de Latitudine Formarum, *Second edition, Padua,* 1486)

more than once within one frame of reference. When Descartes, in his *Geometria* (1637), represented the laws of conic sections by a system of co-ordinates, the Aristotelian-scholastic conception had disappeared and variables had become basic, not only in graphic representation but in mathematics. By means of variables, Descartes interrelates mathematics and geometry.

The Nineteenth Century and the Capturing of Movement

Organic Movement in Graphic Form, c.1860

The nineteenth century makes the great leap and literally learns to feel the pulse of nature. Early in his career, the French physiologist, Étienne Jules Marey, 1830–1904, invented the Spygmograph (1860), which inscribed on a smoke-blackened cylinder the form and frequency of the human pulse beat.

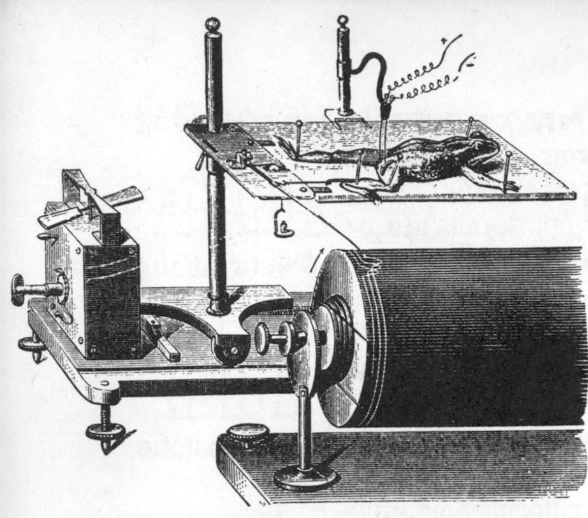

2. E. J. MAREY: The Myograph, Device for Recording the Movements of a Muscle. Before 1868. *Registering reactions of a frog's leg to repeated electrical stimulation.* (*Marey*, Du mouvement dans les fonctions de la vie, *Paris*, 1868)

In this period scientists such as Wundt and Helmholtz were eager to devise apparatus to gauge motion in muscles and nerves (fig. 2). Marey is one of these great *savants*, key witnesses today for the constituent side of the nineteenth century.

Movement, movement in all its form — in the blood stream, in the stimulated muscle, in the gait of the horse, in aquatic animals and molluscs, in the flights of insects and birds — was the ever-returning burden of Marey's research. From the start of his career, when he devised the recorder for the human pulse beat, down to his last studies in 1900, when he investigated the eddies of moving air streams and registered them on the photographic plate; from his first book on the circulation of the blood 'based on a graphical study of the blood,' down to his last and most popular book, *Le Mouvement* (1894), translated into English

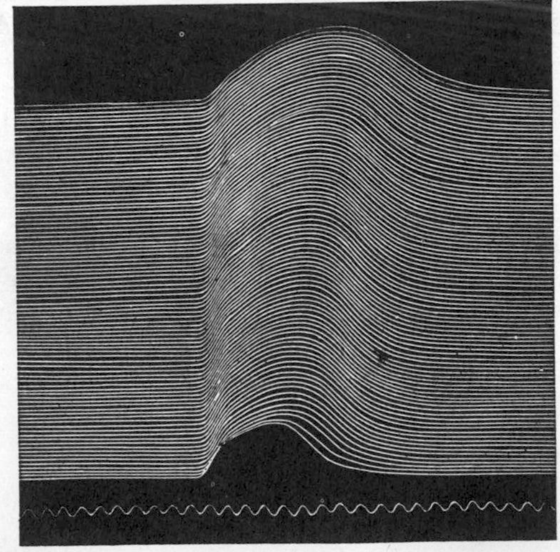

3. E. J. MAREY: Record of the Movement of a Muscle. Before 1868. *Responses of the frog's leg to stimulation by an electric current.* (*Marey*, Du mouvement dans les fonctions de la vie, *Paris*, 1868)

the following year, Marey's thought ever revolves around a central concept of our epoch: Movement.

Marey quite consciously looks back to Descartes,[7] but instead of graphically representing conic sections he translates organic movement into graphic form. In his book *La Méthode graphique dans les sciences expérimentales*, which reflects his mastery of the subject and his universal outlook at its most brilliant, he acknowledges his spiritual ancestors [8] with the respect that only the great can give.

The eighteenth century had witnessed early efforts to extend graphic representation to new domains. The object was to make intelligible a movement of historical dimensions, as Playfair did in 1789 when he charted the fluctuating national debt between 1688 and 1786 in curves that clearly betrayed the effect of wars. Later the phases of the cholera epidemic of 1832 were traced by the same method. The drawing of contour lines on maps was attempted, according to Marey, as far back as the sixteenth century, but only became current in post-Napoleonic times. Marey also mentions an eighteenth-century attempt to represent the successive phases of the horse's gait (fig. 11).

James Watt, inventor of the steam engine, has some claim to be called Marey's direct ancestor. For Watt, Marey reports, 'introduced the first registering device in mechanics, penetrated at first blow one of the most difficult problems: to measure graphically within the cylinder the work developed by steam.' [9] These indicators, diagrammatically registering the movement of the steam,

[7] Marey, *La Méthode graphique dans les sciences expérimentales*, Paris, 1885, p.iv.
[8] Ibid. pp.11–24.
[9] Ibid. p.114.

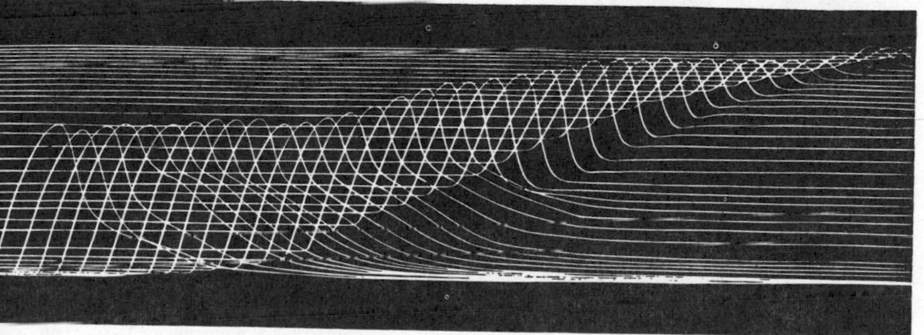

4. E. J. MAREY: Trajectory of Responses in a Frog's Leg. Before 1868. *Coagulation of the muscle and gradual loss of function as the effect of rising temperature.* (*Marey*, Du mouvement dans les fonctions de la vie, *Paris*, 1868)

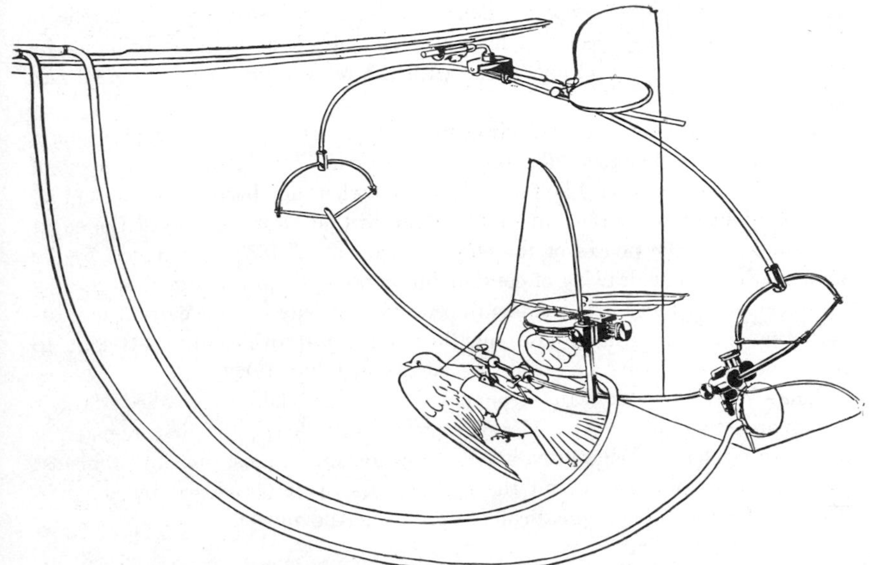

5. E. J. MAREY: Recording Larger Movements — Flight, 1868. *To trace the more extensive movements of a bird in flight, Marey harnessed a pigeon to the arm of a merry-go-round. The wings, connected to pneumatic drums, record their trajectory on a cylinder.*

form a bridge to Marey's activity. Marey unites the genius of the experimental physiologist with that of the engineer. He is inexhaustible, in the first half of his career, as an inventor of a 'recording apparatus' (fig. 2) whose needles register the movement on smoked cylinders.[10] The forms that develop often have a fascination all of their own (figs. 3,4). These curves, says the savant, might be called the 'language of phenomena themselves.'[11] Early in the 'eighties Marey began to use photography.

---

[10] When Marey studied the flight of birds he constructed a working model of a monoplane having two propellers (1872) driven by a compressed air motor (today at Musée de l'Aeronautique, Paris). In 1886 he invented daylight-loading film. And with the first movie camera (which contained all essential parts), he made a brief scene of a man climbing off a bicycle in the Champs-Elysées.

[11] Marey, op.cit.

Finally Marey comes to the domain that is of particular concern to us: rendering the true form of a movement as it is described in space. Such movement, Marey stresses again and again, 'escapes the eye.'

He first attempted a graphic portrayal of movement in the late 'sixties. A dove harnessed to a registering device (fig. 5) transmits the curve of its wing beats to smoked cylinders. From these the form of the movement is plotted out point by point.

At the beginning of the 'eighties, Marey began to use photography for the representation of movement. The idea occurred to him in 1873, when an astronomer showed the Académie des Sciences four successive phases of the sun on a single plate. Another hint he found in the 'astronomical revolver' of his colleague Janssen, who — approximately at the same time — caught on its revolving cylinder the passage of the planet Venus across the sun. Marey now tried using this procedure for terrestrial objects. He devised his 'photographic gun' (fig. 6) to follow flying sea gulls. Instead of stars in motion he portrayed birds in flight.[12]

The astonishing photographic studies of motion that Muybridge was performing in California also stimulated Marey to work along these lines, although their methods, as we shall see, differed considerably. Muybridge arranged a series of cameras side by side so that each camera caught an isolated phase of the movement. Marey, as a physiologist, wanted to capture movement on a single plate and from a single point of view, to obtain the undisguised record of continuous motion as he had graphically registered it on his smoked drums.

---

[12] Marey also devised the first movie camera with film reels (1886), and showed Edison his first short 'movie' during the Paris Exhibition of 1889. Like most of the great nineteenth-century scientists, Marey was not interested in the market value of his ideas. The practical solutions came from Edison in the beginning of the 'nineties and from Lumière in 1895.

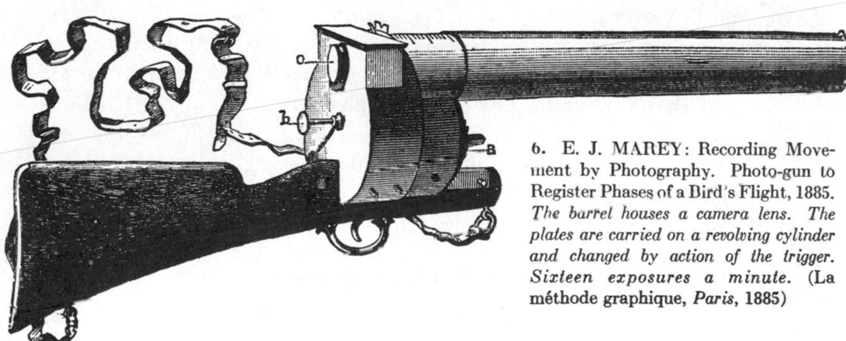

6. E. J. MAREY: Recording Movement by Photography. Photo-gun to Register Phases of a Bird's Flight, 1885. *The barrel houses a camera lens. The plates are carried on a revolving cylinder and changed by action of the trigger. Sixteen exposures a minute.* (La méthode graphique, *Paris*, 1885)

Marey invited Muybridge to visit him in Paris (1881), and introduced him in his house to a gathering of Europe's most brilliant physicists, astronomers, and physiologists, who welcomed Muybridge's straightforward tackling of the problem.

Muybridge's photography of flying birds did not entirely satisfy Marey, who wished to gain full insight into the three-dimensional character of flight — as Descartes had projected geometrical forms: for the flight of insects and of

7. E. J. MAREY: Recording a Gull's Flight in Three Projections Photographically. Before 1890. *At Marey's laboratory in the Parc des Princes, Paris, three still cameras placed at perpendicular angles to the line of flight simultaneously record a seagull's passage before black walls and over a black floor.* (Le vol des oiseaux, *Paris*, 1890)

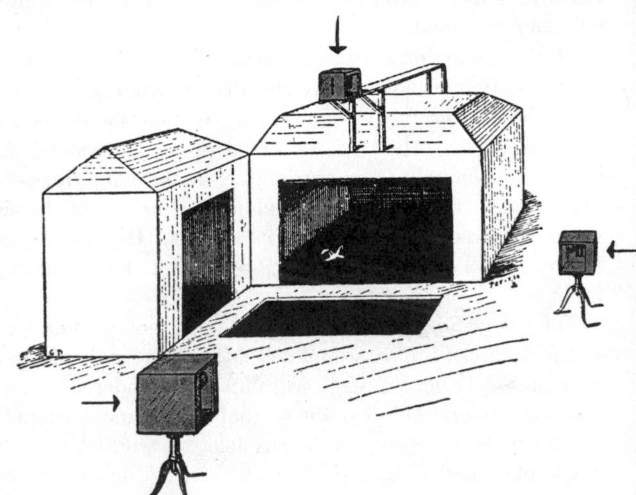

birds is spatial. It evolves freely in three dimensions. Around 1885 Marey pointed three cameras in such a way as to view the bird simultaneously from above, from the side, and from the fore (fig. 7). At his laboratory in the Parc des Princes, Paris, he set up a vast hangar, before whose black walls and ceiling the sea gull flew over a black floor. These simple realities, normally hidden to the human eye, have an impressiveness that needs no further explanation.

For better knowledge of the bird's flight, Marey later drew diagrams in which he separated the overlapping phases of the photograph (figs. 8–10). He even modeled the sea gull in its successive attitudes (fig. 9) — sculpture that would have delighted Boccioni, creator of the 'Bottle evolving in Space' (1912) and of the 'Marching Man' (1913). In his later research [13] Marey made extensive use of the movie camera, which proved not especially suited to this purpose.

---

[13] Marey, *La Chronophotographie*, Paris, 1899, pp.37ff., or as he calls it 'images chronophotographiques recueillies sur pellicule mobile.'

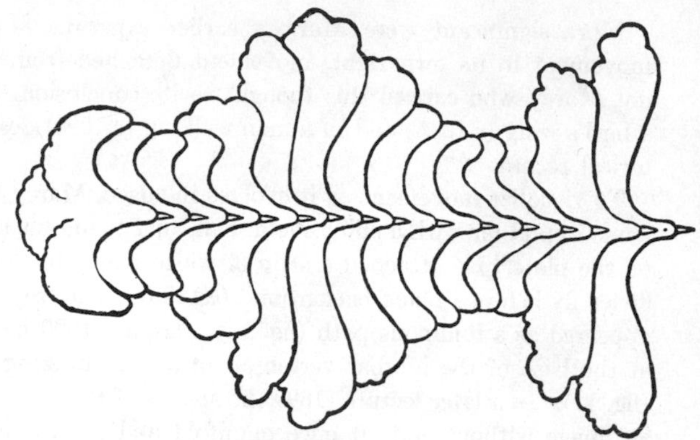

8. E. J. MAREY: Horizontal Projection of the Flying Seagull. Before 1890. (Le vol des oiseaux)

9. E. J. MAREY: Bronze Model of the Flying Seagull. (Le vol des oiseaux)

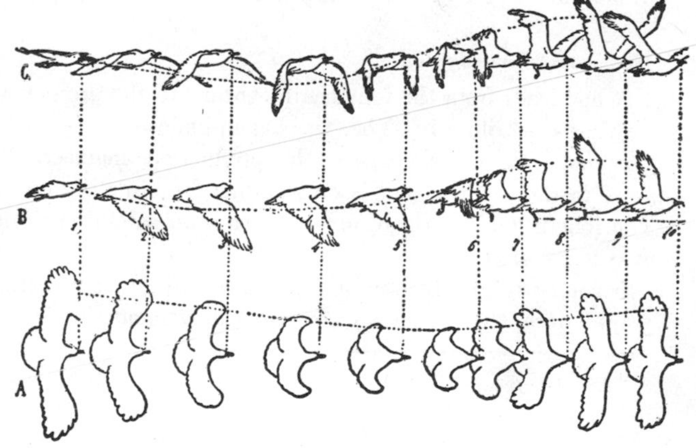

10. E. J. MAREY: Gull's Flight Recorded in Three Projections by Apparatus Shown in Fig. 7. *The sinuous line represents projection on the vertical plane. The dotted lines connecting the heads mark identical phases. For the sake of clarity the distance between phases is exaggerated on the diagram.* (Le vol des oiseaux)

More significant were Marey's earlier experiments with the portrayal of movement in its own right, movement detached from the performer. It was not Marey who carried this thought to its conclusion. But his trajectories of a bird's wing (*c.*1885) and of a man walking (*c.*1890) deserve a place in the historical record.

To visualize movement as it evolves in space, Marey first tried describing his name in mid-air with a shiny metal ball, and found his signature clearly written on the plate. He attached a strip of white paper to the wing of a crow, which he let fly before a black background (*c.*1885). The trajectory of each wing beat appeared as a luminous path (fig. 18). Around 1890 he placed a brilliant point at the base of the lumbar vertebrae of a man walking away from the camera (fig. 17). In a later lecture (1899) he speaks of these curves as 'a luminous trail, an image without end, at once manifold and individual.'[14] This scientist sees his objects with the sensibility of a Mallarmé. Marey called his procedure 'time photography' (*chronophotographie*); its object is to render visible 'movements that the human eye cannot perceive.'

For lack of technical means these early promises did not reach full maturity. The fulfilment was to come from elsewhere, from the industrial sphere. This occurred around 1912, in 'scientific management.' The object was to record a given motion cycle in utmost detail. Only thus could one accurately observe the work process. For the first time, images of pure motion are obtained with entire precision — images giving a full account of the hand's behavior as it accomplishes its task. We see into a closed domain. Frank B. Gilbreth, the American production engineer, built up this method step by step around 1912 and achieved the visualization of movement. How this investigation proceeded, and what parallels simultaneously arose in painting, the section on Scientific Management and Contemporary Art will attempt to show.

Movement Investigated

A line leads from the fourteenth century to the present: Oresme — Descartes — Marey — Gilbreth: The theologian-philosopher — the mathematician-philosopher — the physiologist — the production engineer. Three of these men arose in the country that is outstanding for visualization in all of its domains. The fourth, an American, appeared as soon as efficiency demanded knowledge of 'the one best way to do work.'

Nicolas Oresme, Bishop of Lisieux, was the first investigator to represent in graphic form the ceaselessly changing: movement.

---

[14] Ibid. p. 11.

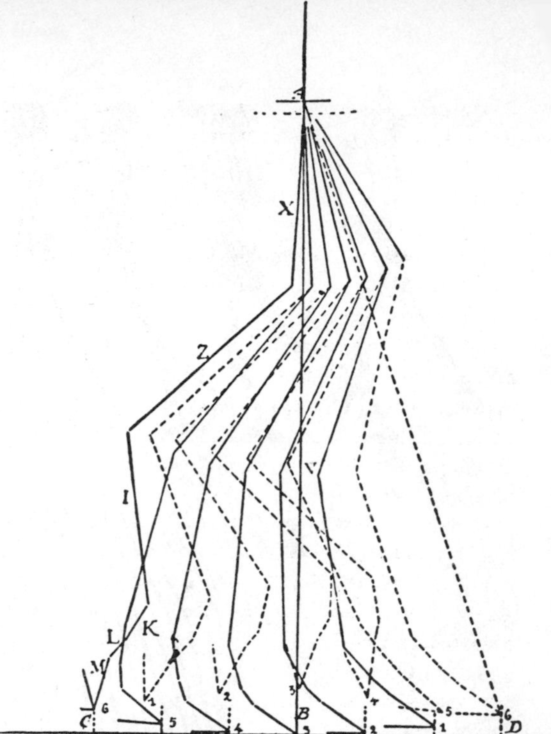

11. GRIFFON AND VINCENT: Graphic Representation of a Horse's Gait, 1779. *One weakness of this method, Marey points out, is that the motion is shown as if centering around a static point.* (*Marey,* La Méthode graphique)

Frank B. Gilbreth (1868–1924) was the first to capture with full precision the complicated trajectory of human movement.

We do not wish to strain the comparison. Nicolas Oresme marks at a decisive point the schism between the ancient and modern world. A task so easy in appearance as the representation of movement demands a faculty of thought and abstraction hard for us to grasp today. The American production engineer, Frank B. Gilbreth, is but one link in the great process of mechanization. But in our connection we do not hesitate to point out a bridge between Nicolas Oresme and Gilbreth. Oresme realized the nature of movement and represented it by graphic methods. Gilbreth, about five and a half centuries later, detached human movement from its bearer or subject, and achieved its precise visualization in space and time (fig. 19). Gilbreth is an innovator in the field of scientific management. His thinking and his methods grow out of the great body of nineteenth-century science.

A new realm opens: new forms, new expressive values, transcending the domain of the engineer.

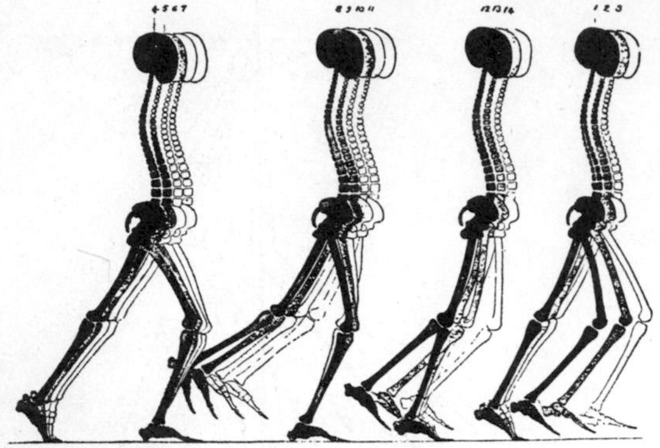

12. Successive Positions in a Human Step. (*From* The Mechanism of Human Locomotion, *by the German anatomists and E. H. Weber*, 1830's. (*Marey*, La méthode graphique)

13. E. J. MAREY: Oscillations of the Leg in Running. Before 1885. *The model to be photographed was clothed in black, with a bright metallic strip down the side of the arms, body, and legs.*

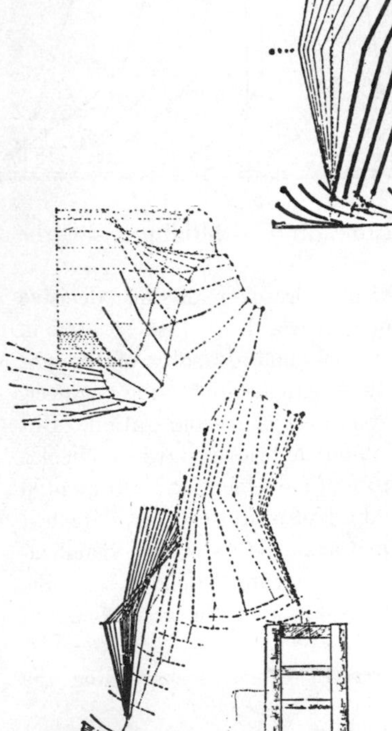

14. E. J. MAREY: Jump from a Height with Stiffened Legs. c.1890. *Diagram from a photograph made by the same method as in Fig.* 13.

15. MARCEL DUCHAMP: 'Nude Descending the Staircase,' 1912. (*Arensberg Collection, Hollywood, Cal. Courtesy Museum of Modern Art, N. Y.*)

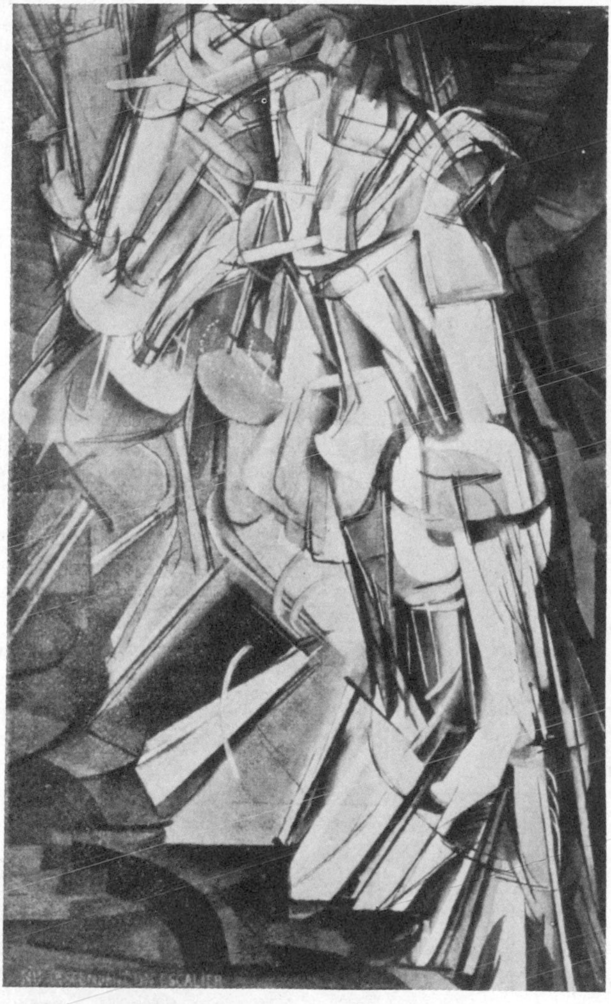

16. EADWEARD MUYBRIDGE: Athlete Descending a Staircase. *c.*1880. *Muybridge set up a series of cameras at twelve-inch intervals, releasing their shutters electromagnetically to obtain a sequence of motion phases. Each picture showed an isolated phase.* (The Human Figure in Motion, *6th ed., London, 1925*)

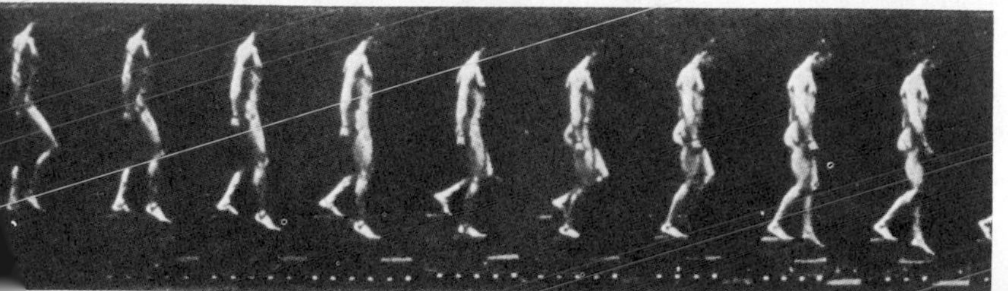

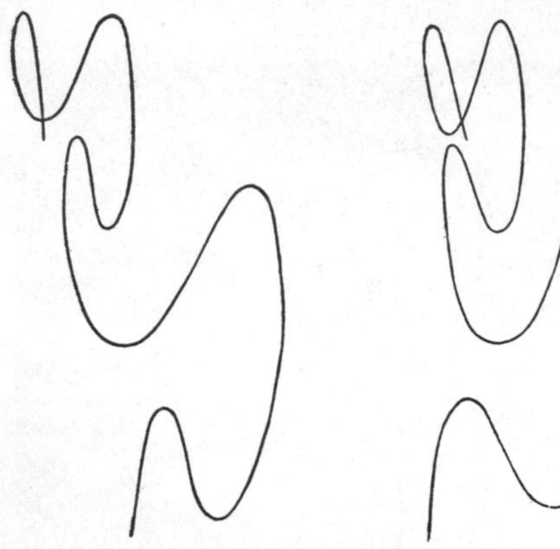

17. E. J. MAREY: Man Walking Away from the Camera. Stereoscopic Trajectory of a Point at the Base of the Lumbar Vertebrae. *c.*1890. *'A luminous trail, at once manifold and individual.' — Marey.*

Movement, the ceaselessly changing, proves itself ever more strongly the key to our thought. It underlies the concept of function and of variables in higher mathematics. And in physics, the essence of the phenomenal world has been increasingly regarded as motion-process: sound, light, heat, hydrodynamics, aerodynamics; until, in this century, matter too dissolves into motion, and physicists recognize that their atoms consist of a kernel, a nucleus, around which negatively charged electrons circle in orbits with a speed exceeding that of the planets.

A parallel phenomenon occurs in philosophy and literature. Almost simultaneously with Lumière's cinematograph (1895–6), Henri Bergson was lecturing to the Collège de France on the 'Cinematographic Mechanism of Thought' (1900).[15] And later James Joyce split words open like oysters, showing them in motion.

---

[15] Cf. Bergson, *Creative Evolution*, Eng. trans., New York, 1937, p.272.

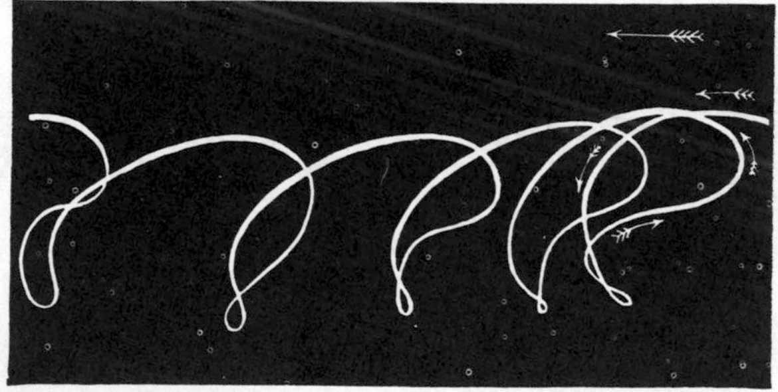

18. E. J. MAREY: Photographic Trajectory of a Crow's Wing. *c.*1885. *Five wing beats. Marey attached a strip of white paper to the wing of the bird and allowed it to fly before a black background.*

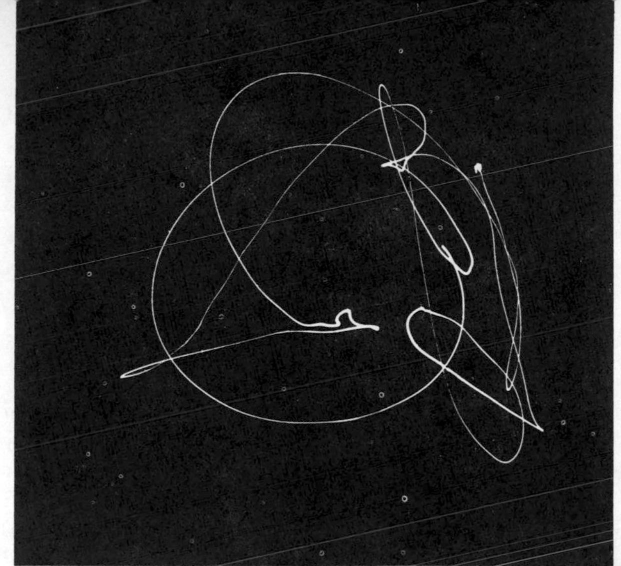

19. FRANK B. GILBRETH: Cyclograph Record of the Path of the Point of a Rapier Used by an Expert Fencer. 1914. '*This picture illustrates the beautiful smooth acceleration and deceleration and complete control of the motion path.*' (*Photo and caption by courtesy of Lillian M. Gilbreth*)

20. WASSILY KANDINSKY: Pink Square. Oil, 1923. (*Courtesy Buchholz Gallery, New York*)

Perhaps our epoch, unaccustomed to translating thought into emotional experience, can do no more than pose the question: Are the trajectories, as recorded by a production engineer, 'to eliminate needless, ill-directed, and ineffective motions,' in any way connected with the emotional impact of the signs that appear time and again in our contemporary art? Only in our period, so unaccustomed to assimilating processes of thought into the emotional domain, could serious doubt arise.

THE CREED OF PROGRESS

ONCE more the contrast should be stressed between the ancient and the modern outlook. The ancients perceived the world as eternally existing and self-renewing, whereas we perceive it as created and existing within temporal limits; that is, the world is determined toward a specific goal and purpose. Closely bound up with this belief that the world has a definite purpose is the outlook of rationalism. Rationalism, whether retaining belief in God or not, reaches its ideological peak in thinkers of the latter half of the eighteenth century. Rationalism goes hand in hand with the idea of progress. The eighteenth century all but identified the advance of science with social progress and the perfectibility of man.

In the nineteenth century the creed of progress was raised into a dogma, a dogma given various interpretations in the course of the century.

In the first decades industry increasingly assumes the prestige held by science. For Henri de Saint-Simon industry is the great liberator. It will sweep away nationalism and militarism. An army of workers will girdle the earth. The exploitation of man by man will disappear. The greater part of Saint-Simon's life was spent in the eighteenth century. His conceptions rest on universal grounds. He sees in mechanization not what was made of it, but what it might become.

Beginning with the nineteenth century, the power to see things in their totality becomes obscured. Yet the universalistic outlook did not fail altogether to live on. It would be a rewarding task to follow the survival and dying-out of this tendency down to the filtering of isolation into the various branches: in the state (nationalism); in the economy (monopolism); in mass production; in science (specialistic approach without heed to universal implications); in the sphere of feeling (loneliness of the individual and isolation of art). This much is certain: the universal outlook is still manifested in remnants around mid-century. It can sometimes be felt in public life. The first of the world expositions at the close of the revolutionary years (London, 1851) was to be a manifestation of world peace and of industrial co-operation. The closely connected idea of free trade reached its short peak under Gladstone in the next decade.

A glimmer of universality is also found in the writings of the great savants, such as Claude Bernard's *Introduction à la physique expérimentale*, 1865.

Herbert Spencer, most influential spokesman for the creed of progress as the second half of the century came to understand it, surely did not intend his evolutionary teachings in the sociological sphere (before Darwin) as license for commercial irresponsibility in the name of *laissez faire*. Evolution is now used interchangeably with progress, and natural selection with the results of free competition. In this roundabout way Herbert Spencer was turned into the philosopher of the ruling taste. He provided the theoretical bulwark. A sociologist has recently observed that over 300,000 copies of Spencer's works were sold in America in the space of four decades.[1]

Eighteenth-century faith in progress as formulated by Condorcet started from science; that of the nineteenth century, from mechanization. Industry, which brought about this mechanization with its unceasing flow of inventions, had something of the miracle that roused the fantasy of the masses. This was especially true in the time of its greatest popularity and expansion, the latter half of the century. The period in which the great international expositions are historically significant — from London, 1851, to Paris, 1889 — roughly delimits that time. These festivals to the ideas of progress, mechanization, and industry fall off as soon as faith in the mechanical miracle becomes dimmed.

Belief in progress is replaced by faith in production. Production for production's sake had existed ever since the Lancashire cotton spinners first showed the world what mechanization on the grand scale was capable of doing. With the waning of faith in progress, floating as a metaphysical banner over the factories, there entered that faith in production as an end in itself. Fanaticism for production as such was heretofore confined to the manufacturing groups. In the time of full mechanization, faith in production penetrated every class and ramification of life, thrusting all other considerations into the background.

ASPECTS OF MECHANIZATION

Mechanization, as envisaged and realized in our epoch, is the end product of a rationalistic view of the world. Mechanizing production means dissecting work into its component operations — a fact that has not changed since Adam Smith thus outlined the principle of mechanization in a famous passage of his

[1] Thomas Cochran and William Miller, *The Age of Enterprise, A Social History of Industrial America*, New York, 1942, p.125. Cf. the entire chapter, 'A Philosophy for Industrial Progress,' ibid. pp. 119–28.

Wealth of Nations in 1776: 'The invention of all those machines by which labor is so much facilitated and abridged seems to have been originally owing to the division of labor.' It need only be added that in manufacturing complex products such as the automobile, this division goes together with a re-assembly.

The rationalistic approach to things came to the fore in the Renaissance. Complex events — the movement of bodies for instance — were dissected into their components and united in a resultant (parallelogram of forces). The nineteenth century and our century expanded to the gigantic this principle of division and re-assembly, until the whole factory became an organism with division and assembly occurring almost automatically.

The second half of the sixteenth century, especially in Italy, saw an increase of technical books. They are practical, and offer great variety of schemes to raise the efficiency of manual labor or to replace it by mechanical power. Archimedes screws, waterwheels, pumping machinery, and gear transmission were developed considerably. In hardly a point, however, did they advance beyond Hellenistic times. On the whole their devices were incomparably more primitive. They are but spelling exercises in mechanization. And even more remarkable to a later period: the mechanizing of production was not attempted. Mechanization could not become a reality in an age of guilds. But social institutions change as soon as the orientation changes. The guilds became obsolete as soon as the rationalistic view became dominant and moved continually toward utilitarian goals. This was the predestined hour for mechanization.

Invention and the Miraculous

Our present-day point of view tends to identify the inventive impulse with the mechanizing of production — an identity that cannot be taken for granted. The Ancients thought along altogether different lines; they placed their inventive gifts in the service of the miracle. They created magical machinery and automatons. Admittedly, they used their mathematical and physical knowledge for practical purposes too. Hero of Alexandria, whose writings are preserved, and whose name has become a sort of generic name for Hellenistic invention, built and improved oil-presses, fire-fighting pumps; invented lamps with automatically advancing wicks, or water-tube boilers for heating baths. The technical equipment of the later Roman thermae, recent excavations give reason to believe, originated in Egypt in the time of the Ptolemies. We shall return to this point when dealing with the mechanization of the bath.

In a practical direction the sole systematic application of the Ancient's physical knowledge was to warfare. The Alexandrian inventors built cannon working by compressed air, with bronzen barrels bored so accurately that fire spurted as the charge was released. But completely foreign to their outlook was the idea of placing their great inventive talents in the service of production.

This book's subject compels us to pass over the period which by its experimentation is closer than almost any other to the nineteenth century — Hellenistic Alexandria, of the third and second centuries B.C.[1]

Among the most fertile ideas of Alexander the Great was that of Hellenizing the East, and for this he founded the city of his name on the Nile Delta, much as, earlier, the Greeks had founded Miletus or any of their colony cities. Here, through Greek thinkers and scientists, emerged a civilization oriented toward precise science. Its doctors laid down the bases of brain anatomy, gynaecology, and surgery. And similarly with the foundations of geometry (Euclid) and astronomy (Ptolemy).

Amid this atmosphere, under the Ptolemies, throve the Alexandrian School of inventors, whose writings, schemes, and experiments reflect the calm leisure as well as the complex character of this Hellenistic city: on one hand the precision of Greek thinking, on the other the love of the marvelous that flourished in the Orient.

The Alexandrian inventors were masters in combining the so-called 'simple machines,' such as the screw, the wedge, the wheel and axle, the lever, the pulley, powered by combinations of water, vacuum or air pressure, to carry out complicated movements or manipulations. Thus the temple gates swung open automatically as soon as fire was kindled on the altar and swung to when the flame died. Religious plays, several acts in length, were staged with mechanically moved figures, which, to minimize friction, Hero put on wheels gliding over rails of wood. So far as we know, no sign of an application to practical transportation has been found. Wooden rails are said to have appeared in English mines in the early seventeenth century. Here they eased the hauling of coal wagons. Only about 1770 did the general use of rolling stock on wooden rails astonish continental visitors to English coal mines.[2]

Economic reasons can easily be given to explain the lack of interest in production: the ancients had cheap labor at their disposal in the form of slaves. But this fails to explain why they did not apply their knowledge practically; did not use their rails to speed the vehicles on their highways; used their automatons to dispense consecrated water and did not commercialize them for selling beverages; did not put to everyday use their facility with vacuum, air pressure, and mechanical contrivances.

---

[1] The following remarks are based on unpublished studies by the author on The Inventive Impulse.
[2] T. S. Ashton, *Iron and Steel in the Industrial Revolution*, London, 1924, p.63.

The fact was that they possessed an inner orientation, an outlook on life different from ours. Just as we were unable to invent a form of relaxation suited to our way of life, the ancients gave little thought to lending their inventive powers to practical ends.

Inexhaustible are the proposals for birds that move their wings and chirp when water pressure drives air through hidden pipes; for water organs built on the same principle; for series of magic vessels with intermittent flow; for automatons that alternately pour water and wine or deliver a quota of consecrated water when a coin is inserted.

This love of the miraculous was passed on to the Arabs. Conspicuous in Islamic miniatures are the automatons, all based on Alexandrian principles.

The urge to put invention in the service of the miracle survived throughout Islam down to the eighteenth century. What created a sensation in the late eighteenth century was not the new spinning machinery, but the manlike automatons who walked, played instruments, spoke with human voices, wrote, or drew. They were shown before the courts of Europe, and finally toured from fair to fair, well into the nineteenth century. The perfecting of automatons in the eighteenth century is related to the high standard of the crafts and especially to the refinement of the clock-making industry. They are based on a minute decomposition and reintegration of movements, which formed the best of disciplines for the invention of spinning machinery.

The Miraculous and the Utilitarian

To go one step further: observing the constituent elements of these tools that were decisive for the first period of mechanization, textile machinery, and steam engines, we find them to be the last term of a development extending from Alexandrian times onward. What has changed is the orientation, from the miraculous to the utilitarian. The steam engine, as left by James Watt, combines utilization of the vacuum (condenser) with transmission of movement; and the machines of the textile industry show the same cunning mind for decomposing and recombining movements that created the man-like automatons.

To illustrate in a simple way how the miraculous and the utilitarian co-existed in the eighteenth century, we shall recall one of the great inventors of the Rococo: Jacques de Vaucanson, 1709–82. He is a mechanical genius whose lifetime runs parallel with Louis XV and Buffon. In him the two opposite conceptions dwell side by side. His automatons bear witness to an astonishing capacity for turning machines into performers of complex organic movements. Vaucanson had studied anatomy, music, and mechanics, all of which he intimately fused in his most famous automatons, the flutist, the drummer, and the mechanical duck.

The flutist, which Vaucanson submitted to the Paris Academy of Science for examination in 1738 and which, says Diderot, was seen by all Paris, possessed lips that moved, a moving tongue that served as the air-flow valve, and movable fingers whose leather tips opened and closed the stops of the flute. On the same principle Vaucanson constructed a drummer, who at the same time played a three-holed shepherd's pipe. Even more admired was the mechanical duck. It could waddle and swim. Its wings imitated nature in every detail and they beat the air. It would wag its head, quack, and pick up grain, the passage of which could be observed in swallowing movements. A mechanism inside ground up the grain and caused its exit from the body much as in natural circumstances. 'It was necessary in a little space to construct a chemical laboratory, to decompose the main constituents [of the grain] and cause them to issue forth at will.' It was thus described in the *Encyclopédie* of 1751 [3] by no less a contributor than the mathematician D'Alembert. Vaucanson had exhibited his duck in 1741, according to the *Encyclopédie*, whose report directly reflects the impression made upon the most advanced contemporaries by this marvelous mechanism. D'Alembert, in his description of the flutist,[4] points out that he is reproducing the greater part of Vaucanson's own account,[5] 'which seemed to us worthy of preservation,' and the acute critic Diderot cannot but exclaim with unwonted enthusiasm at the end of D'Alembert's article, 'What finesse in all these details; what delicacy in all the parts of this mechanism. . . .' [6] Indeed, in addition to a love of the marvelous, Vaucanson's automatons and the long line of similar creations by others reflect the extraordinary mechanical subtlety of the eighteenth century.

The philosopher Condorcet, who succeeded Vaucanson in the Académie des Sciences, mentions in his éloge that Frederick the Great had sought to attract him to the Potsdam court in 1740.[7] But in 1741 Cardinal Fleury, the real ruler of France, named Vaucanson 'Inspector of the Silk Manufactures.' It is then that his genius turns to the mechanizing of production. He makes numerous improvements in spinning and weaving, and proves himself a foresighted organizer. About 1740 he constructs a mechanical loom for figured silks. Its heddles are automatically raised and lowered by means of a drum pierced with holes, on the same principle that controlled the air supply and the selection of notes in his flutist. In Alexandria we already find mechanisms being released by

[3] *Encyclopédie ou Dictionnaire raisonné*, vol. I, p.196.

[4] Ibid. under 'Androide,' pp.448–51.

[5] J. de Vaucanson, *Mécanisme d'un fluteur mécanique*, Paris, 1738.

[6] *Encyclopédie*, p.451.

[7] Condorcet, 'Éloge de Vaucanson,' in *Histoire de l'Académie Royale des Sciences, Année* 1782, Paris, 1785.

means of pins or grooves. Vaucanson's looms place him in the long series of inventors who, from the seventeenth century on, attempted to solve the automatic manufacture of fabrics. Vaucanson's loom did not have immediate consequences. In 1804 the inventor Jacquard of Lyons assembled the fragments of Vaucanson's loom in the Paris Conservatoire des Arts et Métiers [8] and thus invented his weaving automaton, the Jacquard loom, which has remained standard to this day, and reproduced mechanically even the most fantastic patterns.

It is Vaucanson's practical activities that are historically the most interesting. In 1756 [9] he set up a silk factory at Aubenas near Lyons, improving or inventing every detail of the building and of the machinery, even to the reels, which most ingeniously joined the threads from the cocoons as they lay in the bath, and the twisting frames that spun them. To the best of our knowledge this is the first industrial plant in the modern sense, built nearly two decades before Richard Arkwright founded the first successful spinning mills in England. Vaucanson had insight into the fact that industry could not be housed in wooden shacks or in random buildings, but required a concentrated plant where every detail was carefully thought out, and whose machines were moved by a single power. His treatise gives full details of the plan.[10] The factories — he later built a second factory — are three stories high, and well planned in every detail. The source of power is a single overshot water wheel. He calls for softened light, which is obtained from windows with oiled paper. Primitive ventilation and vaulting insure to some extent the moist and temperate atmosphere necessary for spinning the silk. Vaucanson set up his spinning machines (*moulins à organsiner*) in large, well-lighted halls. The small models preserved in the Conservatoire des Arts et Métiers, Paris, show a striking elegance of construction and have an imposing number of vertical spindles. The 'flyers' of the turn of the century are anticipated here. What a contrast with the unwieldy four or eight spindle constructions used in the first cotton spinning machines of England!

Yet these efforts came to nothing. Eighteenth-century France was a testing ground in almost every domain. Ideas arose that could become reality only in the nineteenth century, for they were unable to sink roots in Catholic France under the Ancien Régime. Mechanization was among these.

---

[8] Vaucanson himself began a collection of machine models of various kinds, which became the nucleus of the Conservatoire des Arts et Métiers during the Revolution.

[9] We give the date as 1756, since in his *Mémoires*, 1776, Vaucanson speaks of an experiment made at Aubenas twenty years previously. Cf. J. de Vaucanson, 'Sur le Choix de l'Emplacement et sur la Forme qu'il faut donner au Bâtiment d'une Fabrique d'Organsin,' in *Histoire de l'Académie Royale, Année* 1776, p.168.

[10] Precise illustrations of Vaucanson's installation are given. See especially Planches v et vi.

The Mechanizing of Production

To carry through the mechanizing of production, another class of inventors, another class of doers, other sociological conditions, and another textile proved necessary.

Silk was a luxury textile for a luxury class. The English experimented with cotton from the start, and constructed all their machines with cotton in mind. Here was the road to mass production. And just as the textile itself was rougher, of a rougher fiber too was the class and the environment that pushed forward its mechanization.

Here the inventors were neither nobles nor savants. No academy published their experiments, and today's knowledge of the beginnings has to be pieced together from fragments. No government set up privileged factories: the mechanizing of production began in the North, in Lancashire, far from the ruling classes and the High Church of England. Lonely spots like Manchester — which did not attain corporate status before the nineteenth century and was without hampering guild restrictions — and a proletarian class of inventors were needed. One of the earliest of Manchester's large manufacturers observed these facts by 1794. 'Towns where manufactures are most flourishing, are seldom bodies corporate, commerce requiring universal encouragement instead of exclusive privileges to the natives and freemen of a particular district. Those who first introduced the cotton manufacture into Lancashire were Protestant refugees, who probably found small encouragement for themselves and their industries amongst the corporate towns of England.' [11]

John Wyatt, who stretched the yarn between pairs of revolving cylinders instead of by hand and set up the first small mill in a Birmingham warehouse in 1741, landed in debtors' prison. James Hargreaves, inventor of the spinning jenny between 1750 and 1757, was a poor weaver. And Richard Arkwright, 1732–92, the first successful cotton spinner, who turned to advantage ideas upon which other men had foundered, was by trade a barber. Not before 1767 did he turn from his normal calling, which consisted in buying up dull hair and by some process making it usable. In 1780 twenty factories were under his control, and at his death he left his son a large fortune. Climbing from below — he was the thirteenth child of a poor family — armed with an unbreaking will to conquer, and possessing a flair for success, he exemplifies in every trait the type of the nineteenth-century entrepreneur. In a hostile environment, without protectors, without government subsidy, but nourished by a relentless

[11] T. Walker, *Review of Some of the Political Events Which Have Occurred in Manchester During the Last Five Years*, London, 1794. Quoted in Witt Bowden, *Industrial Society in England Toward the End of the Eighteenth Century*, New York, 1925, pp.56–7.

utilitarianism that feared no financial risk or danger, the first mechanization of production was accomplished. In the following century the mechanization of cotton spinning became everywhere almost synonymous with industrialization.

The Simple and the Complicated Craft

First experiences are often decisive for the future development. Of mechanization this is certainly true in more than one respect. What distinguishes European from American mechanization can be observed in the eighteenth-century beginnings as it can a century and a half later. Europe began with the mechanizing of the simple craft: spinning, weaving, iron making. America proceeded otherwise from the first. America began with the mechanizing of the complicated craft.

While Richard Arkwright, around 1780, was fighting his way upward to a power without precedent, Oliver Evans, on the banks of a solitary creek not far from Philadelphia, was mechanizing the complicated craft of the miller. This was achieved by continuous line production, in which the human hand was eliminated, from the unloading of the grain to the processed flour.

At that time there was no American industry. Trained workers were scarce. The well-to-do imported from England their fine furniture, glassware, carpets, fabrics; the pioneer farmer of the hinterland made his own utensils and furniture.

The sudden leap from Robinsonian conditions amid the virgin forest into an advanced stage of mechanization is a phenomenon that recurs again and again in this period. The impulse behind it was the necessity to economize labor and the dearth of skilled workers. The way in which, simultaneously with the opening of the prairie to agriculture around 1850, the necessary machinery was created and the complicated craft of the farmer increasingly mechanized forms one of the most interesting chapters of the nineteenth century. But the impulse was there even earlier. Only thus can we understand that by 1836 two mid-western farmers had on the field a harvesting machine (fig. 89) that performed in a continuous production line the entire harvesting task of threshing, cleaning, and bagging the grain. It appeared about a century ahead of its time. These symptoms assert the orientation from which sprang the whole development of the United States. The dimensions of the land, its sparse population, the lack of trained labor and correspondingly high wages, explain well enough why America mechanized the complicated craft from the outset.

Yet an essential reason may lie elsewhere. The settlers brought over their European mode of living, their European experience. But from the organization of the complicated craft and the whole culture in which such institutions had

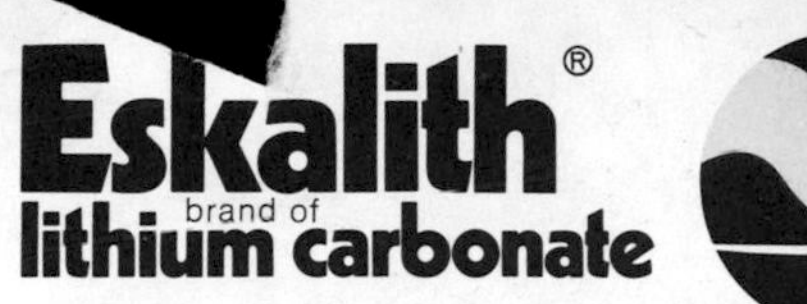

GID clinic

726-2000

grown, they were suddenly cut off. They had to start from scratch. Imagination was given scope to shape reality unhindered.

The Gothic Roots of the Highly Developed Craft

Strife and turmoil notwithstanding, the European development had flowed on unbroken until mechanization entered upon the scene. The highly developed craft has its roots in the late Gothic period. Its rise is inseparably bound up with the revival of municipal life. The need for organized living within a community explains why in the thirteenth and fourteenth centuries city life that had dwindled more and more began to function again, and why, on both old and new cultural soil, cities were founded in numbers exceeded only by the nineteenth-century development in America. The modest timber houses of the Gothic towns, each with its similar front, and built on an equal lot, formed the birthplace of the highly developed handicraft.

Only as the Gothic period was nearing its close, after the raising of the urban cathedrals, did the new burgher class set about the creation of an adequate domestic setting — the burgher interior. Down to the nineteenth century this late Gothic interior continued as a core of further development. Parallel with this, the culture of handicrafts underwent continuous refinement down to the time when mechanization finally set in.

Then a remarkable symbiosis occurs. Handicraft lives on side by side, or intermingled with, industrial production, for the Gothic roots did not perish altogether. A token of this was the obligation to pass through the traditional stages from apprentice to journeyman and master. Even the factory mechanic was trained in a similar way. This careful formation in all branches yielded excellently qualified workers, and led to the basic divergences, for better and for worse, between America and the Continent. The butcher, the baker, the joiner, the peasant, have persisted since Gothic times. In a few countries like Switzerland, besides the Gothic nucleus of the city, many usages have remained alive, even to the way of speech. An inner resistance to mechanization keeps it from penetrating over-far into the sphere of intimate living. And when this does occur, it is likely to be after hesitation and in the wake of America.

The complicated handicraft tends however to give to life a certain rigidity and slowness. In America, where it is lacking, its absence is compensated for by the habit of tackling problems directly. The axe, the knife, saw, hammer, shovel, the household utensils and appliances, in short the panoply of instruments whose form had remained static for centuries in Europe, are taken up and shaped anew from the first quarter of the nineteenth century on. America's original contribution, the mechanizing of the complicated craft, sets in vigorously after mid-century, especially in the early 'sixties, with a second wave of advance between 1919 and 1939. We shall briefly discuss the significance of these decades.

Profile of the Decades

The 'Sixties

In every domain there are times that foreshadow future developments with extraordinary swiftness, even if a tangible outcome, an intense follow-through, is not immediately achieved. The 'sixties in America were such a time. Not in great names or in great inventions. But to the period after 1850 we shall again and again, in this book, trace impulses and trends that have strongly influenced our epoch.

A collective fervor for invention seems to course through this period. In the seventeenth century the inventive urge was possessed by a limited group of scholars — philosophers and savants like Pascal, Descartes, Leibnitz, Huygens, or further back, the universal man of the Leonardo type. The orientation that was later to sway the masses of the people first takes shape in the minds of the few. Until late in the eighteenth century, inventive activity, so far as it found record in the British Patent archives, was no more than a trickle. Toward the mid-nineteenth century it gained its hold over the broad masses, and perhaps nowhere more strongly than in the America of the 'sixties. Invention was in the normal course of things. Everyone invented, whoever owned an enterprise sought ways and means by which to make his goods more speedily, more perfectly, and often of improved beauty. Anonymously and inconspicuously the old tools were transformed into modern instruments. Never did the number of inventions per capita of the population exceed its proportion in America of the 'sixties. But we must beware of assuming an identity between the inventive urge and the degree of industrialization. Such was by no means the case. Taking the key industry of the nineteenth century as an index, Europe and particularly England are seen to have been well in the lead. Around mid-century, according to the *Revue des Deux Mondes*,[12] America had 5.5 million power spindles, France 4 million, and England 18 million. Greater still, even at a later time, was the weaving potential of Europe. In 1867 America had over 123,000 power looms, France 70,000, and England 750,000.[13]

Whoever wishes to know what was going on in the American psyche at this

---

[12] *Revue des Deux Mondes*, 1855, IV p.1305.

[13] Blennard, *Histoire de l'industrie*, Paris, 1895, vol. III p.60 ff.

time will find evidence not only in American folk-art. The activity of the anonymous inventor is more revealing. But only a fraction of the popular habit of invention is preserved in the Patent Office. If we turn so often to the patent drawings, it is as objective witnesses, although the drawings in themselves often have an artistic directness that distinguishes them from the technical routine of a later time. In them no small portion of folk-art lies concealed.

In the American patent lists of the late 'thirties, few schemes for the improvement of steam engines or of textile manufacture are to be found, whereas ideas for facilitating the complicated handicrafts and initial efforts to mechanize human surroundings are conspicuous. This becomes truly evident in the 'sixties, in agriculture, in breadmaking, in the mass processing of meat, in the household. Mechanization penetrated many areas with success. For others, like the household, the time had not yet come. From this period, however, it was but a step to the time of full mechanization, which realized what the 'sixties had foreshadowed.

The Time of Full Mechanization, 1918–39

We designate the period between the two World Wars as the time of full mechanization. The development is too fluid to be tied within strict limits. Before 1918 full mechanization was already setting in, and it was by no means ending in 1939. Even within these years there are times of widely varying intensity. Yet with good warrant one may call the era between the wars the time of full mechanization.

Our point of view is too close to allow a total reckoning of what happened in these two decades, or of what the consequences may be to us. This much, however, is certain: at one sweep, mechanization penetrates the intimate spheres of life. What the preceding century and a half had initiated, and especially what had been germinating from mid-nineteenth century on, suddenly ripens and meets life with its full impact.

True, changes affected living as soon as mechanization announced itself in the early nineteenth century; yet the influence was limited to fairly narrow areas, to those places such as Manchester, Roubaix, Lille, where the large textile factories began to flourish and, with their slums, undermined the structure of the whole city. The greater body of life was left undisturbed.

Never, as we shall see later, was the standard of English agriculture more enthusiastically praised than around mid-nineteenth century. On the Continent too the farming population, even of the industrialized nations, outnumbered that of all other occupations. In the United States in 1850, about 85 per cent of the population was rural, and only 15 per cent urban. This ratio began slowly to decline around the end of the century. By 1940 less than 1 in 4 of the total population lived on farms.[14]

In the latter half of the nineteenth century, with the widening of the railroad network, the accelerated growth of metropoli, and, in America, the mechanizing of many complicated crafts, the influence of mechanization was already reaching deeper into life.

Now, around 1920, mechanization involves the domestic sphere. For the first time it takes possession of the house and of whatever in the house is susceptible of mechanization: the kitchen, the bath, and their equipment, which capture the fantasy and arouse the acquisitive instinct of the public to an astonishing degree. In the time of full mechanization more appliances grew into household necessities than had been introduced in the whole preceding century. They absorb an unprecedented share of space, cost, and attention. To establish at what moment the various electrical appliances became popularized we addressed a questionnaire to one of the large mail-order houses;[15] it appears that the minor appliances — fans, irons, toasters, wringers — entered the catalogues in 1912; the electric vacuum cleaner in 1917; the electric range in 1930; and the electric refrigerator in 1932.

The mechanization of the kitchen coincides with the mechanizing of nutrition. As the kitchen grows more strongly mechanized, the stronger grows the demand for processed or ready-made foods.

Around 1900 the canning industry — meat packing excepted — was still in a rather chaotic state in regard both to production and to quality. The time of full mechanization brings an enormous increase in the output and varieties of processed foods: from excellent canned soups, spaghetti in sauce, and strained baby food, to canned dog, cat, or turtle food. The time of full mechanization is identical with the time of the tin can.

The phenomenon of submitting food to mass production is likewise seen in the development of chain restaurants. A single enterprise in a single building in New York prepares food for 300,000 people daily. Doughnuts swimming in hot fat are transported on the endless belt, and the march of apple pies goes on continuously through the immense tunnel oven by military rows of twelve.

We shall confine ourselves almost exclusively to mechanization's advance into the private sphere, and to the simpler things, such as the kitchen, the bathroom, and their appliances. But mechanization implanted itself more deeply. It impinged upon the very center of the human psyche, through all the senses.

---

[14] *Sixteenth Census of the United States*, 1940, 'Agriculture,' vol. III, p.22.

[15] We owe this information to Professor Richard M. Bennett, who was for a time with Montgomery Ward in Chicago.

For the eye and the ear, doors to the emotions, media of mechanical reproduction were invented. The cinema, with its unlimited possibility of reproducing an optical-psychic process, displaces the theater. The eye accommodates itself to two-dimensional representation. The adding of sound and of color aims at an increasing realism. New values are born with the new medium, and a new mode of imagination. Unfortunately, the demand for mass production caused the medium to be used along the path of least resistance, to the debasement of public taste.

For the reproduction of sound through space even greater potentialities were opened. More than any other medium, the radio acceded to power in the time of full mechanization, influencing every aspect of life. Now music is mechanized in its full tonal range. The phonograph, originating in the eighteenth century, was but a forerunner of this mechanization. Its refinement occurred parallel to the introduction of the radio. As sound was added to the moving picture, so sight was added to radio — television.

To close the circle, transportation breaks into intimate living. Transportation was one of the favorite objects of nineteenth-century mechanization. But the locomotive is a neutral vehicle. The automobile is a personal appurtenance which comes to be understood as a movable part of the household: one the American is least willing to give up. With the exaggeration permitted to a moral critic, John Steinbeck remarks, in 1944, that most of the children 'were conceived in Model-T Fords and not a few were born in them. The theory of the Anglo-Saxon home became so warped that it never quite recovered.' [16]

At all events, the highway network was adapted to the automobile in the decades between the World Wars. The automobile is a harbinger of full mechanization. Its mass production began in the second decade, but took decisive effect only at the beginning of full mechanization. First concrete highways, later parkways, made cruising so effortless that one is led to drive for driving's sake, to overcome one's inner restlessness, or to escape from oneself by depressing the gas pedal. This trend can be observed everywhere, but nowhere so strongly as in America. In the land where in the 1840's Henry Thoreau profoundly but unsentimentally described the life of the tramper, based on the close contact of man with nature, the automobile has almost crowded out the pedestrian. Walking, relaxation for its own sake, because the body demands it, or because the brain requires a pause in which to recuperate, is increasingly eliminated by the motor-car.

To investigate the sociological implications of the automobile or the psychic

---

[16] John Steinbeck, *Cannery Row*, New York, 1944.

effects of the radio and cinema is an inviting task. But such research pertains to fields other than ours and demands the teamwork of many disciplines.

In the time of full mechanization still newer developments set in, whose drift and implications cannot be foreseen. It is no longer replacement of the human hand by the machine, but of intervention into the substance of organic as well as of inorganic nature.

In the inorganic, it is the exploration of the structure of the atom and its use for as yet unknown ends.

One sphere is already taking clearer shape: one that intervenes directly into organic substance. Here the demand for production delves into the springs of life, controls generation and procreation, influences growth, alters structure and species. Death, generation, birth, habitat undergo rationalization, as in the later phases of the assembly line. The host of unknowns that these processes involve makes uneasiness hard to dispel. Organic substance or inorganic, it is experimentation with the very roots of being.

What occurs in art in this period gives the most intimate insight regarding how deeply mechanization penetrated man's inner existence. The revealing selection in Alfred Barr's 'Cubism and Abstract Art' (N. Y., 1936) tells in what different ways the seismographic artist responded to the beginning of full mechanization. At this point we can no more than give a few hints of the many-sidedness of this perception.

Mechanization has penetrated down to the artist's subconsciousness. The dream Giorgio de Chirico reports his most obsessive (1924) intermingles the image of his father with the daemonic strength of the machine: 'I struggle in vain with the man whose eyes are suspicious and very gentle. Each time I grasp him, he frees himself by quietly spreading his arms . . . like those gigantic cranes. . . .' (J. Thrall Soby, *G. de Chirico.*)

The same anxiety and loneliness pervade the melancholic architectures of his early period and his tragic mechanical dolls, portrayed in every detail, yet disquietingly taken to bits.

On the other hand there are Léger's large canvasses, around 1920, building the city's image out of signs, signals, mechanical fragments. There are Russians and Hungarians, themselves far from mechanization, yet inspired by its creative power.

In the hands of Marcel Duchamp and others, machines, these marvels of efficiency, are transformed into irrational objects, laden with irony, while introducing a new aesthetic language. The artists resort to elements such as machines, mechanisms, and ready-made articles as some of the few true products of the period, to liberate themselves from the rotten art of the ruling taste.

PART III MEANS OF MECHANIZATION

21. Serial Production by Handicraft Workers in the Eighteenth Century: The Art of Converting Red Copper. 1764. *This engraving entitled 'The Artisans at Work' is from the* Descriptions des arts et métiers, *one of our most valuable sources for eighteenth-century mechanization. The large flat trip hammers beat with varying force and speed as the volume of water falling on the wheel is greater or less. Artisans shape the metal into strips, plates, or vessels.* (*Duhamel du Monceau,* L'Art de convertir le cuivre rouge. Descriptions des arts et métiers, *vol. V, pl. X, Paris,* 1764)

THE HAND

Beyond enumeration are the domains of mechanization and all the techniques that have gone to build up the life we know today. But the method that forms the basis of all mechanization is amazingly simple.

The human hand is a prehensile tool, a grasping instrument. It can seize, hold, press, pull, mold with ease. It can search and feel. Flexibility and articulation are its key words.

The triple-articulated fingers, the wrist, the elbow, the shoulders, and, on occasion, the trunk and legs heighten the flexibility and adaptability of the hand. Muscles and tendons determine how it will seize and hold the object. Its sensitive skin feels and recognizes materials. The eye steers its movement. But vital to all this integrated work is the mind that governs and the feelings that lend it life. The kneading of bread; the folding of a cloth; the moving of brush over canvas: each movement has its root in the mind. For all the complicated tasks to which this organic tool may rise, to one thing it is poorly suited: automatization. In its very way of performing movement, the hand is ill-fitted to work with mathematical precision and without pause. Each movement depends on an order that the brain must constantly repeat. It wholly contradicts the organic, based on growth and change, to suffer automatization.

Frank W. Gilbreth, the master of motion studies, who probed so deeply the nature of manual activity, stresses once again in his last essay, *A Fourth Dimension for Measuring Skill* (1924), that no movement can exactly repeat another.

The hand can be trained to a degree of automatic facility. But one power is denied it: to remain unvaryingly active. It must always be grasping, holding, manipulating. It cannot continue a movement in endless rotation. That is precisely what mechanization entails: endless rotation. The difference between walking and rolling, between the legs and the wheel, is basic to all mechanization.

STANDARDIZATION AND INTERCHANGEABILITY

THE first phase of mechanization consists in transforming the pushing, pulling, pressing of the hand into continuous rotation. The second phase concerns the means of mechanization: By what procedures are objects to be mechanically reproduced? As early as the first decades of the nineteenth century, mechanical reproduction was effectuated in diverse ways, by stamping, pressing, embossing, and other methods, as described, for instance, by Charles Babbage, 1832, or

22. Serial Production in the Second Half of the Nineteenth Century: Wholesale Grange Supply House, Chicago. 1878. *Hat and clothing parts cut by mass production methods are stacked on the tables. 'In front is one of our salesmen showing Buffalo Robes. Today America excels in mass-production clothing, especially in cheap and sturdy work clothes made from a minimum number of pieces. These had their beginning in the nineteenth-century endeavor to create satisfactory work clothes.* (*Montgomery Ward*)

23. Early Use of the Hydraulic Press and Large Dies: Forming Halves of Metal Lifeboats. 1850. *Joseph Bramah invented the hydraulic press about* 1796. *As mechanization advanced, stamping, pressing, and embossing became more and more prominent — from cheap interior adornment in the 1830's to the pressing of whole automobile bodies in Detroit about* 1920.

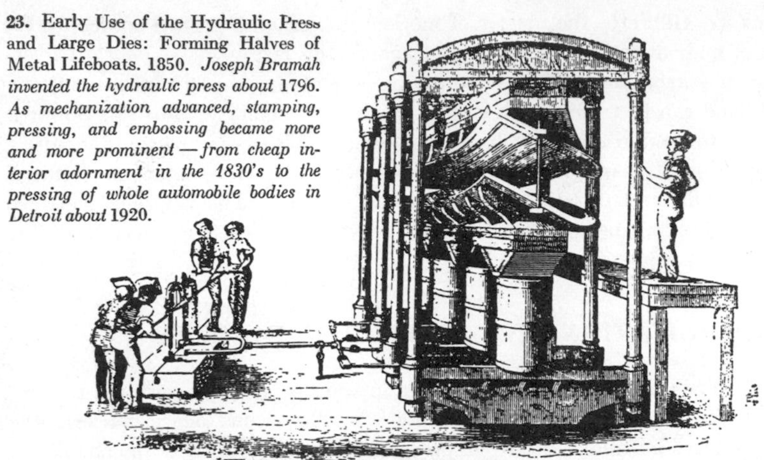

HYDRAULIC PRESS.

The engraving of the Hydraulic Press, is to give the reader some idea of the method of construction. Sheets of Galvanized Iron are laid between the enormous dies, grooved to fit each other, one of which rests upon the Cylinder, and which when brought together by the Hydraulic Pressure of *eight hundred tons*, corrugates the Iron, which gives it great strength, and at the same time the shape and curve of the Boat; the sheets are then riveted together, and finished with the usual gunwale, &c.,

by Peter Barlow, 1836. Dies become of growing importance: from the stamping of coins (fig. 200) to the pressing of metal lifeboat halves, achieved around 1850 (fig. 23). 'Sheets of galvanized iron are laid between enormous dies, grooved to fit each other.' This procedure was not exploited on a grand scale until the time of full mechanization, in the automobile industry. Side by side with the differentiation and reshaping of age-old tools, a simultaneous transformation

24. Interchangeable Parts: Replaceable Saw-teeth. 1852. *A California saw mill superintendent 'realized while engaged in his work how very great are the objections to the use of solid-tooth saws in districts remote from saw factories . . . Circular saws with inserted teeth will do more work with less expense.'* (Manufacturer and Builder, *New York, January* 1869)

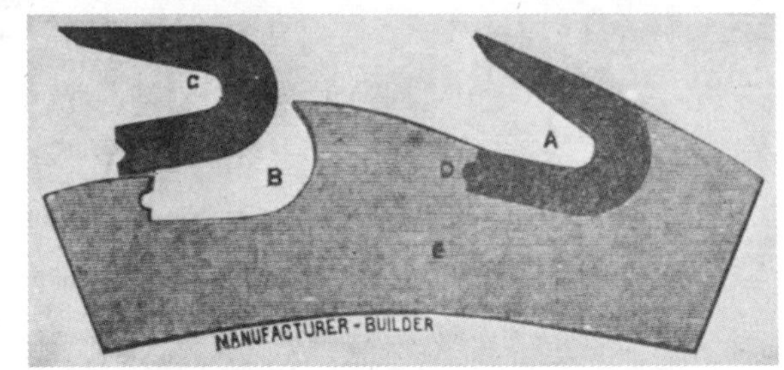

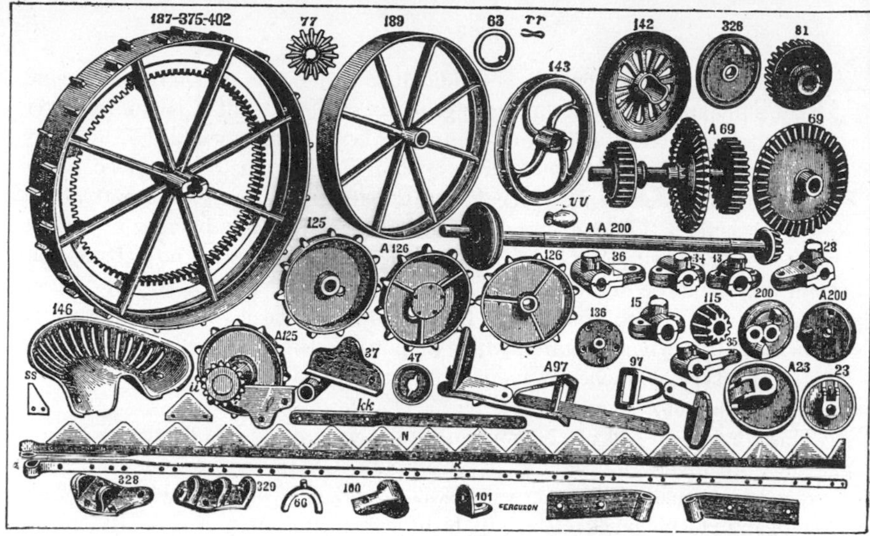

25. Early Use of Interchangeable Parts for Large Machines: Reaper Parts, 1867. *Interchangeable parts for small articles — pistols, guns, clocks — had been in use since the beginning of the nineteenth century. But the now rare catalogue of Walter A. Wood, the enterprising designer of agricultural machines, Hoosick Falls, N. Y., shows a broad range of replaceable parts half a century before Henry Ford brought standardization to the automobile industry.* (*Courtesy McCormick Historical Society, Chicago*)

occurred in their production: It was by dies that hammers, axes (fig. 71), saws, scythes [1] were given their shapes.

Pressing, stamping, casting result in standardization and, closely connected therewith, the interchangeability of parts. Of the early beginnings some facts and fragments are generally known. Eli Whitney, inventor of the cotton gin, is held the first to have introduced interchangeability of parts in gun manufacture at his Whitneyville factory; Simeon North, the pistol maker who had his workshop in near-by Middletown (Conn.), worked on the same principle. That is, the idea was in the air. In France, Thomas Jefferson in an often-quoted letter observed that a mechanic was manufacturing guns from interchangeable parts (1782). We have but scanty knowledge, however, about what late eighteenth-century France accomplished in this sphere, and systematic research is still needed. The machines that Brunel invented or combined with existing ones for the production of pulley blocks based on standardization and interchangeability are described and illustrated in full detail in the early nineteenth-century editions of the *Encyclopaedia Britannica.*

[1] This concomitance of new form with new production methods can be established from the thirties on. The only example we show here is a scythe blade invented in 1834 (fig. 73).

America, for reasons that are not difficult to understand, was a fertile ground for the standardization and interchangeability of parts. But it is still a matter of small dimensions even in mid-century, when clocks assembled from interchangeable parts were manufactured by the Waltham factory. Skilled workmanship was needed for clock repair and the interchanging of clock parts.

Proposals for the interchangeability of larger parts were advanced in various spheres at the beginning of the 'fifties. The idea of saws with interchangeable teeth (fig. 24) arose in a California sawmill extremely remote from any factory where damaged teeth could have been repaired. The inventor subsequently returned to the Atlantic States, where he put his idea into practice.[2] A circular saw of this type, 80 inches in diameter, was exhibited at the Paris International Exhibition of 1867.

This whole field will not be gone into further here, for mainly technical procedures are involved. Besides, to investigate it with the necessary precision demands interrelated research, which will doubtless be accomplished only when American industry has overcome its historical bashfulness.

Only one point need be touched upon here: Interchangeability becomes an interesting question as soon as it is applied to larger machines, and when interchange can be performed independently of skilled labor. One of the very rare catalogues from the 'sixties, the *Circular for the Year* 1867 of the most elegant constructor of agricultural machinery, Walter A. Wood, Hoosick Falls, N. Y.,[3] publishes six 'diagrams of parts' (fig. 25) for his mower and Handrake Reaper, each part being illustrated and numbered, so that the farmer need only write for the necessary part by number. From the first, the mechanically minded farmer was accustomed to assemble the machines himself. McCormick, for instance, sent out his reaper in four numbered crates.

So far as we can yet ascertain, Walter A. Wood, whose name we shall again encounter, was the first to institute the interchanging without technical help of parts for large machines. This catalogue of 1867 gives more space to the representation of interchangeable parts than to the machines themselves. This was half a century before Henry Ford in the automobile industry familiarized the broader public with the same principle.

As we soon shall see, the advent of interchangeable parts for the larger machines and the elimination of skilled labor fall within the same period as the beginnings of the modern assembly line in the meat packing industry.

---

[2] *American Manufacturer and Builder*, New York, Jan. 1869.

[3] The Walter A. Wood Mowing and Reaping Machine Company, Hoosick Falls, New York, *Circular for the Year* 1867, Albany, 1867.

MECHANIZATION OF A COMPLICATED CRAFT

The Craft of the Locksmith

For some centuries after the late Gothic period, the locksmith was known as the artisan of a most elaborate handicraft. He united mastery of hand with the gift of untiring inventiveness. His work included, besides locks, all sorts of artistically wrought ironwork: gates, grilles, knobs, handles, and the fantastic iron ornamentation of chests.

The Gothic period was very sparing of bodily comfort but felt strongly that imagination should animate the objects of man's surroundings. The woodwork of a door is rough and not highly finished; the craftsman spent all his pains on the sensitive area of the door: the keyhole. He framed it with delicate ornamentation as if he were illuminating a manuscript. And the handle that draws the latch he transformed into an abstract serpentine shape ending in an animal head, as in the lock from a house at Visp, Switzerland (fig. 26). Later, in the eighteenth century, the last period of refined handicraft, craftsmen turned their energy to the creation of large-scale works like the wrought-iron grilles, screening choir from nave in monastery churches, surrounding parks, or forming the gates of public squares. They wove transparent iron veils before the altar or the park. In one case the artist-locksmith binds into the architectonic space his high iron structure, the water curtains of the sculptured fountains, and the green beyond.[1]

The development of this artistry ran parallel with the achievement of eighteenth-century furniture and comfort beginning with the last years of Louis XIV and the Regency.[2]

Louis Sébastien Mercier, the remarkable critic of the end of the *Ancien Régime*, was one of the first to see a city from a sociologist's point of view. It has been said that he described the cellar and the attic but forgot the salon. When he comes to the refined handicraft, the critic is carried away. Mercier describes with the directness of a contemporary the high standard of craftsmanship a few years before the French Revolution: 'Our smith has become an artist. Art has so wrought the metal as to fuse it with architecture; it has been developed into superb grilles which have the advantage of enhancing the view without

---

[1] It was Jean Lamour (1698–1771) who accomplished this in Nancy, when he adorned the three most elaborate squares of the late Baroque. In one of them, the Place Stanislas (1751–5), he spans the open side between two of its corners with hovering iron grilles. (Cf. Lamour, *Recueil des ouvrages de serrurerie sur la Place Royale de Nancy*, Paris, 1767.)

[2] Cf. the work of the master locksmith, Louis Fordrin, *Nouveau livre de serrurerie*, Paris, 1723, reprinted in facsimile by A. de Champeaux, Paris, 1891. Especially interesting are plates 19, 23, 27, depicting the various parts of great church grilles.

destroying it. Iron has become as supple as wood. It is twisted at will and changed into light and mobile leaves; its coarseness removed, it is animated with a sort of life.'

But it all died out as the Industrial Revolution set in. What the smith had formerly forged by hand out of iron was then entrusted to the mold. Between 1825 and 1845, as observed in the report of the jury of the Paris International Exhibition of 1867, the highly skilled smiths disappeared from the big cities. Grilles, railings, and balconies had come to be made of cast iron. By the time of Haussmann's transformation of Paris under the Second Empire, large firms had sprung up, offering stocks of cast-iron pieces, from the continuous balconies of the boulevards to cast-iron copies of Michelangelo's sculpture. Their catalogues were like textbooks of art history, and expanded to three or four hundred pages.

But we shall not deal further here with this aspect of mechanization in the locksmith's trade. It was unfruitful from the historical point of view, for it followed the easy way of mechanization, the sole aim of which is to make copies as cheaply as possible. Mechanization in the locksmith's sphere is of historical interest only when it chooses the hard way: when it is achieved by creating new methods and new aims. There is no creativeness in the mechanical production of cast-iron grilles and ornaments.

To gain an insight into the real nature of mechanization we shall have to confine ourselves to the lock. Nowhere else in this respect did the transition from handicraft to mechanical production take place with such speed and efficiency as in the United States. The steps in this change occurred during the two decades from 1830 to 1850, decades of outstanding importance in the formation of American industry's distinctive features. At first, the European practice of using wrought iron for the various parts of the lock was followed in America, but almost from the beginning a differentiation began by the substitution of 'cast material in place of wrought. . . . This change of material greatly reduced the cost of production, and soon led to changes in design. . . .'[3]

From Handicraft to Mechanical Production

The change from manual to mechanized production has another starting point as well — in bank and safe locks. Out of experience in the construction of these expensive locks, costing from \$100 to \$400, there evolved in the 'sixties of the last century a new type of efficient and inexpensive mechanized locks. From the late eighteenth century onward, the problem of the burglar-proof lock

[3] Henry R. Towne, *Locks and Builders Hardware, a Hand Book for Architects*, New York, 1904, p.39.

→

26. Late Gothic Lock of a House at Visp, Switzerland. *The woodwork is relatively rough. The craftsman spent his care in accentuating with iron work the significant part of the door, the keyhole.*

27. Watercolor Sketch for a Fireproof Safe Advertisement. Early 1850's. *Removing documents after a fire. A rare specimen preserved in the Bella C. Landauer Collection, New-York Historical Society.*

fascinated the minds of inventors almost as much as did the solution of the revolving-pistol problem in the late 'thirties, when the most extravagant solutions were proposed for the automatic change of bullets.

Of the multitude of answers offered for the lock problem, we shall isolate one which was developed by Linus Yale, Jr. It came about with the great flood of inventions of the 'sixties, and may stand as a symbol of the transition to mechanical production in lockmaking. Minor details of Yale's lock have changed with time, but, as far as the principle is concerned, his final solution of the lock problem was found from the beginning.

We are choosing this lock for discussion because in it the principle of the handmade lock is completely changed. It translates ancient as well as recent traditions into terms of elaborate mechanical production.

This interplay of things stemming from Antiquity with more recent developments has a counterpart in the art of our day. The direct expressions of quite diverse periods, from caveman painting to African Negro sculpture, has helped modern artists find a pathway to our own subconscious life.

28. Herring's Fireproof Safe. Advertisement, 1855. *Demonstrating his safe at the London Exhibition of* 1851, *the patentee locked a thousand dollars in gold in it and challenged all the picklocks of the world to help themselves to the money. No one succeeded.*

The Early Stage: The Safe and Burglar-Proof Bank Locks

The history of the pin-tumbler cylinder lock, known as the 'Yale lock,' [4] is closely bound up with the creation of safes and safe locks for preserving valuables from fire and theft.

Cast-iron chests for common purposes were made in England about 1780, when cast-iron was first being used in columns and even in coffins. The first portable fireproof chests were constructed in France around 1820. Their walls consisted of two iron plates with a layer of heat-resistant material between them.[5] Before long they were introduced into the United States.

In the late 'twenties and the early 'thirties, the Americans tried to improve the construction of the safe and the insulating material of its walls.

Its first success was registered in the early 'thirties on the occasion of a big fire; the public was greatly impressed to see a safe that had survived, with its contents unharmed, the gutting of a building. They spontaneously dubbed it the 'Salamander,' [6] but its official name was at first 'fireproof' (as in the Philadelphia Directory of 1838) and later, in the 'fifties, 'iron-safe' (figs. 27, 28).

[4] 'Pin-tumbler cylinder lock' is the technical name for Linus Yale's lock, but outside of specialists nobody calls it thus.

[5] Even in the 'thirties this French safe was not very different from the ancient chests closed with a lid. Several examples of these will be found in: *Musée industriel, description complète de l'exposition des produits de l'industrie française en* 1834, Paris, 1838.

[6] *One Hundred Years of Progress*, Hartford, 1871, p.396.

It was in the 'fifties that the fireproof safe reached its standard form. Widely advertised as an excellent American product, it spread from banks, insurance companies, and factories into the ordinary store and private house. But some wonderment even then, it seems, clung to the idea of a catastrophe-resistant container.

Wood's store in this place has been consumed by fire last night. . . . The heat melted the hinges of the doors, a smoke of heat was coming out of the safe containing all our books and money . . . a crowd gathered around to see it opened . . . but to their astonishment every book, paper and the money came out perfect as far as the paper and the writing was concerned.[7]

The development of the fireproof safe and of bank locks coincides with the rise of industry, large-scale banking and finance, the growth of the stock exchange, expanding wealth, the multiplication of fortunes. As the first opulent residences were being built along Regent's Park in London for the anonymous rising class established around 1825 through the development of industry and trade,[8] fireproof chests and burglar-proof locks were at hand.

The Refinement of the Bank Lock

On the technical side, the mechanized lock of Linus Yale has its roots in the complicated mechanism of burglar-proof bank locks.

The French excelled in everything connected with refined handicrafts, from furniture and painting — the highest skill of the human hand — to amazingly cunning automatons.

The lock, as normally used since the fifteenth century, keeps the door closed by means of a bolt held fast by a spring. The key, passed through the keyhole, directly acts with its winged end on the bolt so that by twisting the key one moves the bolt that locks or unlocks the door. Its principle is that the bit of the key acts directly, without any intermediary, on the bolt.

The eighteenth century made locks more complicated by inserting, between key and bolt, a set of movable plates on pivots. These parallel plates had to be aligned by the key before they would allow the bolt to be shot.

Soon, still in the eighteenth century, England took the lead, keeping it well into the middle of the nineteenth, when the United States came to the fore. The English developed still more complicated interplay between tumbler and bolt, providing the key end tumbler with slits and notches.[9]

---

[7] *Herring's Fireproof Safe.* Interesting and important information respecting the preservation of books, papers, etc., New York, 1854, p.36.

[8] S. Giedion, *Space, Time and Architecture*, Cambridge, 1941, pp.460ff.

[9] The Barron lock, 1778, forerunner of modern bank locks.

29. The Elder Yale's Door Lock, Patented 1844. *The door lock of the elder Yale represents a transition from the complicated bank lock to the simple mechanized door lock of Linus Yale Jr. Its four tumblers are packed radially around the movable cylinder pierced with holes to take them. Each of the tumblers (still called pistons) is composed of two pieces that springs (G) keep pressed toward the center. The key, which moves the tumblers outward, is cylindrical in shape, and in many ways resembles Bramah's key. It acts on the 'pistons' (D,F) much as Bramah's key acted on his 'sliders.'*

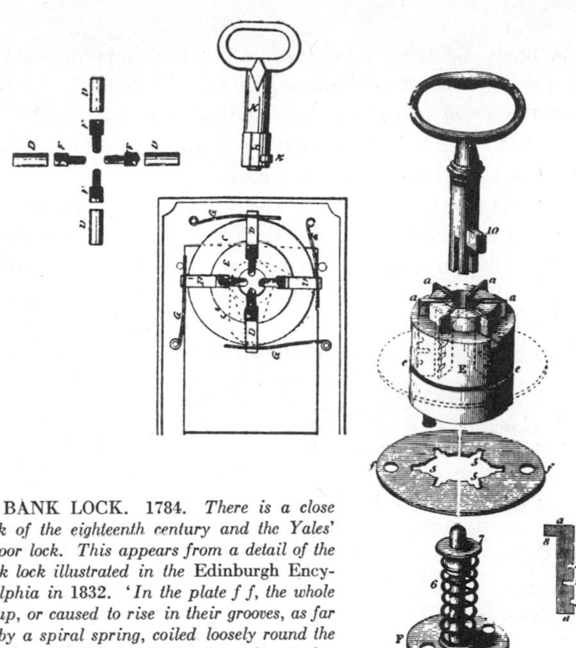

30. JOSEPH BRAMAH'S BANK LOCK. 1784. *There is a close relation between the bank lock of the eighteenth century and the Yales' solutions for the mechanized door lock. This appears from a detail of the famous eighteenth-century bank lock illustrated in the* Edinburgh Encyclopedia *published at Philadelphia in* 1832. *'In the plate f f, the whole number of sliders are pressed up, or caused to rise in their grooves, as far as the top of the Cylinder E, by a spiral spring, coiled loosely round the pin, b. The first locks were made with a separate and independent spring to each slider; but it is a very great improvement, the introduction of one common spring to raise up the whole number.'*

The lock (invented 1784) that is connected with the name of Joseph Bramah, inventor of the hydraulic press became *the* burglar-proof lock of its period, and its fame lasted throughout the first half of the nineteenth century (fig. 30). Its principle is that of the earlier locks, but the interior arrangement is entirely altered. It already anticipates the bank lock in the way, for instance, that the tumblers are circularly packed around the key, thus solving the problem of the safe lock before the safe actually existed. And although Bramah's lock was at last picked at the great Exhibition of 1851 in London, it yielded only to hard work such as could not be hurriedly performed.

It was a Mr. A. G. Hobbs of New York who won the two-hundred guineas the manufacturers of Bramah's lock had put up for anyone who could manage to pick it. Hobbs, who according to his boast 'could pick any lock in England in a few minutes,' had distinguished himself by picking another famous lock after a brief struggle. But Bramah's lock fully occupied him for nearly a month, from 24 July to 23 August, when he finally succeeded. Hobbs thus proved that 'any lock which leaves its tumblers exposed to sight or feeling through the keyhole can be opened.'

Hobbs's theatrical procedure was at the same time a brilliant advertisement for the lock he was exhibiting for Day & Newell, New York (fig. 31), which won the Prize Medal at the London Exhibition. This was the 'Parautoptic lock,' for which his firm offered a reward of two-hundred guineas to anyone who could pick it. But no one succeeded.

A. G. Hobbs had invented a way of fastening glass doorknobs into their sockets. But first and foremost he was the crack salesman of Day & Newell, New York, and had become most dexterous in picking rival manufacturers' locks to sell those of his own firm. Day & Newell's 'Parautoptic lock' ('parautoptic' meant preventing internal inspection) had come into use in America in the mid-'forties and was also known in Europe before the London Exhibition of 1851.[10]

[10] *Report of the National Mechanics Institute of Lower Austria on Newell's Parautoptic Combination Lock*, Awarding the Institute's Diploma and Gold Medal, New York, 1848. The Newell, or parautoptic, lock was first manufactured in 1836.

31. American Bank Lock: Day and Newell's 'Parautoptic Lock,' 1851. *Introduced in America in the* 1840's, *it was indeed the champion of the day, 'from which no impressions could be taken.' Its salesman, A. C. Hobbs, became famous by picking Bramah's lock during the Great London Exhibition of* 1851. *A few years later* (1856) *the Champion Parautoptic was in turn picked by Linus Yale, Jr., who claims to have cut a wooden key for it 'solely by inspection through the keyhole.' Note the free yet sensitive typography of this advertisement of the* 1850's.

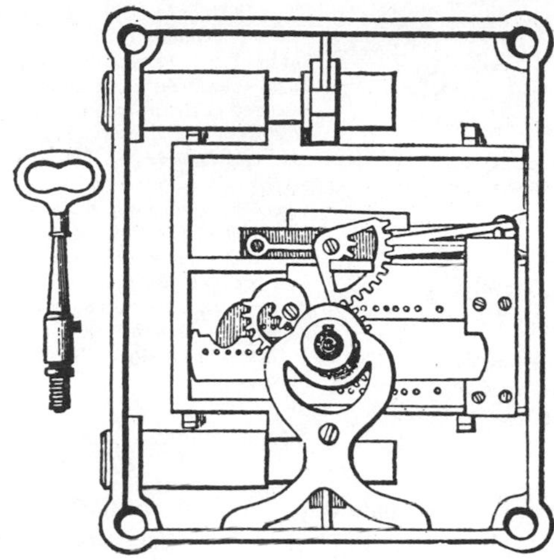

32. LINUS YALE, JR.: The Magic Infallible Bank Lock. *Linus Yale, Jr. reduced the key to a compact minimum, completely filling the keyhole. From the keyhole the bits were carried to a remote part of the lock to act upon the tumblers.*

It had a key made up of mobile combination parts. According to Newell's report, the owner 'can with the greatest facility change at pleasure the interior arrangement of his lock at every moment simply by altering the arrangement of the bits in the key.' The report continues: 'No impression of the lock can be taken, not even by the maker himself. . . . It has triumphantly resisted all efforts of the most skillful and ingenious to open it.' [11] And in truth it was, as Day & Newell advertised, the 'Champion Bank Lock' of its day.

Hobbs's success in London was complete, and soon English banks were installing American locks. Suddenly American products were coming to the fore. The Colt Revolver, Goodyear's rubber products, and American tool-making machinery were among those introduced at the Great Exhibition to an astonished European public.

Linus Yale's Bank Locks

In Philadelphia, in the mid-'fifties, there lived a young locksmith, a native of New England, Linus Yale, Jr. During these years in Philadelphia (1855–61), he made a name for himself with his burglar-proof devices. Linus Yale, Jr. did not agree at all with Mr. Hobbs's assertion that 'no impressions can be taken, not even by the maker himself.' He 'saw a defect which he thought a vital

[11] Ibid. pp.8 and 18.

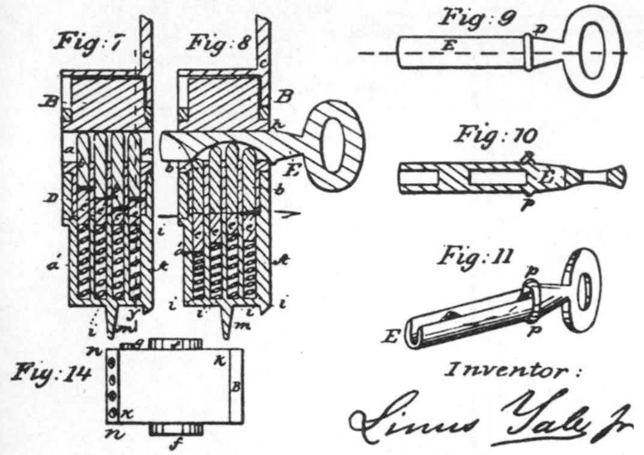

33. LINUS YALE, JR.: First Pin-tumbler Cylinder Lock. Patented 1861. *The basic ideas of the pin-tumbler cylinder lock are fully developed in the first patent: tumblers aligned one behind another in a single row; and lock divided into a fixed cylindrical lock-case (escutcheon) and a smaller, eccentrically placed cylinder (plug). The pin chambers are formed by corresponding holes in the lock case and in the plug. To align the tumblers, however, Yale still uses a round key inserted groove downward in the traditional way.* (*U. S. Patent,* 29 *January* 1861)

error,'[12] and after some trials he opened one parautoptic lock after another with ease. 'The method for picking the best parautoptic lock,' so he assures, 'is so exceedingly simple that any smart lad can make a wooden key which will open these locks and re-lock them again.'[13] Yale's own booklet gives many accounts by different bankers showing how Yale proceeded. One of these affords some insight into the situation: A New York banker, whose Day & Newell lock — popularly called Hobbs's lock — had been picked, writes on 12 January 1856:

> Mr. Yale picked my ten-tumbler lock, the finest of its kind, for which I paid three hundred dollars . . . he cut a wooden key solely from inspection of the lock through the key-hole, which turned the bolt back as readily as my key would have done. And then, to complete my discomfiture, he cut away one bit of his wooden key and locked it so that I could never have un-locked it with my own key.[14]

In 1851, the year Mr. Hobbs carried off his greatest success by opening the famous bank locks of England, Linus Yale constructed a bank lock to which he gave a new name: the 'Infallible Bank Lock' or the 'Magic Lock.' Indeed, one cannot deny that there was something magical about it.

The key for this lock, in contrast to the complicated winged keys, was extremely simple. At first glance it looked rather like a clock winder or a sardine-can opener (fig. 32). It consisted of a round shank terminating in a smaller,

---

[12] *A Dissertation on Locks and Lock-picking* and the principles of burglar proofing showing the advantages attending the use of the magic infallible bank lock . . . invented by Linus Yale, Jr., Philadelphia, 1856.

[13] Ibid. p.16.

[14] Ibid.

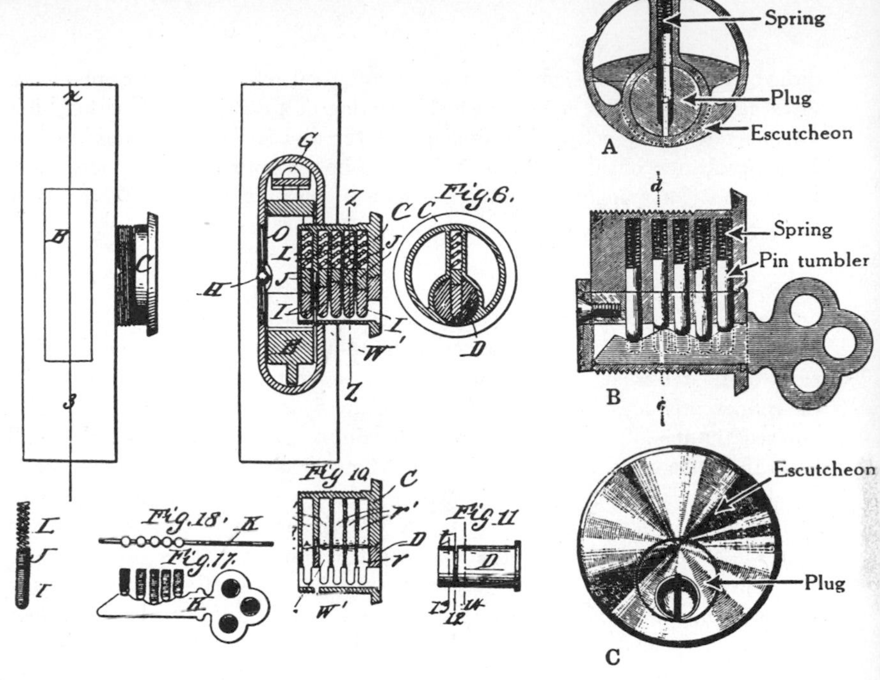

34. LINUS YALE, JR.: Second Pin-tumbler Cylinder Lock. Patented 1865. *Minor changes apart, Yale's lock has reached its final stage. The key is 'a thin slip of steel properly shaped to bring the lines of division between the tumblers into the same line.'* (*U. S. Patent, 27 June* 1865)

35. Yale Lock, 1889. (*A*) *Transverse section taken through one of the pinholes.* (*B*) *Longitudinal section. The key is shown in the plug raising up the pins, or tumblers, to the height where the cut in the pins is flush with the division of plug and tumbler case, leaving the plug free to revolve.* (*C*) *Front view showing keyhole and plug.* (*Yale and Towne Manufacturing Company Catalogue* #12, 1889)

more elaborate cylinder. Once this little instrument was inserted into the keyhole, which it completely filled, its smaller end was taken up by a pin. 'A set of wheels carried the bits — which formed the small end — to a remote part of the lock out of any possible reach of picking tools, where it acted on the tumblers and opened the bolt. This done, they were carried back automatically to the handle or shank.'

Linus Yale now announced a prize of $3000 to anyone who would pick his 'magic infallible bank lock.' Mr. Hobbs never won it.

Linus Yale himself was not completely satisfied with his lock. He finally declared that any lock based on a key and keyhole is in ultimate danger of being picked. He reached the solution of using no key at all. His 'dial combination locks' had two handles or knobs which, meeting in a certain combination, shot a number of heavy bolts. The principle of the dial lock was not unknown to former centuries, but it was Linus Yale, Jr., who made this primitive idea function as part of a highly complex mechanism, opening the way for all later developments.

Linus Yale's Invention

These intricate bank locks do not yield the necessary insight into the change from manual to mechanical production in the sphere of the locksmith. The parts of their complex mechanisms are almost entirely handmade. They are the refined product of elaborate craftsmanship, *haute serrurerie*. What revolutionized the manufacture of locks was the simple familiar door lock that still bears the name of its inventor, Yale. The change that concerns us is not one of merely producing by machine the parts that formerly had been made by hand. The interesting thing, in this case, is the transformation of the whole interior organism of the lock, from its technical construction down to its key.

It is not easy for man to leave the beaten track: to do so often means breaking so deeply rooted a habit as opening or closing his desk drawer or his front door in a customary way. Yet this was the very change wrought by Linus Yale, Jr., with his pin-tumbler cylinder lock. Save for the specialists, few know the device by its technical name; rather, it has been indiscriminately and simply called 'Yale lock.' Nevertheless its use spread slowly. It is not mentioned in Pitt-Rivers' excellent book, *On the Development and Distribution of Primitive Locks and Keys*, published in London in 1883. In Europe, this lock has come into general use only in the course of the last two decades, even in countries having, like Switzerland, a high standard of living. Presumably the introduction of American automobiles in Europe is connected with the spread of the lock on the Continent. Linus Yale's bank lock of 1851, on the other hand, became known in England soon after it was invented.

Linus Yale, Jr., was born in 1821 in Salisbury, Conn., where his father kept a locksmith's shop. Young Yale was reared in the atmosphere of lockmaking and invention, then breathed everywhere in the northeastern United States. We know but little concerning his brief life.[15] He died of heart failure suddenly, at the age of 47, while away on business in New York in the Christmas of 1868. His financial position seems never to have been rosy. In July 1868, six months before his death, he met Henry R. Towne, and in October they organized a

[15] No study of his life has been published. The account of him in the *Encyclopedia Americana*, vol. XXIX (1940 edition), contains inaccuracies and makes no mention of his great invention.

corporation for the manufacture of locks. This has become the large enterprise known as the Yale and Towne Manufacturing Company, Stamford, Conn., whose trademark is the name 'Yale.' But Yale was fated never to see the plant where his new and mechanized door locks were to be produced by machine.

Linus Yale, Jr., was never a shrewd businessman. He was absorbed in his inventions. His attitude toward life was more akin to the spirit of Concord, of Thoreau and Emerson, than that of the brisk businessman of the latter part of the century. The few facts that we know about his life tally with the portrait we have of him. His is a small face with deep-set, inward-looking eyes. The smooth, relaxed features indicate the musician or the artist rather than the efficient manager. And indeed, Linus Yale, Jr., wanted at first to become a painter, a portrait painter. Had he been born in France, he might well have found his way to the Quartier Latin, for he certainly did not lack the rare gift of fantasy. But the most creative forces of the America of that day did not go into painting. They were moved by the urge to invent and to act in the great revolution that transformed human activity in every sphere.

Linus Yale's father [16] was already famous as a maker of bank locks. The son did not remain with him for long. Soon becoming independent, Linus, Jr., spent his most creative years in Philadelphia. Here he lived and here he had his shop from 1855 to 1861,[17] during which years he brought out most of his own bank locks. Here, too, in 1856, he submitted his 'Magic Infallible Bank Lock' for examination by the Franklin Institute's committee on science and arts. It is still on show in the Franklin Institute, bearing the autograph of its inventor.[18] Here also he conceived each of the successive designs that led him step by step to the safe lock without a keyhole — the combination lock — the principle of which is in such widespread use today. And here, finally, he invented the famous pin-tumbler cylinder lock. He filed the specification of his first patent on this lock in 1861. By this time he was known throughout the country and his firm was considered the leading one in Philadelphia.[19]

[16] The family came to Connecticut in the seventeenth century. Elihu Yale, for whom Yale University was named, was a brother of an ancestor of Linus Yale.

[17] Linus Yale, Jr., was listed in the Philadelphia Directory from 1856 to 1861. In the first year, he was entered as 'Yale, Linus Jr. — Safes'; in 1857 and 1858, as 'Yale, Linus Jr. & Co. — Safes and Locks.' From 1856 to 1859, he lived at Milestown and his shop was at various addresses on Chestnut and Walnut streets. In the last three years, 1859 to 1861, his business address was 248 North Front Street and his home was at 142 North 15th Street. I am indebted for this information to Mr. Walter A. R. Pertuch, librarian of the Franklin Institute, Philadelphia.

[18] This lock was already widely used then, as is proved by references in Linus Yale, Jr.'s *Dissertation on Locks and Lock-Picking*, Philadelphia, 1856. It was patented as No. 9,850 on 12 July 1853.

[19] Edwin T. Freedley in *Philadelphia and Its Manufactures*, 1859, p.332, speaks highly of the permutation and bank lock made by 'Mr. L. Yale Jr. and Company,' calling it the most celebrated lock of modern times.

The pin-tumbler cylinder lock invented by Linus Yale, Jr., includes the following essential parts:

First, the lock's closing mechanism — with the exception of his first patent of 1861 (fig. 33) — consists of a set of five tumblers, an arrangement that has never since been altered. The tumblers are called 'pin tumblers' because they are extremely thin when compared to the parts normally used in lockmaking. They are thin steel bars or steel wires and, for reasons we shall see presently, are in two separate sections (figs. 33, 34, 35).

Second, the case enclosing the lock as a whole — a part later called the 'shell' or 'escutcheon' — is cylindrical and can be screwed into the door. It is a hollow cylinder incorporating along its length a rib through which run five vertical holes. The holes form chambers for the pin tumblers (fig. 35). Yale himself, in his patent letter of 1865, describes the 'tumbler-case' as having 'a cylindrical bore through it.' The boring is done eccentrically.

Third, into this boring is fitted a smaller cylinder, later described as a 'plug.' This also has, in the words of Yale, 'holes bored through it in planes perpendicular to its axis.'[20] The holes in the plug correspond with those in the rib of the fixed tumbler case and prolong them. In certain circumstances, however, this second cylinder may revolve. Hence Yale's lock derived its technical name of 'cylinder lock,' distinguishing it from the lock mechanism in use since the fifteenth century.

To sum up the elements of Yale's lock, we have: the fixed cylindrical lock case, or escutcheon; the smaller, eccentrically placed cylinder, or plug (both cylinders having corresponding holes); and, fitting vertically into these holes, five round pins, each in two sections. (The upper section was later called the 'driver,' and only the lower member retained the name of 'pin.') Constantly pressing the pin tumblers downward are five small spiral springs set into the uppermost part of the holes.

Thus the pin chamber is partly in the lock case (fixed cylinder) and partly in the plug (movable smaller cylinder). The pin tumblers, under pressure from the springs, hold the lock case and plug together, just as nails running through two pieces of wood prevent them from sliding. In this position the plug is immovable. The mechanism is locked.

To unlock this mechanism, a small flat key is inserted into a narrow slit in the plug. It passes under the downward-pressing pin tumblers and raises them

[20] Specification for Patent No. 48,475, 27 June 1865.

36. FERNAND LÉGER: The Keys. Oil, *c.*1924.

to a point at which the junctures between the pin tumblers — divided as they are into two separate sections — correspond exactly with the juncture between the lock case and the plug, that is, just between the fixed and the mobile cylinders (fig. 35). When they have reached this precise point, they no longer oppose the rotation of the plug, which will now go around as one turns the key. The mechanism is unlocked.

Practically nothing remained of the ancient type of key after Yale's innovations. As Yale himself described it for the first time, in his patent letter of 1865, the key is a 'thin slip of steel properly shaped to bring the lines of division

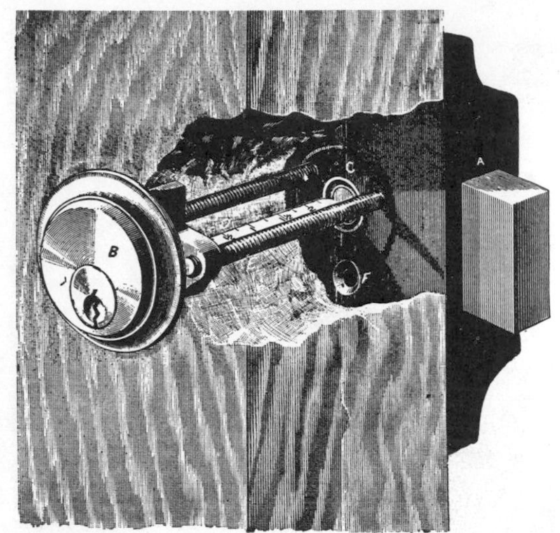

37. Yale's Lock Independent of the Door's Thickness. *The key need no longer extend through the door. Rotated by the plug, a steel bar, on which this catalogue illustration of 1889 marks the inches, passes through the thickness of the door to connect the compact lock mechanism with the heavy bolt. (Yale and Towne Manufacturing Company, Catalogue #12,* 1889)

between the tumblers into the same line.' Thus the key acts only to adjust the pin tumblers. The key's small inclined planes serving this purpose made it, in the words of a contemporary, 'resemble a worn-out saw.'

At the same time the square tang of the key, with its bits, or dentation, has disappeared. The key has become small and thin, and can be punched or stamped in a moment. Above all, its function has changed. It does not act directly on the bolt, as it had done ever since man invented the closing mechanism: it merely turns the revolving cylinder. The key is now a mere handle for that purpose.

'Prior to Yale's invention the size of the key was proportioned to the size of the lock and its length was necessarily such as to enable it to reach through the door.' [21] As Yale conceived it, however, the plug would revolve when acted upon by the key, while the bolt could be placed independently of it. Thus the door could be of any thickness, the lock and key remaining unchanged in size and uniform with all other locks and keys of the same type. This led to the universal adoption of standard locks and of standard-sized keys for doors of the most diverse kinds. The painstaking illustration in the Yale and Towne catalogue of 1889 (fig. 37) gives a glimpse into the mechanism by tearing away

[21] The Yale and Towne Manufacturing Company, Catalogue 12, 1889.

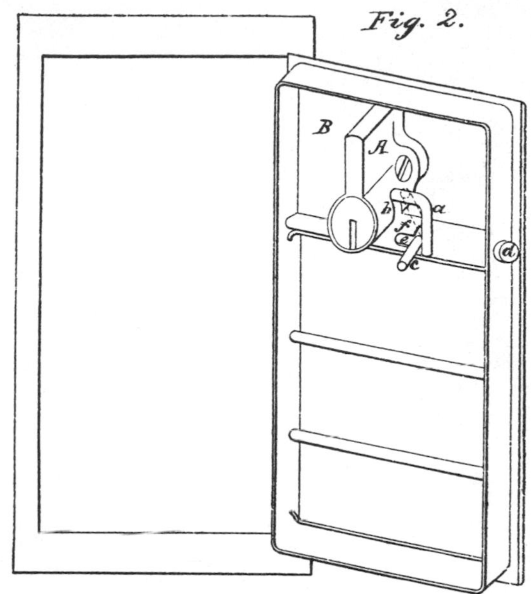

38. LINUS YALE: Lock for Post-Office Boxes. U. S. Patent, 1871. *Linus Yale foresaw the advantages of a key mechanism independent of the bolt. The arm (a) controls the remotely placed bolt (d).*

parts of the wood. It shows how a steel bar attached to the revolving plug can go right through a thick door to act at a distance on the bolt at the other side.[22] Linus Yale, Jr., foresaw this development in his second patent (1865), but in a posthumous patent issued several years after his death (fig. 38),[23] he showed in detail the ultimate advantages to be derived from the independence of the key mechanism from the bolt. Locks for post-office boxes were to be equipped in this way.

Only by stages could Yale throw off his inherited conceptions. When he brought out his first lock, he intended it as a device for cupboards and drawers, not for doors (fig. 33). He still aligned his tumblers with a round key (having a notched groove, or flute, instead of the edge of the later models), and it is interesting to note that he inserted his early key in the traditional manner, groove downward, as if it still had the tongue of ordinary keys. But in his second patent (1865), which frankly claimed to be a door lock, he boldly turned the lock case into its logical position, pins above the plug and weighing down upon it. This meant that the key had to be inserted in an unusual way, dentation

[22] Ibid.

[23] 'Improvement in Locks for Post-Office Boxes.' Patent No. 120,177, 24 Oct. 1871.

39. Iron Key, Ptolemaic Period. 5½ *inches long. From Lord Carnarvon's excavations at Drah abu'l Negga, Thebes. Yale's lock cannot have been derived from the so-called Egyptian lock, as is generally believed. This complicated key shape stems from the highly technical Ptolemaic period — third or second century* B.C. *It more closely resembles Greek than Egyptian ancestors. (Courtesy Metropolitan Museum, N. Y.)*

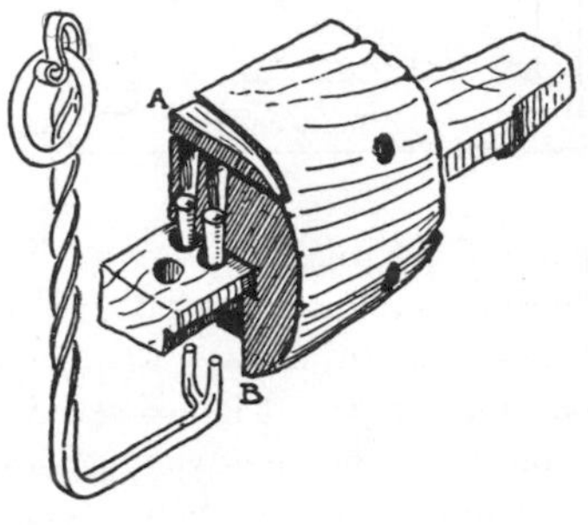

40. Sycamore Wood Lock, *c.*A.D. 800, from the Monastery of Epiphanius, at Thebes. *Over a thousand years after the Ptolemaic example, the lock's principle is unchanged. In neither case are the tumblers aligned in the direction of insertion of the key, as in the wooden key type of the Faroe Islanders or Pennsylvania Dutch, who use an altogether differently shaped key.*

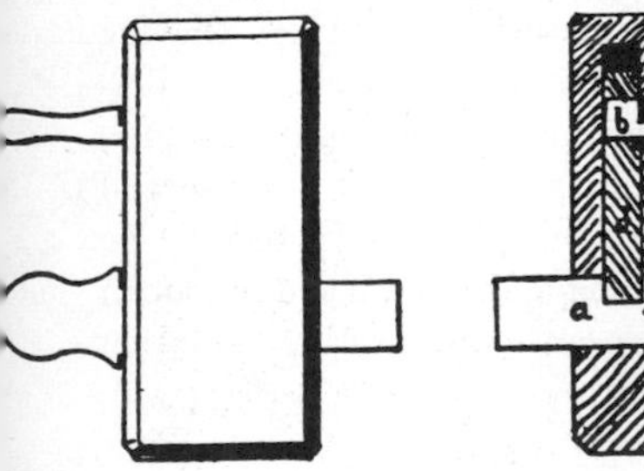

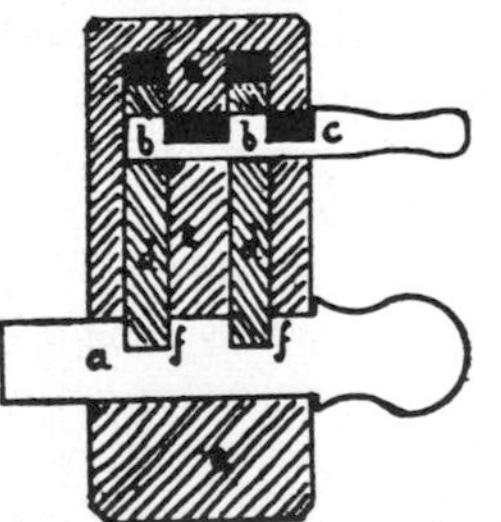

41. Wooden Two-tumbler Lock, Faroe Islands. *Profile and section. Its two tumblers (d,d) fall into holes (f,f) of the bolt (a) to block the mechanism, as in the Pennsylvania Dutch lock (opposite, top). The two locks differ but slightly: the Pennsylvanian lock lifts its key beneath the tumblers; the Faroe lock passes its key (b,b,c) through a groove higher in the lock. (Pitt-Rivers)*

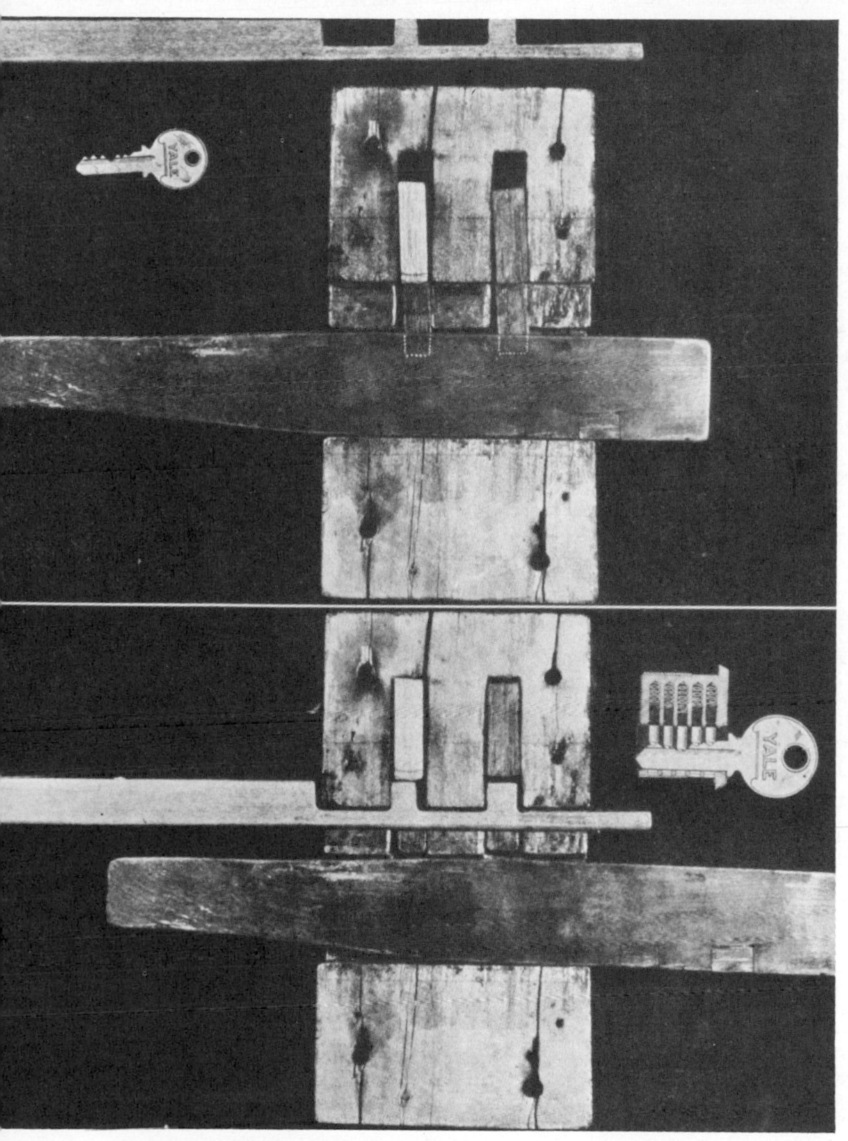

42. Pennsylvania Dutch Wooden Lock. (*Above*) *Locked, key out of lock. The two tumblers are resting in the grooves of the bolt (dotted lines), securing it as if they were nails.* (*Below*) *Unlocked, key inserted and raised, lifting the tumblers and releasing the bolt. The modern lock is shown in the same phase: the key has aligned the joints of the tumblers, allowing key and plug to rotate.*

uppermost. Thus even the manner of closing the door violated habit, for one had to turn the key in the direction opposite to that which has become instinctive.

Each part of the lock was finally conceived so as to be manufactured by machine tools. The flat key was punched or stamped by dies from the outset. The pin tumblers may have been cut by machine from the first. They were eventually manufactured by automatic screw machines, cut and shaped all in one operation. Springs were already at hand, produced by machine. Even the two cylinders, inner and outer, called for no manual intervention. Castings at first, they were later made by machine, like all the other components, automatically.

Linus Yale, the younger, shaped the lock for our time. The ingenuity with which this was done recalls a certain stage in the development of watches when, in sixteenth-century Nuremberg, clocks were reduced to pocket size by the use of springs. Linus Yale's transformation was even more radical.

How did it come about? His father, Linus Yale, patented a curious door lock in 1844 (fig. 29). Its mechanism included a cylindrical ring (*c* in the figure), 'said cylinder being pierced from the outer to the inner circumference with round apertures in which are placed cylindrical pistons.'[24] (What the elder Yale called 'pistons,' after the heavy pistons of the bank lock, became the 'pin tumblers' of his son.) These pistons, in the elder Yale's words, 'pass through said apertures and enter *corresponding apertures in a revolving cylinder*' (*E*). They are packed *radially* around the cylinder, and each piston is made in *two separate pieces*, 'said pistons being kept pressed in toward the center by springs (*G*) attached to the frame plate of the box.'[25]

This lock, conceived from the beginning as a door lock, was derived from the heavy bank locks. Even in Joseph Bramah's celebrated safe lock of 1784 (fig. 30), 'the tumblers [were] packed round the cylinder of the key . . . by springs.'[26] The related idea of a 'revolving plate pierced with a series of holes and having a pin which moved the bolt' as well as a 'series of springs each having a pin at one end'[27] was not unusual even much earlier.

The essential elements later to be used by Yale's son were already present in 1844 (fig. 29): the tumbler divided into two parts; the springs; one fixed and one revolving cylinder; and a key (*K*) without bits, acting directly to adjust

[24] Specification of Linus Yale, Sr., Patent No. 3,630, 13 June 1844.

[25] Ibid.

[26] Pitt-Rivers, op.cit. p.25.

[27] Compare, for instance, Charles Tomlinson, *Rudimentary Treatise on the Construction of Locks*, London, 1853, p.83, in which he mentions 'Stanbury's lock invented in the United States about forty years ago.'

the tumblers. The bitless key is 'a cylinder, containing as many wedge-shaped cavities or grooves (X) on its periphery as there are pistons.' [28] Does not this patent letter of 1844 read like a description of the younger Yale's achievement?

> In order to lock the bolt the key must be pushed in as far as it will go, the inclined plane of the key comes in contact with the pistons (F) and forces them back until their place of union between the two parts of the tumbler is coincident with the joint between the inner revolving cylinder and the fixed outer cylinder which can be turned now by the key.[29]

Archetypes

When the question arises where the lock of Linus Yale, Jr., came from, time and time again the reply has been, 'It came from the Egyptian lock.' Yet even the most recent excavations do not reveal much concerning the old Egyptian lock and how it developed. The so-called Egyptian lock certainly falls into the category of tumbler locks, but it lacks one essential feature of the tumbler lock of medieval times: Its tumblers are not aligned in one row; the iron pins project in various planes across the width of their horizontal holder, like the bristles of a brush. It is still used in this form in humbler Egyptian dwellings.

Howard Carter, who discovered the tomb of Tutankhamen, found some metal keys (fig. 39) in the course of Lord Carnarvon's expedition.[30] According to Carter, they date from the Ptolemaic period (323–30 B.C.). The metal is bent in the shape of an L and the pins are disposed along a sinuous line on the short arm. The lock it fitted is the product of a technically advanced period that flourished under the Ptolemies, when Egypt became the center of Greek science and invention. Actually, this is a post-Egyptian period.

More than a millennium later, the 'Egyptian lock' seems unchanged in principle: A wooden lock, its case carved from a block of sycamore wood (*c.*A.D. 800), was found by the expedition of the Metropolitan Museum, buried among the rubbish of a cell in the monastery of Epiphanius at Thebes (fig. 40). [31] It is of the same type as the lock of the Ptolemaic period, but greatly simplified. It, too, is L shaped, but its pins, although only two in number, are not aligned. To unlock, one had to raise the bolt from beneath by inserting and lifting the iron key. Since this type has persisted — it is still in use on modest dwellings

---

[28] Linus Yale, Sr., Patent Letter, 1844.

[29] Ibid.

[30] We owe this information to the kindness of Ambrose Lansing, curator of the department of Egyptian art at the Metropolitan Museum of Art, New York.

[31] Herbert E. Winlock and Walter E. Crum, *The Monastery of Epiphanius at Thebes*, New York, 1926, Part I, p.57.

in Egypt — it would seem that the medieval tumbler lock, with its tumblers lined up one behind another and with its flat notched key, originated outside Egypt. Archaeologists even doubt whether any tumbler lock originated in that land at all. Locks built on the tumbler principle (the Laconian lock) seem to have been used in Greece from the sixth century B.C. onward and to have been carried to Egypt in Greek or Roman times.[32]

Evidence in regard to where this 'Egyptian' lock originated — in Babylonia, in Egypt, or in Greece of the fifth century B.C. — yields only ambiguous interpretation.

On Babylonian cylinder seals dating as far back as the third millennium B.C., it has been noted, the Sun-God carries a jagged symbol.[33] Some archaeologists have interpreted this symbolic instrument as a saw, others as a key. It is not for laymen in the field to hazard an opinion; we shall merely point to the various interpretations and to the uncertainty of its past.

As we have seen, it cannot be traced with certainty even to Egypt. Tangible evidence begins only with the Hellenistic period, but suppositions regarding its time of origin vary within the range of a millennium.

Concerning the Greek lock of Homeric and post-Homeric periods, carefully gathered information is available.[34] Vase paintings and Attic tomb reliefs confirm the accuracy of Homer's description when Penelope unlocks the door of the chamber in which Odysseus' bow is stored, 'and took the well-bent key in her strong hand, a goodly key of bronze, whereon was a handle of ivory . . . anon she quickly loosed the strap from the handle of the door, and thrust in the key, and with a straight aim shot back the bolts.'[35]

This early Greek key was no more than a sort of bolt-rammer. The priestesses carried such a long heavy key of bronze over their shoulders. Its two **L** bends and long-shafted crank somewhat recall the handle of an automobile jack. Just as the cranked shaft must search under the car to find the jack, so the Homeric key had to pass through a hole high up in the door in order to find the bolt on the inside and ram it. Later, its sharp angles were softened into an easy **S** curve, resembling the human collar-bone, which thus gained its name of key-bone or clavicle.[36]

---

[32] Compare Daremberg and Saglio, *Dictionnaire des Antiquités grecques et romaines*, article 'Sera.'

[33] Felix von Luschan, 'Ueber Schloesser mit Fallriegel,' *Zeitschrift fuer Ethnologie*, Berlin, 1916, 48 Jahrgang, p.423.

[34] Hermann Diehls, *Antike Technik*, Berlin, 1914; cf. chapter on 'Ancient Doors and Locks,' pp.34ff., illustrated with reproduction of vase paintings and reliefs; contains a convincing reconstruction of the Homeric lock, or, as we here term it, 'bolt-rammer.'

[35] *Odyssey*, XXI, Butcher and Lang transl.

[36] Diehls, op.cit. p.40, depicts side by side key-bone and temple key. One such key of a celebrated sanctuary of Artemis of the fifth century B.C. has been retrieved.

As soon as we draw near to the appearance of the Greek tumbler locks in the fifth century, certainty again vanishes. Aristophanes' women, as has more than once been pointed out,[37] complain that the bad men have closed the larder door with the aid of a three-pronged Laconian 'secret key.' This merely indicates that the Laconian lock was a type of tumbler lock. Its three prongs and more especially its later name — 'Ballanos' or acorn lock [38] — liken it to keys belonging to the Hellenistic period found by Carter and others. This lock had cylindrical tumblers whose head, to prevent them from falling through, might be somewhat broadened in acorn shape; [39] whereas the wooden tumbler lock, which has spread almost the world over, had tumblers square of section, in no way suggestive of an acorn. It is hardly likely that the Greek tongue, with its precise and plastic figures of speech, should use the word acorn to describe a square peg.

In fifth-century Greece this type was called the 'Laconian lock,' [40] for it was from Laconia, the Greek mining center, where the metal industry flourished, that it spread to Athens and the rest of the Hellenic world.[41] To Laconia, some venture to think, its route may have been from Egypt through Ionia and the Greek Isles.[42]

The Wooden-Key Type

Of more direct interest to us here is the origin of the wooden-key type, which stacks its tumblers in aligned vertical grooves and raises them with a flat, wooden key. Ethnologists have felt that with certain locks in which the tumblers are aligned in one row a 'new moment' is reached,[43] although they do not distinguish it in principle from the so-called 'Egyptian' lock. Nevertheless, this is a distinct type, pointing to a different origin.

No real evidence is available concerning where and when it was developed. The time and country of its origin are a riddle. But certain symptoms are suggestive.

---

[37] Ibid. p.46.

[38] Ibid. *Ballanoi:* acorns. The word *ballanos* was in general use in Aristophanes' time. Cf. Joseph Fink, *Der Verschluss bei den Griechen und Roemern*, Regensburg, 1890, p.28.

[39] Padlocks of Pompeiian time having tumblers of acorn shape have been preserved. Illustrated in Daremberg and Salio, op.cit. p.1247.

[40] Fink, op.cit. pp.22–31, investigates in detail the Laconian lock.

[41] Daremberg and Salio, op.cit. p.1244, article 'Sera,' with illustrations.

[42] Even less conclusive concerning questions of origin are the specimens found today on the Greek Isles. Belonging mostly to the wooden-key type of tumbler locks, they are offshoots of a worldwide dissemination. Cf. R. M. Dawkins, 'Notes from Karpathos,' *Annals of the British School of Athens*, IX, 190ff. As Dawkins points out (p.195), there is also found there a composite type, with two keys, one of which is used to ram the bolt: 'a descendant of the Homeric lock.'

[43] Luschan, op.cit. p.409. Even if one cannot always concur with his conclusions, Luschan's exposition is of the soundest.

One is that the various specimens of the wooden-key type as it appears in the most diverse cultures and periods are strikingly alike. It can be no accident that locks of the Faroe Isles in northern Britain (fig. 41) so resemble locks from the Greek Isles or from an old Arab house on Zanzibar Island that they might have been manufactured in the same village. They must surely possess a common ancestor. They must be traceable to an archetype other than the bent metal-key type or the so-called 'Egyptian' lock, whose bent key with its complicated arrangement of prongs is the product of a differentiated culture, experienced in the working of metals.

The wooden-key type is found all over Asia: in China, India, in Arabia. Some would link its diffusion to Arab raids into tropical Africa,[44] Moorish conquerors bringing it to the north of that continent. On the other hand, the type has been retrieved in German forts dating from the Roman Empire.[45] It has been assumed that the wooden-key type was carried throughout Europe by the westward marching peoples of the Great Invasions. To close the circle, it came to America along two ways: through German, Scottish, or Swiss settlers to Pennsylvania, and through Negroes to Guiana.[46]

Following these radiations backwards, they converge upon one center of origin: the inner core of Asia; there, in the steppes, without records or history, was most probably the birthplace of the wooden-key type.

One more thing also points to the interior of Asia. The closer one becomes acquainted with the flat, wooden-key-type tumbler lock, the more is one likely to conclude that it is not merely a simplification of the 'Egyptian' lock or its transposition into the woodworker's technique. The whole mechanism is conceived in wood. Strictly avoiding curves, every part of it can easily be shaped by peasants, shepherds, or Nomads. It requires no skilled labor, as the bent metal key does. The wooden-key type arose within a primitive culture and in a region that relied upon wood as the basic material for its buildings, and, so far as possible, for its tools.

We conclude that the flat wooden-key type was the earlier stage; that the more complicated bent metal-key type was patterned from it, in keeping with the more highly organized Mediterranean culture. But, compared to the wooden-key type, it never traveled very far.

The question remains: Whence came the lock that displaced the age-old

---

[44] Luschan, op.cit. p.430.

[45] L. Jacobi, *Das Roemerkastell Saalburg*, Homburg v. d. Hoehe, 1897, pp.462ff. But even here uncertainty prevails: the keys of the Saalburg fort in Germany — flat keys in bronze, probably copied from wooden models — might date from Augustan times or from the late third century. Whence the Romans might have got it is an open question, for they themselves favored skilfully fabricated rotary door locks.

[46] Luschan, op.cit. p.430.

types? The lock that Yale's father invented was also a pin-tumbler cylinder lock, with its tumblers divided into two sections, with its revolving inner cylinder and its fixed outer cylinder, with its springs driving on the tumblers. Over two decades elapsed before the elements that Yale's father had used in his door lock found their final shape in the lock of the younger Yale. The facts at our disposal may suggest the broad outlines of this process.

In the 'fifties, the younger Yale was wholly absorbed in the problem of the burglarproof bank lock, unsolved at the time. Each of his bank locks was successfully received, but he was not satisfied until he had reached a solution that he himself recognized as reliable. As we have seen, this was the combination lock with no keyhole at all.

Every day as he handles the heavy key to his workshop door, he wonders if it cannot be made more simple and convenient. Is it not ridiculous? — the key that opens his 'Magic Bank Lock' is scarcely as large as the key that winds the mantelpiece clock. Something is wrong if an ordinary house door calls for so clumsy an implement, while the foot-thick door of a safe can be opened with a key small enough to fit one's waistcoat pocket.

Strange as it may seem, it is easier to conceive intricate bank locks, when this invention is in the air, than it is to resolve a problem like that of the door lock, which had been at a standstill for centuries.

Could one progress no further along the way of his father? Pin tumblers were usable; but when set in this way, they were not reliable in operation. What good was a complicated, radial array of tumblers on a simple house door? What is adequate for the heavy door of a safe is not necessarily suitable for household use. And worse, the tumblers as arranged lay radially behind the keyhole, within range of sight and touch, to the delight of any tamperer. It was an easy matter to insert a tool and probe until one reached the right spot. A new door lock had to be more burglar resistant than the old, or it would be useless. In his bank lock, the younger Yale pushed the mechanism far back inside, beyond the picker's reach. He wished to follow this principle in his door lock as well, but complicated mechanisms were out of the question. A different approach was needed.

His father's idea not to use the key for shooting the bolt, as in the old door locks, met his need. The younger Yale tried in turn to confine the function of the key to aligning the tumblers so that a rotation could take place. But how to stack the pin tumblers simply, in depth, so as to make it even more difficult for the picker? No archaeological research was necessary for this purpose. It would have led him nowhere, for to this day we do not know much about the Egyptian lock which, as reputation has it, inspired Yale.

The Wooden-Key Type in Pennsylvania

Everywhere in Pennsylvania, on barns and, perhaps in his day, still on farmhouses, Yale could see the wooden tumbler locks brought by the settlers from Scotland, Germany, or Switzerland. Their tumblers were aligned in a single row (fig. 42). This type is a survival of Gothic life, as were the tools and furniture of the first settlers. The Pennsylvania Dutch often expressed their playfulness in inventing new devices which gave further variety to their wooden locks. But they had one type of wooden lock which had closed medieval barns and houses. This wooden tumbler lock, with its aligned tumblers and flat, notched key, had long served as the lock of mankind. Its plain wooden frame, its simple grooves, the tumblers, and the key, all could be shaped by the most primitive tools.

It bespeaks the elemental vigor of this type that it remained current down to the nineteenth century, and could supply a decisive impulse when the mechanized lock of our period had to be invented. It was the rustic simplicity of this lock that provoked the stroke of genius in Linus Yale's invention: to align the tumblers one behind another in a row, so simply and efficiently that the scheme has never since been altered.

THE ASSEMBLY LINE AND SCIENTIFIC MANAGEMENT

THE assembly line [1] is one of mechanization's most effective tools. It aims at an uninterrupted production process. This is achieved by organizing and integrating the various operations. Its ultimate goal is to mold the manufactory into a single tool wherein all the phases of production, all the machines, become one great unit. The time factor plays an important part; for the machines must be regulated to one another.

More recently the assembly line has been brought under a broader heading: line production. 'Line production is characterized by the continuous regular movement of materials from the stockpile through the necessary stages of fabrication to the finished product. . . . Line production requires a rational layout and frequently, but not necessarily, involves the use of conveyor systems. . . .' [2]

In what follows we shall usually employ the term assembly line, which has become almost a synonym of full mechanization.

Humanly and technically, the problem of the assembly line is solved when the worker no longer has to substitute for any movement of the machine, but simply assists production as a watcher and tester. This was done, quite suddenly, toward the end of the eighteenth century in Oliver Evans' mechanization of the grain-milling process. But in the large-scale manufacture of complicated machinery (automobile chassis), the fully automatic production line was not achieved until 1920.

In the transition phase, still predominant in industry, man acts as a lever of the machine. He must perform certain operations that are not yet carried out by mechanisms. True, the tempo of work is geared to the human organism; but in a deeper sense, the inexorable regularity with which the worker must follow the rhythm of the mechanical system is unnatural to man.

The growth of the assembly line with its labor-saving and production-raising measures is closely bound up with the wish for mass-production. We find it used shortly after 1800 for complicated products, such as the manufacture of biscuit in a victualling office of the British Navy, on a purely handicraft basis, i.e. without the use of machinery. A quite similar process was developed in the 'thirties in the great Cincinnati slaughterhouses, where without mechanical auxiliaries systematic teamwork was introduced in the killing and dressing of

---

[1] The term 'assembly line' is of recent date. Only in the supplement of the *Oxford English Dictionary* (1933) was there added this further meaning of *assembly:* 'The action or method of assembling a machine or its parts' (1897); the *assembly line* is not listed; *assembly-room*, however, is defined as 'a room in a workshop where the parts of some composite article are assembled.' An American source of 1897 is referred to.

[2] As defined in *Wartime Technological Developments*, U.S. Senate, subcommittee monograph No.2, May 1945, p.348.

hogs. The assembly line attitude is present before it can be applied in mechanized form to complicated machine processes.

The assembly line is based upon the speediest, most nearly frictionless transportation from each fabrication process to the next. Conveyor systems are employed to this end. It was Oliver Evans who first incorporated the three basic types of conveyor, as still used today, into a continuous production line.

Toward 1830 a new influence appeared: the introduction of railways. They aroused the imagination of the world. The rail and carriage seemed the most perfect means of transportation. Attempts were soon made to use them in the most diverse branches of industry.

In 1832 the patent was granted in France for a continuous oven 'in the form of a large circular track. The bread was taken around and baked in the course of the trip.' [3] It may be regarded as symptomatic. But in England during that decade, important inventions were made, based on the use of tracks and trolleys. Among these is the traveling crane — apparently invented by Johann Georg Bodmer in 1833 — which could move weights along a horizontal path high overhead. It was Bodmer who, as we shall see, laid down tracks within a Manchester factory, on which the material was moved in cars directly to the machines.

The horizontally traveling crane forms a step toward the overhead-rail systems that appeared on a large scale in American slaughterhouses of the Middle West during the late 'sixties and finally came into use in the mass fabrication of automobiles (Henry Ford, 1913).

The assembly line in the present-day sense was originally used in food processing when Oliver Evans first applied it in 1783 to grain-milling. In 1833 biscuit manufacture was mechanically performed in an English 'victualling office,' the baking trays being conveyed from machine to machine through the oven and back to their starting point on continuously moving roller-beds. In the late 'fifties the more difficult process of bread baking became mechanized at various places in England and America; and in America, at this time, even fruit was dried in steam chambers with the help of a conveyor by a now forgotten method (Alden process); in the late 'sixties overhead rails, in combination with various machines, are found in the great meat-packing houses of the Middle West.

Every detail of conveyor systems of interest to the engineer or the manufacturer possesses an almost endless literature; — but one not very helpful for our purpose. The origin of the assembly line, its almost unnoticed growth through an entire century to virtual dictatorship over everything and everyone, is above all a historical, a human problem. Perhaps that is why we are so ill-

[3] Aribert's patent.

informed about its growth. We have no broad survey of the subject, or, apparently, any article outlining the history of this pre-eminent tool of production.

Intimately connected with the assembly line is a problem that has slowly grown to importance since 1900: *scientific management.* Scientific management like the assembly line has much to do with organization. Very early in his experiments during the 'eighties, its founder, Frederick Winslow Taylor, was regulating the speed of various machines by means of individual drive, and became one of the first to use electric motors for this purpose. But of greater significance is scientific management's investigation of the way human work is performed.

Its development has led partly to the alleviation of labor, partly to heedless exploitation of the worker.

Its finest result was the new insight into the nature of work and motion arising from investigations such as Frank B. Gilbreth's. The way Gilbreth made visible the elements as well as the path of human motion is masterly both in the method and the boldness of its application. This aspect of the research, deeply probing the human element, will, we believe, prove the most significant in the long run.

The Continuous Production Line in the Eighteenth Century

Oliver Evans

What is most typical of American industry today, production in continuous flow, was a central preoccupation from the first. Before any American industry had come into being, and long before it was building complicated machines, a solitary and prophetic mind set about devising a system wherein mechanical conveyance from one operation to another might eliminate the labor of human hands.

In the last quarter of the eighteenth century, Oliver Evans (1755–1819) [4] built a mill in which the grain passed smoothly and continuously through the various milling processes without the help of human hand. It flowed in a smooth and continuous production line.

Oliver Evans introduced the endless belt and different types of conveyors, regulated to one another in all stages of production. The 'endless belt' (belt conveyor), the 'endless screw' (screw conveyor), and the 'chain of buckets' (bucket conveyor), which he used from the very start, constitute to the present day the three types of conveyor system. Later these three elements became exhaustively technified in their details, but in the method itself there was nothing to change.

---

[4] Particulars on the inventor's life and work will be found in the painstakingly documented work of Greville and Dorothy Bathe, *Oliver Evans*, Philadelphia, 1935.

43. AGOSTINO RAMELLI: Machine for Raising Water by the Archimedean Screw. 1588. *Interest in mechanics underwent a revival in the late Renaissance. This is reflected in many devices, such as the so-called Archimedean screw, which is no other than the screw-conveyor of today. To raise water Ramelli employs three Archimedean screws powered by the stream itself.* (*Ramelli,* Le Diverse Artificiose Machine, *Paris,* 1588)

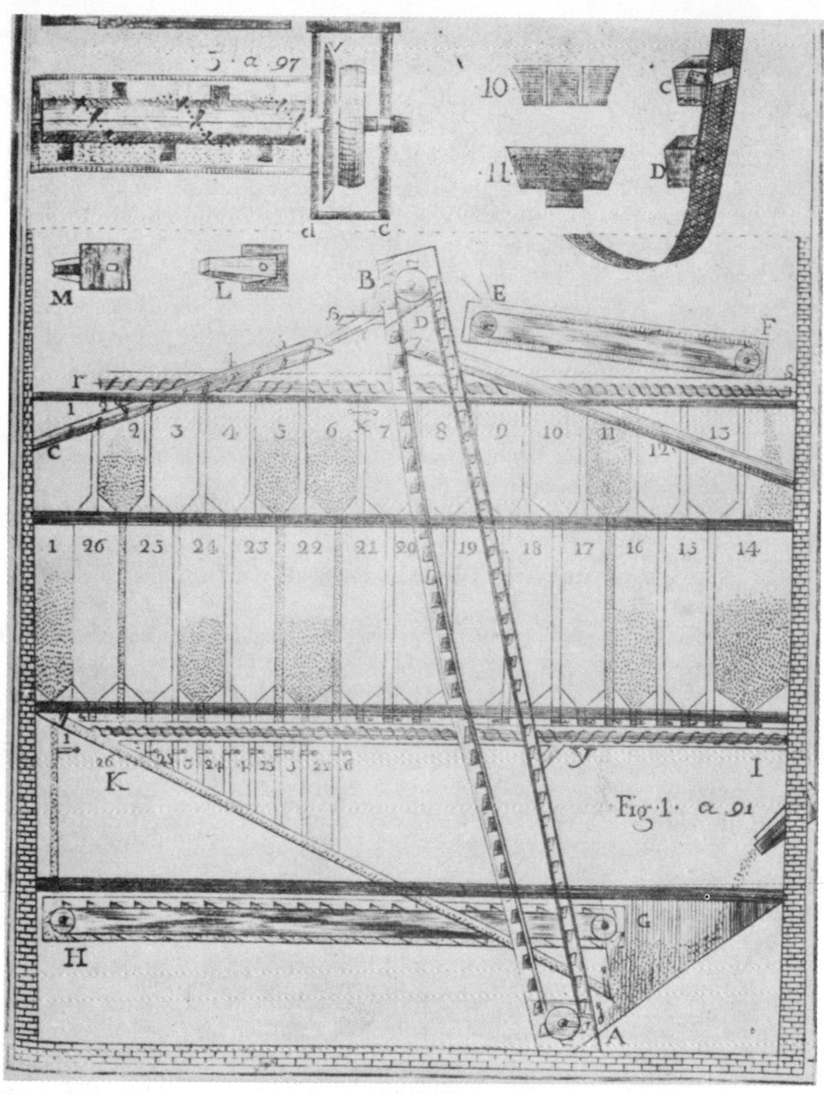

44. OLIVER EVANS: Archimedean Screws and Bucket Conveyor for Elevating and Transporting Grain. 1783. *Inventor of the production line, Evans uses the Archimedean screw within a system of belt and bucket conveyors, to move the material (grain) from process to process unaided by the human hand. 'An endless screw of two continued spires' moves the grain horizontally. The 'elevator for raising vertically' is an endless belt of sheet-iron buckets (CD). The descender (EF) is 'a broad endless strap of very thin pliant leather, canvas or flannel revolving over two pulleys. . . . The grain by its own gravity sets the machine in motion. This machine moves on the principle of an overshot water wheel.'* (*Evans,* Young Millwright and Miller's Guide, 1795)

In 1783 the model of the automatic mill was complete and in the two following years, 1784–5, the mill itself was built in Redclay Creek valley (figs. 44, 45). This mill could load from either boats or wagons; a scale determined the weight and a screw conveyor (or 'endless Archimedean screw' as Evans calls it) carried the grain inside to the point where it was raised to the top storey by a bucket conveyor (or 'elevator for raising vertically'). It handled three hundred bushels an hour. From this elevator, the grain fell on the mildly inclined 'descender — a broad endless strap of very thin pliant leather, canvas or flannel, revolving over two pulleys.' This belt was set in motion by the weight of the grain and, as Evans adds, 'it moves on the principle of an overshot waterwheel.' A prominent mechanical engineer remarks a century later: 'It is the prototype of belt conveyor of the present day, usually used for horizontal movement.' [5] After intervening operations, the grain was carried down to the millstones and from the millstones back to the top storey. Thus it made its way — which interests us here — through all the floors, from bottom to top and top to bottom, much as the automobile bodies in Henry Ford's plant of 1914.

People refused to believe it would work. How could human hands be thus suddenly superseded? In a rather obscure passage written as a footnote to one of his books twenty years later, Oliver Evans could not keep himself from this comment:

. . . The human mind seems incapable of believing anything that it cannot conceive and understand . . . I speak from experience, for when it was first asserted that merchant flour mills could be constructed to attend themselves, so far as to take meal from the stones, and the wheat from the wagons and raise them to the upper storeys, spreading the meal to cool and gathering it by the same operations into the bolting hopper, etc. until the flour was ready for packing, the projector was answered: You cannot make water run up hill, you cannot make wooden millers.[6]

But the mill Oliver Evans built for himself and his partners on Redclay Creek, 1784–5, did work. The millers of the region came to look and 'they saw that all the operations of milling were going on without the care of any attendant — cleaning, grinding and bolting . . . without human intervention.' [7]

On their return home they reported that 'the whole contrivance was a set of rattle traps unworthy the attention of men of common sense.' [8] But soon the economic advantages became clear. The mechanization of milling was soon accepted. Oliver Evans obtained a patent in 1790 for his 'method of manu-

[5] Coleman Sellers, Jr., 'Oliver Evans and His Inventions,' in *The Journal of the Franklin Institute*, Philadelphia, vol. XCII (1886), p.4.

[6] In a short history of the steam engine in *Young Steam Engineer's Guide* (Philadelphia, 1804), where he compares himself with the Marquess of Worcester, adding the above passage.

[7] Coleman Sellers, Jr., op.cit. p.2.

[8] Ibid.

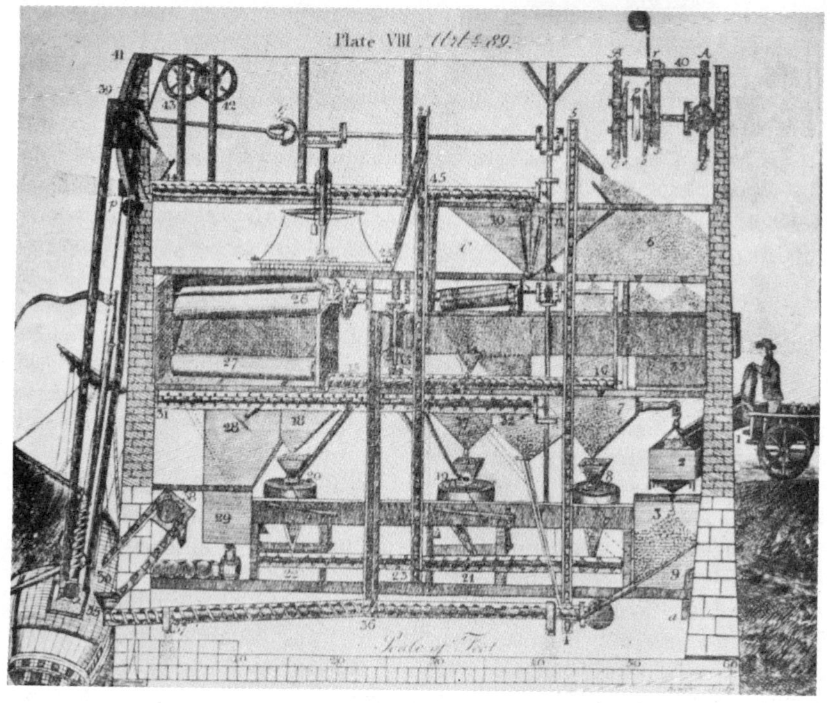

45. OLIVER EVANS: Scheme of the Mechanized Mill, 1783. *The first complete production line, achieved before American industry really existed.* (*Evans,* Young Millwright and Miller's Guide, 1795)

facturing flour and meal.' New difficulties arose. We shall return to them presently.

How did this invention come about?

Oliver Evans grew up in the country, in the state of Delaware. The ruins of his father's farmhouse are still standing. When he moved to the city, Philadelphia, then the leading center of culture in America, he was nearly fifty. Evans never went to Europe, and carried on no correspondence with the great scientific personalities of his day. He had to rely solely on his own powers. He dwelt in an agricultural land where farming was carried on by the most primitive methods. His reading was the popular textbooks on the basic laws of mechanics, the mechanics of solids and fluids. These laws, by then long taken for granted, became as new and exciting as they had been in Renaissance time. They took on a fresh vitality, as when an artist infuses with new plastic life objects that had become dull and commonplace.

This is no empty conjecture. Going through his book on the mechanization of the milling process, *The Young Millwright and Miller's Guide*,[9] one finds that about half of it deals with the laws of 'Mechanics and Hydraulics.' The reader can follow almost step by step as the simple theorems, the 'laws of motion and force of falling bodies, of bodies on inclined planes, the laws of the screw and circular motion,' are transformed into mechanical devices, whence is composed the mill that runs by itself, the mill without workers, the automaton.

The paddles of the mill wheel, whose laws of motion under the influence of water Evans studied, are changed into baskets, into buckets on an endless belt, carrying products from a lower to a higher, or from a higher to a lower level. The water on the paddles of the overshot wheel is changed to grain, moving and moving ever onwards; but it does not drive, it is driven.

The difficulties which arose, leading to quarrels and finally to a conflict with the Congress, came from the millers. Aware of the advantages of the mechanized mill, they did not wish to pay royalties to Oliver Evans, and later (1813) attacked the patent in a 'Memorial to Congress.' They asked for 'relief from the oppressive operations' of Oliver Evans' patent.[10] Thomas Jefferson was called in by an expert. His opinion of Oliver Evans' devices was low. He saw only the details, not the thing as a whole. 'The elevator,' he declared, 'is nothing more than the old Persian Wheel of Egypt, and the conveyor is the same thing as the screw of Archimedes.'[11]

If Oliver Evans' invention be split into its simple components, Jefferson is of course right. The chain of pots was used throughout the Ancient World — from Egypt to China — for raising water;[12] and the endless Archimedean screw, the screw conveyor, is found in almost every late Renaissance book dealing with machinery. In the Renaissance it served as a means of 'screwing' water from a lower to a higher level. Thus Agostino Ramelli used a series of

---

[9] *The Young Millwright and Miller's Guide*, Philadelphia, 1795, with an appendix on business management by his partner Elincott, also translated into French, saw fifteen editions up to 1860. They have been carefully collated by Greville Bathe. The book was used as a standard work for more than half a century.

[10] G. Bathe, op.cit. pp.189–90.

[11] Ibid. p.91.

[12] Recent studies have noted from a drawing of Pieter Breughel that the chain of pots 'were used in Holland as dredgers during the digging of a canal in 1561.' Zimmer, 'Early History of Conveying Machines,' in *Transactions of the Newcomen Society* (London, 1924–5), vol. 4, p.31.

Archimedean screws for the raising of water [13] (fig. 43). But Oliver Evans was, so far as we know, the first to use it horizontally, for the transportation of *solids*.

The Renaissance theorists are concerned with simple operations: they aim to raise a heavy load or to transmit force with the aid of lever, gear, or pulley systems. Their work sometimes may assume grandiose form, as when Domenico Fontana (1543–1607), architect, engineer, and town-planner to Sixtus V, lowered the Vatican obelisk on the south side of Saint Peter's, transported it, and raised it on its present site. In contrast to the clumsy proposals of his rivals, Fontana in 1586 used forty sets of windlasses driven by horses to swing the monolith around its center of gravity, while all Rome watched in silence.

All these were tasks of simple lifting and moving, a class to which modern cranes for the handling of coal, minerals, and other goods in harbors, factories, or freight yards also belong.

For Oliver Evans, hoisting and transportation have another meaning. They are but links within the continuous production process: from raw material to finished goods, the human hand shall be replaced by the machine. At a stroke, and without forerunner in this field, Oliver Evans achieved what was to become the pivot of later mechanization.

Evans' method had no analogy in its time. Yet nothing is harder for man than to frame ideas for the barely conceivable future; by nature we tend to approach all things by analogy, be it science and production methods, or emotional phenomena, as in art.

Arthur Schopenhauer once described talent as hitting a mark which ordinary man cannot reach; genius as sighting a point which others cannot even see.

Outwardly Oliver Evans' invention was, as his contemporaries said sneeringly, 'a set of rattle traps.' Moreover, Evans was not, like Benjamin Franklin, a master in dealing with men. Nothing favorable came of his other inventions, among which one at least is of a vision that takes us somewhat aback.[14]

His late successors were far more fortunate in achieving continuous line production. They had an advanced technology to work with and were assisted by an age bent upon nothing more strongly than production.

To the historian it does not matter whether a man joins the successful or the stranded, whether he himself carries his invention from conception to the last

---

[13] Agostino Ramelli, *Le Diverse et Artificiose Machine Del Capitano Agostino Ramelli*, A Parigi, 1588.

[14] We are thinking not so much of his 'amphibious digger,' a steam-dredging machine for cleaning the docks of the city (1804, cf. G. Bathe, op.cit. p.108), or of his high-pressure steam engine, as of the astonishing precision with which he laid down a method for mechanical ice making that remained current during a half century. See below, p.599.

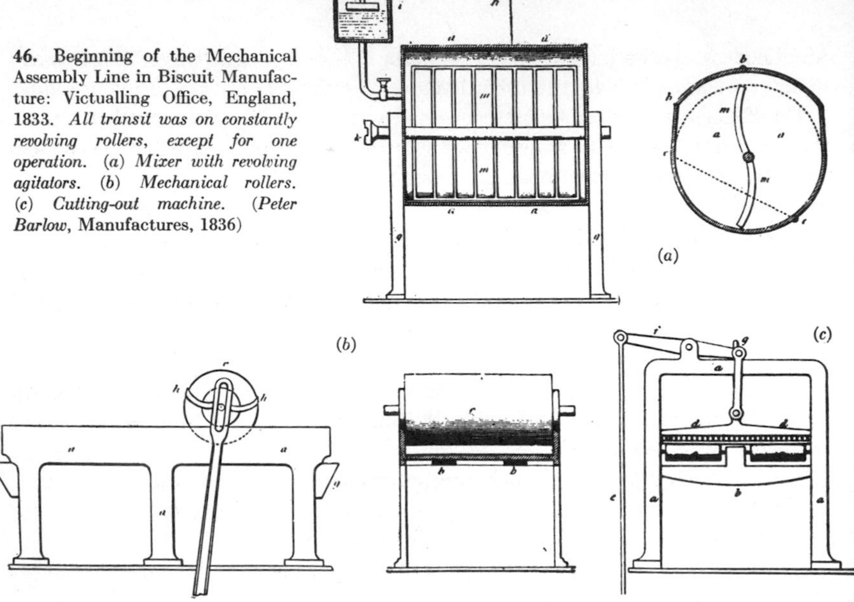

46. Beginning of the Mechanical Assembly Line in Biscuit Manufacture: Victualling Office, England, 1833. *All transit was on constantly revolving rollers, except for one operation. (a) Mixer with revolving agitators. (b) Mechanical rollers. (c) Cutting-out machine. (Peter Barlow,* Manufactures, 1836)

cog-wheel, or has a staff of thousands of engineers to work out his ideas. What matters is the power of his vision. From this standpoint, Oliver Evans' invention opens a new chapter in the history of mankind.

The Beginnings of the Assembly Line

Oliver Evans disassembled a complex material (grain), mechanically fabricating a new product therefrom (flour). In the nineteenth century also the problem was to fabricate a product mechanically — a machine for instance. Here the parts are 'assembled' and combined into a new whole. But this is no rule. A whole is often disassembled into its parts as in Evans' mill (in mechanized slaughtering for instance). What marks this period is the unperfected state of the machinery. Men had to be inserted in the mechanisms, as it were, to ensure an uninterrupted production line.

The assembly line forms the backbone of manufacture in our time. The problems involved are no less deeply human than they are organizational and technical. Its slow growth is imperfectly known. In what follows, we shall take at random only a few cross sections from the nineteenth century.

From the nineteenth century on, the assembly line, beyond its labor-saving mechanisms, consists first and foremost in the rationally planned co-operation of groups, teamwork. This is achieved by the division of labor, which Adam Smith in the eighteenth century recognized as the basis of all industry, into tasks regulated to one another in regard to both time and succession.

Systematic beginnings of line production appear in hand methods before the advent of mechanization.

1804

Two decades after Oliver Evans' automatic mill, a human assembly line was established in an English naval arsenal to speed up the production of biscuits. The work was divided into various phases, and the hand operations of the different workers were timed to one another.

A source of 1804, the *Book of Trades*,[15] gives a clear account of this early form

[15] *The Book of Trades, or Library of the Useful Arts*, London, 1804, pp.107–8. The first American edition of this source appeared in Philadelphia, 1807.

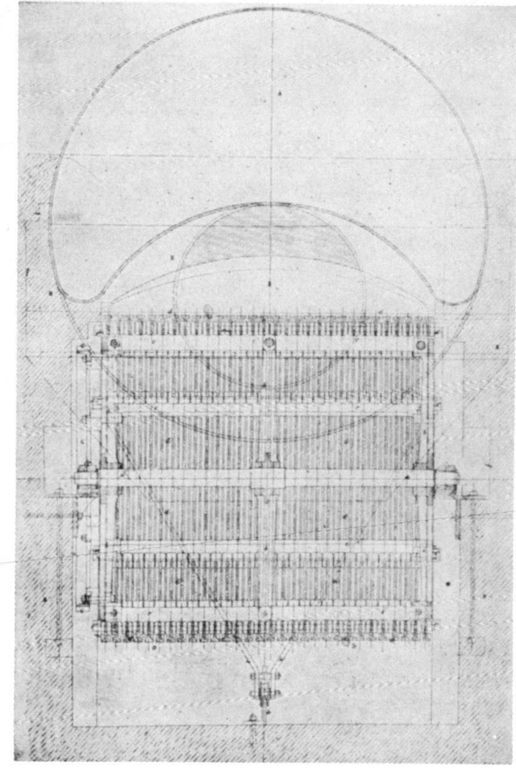

47. J. G. BODMER: First Traveling Grate for Boilers, British Patent, 1834. *This Swiss engineer, active in England during the 1830's, brought new methods to the manufacture of machine tools and complicated machines; he is said to be an inventor of the overhead traveling crane. We have no view of his machine shop at Manchester, but detailed patent specifications exist. Like Evans, Bodmer was preoccupied with the endless belt, using it to carry heavier material and for new purposes. His traveling grate made in articulated sections was for the continuous stoking of furnaces.*

48. Sweet's Project for a Railroad over Broadway. 1850's. *The overhead traveling crane moves a heavy load through the air. The 'sixties were fascinated by the idea of hovering transportation: there are patents for conveying materials for cable railway, and fantastic schemes such as that for a balloon railway to the top of Mt. Rigi* (Fig. 95), *or for a railway on the principle of the traveling crane over Broadway in New York.* (The Scientific American, 15 *October*, 1853)

of assembly line. A work team of five bakers is to turn out seventy ships' biscuits a minute: twelve ovens; 'each will furnish daily bread for 2040 men.'

> The process of biscuit-making, as practiced at the Victualling Office at Deptford, is curious and interesting.
>
> The dough, which consists of flour and water only, is worked by a large machine. . . . It is handed over to a second workman, who slices them with a large knife for the bakers, of whom there are five. The first, or the *moulder*, forms the biscuit two at a time, the second, or *marker*, stamps and throws them to the *splitter*, who separates the two pieces and puts them under the hand of the *chucker*, the man that supplies the oven, whose work of throwing the bread on the peel must be so exact that *he cannot look off for a moment.* The fifth, or the *depositor*, receives the biscuits on the peel and arranges them in the oven. The business is to deposit in the oven *seventy biscuits in a minute* and *this is accomplished with the regularity of a clock*, the clacking of the peel, operating like the motion of the pendulum.

This biscuit bakery of the British Navy at Deptford seems to have been well-known. More than thirty years later,[16] an observer still found it worthy of detailed description. His account adds nothing essentially new, but does give a more precise picture of the installation which already approximates the idea of the later assembly line: 'The baking establishment consists of two long buildings each divided into two baking offices with six ovens in each, which are ranged back

[16] Peter Barlow, *Manufactures and Machinery in Britain*, London, 1836.

49. Origin of the Modern Assembly Line. Cincinnati, c.1870. *The modern assembly line has its origin in the late 'sixties, probably in the packing houses of Cincinnati. The principle of the modern assembly line entered at a specific phase of the slaughtering process. After catching, killing, scalding, and scraping, the hogs are hung from the overhead rail at twenty-four-inch intervals and moved continuously past a series of workers. Each man performs a single operation. 'One splits the animal, the next takes out the entrails, the third removes heart, liver, etc., and the hose man washes it out.'* **(Harper's Weekly, 6** ***Sept.*** **1873)**

to back. . . . The kneading troughs and kneeling boards are arranged round the outside walls of the building, one opposite each other.'[17]

About this time the 'hand process' came to be replaced by 'a highly ingenious piece of machinery.'

1833

The Superintendent of the Deptford Victualling Office, a Mr. Grant who had devised this 'highly ingenious piece of machinery,' thus brought about what was probably the first assembly line in the food industries (fig. 46). Only one operation, the removing of the dough from the kneader, was performed by hand. All other conveyance from operation to operation took place mechanically, on continuously rotating rollers.

The arrangement of the several machines should be as near together as possible in order that the boards may pass from one to the other on rollers. . . . [Doesn't this sound

[17] Ibid. p.801.

like a doctrine of Henry Ford?] A series of rollers should be fixed against the wall for the purpose of returning the boards to the first table after they have been emptied. At Portsmouth [England] this series of rollers was kept constantly revolving by the steam engine, so that when the empty boards were *placed upon any part of the line* they traveled upon the mixer without further attention.[18]

Several other fields show a like division of the production process into phases, as made famous by Adam Smith's account of the division of labor in a Birmingham needle factory. In the United States, where department stores had slowly been developing since the 'forties, ready-made clothes, in contrast to Europe, were produced from the start. This, before the introduction of sewing machines, led at an early date to a division of labor by teamwork, as in the English biscuit manufactory.

We shall look into one example only: the packing industry, for we shall presently meet with its later development. In Cincinnati, Ohio, where large-scale slaughterhouses originated, travelers as early as the 'thirties were reminded of Adam Smith's division of labor as they observed the slaughtering process and its organization.[19]

By 1837 the point seems to have been reached where, without machinery, a team of 20 men could kill and clean, ready for the cutting-knife, 620 pigs in 8 hours.[20]

By mid-century, 'it was found economical to give each workman a special duty . . . one cleaned out the ears; one put off the bristles and hairs, while others scraped the animal more carefully. . . . To show the speed attained at Cincinnati in 1851 the workmen were able to clean three hogs per minute.' [21]

1839

Beginnings of flow work in the building of intricate spinning machinery are discernible in England around 1840. What was taking place in America at this time is still largely unknown. A Swiss inventor, Johann Georg Bodmer (1786–1864),[22] equipped a machine-tool factory which both by its layout and by the construction of its machines was to save movement, labor, and energy

[18] Peter Barlow, *Manufactures and Machinery in Britain*, London, 1836, p. 804.

[19] Harriet Martineau, *Retrospect of Western Travels*, New York, 1838, vol. 2, p.45. Quoted in R. A. Clemen, *The American Livestock and Meat Industry*, New York, 1923.

[20] R. A. Clemen, *The American Livestock and Meat Industry*, New York, 1923.

[21] Ibid. p.121.

[22] The rediscovery of Johann Georg Bodmer in our time is due to J. W. Roe, who in his book *English and American Toolbuilders*, New Haven, 1916, pp.75–80, accords Bodmer the place he deserves. He bases his article on the *Minutes of the Institution of Civil Engineers*, London, 1868, XXVIII, 573ff., which shortly after Bodmer's death printed a detailed memoir ending with an eight-page list of his patents.

in conveyance. The principle given by Henry Ford in *My Life and Work* (1922), to 'place the tools and the man in sequence of operations,' was here followed to a surprising degree.

It was a sort of model workshop, for which almost everything was newly constructed. Nearly every machine was a patent. What improvements were made in the various machine tools are still accurately recorded in Bodmer's patent drawings.[23] Normally a patent runs to only a few pages, here one specification fills fifty-six pages, almost a mechanical catalogue: 'Tools, or Apparatus for Cutting, Planing, Drilling and Rolling Metal' and 'novel arrangements and construction of the various mechanisms.' [24]

Between 1830 and 1850 England was hard at work perfecting these machine tools. It was on this basis that the intensive industrialization proceeded in most branches between 1850 and 1890. What interests us in this connection is how far around 1830 the construction and disposition of machine tools, and means of conveyance was aimed at a unified production line.

In construction: 'the large lathes being provided overhead with small *travelling cranes* fitted with pulley blocks for the purpose of enabling the workmen more *economically and conveniently to set the articles to be operated on in the lathes* and to remove them after being finished.'

'Small cranes were also erected in sufficient number within easy reach of the planing machines.'

In disposition: 'Gradually nearly all of these *tools* were constructed and were *systematically arranged in rows*, according to a carefully arranged plan.'

In conveyance: 'Several lines of rails traversed the shop from end to end for the easy conveyance on trucks of the parts of machinery to be operated upon. Such arrangements were not common in those days [1839] whatever may be the case now [1868].' [25]

In the first half of the nineteenth century and especially between 1830 and 1850, inventive minds appeared everywhere, measuring themselves against the most diverse problems of industry. Extreme specialization — except in the highly developed spinning machines — was far off. The times still offered the freshness of unfulfilled tasks. Bodmer was one of these versatile inventors; he worked on water wheels, steam engines, locomotives, machine tools, spinning machines;

---

[23] British Patent No. 8070, A.D. 1839 — British Patent No. 8912, A.D. 1841.

[24] British Patent No. 8070, A.D. 1839, p.2.

[25] The best picture is given by the untouched contemporary account, Institution of Civil Engineers' memoir on Bodmer, op.cit. p.588.

even on the mechanical production of beet sugar. But one problem occupied him from beginning to end: that of *conveyance within production.*

It began as early as 1815 when he built a mill for his brother in Zurich 'with some essential particulars . . . of a hoist of simple construction consisting in fact only of a large and broad flanched strap-pulley and ropedrum . . . the sacks of grain could be made to ascend or descend at pleasure and the operatives could pass from floor to floor by simply tightening or releasing the rope.'[26]

Installing a small factory for the manufacture of textile machines in Bolton (1833), Bodmer constructed 'what is now called a *travelling crane.*'[27] It was, as Roe remarks, one of the first, if not the first traveling crane.[28]

Bodmer, like Oliver Evans, was much interested in the endless belt. He used it (1834) to convey heavier materials and to serve new ends. He was the first to employ it for continuous fueling. It was he who invented the traveling grate for boilers (fig. 47) and furnaces,[29] 'to obtain the greatest possible degree in economizing pitcoal.'[30] Just as later in the assembly line the speed of the conveyor belt must be regulated to the pace of the worker, here the speed of the traveling grate is regulated to the rate of combustion. 'It was necessary to supply the furnace with fuel at a slow rate and continuously. These considerations led Mr. Bodmer to the adoption of a *traveling grate surface.*'[31] Having divided the rigid grate into movable sections, he goes on to make the most diverse suggestions for his chain grates, for traveling or propelling grates, drum-fire grates, thus broaching the domain of automatic stoking. He tried out a boiler stoked by his traveling fire grates in the Manchester machine-tool factory in 1839. After a while the experiment was dropped. It was still too early. Two decades later, about 1850, the endless belt found a place in American mechanical bakeries (fig. 100), to carry the loaves slowly and continuously through the oven, thus reviving the idea applied by Admiral Coffin in 1810, to which we shall return in the section on the oven and the endless belt.

Bodmer seems to have been still concerned with the problem of the traveling grate. One of his comprehensive patents (1843)[32] brings out further proposals in this field.

Bodmer, as we have mentioned, used his traveling cranes in close co-ordination with large lathes and planing machines in the Manchester machine-tool factory (1839); to this was added a rational arrangement of the machines, and the moving of the material on rails to the machine where needed.

[26] Institution of Civil Engineers' memoir on Bodmer, op.cit. p.579.

[27] Ibid. p.581.

[28] J. W. Roe, op.cit.

[29] British Patent No. 6617, A.D. 1834.

[30] Institution of Civil Engineers, op.cit. p.584.

[31] Ibid.

[32] British Patent No. 9899, A.D. 1843. The specification runs to 17 pages.

Johann Georg Bodmer was a restless inventor of a type often found in his day. He was spurred from country to country, from invention to invention, as if he might thus bring the times to ripen with the pace of his ideas. He seems to have been sought out for advice,[33] but flourishing success he did not know. He finally died at the place whence he had set out, Zurich. The problem Bodmer attacked time and again, conveyance within production, yielded him true advances as early as 1830, toward the integrated management that was later to find its elaboration in the assembly line.

The 'Sixties

The division of labor, which Adam Smith regarded as the pivotal point of industrialization after mid-eighteenth century; Oliver Evans' sudden achievement of the continuous production line, 1783; the manufacture of ships' biscuits as organized in the Victualling Offices, 1804 and 1833; J. G. Bodmer's layout of a Manchester machine-tool factory, with traveling cranes and rails to convey the material to the convenient spot, 1839 — all these were steps toward the assembly line.

Despite scant knowledge of nineteenth-century anonymous history, we can, passing over many facts, tell when, why, and how the specific form of the present-day assembly line first appeared. This is no mere date. It marks the putting into practice of the dominant principle of the twentieth century: industrial production based on efficiency.

The present-day assembly line had its origins in the packing industry. It originated there because many of its devices were invented in the late 'sixties and 'seventies, when slaughtering and its manifold operations had to be mechanized.

These inventions — kept in the Patent Office at Washington, and some of which we have chosen to illustrate the industrialization of slaughtering — proved, with few exceptions, unfit for practical use. They did not work; in the slaughtering process the material to be handled is a complex, irregularly shaped object: the hog. Even when dead, the hog largely refuses to submit to the machine. Machine tools for planing iron, undeviating to the millionth of an inch, could be constructed around 1850. Down to the present day, no one has succeeded in inventing a mechanism capable of severing the ham from the

---

[33] 'It was about this time [1834] that the formation of a railway between London and Birmingham was contemplated. One of the directors invited Mr. Bodmer to give his views as to the best system of carriages. On this occasion Mr. Bodmer proposed the construction of carriages since adopted in the U.S.A., in parts of Germany, in Switzerland, and the distinctive feature there is a longitudinal passage through the middle of each carriage, so that the guard can pass from one end of the train to the other with greatest ease and security.' Minutes of the Institution of Civil Engineers, op.cit. p.585.

carcass. We are dealing here with an organic material, ever changing, ever different, impossible to operate upon by revolving cutters. Hence all the essential operations in the mass production of dressed meat have to be performed by hand. For the speeding of output there was but one solution: to eliminate loss of time between each operation and the next, and to reduce the energy expended by the worker on the manipulation of heavy carcasses. In continuous flow, hanging from an endlessly moving chain at twenty-four-inch intervals, they now move in procession past a row of standing workers each of whom performs a single operation. Here was the birth of the modern assembly line [34] (fig. 49).

This production line in slaughtering comes only in the third act, after the hog has been caught and killed, scalded and scraped.[35] It begins as soon as the carcass, with a gambrel through its hind legs, is switched onto the overhead rail, where, drawn by the endless chain, it is ready to be opened, all but beheaded, to be disemboweled, inspected, split, and stamped. This is the sole phase of slaughtering in which continuous line production could be carried out. The killing and the cleaning could not be done in complete mechanization. Neither, after a sojourn in the chilling room, could the fourth phase, the final dressing and cutting, be mechanically performed.

In the literal sense, Thomas Jefferson, who himself delighted in devices to open doors automatically or to convey bottles from his Monticello wine cellar, was right in stating that Oliver Evans' elevators and conveyors were known from Antiquity, from pre-Roman times. In the literal sense, too, there is nothing in the mechanism of the assembly line, or in the aligned workmen in the packing houses, that could not have been invented in Antiquity: a slaughtered pig hung on a moving chain and in some way aided by wheels or rollers required no new discovery and could equally well have been set up in one of the large Roman slaughterhouses. The devices themselves — influenced, it is true, by suspended or aerial railways — were extremely simple. What was revolutionary and what could not have been invented in earlier periods, in other countries, or even in other industries, was the way they were used to speed into mass production an organic material which defies handling by purely mechanical means.

All that remains, so far as we know, to bear witness for the early period, is a panoramic painting which the Cincinnati packers sent to the Vienna International Exhibition of 1873 (figs. 49, 109), and which, with some liberties in the disposition, as observed by *Harper's Magazine* in September of that year,[36]

---

[34] It matters little that the process here is one of disassembling, not of assembling, as in the automobile industry. The method of mass production which forms the common denominator is what counts.

[35] Cf. pp.228–9.

[36] *Harper's Magazine*, 6 Sept. 1873, p.778.

records the hog-slaughtering process through all its stages, from the catching of the pig to the boiling out of the lard. What interests us at the moment (the fuller description will be found in our chapter 'Meat') is a single phase in which lies the genesis of the assembly line. If one defines the assembly line as a work method wherein the object is mechanically conveyed from operation to operation, here is indeed its origin.

Despite careful investigation and the help of Cincinnati's local historians, no other pictorial evidence for the birth period of the assembly line could be found. It was explained, not too convincingly, that Cincinnati was at first ashamed to trace its wealth to pork packing. All the city's activities, its musical life for instance, can be accurately followed. But in tracing the first mechanization of the butcher's trade and the beginnings of the assembly line we have no foothold.

Thus far we can only speculate, as if we were studying some faintly known epoch that has left no documents. The hypothesis is that the assembly line arose in Cincinnati. Devices for use in connection with it, patented in the late 'sixties, stem from Cincinnatian inventors. They indicate that overhead rails fastened to the ceiling were not unusual at this time.

Over forty packing-houses were operated in Cincinnati in the 'fifties. The city remained the center of the industry down to the Civil War, and most of the patents lead back to it.

1869

The overhead rail systems in the great slaughterhouses ultimately led to the conveyor system, which did not reach full development until the following century. The track, high above head level, carries small wheeled trolleys which are either drawn by chains or rolled by their own weight down an incline. Invented by a Cincinnatian in 1869[37] (fig. 50), a hog-weighing device for pork-packing houses shows how overhead rails — as had appeared in J. G. Bodmer's traveling cranes by about 1830 — have now developed into whole railways. 'The hogs are transferred from drying-room to cutting-block by means of an *elevated railway*.'[38] The inventor plainly speaks of improving equipment already current: 'My improvement consists in providing the railway with a detachable section, that is connected to the weighing scale . . . the hog is *suspended from a carriage or truck* which is permitted to run down an inclined portion.'

The patent's well-thought-out overhead tracks, hoveringly suspended from the ceiling, betray that this is no longer a novelty. There had already been experimentation along these lines. In the 'fifties the thought of building an

[37] T. Morrison, Hog Weighing Apparatus, U.S. Patent No. 92,083, 29 June 1869.
[38] Ibid.

'Elevated Railroad' over Broadway in New York was played with by engineers. 'A locomotive is to run on the rails and carries a suspended car which will pass between the space of the supporting arches . . .' [39] (fig. 48).

The Appearance of Scientific Management

Around 1900

The position is clear. Competition is growing. Wage-cutting has proved impractical as a means of lowering production costs. The machine tools are at hand. They will become continually further differentiated and more specialized, but few real improvements seem likely to raise productivity.

The question is narrowing down to: What can be done *within* the plant to lower costs and raise productivity? Before the turn of the century, the attention of industrialists was being claimed not so much by new inventions as by new *organization.* Work in factories was computed by rule of thumb. Scientific methods should take the place of inventions. Hence the question: How is work performed? The work process is investigated, as well as each movement and the manner of its performance. These must be known to the fraction of a second.

In the last decades of the century, a number of men, often independently of one another, took up the problem of rationalizing operations within the factory. Beyond question it was the unremitting effort of Frederick Winslow Taylor (1856–1915) and his circle that, within a quarter of a century, laid the foundations of that ever-growing field they themselves named *scientific management.*

By 1880, when after two years as a worker Taylor became foreman in the Midvale Steel Company (Philadelphia), he resolved to investigate the work process through time studies. He recalled one of his school teachers who had used a stop watch to determine how long different pupils took to finish an exercise. As a youth Taylor spent several years in Europe with his family; he received a high school education, and served an apprenticeship as a molder and tool maker in a small Philadelphia factory. In 1878 he started as a worker in the Midvale Steel Company, where he was promoted to foreman, master, and engineer, until in 1889 he began reorganizing factories of various types. Meanwhile he had completed his engineering studies at night. His name was already known when, for three years, 1898 to 1901, he was in close collaboration with the Bethlehem Steel Works. This was his most fertile period, both in production

[39] *The Scientific American* (New York), vol. IX, Pt. I, 15 Oct. 1853.

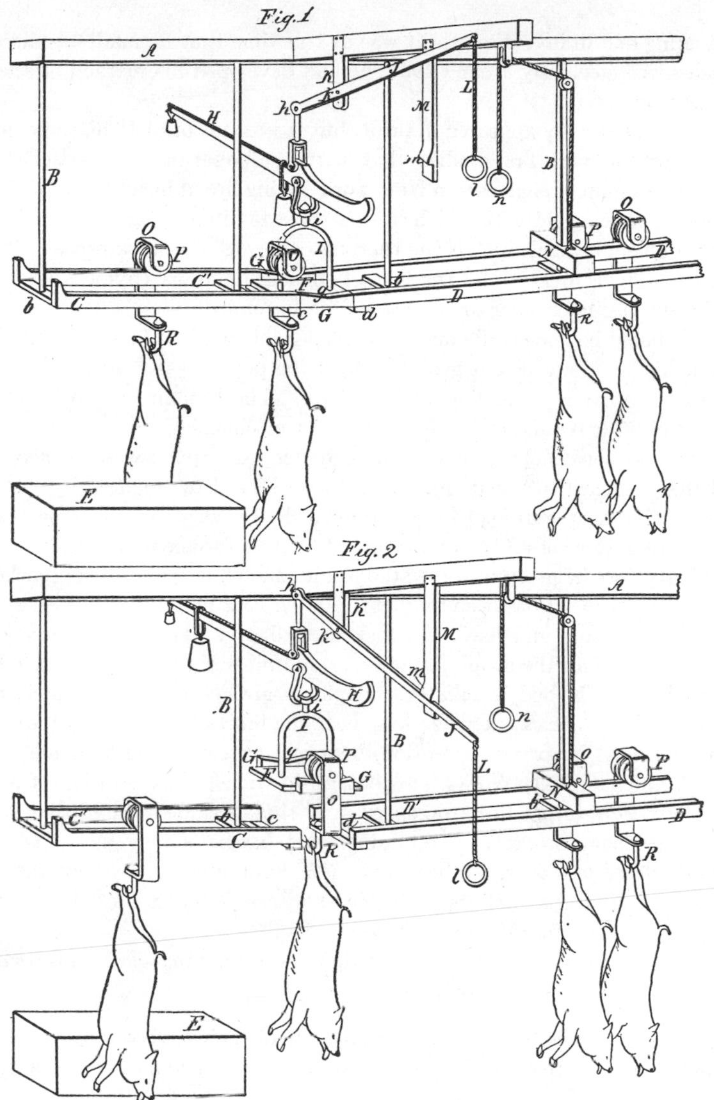

50. Automatic Hog-Weighing Apparatus for Use in Packing Houses. Cincinnati, 1869. *This device invented by a Cincinnatian shows that the late 1860's had considerable practice in combining the overhead railway with sections of the assembly line.* (*U. S. Patent* 92,083, 29 *June* 1869)

engineering and in invention, for it was at this time that he made his discovery of high-speed steel. By around 1900, he had developed his method of scientific management.

Taylor had already appeared in print, but it was not until 1906, some quarter of a century after his first studies, that he read a paper on 'The Art of Cutting Metal' to a group of engineers in New York, giving broad insight into his accomplishments in the field with which he was most familiar.

The problem he deals with is the thorough analysis of a work process. Everything superfluous must go, for the sake of efficiency and, as Taylor is ever stressing, for the easing of labor, its functional performance.

Work should be done easily and so far as possible without fatigue. But always behind this lies the constant goal to which the period was magically drawn — production, greater production at any price. The human body is studied to discover how far it can be transformed into a mechanism.

Taylor once constructed a great steam hammer, whose parts were so finely calculated that the elasticity of its molecular forces served to heighten its efficiency. The steam hammer 'was kept in its alignment by the elasticity of its parts which yielded to the force of a blow and returned to their former positions.' [40]

Similarly does he proceed in the study of human efficiency: He approaches the limit of elasticity. It has been frequently noted that he picked the best workers for his experiments and fixed the task accordingly. The human organism is more complex than the steam hammer, whose inner forces may be included in the reckoning. The body retaliates, though not always in an immediately recognizable manner, when worked too long near the limit of its capacity.

Taylor's most important invention, high-speed steel, which he made in 1898 in the Bethlehem Steel Works, also has to do with the exploration of a limit. When tools were run at their top speed until they became red hot, they showed an 'extraordinary property of retaining what hardness they have. It turned out that at a certain degree of heat [over 725° Fahrenheit], they kept the sharpness of cutting steel as well as their "red-hardness," the greatest improvement taking place just before the melting point.' [41]

The stretching of human capacities and the stretching of the properties of steel derive from the same roots.

Organization proceeds thus: the managers pool their experience to survey the field and if possible to recognize already known rules. The most capable workers

[40] *Iron Age*, New York, vol. 96, p.1029.

[41] Frank Barklay Copley, *Frederick W. Taylor, Father of Scientific Management*, New York, 1923, vol. 2, p.84. The term 'red-hardness' from F. W. Taylor, *The Art of Cutting Metal*, New York, 1906, p.223.

are chosen for experiments. By constant observation wrong or slow-working methods are replaced by rational ones. This, Taylor says,[42] means a division of labor between the management and the operatives. One labor technician in the planning or distributing office was often necessary for every three workers in the factory.

A methodical system develops, in the beginning at least, which Taylor himself calls the 'military type of organization.' 'As you know,' he said in his Harvard lectures (from 1909 on),

> one of the cardinal principles of the military type of management is that every man in the organization shall receive his orders directly through the one superior officer who is over him. The general superintendent of the works transmits his orders on tickets or written cardboards through the various officers to the workmen in the same way that orders through a general in command of a division are transmitted.[43]

Taylor and his successors do not want to command only. They provide for departments through which the worker himself can suggest improvements and share in the economies. The gifted workers may perhaps benefit, but the average man cannot escape automatization.

The hierarchy from general superintendent to worker, the soldierly discipline for efficiency's sake, doubtless offer industrial parallels to military life. But let there be no mistake: Taylorism and military activity are essentially unalike. The soldier indeed has to obey. But when under greatest stress, he faces tasks which demand *personal* initiative. His mechanical weapon becomes useless as soon as there is no moral impulse behind it. In the present situation where the machine is not far enough developed to perform certain operations, Taylorism demands of the mass of workers, not initiative but automatization. Human movements become levers in the machine.

The Factory as an Organism

Taylor organized industries of the most diverse types: steel mills, arsenals, ferro-concrete constructions, ball-bearing works. He would have his 'fundamental principles of scientific management' worked out in every sphere of life, in 'the management of our homes, farms, of the business of our tradesmen, of our churches, of our governmental departments.' [44]

The significance of his work lies in a further increase of *mechanical efficiency*. He is a specialist of the 1900 type: He conceives the object of his research —

[42] Compare Taylor's basic publication *Shop Management*, 1903, and *Principles of Scientific Management*, 1911.

[43] F. B. Copley, op.cit. vol. 2, p.213.

[44] F. W. Taylor, *The Principle of Scientific Management*, New York, 1911, p.8.

the factory — as a closed organism, as a goal in itself. What is manufactured in it and for what purpose are questions beyond his scope.

He owned shares in factories, received income from patents and his organizing work, but he seems never to have been tempted to become a big businessman himself. Taylor was eminently at home in the practical world. But by virtue of his analytical talent, his was one of those laboratory minds bound to the hardships and delights of research. By 1901, already having earned what he judged sufficient for his needs, he retired to devote himself wholly to his investigations.

Freud, the founder of psychoanalysis, by the exceeding penetration of his diagnostic and therapeutic methods, opened new access to the structure of the psyche. That F. W. Taylor was born in the same year as Freud, 1856, is of course coincidental. But a common trait of the scientific and artistic groups around the turn of the century was to employ an unprecedented sharpness of analysis in revealing the inside of processes.[45]

Space-Time Studies in Scientific Management

By the weight of all his energy Frederick Taylor opened the way for further elaboration of his method. Refinements soon appeared. There followed an alliance between scientific management and experimental psychology. Independently of scientific management, psychology had already devised tests to determine the person best suited to certain occupations. The basis of these tests was the time taken to react to a given impression. These techniques had been developed in psychological laboratories. Hugo Muensterberg, German psychologist who taught at Harvard, was among the first to survey the results of scientific management, then (1912) coming into its own, and to point out that from the psychological standpoint it was still reckoning by rule of thumb.[46] Testing was also experimented with in America — Stephen Calvin on schoolwork.

Scientific management's approaching of psychology was connected with the giving up of Taylor's stop-watch methods. Frank B. Gilbreth (1868–1924) and his wife, the psychologist Lillian M. Gilbreth, often in collaboration, developed methods which led to a visual representation of the work process. Gilbreth

---

[45] Freud published his studies on hysteria at the same time (1895) as Taylor was delivering his first lectures to American engineers.

[46] Hugo Muensterberg, *Psychology and Industrial Development*, Boston, 1913. This book was important also for Muensterberg's experiments for the improvement of electric railway and telephone service, the examination of ship's officers not able to meet emergencies, and for his research in the field, much further developed since, of advertising, display, and salesmanship.

began his studies while working as a large-scale contracting engineer in Boston. He investigated the best way of doing work — in industry and handicrafts indifferently.

The freshness and directness with which the age-old manipulations were observed — Taylor studied the coal-shoveler, Gilbreth the bricklayer — form perhaps the closest parallel to the functional improvement of such traditionary tools as the hammer, saw, spade, or plane in America from around 1830. Gilbreth gives us a step by step account [47] of how without elaborate apparatus he proceeded in rationalizing the most traditionary trade of bricklaying. An adjustable scaffold for piling up the bricks was all he used. It did away with the workman's need to 'bend over and raise the weight of his body a thousand times a day,' thus almost tripling a man's daily output, from 1000 to 2700 bricks.

The method responsible for this was the study of motion. From the question: 'How long does it take to do a piece of work?' one came to a representation of the path and elements of a movement. Soon the stop watch was eliminated, to be replaced by objective recording apparatus. The Gilbreths were thus led deeper and deeper toward the inside of human motion and its visualization. This was accomplished through time and space studies.

Scientific Management and Contemporary Art

Scientific management, like the assembly line, is deeply concerned with organization. But its most significant achievement is the study of the *human work process*, the way work is performed by the worker.

The purpose of research in scientific management is: 'Analyzing the motions of the workmen in the machine shop . . . all the operations for example which were performed while putting work into or taking work out from the machine.' [48]

This should eliminate unnecessary motions and reduce the time of an operation to a minimum. If we temporarily set aside all technical details and inquire into the essence of the methods employed, we find that they center around space-time studies. Their purpose was to determine the path of a motion through space and its duration in time.

In formulating the laws of mechanics, the physicists of the Renaissance investigated the relation between motion and time. The laws of human work are now investigated in a similar way, so that rough guessing and rule of thumb may yield to precise laws, so far as is possible in the human sphere.

What interests us here is the plunge *inside* the working process.

---

[47] Frank B. Gilbreth, *Bricklaying System*, New York, 1909.

[48] F. B. Copley, op.cit. vol. I, p.223.

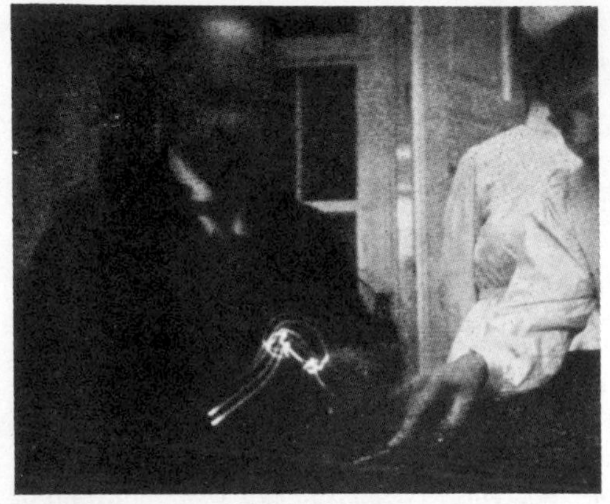

51. FRANK B. GILBRETH: Cyclograph of an Expert Surgeon Tying a Knot. 1914. *Carrying further the line of Marey's experiments, although he may not have been acquainted with them, Gilbreth was the first to give a representation of movement in space that could be precisely measured. He made this photograph while in Germany in 1914. 'The path of the motion is shown, but not the speed or direction. The record does show the beautiful smooth repetitive pattern of the expert.' (Quotation and photo by courtesy of Lillian M. Gilbreth)*

Frank B. Gilbreth succeeded in extending and refining the study of time and motion. 'Time study,' he says in his popular *Primer of Scientific Management*, 'is the art of recording, analyzing, synthesizing the time of the elements of any operation.' [49]

Stop-watch methods were not precise enough for Frederick Taylor's successors. The stop watch is mute and can say nothing about how a motion is performed. The human eye is untrustworthy; reaction time varies with the observer. The form of the movement remains invisible and cannot be investigated. Gilbreth's problem was to portray its elements, to delineate its path.

In his earlier research the goal is not yet clear. His study of ferro-concrete building (1908) lays down some four hundred rules, a sort of military dispatch system as preferred by Frederick Taylor. New conceptions already announce themselves in his large square book, *Concrete System*. It is saturated with pictures illustrating the different phases: 'almost a stenographic report of what a successful contractor said to his workmen.' [50] But in his *Bricklaying System* of the following year, he clearly states what he wishes to inaugurate — an era of motion study. 'The motion study in this book,' he declares, 'is but the beginning of a motion study era.' [51]

*The Precise Recording of Movement, c.*1912

It is not surprising that Gilbreth made use of the motion-picture camera as soon as it appeared in France. For further insight into the process of movement,

[49] F. B. Gilbreth, *Primer of Scientific Management*, New York, 1914, p.7.
[50] Gilbreth, *Concrete System*, New York, 1908.
[51] Gilbreth, *Bricklaying System*, New York, 1909, p.140.

he used a black background with a net of co-ordinates to ascertain the various phases.

But this was not a satisfactory solution. It did not make the trajectory of the movement clearly visible, and portrayed it only in conjunction with the body. To accomplish the separation, Gilbreth constructed a device of appealing simplicity. An ordinary camera and a simple electric bulb were all he needed to make visible the absolute path of a movement. He fastened a small electric light to the limb that performed the work, so that the movement left its track on the plate as a luminous white curve. This apparatus he called a 'motion recorder' — Cyclograph. The very form of the movement, invisible to the naked eye, is now captured. The light patterns reveal all hesitation or habits interfering with the worker's dexterity and automaticity. In a word, they embrace the sources of error as well as the perfect performance.

Later Gilbreth translated the image of the movement into models constructed of wire. These wire curves, their windings, their sinuosities, show exactly how the action was carried out. They show where the hand faltered and where it performed its task without hesitation. Thus the workman can be taught which of his gestures are right and which are wrong. For Gilbreth these

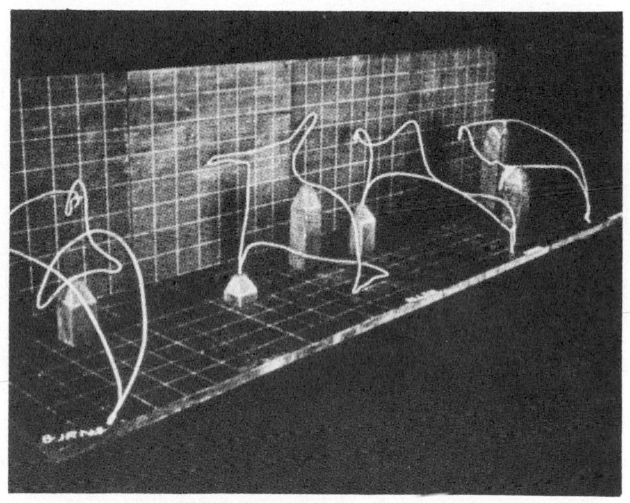

52. FRANK B. GILBRETH: Movement Translated into Wire Models. c.1912. *Gilbreth modeled the path of the motion in wire constructions. The worker, enabled to see his own gesture in space-time representation, should become what Gilbreth calls 'motion minded.'* (*Courtesy Lillian M. Gilbreth*)

models were a means of making the worker motion-minded. They revealed the character of the individual's own work. The worker might compare the record of his motions to the wire models, and correct his inefficiencies. Moreover, the gestures captured in wire a life of their own. It is no accident that modern artists sometimes turn to the same material in constructing their airy sculpture.

What followed Gilbreth's Cyclograph was but an elaboration of the method. The principle remains unchanged.

Frank B. Gilbreth investigated the forms of movement. It is not surprising that their trajectories became for him entities with independent laws.

He began to study the similarities of human activities. He believed 'that the skill in trades and in all forms of athletics, and even in such professions as surgery, is based on one common set of fundamental principles.' [52]

He made Cyclographs of champions in widely varying fields — champion fencers (fig. 19), champion bricklayers, expert pitchers, famous surgeons (fig. 51), and the champion oyster opener of Rhode Island — to find 'the points of similarity between their motions.' [53]

The light curves and the wire models reveal the motion in full plasticity. Motion acquires a form of its own and a life of its own. For eyes trained by contemporary art, there is a direct emotional appeal in these shapes, which the eye does not find in nature.

The light curves that visualize the movements of 'a girl folding a handkerchief' (fig. 60), showing all the unconscious intricacies, belong to that type of phenomena in which the motion means everything, the object performing it nothing.

We have found no mention of Marey's work in Gilbreth's studies. But it matters little, for our purpose, whether Gilbreth had heard of it or not. Marey had recorded trajectories on a single plate, and mentioned that a Geneva scientist used incandescent lamps for the same purpose. Gilbreth, with his Chronocyclograph, was the first to give us intimate insight into the pure path, as well as the time element, of a movement.

---

[52] Frank B. and Lillian M. Gilbreth, *Motion Study for the Handicapped*, London, 1920, p.15.

[53] Ibid. p.16. 'A prominent surgeon,' writes Gilbreth in connection with one of his experiments, 'is perfectly willing to be photographed performing a delicate operation but when the fact is mentioned that this is being done to find the similarity between his actions and other skilled workers, he becomes scornfully incredulous. How can such a thing be? He, a skillfully trained, highly developed product of long years of study to be likened to a bricklayer!' With the same contemptuous incredulity, a well-known physicist rejected the idea of a relation between the methods of present-day physics and the methods of contemporary art.

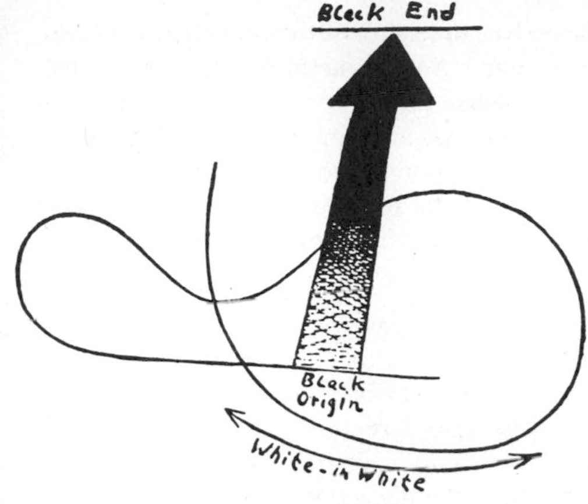

53. PAUL KLEE: 'Formation of the Black Arrow.' 1925. *Better perhaps than any other painter, Paul Klee has the secret of projecting psychological movement. In Klee's work the pointer arrow in the shape of a rectangle headed by a triangle first appeared — an artistic symbol before it became internationally familiar in ordinary use. 'The given white is accepted by the eye as customary, but the contrasting strangeness of action (black), sharpens vividness of vision for the climax, or end.' (Klee,* Pedagogical Sketchbook, *tr. Sybil Peech, Courtesy Nierendorf Gallery, New York)*

54. FRANK B. GILBRETH: Perfect Movement, Wire Model, *c.*1912. *(Courtesy Lillian M. Gilbreth)*

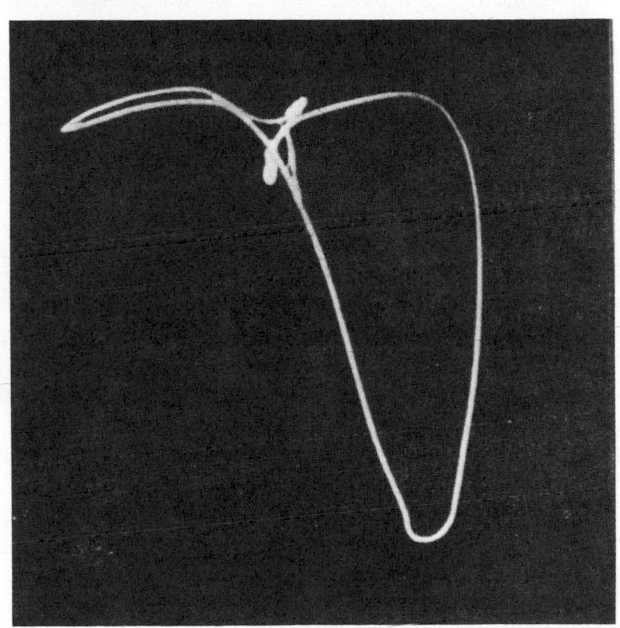

Problems of motion presented themselves to scientists, to production engineers, and to artists. Independently they found similar methods of solving them. Unexpectedly, we encounter the same tendency in art and in scientific management as soon as the latter touches on absolutes and illuminates the structure of manual operations by penetrating the elements and the path of the motion.

The fact that a similarity of methods can be found arising unconsciously in such heterogeneous fields is among the most hopeful symptoms of our period.

This research takes a new starting point. It uses the time factor in making visible the elements of a motion. 'The timing . . . is done on the elements of the process.' [54] Space-time relations form the very basis of the method: Motion is dissected into phases so as to reveal its inner structure.

This characteristic is not limited to scientific management. It is deeply rooted in our epoch. About the same time the dissection of movement appears quite independently as an artistic problem in painting. From the standpoint of motion we can distinguish a close succession of two stages in contemporary art.

First, movement is dissected into separate phases so that the forms appear side by side or overlapping. This occurs around 1910.

The second stage makes the *form* of movement into an object of expression. Scientific management does this for purposes of analysis. In art, calligraphic forms are endowed with the power of symbols. This occurs around 1920.

The development continues into a third stage, of which we know only the beginning. During the 'thirties motion forms increasingly become a pictorial language to express psychic content.

***Movement in Successive Phases, c.*1912**

The Italian Futurists attempted to represent movement in successive phases — Carlo Carrà with his 'Rattling taxi,' Giacomo Balla with his 'Dog on the leash' (1912).

The boldest handling of phase representation was Marcel Duchamp's 'Nude descending the staircase' (fig. 15). The sequence of movements — which the eye but summarily perceives — forms the starting point of the picture. From their succession, a new synthesis, a new artistic form emerges, giving representation to the heretofore unrepresentable: movement in its phases.

One easily recognizes in this picture the influence of the Futurists, of Archi-

---

[54] Frank B. and Lillian M. Gilbreth, *Motion Study for the Handicapped*, London, 1920, p.7.

penko's early sculpture with its hollowed forms, and of Cubism at its peak. Yet the question of influence is overshadowed not only by the masterful rendering, but by the more universal issue: What attempts are made from other sides to solve Marcel Duchamp's problem? What do the scientists have to say about it? Looked at it in this way, Duchamp's problem appears deeply interfused with the period. How early the physiologists showed interest in these problems, we have already seen. In his celebrated studies of the 'seventies on the motions of men and animals, Eadweard Muybridge set up a series of thirty cameras at twelve-inch intervals, releasing their shutters electromagnetically as soon as the moving object passed before the plate. Muybridge attempted — and from several sides simultaneously — to record the phases of simple movements such as rising, sitting, and walking downstairs. He thereby obtained a sequence of motion phases. Each picture showed the object in an isolated phase as arrested by each camera (fig. 16).

Etienne Jules Marey came closer to reconstructing the path of a movement from its phases. He used but a single camera and, in his research of greatest interest today, a single plate. At the beginning his movers wore white garments against a black background. But this resulted in an overlapping series. He therefore clad his model in black, with a bright metal strip extending along the feet and up the torso and arms. This gave a coherent motion sequence in which the forms no longer obliterated one another [55] (figs. 13–14). A half century later H. E. Edgerton invented the stroboscope, whose highly perfected technical equipment (radio interrupter) could freeze motion to the millionth part of a second. The problem was conceived by both Marey and Edgerton along lines that are methodologically similar.

Although Marcel Duchamp's 'Nude descending the staircase' created a sensation when exhibited at the New York Armory Show of 1913, it lay beyond the public's comprehension — a failure of understanding not limited to one place or one country. It is not enough to say that the American public was here making its first acquaintance of the new trends. The reason must be traced to the deeply ingrown fallacy that problems of feeling have nothing to do with problems of science, notwithstanding the fact that every true culture has taken it for granted that thinking and feeling are interdependent.

Movement in Its Own Right, c.1920

In the second phase *the pure form of movement* becomes an artistic object in its own right. It does not have to reproduce naturalistically an outside object.

[55] E. J. Marey, *La Méthode graphique dans les sciences expérimentales*, with appendix: 'Développement de la méthode graphique par l'emploi de la photographie,' Paris, 1885, p.34.

55. JOAN MIRO: Composition. Oil on Sandpaper, 1935. Detail.
(*Courtesy Pierre Matisse Gallery, New York*)

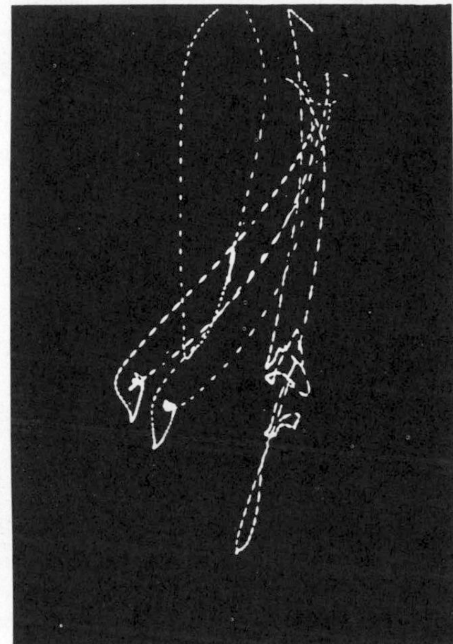

56. FRANK B. GILBRETH: Chronocyclograph of a Motion.
(*Courtesy Lillian M. Gilbreth*)

Every age has known the impact upon feeling of lines, curves, signs. All good ornament stands witness to this.

And this is no less true of movement in space; it too can be experienced as an absolute, likewise disengaged from the performer.

Is not the endless flow of movement in skating more significant than the body of the skater? As we watch a fireworks display, is it merely the luminous trajectory against the dark background that arrests us? Is it not rather the disembodied movement of the rockets through space that so appeals to our imagination?

What occurs in painting around 1920 is but the artistic extension of this faculty. For a work process to be understandable, it must be made visible; for he who performs it does not know his own movement. And this holds good for our subconscious processes.

These symbols of movement are spontaneous condensations, like the sound-poems of the Dadaists and, later, the Surrealists' quest for an 'automatic writing' (1924). A poet such as Paul Eluard confirms this (1939), as he comments on the 'integral truth' (*vérité totale*) sought by Picasso and every real artist of the time. 'Picasso has created fetishes, but fetishes possessing a life of their own. Not mere intermediary signs but signs in motion. Their motion makes them concrete things.' [56]

Signs in movement, movement in signs. Paul Klee, perhaps the boldest explorer of the subconscious, held that 'pictorial art springs from movement, is in itself interrupted motion and is conceived as motion.' [57]

Klee's *Pedagogical Sketchbook* emerges ever more clearly as a key to contemporary art. This pithily worded notebook summarizes his teaching at the Weimar Bauhaus. Here the master does more than teach; he admits us into the workshop.

57. JOAN MIRO: 'Ecritures, Paysages et Têtes d'Hommes,' 1935. Detail. *Miro, whom Klee regarded as the painter closest to himself, uses movement in signs and symbols to achieve an astonishingly direct expression, without interposition of philosophical or reflective motifs. (Courtesy Pierre Matisse Gallery, New York)*

[56] Paul Eluard, *Picasso*, London Bulletin 15, 1939.
[57] W. Grohmann, *The Drawings of Paul Klee*, New York, 1944.

58. PAUL KLEE: 'The Queen of Hearts,' Lithograph. 1921.
(*Courtesy Buchholz Gallery, New York*)

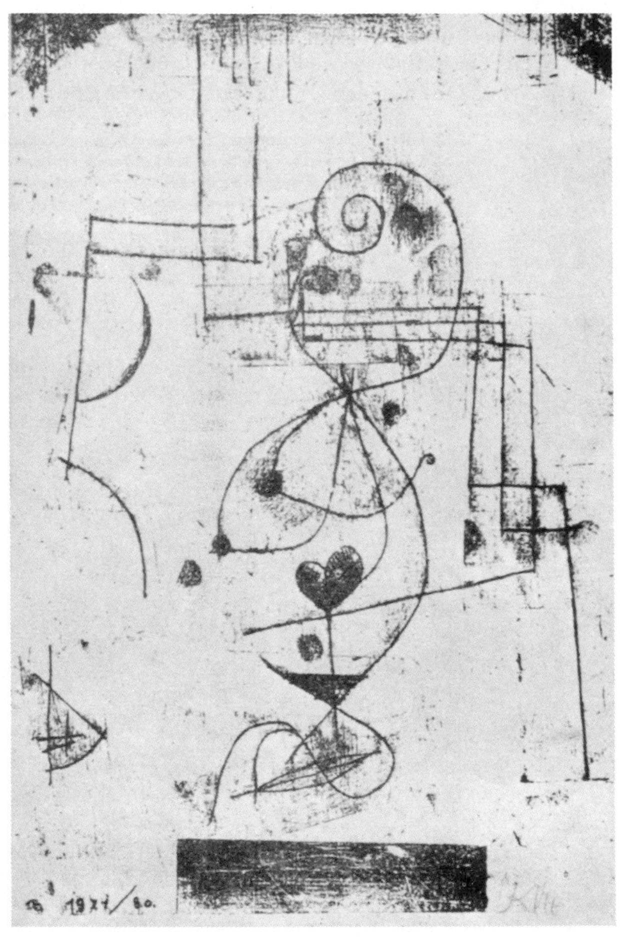

Klee's elucidation of an artistic problem comes astonishingly close to the framework of Oresme's thought. Nothing is static. A line, he begins, 'an activated line, a line moving freely along, is a stroll for strolling's sake. Its performer is a point in transit.' [58] Everything for him is the outcome of motion, even the circle, which, plastically speaking, seems to rest in itself — and which geometry defines as a curve whose points are at an equal distance from the center. For Klee the circle originates in the rotation of a pendulum. And from the circle Klee develops 'The Spiral' (fig. 59), 1925, a spiral-head crowns the 'Queen of Hearts' (fig. 58), 1921.

[58] Paul Klee, *Pedagogical Sketchbook*, first issued as second *Bauhausbuch* under the direction of Walter Gropius and L. Moholy-Nagy, English ed. New York, 1944.

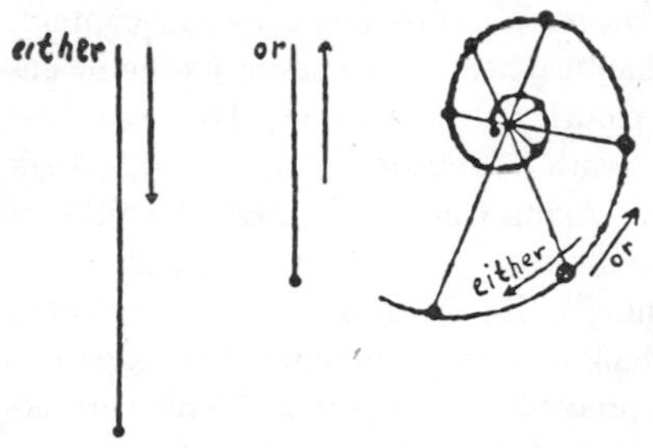

59. PAUL KLEE: 'The Spiral,' 1925. *'The moving spiral originates with the lengthening radius. Shortening the radius progressively narrows the circumference till the beautiful spectacle dies suddenly when it reaches a point of stasis. Movement no longer being infinite, the question of direction becomes decisive.'* (*Klee,* Pedagogical Sketchbook, *tr. Sybil Peech. Courtesy Nierendorf Gallery, New York*)

60. FRANK B. GILBRETH: Girl Folding a Handkerchief. *All the unconscious intricacy of a motion's progress is registered in curves of light.* (*Courtesy Lillian M. Gilbreth*)

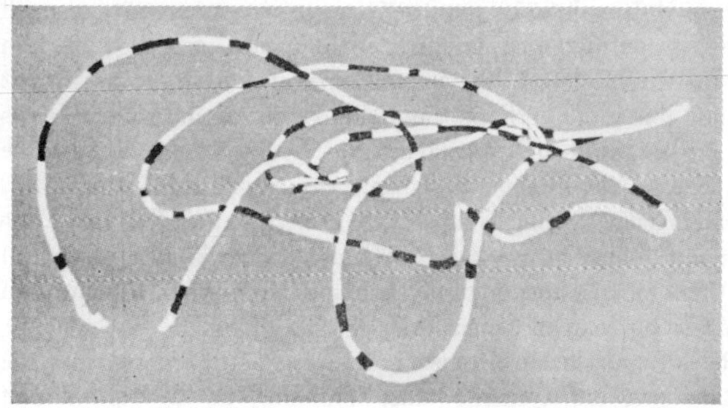

Surely it is no accident that in Klee's work first appeared the direction-pointing arrow as a rectangle headed by a triangle, a form that gained international currency. In his *Pedagogical Sketchbook* Klee explains in his way, which is at the same time symbolic and direct, the coming about of this form (fig. 53). Kandinsky's canvas 'Pink Square' (1923) (fig. 20) is a cosmic storm, a cosmogony of shooting lines, of arrows, of planetary rings, and the figure '3' expanded in sickle form.

Drawings and lithographs, Paul Klee's favorite expression around 1920, offer the natural medium for rapidly executed and continuous motion. Very soon his motion symbols extend into the organic. A bold step it was in 1921 to form the image of man out of the symbols of movement, as if to portray him by the things he does and thinks.

A third stage announces itself, a development of which we know only the beginning: the form of movement becomes a means of expression in painting just as perspective had formerly been the means of expressing a specific content, an isolated scene. When motion rather than perspective is chosen as the means of expression, it yields instead of a static picture a dynamic one. The titles that Klee gives his pictures — 'Lady in the South,' 'Spinster,' 'Anchored,' 'Park with Birds,' 'Temple Reflected in Water,' 'Aging Couple' — might be titles of the static genre pictures of the ruling taste.

Here the same title stands for something quite different. Just as Gilbreth made visible the form and the true meaning of bodily movement, so Klee was able to give visible form to the innermost processes of the psyche. This perspective cannot do. The search now is for relations that are manifold, fluctuating, and far from static.

The whole picture becomes motion process.

Let us take a picture of Klee's late period — 'Aging Couple' (fig. 61) for instance. In truth it hardly needs a title. It lives in its motion-form with a life of its own. As in a good Renaissance painting, its power stems not so much from its content as from distinguished handling of the means of expression. An eye not yet accustomed to the pictorial language based on motion process will at first see no more than this, and perhaps the striking interaction of the colors — brilliant yellow, brown, pink-violet, and green. Whoever has learned the pictorial language based on symbols will see portrayed all that is masklike, antagonistic, and evil in this 'Aging Couple' and how, in a single circuit, the movement embraces and binds the two faces. Without Picasso's pitiless surgical intervention and without his pathos, anatomy is made submissive to expression and movement. This is the year of 'Guernica.'

In less than two decades, art learned to use motion forms to represent psychic processes with lapidary cast and dynamic color. This may be the beginning of

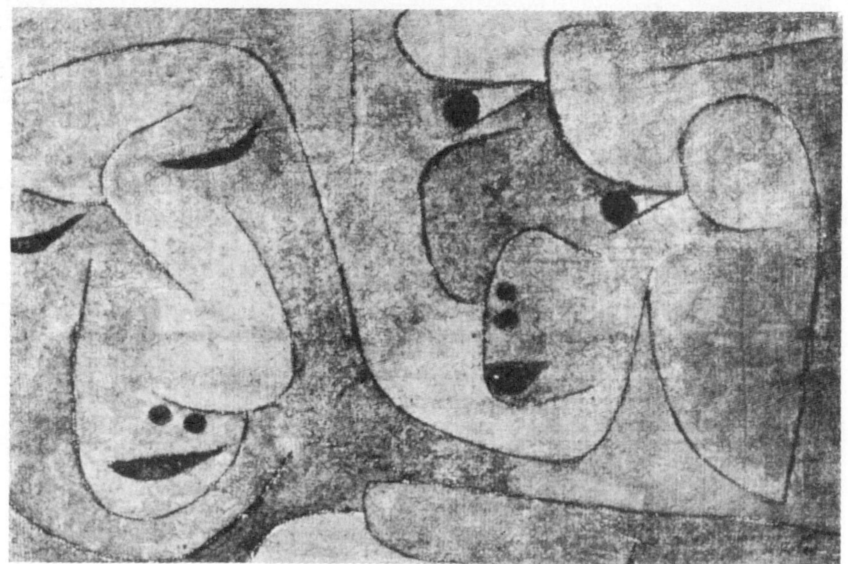

61. PAUL KLEE: 'Aging Couple,' Oil. 1931. *Black-and-white reproduction does not render Klee's luminous color relationships, but sufficiently shows how he uses motion forms as a plastic language to interpret a psychic process.* (*Courtesy Nierendorf Gallery, New York*)

a third step, leading toward mastery of symbolic language free of atavistic reference.

In Joan Miro's painting, around 1924, appear signs, numbers, and serpentine curves. Their use is hesitant at first, haphazard and Dadaistic. Toward 1930 they gain in power (figs. 55, 57). The faculty awakens in Miro to endow color, both by the shape it fills, and by its relation to the whole image, with a luminous quality bordering on the magical. Miro's forms, which used to flutter lightly like paper streamers through space, take on weight and definition. What was a boldness in 1921, when Klee lithographed his 'Queen of Hearts,' is now taken for granted. Personages, animals, erotic constellations, turn into signs, motion forms imbued with the force of symbols; and this artist of the post-Kleeian generation seems almost predestined to translate them into murals.

By signs and forms, the artists express the unknown within us, to interpret the winding paths of the mind as really and efficiently as motion-curves serve scientific management.

Both lie equally rooted within us, for movement and the symbols of movement become of one flesh with our being.

Forerunners, Successors?

Charles Babbage

Do time and motion studies have any historical forerunners?

It was pointed out (1912)[59] that the early nineteenth and even the eighteenth century had known approaches to Taylor's method. Cited as chief witness was a disciple of Adam Smith, Charles Babbage, professor of mathematics at Cambridge. His book *On the Economy of Machinery and Manufacture* (Cambridge, 1832, and often reprinted) gives tables 'for the cost and time of each operation' in needle manufacture. Babbage quotes the tabulation of the Frenchman Perronet,[60] who in 1760 timed by the clock and computed the cost of each operation in the manufacture of twelve thousand needles.

It would be straining the truth to regard these men as precursors of Taylor's method, or to suppose that they anticipated it. The using of a watch is an external. Babbage employs it only to make clear the advantages of the division of labor; it occurs in his chapter on that topic.

Taylor was perfectly right in giving the simple answer: 'Time studies began in the machine shop of the Midvale Steel Company and in 1881.' [61]

Babbage's time measurements were to show the advantages inherent in the division of labor. The time factor in scientific management serves to reveal the very elements of motion.

Charles Bedaux

Is the success of Charles Bedaux, mainly in the 1930's,[62] to be regarded as a further development of scientific management? Doubtless his 'close analysis and systematic observation of industrial operations' were taken over from Taylor and especially from Gilbreth, but the main purpose was to establish more perfect wage systems. Bedaux, who came to New York from France in 1911, said that he applied 'corrections for speed of performance.' To this end, he introduced a unit of human power similar to the 'dyn,' which the physicists use to measure mechanical work. Bedaux calls this unit a '*B*.' And he defines it: 'A "*B*" is a fraction of a minute of work plus a fraction of a minute of rest always aggregating unity but varying in proportion according to the nature of strain.' [63] His

[59] By the sub-committee on Administration of the American Society of Engineers.

[60] Babbage, op.cit. p.146.

[61] Copley, op.cit. vol. 1, p.226.

[62] The Bedaux Company, *More Production, Better Morale*, A Program for American Industry, New York, 1942. In 1942, 720 corporations with 675,000 workers adopted the Bedaux system.

[63] Charles Bedaux, *Labor Management*, a pamphlet, New York, 1928 (many subsequent editions).

'*B*' forms the basis of a wage system which has aroused greater hostility among workers than any other measure in scientific management, since it can be used to exploit labor with unusual severity.

The aims have shifted. With Taylor and his successors the stress fell on analysis and organization of operations; with Gilbreth and the elucidation of human work processes by the visualization of movement, the human factor comes to the fore: elimination of waste motion, the reduction of fatigue, the training of the handicapped. With Bedaux, attention centers upon 'labor measurement,' on the wage scale. It stands for a much earlier conception of business enterprise. The suspicion of espionage under which he came, and his inglorious end during the Second World War, show Bedaux's methods in an even more crudely materialistic light.

The Assembly Line in the Twentieth Century

1913–14

This is the time when Henry Ford brings the assembly line into the limelight of success. The assembly line was in full stride at Ford's Highland Park plant by 1915, the year of F. W. Taylor's death. Two methods overlap. Henry Ford does not mention Taylor; he is the self-taught man, who does everything by himself. The results Taylor had attained by decades of perseverance have become common knowledge. The instruction cards on which Taylor set so much value Ford is able to discard. The conveyor belt, the traveling platform, the overhead rails and material conveyors take their place. These are automatic instructions that work more efficiently than Taylor's written cards. Motion analysis has become largely unnecessary, for the task of the assembly-line worker is reduced to a few manipulations. Taylor's stop watch nevertheless remains, measuring the time of operations to the fraction of a second.

When the assembly line was introduced in Cincinnati and then in Chicago, over thirty years before Henry Ford, the stimulus arose in the mechanization of a manual trade, slaughtering. In this period, much experience was gathered regarding the speed at which the moving-line should travel and how the workers conducted themselves toward it. By 1900 conveyor systems were used even in department stores, but without affording continuous flow.

After 1900 the machine industry lapsed into that routine which leads to a crippling of the creative impulse. Its experience seems to have become irrevocably frozen into formulae. This is the period when experts appear with analogies, and argue the impossibility of all that lies beyond their routine. No one has written more amusingly of this than Henry Ford himself.[64] In such periods, every problem seems solved and every path trodden. Nothing remains of the morning freshness of the 'thirties, when a J. G. Bodmer could invent and construct from beginning to end both the machines and the tools with which to fabricate them. A new impulse could spring only from a new product, one that had to be created from the ground up: This around 1900 was the automobile.

Henry Ford's function is to have first recognized democratic possibilities in the vehicle that had always ranked as a privilege. The idea of transforming so complicated a mechanism as the motorcar from a luxury article into one of common use, and of bringing its price within reach of the average man, would have been unthinkable in Europe.

The belief that the automobile could be made an article of mass production, and from this conviction the complete revolutionizing of the manufacture of the product assure Henry Ford his historical position.

Like mass production in butchering, mass production of a new means of transportation, the automobile, became a stimulus for the assembly line, which from there spread to the inflexibly routinized machine factories.

'The Ford shop's assembling practice is to place the most suitable components on elevated ways or rails and to carry it past successive groups of workmen, who fix the various components to the principal component, until the assembling is completed.'[65] How this was carried out in Ford's Highland Park factory at Detroit in 1913–14; how, in April 1913, 'the first experiment of an assembly line on assembling the fly-wheel of a magneto'[66] was attempted; how the motor assembly was split into eighty-four different operations, taking a third of the former time; how the chassis was first placed on rails, operated by a rope and pulley, can be read in Ford's own book or in detailed accounts printed as early as 1915.[67]

To realize his conviction that the automobile must become a people's vehicle Henry Ford employs the means and the ideas of his time. He uses them like building-stones, often with fresh meaning, and simplifying them wherever possible. The assembly line supplants Taylor's motion studies and the yet more complex fatigue studies of his successors. The interchangeability of parts, already known in the field of agricultural machinery in the 'sixties for maintenance of the reaper, takes on another nuance in Ford's hands. He stresses its usefulness for the automobile: 'The machinery of today, especially that which

[64] Henry Ford, *My Life and Work*, New York, 1922, p.86.
[65] Horace Lucien Arnold and Fay Leone Fanrote, *Ford Methods and the Ford Shop*, N. Y., 1915, p.102.
[66] Henry Ford, op.cit. p.80.
[67] Arnold and Fanrote, op.cit.

is used in general life away from the machine shop, has to have its parts absolutely interchangeable, so that it can be repaired by non-skilled men.' [68]

He follows Taylor's method, unusual for the time, of so far as possible reducing working hours and raising wages. Here too the foreman retains his function. But when Taylor, in his famous experiments on shoveling, tells his laborers in the yard of the Bethlehem Steel Company: 'Pete and Mike, you fellows understand your job all right, both of you fellows are first class men, but we want to pay you double wages,' [69] he still is set upon raising production within the factory. Henry Ford goes further, and regards low wages as 'the cutting of buying power and the curtailment of the home market.' [70] Indeed Henry Ford views production and sales as a unit and, long before the high-pressure salesmanship of the 1930's, builds a world-wide organization to distribute his products. The efficiency of the sales force is as precisely worked out as the tempo of the assembly line.

A further broadening of the circle might take up the question: How has the automobile affected living habits? In what measure has it stimulated and in what measure has it destroyed? How far, then, is its production to be encouraged and to what extent curbed?

As a phenomenon, Henry Ford crystallizes anew the independent pioneering spirit of 1830 and 1860. In a period of elaborate banking and credit institutions, a period governed by the stock exchange, when the lawyers are needed at every move, Henry Ford trusts none of them and operates without banks.

In an age when anonymous corporations grow to giant proportions, he would exercise patriarchal power over his worker force, like a master over his journeymen. He would be independent of everyone in everything. He gathers in his own hands forests, iron and coal mines, smelting furnaces, rubber plantations, and other raw materials.

But just as great cities become increasingly ungovernable when they overgrow themselves, great industrial concentrations elude the patriarchal hand when they develop to the gigantic.

Ford did not have to spend his life, like Oliver Evans, furthering ideas ungrasped by his contemporaries. He may have had the same indomitable energy; but he also had the advantage of coming not at the start but at the end of the mechanistic phase. Success does not depend on genius or energy alone, but on the extent to which one's contemporaries have been prepared by what has gone before.

The assembly line too, as conceived by Henry Ford, forms in many ways the fruition of a long development.

---

[68] Henry Ford, *Moving Forward*, New York, 1930, p.128.

[69] Copley, op.cit. vol. 2, p.58.

[70] Henry Ford, *My Life and Work*, chapter on wages.

The Automatic Assembly Line, c.1920

Toward the end of the eighteenth century, Oliver Evans at one stroke achieved continuous line production, an automatic unit in which man acted only as an observer.

More than a century and a half later the curve gradually closes. Again we are approaching the point where a continuous production line, with man serving only as an observer, is the objective. Now it is not for the automatic grinding of grain, but for the building of complicated machinery, involving hundreds of different operations.

It is increasingly clear that the assembly line, as developed from the packing houses, through the automobile industry, and beyond, forms an intermediate stage: Man has still to perform whatever movements the engineer cannot yet delegate to the machine. Quite possibly this form of mechanical work will in some future day be pointed to as a symptom of our barbarism.

The impulse toward a new phase, the automatic assembly line, again has its starting point in the automobile industry. The reason is plain: for the first time an industry was faced with the problem of building a most complex mechanism by the million. A new scale was thus introduced.

After Ford's assembly line was in operation, L. R. Smith, Milwaukee manufacturer, raised the question (1916): 'Can automobile frames be built without men?'

'Its answers rested in the subconscious mind of engineers. We set out,' he says,[71] 'to build automobile frames, without men. We wanted to do this on a scale far beyond that necessary to meet the immediate requirements of the automobile industry.'

Now the question that could not be permanently evaded is raised, from within the industry, not from outside influences: 'It is highly probable that watching our workers do the same thing over and over again, day in and day out, sent us on our quest for the 100% mechanization of frame manufacture.'[72]

It was this often clairvoyant optimism which, at a time when the industry as a whole was producing no more than a million and a half automobiles a year, conceived, and within five years built, a single plant to produce more than a million yearly. 'A completed frame leaves the conveyor end, brushed and cleaned for the paint line, every ten seconds of the production shift. It takes ninety minutes from the strip of steel as received from the mill to the delivery of an enameled automobile frame into storage.'[73]

[71] L. R. Smith, 'We Build a Plant to Run without Men,' *The Magazine of Business*, New York, February 1929.

[72] Ibid. [73] Ibid.

62. Fully Automatic Assembly Line: Rivet-Setting in a General Assembly Unit. *In the time of full mechanization the assembly line becomes a synchronized automatic instrument. The entire factory mechanism must function like a precision watch accurate to the split second. A long development begun by Oliver Evans culminates here, when production is accomplished without hands. Man, no longer compelled to repeat his movement endlessly, stands by and supervises.* (*Courtesy A. O. Smith Corp., Milwaukee, Wis.*)

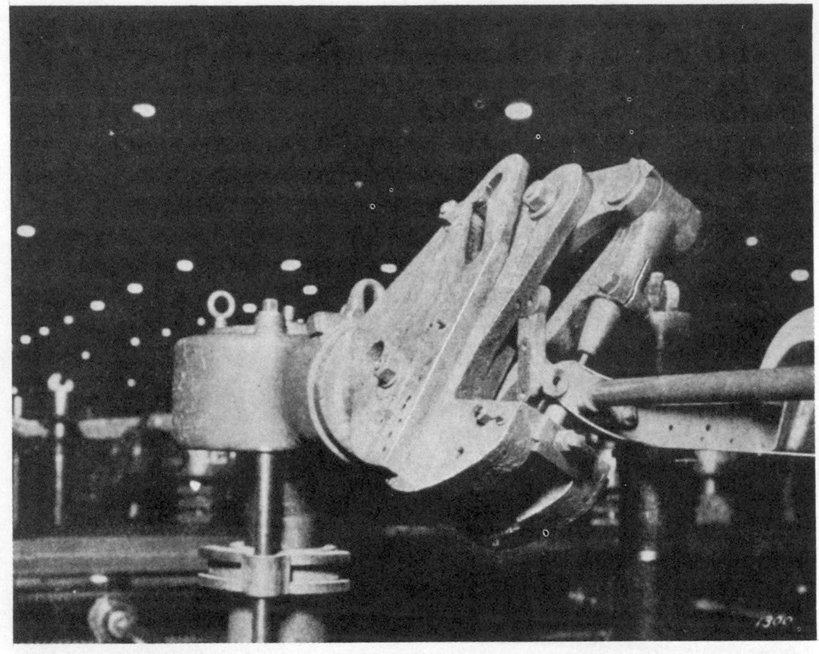

63. Fully Automatic Assembly Line. Close-up of Riveting Heads. *A series of automatic riveters, with enormous jaws like heads of mythical birds, press the rivets at a single bite. This is the final assembly station, following* 552 *automatic operations.* (*Courtesy A. O. Smith Corp., Milwaukee, Wis.*)

Here scientific management, so far as it is the analysis of human motions, is replaced by new tools of production. Five hundred engineers transform a factory into an automatic unit, producing more quickly, cheaply, and profitably, and freeing man from mechanical movement.

This automatic assembly line begins with an 'inspection machine,' which 'straightens and checks every piece of strip steel as received from the mill.' [74] The material is worked upon and moves back and forth through the factory on the most varied types of conveyor systems in an uninterrupted process. First in a sub-assembly line, often in parallel operations, the steel bars are cut, punched, and formed. A second group of machines assembles the various parts until they are finally clamped together in the general assembly line (fig. 62).

[74] Sidney G. Koon, '10,000 Automobile Frames a Day,' in *The Iron Age*, 5 June 1930.

'Automatic rivet feeding heads swing into position and rivets are shot into the holes waiting to receive them. Air pressure accomplishes this task.' [75] The rivets are pressed into rows of automatic riveters with enormous jaws like the heads of mythical birds (fig. 63). Cleaning and painting follow.

Something of the 1830 spirit of Johann Georg Bodmer lives on in the way manufacturing tools — presses, riveters, conveyor systems — are freshly invented, constructed, and integrated. No longer is the individual machine alone automatized, as is usual in bulk manufacture. Here, extremely precise time charts guide the automatic co-operation of instruments which, like the atom or a planetary system, consist of separate units, yet gravitate about one another in obedience to their inherent laws.

The Human Aspect of the Assembly Line

It is not easy to take a historical view of recent periods, especially in so sensitive and ramified an aspect as the inquest into human work.

The assembly line and scientific management are essentially rationalizing measures. Tendencies in this direction extend relatively far back. But it was in the twentieth century that they were elaborated and became a sweeping influence. In the *second decade* (with Frederick Taylor as the central figure), it was scientific management that aroused the greatest attention: the interest of industry, the opposition of workers, public discussion, and governmental enquiries.[76] This is the period of its further refinement and of its joining with experimental psychology (Frank B. Gilbreth, central and most universal figure).

In the third decade (Henry Ford, the central figure), the assembly line moves to a key position in all industry. Its scope is constantly growing. In the time of full mechanization, the production engineer gained sway over manufactures of the most diverse types, seeking every possible opening in which an assembly line might be inserted. The forming of a more comprehensive picture would well reward the effort, for the assembly line becomes almost a symbol of the period between the two world wars.

Looking at the impact of mechanization on man, we must stress those aspects which bear upon man's very nature. We must sharply distinguish the impulse that gave rise to the assembly line and scientific management from the human repercussions. The impulse sprang from the epoch's imperious demand: production, ever-faster production, production at any cost. As soon as evaluation is called for, we find often diametrically opposed views: on the one side, a disgruntled worker; on the other, the enthusiastic promoter of the idea.

[75] Ibid.

[76] *Hearings before special committee of the House of Representatives to investigate Taylor's and other systems of Shop Management.* 3 vols. Government Printing Office, 1912.

64. Fully Automatic Assembly Line: Storage of Automobile Frames. *One frame every eight seconds. Ten thousand a day. 'We have accomplished what nobody has accomplished before,' says the manufacturer. (Courtesy A. O. Smith Corp., Milwaukee, Wis.)*

Taylor, 1912: 'After a long struggle, worker and employer regard one another as friends.' [77]

Complains the *worker:* '. . . driven at an inhuman pace by foremen picked for their brutality.' [78]

The *advocate of scientific management*, 1914: 'The speed boss does not drive the men at all. He is their servant. . . . The correct speed is the best speed at which the men can work day after day, year after year, and continuously improve in health.' [79]

Complains the *worker:* 'There was never a moment of leisure or opportunity to turn my head. . . . The men have no rest except for fifteen or twenty minutes at lunch time and can go to the toilet only when substitutes are ready to relieve them.' [80]

---

[77] *Bulletin of the Taylor Society*, June–August 1912, p.103.

[78] Robert L. Cruden, *The End of the Ford Myth*, International Pamphlets no. 24, New York, 1932.

[79] Gilbreth, op.cit. p.65.

[80] R. L. Cruden, op.cit. p.4.

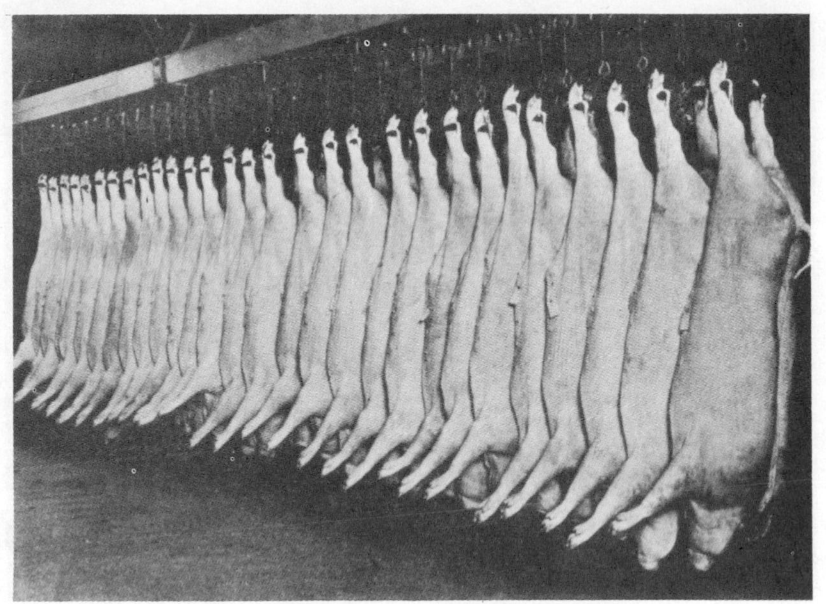

65. Carcasses in Chicago Slaughter House.
(Courtesy Kaufman and Fabry)

These are personal utterances picked at random. The unions were hostile to scientific management. Trade-union organization was late in permeating the United States. In the Bethlehem Steel Works, for example, in which Taylor carried out his famous shovel and high-speed steel experiments, 'not a single employee was a member of a union' even ten years later (1910).[81] The unions saw their tactics endangered 'through building up loyalty to the management,'[82] and above all, they saw scientific management as a new means of exploitation.

Later a change in trade-union policy led to reformulation of the program. 'Labor is fully conscious that the world needs things for use and that the standards of life can improve only as production for use increases. Labor is conscious to work out better methods of industry.'[83]

Not to be overlooked are those aspects which have to do with the class struggle. They, however, lie outside the actual problems of this book, whose task is to

[81] Drury, *Scientific Management*, New York, 1915, p.176.

[82] Ibid. p.175.

[83] Ibid. p.27.

66. Man in the Assembly Line. Charlie Chaplin in 'Modern Times.' 1936. '*The mechanized individualist goes mad and proceeds to turn the factory into the madhouse it has always been.*' (*Courtesy United Artists Corp.*)

describe the impact of a mechanized world on the human organism and on human feeling.

In a Chicago packing house, hogs, hanging head downwards, moved uninterruptedly past a staunch Negro woman at the curve of the conveyor system. Her task was to stamp, with a rubber stamp, the carcasses examined by the inspectors. With a sweeping movement she smacked the rubber stamp on each skin.

Perhaps we start from false premises; but in an outside observer a strange feeling was aroused: a creature of the human race trained to do nothing else but, day after day, and eight hours each day, stamp thousand after thousand of carcasses in four places.

Henry Ford tells (1922) [84] of a worker who had to perform a particularly monotonous task, actually one single motion of the hand. At his request, he

[84] Henry Ford, *My Life and Work*, in the chapter on 'The Torture of the Machine.'

was moved to another position, but after a few weeks he asked to be put back in his old job. Here Henry Ford hits on a phenomenon known to every urbanist who has slum-dwellers to resettle: No matter how primitive and unsanitary conditions may be, a certain number will always be found who refuse to leave their slum for new houses, and who prefer by far their old and familiar conditions.

The modern assembly line as it appears, probably for the first time, in the packing houses of Cincinnati, and certain measures of scientific management, which use man as part of an automatic process, are transitional phenomena, prevailing only so long as machinery is unable to perform certain operations of its own accord.

A document that translates the human response to this phase into artistic symbols is Charlie Chaplin's film *Modern Times* (fig. 66).[85] When the picture was first shown in New York, in February 1936, a radical periodical took the

[85] Chaplin worked for five years on this silent film. He began in 1931 at the time when René Clair in *A Nous la Liberté* brought the endless belt and the mechanized man into the film. But a somewhat primitive romanticism and too superficial comparisons — prison life and assembly line — destroy the symbolic force of Clair's satire.

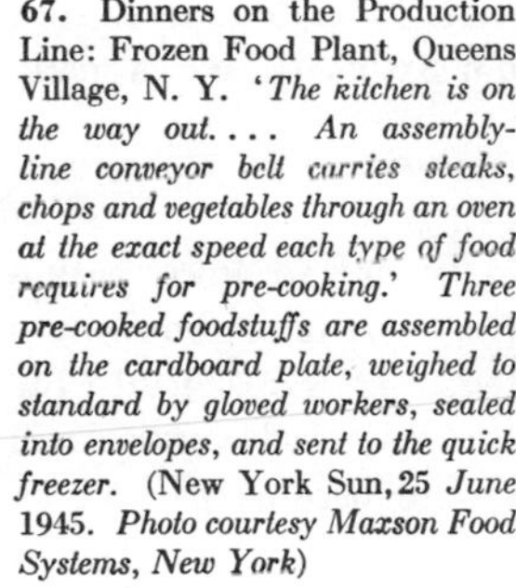

67. Dinners on the Production Line: Frozen Food Plant, Queens Village, N. Y. '*The kitchen is on the way out. . . . An assembly-line conveyor belt carries steaks, chops and vegetables through an oven at the exact speed each type of food requires for pre-cooking.*' *Three pre-cooked foodstuffs are assembled on the cardboard plate, weighed to standard by gloved workers, sealed into envelopes, and sent to the quick freezer.* (New York Sun, 25 *June* 1945. *Photo courtesy Maxson Food Systems, New York*)

attitude: 'What his political views are I don't know and I do not care. . . .'[86] The decisive point in this document is the revolt against subordination to the machine.

It is the story of an individual who, eight hours a day, year in and year out, must perform the same motion, and for whom the whole world is transformed into nuts to be turned by his wrench. The monotony and compulsion of the high-speed conveyor belt destroy his mental balance. 'The mechanized individualist goes mad and proceeds to turn the factory into the madhouse that it really always has been.'[87] He loosens dangerous screws that accelerate the assembly line to a mad pace. In the nose of a foreman, the buttons of an office girl, the breasts of a fat woman, everywhere he sees nuts that have to be tightened. By grotesque exaggeration the human core of the problem is revealed. What is this automatism, this reflex movement of screw-tightening, but the observation which can be made every day upon the workers streaming from the factories, who have the machine in their very gait?

It is the ceaseless mechanizing drive that leads Chaplin to invent the eating machine, which feeds the worker automatically without loss of time; he does not need to stop for lunch, and the assembly line goes on.

All this, though intensified to the grotesque, has a glint of that inner truth which dwells in Shakespeare's comedies.

True, the eating machine is rejected by the manager as too complicated. But a few years later, does not reality begin to approach that symbol of eating in factory tempo? At lunch counters, do not endless belts carry hot plates from kitchen to customer? In drug stores and in the basements of 5- and 10-cent stores do not counter after counter wind like mountain paths to feed as many men as quickly as possible?

The assembly line and scientific management can be put to work within quite opposite economic systems. Their implications, like those of mechanization as a whole, are not unilaterally tied to any one system. They reach into the depths of a basic human problem — labor — and the historical verdict will depend on how far one may expect the human being to become part of an automaton.

Before these methods had come into being, the Reverend William Ellery Channing, one of the great New England preachers of the 1830's, formulated

[86] *New Masses*, 18 Feb. 1936, vol. 18, no. 6.
[87] *Herald Tribune*, New York, 7 Feb. 1936.

with finality the problem of the assembly line and of any purely mechanical use of man: 'I do not look on a human being as a machine, made to be kept in action by a foreign force, to accomplish an unvarying succession of motions, to do a fixed amount of work, and then to fall to pieces at death. . . .' [88]

[88] Rev. William Ellery Channing, *Self Culture*, Introductory address to the Franklin Lectures, delivered at Boston, Sept. 1838.

68. Poultry on the Production Line. 1944. *After the perfecting of line production of machinery full mechanization was applied to so delicate a material as poultry.*
(Courtesy Berenice Abbott)

PART IV MECHANIZATION ENCOUNTERS THE ORGANIC

MECHANIZATION AND THE SOIL: AGRICULTURE

The Farmer in Structural Change

THE structural changes which mechanization has brought about are nowhere easier to follow than in the agricultural sphere, but only so far as the machines are concerned. It is otherwise with mechanization's impact upon the structure of the farmer. This may hold implications for society transcending the purely economic.

We survey too short a span and our experience is still too brief for the voicing of assured judgment. A bare century of agricultural mechanization lies behind us. Our experience is limited to capitalistic conditions. What mechanization has wrought upon the farmer in the Kolkhoz is even harder to judge with finality.

In the industrial domain, we can more approximately see what the change from handicrafts to mechanization has meant. In the agricultural domain, questions arise that still lack any answer. Man's relation with the soil is involved; not in the sense of ownership, for the structural change is manifest in the United States and the Soviet Union alike. The farmer, symbol of continuity, has been drawn into flux.

Within society the tiller of the soil is a link, a bond of union between man and the vitality of nature. The craftsman and the industrial worker shape artifacts — clothing, mechanisms, houses. The farmer tends organic growth: animal, plant, and soil.

Thus the tiller of the soil is understood as the constant element within a civilization. This has not changed since Homer's contemporary Hesiod praised the farmer's calling as one blessed above all others, overranking the trader's and even the warrior's. The attitude is re-echoed with striking consistency and the more so in highly civilized periods, as under Rome of the Empire or during the eighteenth century. It little matters that in contrast to court and urban life the tiller of the soil becomes simplified in the imagination of moralists and poets.

The farmer does not shine in a civilization. But he is as the stabilizing lead stowed deep within the keel. Cities form the content of a culture, the cargo. It is the function of the farmer invisibly to resist the cross winds of destiny. When disaster overtook Antiquity, not the least factor, it has been pointed out, were those forces which, from the third century on, conspired to drive the Roman peasant from his holding and led to the forsaking of the land.[1]

Until late into the nineteenth century the farmer was everywhere a home producer and home consumer, still embodying the archetype of sedentary mankind. When Emerson delivered his address on farming, 'The Man with the Hoe,' at a Massachusetts cattle show in 1858, one could imagine that it was one of the physiocrats speaking:

> The glory of the farmer is that, in the division of labors, it is his part to create. All trade rests at last on his primitive activity. . . .
>
> . . . He is permanent, clings to his land as the rocks do. In the town where I live, farms remain in the same families for seven and eight generations; and most of the first settlers [in 1635], should they reappear on the farms today, would find their own blood and names still in possession.

The agriculturalist as Emerson thought of him was the handicraft farmer, the 'man with the hoe.'

In that same year (1858) McCormick manufactured 4,095 reapers. By then the Middle Western farmer had already changed in structure, and in the hills of Vermont were deserted farmsteads whose owners had gone West.

Mechanization forever altered the structure of the farmer. From home producer and home consumer, carrying his surplus directly to market and dealing with the customer, he became a commercial producer altogether dependent upon the profit of his goods. The narrow circle of home production is broken as soon as mechanization sets in. In its place enters dependence on the international market, on the ups and downs of world trade. Now the farmer and his produce are exposed to the financial power of all the organizations influencing the price level.

The structural change from self-sufficiency to specialization is irresistible. To remain in competition, the farmer must narrow himself to specific products. In America this trend to specialization set in about a century ago, when cheaper wheat from the Middle West appeared in the Eastern states, and converted tilled land into pasture.

Whole regions came to specialize in cattle raising and in dairy farming.[2] The

---

[1] Michael Rostovtzeff, 'The Decay of the Ancient World,' *Economic History Review*, London, 1929, vol. II, p.211. Setting aside theories of decline caused by exhaustion of the soil or climatic change, Rostovtzeff regards the flight from the soil as a decisive factor.

[2] Russell H. Anderson, 'New York Agriculture Meets the West, 1830–1850,' *Wisconsin Magazine of History*, 1932, vol. 16, p.186. 'By 1840 the wheat which arrived at Buffalo alone was equal to about 30% of the New York crop. By 1850 it had increased to over 70%. . . . The New York farmers, with higher priced land, poorer soils and increased competition from the cheap lands of the West, were forced to change [p.292] . . . the forties saw a shift of emphasis from grain to livestock [p.293].'

same process is seen in Europe as soon as countries with a high standard of living find that the cheapness of world wheat makes the growing of domestic wheat unprofitable.

The structural transformation of the farmer from self-sufficiency to specialization occurs in all lands, wherever industrialization runs its course; but in America this process can be observed as clearly as in a laboratory. Here mechanization could deploy untrammeled by dimensions, terrain and social structure.

In Europe today the farmer can stand on his own legs as a home producer and consumer only in countries where the standard of living is low. In countries such as Switzerland, where the living standard comes closer to the American, the farmer must be shielded by subsidies of all kinds. To appearances nothing has changed. The old stock remains in possession of the same holdings which, as Emerson claimed for the New England farms in 1858, may not have changed hands for centuries. The meadows are as carefully kept as the houses, each of which seems to have a physiognomy of its own. But economically the existence of the farmer is in danger, for his products cannot compete in the world market. His survival on the old basis is felt as a social imperative. The legislature provides for him and protects him. In America the authors of the laws served the interest of businessmen, bankers, railroads; legislation for the farmer's benefit (Homestead Act, 1862) was later interpreted in favor of the trusts and railroad companies.[3]

Specialization goes on without respite. If he is to remain in competition, the farmer must increasingly narrow his produce to a specific type of corn, tomato, cattle, or poultry. Even within the product itself he is forced into stricter and stricter standardization. The commercial fruit farms grow tens of thousands of fruit trees of a kind. This is the result of more systematic cultivation of the trees: careful guarding from parasites, better exposure to sunlight, the pruning away of superfluous branches, the discarding of useless blossoms. The climate too plays its part. By the middle of the last century, North America had earned the title 'a grand laboratory of nature for the production of new ameliorated fruit.'[4]

The influence of mechanization — or more accurately, here, of mass production — leads to standardization of the fruit into few varieties. A million peach trees, it is claimed, grow on one commercial farm. We have seen an orchard of 42,000

---

[3] Allan Nevins and Henry S. Commager, *The Pocket History of the United States*, pp.372–3. 'Men who wrote the national laws were much more zealous to serve the interests of manufacturers, bankers and railroad men than to take care of the farmers and legislation reflected this zeal. . . . Laws designed to regulate trusts and railroads were so written or interpreted that they caused little inconvenience.'

[4] *The Rural Cyclopedia*, Edinburgh, 1854, vol. I. p.222.

McIntosh trees; and the apples were so uniform that they might have been stamped out by machine.

The consumer is educated to remain content with little variety. The large red apple, which attracts the customer's eye, is especially favored, and bred less for bouquet than for a resistant skin and stamina in transit. The flavor is neutralized, deliberately, it would seem. The multiplicity of flavors from mildly sour to sweet, and appreciation for the various qualities of the flesh has, we believe, nowhere been more poetically expressed than in Nathaniel Hawthorne's *Mosses from an Old Manse* (1846):

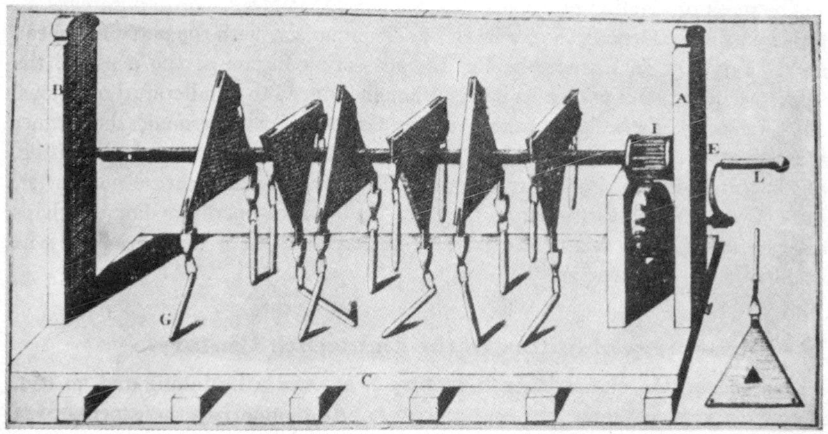

69. Beginning of Mechanization: Threshing Machine. 1770's. *This device typifies the early phases of mechanization in agriculture. It multiplies the number of flails and imitates by mechanical rotation the motion of the human arm. The threshing machine came into practical use in late eighteenth-century England, and was the first successful instrument of mechanized agriculture.* (Pennsylvania Magazine, *Philadelphia,* 1775)

> He loved each tree, doubtless, as if it had been his own child. An orchard has a relation to mankind and readily connects itself with matters of the heart. The trees possess a domestic character. They have lost the wild nature of their forest kindred, and have grown humanized by receiving the care of man as well as by contributing to his wants. There is so much individuality of character, too, among apple trees. . . . One is harsh and crabbed in its manifestations; another gives us fruit as mild as charity. One is churlish and illiberal, evidently grudging the few apples that it bears; another exhausts itself in free-hearted benevolence.

Hawthorne was not using poetic exaggeration when he spoke of the peculiar relation between apples and men. His contemporary, Andrew Jackson Downing, noted landscape architect of the first half of the century, recommends in *The*

Fruit and Fruit Trees of America[5] 186 varieties of apple and 233 varieties of pear. For the keeper of a small orchard he recommends among other trees thirty kinds of apple 'to ripen in succession' — names for the most part still current in Europe. Among them is the distinctive Canada Rennett, a delicate apple of especially subtle flavor, which seems to have become extinct in the United States. These views are not merely literary. 'North America has for a considerable period been celebrated for the great number and surprising richness of its varieties of apple trees,' writes the *Rural Cyclopedia*, in 1854.[6]

The mass production of apples, peaches, corn, tomatoes, cows, pigs, eggs, or poultry by the American farmer is out of all comparison with the petty European scale. Yet even in Europe, behind the reassuring façade of the peasant, the same specialization is taking its path, although reduced to handicraft dimensions. Thus in many of the high valleys of the Grisons in Switzerland, the farmer increasingly concentrates upon one product, milk. His branch is cattle raising, and within cattle raising, dairy farming. He makes neither cheese nor butter, but delivers milk in summer from the high Alp to his co-operative dairy, perhaps many miles distant, where the product is processed. For his own family he frequently buys margarine.

The Rediscovery of Nature in the Eighteenth Century

Like all periods, the eighteenth century is at once a beginning and an end. It opens highways to the nineteenth century. It summarizes the experience of earlier times. The wonderful gift of the eighteenth century is that of apprehending things universally, as only late periods can. We shall look more closely into its ways when examining a single case, the furniture of the Rococo.

Natural Science

In the eighteenth century, nature is rediscovered and probed from all sides — the nostalgic, the economic, the agricultural, to the classification of the entire realm of creation. The lives of the great naturalists of the period — Count Buffon (1707–88), Charles Linné (1707–78) — run with the century. The Swedish naturalist, in his *Systema Naturae* (1735), sweepingly carries through the binary nomenclature of plants, naming them by clan and family.

Buffon, with typically late Baroque outlook, is against sharp cleavages, and points to the often imperceptible merging of animal species. He has a supreme

[5] A. J. Downing, op.cit. (9th ed., 1849) p.148.

[6] *The Rural Cyclopedia*, p.222.

awareness for the continuity of phenomena, in the body as in the cosmos. Many of his hypotheses, such as that which would place the seat of life in 'organic molecules,' no longer appear as grotesque today as they did in the nineteenth century.

René Antoine Ferchault de Réaumur (1683–1757) observes the life of insects. His *Mémoire sur la vie des insectes* was planned as a work in ten volumes, each running to over five hundred pages; six of these left the press between 1734 and 1742. He was older than both Buffon and Linnaeus, but like them first claimed attention during the 'thirties. Réaumur's name is closely associated with the thermometer. Here again his work was one of classification, starting from two fixed points, the freezing point and the boiling point of water, the interval being divided into eighty degrees (1730). This was but a by-product of his studies. It was Réaumur who recorded the insect world in all its elusive breadth. Jean-Jacques Rousseau was an enthusiast of his studies, and Thomas Henry Huxley accounted him the only naturalist on a rank with Darwin.[7] Réaumur and Buffon possessed that gift of universal men, to be at once simple and scientifically precise.[8] The naturalists form the cornerstones in the rediscovery of nature.

The Soil

The earth, so long accepted in its complexity as something wherein one lays seeds and which is tilled by traditional rules, becomes an object of scientific inquest. Questions are raised: Whence do the plants derive their sustenance? Do they draw water from the earth, or 'nitrate'? Or do they suck up tiny particles of the soil? That plants live on minute fragments of earth was the belief of Jethro Tull, 1674–1740. On it he based his revolutionary theory of tillage: 'Division of the parts of the soil' was the one way of increasing fertility. Dunging and the rotation of crops, he held unnecessary. The first workable drill was invented in fulfilment of this idea. Jethro Tull's device allowed the grain to be sown in perfectly straight rows between which the earth was to be tilled six times within the growing period. This called for his second invention, the horse-drawn hoe.[9] On his own farm, Jethro Tull proved that it was possible to raise wheat on the same field thirteen years running.

Tull, who was musically inclined, became heir to a small estate and studied at Oxford. The mechanism of the organ inspired his drill. He became a prac-

[7] 'I know of no one who is to be placed in the same rank with him except Réaumur.' Quoted in Will Morton Wheeler, *The Natural History of the Ants*, from an unpublished manuscript in the Academy of Sciences [Paris] by René Antoine Ferchault de Réaumur, New York and London, 1926.

[8] Jean Torlais, *Réaumur, un esprit encyclopédique en dehors de l'Académie*, Paris, 1936, gives insight into the many-sidedness and inventive gifts of an eighteenth-century scholar.

[9] Critical treatment of Jethro Tull and reference to his predecessors in T. H. Marshall, 'Jethro Tull and the New Husbandry of the Eighteenth Century,' *Economic History Review*, vol. II, London, 1929, pp.41–60.

tical farmer, a direct observer who did not bother with contemporary theory until, late and reluctantly, he set down his ideas in *The New Horse Hoeing Husbandry*, 1731. This was the time when the theory of agriculture was drawing ever-greater attention.

In France a new impulse was supplied by the generation born around 1700. These men were scholars like Réaumur, whose interest extended to agricultural problems, and like Henri Louis Duhamel Dumonceau, 1700–1782, who first built up a systematic physiology, or 'physics' as he called it, of plants. We must restrain ourselves from quoting Duhamel's *Physique des arbres*, 1758, or his much-read *Eléments d'agriculture*, 1762, where, with that wonderful capacity for observation and directness of the eighteenth century, he reveals the laws governing the growth of plants: their root patterns suited to the type of soil, the transformation of their twigs into roots, the formation of bark, the circulation of sap, the respiration of leaves.

Duhamel, youngest son of a French nobleman, was an engineer and Inspector General of the Navy and author of a standard treatise on naval architecture. His passion was the study of agriculture. On his father's estate he investigated the nature of the soil, washing it, analyzing the remaining elements, and from 1740 on was apparently the first to keep a meteorological diary. He honors Jethro Tull and, although strongly opposing the substitution of tillage to manure[10] and preferring to illustrate the French type of drill,[11] names his six-volume work, 1751–60: *Traité de la culture des terres suivant les principes de Mr. Tull.*

Agriculture, Man's Native Calling

Attention increasingly turned to agriculture. To it all other occupations were subordinated. When the Physiocrats worked out a scientific economic theory toward the end of the Rococo period, between 1758 and 1770, they took the most extreme view regarding the sovereignty of agriculture over the quite secondary activities of finance, commerce, and industry. Agriculture was the source of all wealth and the mainstay of economic life. It accounted for five-sixths of the national wealth. 'Agriculture is productive, industry is sterile.'[12] Finance, commerce, and industry were thus seen as opposed to the ways of nature.

The Physiocrats were no romantic idealizers of the peasant. They were spokesmen for *la grande culture*, and advocated 'in the culture of cereals large

---

[10] Ibid. pp.51–2.

[11] Duhamel Dumonceau, *Eléments d'agriculture*, Paris, 1762, vol. II, p.37. 'Ces machines,' he says, referring to Tull's apparatus, 'étoient trop compliquées et d'une trop forte dépense.'

[12] G. Weulersee, *Les Physiocrates*, Paris, 1931, p.62.

farms at least 100 hectares in extent.' [13] In other words, they wished large-scale landowning and mechanization. 'Who, if not a rich landowner,' they argued, 'will have available the implements needed for the obtaining of a better product at lower cost?' [14]

The Physiocrat attitude toward other occupations re-echoed the complaints of Roman authors under the Empire, such as Junius Columella's *De Re Rustica* (On Husbandry), then to be read in English and French translations. Finance was 'odious'; the military vocation, one of blood and slaughter; the legal profession, one of 'barking and snarling.' [15]

Natural law and natural rights are also reflected in Jean-Jacques Rousseau's writings at this time, but in another direction. To Rousseau, nature stands for all in man that is inborn, non-artificial, and uncultivated. He too does not look to the peasant, but to primitive man, then known as the 'savage,' obedient to his own instinct. And instead of extolling the large landowner, Rousseau holds that the man was founder of society who first sowed a piece of ground, saying 'This land is mine,' and found others to believe him. We mention this to show how the approach to nature furnished the ideological basis for most varied phenomena, from poets and economists, to pedagogues, kings, and the first industrial theorists.

Adam Smith, who first recognized the division of labor as the basis of industry, also recognized the farmer as a mainstay of society and the farmer's work as 'the most productive of economic enterprises and the fundamental type of them all.' [16] This economist, who composed his *Enquiry into the Nature of the Causes of the Wealth of Nations* within the two decades prior to its issue in 1776 — that is, while the Physiocrats were at their peak and Rousseau was in his most fertile period — also valued the 'security and tranquillity of the farmer's life.'

Looking backwards, the perspective becomes all too easily foreshortened. The preparation of mechanized spinning and weaving did not take place in the limelight. It was an inconspicuous process. Industry as later understood had no status in the eighteenth century. Industry was synonymous with handicraft. The highly refined crafts of the period were taken quite for granted by contemporaries. The Encyclopedists, to whose engravings we owe much of our insight into the anonymous history of the century, were performing an unusual task. Diderot, in the *Discours Préliminaire* to the *Grande Encyclopédie*, 1751, tells us that no

[13] Ibid. p.88.

[14] Ibid. p.83.

[15] Paul H. Johnstone, 'In Praise of Husbandry,' *Agricultural History*, Wisconsin, 1937, comprehensively surveys the literature from Antiquity onwards. For more recent times in England and France, see the same author's 'Turnips and Romanticism,' ibid. vol. XIII, 1938, pp.244–55.

[16] Johnstone, 'Turnips and Romanticism,' ibid. p.245.

dates or facts for the various trades were then on record. He and his collaborators had to learn these *viva voce* from the workers themselves.[17] At the time when the Physiocrats, J.-J. Rousseau and Adam Smith, were at work, and the *Encyclopédie*, 1751–72, was slowly being brought forth volume by volume despite strong opposition, a few poor handicraftsmen of Lancashire, men of the lowest social class, were devising apparatus for mechanical spinning, and James Watt was completing the invention of a workable steam engine. What was later to become synonymous with industrialization was then embodied in experiments among hundreds of others, which never saw daylight.

If in the first volume of the *Transactions of the Society of Arts*, 1783, we compare the models exhibited in the 'repositories' of the Society thus far in the course of its career, we find 63 examples in class I, 'machines and models belonging to agriculture,' [18] as against the some 20 examples in class III, 'machines and models belonging to the manufacturer' — a few spinning wheels, reels, etc., but not a single important industrial innovation. These numbers well reflect the proportionate interest taken in agriculture and in industry.

The New Husbandry

The theoretical edifice of the French Physiocrats, soon burned down in the Revolution, became a reality in England.

Unlike the French aristocracy, the landed gentry of England were at no time more active than in the waning eighteenth century. The result was that the *aristocrates* lost their heads or became impoverished, while the British landowners gained power and wealth. The productive energy that ran through all classes and callings in England also touched the gentleman farmer. Some of these devoted their efforts to a particular aspect of agriculture. Lord Townsend studied the rotation of crops. Robert Bakewell, 1725–95, specialized, around 1760, in the systematic breeding of sheep and cattle for slaughter; he re-invigorated the breed of farmhorses with excellent results. In the hall of his house the skeletons of his most celebrated animals were set up. Bakewell never made his principles public. He regarded them as trade secrets. Essentially they consisted in mating the best specimens of various breeds and in taking care not to mix good stock with inferior.[19]

---

[17] 'Tout nous déterminait donc à recourir aux ouvriers.'

[18] *Transactions of the Society, Instituted at London, for the Encouragement of Arts, Manufactures and Commerce, with the Premiums Offered in the Year 1783*, London, 1783, vol. I, p.309. Agricultural implements: machines for sowing turnips, drills for beans and wheat, plows with shares, drill plows, machines for cutting straw, threshing and winnowing machines, etc.

[19] Lord Ernle, *English Farming Past and Present*, new ed., London, 1936, pp.176–89.

William Coke, Earl of Leicester, 1752–1842, inherited the Holkham estate, 48,000 acres of poor Norfolk soil, and took over its management. He succeeded in rendering it fertile by turning the subsoil topmost. His vast estate, surrounded by a ten-mile wall, became the first experimental farm, on which Coke tried out crops of every type. The revenue of the land rose, through his efforts, from £2,200 to £20,000. His sheep shearings, held in Holkham down to 1821, drew a European attendance. It is consonant with the vigor of this gentleman farmer that his marriage at the age of sixty-nine with a girl of eighteen gave him five sons and a daughter.[20] None of these gentlemen farmers wrote on agriculture.

The transformation of the feudal lord into a large-scale entrepreneur went hand in hand with the expansion of his wealth through the enclosure of the common lands. This was the surrounding of a piece of land with hedges, ditches, and other barriers to the free passage of men and animals, its collective use being abolished.[21] Thus the laborer was disenfranchised and became entirely dependent on wages. The dispossession of the free yeoman and management by the landowner gained impetus through the eighteenth century; the movement reached its peak in the opening of the nineteenth.[22] The outcome is well known. Here we would make but one point: The concentration of the workers upon large estates might seem to foretell a mechanization of agriculture similar to the one that was being prepared in this period in the textile industry. The work of the anonymous, as well as of the gentlemen farmers, was to improve the soil and its produce. Mechanization had little to do with this change.

The literary spokesmen, Arthur Young, 1741–1820, and Sir John Sinclair, 1754–1835, came in the wane of the gentleman-farmer movement. They witnessed its peak and its decline. Their writings and influence spread far and wide, from Russia and Catherine II to Washington and Jefferson in North America. Arthur Young was a son of the middle class; Sinclair, a scion of the Scottish landowning gentry. Arthur Young, hardly more successful as a farmer than his contemporary the educator Pestalozzi, 1746–1827, but like him fanatically attracted to the land, roused widespread attention by his agricultural travels, the *Tours*, and through his *Annals of Agriculture*, to the volumes of which the foremost authorities contributed. In addition to tending his estate, Sinclair compiled a *Statistical Account of Scotland* in 21 volumes, 1791.

Sinclair's name is associated with the foundation of the semi-official Board of

---

[20] William MacDonald, *The Makers of Modern Agriculture*, London, 1913.

[21] Gilbert Slater, *The English Peasantry and the Enclosure of Common Fields*, London, 1907, pp.1, 2.

[22] Ibid. p.267. Statistics are given for the yearly enclosures at different periods from 1727 to 1815.

Agriculture, 1791.[23] Arthur Young was its secretary. Their intention was to educate the country in the fundamentals of agriculture. But when farming sank into a mood of resignation in the 'twenties, the board lost its vitality. The moral prestige of this body may have inspired the United States Department of Agriculture, which since its beginnings in 1862 has increasingly shaped the theory and practice of American farming, fulfilling a more effective role than similar bodies in other countries. For the beginnings of the textile industry, we must fall back upon fragmentary clues. For the state of English agriculture, we have the thorough documentation of its spokesmen, Young and Sinclair.[24] Conservative in outlook, Sinclair had at the same time cosmopolitan plans. He wished for international control of inventions 'with the purpose of spreading knowledge of new invention and discoveries throughout the world for the free use of all' (1795).[25]

Of mechanical inventions for agriculture, there was no dearth. All the elements of the McCormick reaper had been embodied in English patents by the end of the eighteenth century and the first decades of the nineteenth. But no power was present to draw them together. They remained unexploited. Neither did the expansion of the estates alter this situation. Around 1830 the movement ended in temporary resignation, while the textile industry, that outsider, began to show a power the equal of which was never before seen in any domain of production. Yet the eighteenth century's efforts to intensify agriculture did not remain fruitless. English agriculture had risen to an extraordinary status. 'Rarely will the traveller come upon a land where the aspect of the countryside impresses the beholder more favorably,' writes a German agriculturalist in 1845. 'Seen from any height, an English agricultural county has the appearance of a vast rich garden: the large fields . . . surrounded by growing hedges, the powerful teams drawing elegant and handsome implements, the fine herds of milch cows at pasture . . . the cleanly dwellings of the tenants amid the orchards and grain fields. . . .' [26]

What a contrast with the American landscape at this time! Boundless stretches of wilderness, virgin soil — this, after all, is what seemed indispensable for the

---

[23] John Sinclair, *Account of the Origin of the Board of Agriculture and Its Progress for Three Years after Its Establishment*, London, 1793.

[24] Cf. Collection in the British Museum referred to in Witt Bowden, *Industrial Society in England Towards the End of the Eighteenth Century*, New York, 1925, pp.316–17.

[25] Ibid. pp.34–5.

[26] Wilhelm von Hamm, *Die Landwirtschaftlichen Maschinen und Geraete Englands*, Braunschweig, 1845.

mechanization of man's most ancient calling. It is no accident that even within the American continent the early-settled Atlantic States remained comparatively passive, while the mechanization was carried through on soil that no plowshare had hitherto touched: the Middle West.

The sudden leap from wilderness to an advanced stage of mechanization, intermediary phases being passed over, is observable not only in agriculture. It is one of the most curious phenomena of the American development, whose repercussions deserve the close study and teamwork of sociologists, psychologists, and historians.

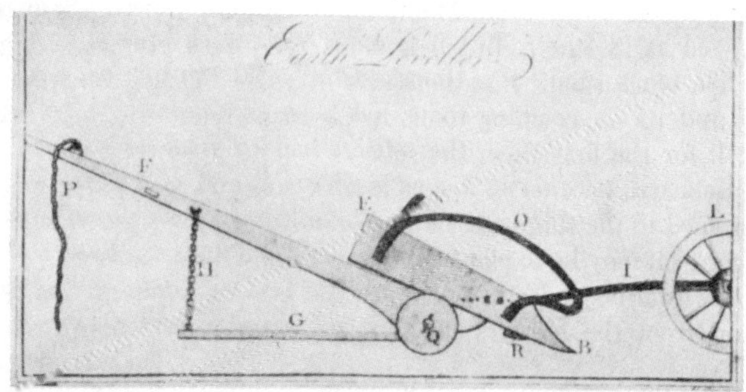

70. 'Machine for Removing Earth Short Distances by the Force of Cattle,' 1805. *Early nineteenth-century America saw many attempts to replace the hand shovel by mechanisms — a trend that led to the bulldozer of our time. This machine is drawn by three horses. It 'can do more work than twenty men.' (S. W. Johnson, in Oliver Evans,* Young Steam Engineer's Guide, *Philadelphia,* 1805)

The Middle West and Mechanized Agriculture

The revolutionizing of agriculture by mechanization is bound up with a specific region, a specific era, and a specific layer of society. It is explained by the meeting of these three factors. Hence it stands closely linked to the theater in which it was carried through: the Middle West.

Just as the origin of the planned Greek city is bound up with Ionia, the Gothic with the Isle de France, and the Renaissance with Florence, so the mechanization of agriculture is indivisibly connected with the prairies of the Middle West.

The Prairie

The Middle West embraces the broad prairie landscape spreading out like a fan from the basin of the Great Lakes, from Lake Michigan, to the Northwest and Southwest. The irregular outline of the Prairie crosses several states, losing self to the north in Canada and to the south in the Great Plains of Texas. Illinois forms the heart and the beginning of the Prairie, just as Chicago became the economic and industrial center of the Middle West.

In his message to the Congress 1 December 1861, Abraham Lincoln, himself born in a log cabin of the prairies, defines the Middle West in phrases equal to their subject: 'The Egypt of the West . . . the great interior region bounded east by the Alleghenies, north by the British dominions, west by the Rocky Mountains and South by the line along which the culture of corn and cotton meets.'

The prairies were virgin soil. The nature of this soil varies. Sometimes it is loamy and red as in Italy. But it is more often dark brown, crumbling, and shot with fine black sand. For thousands of years the humus, remains of the dead grass and its far creeping roots, has been accumulating. To cut through this network for the first time, the settlers had to yoke six oxen to the plow; thereafter the earth became as fine as garden soil and of a surprising fertility. One accustomed to the thin layer of humus in Europe is surprised when he takes a post digger — it may be to plant fruit trees — and finds the loose soil extending four feet downwards, and still no end. The bountifulness of this earth drew farmers first from the hillsides of Vermont, later from Britain and Western Europe.

Other great plains had been brought under the plow. But the opening of the Russian plains and of the vast tracts of China extended over centuries. Compared to these the development of the Middle West took place within a few decades, almost by elimination of the time factor.

When, through the Pullman window, a traveler sees the sun sink beneath the cornfields of Illinois, and the next morning rise again on cornfields as if the train had not moved from the spot, he experiences the meaning of dimension as figures can but thinly convey it.

This elimination of time, together with the mystery of dimension, produced the mechanization of agriculture.

How did the development proceed? How did the prairies of Illinois appear in this initial stage, in 1833? One of our best accounts is that of a Scotsman who surveyed the yet undisturbed land with the searching eyes of a farmer. Patrick Shirreff of Mungoswells, East Lothian, journeyed across sections of Canada and of the United States, mainly to see if his brother might find a means of existence. He travels from Detroit to Chicago, partly by post, partly by ox-cart. From Chicago Shirreff traverses the prairie to the south, on foot, for there was as yet no full connection with St. Louis. It was then that the charm of this landscape impressed itself upon him:

> I became fully sensible of the beauty and the sublimity of the prairies. They embrace every texture of soil and outline of the surface, tall grass interspersed with flowering plants of every line . . . occasionally clumps of trees stood on the surface like islands on the sea.
>
> Sometimes I found myself amidst of the area without trees or object of any kind within the range of vision . . . the surface clothed with interesting vegetation around me, appearing like a sea, suggested ideas which I had not then the means of recording and which cannot be recalled.[27]

He travels from homestead to homestead. He has to share the bed of others or to sleep on a dirty tick, which, placed on the ground, formed the couch of five people. 'I laid my head on my knapsack.' [28] What he tells of the interiors recalls the slums of the industrial cities of England or France at the time. It is a subsistence level. 'The farmer,' he says elsewhere, 'seemed contented to live . . . there were no barns to be seen, everywhere the wheat was threshed in the open air or on the bare earth.' [29]

These temporary conditions do not deceive him, and it is interesting to observe how keenly this Scot farmer sees through the theories of Malthus: 'The wide expanse [of the prairie] appeared the gift of God to man for the exercise of his industry, and there being no obstacle to immediate cultivation, nature seemed inviting the husbandman to till the soil and partake of her bounty. Mr. Malthus' doctrine that population increases faster than the means of subsistence appeared more than doubtful.' And he compares the prairie, 'where cultivated fields form a mere speck on the surface,' against conditions in Britain: 'I felt grateful at beholding a field so well fitted to relieve the depressed and starving population of Great Britain and Ireland, while the conduct of their landowning and tithe-eating legislators, in restricting the circulation of nature's bounty, appeared sinful.' [30]

Time and the Social Moment

In comparison with Ohio to the South, the Middle West slumbered almost until mid-century. Even in 1850 the population-density in many parts of Illinois varied between two and six inhabitants per square mile,[31] and in 1859, that is

---

[27] Patrick Shirreff, *A Tour through North America*, Edinburgh, 1835, p.244.

[28] Ibid. p.237.

[29] Ibid. p.225.

[30] Ibid. p.245.

[31] P. W. Bidwell and John L. Falconer, *History of Agriculture in the Northern United States*, Washington, 1925. Cf. maps showing population densities, 1790–1840, pp.148–51.

during the time of the great expansion, an English source assures emigrants: 'Not a tenth of the soil is yet cultivated.' [32]

The leap from a primitive, colonial mode of living into highly organized mechanization is typical for the whole American development. Two centuries elapsed before this leap became possible.

Once again, but compressed within a few decades, the process was repeated when the pioneers advanced into the Middle West early in the nineteenth century. Almost as in the seventeenth, these settlers were left upon their own resources, without help and without communication. They were content to survive. Whatever the pioneers needed, they had to bring in with them. 'Their oxcarts were loaded with tools, seeds, poultry, utensils and simple furniture, livestock were driven along.' They were self-sufficient and lived from hand to mouth. They settled near the fringes of the woods. There was game in abundance. In Autumn, it is said, they sometimes burned down woods, or set fire to the prairie for easier hunting.[33]

And, as in colonial times, the settlers used wooden implements and utensils, wooden plows, wooden harrows with hickory sticks, mostly of their own fashioning. The primitive prairie plow, the bull-tongue plow, was used in southern Illinois, it is said, down to 1850.[34] 'Most cultivators do everything for themselves,' observes an Englishman who traveled through Ohio in 1818, 'even to the fabrication of agricultural implements.' [35]

The mid-century in the Middle West brings the sudden leap from home economy to mechanized production. A mechanization of agriculture sets in, such as had existed nowhere before. To the account of his journey through southern Illinois in 1833, Patrick Shirreff appends this remark: 'A reaping machine was used at Jacksonville in 1834 and it is on the lawned surface of the prairie where this and almost every other description of agricultural machinery can be used with advantage.' [36] Here too the Scot farmer saw unerringly: it was the smooth, lawn-like surface of the prairie that called for mechanical reapers and 'every other description of agricultural machinery.'

This solitary reaper of 1834 is quite comparable to the 78 bushels shipped from Chicago in 1838. The amount of grain produced grows in ratio with the number of machines. The curve begins sharply to rise in the mid 'fifties. Chicago shipped ten million bushels in 1860; twenty million in the Civil War years.

---

[32] James Caird, M.P., *A Brief Description of the Prairies of Illinois*, London, 1859, p.4.

[33] Hubert Schmidt, 'Farming in Illinois a Century Ago as Illustrated in Bond County,' in *Journal of Illinois State Historical Society*, Springfield, Illinois, vol. 31, 1938, p.142.

[34] Ibid.

[35] *The Farm Centennial History of Ohio*, 1803–1903, Dept. of Agriculture, Springfield, Ohio, 1904, p.10.

[36] Shirreff, op.cit. p.463.

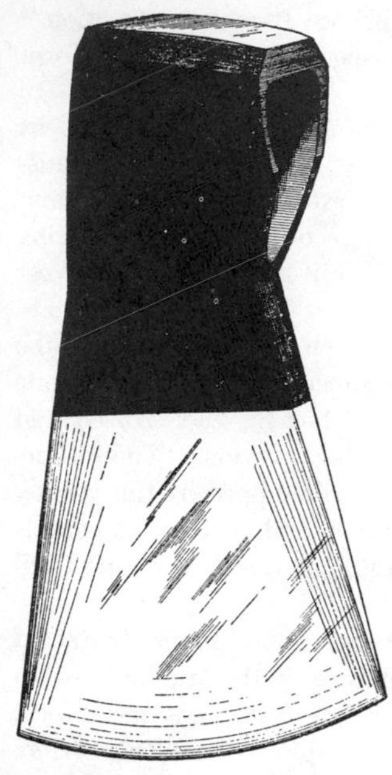

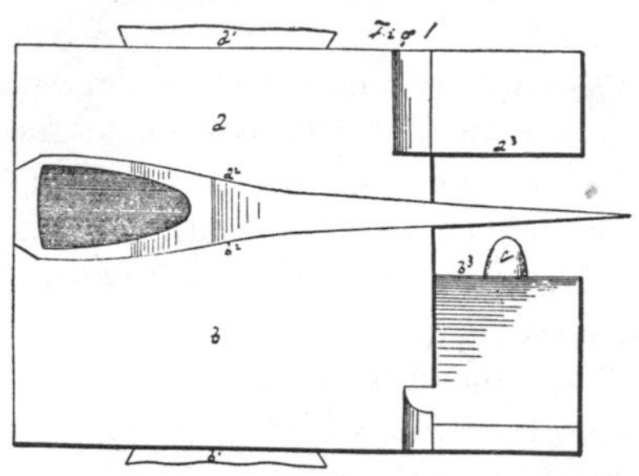

71. The Reshaping of Hand Tools in America: Die-cast 'Spanish Axe.' *Here mechanical production goes hand in hand with refinement of form.* (*U. S. Patent* 172,251, 18 *January* 1876)

Correspondingly, 70,000 reapers were built in 1864, or twice as many as in 1862. The demand was so great that industry could not keep up with it.[37] Around 1860 the development was in full swing; the Civil War only intensified it. It was already possible to supply both Armies and the world market.

We can now understand why, in 1859, a British Member of Parliament advised emigrants to take nothing with them but a trunkful of clothes. In Illinois they would find better tools than in England. Reapers and threshers were for hire, and an acre could be cut for 2*s.* 6*d.* Machines would reap 14 acres, and thresh 300 bushels in a day. Moreover it was 'customary for a number of farmers to join together in purchasing the expensive implements.'[38] The railroads ran 'within sight of the homestead, with excellent markets for the products.' 'Fresh unexhausted prairie soil' awaited cultivation. Finally, prefabricated houses 'can be contracted in Chicago and put up anywhere within reasonable distance from the railroad in less than 30 days from the date of order.'[39] These, of course,

[37] E. D. Fite, 'The Agricultural Development of the West during the Civil War,' *Quarterly Journal of Economics*, Boston, 1906, vol. 20, p.260.

[38] James Caird, M.P., *A Brief Description of the Prairies of Illinois*, London, 1859, pp.16, 20.

[39] Ibid. p.4.

were for the most part of the exceptionally light 'balloon frame' construction [40] invented in Chicago during the 'thirties and transportable in packaged form everywhere.

The impetuous mechanization of agriculture in the Middle West came about by a coinciding of developments at one point in time. Among these was transportation. The canal system, linking the Middle West with the Hudson and New York on the one hand and with Quebec on the other, came into being between 1825 and 1850. But it was by means of the rail that the Middle West was truly conquered.

When around 1850 the first miles of track sprang forth from Chicago into the Prairie, the signal was given for an irresistible development.[41] Within one decade a dense network of railroads, all converging upon Chicago, had crossed and recrossed the prairie.[42] The lines were laid down in short sections. The settlers are reported usually to have reached the area about to be tapped by the railway shortly ahead of the tracks.[43] The most energetic period of development is crowded in the short interval between 1855 and 1865, at the close of the Civil War.

The Trans-Siberian railroad, built between 1891 and 1905, likewise attracted settlers and expanded the area under cultivation. Here, as in the Middle-Western prairie, the soil was fertile and shot with fine black sand. But it was only a local event confined within the near-hermetically sealed empire of the Tzar. Here came no bold agricultural adventurers or new methods. Beside what occurred in the Middle West, the Trans-Siberian railroad remained a solitary track crossing the wilderness.

The Carriers of Mechanization

The Reshaping of Tools in America

Agriculture comes within the sphere of complicated handicrafts. Animals, plants, and earth embody within themselves all the variety and all the riches of nature. Bringing machines to perform the work of the human hand proved a more difficult and wearisome task here than in industry, which deals with the processing of materials.

---

40 S. Giedion, *Space, Time and Architecture*, pp.269–77.

41 Some remarks thereon will be found in our chapter 'Meat,' pp.218–19.

42 The development of the railroad network down to 1860 has been clearly represented on a number of maps by P. W. Bidwell and J. L. Falconer, op.cit.

43 Joseph Schafer, *A History of Agriculture in Wisconsin*, Madison, Wis., 1922, p.42. 'The Milwaukee and Mississippi Railroad, begun in 1849, built gradually westward by short sections and sent its surveyors forward ahead of the construction parties. Our record of land entries shows that prospective settlers reached an area about to be tapped by the railway very soon.'

About a century and a half had to elapse before the American farmer — under his wide-brimmed hat — could drive his tractor in long four-cornered swathes around the field, and so reap his harvest. He has little more to do — beyond keeping watch — than to guide the steering wheel. The work requires a machine of manageable size, able to perform in concentrated line production all the operations from reaping the grain to pouring it into sacks. The farmer, if need be, can complete his harvesting singlehanded. Otherwise it suffices for a lad of ten to stand on the platform and see that the sacks are being correctly filled. Increased production, freedom from exertion, human and animal, and gratifying work, seldom are all these so happily combined.

A few typological remarks may help to situate the development in historical space. As soon as one has grasped the principle of all mechanization — replacing, motion by motion, the activity of the hand, the sequence becomes clear. We need only state the phases of the development.

During the second quarter of the nineteenth century, America intensively reshaped the tools of every trade (fig. 71). Agricultural implements also were given a new standard form and greater differentiation (figs. 72, 73). Quite late, in the 'seventies, European museum directors, visiting the expositions, realized that 'a display of American axes could be the source of esthetic delight as strong as an actual work of art.' [44] This high standard was already reached in the second quarter of the century. It was immediately recognized by the specialists. The American axe, as it is described in the *Handbook for Settlers in the United States* (Frankfurt a.M., 1848), clearly brings out the contrast with the European implement, which even today retains its rigid handle and unregulated balance, hardly changed since late Gothic times:

> The axe, this implement so essential to the settlers in our woods, has here [America, 1848] been perfected to a high degree. Its curved cutting edge, its heavier head, counterbalanced by the handle, gives the axe greater power in its swing, facilitates its penetration, reduces the expenditure of human energy, speeds up the work. . . . The handle of the axe is curved, whereby it is more easily guided and more forcibly swung [Kentucky axe].

Implement after implement was in like manner reshaped and differentiated for the more exacting American environment. True, differentiation of the plow

---

[44] For this and other utterances, cf. Giedion, op.cit., pp.262ff.

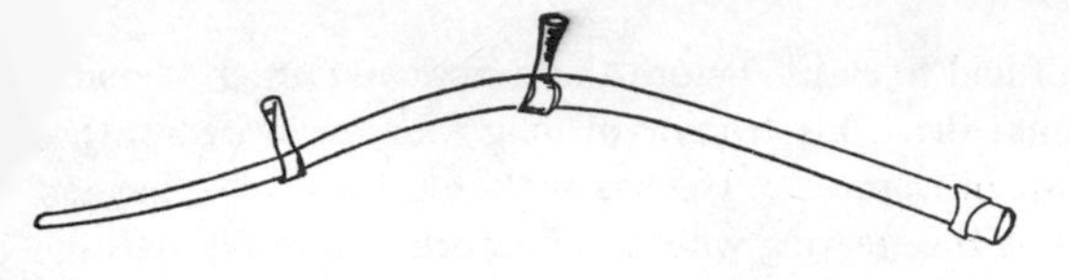

72. Refinement of the Scythe: Curved Thole and Movable Handle. 1828. *Originating in continental Europe, the curved thole was rapidly perfected in America. (U. S. Patent,* 28 *December* 1828)

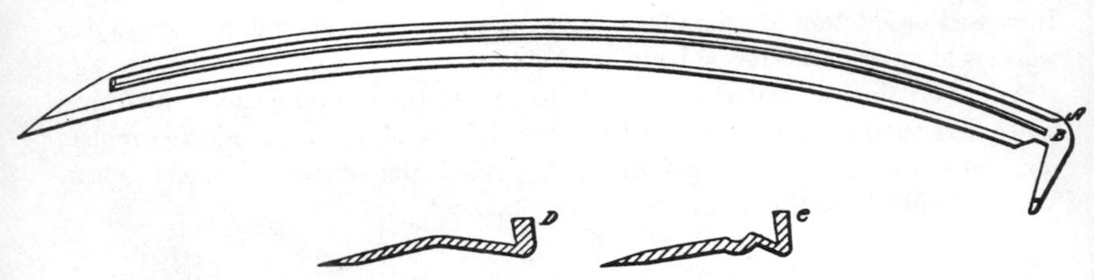

73. Refinement of the Scythe: 'Raising a Ridge on the Upper Surface of the Plate' by Dies. 1834. '*Made with less stock and cheaper and much stiffer.' The American scythe reached its standard form in the* 1830'*s. (U. S. Patent* 56, *Reissued* 17 *December* 1843)

74. Differentiation of the Scythe: 'For Every Kind of Grass or Grain.' 1876. (*Asher and Adams*, Pictural Album of American Industry, *Philadelphia*, 1876)

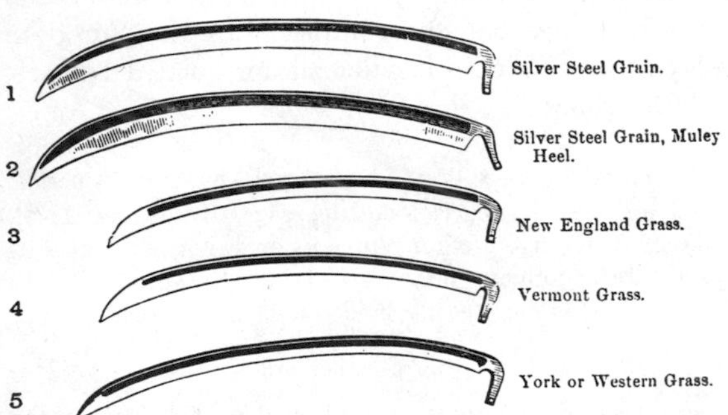

BEARDSLEY SCYTHE COMPANY,

Manufacturers of

GRAIN, LAWN, BUSH AND WEED SCYTHES.

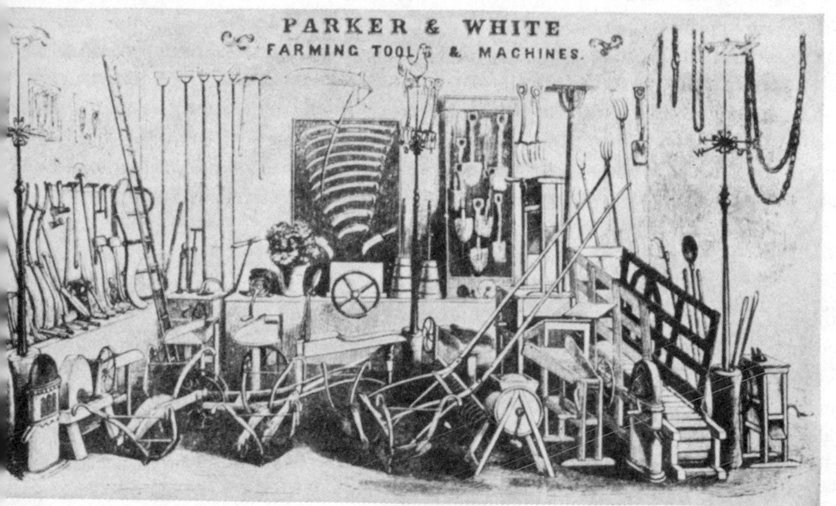

75. Standard Agricultural Implements. *c.*1850. *America's reshaping of tools that had remained unchanged for centuries is almost at its peak by 1850. This mid-century advertisement shows the 'Variety of Ploughs, Hay and Stalk Cutters, Thrashing Machines, Bark-Mills, Sausage Meat Cutters, Chains of every pattern.' There are axes, scythes, hoes, hammers suited to a variety of purposes.*

had begun in England and France during the second half of the eighteenth century.[45] But by the middle of the nineteenth, over sixty different plows — 'generally made of cast iron' — had been shaped for specific purposes, including 'rootbreakers, prairie, meadow, stubble, selfsharpener, corn, cotton, rice, sugar cane, as well as plows for subsoil and hillside land.'[46]

Differentiation for the various types of grass, grain, or shrubbery occurred in the sickle, the scythe (fig. 74), and later the hoe. All attained a new standard form around mid-century, and took on a new vigor of aspect (fig. 75).

Reaping Mechanized

Here, where we are concerned with methods, not with technological detail, we have to decide which of all the implements will yield clearest insight into the replacing of the hand by a mechanism. The choice is not difficult. The reaping machine was to the mechanization of agriculture what the selfactor had been to that of spinning. Both radically increased production. Both are

[45] Examples in Henri Duhamel du Monceau, *Eléments d'agriculture*, Paris, 1762, vol. II.
[46] A. and B. Allen & Co., Catalogue, New York, 1848.

late types within their respective spheres. The selfactor reaches standard form around 1830; the reaper, completed by its accessory mechanisms, around 1880. These dates mark the time interval between the mechanization of spinning and the mechanization of agriculture.

The reaper in many respects seems the more crucial of the two. Rapid harvesting is a necessity; it must go ahead as soon as the grain is ripe and the weather favorable. Here the intervention of a mechanism, instead of the need to call in helpers at the last moment, brings a double benefit.

REAPING

In 1783 the 'Society for the Encouragement of Arts' in London offered a golden medal for 'inventing a machine to answer the purpose of mowing or reaping wheat, rye, barley, oats or beans, by which it may be done more expeditiously, and cheaper. . . . The machine with certificates that at least three acres have been cut by it, to be produced to the Society on or before the second Tuesday in November 1783. . . . Simplicity and cheapness in the construction will be considered as principal parts of merit.' [47]

Jethro Tull devoted his fortune and fanaticism to the improvement of agriculture and the realization of his drill (1701) and horse-drawn cultivator (1716). In 1732 the first threshing machine made its appearance, which, when the Society of Arts held its contest half a century later (1783), had already been given essential improvements, and had become a practical instrument.[48]

Why should not reaping by machine be likewise possible? Pliny's description of the Gaulish header, which plucked off the ears and left the straw standing, had appeared in English and French translation and was generally known. The Society of Arts demanded more: The machine should lay the swathes 'in such a manner as may be easily gathered up for binding.' [49]

For a time nothing workable was offered.

Yet in the last years of the eighteenth century a time of intensive invention set in, which created important, even if unexploited, mechanisms.[50]

How might the motion of the hand be supplanted? The English washing machines of that time attempted, as we later shall see, to find mechanisms that would directly imitate the rubbing and pressing of the hand. The reapers, from

[47] *Transactions of the Royal Society of Arts*, vol. I, p.107 (1783).

[48] The first truly practical machine was invented by the Scot Andrew Meikle, in 1786. The stationary thresher, powered by oxen, was the first mechanical implement to become popular on the farm.

[49] *Transactions*, op.cit., vol. I, p.107.

[50] Bennett Woodcroft, *Specifications of English Patents for Reaping Machines*, London, 1853; *The Evolution of the Reaping Machine in the United States*, Dept. of Agriculture, Office of Experimentation Bulletin no. 103, Washington, 1902; William T. Hutchinson, *Cyrus Hall McCormick*, New York–London, 1835, pp.49–73.

the very start (1786), came to the principle of continuous rotation, the goal of all mechanization. In 1811 there was patented a reaper (fig. 76) with a circular cutting blade set on the periphery of a conical drum.[51] In other words, the principle of the circular saw [52] was here applied to the cutting of wheat. Wheat stalks, however, are neither trees nor planks. Although attempted again and again, continuous rotation did not lead to the goal.[53]

76. Introduction of the Mechanical Reaper. British Patent, 1811. *One of the many efforts to mechanize reaping, which failed because of too simple an approach. The large rotating drum edged by a circular blade was an attempt to borrow the principle of the circular saw.* (The Edinburgh Encyclopedia)

The stalks would have to be cut as the hand implement cut them: stroke by stroke, along a steady line of progress. The sickle-wielding hand cuts a segmental swathe. With the machine this could become a straight one. Instead of the scythe, short triangular teeth were aligned side by side. Fixed iron fingers held the stalks while the teeth cut them down, but just as with the scythe: stroke by stroke. At intervals a large reel laid down as many stalks as the teeth could cut in one motion. And so it has remained to this day.

It soon became evident that grass behaved differently from the hollow stalks, and could be more effectively cut when longer fingers were used.[54] These long-

[51] One invented by Kerr, another by Smith.

[52] Invented by General Bentham, 1790. Improved, 1804.

[53] Concerning the history of agriculture and the growth of reapers, including the American phase, we are incomparably better informed than in the case of mechanization in industry. The bibliography prepared by Everett E. Edwards, published by the Dept. of Agriculture, Washington, gives some idea of the breadth of the material. We are indebted in the first line to our friend and director of the McCormick Historical Association, Herbert A. Kellar, who during our research at the Institute unselfishly opened to us this richest repository of source material for the history of agriculture. Neither should we forget the farmers of Rouses Point, in the north of New York State, who acquainted us with the advantages and drawbacks of their agricultural machinery, and Mr. Earle Woodroffe, farmer, of Perkasie, Buck's Co., Pa., with whom we reaped corn.

[54] Obey Hussey's machine, which at first outstripped McCormick's reaper, is based on this arrangement.

fingered reapers work rather on the shearing principle as later used in hair clippers. Grass and hair, both well rooted, are structurally closer akin than stalks and timber, and can thus be dealt with by the same principle.

Cyrus McCormick's cutting instrument consists, to the present day, of short triangular knives, having small cutting edges serrated with sharp ridges. They resemble sharks' teeth and like them are excellently suited to biting into the material.

By 1783 the idea of the reaper was formulated. McCormick obtained his patent half a century later (1834) (fig. 79). The reaper still numbered among the shelved inventions. In 1854 a Philadelphia chronicler to whom we owe valuable insight into this period reports: 'scythe and cradle continue to be the principal instruments in use for the cutting of hay and grain in Europe and in America. . . . All the attempts to introduce machinery have failed, more, it may be stated, from the disinclination of the public to encourage them, than from want of merit.' [55] Only recently had the machine come to the fore through the success of the McCormick reaper.[56]

The reaper was not alone in having to await the mid-century. The full expansion of industry — other than iron and textiles — dates from this time. C. W. Marsh, who took the next step after McCormick in perfecting the reaper, stresses that unusual daring was shown by the factory which in 1846 ventured to build a series of a hundred reapers (fig. 77).

> It was difficult indeed to find parties with sufficient boldness, or pluck and energy, to undertake the hazardous enterprise of building reapers, and quite as difficult to prevail upon farmers to take the chances of cutting their grain with them, or to look favorably upon such an innovation. But the hundred machines made that year operated successfully . . . and the advent inaugurated a revolution in the manner of cutting and harvesting grain.[57]

As soon as McCormick moved West and founded his factory in Chicago the yearly output sharply rose.[58] The standard form had been reached, regardless of the many modifications later brought to it.

The mechanical reaper was not the invention of one man. C. W. Marsh, drawing on his long experience, thus expresses himself: 'A practical reaper was

---

[55] Edwin T. Freedly, *Leading Pursuits and Leading Men*, Philadelphia, 1854, p.29.

[56] Between 1846 and 1854 over 8000 McCormick reapers were sold and used, principally in the Middle West. (Communicated by Herbert A. Kellar.)

[57] R. L. Ardrey, *American Agricultural Implements*, Chicago, 1894, p.229. They were made in 'The Oldest Reaper Factory in the World,' that of Seymour and Morgan, Brockport, N.Y. These machines were built under license from McCormick.

[58] In 1849, 1500 machines; in 1856, 4000; in 1874, 10,000; in 1884, the year of McCormick's death, 80,000.

produced by degrees . . . one invented a machine having, perhaps but a single useful feature; his machine died, but this feature lived on.'[59] The seven essential elements of McCormick's reaper, as we have mentioned, had already appeared in English patents of the first quarter of the century. Whether he knew of these or not is immaterial, and the copious arguments that would portray him as a heaven-sent genius belong to the less admirable side of historical writing. That he had true inventive talent, not, as Pullman, his contemporary in Chicago, merely a flair for things promising of success, may be judged from his whole patterning of the reaper and of the shark-toothed cutting mechanism, maintained to the present day. He possessed the American secret of making things work and at the same time exploiting them. No other inventor came from a Southern farm. Had he stayed in Virginia instead of removing to Illinois in 1847 — the year after the pioneer firm built one hundred of his reapers in a series — he might easily have dwelt forever in the long roll of anonymous inventors. He was cautious, even conservative. In later years, he accepted inventions only when he could be sure they would function and when little risk was involved. Yet he was no latecomer, and knew when it was time to act. Thus in 1851 he traveled personally to the London Great Exhibition, where the nations were to meet. His chief rival, remaining in America, suffered a decisive setback. The London *Times* scoffed at the grotesque aspect of McCormick's reaper, 'this cross between an Astley chariot, a wheel barrow and a flying machine.' But the view was quickly revised when the machine proved its unrivaled superiority in the field. McCormick united in his person the inventor, manufacturer, financier, sales and public relations man. In the 'fifties he was one of the first businessmen to locate his agents systematically through the land.

REAPING, RAKING, AND BINDING

Reaping had been solved. The next step was to eliminate the man who, walking alongside the platform at first, and later standing upon it, raked the grain at intervals onto the ground. Self-rakers of various types took his place.[60] This was done around mid-century.

Solution by the endless belt: The grain lay on the ground; only its reaping had been successfully mechanized. The remaining tasks still had to be done by hand. The first step was to combine reaping with binding — that is, to bind the grain into sheaves before it reached the ground. This was attempted in a variety

[59] R. L. Ardrey, op.cit. p.47.

[60] The early English patents already had such devices, but only now does the self-raker become prominent. First tried out were mechanisms imitative of the human hand (1852). They swept across the platform at regular intervals. Later (1860) the raking device was connected with the 'reel' that laid down the stalks.

M'CORMICK'S PATENT VIRGINIA REAPER.

77. McCormick's Reaper. 1846. *This 1850 order form shows the first model of the 'Virginia Reaper,' as it was still called, of which a series of a hundred was manufactured in 1846. The driver rides one of the horses, while the second man, riding backward on the machine, rakes the grain to the ground in piles.* (*Library of the McCormick Historical Society, Chicago*)

78. WALTER A. WOOD: Reaper with Self-Raker. 1864. *Mechanical reaping was solved. Now the problem was to do away with hand labor in raking. The earliest mechanized raker, replacing the man on the platform, and sweeping in the manner of a human arm, dates from 1853. Soon the driver is sitting on the cantilever seat at the rear. His weight helps to balance the machine and he can supervise its work.* (*Walter A. Wood's Self-Raking Reaper*, 1864, *Catalogue. McCormick Historical Society, Chicago*)

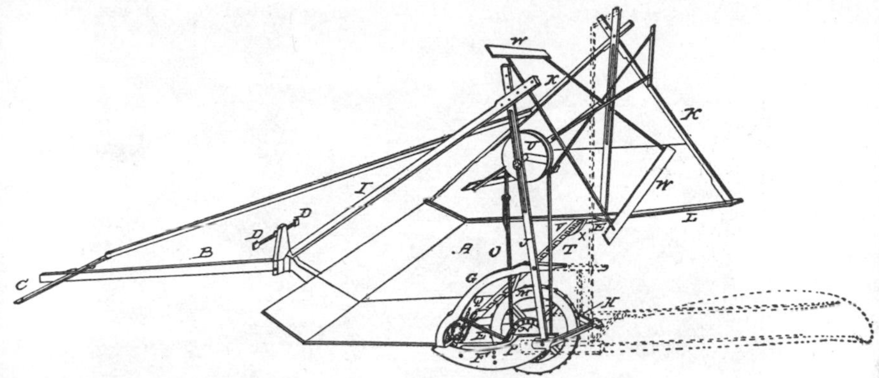

79. McCormick's First Reaper Patent, 1834. Invented 1831. (*U. S. Patent*, 21 *June* 1834)

80. Wood's Self-Raking Reaper, 1875. *Movability in agricultural machines.* '*The Bar and Platform can be turned up in a few minutes. Thus arranged the Machine will pass through a Gateway* Four *feet in width. The most successful Reaper ever introduced. A few were made in* 1872, *about* 1,000 *in* 1873, *and nearly* 4,000 *for* 1874.' (*Walter A. Wood, English Catalogue*, 1875. *McCormick Historical Society*)

The above Cut shows Wood's New Self-Delivery Reaper on the Road.

Marsh Harvester.

81. Elimination of the Self-Raker: The Marsh Harvester in 1881. *Endless belts transport the grain from the platform up to the binding table on the reaper. Two men (not shown in picture) bundle it before it touches the ground, as shown in Fig.* 83. (*Manufacturer's Catalogue, William Deering, Chicago. McCormick Historical Society*)

of ways. Finally two young farmers from Illinois, C. W. and W. W. Marsh, succeeded. On their solitary farmstead, in 1858, they constructed, with that adventurous spirit distinguishing the Middle-Western from the European farmer, a rough model of a mechanical reaper, on the platform of which they fixed a table. An inclined endless belt delivered the stalks to the table top; standing on the platform, two men bound the sheaves and cast them from the advancing machine to the ground.

The essential idea of the Marsh brothers, which to this day has not been abandoned, lay in conveying the grain to a higher level (elevated delivery). The belt conveyor, so closely bound up with mechanization in America — Oliver Evans, 1784 — was used here again with almost magical effect. Actually there were two, a lower conveyor carrying the grain from the platform; an upper conveyor close above (fig. 82). The stalks were transported between them up an incline and down the other side to the working surface. This roof-shaped arrangement (fig. 81) was to become the distinctive feature of later reapers, even when, replacing the two men, an automat took over the binding and knotting. Thus around 1890 the inventor could remark with understandable pride that the Marsh Harvester 'has never changed materially, in principle or form, since; and if the same old machine as used in 1858 and painted as others now are, were seen stand-

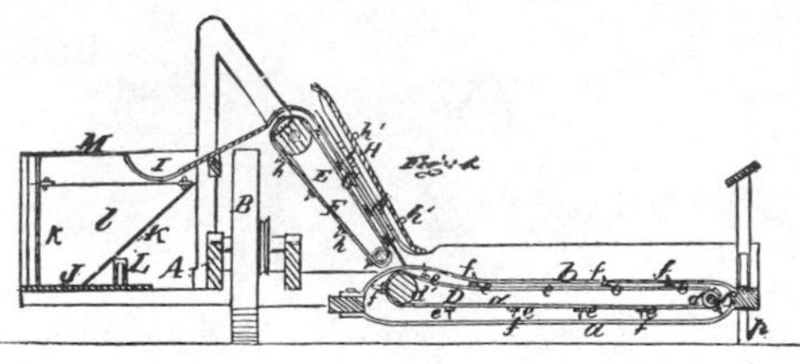

82. The Marsh Brothers' First Harvester Patent, 'Harvester Rake.' 1858. *This pivotal invention replaced the platform rake by 'endless bands of rakes, formed of straps D, E,' which carry the grain to a table where two men bind it in sheaves.* (*U. S. Patent* 21,207, 17 *August* 1858)

ing today in any field in America, Europe or Australia with binders' table off'[61] the models, wherever built, would be hardly distinguishable. Indeed, all the manufacturers had to fall in with this type. 'Harvester,' the name given it by Marsh, soon became the categorical term for machines that did more than simply reap the grain. C. W. Marsh numbers among those American inventors who, like Oliver Evans, lack the talent for converting their ideas into dollars. In the end Marsh became editor of *The Farm Implement News.* His historical

[61] Invented in 1858, the Marsh Harvester slowly came into use in the latter half of the 'sixties. Twenty-five were manufactured in 1865, a thousand in 1870. Cf. Ardrey, op.cit. pp.58–9.

83. McCormick's Two-Man Hand-Binding Harvester. 1880. (*Catalogue of McCormick Harvesting Machine Co., Chicago,* 1880. *McCormick Historical Society*)

THE McCORMICK HAND-BINDING HARVESTER AT WORK.

84. Binding Mechanized: Harvester with Wire Self-Binder, Walter A. Wood. 1876. *The two men have disappeared from the platform: an automaton now fastens the wire. Patented in* 1871, *the wire-binder on Wood's machine was on the market by* 1873. *McCormick's wire-binder was developed at the same time.*

essays written for this journal, wherein he elucidates for himself and others the significance of the various inventions, form one of our indispensable sources. The slender volume, *American Agricultural Implements* (Chicago, 1894), in which they were collected by R. L. Ardrey, and to which we turn again and again, serves as a Vasari for the key years of American agriculture.

The mechanical knotter: No device for tying knots was available from the textile industry. The idea presented itself of using twine to bind the sheaves, but no satisfactory solution came to hand.[62] The self-binding harvester was a burning problem of mechanization. C. W. Marsh gives some insight into the extent of the ill-fated attempts, when he reports: 'It was twenty-five years before they had become perfect in design and operation so that they could be manufactured for general use; and during this time as much capital was lost in fruitless efforts as there is invested in the industry at the present time.'[63]

The stiff material, wire, offered fewer difficulties, and at the beginning of the 'seventies there emerged a workable automat that secured the sheaves by means

[62] By 1851, a patent attorney, well versed in agricultural machinery, together with several inventors took out a patent on a reaper, protecting everything that they thought of possible interest in the future development of the reaper. Correctly anticipating the next step, they were mainly concerned with the sheaf-binding mechanism.

[63] Ardrey, op.cit. p.115.

Novel in every feature, perfectly automatic. Grain compressed and delivered in sheaves of uniform size.

NEW AUTOMATIC

STRING SHEAF BINDER.

Awarded the FIRST PRIZE at the Trial of BINDERS, near Dunedin, New Zealand, February 10th, 1880, SEVEN MACHINES COMPETING.

Price, with Two Knives and extras . . . £65

85. Binding Mechanized: Walter A. Wood's First Twine Binder. 1880. *The brief time of the wire binder came to an end when a satisfactory twine binder was invented.* (*Wood's English Catalogue for* 1880. *McCormick Historical Society*)

of wire (fig. 84).[64] But metal did not seem agreeable for this purpose. The complaint that pieces of wire remained in the fodder may have been less decisive than the dislike of having to deal with so refractory a material.

Wire was to be replaced by twine. By 1880 the twine binder was ready. John F. Appleby, the third name and important milestone in the mechanization of reaping, had patented, by 1858, a device for binding sheaves with twine, had abandoned it in favor of wire, finally returning, around 1875, to the original idea.

86. Walter A. Wood's Trade Mark, Registered 1875. *Walter A. Wood constructed the most elegant agricultural machinery in the second half of the nineteenth century. He too was one of the first trail blazers in the use of interchangeable parts in large machines* (*Fig.* 25). *This firm closed in* 1904 *and its archives were destroyed.* (*Wood's Circular for the Year* 1876)

[64] In 1871, by the pioneer firm of this period: Walter A. Wood, Hoosick Falls, N.Y. This manufacturer produced machines of strikingly elegant construction and was the first out with many of the most interesting inventions. Among these was the use of tubular steel frames in agricultural machines. On the firm's dissolution in 1904, the new owner, it is said, dumped its archives into the river. Thus was lost one of the most precious sources for the history of mechanization. His behavior appears less strange when one recalls that the Patent Office did not act much differently when it ridded itself of its models in 1926, with the sanction of Congress.

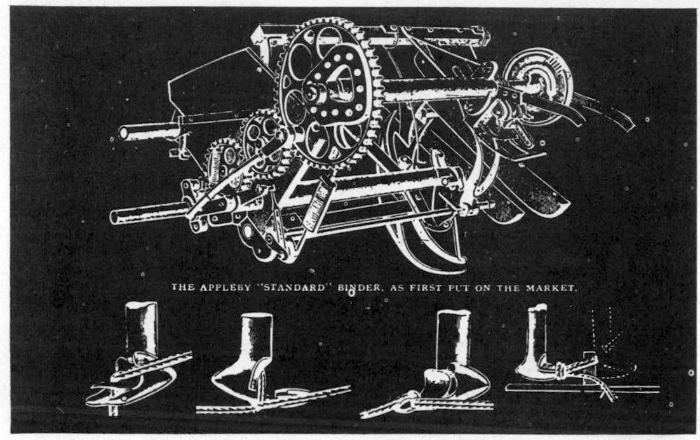

87. The Successful Twine Binder: Appleby's Binder and Knotting Device. Forming the Knot. '*No machine ever swept the world with such overwhelming rapidity,' writes R. Ardrey, the Vasari of agricultural mechanization* (1894). *Both Appleby and Wood brought their devices, which could be added to the Marsh-type harvester, onto the market in the same year,* 1880. (*Ardrey,* American Agricultural Implements, 1894)

88. Twine Binder. 1940's. *The standard twine binder achieved by* 1880 *remained essentially unchanged down to the time of full mechanization, when the small combine appeared.* (*Photo by Martin James*)

Appleby's binder (fig. 87), like McCormick's reaper, happily combined the pioneering work of various inventors, so effectively that to the present day no real departure from the principle has been necessary. 'No machine,' Marsh adds, 'ever swept over the world with such overwhelming rapidity.' [65]

Today harvesters with the roof-profile still reap the fields. The endless belts carry the cut grain up one side and down the other, where, instead of the two men, an automat is mounted. The grain gathers and is pressed into a full sheaf. At that instant the mechanism is tripped (fig. 88). A length of manila twine is carried round the bundle, knotted, and cut; a discharging arm throws the sheaf clear.

The knotter (fig. 87) has about the size and shape of a chicken's beak. To knot the cord it turns this way and that, wherein its movable tongue that loops the twine plays an important part. All the manufacturers, with a single exception, became licensees of John Appleby.[66] The success of the automat rests in greater production. 'This machine,' it is said in retrospect, 'has more than any other made it possible to increase production.' [67] With the automatic knotter around 1880, the standard of agricultural mechanization was reached. This is the time when four-fifths of the wheat grown in the United States are reaped by machine. Parallel with the reaper, other implements — plows, disk and spring harrows, drills — were improved and mechanized.

In the time of full mechanization, a new type took its place next to the binder, combining all the operations from reaping to threshing in a continuous process. But this did not rob the Appleby binder of its value, for only in regions that have an equable climate can grain be conveyed directly from the ear to the sack without danger of fermentation.

Retrospect: Starting from the time mechanization became an influence in production, three phases may be distinguished.

Reaping: about 1850. McCormick Reaper (invented 1831).

Reaping with hand-binding: about 1870. Marsh Harvester (first model 1858).

Automatic binding: about 1880. Appleby's Twine Binder (idea by 1858).

Thus the standard is attained. Down to the advent of full mechanization, agricultural machines were improved in lightness, efficiency, and stability (steel frames). The improvement of the mechanisms was reflected in the gradual and constant rise of production in the period 1880–1920.

Seen in the dimension of time, the mechanical reaper was perfected between 1850 and 1880 with bewildering speed, with its most interesting period from the

[65] Ardrey, op.cit. p.77.

[66] Only the firm of Walter A. Wood went its independent way, until its end in 1904.

[67] Thomas N. Carver, quoted in *Yearbook of Agriculture*, 1940, p.230, U.S. Dept. of Agriculture, Washington, D.C., 1941.

late 'fifties into the 'seventies. As we shall see, this also applies to other spheres of activity in the United States of the period.

Agriculture in Full Mechanization

Phase by phase the operations of the hand were replaced by mechanisms. But the succession of processes remained what it had been in handicraft methods: reaping and binding the sheaves.

In 1880, it is estimated, 20 man-hours were needed to harvest an acre of wheatland. Between 1909 and 1916, this number was reduced to 12.7 man-hours, and between 1917 and 1921 — that is, with the advent of full mechanization — to 10.7 hours. The following decade cut the figure to 6.1 (1934–6),[68] that is, to almost the same extent as in the four decades preceding.

The Tractor

This leap in productivity was brought about from the outside: one mobile power, the small electric motor, made possible the mechanization of the household; another mobile power, the internal combustion motor, made possible the full mechanization of agriculture. Around 1905 the first tractors appear. They are monsters, like the electric ranges of the time. The tractor was made possible by the cheaper production of the automobile. But how cautiously it was broached. Even in 1915, when in December of that year the International Harvester Company (McCormick) put out the first issue of *Tractor*, the uniqueness of the periodical was stressed as 'the first publication devoted exclusively to tractor-farming.' Such questions are raised as: 'Is it difficult to operate a small farm tractor?' 'Will it pay to buy a tractor now?' The tractor is contrasted with the horse. 'This power does not eat a cent when idle.' And finally, to rouse the farmer's imagination, a tractor and an airplane are shown side by side with the comment: 'This butterfly and this ant are sisters under the skin.' It was the time when Henry Ford had attained the output of a million automobiles yearly. Within a few years came the great leap in the tractor's popularity. From 80,000 in the year 1918, the number was doubled to 160,000 in the following year, rising to 1.6 millions by 1939. A tenfold increase had occurred in the time of full mechanization (1919–39).

The progression from the clumsy locomobile, which the English applied to their steam plows in the 'sixties and 'seventies, to the larger and, eventually, lighter tractors, reflects the normal phases of mechanization. The popular instrument for the ordinary farmer is the light all-purpose tractor. Instead of

---

[68] *Technology on the Farm*, U.S. Dept. of Agriculture, 1940. p.63.

steel wheels, it received balloon tires (1932), so that no time need be lost in field-to-field transit.

Decisive in the tractor is its concentration of power in a light unit. It works not only faster but with greater output than the three horses harnessed to a reaper. It can haul more machines than they, and serve a greater variety of them.

Combined Processes

We are in the time when the assembly line or production line extends into every sphere. Even if nature refuses to merge beginning and end in one swift process, and needs time to grow and ripen, ways and means are nevertheless found to integrate the beginning — plowing-sowing-fertilizing — and the end — reaping to bagging — into line production.

The grain lies on the ground. For drying, the sheaves must be set up by hand. Further time is lost in transporting the grain. The combined harvester-thresher, known simply as a 'combine,' gathers these operations into a single one (fig. 90). In 1936 — at this time fast tractors on tires came to the fore — there was built a combine suited to the needs of the family-type farm. It cuts the grain like the reaper, in the customary five or six foot swathe. Under favorable circumstances, it is said [69] to travel four to five miles an hour, reaping, threshing, and pouring the wheat into sacks. This combination is known as the 'baby combine.'[70]

The idea of harvesting in a single operation is of early date. It was one of the temporarily shelved inventions. The first patent for combined processes was taken out in 1828 — before McCormick had built his earliest reaper — but nothing is known of it beyond the specification. The first 'machine for harvesting, threshing, cleaning and bagging grain' was built in 1836 (fig. 89),[71] so that a hundred-year waiting period intervenes between the creation of the type and its introduction upon the one-family farm. The reasons are easy to understand. Not only did the machines drawn by a team of twelve oxen cost several thousand dollars; they called for an equable climate and well-organized commercial farms. These were lacking in the Midwest. In keeping with the spirit of the prairie, this 'combine' of 1836 was built by two prairie farmers and sprang up directly in the wilderness.

---

[69] Ibid. p.14.

[70] New agricultural machines did not have to be invented for these, only 'new combinations.' The internal-combustion motor made it possible to combine existing mechanisms into a production line on wheels. The 'baby combine' followed in 1939. It was followed in turn by a further reduction in scale, the 'midget combine,' cutting swathes of 40 inches.

[71] By H. Moore and J. Haskell, U.S. Patent, 28 June 1836. Thoroughly described in Ardrey, op.cit. pp.54–5. It had a reaping mechanism, an endless belt which carried the grain to the thresher, a winnowing mechanism, fan, and sack-filling apparatus.

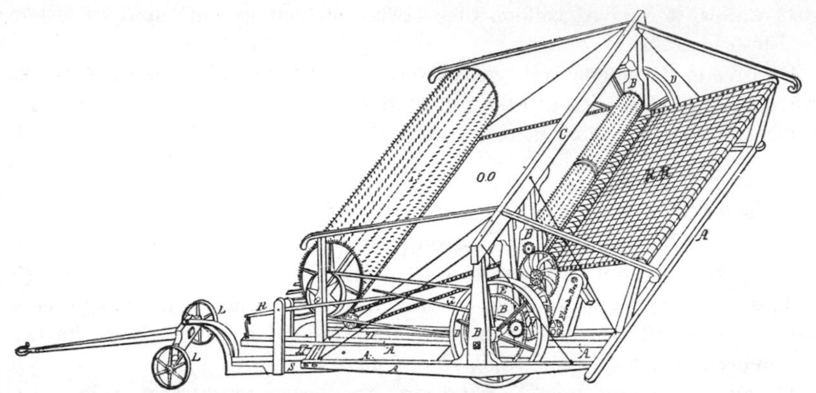

89. Continuous Production Line: U. S. Patent, 1836, 'Machine for Harvesting, Threshing, Cleaning and Bagging Grain.' *Constructed in the wilderness of Michigan in* 1836, *this earliest combine, harvesting without human hands, manifests the same trend as Oliver Evans's achievement in the milling production line,* 1783. *About a hundred years had to pass before the combine, which automatically reaps, threshes, and bags the grain, became available for the family-size farm.* (*U. S. Patent,* 20 *June* 1836)

In the 'eighties, the 'harvester-thresher' appeared in California. Here an equable climate prevailed, and there were giant bonanza farms where large machinery paid. As many horses were harnessed to these automats as might be used for the shifting of an obelisk. And the locomobile did not solve the problem.

The tractor alone had the adaptability that was needed. Around 1920, there was continuance of the Californian giants, which cut a 16- to 20-foot swathe. Their size and their price were progressively lessened, until, by 1939, the midget combine was introduced, which cuts 40-inch swathes, costs little more than a grainbinder, and gives to the small farmer 'an advantage in harvest-costs heretofore held by operators of large holdings.' [72]

Comparable machines are used at the start of production. The wheat-harvesting combine is but an exponent of the ruling trend: simultaneous performance of formerly distinct operations. Whether to sow wheat or to plant potatoes, the tilling, the preparation of the seed-bed, the fertilizing, all are made to flow in a continuous production-line.

The Homestead and the Factory Farm

Yonder, in the vast gambrel-roofed barn, stands the machinery of the American farmer. And near by, 160 acres of grass, wheat, or corn land are ready to be reaped. Three people suffice to carry on the work. Twenty cows in the stalls are milked by machines, which automatically stop as soon as the udder runs dry.

[72] *Technology on the Farm,* op.cit. p.14.

The farmer does not have to be in the fields at five in the morning. He sometimes leaves the house between nine and ten, to sow or to harvest.

For the first time since it has been tilled by man, the soil no longer exacts sweat and unceasing tenacity. Mechanisms perform the work. What the eighteenth-century theorists did not foresee even in visions has now become an everyday matter. If mechanization has ever worked to relieve man of drudgery, it has here. The worker is not condemned to repeat endlessly the same movements. The wonderful multiplicity of labors remains as always: contact with the great natural forces, with the changing seasons, with wind and sun, with the animal and the soil.

One-hundred-sixty acres was the area of the farm with which we became acquainted. This is no accidental number. One-hundred-sixty acres, according to the provisions of the Homestead Act signed by Abraham Lincoln, were to be made over on request to any citizen of the United States or any person who had applied for citizenship. The only condition was that the land should be brought under the plow and built upon for a period of five years. Land thus granted

90. Continuous Agricultural Production Line, 1930's: The Small Combine. *Before fully mechanized harvesting could come to the small farm, size and price had to be cut down, and a new power perfected — the gasoline tractor. From immense Californian harvester-threshers, cutting twenty-foot swathes, came the baby combine* (1936) *and finally the forty-inch-swathe midget combine* (1939), *suited in size and price to the family-type farm. The compact gasoline motor had a role in agriculture similar to the small electric power unit in the household.* (*International Harvester Co., Chicago*)

under the Homestead Act was in no circumstances to become liable for earlier debt.

Supporting this measure were America's broad unopened spaces and democratic will. 'Instead of baronial possessions let us facilitate the increase of independent homesteads. Let us keep the plough in the hand of the owner.' [73]

The situation at that time favored the rise of the free farmer. The agricultural ladder, as this ascent from farmer lad to independent farmer was called, worked so well that the farmers complained of a lack of help. 'Good farm labor is very scarce, from the fact as soon as a young man gets ahead in this country of cheap land, they make arrangement to secure a farm of their own.' [74]

Grain was already being reaped by machine at this time, and mechanization had reached an advanced stage. Textile mills demanded large accumulations of capital. A reaper cost only $125. It was the pre-eminently democratic tool.

As everywhere, mechanization intervening, the situation becomes involved. Lingering depressions darkened the agricultural picture. This was the price paid for access to the world market. As grain, meat, fruit were exported after the Civil War, the slumps set in, and with them a new unrest such as agriculture had not before known. It was no longer a matter of disenfranchised peasant masses, as in the time of the Reformation, but of free farmers, gathered in various political and organizational struggles against the dictatorship of the great corporations and the middle-men. It was a campaign against price fixing from without at sub-market levels.

The reduction of work hours, rising productivity, and complicating of social conditions entered hand-in-hand with the change in social structure of the farmer. Mechanization had a decisive influence upon the expansion in size of the farm as observed from 1880 on.

'Times are changing mister, don't you know? Can't make a living. Crop land isn't for little guys like us any more. . . . Nothing to do about it. You try to get three dollars a day some place. That's the only way.' [75]

The commercialization of the farm is pointed out by Californian agriculturalists, 1926: 'We no longer raise wheat here, we manufacture it. . . . We are not husbandmen, we are not farmers. We are producing a product to sell. . . .' [76]

---

[73] Quoted in Carey McWilliams, *Ill Fares the Land, Migrants and Migrating Labor in the United States*, Boston, 1942, p.301.

[74] Quoted in *Yearbook of Agriculture*, 1941, p.150.

[75] John Steinbeck, *The Grapes of Wrath*, Viking, New York, 1939.

[76] Carey McWilliams, op.cit. pp.301–3.

This satisfied comment upon the structural change of the farmer into a businessman also has its dark side. Farm produce lies at the mercy of the fluctuating stock exchange. Agricultural prices were first to suffer in the downward trend.[77] Farm income fluctuates in mad curves. Economic uncertainty no longer stems from failure of the harvest, but from overproduction.

The position of the independent farmer is severely menaced in the great production areas of the Midwest. When the farmers were unable to meet their debts in the trying days of the early 'twenties, the banks formed 'Farm Management Companies' which sent in hard-boiled managers from elsewhere to cultivate the ruined farmers' land. One of these companies expanded its holdings from seven hundred acres to a quarter-million acres in a few years. A process — now magnified to gigantic dimensions and without creative impulse — recalls the enclosure of the common lands by feudal owners in the eighteenth century. Here, as earlier, unemployment followed and uprooted populations.

More than erosion and dust storms, the tractor and combines were blamed for the uprooting of farm families. John Steinbeck pictures the process in close-ups in his *Grapes of Wrath*, when the tractor has to clear the fields and run down the houses of the now superfluous tenants.

'And that reminds me,' says the man on the tractor, 'you better get out soon. I'm going through the dooryard after dinner.'

'But if we go where'll we go? How'll we go? We got no money.' This is the question that the tenants ask of the owners. But they in turn know only that the land must be handed over to the bank.

From these dispossessed farmers and tenants came the 'Okies,' migrant farm workers traveling from one state to another, from strawberry to grapefruit, from peaches to oranges or cotton: nomads in their own land.

The Human Implications

As we said in opening, the structural change precipitated by mechanization is nowhere more conspicuous than in the sphere of agriculture. The consequences, however, are harder to survey. The figure of the wanderer in his own land, the migrant farm worker, may be abolished. The Second World War proved this. Yet the phenomenon remains. The farmer has been drawn into flux. He has been altered in his relation to the soil. The relationship has become neutralized. Mechanization hastened the process. There can be no doubt of

---

[77] 'Agricultural prices were the first to break in 1920. . . . The blow struck the farmers at about the same time the grain crop of the United States was coming on the market. . . . In contrast there was no noticeable drop in non-agricultural products until near the end of the year.' Chester C. Davis, 'The Development of Agricultural Policy since the World War,' in *Yearbook of Agriculture*, 1941, pp.298–9.

that. We shall see later[78] how phenomena often regarded solely as the outcome of mechanization had already appeared before mechanization took effect. The relation to the soil began to alter when, early in the nineteenth century, before mechanized agriculture had come into being, the settlers abandoned the old Atlantic States and migrated westwards.

Then the tiller of the soil entered into flux. Mechanization did no more than magnify a latent trend into the gigantic. Does the changing farmer reflect, but more conspicuously, a process that is everywhere at work? Can what is taking place in the farmer be a projection of something that is going on throughout? Does the transformation into wandering unemployed of people who for centuries had tilled the soil correspond to what is happening in each of us? In this process, has movement, the basic concept of our world-image, been transposed, in distorted form, into human destiny? During and after the Second World War the violent uprooting of millions has become a coolly accepted practice.

Other periods too have had their mass displacements, whether by free will, violence, or force of circumstance. Yet in due time the people came to rest. Is what we are witnessing today the convulsions of a transition period, different from earlier periods, yet penetrated like them with the need for continuity? Or does it represent a remolding of life into ways for which a form is as yet lacking, and of which the structural alteration of farming, man's basic calling, stands as the first symptom?

These are questions that as yet cannot be unequivocally answered. They transcend differences of economic system, and are bound up with the great human constants. These constants change as little as our organism does, within narrow limits. Down to the present no fruit, no work, no culture has grown otherwise than through intentness and concentration.

---

[78] In our chapter 'The Beginnings of Ruling Taste.'

MECHANIZATION AND ORGANIC SUBSTANCE: BREAD

Food is one of man's most immediate points of contact with nature. Man's sustenance must be suited to the laws that govern his body. Our ability to adapt cannot stretch beyond narrow limits. When these limits are exceeded, our organs rebel — depending on the dosage — either immediately, or later in life, or, it may be, imperceptibly and in the course of generations.

No field within the entire scope of mechanization is so sensitive to mishandling as that of nutrition. Here mechanization encounters the human organism (whose laws of health and disease are still incompletely known). The step from the sound to the unsound is nowhere so short as in the matter of diet.

This is not always immediately perceptible. The ultimate effects cannot usually be foreseen. If man deviates too long from the constant of nature, his taste becomes slowly vitiated and his whole organism threatened. Unwittingly, he impairs judgment and instinct, without which balance is so easily lost.

The Mechanization of Kneading

Toward the end of the handicraft era, the pharmacologist and agronomist Antoine Augustin Parmentier (1737–1813), who in the universal manner of his time combined scientific precision with a knowledge of the crafts, came to this definition: 'Kneading is an operation by which the mixing together of yeast, flour, water, and air yields a new substance with special properties, soft, flexible and homogeneous.' [1]

This kneading of dough is a strenuous activity, consisting at once of pulling, pushing, and beating. It was performed by hand and, for large quantities of dough, with the feet as well. With the advent of industrialization, the end of the guilds, and the expansion of cities, there arose a demand for machine kneading. The mechanical kneader can produce more quickly and more hygienically.

The beginnings reach a long way back. The Romans used rotating kneaders, and we have a number of experiments from the late Renaissance, with its penchant for applied mechanics.[2] All these are primitive implements, which, among the various phases of kneading, are restricted almost entirely to striking. Boards or wooden bars attached to a crank shaft strike the dough. Elementary kneading devices are found even in pre-industrial times. There is, for example, the Castilian *braga*,[3] a large roller suspended from the ceiling, which swings back

[1] Parmentier, *L'Art du boulanger*, Paris, 1778, p.361.

[2] *Baker's Weekly*, 18 Aug. 1923.

[3] 'This device which resembles the kneading rollers used in several British seaports for biscuit-making, would seem to have provided the idea for the machine employed at Portsmouth and at Plymouth.' Cf. Augustin Rollet, *Mémoire sur la meunerie, la boulangerie et la conservation des grains et des farines*, Paris, 1847, p.383.

and forth over enormous bread boards. This Renaissance idea was used in the Vatican kitchens, although here the dough was worked by boards instead of rollers. Certain characteristics, which became more and more pronounced in the latest stages of mechanized bread making, can already be observed in the product of this simple Spanish machine; the bread was 'whiter than that kneaded by hand; its crust is not crisp but extremely delicate and not too elastic.'[4]

Late in the eighteenth century, Italy, the land of floury foods, began to employ kneading machines on a larger scale. By 1789 kneading machines were operating in the municipal bakeries[5] of Genoa. Here already a rotary mechanism was used. A tread wheel, such as we shall find in the first mechanical bakery in Paris toward the middle of the nineteenth century, drove vertical bars placed at intervals in the tub. This procedure, it was stressed, could provide a 'pain léger et délicat.'[6] The bread of the municipal bakeries of Genoa was the only one sold on the market. And even today large-scale bread manufacture in Europe has been adopted mainly by co-operatives.

In 1796 a Paris baker, J. B. Lembert, began work on a kneading machine, which he did not make public until 1810 when the Société d'Encouragement pour l'Industrie Nationale offered a prize of 1500 francs for the machine that could produce 'the most perfect dough.' Lembert employed the principle of the churn. A great cylinder, with tight-fitting covers, revolved seven or eight times a minute around a horizontal axle; in about half an hour, the dough seems to have been adequately mixed (fig. 91).[7]

J. B. Lembert's machine is often regarded as the beginning of mechanical kneading, and, though his principle was not retained, it does seem to have yielded the best results at first. Several decades later, a model successfully applying Lembert's idea of a trough revolving on an axle is mentioned as the best kneading machine.[8] Lembert had few competitors. Not until the end of the 1820's, as France slowly ripened for industrialization, did anyone attempt to mechanize baking ovens and mixers. In 1829 five French patents for kneaders were registered. From then on, almost every year saw new proposals and combinations to replace the various kneading motions — pushing, pulling, and striking — by mechanical operations. Sometimes this was done by means of iron arms rotating in a closed cylinder, sometimes by an Archimedean screw or by interlocking cones, which slowly drive the dough from the circumference to the

[4] Benoit, Fontenelle, and Malpeyre, *Nouveau Manuel du boulanger*, Paris, 1778, vol. 2, p.47.

[5] Ibid. vol. 2, p.48.

[6] Ibid.

[7] Ibid. vol. 2, p.47.

[8] Fontaine's kneading machine, cf. C. H. Schmidt, *Das Deutsche Bäckerhandwerk in Jahre 1847*, Weimar, 1847, p.234.

center. Others again, seeking to imitate the movements of the human hand, made the agitator swing like a cradle. One innovator, Rollet, whose *Mémoire sur la Meunerie*, 1847, is a source of meticulous information on the mechanical development up to mid-century, built a kneader which both struck and pushed. It was a time of experimentation in the most diverse directions, to the end of performing the complex work of the human hand by mechanical means. Invented shortly before mid-century (1847)[9] was a mixer embodying the principle that subsequent decades were to adopt.

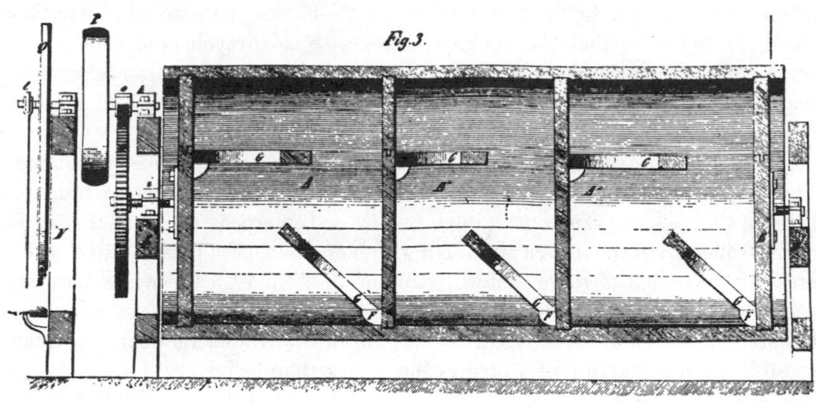

91. Kneading Machine, 1810. J. B. Lembert. *A kneading machine on the churn principle, with a large wooden cylinder rotating on a horizontal axis, was invented by the French baker Lembert toward the end of the eighteenth century. The device proved successful, and many mechanical kneaders followed. Before* 1850 *the principle of the modern kneader was developed in France. However, the ordinary needs of the European baker were not large enough for the advantageous use of machines.* (*C. H. Schmidt,* Das deutsche Bäckerhandwerk in Jahre 1847, *Weimar* 1847)

The inventions, despite their astonishing number, were extremely slow to be adopted. The reason given for this is that 'the ordinary needs of the baker were not large enough for the advantageous and profitable use of machines; for even with machines, many stages of dough-making must be performed by hand.' [10] This observation, referring to conditions in Germany in the 'forties, does not essentially differ from a report, in the *Scientific American* for 1885, on a French mixer then to be seen in operation at a fashionable bakery on the Avenue de l'Opéra in Paris: 'kneading by hand usually employed in all bakeries, is here replaced by machinery.' [11] Indeed, the first rotary mixer was not

[9] French Patent 2754. *Description des brevets d'invention*, vol. 10, p.216. Boland, 15 Jan. 1847.
[10] Christian H. Schmidt, op.cit. p.230.
[11] *Scientific American*, 17 Oct. 1885

patented in America until the late 'sixties, at the time when attempts were being made to carry mechanization into every sphere of daily life.

More than half a century was needed before the decisive step could be taken toward complete mechanization. This came with the introduction of the high-speed mixer, which did not enter general use until surprisingly late: after 1925.[12] The high-speed mixer no longer attempts to imitate the various movements of the human hand. The agitator usually consists of two arms attached to simple steel bars, which perform sixty to eighty revolutions a minute. 'High speed' refers to the greater number of revolutions, but even more to the incredible speed and agitation that the dough receives with each revolution, that is, the accelerated mixing speed. The shocks administered in this process are so great that the more delicate European wheat cannot withstand them. High-speed mixers have not proved successful in Europe.

But in America they have become one of the mainstays of full mechanization. This is perhaps not only because they allow accelerated production but also because they achieve a more thorough mixing and interpenetration of the ingredients, which are thrown back and forth with incredible speed between steel arms, producing a dough of more uniform structure. If 'in 1925 the whole industry had sold itself on the desirability of the high speed mixer,' as a contemporary has stated,[13] the main reason seems to have been that the energetic mixing made possible the manufacture of a bread even whiter than before.

The Mechanization of Baking

The Baker's Oven in the Handicraft Age

The form of the baking oven has passed down almost unchanged through the centuries. Like the axe and the knife, it is a basic tool of the human inventory. The oven developed into an egg-shaped chamber, which is excellently adapted to retaining and distributing heat.

There have been exceptions, however, as in Apulia in southern Italy, where the baking oven assumed the shape of a domelike vault. This is said to have been more suitable for economic heating by manure or cow dung. But southern Italy is also the land of the *trulli*, those strangely domed straw or stone huts that are related to the graves of the Mycenean kings. When and how these south Italian structures came into being is still uncertain.

Antoine Augustin Parmentier gives us a classic description of the stage of development that the oven had reached in his time: 'Its size varies, but its shape

[12] An early model of high-speed mixer appears in 1898 and a serviceable one is said to have been developed in 1916. Commercial use of the high-speed mixer dates from 1925–7.

[13] On the occasion of an exhibition in Buffalo, 1925.

is fairly constant. It ordinarily resembles an egg, and experience has proved up till now that this form is the most advantageous and the most economical to concentrate and store the necessary heat, communicating it to the object which it surrounds.' [14]

Thus the baking oven was an oval chamber encased in a thick, fireproof vault of clay, brick, or stone. A fire of logs and faggots was built within. Once the stones had stored enough heat, the ashes were raked out; then the dough was put in and slowly baked by the heat which the stones retained. The highest temperature struck the dough when it was first put into the oven, and the heat gradually abated in the course of baking: a natural process, coinciding with the needs of bread baking. Every detail of this simple device — the vaulting, the inclined hearth, the position of the flue — was the outcome of unfathomably ancient experience.

The Influence of Technology: The Indirectly Heated Oven

The method in which the chamber was heated, the embers swept out, and the bread inserted came to be regarded as too slow for the large quantities of bread required by the nineteenth century. No continuous flow of production was possible. The bake oven could not be mechanized in its traditional form. The first step, then, was to make the chamber in which the bread was baked separate from the fire. The baking chamber and the furnace chamber became independent of one another. The hot gases were made to pass, often in ingenious ways, around and over the baking chamber. This indirectly heated type became the basis for future mechanization. Count Rumford (1753–1814), the adventurous New Englander, Bavarian general, horticulturist, founder of the public soup kitchen, and an ingenious pioneer in thermodynamics, was one of the first to bring about fuel economy by drawing the flame and hot gases around the baking chambers of the six ranges in his Munich soup kitchen (fig. 348). These chambers were constructed of cast-iron plates and their flues could be regulated, thus creating the modern range.[15]

The nineteenth century developed the technique of heating air in special chambers before conducting it into the baking chamber. This type was called the *aerotherme*. In principle, this is nothing other than the hot-air heating favored in dwellings throughout the second half of the nineteenth century, with the difference that the aerotherme ovens were a closed heat circuit. The air, heated

---

[14] Parmentier, *Nouveau Cours complet d'agriculture théorique et pratique*, 16 vols., new ed., Paris, 1821–3, vol. 6, p.565, article on 'Four.'

[15] Augustin Rollet, op.cit. p.437. In his sixth chapter, 'Des Fours,' pp.411–78, Rollet gives an excellent account of the development of the oven.

in special channels and reservoirs, did not come into contact with the fire gases. Not only was the method more efficient, but the air in the baking chamber remained entirely pure. This oven was used with success in French hospitals in the 'forties.[16]

The aerotherme oven (1832) of the Frenchman Aribert retains some characteristics of the old baking oven. The bread trays were slowly carried on rails through the straight or circular hot-air tunnels from a hotter to a cooler zone.

92. Mechanized Bakery, Mouchot Bros., 1847. *The first bakery successfully mechanized in France. The partial mechanization found here is characteristic of European bakeries to the present day. Their small-scale equipment permits only the most strenuous tasks to be performed mechanically.* (*C. H. Schmidt,* Das deutsche Bäckerhandwerk)

This aerotherme oven, which shows beginnings of distinctly mechanical operation, was to be found in several French cities around 1840.[17]

Finally, toward mid-century, steam heat was employed.[18] The earliest to do this was Angier March Perkins (1799–1881), foremost exponent of hot-water heating for dwellings. An American living in England, he first worked with hot-air heating, but soon shifted to hot-water coils.[19] He even hoped to use steam in

---

[16] It was introduced in the 'thirties. In 1836 the *Société d'Encouragement pour l'Industrie Nationale* offered a prize for a 'four aerotherme,' with a specially efficient system of heat circulation. Cf. Benoit, op.cit. vol. 1, pp.231ff.

[17] Rollet, op.cit. p.440, states that in Gap, Grenoble, Avignon, and other cities, 'it is heated with anthracite or soft coal.' Cf. plates M and N, and Atlas vol., pl.45.

[18] The idea of 'making the steam of boiling liquors useful for boiling and baking' was patented in the early eighteenth century (British Patent 430, 25 June 1720).

[19] Perkins, Apparatus for heating air in buildings, British Patent 6146, 30 July 1831. Apparatus for transmitting heat by circulating of water, British Patent 8311, 16 Dec. 1839; apparatus for heating by the circulation of hot water, British Patent 8804, 21 Jan. 1841.

iron production. Later, in 1851, he heated the inside of a bake oven by means of inch-thick pipes connected with coils passing through the fire box.[20] 'It has before been proposed to heat ovens by the circulation of hot water in branch channels made in cast plates,' he stresses in his patent. He claims only the 'distribution of heat by a series of branches' of circulating pipes.

This closes the series of types that came to perfection only when bread making reached the fully mechanized stage, mainly after 1910. In contrast to the steam

93. Mechanized Bakery, Mouchot Bros., 1847. *The kneading machines are powered by dogs who work a treadmill outside. Coke-heated, aerotherme ovens. Kneading machines and ovens progressed with the times, but the small scale prevails in Europe to the present day.* (*C. H. Schmidt,* Das deutsche Bäckerhandwerk)

boiler, which, with Wilcox's tubular type (1856), attained a considerable perfectedness by the 'fifties, the bake ovens of the same period are mere beginnings, and, all in all, shelved inventions.

The Oven and the Endless Belt

Aribert, whose aerotherme oven (1832) with its plates running on rails pointed to a clearly mechanizing trend, called his invention a *four continu,* continuously working oven. Around 1850 efforts in this field focused on bringing about continuous operation by means of a moving mechanism within the baking chamber. The ordinary hot-air ovens could be heated continuously, but changing the loaves took too much time. Trained workers were needed to manipulate the peel, the flat wooden shovel with the long handle used to introduce and remove the loaves.

[20] Perkins, Heating Ovens, British Patent 13509, 11 Feb. 1851.

Attempts were made to increase production in two ways.

One was the use of draw plates, which could be thrust into the oven or taken out by unskilled workers with a single motion. This type has been preserved and developed in the most varied forms.

The decisive step toward mass production lies in the use of a continuously running mechanism. Many possibilities were considered for equipping the baking chamber with moving devices. In one variety this was done by means of horizontally or vertically rotating wheels. Wheels revolving around a vertical axle have been retained up to the present time in mechanical pie baking. This means that the hearth plate, which normally was fixed, becomes movable; it is transformed into a wheel. This type of thinking seems to have become possible only in the nineteenth century. The eighteenth century had toyed with the idea of mobility. In 1788 an English patent was issued for a cast-iron oven in which the hearth plate remained fixed, but the oven itself revolved.[21] In 1851, I. F. Rolland invented the modern form of the rotary oven [22] with the movable wheels.

Wheels revolving around a horizontal axle allowed the baking trays to remain horizontal, much like the cars of the giant Ferris wheel at the Chicago Exposition of 1893.

But far more persistent were the efforts to obtain a continuous flow by building a chain conveyor through the baking chamber. Between 1850 and 1860, the most diverse solutions were attempted: chains running horizontally, chains running vertically, singly, or in series, until, by the early 'sixties, the bake oven of 1800 had become a highly complicated mechanism.

The first use of the endless chain occurs surprisingly early. In the first decade of the nineteenth century, Admiral Sir Isaac Coffin (1759–1839) built for the British Navy an oven 'intended for baking sea-biscuits' (figs. 99, 101) which he named the 'perpetual oven.' [23] His invention falls at the end of his long and adventurous career, when, forced out of active service by the consequences of an 'accidental strain,' he had become superintendent of Portsmouth navy yard. The Portsmouth 'victualling office' has been mentioned earlier in connection with important innovations.

Coffin thus explains the name he gave to his oven: 'It is called a perpetual oven because the operation of baking may be continued for any length of time.' It was indirectly heated. An endless belt a yard wide and made of a loose wire

[21] John Naylor, British Patent 1656, 29 July 1788. 'An oven for making bread . . . placed upon or hung over a kitchen fire . . . may be turned around while the bread . . . contained in it remains in a fixed position . . . which I called Rotative Oven.'

[22] I. F. Rolland, *Four de boulangerie*, French Patent 7015, 8 Apr. 1851. *Description de brevets d'inventions*, vol. 23, p.176.

[23] British Patent No. 3337, 15 May 1810.

mesh ran the whole length of the baking chamber. At either end, outside of the oven, the belt ran around large cast-iron rollers, which kept it continually moving.

Coffin's independence of the conventional solutions was quite in keeping with his temperament. Even when court-martialed for disobedience and contempt, he stood fast in refusing to keep inadequately trained officers on his ship. Coffin was born in Boston, Massachusetts, the son of a customs officer. It would be misleading to call this British officer an American; but we may note that he spent his youth in Boston.

Admiral Coffin's proposal of 1810 differs from the long series of patents between 1850 and 1860 in one respect: all the mid-century patents place the endless belt entirely within the baking chamber, so as to prevent loss of heat. The first proposal of this sort,[24] made by a Philadelphia inventor, claims to be the first time an endless-chain platform was combined with a baking oven (figs. 100, 102). Historically speaking, this is certainly not true, but what was new and of future promise was the idea of placing the conveyor within the baking chamber. All successors adopted this feature. Proposal follows proposal for raising production; the belts are multiplied; soon attempts are made with upright chains, the bread's being baked during its short vertical transit through the baking chamber.

Around 1860, the problem of the bake oven seems to have stimulated such outstanding engineers as William Sellers, the machine-tool builder.[25] William Sellers' organization of the interior of the oven, his arrangement of the vertical endless chains so that 'they shall nearly balance each other, to make the reception and discharge of the material automatic,[26] as well as his mode of heat regulation, all reveal the expert engineer.

At the time these automatic ovens came into being, Boston, Chicago, New York, and especially Philadelphia had mechanical bakeries using ovens, sometimes several storeys high, fed by an endless belt. Some of these were successful, others ill fated, either burning down or, when they failed to pay their way, passing from hand to hand. But successful or otherwise, they were on the whole show pieces. Small bakers were the rule, and, much longer than the European, American housewives continued to make their bread at home.

---

[24] H. Ball, Bake Oven, U.S. Patent 7778, 19 Nov. 1850.

[25] William Sellers (1824–1905) of Philadelphia belongs to the early generation of American industrialists, in which the manufacturer and inventor were combined in one person. He was active in many fields, from tool making to bridge building and skyscraper construction. As president of the Midvale Steel Co., he was Frederick Winslow Taylor's chief; it was he who enabled Taylor to develop his system in Midvale Steel.

[26] W. Sellers, Improvement in Ovens, U.S. Patent 31192, 22 Jan. 1861.

There was another factor, too: the automatic manufacture of bread is an unusually exacting task. In the second half of the nineteenth century only the first and last phases of the process were at hand: kneading machines and conveyor ovens. The middle links were lacking: machines to weigh the dough automatically, to divide it, to make it into balls, roll it, and carry it on endless belts through glass-paneled passages exactly controlled for warmth and humidity. And modern yeast, which cuts fermentation time almost by half, was not yet available.

After 1900, as mechanical baking approached readiness for final mechanization, all experiments had to go back to the beginning. The astonishingly diverse baking ovens of the 'fifties and 'sixties, which clearly developed the principles underlying all types, had been forgotten. They belonged to the great realm of shelved inventions. This broken continuity impresses the historian much as a mine shaft left unworked and unexploited.

Around 1907, before a Canadian bakers' convention, a Mr. Roberts, representative of a London baking-oven firm, envisioned what he called an 'oven of the future' in which the dough would be put in at one end and the finished bread come out of the other.[27] These are the very words we read in the specifications of 1850. In his audience was an enterprising baker, Dent Harrison of Westmount, Quebec, who became the initiator of the present-day development. At that time traveling ovens existed, but they were used only in biscuit-making factories. In one of these, at Montreal, Harrison and Roberts baked experimental batches on the traveling oven. The loaves coming out of the other end were burned black. Dent Harrison nevertheless continued to think the 'new' idea practicable, and gave Roberts an order 'for the first travelling oven in the world for baking bread.'[28]

In 1913 this oven, constructed in England, was set up in Montreal. Its baking plate was 50 feet long and 6 feet wide. Fired with coal, it functioned from the very start. Thus a century had elapsed between the 'perpetual oven' (1810), invented for the British Navy by Isaac Coffin, and this tunnel oven, finally marking full mechanization of the process.

Baking companies bent upon large-scale production were on the increase and began to experiment with similar ovens. Such an oven built in Chicago in 1914–15 had to be torn down several times. All were heavy ovens with massive walls of brick, weighing heavily on the floor and calling for special foundations.

Soon gas took the place of coal in heating the ovens; in 1917 a series of gas

---

[27] Gordon E. Harrison, 'The First Travelling Oven,' *The Baker's Helper*, 50th Anniversary Number, 17 Apr. 1937, p.832.

[28] Ibid.

burners was placed at fixed intervals above and below the hearth plate throughout the length of the oven.

Finally, in the 'twenties, high pressure steam was used, which circulated through a series of tubes around the hearth.[29] It seems that gas explosions led to this measure, yet it should not be forgotten that this most recent device renews the principle which Angier March Perkins in 1851 modestly claimed as his: exact control of the baking temperature by direct radiation from steam pipes.

The heavy brick walls now disappear in favor of insulated steel plates, which allow more accurate regulation of temperature, greater flexibility, and a reduction of the heating time to one quarter; and electric lighting is installed in the baking chamber.

The Mechanization of Bread Making

Thus far we have been dealing with individual phases in the process of bread manufacture. So long as an uninterrupted production line was lacking, mass production remained impossible.

The first assembly line came into being, as we recall,[30] in an English 'victualling office,' when the various machines for making ships' biscuits were interrelated. This was in 1833, just a half century after Oliver Evans had devised his mechanical mill. In this royal victualling office, the amounts of flour and water flowing into the mixer, as well as the rolling of the dough, were automatically regulated (fig. 46). 'Heavy cast iron rollers . . . run alternately with great rapidity from one end of a table to the other by means of a beam connected with the steam-engine below.'[31] These heavy rollers were inspired by the Castilian *braga*, French writers say. 'When this operation is finished, the dough is conveyed on rollers to a second table' — where it is divided into pieces — 'and finally, still running on friction tables, to the machine which at the same moment cuts and stamps the biscuits.'[32]

Thus the three main phases of modern mass production — mixing, rolling, and molding — were at once mechanized, and connected in a single production line.

The unfermented dough of flat ships' biscuit is of far simpler structure than the sensitive dough of bread. But it was not long before bread too was being turned out in continuous manufacture and even in mass production. The French had such establishments successfully operating as early as the 1840's. The machine

[29] V. C. Kylberg, 'Baking for Profit,' *The Northwestern Miller and American Baker*, 6 Oct. 1937, Minneapolis.

[30] Cf. p. 89f.

[31] Barlow, op.cit. p.803.

[32] Rollet, op.cit.

bakery of the Mouchot brothers in Paris (figs. 92, 93) won continental fame. It used the latest hot-air ovens and large efficient kneading machines. These kneaders were driven by a tread wheel, as used in the Renaissance and in the municipal bakeries of Genoa in the late eighteenth century. The wheel was suspended outside the baking room and was trodden by well-drilled dogs. When the kneader had completed the necessary revolutions and the mixing was completed, a whistle automatically blew and the animals ceased their labor. The new aerotherme ovens were heated by coke (fig. 92), which was 50 per cent cheaper and offered greater 'production capacity.'[33] Two bake ovens turned out 6240 kilograms of bread in 24 hours. The gas used to illuminate this cellar bakery was manufactured by the ingenious baker himself.

In England at this time one could have found no Renaissance tread wheels for bread making. In 1850 a mechanism was put into operation in Glasgow,[34] which was said to manufacture one and a half tons of bread an hour, or approximately four times as much as the Paris bakery of the Mouchot brothers. This was a bread factory packed within a few square yards. Everything was automatic and concentrated in one machine. A fly-wheel regulator, as used in steam engines, controlled the flow of flour and water into the mixer; rotary or sliding knives cut the dough into pieces which were mechanically molded into loaves and propelled into the oven. This bread factory in miniature recalls those queer musical contrivances that unite a whole orchestra in one instrument. But this grotesque scheme embraced two ingenious ideas: coiled pipes were used to heat two of its four baking chambers, and soda water to saturate the dough. In France this device would have been unthinkable, for the people would never have accepted such bread. Nor did it enjoy much success in England. It is one of the starting points, however, for more refined methods.

Bread and Gas

To make the dough tasty and porous, two kinds of ferment were generally used: leaven and yeast. In bread making with leaven, some of the dough from one baking is set aside and used for the next. The leaven acts as a sort of starter. It yields a full-bodied and tasty bread, with the slightly sour aroma that many people still prefer.[35] Leaven was used throughout the Middle Ages, and long after. The Italians still insist on leaven for their white bread, the Germans for their mixed rye breads,[36] the Russians for their black bread.

[33] Detailed description in C. H. Schmidt, op.cit. pp.320ff.

[34] G. A. Robinson and R. E. Lee, Manufacture of bread, British Patent No. 12703, 10 July 1849.

[35] Some modern authorities seem to prefer leaven. L. Boutroux, in *Le Pain et la panification*, considers bread made with leaven more healthful than that made with yeast, because the acids it contains aid in its digestion. Quoted in Emil Braun, *The Baker's Book*, New York, 1903, p.52.

[36] Pumpernickel and Schwarzbrot.

In many highly mechanized countries, leaven has been altogether supplanted by yeast. First brewer's yeast was used. Opinions vary about when this began. Some say that yeast did not come into general use until the middle of the nineteenth century,[37] while others point out that brewer's yeast was used in Paris bakeries as early as the seventeenth.[38] Yeast dough, like leaven dough, is left to rise overnight. During this time it slowly rises as a result of the gas formed by fermentation, and a natural warmth develops.

On the Continent, special high-fermenting types of yeast were later developed and sold in compressed form. These ultimately led to the modern bakery yeast, which American concerns produce in large quantities. High-fermenting yeast reduces the time of fermentation from ten hours to five.

Prior to the mechanization of baking, the bread's aroma was held in great esteem. It comes from the natural bouquet of baked grain, from the volatile esters developed in fermentation or during baking, and sometimes from added aromatic herbs (caraway seed). These volatile esters, together with carbonic acid gas, are slowly produced in the course of fermentation. Chemists have stressed that a large and rapid generation of carbonic acid results in a loss of flavor.[39]

In the 'fifties, bread, in its very substance as a material, was attacked by mechanization. For the sake of increased production, carbonic acid, instead of the slower-working ferments, was mixed with the dough.

From mid-eighteenth century on, chemicals were resorted to in bread manufacture in order to make the bread weigh more than its flour content would allow, or to make it look whiter than was to be expected from the quality of the flour: plaster, alum,[40] sulphate of copper — 'a liqueur glass of weak copper sulphate solution for 200 loaves of bread'[41] — or such substitutes as potato or bean flour.[42] This tampering gave the illusion of greater quantity or of better quality. Punitive measures were taken to reduce or eliminate adulteration.

In the 1850's, attempts to increase production resorted not only to mechanical means, but also to the natural sciences. The laws of the expansion and contraction of gases, which John Dalton and Gay-Lussac discovered shortly after 1800,

---

[37] J. C. Drummond and Anne Wilbraham, *The Englishman's Food*, London, 1939, p.353.

[38] E. and L. Bunyard, *The Epicure's Companion*, London, 1937.

[39] *Arkady*, a collection of articles reprinted from the *Arkady Review*, Manchester, England, 1938.

[40] 'Alum was used in the town bakeries as much as four ounces to the sack of flour; this chemical increases the size and at the same time the texture and the colour of a loaf baked from inferior flour.' Drummond and Wilbraham, op.cit. p.342.

[41] Schmidt, op.cit. p.146.

[42] Sylvester Graham writes in his *Treatise on Bread and Breadmaking*, Boston, 1837, that in 1829 25 bakers were punished for the use of copper sulphate. The first to attack the adulteration of food was F. Accum, *Treatise on the Adulteration of Food*, London, 1820. His description of 'illicit methods' did him no good. He was forced to leave England.

THE BOSTON AERATED BREAD BAKERY.

94. Bread and Gas: Dr. Dauglish's Bread-Making Apparatus, Early 1860's. *Bread making is reduced from ten hours to a few minutes. The first experiment in mechanizing bread manufacture on a large scale was by John Dauglish, a British physician, in 1856. Dauglish injected carbonic acid gas into the dough under pressure, reducing the nine-hour fermentation period to twenty minutes. Failing to generate the natural warmth of fermentation, this gave a homogeneous mixture permeated with fine bubbles, but cold as a corpse. Serious disadvantages in baking ensued.* (American Artisan and Patent Record, *N. Y., Vol. III*, 9 *May* 1866)

95. Balloon Railway Project for Mt. Rigi. 1859. *The late 'fifties and 'sixties were fascinated by all sorts of experiments that attempted to use balloons for traction purposes. Here a balloon is expected to haul a car, suspended on an overhead rail, to the mountain top.* (Harper's Weekly, 1859)

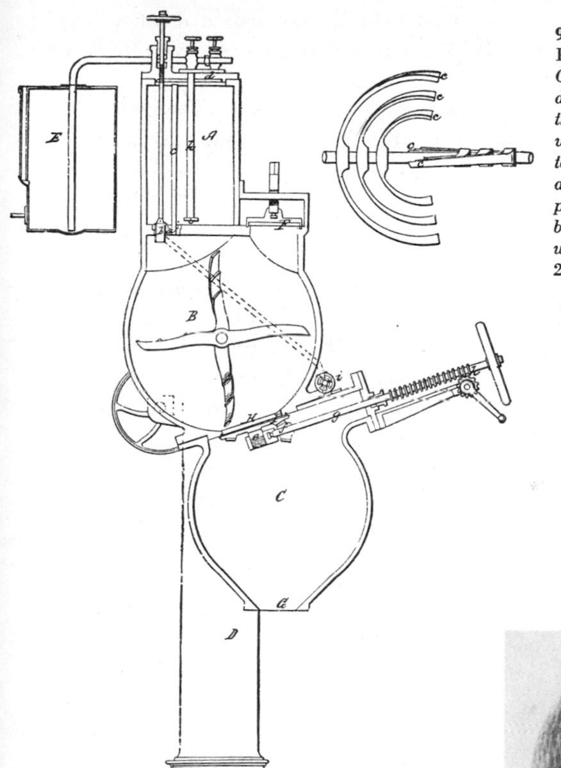

96. Bread and Gas: Dr. Dauglish's High-Pressure Apparatus, Later Patent. *Companion ideas to the idea of saturating dough with gas under pressure appear in the mass production of steel or of soda water. The standard soda-water container was invented in this period* (1851), *and so was Bessemer's mechanized steel-product-making process* (1856). *But bread is a more sensitive product than water or iron.* (*U. S. Patent* 52,252, 23 *January* 1866)

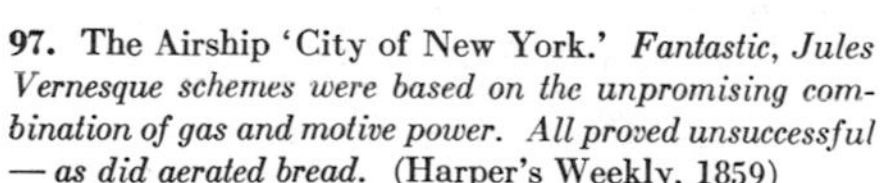

97. The Airship 'City of New York.' *Fantastic, Jules Vernesque schemes were based on the unpromising combination of gas and motive power. All proved unsuccessful — as did aerated bread.* (Harper's Weekly, 1859)

found their practical application in bread manufacture half a century later. John Dalton's researches into the 'Absorption of Gases by Water' (1803) are especially relevant.

The solubility of gases increases in ratio with the pressure. The greater the pressure over a liquid, the more gas it will absorb. Why should this not apply to dough?

Dr. John Dauglish, a British physician (1824–66), proceeded from this idea. While studying in Edinburgh (1852–5), he experimented with driving carbonic acid into dough under a pressure of 10 to 12 atmospheres. In the specification of his *Improved Method of Making Bread*,[43] for which he obtained a patent in 1856, he states that 'water charged with carbonic acid' had been used before in the manufacture of bread, but that the substance of his invention was the mixing of charged water and flour under high pressure. High-pressure apparatus to saturate water with gas had long been used in the manufacture of soda water. There would be little difference, between manufacturing soda water or bread by this process; the apparatus would merely have to be somewhat adapted to material of a different consistency. Dauglish had no monopoly over such endeavors. In the very month of 1857 when his second patent was granted,[44] two Americans came forward with 'Improvements in the preparation of dough [mixing with gas].'[45] A few years later they brought out a pamphlet, its title a striking slogan for the aerated product: 'Bread for the Millions.'[46]

Dauglish too pointed out the advantages of his unfermented bread. In a paper read at the Society of Arts in London in 1860, he showed that it could be kept indefinitely and proved that it was more healthful. The American authors of *Bread for the Millions* go one step further. They raise the alarm against bread made with yeast. 'A ferment or yeast,' they write, 'may be characterized as a body in a rotting condition.'[47] Pasteur, who had not long before (1857) discovered the yeast bacilli, might have shown some surprise at this definition.

John Dauglish was a fanatic who wore himself out crusading for his bread, and died at the age of forty-two. His name is still associated with the idea.

His first apparatus was simple. Soda water and flour were mingled under high atmospheric pressure in a strong-walled mixer. When the kneading was complete, the pressure was removed. This allowed the gas to expand, and within

[43] British Patent 2293, 1 Oct. 1856.

[44] British Patent 2224, 21 Aug. 1857.

[45] George Tomlinson Bousfield, 'Improvements in the preparation of dough,' communicated by Perry and Fitzgerald of New York, British Patent 2174, 15 Aug. 1857.

[46] Perry and Fitzgerald, *Bread for the Millions, a brief exposition of Perry and Fitzgerald's patent process*, New York, 1861. With illustrations.

[47] Ibid.

HARPER'S WEEKLY.

MISTRESS. "Why, Bridget, what *are* you doing—nailing those biscuits down to the tray?"
COOK. "Yes, faith, Mum, or they'd be afther liftin' the tops off your oven, Mum—this Yaste Powdher's so moity powerful."

98. Baking Powder: The Nailed Biscuits. (Harper's Weekly, 1865)

a few minutes its tiny bubbles would raise the dough. The high pressure and sudden expansion caused coldness to spread through the dough as it might in a corpse. The natural warmth developed when gas is generated by fermentation was lacking. Formerly, however, the dough would rise in six to eight hours. Now it rose instantaneously.

What track did these inventive minds follow?

Is there any relation between the curious idea of making bread by carbonic acid and contemporary invention in other fields? The 'fifties, and more so the 'sixties, were particularly fascinated with the harnessing of vapors, steam, and gases to unwonted ends. The balloon had been invented long before. But now fantastic plans appeared. The popular diversion of the paper-makers Montgolfier (1782) was now to be made dirigible and adapted to aerial navigation. The airship 'City of New York,' for instance, that combination of balloon, basket, and motor-driven lifeboat (1859), was seriously expected to cross the ocean (fig. 97).[48]

This was the time when Jules Verne published *Five Weeks in a Balloon* (1863) his first novel, the great success of which determined the author's career. But real life was also peopled with Jules Vernes, eager to transform their fantasies into reality. In 1863 an American physician projected the 'Aereon,' consisting

[48] *Harper's Weekly*, 1859, p.612.

of three cigar-shaped balloons harnessed together like dogs. 'The discovery made by Dr. Andrews,' if we are to believe the prospectus, 'was simply this: that the attraction of gravity is a sufficient motor for navigation.' One need only know how to exploit it correctly.[49] On the other side of the ocean, there was no lack of similar plans for harnessing the aerial balloon. A balloon railway to the summit of Mt. Rigi, Switzerland, was projected (1859) (fig. 95); its gas bag was expected to hoist a car, suspended from an overhead rail, up the mountainside.[50]

The period also took appreciable interest in the use of steam pressure to preserve milk and fruits. Charles Alden was famous in his day for his experiments in drying and preserving fruit, tomatoes, and milk by a steam process. 'The pneumatic evaporator reduces the whole pulp of the tomato to a condition like that of the dried fig.' [51] The early 'fifties also saw Gail Borden's experiments in condensing milk.[52]

Although soda water had been commercially produced by a Geneva pharmacist in the late eighteenth century (1788), its general use did not begin until around 1850, and in America only at the time of the Civil War. Its first application was chiefly for medicinal purposes and as mineral water. England issued 17 patents between 1840 and 1850, but the French were unquestionably in the lead; though far less given to patents than the English, they registered 34 'appareils à faire des eaux gaseuses' from 1844 to 1851. Toward mid-century, a Frenchman put on the market the present form of soda siphon, with the 'pewter collar having a turn of screw on it.' [53]

Baking powder came into general use during the same period. In 1836, Dr. John Whiting, a reader of Justus Liebig's chemical writings, patented his method for 'preparing certain farinacious food.' [54] This first chemical baking powder for raising dough did not become popular until the 'fifties.[55] Contemporary advertising, in which the biscuits are pictured as nailed down so as not to fly away while baking (fig. 98), indicates that even in the 'sixties the gas-producing powder was still something of a novelty.

A great contemporary was moving along lines similar to John Dauglish's, to obtain more rapid and cheaper production by means of gases and pressure: in 1856 Henry Bessemer first announced his method of steel production that was

[49] *The Aereon, invented by Solomon Andrews*, New York, 1866, with illustrations, p.3.

[50] *Harper's Weekly*, 1859, p.276. With illustrations.

[51] *The Great Industries of the United States*, Hartford, 1872, p.673.

[52] Gail Borden, U.S. Patent 15533, 19 Aug. 1856.

[53] Fèvre, *Brevets d'Inventions* 5981, 16 avril 1851. British Patent No. 13525, 22 Aug. 1851.

[54] British Patent No. 7076, 3 May 1836.

[55] In 1859 the Rumford Chemical Works, Rumford, R.I., put on the market the first calcium phosphate for baking powder. Cf. Albert E. Marshall, "Eighty Years of Baking Powder Industry," *Chemical and Metallurgical Engineering*, New York, 1939.

to have such important repercussions, forcing a blast of air through a pear-shaped convertor that contained the molten metal.

Dauglish in his second patent tried to achieve something similar in the field of baking: abandoning his predecessors' use of soda water, he forced pure carbonic acid from a steel flask into the convertor-shaped container.

His new machine somewhat recalled an upright boiler or perhaps superimposed divers' helmets (figs. 94, 96). The upper spherical vessel was a strong-walled mixer into which water and flour flowed under exact regulation. Into this mixer, the carbonic acid was forced under high pressure. Beneath, and separated by a heavy slide valve from the mixing chamber, lay the second vessel, a receiver from which the dough could flow steadily into the molds. In this way Dauglish achieved continuous flow, which cut the time of baking from ten hours to thirty minutes. 'From the time the flour is emptied from the barrel into the machine, to the time the bread is taken from the baking press, it is not touched by hand.' [56]

These are almost the words in which Oliver Evans expounded the advantages of the uninterrupted production line in his automatic mill. But bread is a more sensitive product. Indeed, Dauglish's dough had a very fine porous texture, the gas bubbles being evenly distributed throughout, but the bread was rubbery, spongy, and destitute of flavor. His contemporaries said as much, and added that it was 'not really bread at all but only an imitation.' To all these charges the doctor found ready counter-arguments.

The gas bread manufactured in various American cities around 1860 never became truly popular. A single company, the Aerated Bread Company, instigated by Dr. Dauglish himself, still sports the letters A.B.C. over its chain restaurants in London.

Dr. Dauglish was not one of the really creative inventors. He did perfect the thought he pursued so fanatically throughout his career, an idea, however, that was not new. There is something quixotic about the goal and the fanaticism of the man who devoted his lifetime to attaining it. His apparatus cannot be dismissed as a mere mechanical plaything. It revealed at an early date how mechanization was later to change the nature of bread.

The Human Aspect: Bread under Mechanization

Two questions will be considered here.

How was flour, the material of bread, affected by the advance of mechanization?

How did mechanization alter the structure of bread, for so many centuries the symbol of human sustenance?

[56] *American Artisan*, New York, 1866, vol. 3, no. 1.

Flour in Mass Production

The flour used by bakers today has a whiteness far exceeding that of 1850. This whiteness is not the result of adulteration with foreign substances (alum, copper sulphate, etc.), but of a revolutionized milling process. The millstones crushed the grain in such manner as to mix inseparably at the first milling most of the components of the berry, the starchy interior, the nutritious layer of gluten cells, and the valuable oily germ or embryo. The oily substance of the germ penetrated the mixture, making it oily to the touch and frequently unpleasant in appearance. Moreover, there was the risk that the oily ingredients would turn rancid in prolonged storage. In this low or flat grinding process, the millstones with their sharp grooves were set as close together as possible.

The millstones, which crushed the grain as small as possible at the first milling, are now replaced by rollers, relatively far apart, which squeeze the grain far more gradually. This 'high grinding' is performed in stages. After every passage through rollers, the grain is separated by sifting machines into its various components. The process is repeated four, six, eight, ten times.

When did this begin?

The gradual reduction of the wheat into flour by means of rollers was called the 'Hungarian system.' Although France and other countries worked on this process, it was systematically developed in a country having much wheat and a fondness for elaborate pastries requiring extra fine flour — Hungary. This took place between 1834 and 1873.[57] In America the transformation of the milling process was carried out between 1870 and 1880 in the wheat-growing Middle West (Minneapolis). It had begun in the late 'sixties with attempts to separate the thin glutinous middlings surrounding the kernel.[58]

The year 1871 brought a cleaner, such as the French had sought around 1860, by which a hitherto poor grade of wheat could be made to yield the most highly priced flour. Minnesota flour was the outcome of this 'new purifying process,' popularly known as the 'new process.' 'Minnesota fancy reigned supreme in every market in which it was introduced as the sharpest, whitest, brightest

---

[57] This Hungarian system' was developed in Budapest between 1834 and 1873, chiefly by three Swiss inventors: in 1834 by Jacob Sulzberger, in 1850 by Abraham Ganz, who introduced chilled iron rollers, and finally in 1873 by Friedrich Wegmann, who used smooth, automatically regulated porcelain rollers. (Cf. Wilhelm Glauner, *Die Historische Entwicklung der Müllerei*, Munich, Berlin, 1939.) The rollers are typical shelved inventions. But it took them two and a half centuries to be developed from Ramelli's portable roller-mill (1588) into a machine. In the eighteenth century, various proposals of this sort, mostly for household use, are found in France and in England. As in the entire field of breadmaking, numerous attempts were made in the 'twenties, but led to no satisfactory solution.

[58] Charles B. Kuhlmann, *Development of the Flour-Milling Industry in the United States*, Boston, 1929, pp.115ff.

flour ever produced,' as an anonymous contemporary pamphlet points out.[59] This cleansing process was devised before the rollers were tried out in America in 1873; but from then on, the tempo as well as the size of the mills increased enormously. Around 1881 all the large Minneapolis mills were adapted to the new process and extensively automatized.

Hand in hand came large-scale production and increasing concentration of ownership. It was the period in which the Chicago packing houses moved toward monopoly.

No radical change had taken place in the century from Oliver Evans' 'new process of flour making by automatic machinery' [60] to the 'new process of middling flour.' Likewise no basic improvement in milling machinery occurred after 1890. Instead there were technical changes in the direction of novelty. Interest centered around obtaining still finer and whiter flour. Efforts bore on elaborate, ever more complicated apparatus for the artificial bleaching of flour. The public — the millers maintained — demanded a flour of greater whiteness than could be obtained by anything but artificial bleaching.[61] This may have been the case. But the decisive reason lay elsewhere. It had formerly been considered necessary to age the flour for a period of months. During this time it lost its natural creamy color and became pure white. But the time factor involved in this aging process was onerous to large-scale production. It meant large warehouses and capital outlays lying idle. 'Millers sought for a way to escape the burden,' specialists inform us. 'The remedy they found was the artificial bleaching and aging of flour.' [62] This was done by high-voltage currents or infiltration with gases (chlorine). Commercial bleaching was first introduced in France around the turn of the century, then successfully carried out in England, finally finding its large-scale application in America.[63] The cabinet in which the bleaching takes place within a matter of minutes is no bulkier than a small chest of drawers. Blown in through tubes, the chlorine gas instantaneously penetrates the whirling particles; and the flour drops another storey downwards straight into its paper sack.

Artificial bleaching was not accepted without debate. There were long and bitter controversies and investigations. The experts often took diametrically opposite stands. It is not for us to judge whether they are right who maintain

[59] *The original inventor for the purifying of middlings*, New York, 1874, p.4. This pamphlet is one of the numerous works about the inventor of the new process.

[60] From Oliver Evans' specification.

[61] Kuhlmann, op.cit. p.283.

[62] Ibid. p.234.

[63] Commercial bleaching apparently dates from a French patent, 1898. Cf. C. H. Baily, *The Chemistry of Wheat Flour*, New York, 1925.

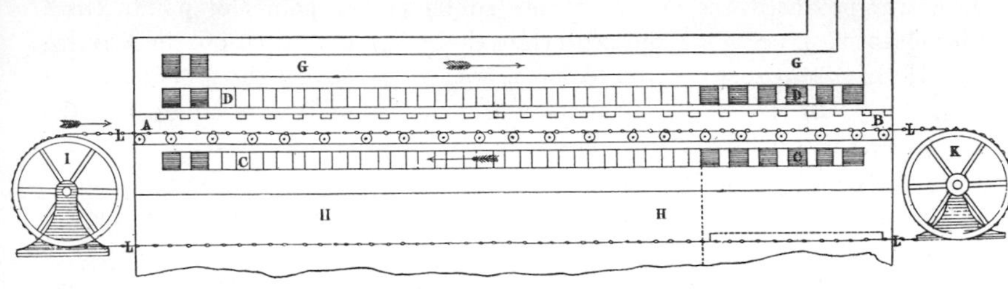

99. First Oven with Endless Belt, 1810. Admiral Isaac Coffin. *Invented by a Bostonian who became a British admiral, this oven for baking sea biscuits supplied a link towards the continuous-production line.*

that the bleaching process causes no deleterious effects,[64] or they who claim that the present milling methods remove the most important nutritional values from the grain. We need only note that the new methods arose in the demand for greater output, the human considerations having little voice in the matter.

Mechanization of the milling process yielded a brilliant façade and a more or less artificial product. The oleaginous germ that formerly made the flour somewhat greasy to the touch, and which contains the most valuable elements, has been rigorously excluded. More recently, we have seen attempts to make good the values removed from the flour by vitamin reinforcements added to the yeast or the dough. The whiteness of the flour remains unspotted. But such measures remind one of a dentist who extracts good natural teeth, filling the void with a bright and handsome set of artificial ones. The device of adding vitamins is a simple one. It consists of a metal cabinet slotted like a letter box. The vitamin paste dropping in small clusters into the flour is thoroughly mixed with it by a screw conveyor such as Oliver Evans used.

[64] Cf. Baily, op.cit. p.213.

100. Oven with Endless Chain. 1850. *The 1850's and especially the 1860's saw many continuous ovens patented, all having an endless belt within the baking chamber. 'The plates upon which the bread, cakes &c. are placed, are made of thin sheets of metal constituting the endless chain platform. The bread when baked is dropped from the end of the endless platform.'* (*U. S. Patent* 7778, 19 *November* 1850)

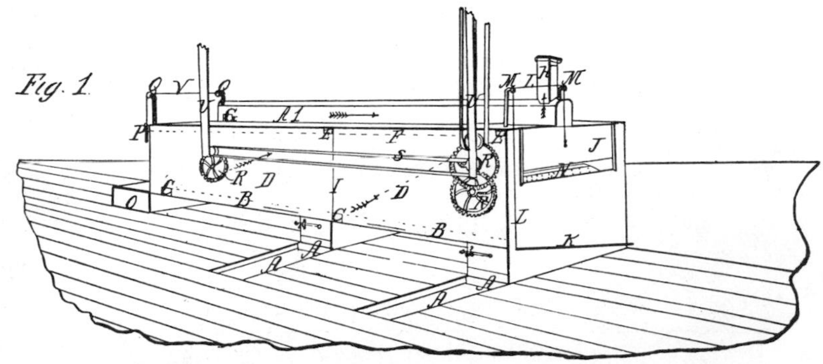

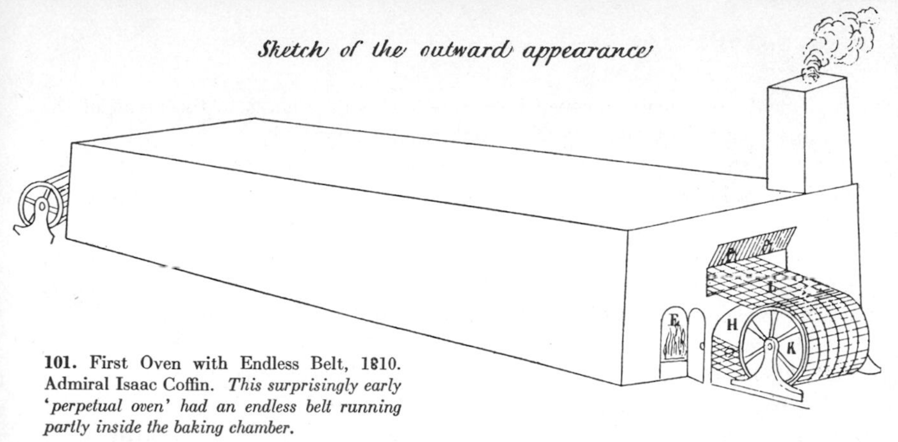

101. First Oven with Endless Belt, 1810. Admiral Isaac Coffin. *This surprisingly early 'perpetual oven' had an endless belt running partly inside the baking chamber.*

Full Mechanization: Bread on the Production Line

Many of the machines by which the mass manufacture of bread and the continuous production line became possible were first devised in Europe. Bread baking is a complicated craft. Although kneading machines and other labor-saving devices were used long before, nowhere was the passage to full mechanization more hesitant than in the food products.

Even in England, where this mechanization had its beginnings, 'bread factories are less numerous than small bakeries. After 1900, the proportion is 80 : 1 in favor of the small bakeries.' [65] Since that time, in comparison with America, things have remained much as they were.

Such is certainly the case on the Continent, even in countries with a high living standard. Their small bakeries are largely equipped with mechanical

[65] Emil Braun, *The Baker's Book*, New York, 1901, vol. 1, p.182.

102. Oven with Endless Chain. 1850. Section. *Some mechanical bakeries appeared in the* 1860's, *after the tunnel oven's construction had been ingeniously refined. Yet none was successful: the production line in bread making only became effective in the time of full mechanization, which perfected automatically controlled tunnel ovens heated by gas or electricity. By this time the earlier experiments were forgotten, and efforts had to start from scratch.* (*U. S. Patent* 7778, 19 *November* 1850)

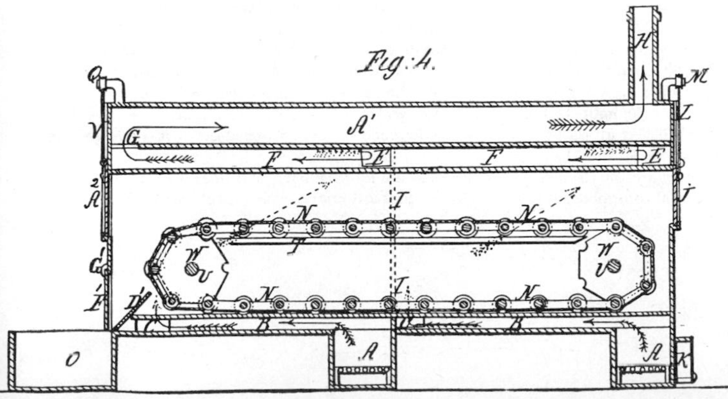

implements and electric ovens. Everyone tastes differences in the bread of the various local bakers and selects his baker accordingly.

Only in countries where the most advanced stages of mechanization have been reached, as in the United States and, in this respect, Canada, has the small baker almost disappeared and mass production become the rule. According to the U.S. Census of 1939, corporate enterprise manufactured bread and other baked goods (biscuits, crackers, and pretzels excepted) to the value of 514 million dollars as against 20 million dollars manufactured by non-corporate, i.e. small establishments.[66] This went hand in hand with the growing mechanization of daily life between 1914 and 1930, and especially in the period 1925–30.

In this period the bread factory was consolidated into a production unit.[67] All operations and machines were co-ordinated and synchronized with clock-work precision. The manufacture of dough became automatized in all its stages; the loaf obtained an extremely even structure and absolute uniformity.

The dimensions of the ovens have increased over those of 1850; this is true of all types — steam ovens, draw-plate ovens, rotary ovens — above all of the endless-belt type, which has grown to the length of 100 to 130 feet. The term 'tunnel oven' is no exaggeration.

Engineers use their thermodynamic experience to insulate the ovens and to regulate the heat with great precision. All dirt is kept out; no stoking or coal-shoveling pollutes the atmosphere, for gas, electricity, or oil have replaced coal. The baking chamber is now as clean as a hydroelectric power plant.

The kneaders with their shiny enamel housings often reveal a surprising beauty of form. All sharp edges and corners disappear, the forms have the fluidity of a melting ice block. We are in the period of streamline design. The assembly line, which rolls almost without human intervention, has developed to a point rarely reached in other fields.

Beyond a doubt there is something impressive in the precision, synchronization, and cleanliness of a modern bread factory with its hourly output of 30,000 loaves. In Philadelphia we visited one of the largest plants of the kind — a five-storey

---

[66] *U.S. Census* 1939, vol. 1, Statistics and subjects, p.234:
Number of establishments in corporate ownership — 1160; in non-corporate — 329.
Wage earners in establishments in corporate ownership — 80,074; in non-corporate — 3561.

[67] The data found in scattered articles on the introduction of the various machines often disagree. Nevertheless the development can be ascertained with a certain accuracy. If we start with the turning points of full mechanization, the high speed mixers and the gas-fired tunnel ovens, it becomes clear that the present-day tunnel oven of light steel plates and the high-speed mixer came into general use after 1928. Parallel to this runs their first appearance in serviceable models: the high-speed mixer in 1916, gas-fired tunnel oven (with brick walls) in 1917.

Associated with these are the devices which perform the intermediary and final operations, such as loaf molders around 1900, wrapping machines 1913–14, and automatic slicing machines 1928.

reinforced concrete building, its façade a vast expanse of glass, its auto park accommodating 500 delivery trucks.[68]

The production method is the same as in almost all modern factories: that is, production starts in the upper storeys; conveyor systems link one operation to another. Oliver Evans, in his mill at Red Clay Creek (1784), was the first to couple the force of gravity with mechanical conveyor systems. In the modern bread factory, the flour is first elevated to the top storey, where batteries of high-speed mixers are aligned. Each of these mixers holds three and a half barrels (or some 600 pounds). 'Mammoth' mixers have been abandoned; they overheated the dough. The plant we visited formerly had the largest mixer of this kind, capable of mixing 30 barrels, or nearly 6000 pounds, of dough at a time. But giant mixers and giant troughs were unsuited to so sensitive a material.

After a few minutes of mixing, the heavy mass of sponge — or first mix — is poured from each machine into a trough. The troughs swing on pivots much as miners' towcars, but much longer, and hang by strong rods from trollies which glide on a monorail close to the ceiling. The system is the same in principle as that used for moving carcasses in packing houses, but far more massive. The troughs are shunted into the next room, where fermentation takes place. Trough follows trough along the ceiling, train after train, monorail after monorail, as in a suspended freight yard. In four and a half hours the sponge rises from the bottom of the trough to the brim. The slowly forming gas bloats the mass like a balloon, and if the elastic, membrane-like layer spanning the vessel is broken open, the warm carbonic-acid gas rushes out and it is possible to look into countless invisibly working gas chambers. At this stage, the living mass still has the irregular hollows, bubbles, and cavities of the hand-made loaf.

After the mass stands for four and a half hours, the train is set in motion. Trough after trough is pushed to the rear of the room and tipped over; the sponge flows through large openings in the floor down to the storey below.

There it goes into a second battery of mixers, where the irregular sponge is given the ingredients it needs to become a uniform mass. Before fermentation, only about 60 per cent of the flour is put in. Now the other 40 per cent is added, along with milk, water, fats, six parts per hundred of sugar, vitamins, and what other ingredients may seem desirable. The dough now has its final composition.

After this second passage through the high-speed mixers, the dough must be allowed half an hour or an hour's rest, to appease the shaken-up molecules. Then it is ready to be divided. Again it drops one storey groundwards, where a divider

---

[68] We are indebted to Mr. W. A. Sieber, manager of the Freihofer Baking Co., Philadelphia, for his obliging guidance and information.

severs the mass into pieces, each the weight of a loaf. A second machine rounds these into balls, as the baker formerly did by hand. This encourages a thin skin to form around the pieces of dough to prevent the gas from escaping, or, as bakers say, to prevent 'bleeding.' The balls of dough fall each into its hollow on the bucket proofer, an endless chain, and glide for a quarter of an hour through warm glassed-in chambers, where they are sheltered against any draft.

The final preparation of the dough takes place in a molder which, mechanically imitating and breaking down the last movements of the hand-baker, rolls the balls into cylindrical shape. Now they are ready to be laid into the pan, an operation that can be automatically performed but which even large plants prefer to do by hand. Fermentation is again stimulated. In pan-proofing cabinets with high humidity, the yeast works vigorously and in the course of an hour drives the dough over the top of its pan.

Now the baking process begins. The pans disappear into the 10-foot-wide slot of the white-walled ovens, standing side by side. For half an hour they travel on their endless belt through the 130-foot tunnel. Fully baked, they are automatically pushed out at the other end. A second time the human hand intervenes, and heavily gloved workers pluck the loaves from the hot pans. A conveyor moves them to the floor below where, in about two hours, they slowly cool in overhead coolers — moving racks in chambers with exact control of temperature and humidity.

Methods appear in the 'thirties by which the cooling time is reduced by division into two stages: 'The first step at atmospheric pressure, and thereafter quicker cooling of the bread by evaporation of moisture under subatmospheric pressure.' [69]

There remains only to slice the loaves, to pack and distribute them.

The automatic slicing machines, which cut sixty loaves a minute into uniform slices, are late comers in bread manufacture. Invented in 1928, hesitantly accepted in 1930,[70] by 1940 they were regarded as indispensable. When in 1942 the United States Government, being at war, banned the use of bread-slicing machines to save steel, this so displeased the housewives that the order had to be canceled.

The idea of cutting a whole loaf of bread at once, we may note, had appeared in America as early as the 'sixties, when a bread-cutting device with ten parallel

---

[69] U.S. Patent 2,012,772, 19 Nov. 1935. As we shall see presently (cf. 'Changes in Structure'), this process was further extended to inject into the bread any desired aroma or color.

[70] 'When slicing bread was first suggested . . . the bakers felt slicing would impair the quality and appearance of their loaves,' E. J. Frederick, 'Slicing latest development,' *Canadian Baker & Confectioner*, Toronto, July, 1938.

sickle-shaped blades attached to a lever was patented.[71] But this machine, like the vacuum cleaner and the dishwashing machine, joined the shelved inventions. There were reasons for this. To work satisfactorily, the modern bread-slicing machine, as a leading expert remarks, requires bread such as only present-day mechanization can produce, loaves of absolute uniformity, soft in crust and regular in crumb.[72]

As a rule the slicers form a unit with the wrapping machines, also introduced relatively late, in 1913–14. From these the wrapped product is conveyed directly to trucks waiting in rows on the ground floor.

Viewing the entire cycle, we find that the time saved by these mechanisms is out of proportion to their complexity. In the double mixing (sponge-dough) method we have described, some eight and a half hours are required before the flour is transformed into finished bread. The main time saving over earlier methods lies in the use of quicker rising yeast, which reduces the fermentation period from nine to approximately four and a half hours. There are quicker ways — the straight dough method — in which one mixes all the ingredients at once. Fermentation time can thus be cut to three and a half hours. But general preference is for the longer, sponge-dough method.

The decisive saving rests not in acceleration of the process but in the enormous output that mechanization and the assembly line render possible.

The bread-making process refuses to be hastened beyond narrow limits; for mechanization here encounters an organic substance whose laws are inviolable. Antoine Augustin Parmentier defined dough (1778) as the soft, flexible, and uniform substance obtained by thoroughly mixing flour, water, air, and leaven (for yeast was not yet used in bread baking). Today one might add that this substance is not a static one, but an organic body ever in flux, a highly sensitive culture whose incubation must be carefully controlled in every phase of its mass manufacture with the aid of thermometers and hot-air chambers. We have had occasion to see how after each mechanical intervention a pause of varying length is required to restore the interrupted activity of the enzymes. In the mechanized process, more subdivisions and pauses, and far greater caution, are necessary than in hand baking.

Wherever mechanization encounters a living substance, bacterial or animal almost indifferently, it is the organic substance that determines the law.

---

[71] W. B. Vincent, Machine for Cutting Bread, Soap and Black Lead, U.S. Patent 52627, 13 Feb. 1866, Boston, Mass.

[72] Julius B. Wihlfahrt, *Treatise on Baking*, New York, 1934.

The Changed Nature of Mechanized Bread

The question still remains: How was bread changed under the influence of mechanization?

Dr. Dauglish's carbonated bread had an extremely uniform, finely porous structure, produced by the stream of gas injected under pressure. The crust was relatively hard, but the inside was elastic as a rubber sponge and completely tasteless. It did little good to mix the dough with wine instead of with water, as was later done in the hope that the acid ingredients would heighten its flavor.

Dr. Dauglish's actual formula did not prevail, but characteristics distinguishing his mechanical bread from that of the pre-industrial period have.

103. Advertisement for Wrapped and Sliced Bread. 1944.

UNIFORMITY

How did it become possible, after 1900, for the large baking corporations to eliminate the small bakers who had hitherto possessed the market? The experts always offer this explanation: the product of the small bakers, they say, was always changing; one day it was such, another day it was such. Mechanization, on the other hand, furnished bread that was entirely uniform. That the public demanded uniformity may be true, but economic factors were doubtless more decisive. After 1900 we enter the period when anonymous corporations penetrate nearly every province of living.

Bread as completely homogeneous as Dr. Dauglish obtained by his gas process remained impossible with yeast, that is, fermentation, until the high-speed mixer was generally introduced (1928). The tremendous beating power of its

→ 104. HERBERT MATTER: Italian Bread, New York. 1944.

agitator scattered the yeast particles throughout the dough. Uniformity and the increasing stress on appearance entered hand in hand.

Today the public demands that their eggs shall have yolks of uniform color. One city prefers a light yellow, another a deep orange. Industry provides the corresponding chicken feed, which, with the help of artificial coloring, never fails to produce yolks of the same shade.

Public taste is not so particular about the color of bread crust, but here too any required tint can be precisely obtained by means of thermostats and added ingredients. The neat wrapper, often highly effective from the advertising standpoint, in addition to keeping the bread clean and fresh, satisfies the demand for uniformity (fig. 103).

CHANGES IN STRUCTURE

The bread of full mechanization has the resiliency of a rubber sponge. When squeezed it returns to its former shape. The loaf becomes constantly whiter, more elastic, and frothier. This is not the result of mechanization alone. With the increasingly complex machinery and greater capital outlays, new ways of pushing consumption had to be devised.

Since mechanization, it has often been pointed out, white bread has become much richer in fats, milk, and sugar. But these are added largely to stimulate sales by heightening the loaf's eye-appeal. The shortenings used in bread, a leading authority states, are 'primarily for the purpose of imparting desirable tender eating or chewing qualities to the finished product.' [73] They produce the 'soft velvet crumb,' a cakelike structure, so that the bread is half-masticated, as it were, before reaching the mouth.

About 6 per cent of sugar is usually added to white bread. This too makes for looseness of structure and imparts a slight sweetness. Moreover it stimulates fermentation. But above all, sugar is 'the source of crust color.' If the amount is reduced, the thin crust becomes 'pale and unattractive' in appearance instead of being infused with that golden-yellow gloss, like those bright red apples whose appetizing exterior has almost driven out other varieties of less dazzling appearance but more delicate flavor.

Mechanization does not stand still. We have mentioned those proposals of the 1930's for cooling the bread more rapidly, under atmospheric, followed by subatmospheric, pressure. In a later patent [74] the inventor turns to good advantage the opportunity of the cooling phase for further work upon the make-up. While the loaf is having its dampness extracted in the vacuum chamber, it is

[73] Julius B. Wihlfahrt, op.cit.

[74] British Patent No. 13974–76, 19 Jan. 1937.

pierced by 'an injector device provided with a needle valve' much as the human skin is pierced by the doctor's hypodermic. One can, the inventor assures us, 'provide any desired penetration.' His discourse has something of Dr. Dauglish's fantasy and seems worth recording for its symptomatic value.

> Another object of the invention is to provide for injecting substances such as lemon, orange, raisin or other flavors or flavoring extracts, colouring materials. . . . Thus bread may be treated with a colouring material so that it will assume the desired tint. This material may have any desired flavor and hence the loaf, in addition to being coloured, will also have its taste fixed. . . . Similarly vitamins may be injected by volatile carriers. . . . For reinforcing the keeping qualities such gases as ozone may be introduced.[75]

As the loaf becomes ever softer and frothier, there is developed the demand for crust of the utmost thinness and for bread that is absolutely fresh. In the 'thirties of the past century, Sylvester Graham, the great reformer whom we are to meet again presently, condemned his countrymen's taste for bread as it comes steaming from the oven. Mechanization may have fostered the wish by using its skills to develop the soft airy texture that is characteristic of freshly baked bread. But it is certainly not the sole cause. Such texture concurs with the whole process of rapid production: long before mechanization set in, Sylvester Graham made it clear that thin-crusted bread, made of finely milled flour, bakes more quickly than any other. Imperceptibly, public taste adapted itself to this fact. Today's arbiter of taste in the bread industry indicates to bakers what he considers the main defects in crust: toughness, thickness, cracks. And he recommends above all tenderness and uniformity.[76]

Extreme freshness has grown into a demand that it does not pay to disregard. 'Storekeepers find stale bread, that is, bread that has stood for a day or even less, unsaleable.'[77] To preserve its fresh-baked quality the bread is wrapped in thick waxed paper bearing a carefully printed design — a usage that was respected through the paper shortage of the Second World War. The housewife, according to an American expert, feels the bread through the wrapper, and if it is not so soft and elastic that her fingers can almost meet in the middle, puts it back. Only thoroughly fresh bread is tolerated in the home — a factor conducive to waste. This schooling in waste works more in favor of expanded production than to the advantage of human digestion.

There has been no dearth of efforts to restore artificially the natural values removed for appearance's sake. In 1916 a large raisin firm began to advertise,

---

[75] Ibid.

[76] Wihlfahrt, op.cit. p.380.

[77] J. S. David and W. Eldred, *Stale Bread as a Problem of the Baking Industry*, Leland Stanford Jr. University, Food Research Institute, Miscellaneous Publications, no. 1, p.11.

urging bakers to use raisins in bread. Within two years the sale of raisins increased over tenfold.[78]

Suggestions for adding vitamins to the dough date from the late 'twenties. They were not carried out on a large scale until 1940, when vitamins were raised into a public preoccupation.[79] 'The American public has been told that they can now obtain a new white bread containing vitamins and minerals natural to whole wheat.' [80]

Mechanization Alters Public Taste

Doubtless fine bread, like many other luxuries, was so cheapened in price through mass production as to become available to all. No King of France had bread of such white and silken quality on his table. But bread's position as the staff of life has been undermined. The complicated machinery of full mechanization has altered its structure and converted it into a body that is neither bread nor cake, but something half-way between the two. Whatever new enrichments may be devised, nothing can really help as long as this sweetish softness continues to haunt its structure.

If the type of bread preferred in the United States were put to the public vote, the verdict would not be hard to foresee. The 1939 Census tells the story: the quantity of white pan bread consumed is about four times that of rye or whole wheat.[81] And we may note that the whole-wheat bread is not unlike the white pan bread in frothiness and flavor, and that as a rule 40 to 50 per cent of highly refined white flour is mixed with rye bread; here too the crust is kept as thin as possible.

The change of taste through mechanization forms an even clearer picture when the quantity of white flour used in bread and other bakery products in 1939 is compared to that of whole wheat (including graham). The ratio is 27 : 1.[82]

The adulteration of taste, similar to the one that accompanied the mechanizing of bread, was witnessed a century earlier in a quite different field. The ruling

---

78 Cummings, op.cit. p.151.

79 'Publicity and promotion by magazines representing 32 millions of readers; 50,000 news items on enriched bread appeared during six months in the daily press.' Cf. *Baker's Weekly*, 21 Sept. 1941.

80 Ibid. 'The future of enriched bread.'

81 Consumption of white pan bread — of whole wheat, rye, and hearth breads

White pan bread	Whole wheat, rye, and hearth breads
7,218,843,271 lbs.	1,731,225,028 lbs.
value: $491,520,741	value: $128,210,418

Cf. *Sixteenth U.S. Census* 1939, vol. 2, part 1, 'Manufactures,' p.164.

82 Consumption breads, cf. *Sixteenth U.S. Census* 1939, 'Manufactures,' vol. 2, part 1, p.165. Consumed in bread and other bakery products (except biscuits, crackers, and pretzels), 1939:

White Flour:	41,867,698 barrels	$188,033,486
Whole Wheat (including graham):	1,949,517 barrels	$ 9,214,166

artistic taste in the nineteenth century was formed by exploiting certain dormant wishes of the public. The public loves what is sweet, smooth, and outwardly appealing. These desires can be strengthened, weakened, or diverted into positive channels. The painters of the ruling taste set out to satisfy this public demand more and more, thus securing a market and rewards. The outcome was a blurring of the instincts in all classes of society, a disorientation that is doing its damage even today.

How ancient instincts were warped when bread met the impact of mechanization cannot be demonstrated in detail. There was an impenetrable thicket of action and reaction, the stimulating of wishes and their satisfaction. The changed characteristics of bread always turned out to the benefit of the producer. It was as if the consumer unconsciously adapted his taste to the type of bread best suited to mass production and rapid turn-over.

Sylvester Graham (1794–1851) *and the Devaluation of Bread*

The demand for fresh bread in the morning led at an early date to night baking. This custom of court and bourgeois society was long believed to have started toward the end of the *Ancien Régime*, when a shrewd Parisian baker sought to put his bread on sale earlier than his rivals. Today we know that work commencing around midnight was already performed in cities during the late Middle Ages. Detailed ordinances regulated night baking in the latter half of the fifteenth century.[83]

This was for the benefit of a small privileged class. Country people baked but once a week, sometimes no oftener than once a fortnight.[84] The loaves were stored on wooden racks up in the air near the ceiling. In many mountain regions, the habit of buying the week's supply of bread still prevails, even when the peasant can get bread fresh each day at the baker's. This is both time-honored usage and economy, for bread stored several days stretches farther than when it is oven fresh.[85]

Such was the common custom everywhere. The Pennsylvanians[86] seem to have used tall barrel-shaped willow baskets 'to contain a week's supply of home-made bread' (fig. 106). Their 'olden time loaves were several times the size of the baker's loaves of today and an oven full would readily fill one of these baskets.'[87]

---

[83] Ambroise Morel, *Histoire illustrée de la boulangerie en France*, Paris, 1924, p.114.

[84] Schmidt, op.cit. p.298.

[85] To relieve the wartime flour shortage, the Swiss Government prescribed that bread be aged 48 hours before selling. This immediately reduced consumption by 10 per cent.

[86] Dutch settlement in Lancaster County.

[87] Cf. *Lancaster Sunday News*, 12 Jan. 1930.

This bread had to be thoroughly baked. It should be neither soft nor spongy. The tough crust formed a natural protection against spoilage and drying out. One masticated it thoroughly and at leisure. It gave the teeth something resistant to bite into.

Often the normal area of the crust was deemed insufficient. Special shapes of bread were devised to increase its area. The bread of an Italian baker in New York shows in its plastic structure, so well rendered by Herbert Matter, the endeavor to enlarge the crust to the utmost (fig. 104).

The Italians are masters at thus extending the loaf's surface, and often draw their products into Baroque shapes. Indeed it was in the seventeenth century that elongated loaves with their greater crust area appeared. The long Paris loaves, the several forms of Vienna fancy bread, the salt twist, the cannon, the Kaiser roll or crescent, all these are rolled or folded from flat strips of dough, thus favoring the formation of crust and allowing the oven's heat thoroughly to penetrate the whole. Such bread is usually broken rather than cut.[88]

Functionally considered this means that the eater must bring his teeth and jaw muscles into play, and that he will experience the full flavor of the loaf.

Bread must have a hard crust if it is to give work to the jaws. During America's important preparatory period between 1830 and 1850, a number of reformers took up the problem of nutrition with the spirit and independence that other of their countrymen brought to the reshaping of age-old tools.

Sylvester Graham (1794–1851) was the leading figure whose name is still associated in all countries with the coarse-ground whole-wheat flour he advocated. Graham was not alone. He initiated a movement that enlisted the support of experts and found an echo in university circles.[89]

'Bread,' Graham writes in 1837,[90] 'should be baked in such a way that it will, as a *general statement*, require and secure a full exercise of the teeth in masti-

---

[88] Excellent explanatory figures on the making of these bread types are found in John Kirkland's *The Modern Baker*, London, 1924, vol. 1, pp.198–202.

[89] *The Boston Medical and Surgical Journal*, no. XIII, 21 Oct. 1835, p.178, thus reviews a lecture 'On the Science of Human Life' which Graham delivered in that city: 'We are utterly amazed at the ridicule with which this gentleman has been assailed in other places. . . . With such strict regard to the positive indications of nature as he exhibits, based upon known physical laws, there is no denying his propositions. Both his language and his illustrations were in accordance with the best medical authors. . . .' Cf. Richard Osborne Cummings, *The American and His Food*, Chicago, 1940, pp.47–8. This book is indispensable for the history of American nutrition. In many cases it has relieved us of the need to go into further detail. The author has combined breadth of outlook with the use of primary sources. He gives a short but pregnant survey of the activity of the American reformers between 1830 and 1850 (pp.43–53). The best insight into the matter is to be gathered from Graham's own writings. Cf. also Richard H. Shryock, 'Sylvester Graham and the Popular Health Movement,' *Mississippi Valley Historical Review*, Cedar Rapids, vol. 18, 1931, pp.172–183.

[90] Sylvester Graham, *Treatise on Bread and Breadmaking*, Boston, 1837, p.87.

cation.' But this is not all. The material of which it is made must be suited to these requirements. It shall be unbolted and coarsely ground wheat. Bread, Graham held, should retain something of 'the delicious flavor and delicate sweetness which pure organs perceive in the meal of good new wheat just taken from the ear.' He goes a step further. He knows how important is the soil in which the grain was ripened and the fertilizer used to enrich this soil. Here he draws close to the investigations of recent times.

Soil, flour, bread, were conceived as forming an indivisible entity in relation with another entity, the human organism. Sylvester Graham wished to restore man's contact with the organic. Nutrition was his medium.

Romantic nature sentiment merges with eighteenth-century back-to-nature trends in a summons to natural living. Graham saw nutrition as the way, just as the Silesian peasant, Vincent Priessnitz (1799–1851), saw water as the means of direct access to what was central in man's nature. When we come to speak of regeneration in the nineteenth century we shall see how Priessnitz, the founder of hydropathy, performed his cold-water cures between 1830 and 1850, using cold rub-downs, baths, and showers to treat chronic maladies, to harden and restore circulation in bodies debilitated by soft living. In their approach, both Graham and Priessnitz follow the lines which Jean-Jacques Rousseau laid down half a century earlier and which by 1830 had broadened into a general consciousness.

Sylvester Graham came of an early settled Colonial family of Connecticut preachers. As a child he was none too sturdy. He knew hard times in his youth, and having tried several vocations became a Presbyterian minister like his father. In Philadelphia, where he had his first congregation, he associated with Quakers and temperance men, although abstinence interested him far less than the way our body interacts with the nutriment it takes in. He studied physiology and anatomy. 'The laws of relation under which man exists' engaged his attention, as did 'the reciprocities and mutual dependencies of mind and body.' [91]

His rise began in 1832 when the cholera was ravaging both Europe and America. This epidemic led to the improvement of London's sewage system and the first housing settlements for the working class. Sylvester Graham, in well-attended lectures at Clinton Hall, New York, advocated a return to natural eating habits as a preventive of disease. He gained a large following.[92] Hotels observing his rules were established in New York and other cities.[93] Graham

[91] Graham, *Lectures on the Science of Human Health*, Boston, 1839, p.12.

[92] Graham, *Aesculapian Tablets of the Nineteenth Century*, Providence, 1834. Some hundred pages are devoted to testimonials which show that his ideas aroused great public interest at the time.

[93] The rules and mode of life in one of these boarding houses are briefly described and explained by Graham himself in [A. Nicholson's] *Nature's Own Book*.

later lived in a small Massachusetts town and acquired a number of active followers in Boston, who, through periodicals and societies, carried on the teachings after his death. Grahamism in diet was later joined in a combined cure with Priessnitzian hydropathy.[94] In various forms this union of diet, exercise, and water treatment has survived in European countries to the present day.

More than half a century before mechanization came to dominate life, Sylvester Graham uttered the sharpest indictment of its effects. What at that time was in its beginnings and mainly limited to the 'vitiated taste of refined society'[95] has since engulfed the broad masses of the people.

Sylvester Graham's interest in nutrition arose from a wish to reconcile man with the constants that govern his organism. Sometimes Graham's ideas border on the extreme; but on the whole his rules, far in advance of his time, are framed with surprisingly sure instinct.[96] He could not know precisely what vital elements were stored in the germ or the husk of the grain, or what was the secret of the raw fruit and whole vegetable he so zealously advocated. But his one great concern is recognizable throughout: food should not be robbed of its most important values in the course of preparation. In like manner, we are to read these lines from the 'Laws of Diet'[97]: 'If man were to subsist wholly on alimentary substances in their *natural state*, or without any artificial preparation by cooking, then he would be obliged to use his teeth frequently in masticating food and by so doing not only preserve his teeth from decay, but at the same time and by the same means, would he thoroughly mix his food with the fluid of his mouth.'

For the same reasons, Graham warns against mashed potatoes, which almost altogether relieve the eater of mastication and reach the stomach as a cloggy and concentrated mass. Mashing, in our day, has visibly outstripped all other modes of preparing this food.

In the course of our century the preference has become ever more marked for foodstuffs that can be swallowed with a minimum of time and effort — from chopped meat (hamburger) to ice cream, both of which deserve the title of national dishes. Fruit is favoritely taken in liquid form (juices) or diced in small cubes (fruit cup). Children, we have noticed, often refuse to eat whole peaches, having been brought up largely on sliced fruits. How these trends took shape

---

[94] Dr. T. H. Trall, New York, was successful in the amalgamation of these two tendencies; his periodical was maintained under different titles for forty years. (*The Water Cure Journal, The Herald of Health, The New York Journal of Hygiene.*) Cf. Shryock, op.cit. p.177.

[95] [Asenath Nicholson] op.cit. 2nd ed., Boston, 1835, p.6.

[96] Ibid., pp.13ff.: 'Rules and Regulations of the Temperance Boarding House in New York, 1832.'

[97] Graham, *Treatise on Bread and Breadmaking*, Boston, 1837, ch. 'Laws of Diet,' p.17.

and how seriously the time-saving compulsion has recoiled upon the people's food are questions for more searching enquiry. If we consider powdered and packaged ingredients for making soups and cakes, coffee sold ready ground in cans, granulated sugar used in preference to the less rapidly dissolving cubes, the limits of this ever-growing field seem almost impossible to draw.

Bread was Graham's starting point, and to bread he always returns. He sings the praises of that 'delicious bread' which, he reminisces, the women of New England baked around 1800: 'There was a natural sweetness and richness in it which made it always desirable.' [98] Such times were past, and Graham sensed this. While bread should be made 'within the precincts of our own thresholds . . . from the best new quality of wheat,' every family being 'furnished with a modern patent hand-mill,' and while even home yeast 'can be made of a far superior quality' to that obtainable from the brewer,[99] Graham himself suspected that these proposals were condemned in the long run and ran counter to the trend of the times.

Not so far from the possible was his recommendation that bread should have a hard protective crust and be kept twenty-four hours before eating. What Sylvester Graham taught in 1832 now reads like a warning against blurred instincts, a warning of the soft, forever fresh, and crustless bread that the ruling taste in most industrialized countries now demands.

Elsewhere Graham sharply attacks American custom:

> It is a general fault of bread of every description made in this country that it is not sufficiently baked. . . . The multitude eat their bread hot and smoking from the oven in a half-cooked state.
>
> Stale bread: this ought to be written in capitals upon every plate. Every child, as soon as it has teeth, should be taught to eat stale hard bread. The crust is far preferable. It answers more than one good purpose. It is better for the teeth, more palatable to a correct taste, more suitable to the stomach.[100]

A century later, at the high point of mechanized bread manufacture, the most reliable guide, we recall, instructs bakers to make the crust of their bread as tender and as thin as possible: 'Some faults in the character of the crust are: too thick, too hard. . . . A desirable character of the crust must be described as tender, even surface and uniformity . . .' [101] A more radical transformation of taste is hard to conceive.

---

[98] Ibid. In a few localities it is still possible to corroborate Graham's remarks. In the high valley of Wallis Canton in Switzerland, along with late Gothic houses and language of late Gothic plasticity, something of the strength of that period has been preserved in the native bread. It has a distinctive content which, as Graham says of the bread of New England, makes it 'always desirable.'

[99] Ibid. pp.39, 49, 131.

[100] Ibid. p.97.

[101] Wihlfahrt, op.cit. p.380.

Sylvester Graham, we may assume, would react to the bread of full mechanization much as a noted French painter who observed of his white bread, 'C'est de la neige, il n'a pas de goût.'

Nutrition was the instrument through which Graham sought to approach the inherent laws of the human organism. In this, bread was for him the central pillar, or, as he put it, 'Bread has been in nearly every portion of the world and every period of time one of the first and most important universal articles of food.'[102] But he does not stop here. In his 'Laws of Diet,' he comes close to the raw-food diet which has widely influenced eating habits in certain countries with a high living standard, such as Switzerland, from about 1930 on. Many of his rules imply this, as does his remark: 'If man were to subsist entirely on food in a natural state he would never suffer from concentrated ailments.'[103]

When certain physicians objected with excessive logic that since Graham's coarse wheaten bread was totally indigestible it should never be allowed to enter the human stomach, he answered as might a modern dietician, who knows that the stomach muscles, like those of our arms and legs, must be given an opportunity for exercise if they are not to grow flabby: 'This objection betrays so much ignorance of . . . final causes and constitutional laws . . . that it scarcely deserves the slightest objection.'[104]

Here he touches on a problem with which he was much preoccupied and which has grown dangerously acute in our time: belief that primary elements lost by improper preparation can be replaced in pill-form. 'Nature produces nothing for the alimentary use of man which is purely concentrated nutrient substance.'[105]

The present-day scientist will find it easy to red pencil the fallacies in Graham's rules. Nevertheless, few reformers of his time have left so much in their teachings that is valid for ours. Pages from the 'Laws of Diet' and the *Treatise on Bread*, with suitable commentation, might well be used in schools and on the radio until they permeate the general consciousness.

The nature of bread has changed but little in the course of centuries. A certain coarseness, as in many things handed down from generation to generation, is one of bread's basic traits. Among foodstuffs, bread has always held a status bordering on the symbolic.

Graham's remarks return again and again to bread's essential nature, and rest on age-old human experience. He understood that a people's bread reveals

[102] Graham, op.cit. p.16.
[103] Ibid. p.53.
[104] Ibid. p.18.
[105] Ibid. p.19.

their whole attitude toward nutrition. No technical advances, no pill culture, no concentrated food — against which he gave such timely warnings — will change anything in this.

Graham was relatively alone in his time. The questions he raised have been raised again, and on a broader plane, in Europe. There, in the very countries that enjoy high living standards, a reaction has set in, not against patent flour alone but against all artificiality in food. It is a revolt too closely bound up with the renewed trend to the organic to be arrested in any land. The trend is appearing in ever-new fields, and should in the long run outlive the dictatorship of production.

105. PABLO PICASSO: 'The Woman with the Loaves.' 1905. *(Courtesy Philadelphia Museum of Art)*

106. Pennsylvania Dutch Basket for Storing Bread. *As in Europe, enough bread was baked for a week's supply. 'The olden time loaves were several times the size of bakers' loaves of today, and an oven-full would readily fill such a basket.' (Courtesy the Landis Valley Museum, Lancaster County, Pa.)*

Mechanization, pure and simple, has passed its crest. A stock-taking has begun, and, at the same time, criticism. The question, 'how did mechanization alter bread?' cannot be put off and no doubt can remain about the answer. Mechanization has devaluated the constant character of bread and turned it into an article of fashion for which new-found charms must ever be devised.

As Graham proclaimed in 1832 with unrestrained zealotry. 'While the people of our country are so entirely given up as they are at present . . . to the unthinking pursuit of wealth it is perhaps wholly in vain for a single individual to raise his voice in a subject of this kind. . . . Whether my voice will be heard or not, I will obey the dictate of my sense of duty. . . .'[106]

As Graham foresaw, his voice went unheard. No one could have stemmed the course of the nineteenth century. Today, his endeavors to reconcile man with the organic take on their full timeliness and urgency.

---

[106] Graham, op. cit. pp.35–6.

MECHANIZATION AND DEATH: MEAT

Centralization and Handicraft

Paris, the Slaughterhouse of La Villette (1863–7)

THE Prefect of the Seine Department, George Eugène Haussmann, so wielded his almost dictatorial powers that in the space of seventeen years he changed the whole aspect of Paris and recast its technical organization from top to bottom. After the steps initiated by Napoléon I, the city had failed to keep pace with the times; Haussmann transformed Paris into a nineteenth-century metropolis.[1] He was the first to perceive the city primarily as a problem in engineering and organization. In keeping with his foresight and his preference for the large scale, he did not hesitate to provide, in his master plan, for a central slaughterhouse demanding an outlay of 23 million francs. And this he accomplished while his downfall was being openly contrived at every step. He began the building in 1863, opening it 1 January 1867, the year of the lavish International Exposition; yet the installation was not complete when the Second Empire collapsed.

The Central Slaughterhouse of La Villette (fig. 107) was erected on the outermost limit of the fortified belt. One side was bordered by manifold railway sidings, another by the harbor-like expanse of the Canal St. Denis, one arm of which flowed through the plant, whose buildings rose on either bank. On the two other sides, the Slaughterhouse was bounded by a broad military road and a lesser thoroughfare.

It was the first central slaughterhouse to cater to a population of millions. Its lairages, as Haussmann pointed out, could accommodate 'the number of beasts needed for Parisian consumption over a period of several days.'[2] In England and in Germany, vested interests stood in the way of any development such as conceived by Haussmann. Nowhere did anything comparable exist at the time. In his *Mémoires*, Haussmann gives his enterprise the prominence it deserves: 'The vast establishment is one of the most considerable works accomplished by my administration, paralleling the great sewer constructions. . . . I should not forget to mention that the millions it cost were in very large measure balanced by the sale . . . of the better situated lots of the old abattoirs that it replaced.'[3]

The 'old abattoirs' to which Haussmann refers in his *Mémoires* were the work of Napoléon I and represented the first endeavor to organize a slaughter-

[1] For the details of this development, cf. Giedion, op.cit. pp.465–501.

[2] George Eugène Haussmann, *Mémoires*, Paris, 1890–93, vol. III, p.561.

[3] Ibid. pp.560 and 561.

house along more hygienic lines. Napoléon's first decree dates from the year 1807, when he ordered the building of public slaughterhouses. The fleshers as a body were pledged to slaughter nowhere else. In this way, five slaughterhouses were erected outside the city walls as they then stood, three to the north and two to the south of the Seine. In 1810 Napoléon issued a second decree, requiring that public slaughterhouses be built in every town of France, and — it was specified — outside the city limits.[4] This sanitary reform was to put an end to the murky doings of previous centuries. In the early years, public slaughterhouses spread rapidly through France and Belgium. With ever-fewer exceptions, they remained municipal property. They were regarded not as sources of revenue, but as centers where the animals could be slaughtered under supervision. This left the position of the small butcher almost unchanged. To this day, in Europe, the areas from which the cattle are supplied have remained preponderantly local.

The 'abattoirs' of Napoléon I also gave their name to the American establishments and were still regarded as models of their kind up to shortly before the opening of La Villette. A pamphlet of 1866 remarks: 'Although the name of abattoir has been given to these erections [American slaughterhouses] — taking the Parisian abattoirs as our models — we neither have perfected arrangements for cleanliness nor protection against fire nor conveniences.' We further learn that Napoléon's abattoirs 'are all conducted in the most rigid manner by a guild or corporate body of butchers. . . . The butchers have all their work done by regular slaughterers at slight cost.' Moreover, the slaughterers retain 'an additional prerequisite in the blood, rough offal, etc.' Of these, the blood is held the most valuable part. It may be noted that by mid-century the blood is already being saved and its value further exploited in industrial establishments. 'It is saved separately in stone wells, afterwards subjected to a scientific process, after which it is used for refining sugar and manuring the earth.' [5]

Just as Haussmann had enlarged Napoléon's Rue de Rivoli, so with the slaughterhouse of La Villette he took up a previously initiated development and pursued it further. Haussmann toiled over the slaughterhouse of La Villette with painstaking care, one might almost say with the consciousness of a mission to fulfil, on a scale so generous that the period has nothing to offer in comparison. It became *the* abattoir, a prototype for the rest of the century, just as the boulevards and public parks of Haussmann's Paris became models from which every growing metropolis of the Continent took pattern.

---

[4] *Handbuch der Architektur*, 4.Teil, 3.Halbband, Darmstadt, 1884, p.182.

[5] Thomas DeVoe, *Abattoirs*, Paper read before the Polytechnic branch of the American Institute, Albany, 1866, p.19.

The whole installation bears witness to the care with which the individual animal was treated. The great lairages (*bergeries*), with their lofts under the high roofs and their careful design, might have stood in a farmyard; each ox had a stall to itself. Dominating the long rows of low slaughterhouses and administrative buildings were three gigantic halls of glass and iron, elegant in design. The central hall, with its nine aisles over 800 feet long (286 m.) served as a 'cattle-shelter' (*abri pour bœufs*). Here the animals were bought and sold. The two flanking iron constructions were intended for swine, sheep, and calves.

Later critics have dealt severely with Haussmann's central slaughterhouse. Around 1900 he was taxed with having 'brought no modification to the dispositions adopted in 1810 for the first five abattoirs.' [6] This is perfectly true so far as the technical scheme is concerned. But such improvements were nowhere to be found in the Europe of 1860. At that time, even in America, mechanical aids to slaughtering had not emerged from the experimental stage.

Certainly this criticism holds good for the methods of operation that prevailed throughout La Villette. A glance into the halls in which the carcasses were quartered attests the calm of the handicraft that no cog-wheel, no conveyor has shaken; and this toward the end of the 'eighties, when in Chicago the assembly line had been developed.

In this curious symbiosis of handicraft with centralization lies the peculiarity of this establishment as well as of many others in Europe. In La Villette — another point of criticism — each ox had a separate booth in which it was felled. This is a survival of handicraft practices, to which the routine of mass slaughtering is unknown. The long houses in which the cattle were slaughtered consisted of rows of single cabins set side by side. Long since, technical installations and slaughtering in large halls have superseded them. It may well be that this treatment in separate booths expresses the deeply rooted experience that the beasts can be raised only at the cost of constant care and attention to the individual animal.

The Great Plains beyond the Mississippi, where free tracts of grassland can be dominated from horseback and where the herds grow up almost without care, are implicitly related to the assembly line. In just the same way the peasant farm, where each cow has its name and has to be attended when giving birth to its calf, is linked to handicraft methods in slaughtering.

La Villette and Union Stock Yards (1864)

This difference between the painstakingly raised animal and the herds growing up at minimum effort on the prairie is likewise reflected in the planning of the slaughtering centers.

[6] *L'abattoir moderne*, 2nd ed., Paris, 1916, p.45.

107. Paris, Slaughterhouse of La Villette. 1863–7. *These iron and glass halls, prototype of the abattoir, were built by Haussmann, prefect of Paris under the Second Empire, on a scale unique in Europe. Each ox rested in a stall before its slaughter in a separate booth. Routinized mass slaughter is alien to this calm, handicraft atmosphere. Europe's strongly rooted feeling that each animal needs individual care explains this symbiosis of handicraft and centralization.*

What was going on in America at the time Haussmann built the slaughterhouse of La Villette?

Chicago was engrossed in its first and wildest expansion. It had the same problem to centralize the cattle lairages, to gather them in one place. This led to the founding of the Union Stock Yards, thenceforth the greatest cattle market in the world. Haussmann, having once opened La Villette, did not again set eyes on the plant during his administration. The decision to found the Union Stock Yards was made late in 1864. 'Work was commenced on June 1, 1865, and by Christmas of that year the yards were thrown open for business. The yards were laid out as a rectangular figure, with streets and alleys crossing one another at right angles. About 120 acres were covered with pens when the Yards were opened. . . . Every railroad entering Chicago is connected with the Stock Yards.'[7] By 1886, when Andreas wrote his history of Chicago, the railroad trackage surrounding the stock yards had grown to a hundred miles.

Here were no iron halls or stalls for the cattle; these animals brought in from the great plains had never known stalls. Summer or winter they could remain in the network of open pens of which the Stock Yards consisted. Thus the yards (fig. 108) formed a collection and market center, from which the cattle were driven directly up an open gangway into the top storey of the packing houses.

Here was no architectonic plan.

Built entirely of wood, and doubtless gradually, no one has ever thought of making a general plan of it. All has been constructed in haste and according to the needs of the

[7] A. T. Andreas, *History of Chicago*, Chicago, 1886, vol. 3, p.334.

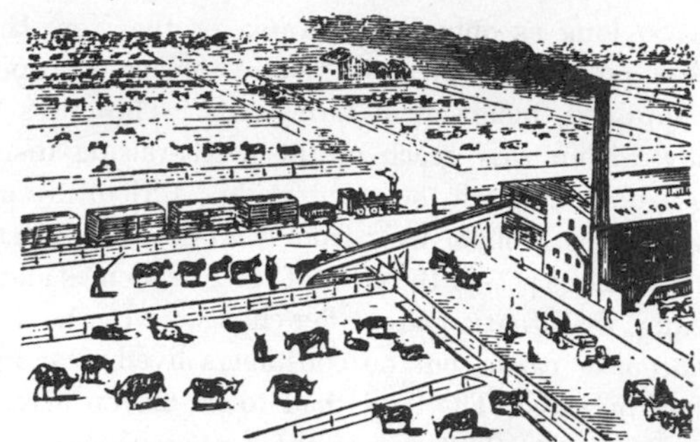

108. Chicago Stockyards in the Early 1880's. *Begun in 1865, while La Villette was still under construction, the Union Stockyards correspond to American conditions. The wild herds brought in from the great plains needed no shelter. Summer and winter, they could wait in open pens; from this assembly point they ascended to the top of the packing house by uncovered gangways.*

moment. It is a true labyrinth of sheds and enormous halls that communicate in various ways by passages, staircases, and suspension bridges, over which pass the workmen and over which runs the railway. Without a guide, one could never find his way in these immense structures.[8]

This description is of the time when the processing of livestock had reached a high point, over five million hogs yearly passed through Chicago's Union Stock Yards. The plants had a processing capacity of some 200,000 hogs daily, a figure which La Villette at that time did not equal in a whole year.[9]

The Mechanizing of Meat Production in America

The American meat industry is rooted in the very structure and dimensions of the land. Only these can explain its origin and its character. Long before industrialization gained this domain, its prerequisites were already framed in the configuration of the land.

[8] *Scientific American*, 21 Aug. 1886, p.120.

[9] These figures alone give a distorted picture of the whole. We have therefore brought the yearly turnover of Chicago and of Paris side by side. The Parisian data are drawn from *La Grande Encyclopédie*, Paris, 1884; the Chicagoan from Andreas, op.cit. vol.3, p.335. Comparison of the yearly requirements not only affords insight into food preferences; it also points up the divergent ways of Europe and America. Paris slaughters twice as many sheep and six times as many calves as Chicago. Chicago slaughters pigs to about thirty-three times and cattle to about nine times the Parisian numbers. One firm alone, Swift and Co., in Chicago processes in this year about twice as many cattle as consumed by Paris in the same period (Swift and Co.'s production for 1884–5: 429,483 head). One also notes that America does not subdivide the heading 'Cattle.' In Europe the flesh of the cow is held in low esteem, hence the lower Parisian figure; that of the ox, on the other hand, is highly prized. But in the United States oxen, used as beasts of draught on small farms, are killed in decreasing numbers.

1883	*Cattle*	*Calves*	*Pigs*	*Sheep*
Chicago	Cattle, 1,878,944	30,223	5,640,625	749,917
Paris	Oxen and Bulls, 184,900 Cows, 43,099	189,490	170,465	1,570,904

So long as only Pennsylvania or the New England States were settled, it was possible to preserve the customary European scale: small-farming, self-contained, independent farmsteads. The cities were modest in compass, but lay within easy reach of the cattle-raising districts; numerous villages were scattered through the countryside. Agriculture and stock farming followed the traditions brought over from Europe. But after the war of 1812, as soon as the settlers passed the crest of the Alleghenies and encountered American dimensions, the situation altogether changed. It was easy to raise great herds of swine, sheep, or cattle, but no consumers lived near by. On the spot, the products had no value: The herds had to be driven across wide stretches and over the mountains to the towns in the East, regardless of all hazards and losses.

These extremes of sparsely populated areas far from the consuming centers persisted in America until well into the latter half of the nineteenth century. Such contrast between urban concentration and gigantic undeveloped regions did not exist in Europe. To this day in Europe the meat supply is largely local, while in America producer and consumer live far apart.

Technical conditions have changed in the course of the century. But, around 1820, as soon as slaughtering tended to concentrate in one locality, Cincinnati, which could not itself consume the products but was forced to export them, the *raison d'être* of the American meat industry became clear. It operates on the assumption that vast areas of the land shall draw their provision of meat from a central place. The meat was either moved on the hoof or shipped, salted in barrels, down the Mississippi. Later on, when Chicago gained ascendancy in the 'sixties, the cattle were loaded into freight cars to be moved East; finally, at the beginning of the 'eighties, the supply system of today was set up, and refrigerator cars distributed the dressed carcasses to the various centers of consumption.

From these beginnings developed the largest industry of the United States, as measured by turnover, 3.3 billion dollars (in 1937), and with a production of some 50 million pounds a day.

The Beginnings of Mechanization: Cincinnati (1830–60)

It is still uncertain how the separate phases slowly emerged to build up a meat industry of continental proportions, the whole form and operation of which make it almost a precision instrument. The drive and inventiveness it represents can be judged by comparison to the same industry in South America. Some insight into the way it evolved is nevertheless possible today.

The industry has its origin in the State of Ohio, center of production during the early nineteenth century; it centers around the city which European observers up to the 'fifties deemed the westernmost point in which settlement was safe. Cincinnati lies on the Ohio River, the most abundant tributary of the Mississippi, about half way between the industrial city of Pittsburgh and the confluence of the two rivers. The river was to Cincinnati what the railroads later became to Chicago, its life artery; the South was the natural consumer; the export trade passed through New Orleans. Throughout the period of Cincinnati's rise — the peak was reached toward mid-century — there existed no convenient mode of transportation to the consumer-centers in the East.

The products were almost worthless at first, even in Cincinnati. 'I have referred to the remarkable fact,' says Charles Cist,[10] historian of Cincinnati, in 1866, 'that there was a period in the West when corn would not, in some sections, command six cents per bushel, and in others was of so little value as to be substituted for wood as fuel.'

In the effort to absorb an abundant corn crop, Cincinnati resorted to condensing it in the form of whisky or hogs. The broadness of the land made it possible to let the hogs run in the woods to feed on acorns and beech-nuts 'until five or six weeks of killing time, when they are turned into the corn field to fatten.'[11] Production figures soon reached a height that seemed no less extraordinary to European eyes than did the method of raising the animals. 'Some of these farmers drive in one season as high as one thousand head of hog into their fields; from 150 to 300 are the more common numbers, however.'[12]

This led directly to overproduction. The packing industry could not cope with the entire bulk of material produced. Here, very early, appears a symptom that in the course of the century becomes ever more conspicuous in American life: surplus production and its artificial dissipation. While first appearing in the agricultural domain and in relatively sparsely populated districts, it was later imparted to nearly all branches of production by a highly intensified industry.

When the large-scale industrialization of meat production set in, surplus production led Cincinnati to use only the most valuable parts and to throw the remainder into the river:

> Not less extraordinary is the fact, within the knowledge of hundreds now in Cincinnati, that in the early ages of pork packing, say in 1828, there was so little demand for any

---

[10] Charles Cist, 'The hog and its products,' *Commissioner of Agriculture Report*, 1866, p.391.

[11] Charles Cist, quoted in C. F. Goss, *Cincinnati, the Queen City*, 1788–1912, Chicago, 1912, 4 vols.; vol. 2, p.334.

[12] Ibid.

portion of the hog, other than hams, shoulders, sides and lard, that the heads, spare-ribs, neck-pieces, backbones, etc. were regularly thrown into the Ohio River to get rid of them.[13]

At that time, Cincinnati processed about 40,000 hogs a year.[14]

It is a far cry from this phase to the meat industry of today, which attempts to utilize all its by-products, down to the pea-sized pineal gland of the bull, 15,000 of which produce one pound of pineal substance; or the gall-stones, which are shipped to Japan to be carried about by individuals as talismans or charms.

In the early days of Cincinnati, slaughtering was conducted as a process distinct from packing and preserving, and the work was performed in separate places. Such a division still marks the European practice. 'The packing houses were located on the wharves or close by, for water transportation, while the slaughter houses were outside the settled city area. The meat for packing was carried through the city streets from the slaughter houses to the packing houses.'[15]

Altogether different was the method of slaughtering and dressing the beasts. As we have noticed,[16] the traveler, as far back as the 'thirties, was struck by the carefully planned organization of the slaughtering. The work could be carried on only in the cool season, the load of an entire year descended on the slaughterhouses in late autumn. Masses of highly perishable products had to be processed with all possible haste. This led to a minute division of labor, step by step, manipulation by manipulation. In much the same way in England at the same period the ship-biscuit bakery substituted mechanical devices wherever the nature of the material allowed. All other considerations were subordinated to the question: How to secure an uninterrupted production line?

Around 1850, slaughterhouse and packinghouse were already united under one roof. William Chambers[17] of Edinburgh, publisher and editor of the *Encyclopedia*, acquaints us with what was then (1854) the largest establishment in Cincinnati. It was four storeys high; an inclined plane led to the top of the building. Up this path the pigs were driven, and slaughtered on the top storey. Thus, in the middle of the century appears the principle of today's packinghouses: to utilize the animal's own weight to transport it downwards from floor to floor by the force of gravity.

William Chambers adds somewhat sarcastically that in England the sufferer is privileged to convey the news of his death to his neighbors by uttering shrill cries. 'In Cincinnati there is no time for this. Each hog entering the chamber

[13] Charles Cist, quoted in C. F. Goss, *Cincinnati, the Queen City*, 1788–1912, Chicago, 1912, 4 vols.; vol. 2, p.391.

[14] Goss, op.cit. vol. 2, p.334.

[15] Malcolm Keir, *Manufacturing*, New York, 1928, p.257.

[16] In the chapter 'The Assembly Line.'

[17] Chambers, *Things as They Are in America*, 1854, p.156.

109. Cincinnati, Hog-Slaughtering and Packing: Panoramic Painting. 1873.

Clutching and slaughtering: '*The ends of the arms of the tong are joined to a chain connected with a pulley resting on an aerial iron rail, suspending the live hog head downwards, and the suspended animals are pushed forward in the presence of the executioner . . .*'

Scalding and scraping: *These are here still performed by hand. The following phase represents the origin of the assembly line:*

Disembowelling: '*The tendons of the hog are slipped over the end of the gambrel placed upon a hook attached to a grooved pulley that runs on a suspended single track railway. One man splits the animal, the next takes out the entrails, the third removes heart, liver etc. and the carcass is washed by the hose-man after which it is rolled along the rail to the drying room.*' (*See Fig.* 49)

Drying room and trimming tables. Curing cellars and lard rendering. (Harper's Weekly, 6 *September* 1873)

of death receives the blow with a mallet on the forehead which deprives him of consciousness and motion. The next instant he is bled to death.'

Frederick L. Olmsted, designer of Central Park in New York and one of the most farseeing landscape architects of his day, visited the packinghouses of Cincinnati around the same time. But he preferred not to witness this part of the procedure. He seems to have seen another plant: 'The vast slaughter yards we took occasion not to visit, satisfied at seeing the river of blood that flowed from them.' [18] The more vividly does he convey his impression of the division of labor, passing over technicalities. He recognizes that here already, even in the absence of cogwheels, men's hands are trained to function like machines.

[18] Olmsted, *A Journey through Texas*, New York, 1857, p.9.

We entered an immense low-ceiled room and followed a vista of dead swine upon their backs, their paws stretching mutely towards heaven. Walking down to the vanishing point we found there a sort of human chopping machine where the hogs were converted into commercial pork. A plank table, two men to lift and turn, two to wield the cleavers, were its component parts. *No iron cog-wheels could work with more regular motion.* Plump falls the hog upon the table, chop, chop; chop, chop; chop, chop, fall the cleavers. All is over. But before you can say so, plump, chop, chop; chop, chop; chop, chop, sound again. There is no pause for admiration. By a skilled sleight-of-hand, hams, shoulders, clear, mess, and prime fly off, each squarely cut to its own place, where attendants, aided by trucks and dumb-waiters, dispatch each to its separate destiny — the ham for Mexico, its loin for Bordeaux. Amazed beyond all expectation at the celerity, we took out our watches and counted thirty-five seconds, from the moment when one hog touched the table until the next occupied its place. The numbers of blows required I regret we did not count.[19]

Mechanization Extended: Chicago (1860–85)

Cincinnati, long after it had been overshadowed by Chicago, remained the place with the widest experience in the packing industry. Here new appliances were tried out and their efficiency put to the test.

Despite the mass of material processed, Cincinnati still relied mainly on local supplies. When the landscape architect Frederick Law Olmsted left Cincinnati for Texas by road, the coach horses were obliged to wade slowly through 'droves of hogs grunting their obstinate way towards Cincinnati and a market. . . . Though the country was well wooded,' he asserts, 'I venture to say we met as many hogs as trees. . . .'[20]

The local provisioning sufficient to Cincinnati's packinghouses contrasts strongly with what occurred later at Chicago. The enormous quantities that this center had to process required a gigantic area of supply. In Chicago we are dealing with dimensions for which there is, even today, no yardstick. A spontaneously growing center of force, it embodies, as few other places do, that brutal and inventive vitality of the nineteenth century. Increasingly it became the most important link between the raisers and the consumers of a vast country.

At the beginning of the 'seventies — just before the world crisis of 1873 — an observer[21] speaks of the incalculable potentialities of this city. This readiness for achievement unlimited in scope gave the necessary impulse for large-scale experimentation. As soon as the industry began to process animals by the million, the necessary instruments lay at hand. Mass production of raw material (grain, cattle) parallel with mechanization of processing (machinery,

---

[19] Olmsted, *A Journey through Texas*, New York, 1857, p.9.

[20] Olmsted, op.cit. p.12.

[21] James Parton, *Triumphs of Enterprise, Ingenuity and Public Spirit*, New York, 1872, ch. II.

assembly line), transportation and storage facilities (railroads, refrigerator cars, and refrigerated storehouses) were developed side by side.

When a modest settlement, Chicago had a local area of supply. In 1839, '3000 head of cattle had been driven in from the neighbouring prairies, barrelled, and exported.'[22] Soon the near-by Midwestern states were included; this area of supply likewise proved inadequate.

The great plains west of the Mississippi, stretching from the Gulf of Mexico almost to the Canadian border, were transformed, in little over a decade, into a gigantic reservoir of cattle. The wave moved from the South upwards. There, the Spanish colonists had already bred their Texas Longhorns. In the brief period from the Civil War to 1876, the herds spread over the plains of twelve states. On the prairie, there were no boundaries, no fences; the range was masterless and free. 'The rapidity of this expansion has perhaps no parallel in all American history.'[23]

The same question that faced Cincinnati about 1830 arises once more in the giant domains of the Cattle Kingdom: What is to be done with the surplus? How are the purchasers to be reached?

Only hazardous trails were available on which to drive the cattle to the buyers. Faced with these almost insuperable distances, even the cattle dealers became planners and strategists. The most talented of them all, the Chicagoan J. G. McCoy, bending over maps, calculated 'where the cattle trail from Texas would cut the railroads then pushing west.'[24] An abandoned settlement, Abilene, in Kansas, north of Texas, seemed the most favorable point. It consisted of twelve shacks; prairie dogs were bred there. Within sixty days McCoy had provided accommodation for over 3000 head of cattle (1867). In autumn of the same year, he shipped 35,000 head. Nearly every train was bound for Chicago. By 1869 the figure had multiplied tenfold, and in 1871, some 700,000 head were consigned to the packinghouses of the Middle West.

THE REFRIGERATOR CAR AND STOREHOUSE

Parallel with the formation of this reservoir of cattle ran many-sided experiments seeking to create the machinery needed for the mass processing of the animals. We shall later examine more closely certain phases of this achievement, for only thus can we gain insight into the methods that were tried.

Chicago remained isolated for a comparatively long while. Not until 1856 did it receive its first railway link with the eastern cities. With the mid-century

[22] Parton, op.cit. p.44.

[23] Walter Prescott Webb, *The Great Plains*, Boston, 1936, p.207.

[24] Webb, op.cit. p.219.

110. Swift's First Successful Storage Refrigerator. New York, 1882. *After twenty years of failure, Gustavus Swift succeeded by careful planning in bringing chilled meat to the markets of a distant metropolis. 'The new departure depressed the market by three to four dollars the hundredweight.'* (Harper's Weekly, 21 *October* 1882)

a more intensive widening of the railroad network began. 'It was in 1849 that the whistle of the locomotive was first heard on the prairies west of Chicago,' if only over a ten-mile stretch.[25] In 1850 a portion of the northwestern prairie in the State of Illinois as far as Galena was also brought in. In the 'sixties repeated spanning of the entire continent was successful. At the beginning of the 'seventies, the Chicagoans boasted of a train leaving every fifteen minutes.[26] In the same decade, the competing lines grew so powerful that a debacle ensued, with open warfare against the railroad companies.

During the 'fifties, to escape the drawbacks of seasonal operation, summer slaughtering was introduced so far as was then possible in Chicago. This called for capacious, cool storehouses stocked with natural ice. Soon these wooden constructions appeared in every town where packing was carried on. In the early 'seventies, gradually began the introduction of refrigeration by artificial means.

The final overthrow of the local supply system came about only with the introduction of the refrigerator car.[27] The experimental period extended over fifteen years, 1867–82: from the first granting of an American patent in 1867, and from the moving of the first shipments between Chicago and Boston, to the decisive success of the marketing of slaughtered carcasses in New York.

[25] Webb, op.cit. p.222–23. [26] Parton, op.cit. p.46.

[27] For further details see Harper Leech and John Charles Carroll, *Armour and His Times*, New York–London, 1938, pp.125–7.

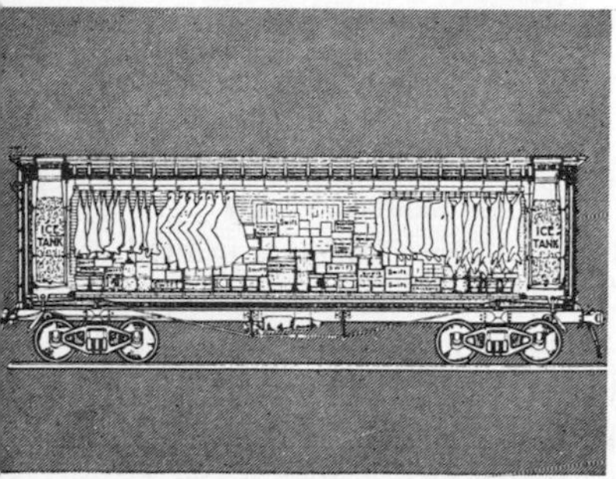
111. American Refrigerator Car.

112. The Farmer and the Packer. (*Courtesy J. Ryerson Collection, Chicago*)

The problem was handled from the first patent[28] by a regulated air-circulation and by evacuating the warm air. Five years later, 1872,[29] the ice was moved from overhead into V-shaped containers at the end of the car. There were also attempts to effect self-cooling through the evaporation of water.

Meanwhile the Frenchman Charles Tellier[30] had succeeded in bringing fresh meat across the ocean on the ship *Frigorifique* (1876). In the ports, and even in Paris, American mutton could be obtained. The South Americans claim primacy in this invention for their countryman, Francesco Lecoq of Montevideo, who was closely associated with Tellier in Paris. Lecoq's refrigerating process was based on the evaporation of ether.[31]

George Henry Hammond was the first packer to recognize the potentialities latent in the refrigerator car. Precisely when he sent his first carload from Chicago to Boston is not certain, but it was either in 1867 or 1868. Because

[28] U.S. Patent 71,423, 1867, J. B. Sutherland.

[29] U.S. Patent 131,722, 24 Sept. 1872, J. Tunstel.

[30] Charles Tellier, *L'Histoire d'une invention moderne, le frigorifique*, Paris, 1910.

[31] Ramon J. Carcano, *Francesco Lecoq. Su teoria y su obra* 1865–1868, Buenos Aires, 1919. The French patent was granted to Lecoq 20 January 1866.

the meat was stored on ice, it discolored slightly, and therefore met with some unpopularity.

Complete success was achieved by Gustavus Swift when he conquered the New York market in 1882. He had made thoroughgoing preparations. The refrigerator car he had constructed with the assistance of a Boston engineer (1879)[32] stored its ice in the ceiling, so that the cold air sank slowly past the hanging meat down to the floor. In similar fashion he equipped the New York storehouse: 300 tons of ice were laid in above its strongly insulated walls (fig. 110).

Such was the success of his first shipment that *Harper's Weekly* printed an abundantly illustrated article, 'Cheaper Beef,' in which the reason for its immediate commercial triumph was brought out: 'The new departure has already depressed the market by three to four Dollars per hundredweight. . . . The present agitation of the beef market which must result in a decided and permanent lowering of the beef prices cannot fail to awake the deepest interest . . . at least this era of cheep beef has begun for New York.'[33]

Statistics show how wholesale transportation of chilled meat took effect. Within one year, the number of live cattle shipped from Chicago suddenly decreased by 170,000.[34] This was in 1884, in a period in which production was almost hectically rising in every sphere, just before the great boom of 1885, of which the first skyscrapers remain the most lasting monument.

Packers and the Packing Industry

Chicago's development was organic, and almost as anonymous at first as that of a gold-mining town. World-famous names do not appear in the packing industry until the most arduous part of its rise is over.

The two greatest packers, Gustavus F. Swift and Philip D. Armour, decided to settle in Chicago hesitantly and comparatively late. G. F. Swift (1839–1903) began the butcher's trade in New England, driving his meat cart from house to house. Later he became a cattle buyer, visiting the main slaughtering centers, Albany, Buffalo, and finally Chicago, to which he came at the age of thirty-six with a family of five. By that time, from a quarter-century of business, he had set aside $30,000, a capital which, as his son relates,[35] 'even in 1875 was not enough' to found a modest-sized packing plant. At first, therefore, he continued in his cattle trade. He was an expert appraiser, who took pride in the sureness

[32] U.S. Patent 215572, Purifying, circulating, and rarefying air, 1879, Andrew J. Chase.

[33] *Harper's Weekly*, 21 Oct. 1882, p.663.

[34] Cf. A. T. Andreas, *The History of Chicago*, Chicago, 1884–6, vol. 3, p.335. Shipments of cattle: 1883 . . . 966,758; 1884 . . . 791,884.

[35] Louis F. Swift, *The Yankee and the Yards, the Biography of Gustavus Franklin Swift*, New York, 1927, p.18.

of his eye. Hampered by insufficient capital, yet driven by a will to rival with the great packers, he chose another path.

In the winter of 1875, the year he came to Chicago, and without backing to speak of, he began to transport in freight cars not livestock but meat.[36] Others before him had already experimented with the refrigerated car. But Swift made it his starting point and used it as a wedge. He saw in it a chance to bridge the gap between his lack of funds and his ambition. As the railroads that transported livestock refused their co-operation, he was forced to ship his meat by a circuitous line, out of the question for normal business. Swift won this line over to his plan, after a wealthy Detroit firm had built ten cars for him in a magnanimous gesture — against certain security.[37] Then his ascent began. It was not an easy one. In his son's book [38] it is told how the cars 'perversely failed to keep their perishable content fresh' and how Swift and his aides tried by simple means to improve them. In the late 'seventies, when successful packers were already established on the spot with their large packinghouses, the whole field seemed fully divided, leaving small chances for an outsider with such ridiculously meager capital.

With the sureness of an expert, Swift threw all his energy into broadening his enterprise. He succeeded because of his powerful analytical gifts joined to a boldness for daring construction.

Philip D. Armour (1832–1901) had, before coming to Chicago, already been a successful packer in Milwaukee, and with his brothers had founded plants outside of that city. A specialist in pork packing, he was also active in the grain market. He was a born speculator. To this must be put down Armour's quarter-century of feverish activities in Chicago. He, too, did not settle there before 1875, choosing Chicago as his base of operations in what chanced to be the same year as Swift, who was seven years Armour's junior. This was the time when, as Swift's daughter puts it, 'Chicago was the place where money could be made right on the ground floor.' [39]

Chicago's miraculous rise began in 1861–2, when the railroads were able to keep the city supplied with livestock and when the industry, processing half a million hogs yearly, was overtaking the old center, Cincinnati. Output nearly doubled in the first few years of the 'sixties. In 1860 the figure was still below 400,000; but by 1862 the million mark was well exceeded (1.34 million). In 1865 the Union Stock Yards were founded in keeping with the new scale of

[36] Ibid. p.185.

[37] Neither was this step accomplished without difficulty, for the packer Hammond attacked the cars on grounds of patent infringement. Swift, op.cit. p.189.

[38] Ibid. ch. 'Never Stay Beaten.'

[39] Helen Swift, *My Father and My Mother*, Chicago, 1937, p.127.

business. Chicago's rise, it has justly been pointed out, was not a result of the Civil War,[40] as is so often said, but of inherent forces.

This first upswing was followed by a *second phase* early in the 'seventies. It was then that original minds fought their way into the packing industry, introducing new things, suited to a big business era: the introduction of refrigerating machines in the storage rooms and strenuous efforts to mechanize the slaughtering process. Of the packers, it was George M. Hammond who, as we have seen, employed the refrigerator car to bring meat to Boston at the end of the 'sixties.

J. A. Wilson, another packer, introduced a new article of food, having 'discovered and tested a method by which meats could be preserved in compact and solid form . . . the meat would come forth in a solid cake, without a particle of gravy, in a natural and palatable condition . . . cooked, ready to be sliced and eaten.' This, of course, was corned beef, a name now passed into many languages and an article found in the canteen of every soldier. Wilson devised a suitable can, shaped like a truncated pyramid (figs. 113, 114), which has been kept almost without change to the present day. As we read in *Frank Leslie's Illustrated Newspaper* in 1878, the 'meat is compressed in cans clear of all bones or gristle,' a weight saving of 3 : 1 over meat packed in barrels;[41] that is, about the same economy as in the transportation of fresh meat instead of livestock.

The entry into competition of Armour and Swift marks the third phase: the conquest of the national and, in a sense, of the world market. This phase brought a further elaboration of the machinery and the perfecting of the assembly line as still used today: The refrigerator car became the offensive weapon in this expansion. Swift and Armour's ascent certainly stems from an irrepressible entrepreneurial drive; yet two advantages were theirs: They came at a time ready for men of giant projects; and they could profit from the intensive experience which the industry had gathered at this place. Actually neither of them introduced new inventions at first. Nevertheless their figures stand out more vigorously than any others, for both center around the very crux of the packing industry: organization. Through organization they attained a scale once inconceivable in livestock processing.

In the packing industry, for reasons about which we shall have more to say, invention plays no great role. What invention could do here to mechanize the handicraft process cannot be compared with what it did in developing precision machinery for spinning. The millowner's problems are almost ended when the thread has been spun. The packer's problems begin when it comes to distributing his perishable product and bringing it to the consumer.

---

[40] Helen Swift, *My Father and My Mother*, Chicago, 1937, p.127.

[41] *Frank Leslie's Illustrated Newspaper*, 12 Oct. 1878, p.95.

113. 'Making Cans for Use in Packing the Meat,' Chicago, 1878. (Frank Leslie's Illustrated Newspaper, 12 *October* 1878)

Swift is said to have crossed the Atlantic over twenty times before finding an outlet for his products in England. How far organization was basic to the enterprise may perhaps appear more clearly from a single incident than from long descriptions. When Swift engineered, with striking success, his 'Chicago dressed beef' in New York, especial care was taken, as *Harper's Weekly* then explained, to station each refrigerator car with 'its door . . . opposite to that of the storage building, and the railways [overhead monorails] of the two are connected, and the meat is easily transferred to the storage room, which is of the same temperature as the car, *without loss of time and without being removed from the hook* on which it was hung when killed.' [42]

[42] *Harper's Weekly*, 21 Oct. 1882, p.663.

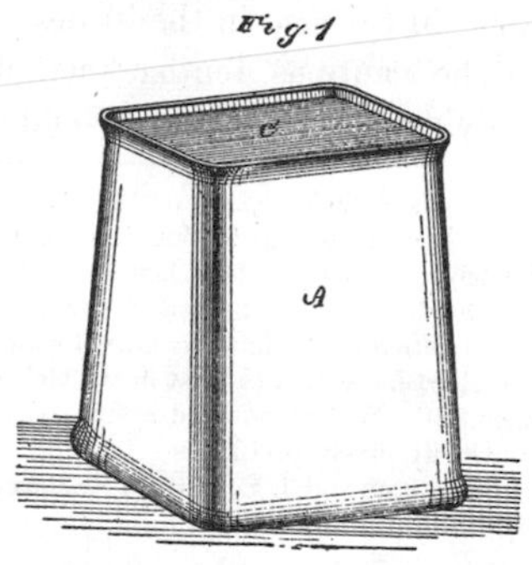

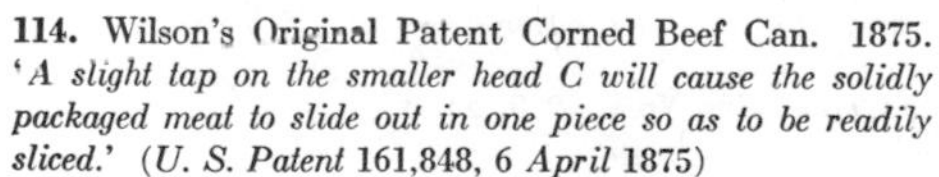
114. Wilson's Original Patent Corned Beef Can. 1875. '*A slight tap on the smaller head C will cause the solidly packaged meat to slide out in one piece so as to be readily sliced.*' (*U. S. Patent* 161,848, 6 *April* 1875)

The financial peril in which Swift found himself more than once has its source in a business expanding faster than the capital behind it.[43] All his attempted expansions center around one aim: by what channels to enlarge his sphere of influence? He demanded the highest precision and operating efficiency,[44] and could judge at a glance the quality of the product and the management of the shop. In keeping with this was his thorough exploitation of the by-products. He is said to have ridden many a time at night to read the thermometer in the storage rooms. This was his approach, too, when, in the late 'eighties, he followed the retreating cattle belt and built branch factories as far south as Texas. Sometimes he chose places viewed as quite unsuitable, but through his attention to the soil, his observation of what grew, and his judgment of what might grow, he could act unerringly.[45] It is a measure of men in any sphere, when they join farsightedness with a care for minute detail.

It was of Armour that Gustavus Swift commented: 'He was exactly what he claimed for himself, a born speculator; he had the faculty to keep a great number of irons within the fire at the same time.'[46] Turbulence and confusion pervaded the Chicago grain market, where the price of the world's bread was decided. Amid this vortex of cracks and crashes, of real or induced panics and semi-panics, Armour passed a quarter-century of overt or concealed operation. Now he would 'join the bulls,' now 'thread against the bulls'; now again there would be a 'raid on the bears,' now he is on 'the bear side of the market.' It was common knowledge that a warrant had been issued for his arrest 'for running a corner in pork.'[47] His transactions were not merely on paper. He built the greatest silos of the world to accommodate them.

The struggle at this time was waged without gloves. It called for the unbroken energy of a first generation. Armour had $100 in his pocket when, sometimes on foot, sometimes by ox-cart, he migrated to California, there to try his luck in 1851. George Hammond began a small meat shop, with $13 cash plus a $50 note, in Chicago in the 'fifties. And Swift began in New England with $25.

The cautious rentier mentality that betrays later generations — be they individuals or nations — could have brought not a single stone to the building

---

[43] Louis F. Swift, op.cit. p.118.

[44] Nevertheless hygienic conditions in the plants were alarming, at least around the turn of the century. Decisive reforms were later instituted. The English periodical *The Lancet* aroused public opinion (7, 14, 21, and 28 Jan. 1905); it was followed by Upton Sinclair's *The Jungle* (1906), and by a congressional investigation (1906) in the course of which Theodore Roosevelt declared, 'The conditions shown by even this short inspection to exist in the Chicago stockyards are revolting' (*59th Congress, 1st Session, Document* 873). We are indebted to Mr. Wayne Andrews for this information.

[45] Swift, op.cit. p.118.

[46] H. Leech and J. C. Carroll, *Armour and His Time*, New York, 1938, p.238.

[47] Ibid. p.251.

of these giant concerns. All this called for men ready for danger, ready to win or to lose. There was no middle course. It was a staking of all against all.

The key to large-scale production in Swift and Armour's time was the refrigerator car. At first it met the opposition of those who stood most to profit by it. The railroads could see no reason to be drawn into doubtful experiments for the packer's benefit, which if successful would cut their freight by half. What would they do with the tremendous pool of rolling stock that conveyed live cattle to the eastern cities? Why should the railroads help to decrease their own profits and at the same time render their equipment obsolete? But the development proved the stronger. Forcing the packers to build their own cars helped little; indeed, it was this that gave rise to the 'private car lines,' [48] which directly and indirectly yielded high returns to the packers.

Then there was the task of converting the butchers in the East from their handicraft into salesmen of chilled meat. This was achieved directly after the refrigerator cars were put into successful operation. The packers can 'sell a superior "cut" at a lower cost than the butcher can sell an inferior "cut" taken from an animal killed in his own slaughter house.' [49]

With the same energy, the struggle was carried on in the home city, and was later extended to the other packing centers. The smaller firms were absorbed, bought out, or in other ways forced to the wall.

Armour's interest in the refrigerator car began only when it had proved its success. Then he went in for it with more than usual energy. The end of the 'eighties saw attempts to bring the fruit of newly flourishing California to the East under refrigeration.[50] Soon enormous profits were promised. This drew Armour's attention (*c.*1890). He entered the contest as in the grain market and — as yet without customers — ordered a thousand cars and more. He formed a partnership with one company, absorbed others, often at high cost, while others he forced into retirement. The company that made the first successful trials in transporting fruit from California fell by the wayside.[51] During the 'nineties the Armour car lines, operating under various names,[52] became the most powerful.

The perspectives broadened, the dimensions grew, until the point came into sight when capture of the whole provision market — fruit, grain, meat — seemed

[48] Louis D. Weld, *Private Freight Cars and American Railways*, Columbia University Studies in History, Economics and Public Law, New York, 1908, vol. 31, no. 1.

[49] J. Ogden Armour, *Packers, The Private Car Lines and the People*, Philadelphia, 1906, p.24.

[50] 'The first refrigerator line of any importance operated only for the fruit traffic, was that of F. A. Thomas in Chicago, a Detroit inventor who built fifty refrigerator cars in 1886.' Cf. L. D. Weld, op.cit. p.18.

[51] Ibid. p.19. Through the cutting of freight rates.

[52] Armour Car Line, Fruit Growers' Express, Continental Fruit Express.

near. The turn of the century marks this point. In the year 1902, J. O. Armour, Gustavus Swift, and his son-in-law, Edward Morris, joined to form a cartel, the 'National Packing Company,' later dissolved by order of the law.

Single Operations in Mechanized Meat Production

The operations of the butcher, slaughtering by handicraft methods, are often so merged into one another as to be difficult to separate. As soon as mass production was used to turn the live animal into salable meat, sharp and thorough division into single operations became necessary, as in all mechanization.

Interest in the rapid conversion of the animal into meat centered from the first around the pig. This was as true of the half-million hogs processed in the United States in 1850 as for the five and a half million about two decades later.[53]

Today some twenty-four separate operations are counted before the live hog has been reduced to two halves traveling on conveyors into coolers. Three phases can be distinguished. Organization set out to make up for the loss of time that nature enforces, and so far as possible to approach continuous flow.

The first phase comprises the slaughtering process: The pig is seized by its hind leg, around which a chain is looped; this is made fast to a great rotating drum some twelve feet in diameter. As the drum slowly revolves (two to three revolutions per minute) the animal is drawn backwards and up until, hanging head bottommost, it has become a defenseless object. It is carried around with the wheel and, after reaching the peak of its ascent, is transferred by a simple device to an overhead rail, on which it glides to the slaughterer's reach. Experience has proved this rotary hog-hoisting method the best means of avoiding 'loss of time in catching and hoisting . . . the most rapid means of raising them to the track bars.'[54] The whole process requires barely half a minute, but a large number of hogs are held in readiness in the bleeding passage.

In the second phase the animal is cleansed of slime, blood, and dirt, and hair and bristles are removed. The scalding barrel of the butcher has become a steam-heated scalding vat. Hot water makes the skin elastic and softens the hairs and bristles. An inclined rail moves the animal to the hog-scraping machine, which almost completely shaves it, even to the head and feet. This second stage ends when the tendons of the hind legs are bared, and a gambrel stretched between them, which is hung to a small trolley connected to the endless chain.

The third stage prepares the carcass for the cooler, where it must lose its animal heat. So far the production process could progress more or less continuously.

---

[53] According to *Harper's Weekly*, Mar. 1872 to Mar. 1873.

[54] William Douglas & Son, *Encyclopedia.* A book of reference for all industries associated with the meat, pork, provision, and general food trade, London, 1903, p.451.

It has taken place on rising and descending planes and on various levels, like a switchback railway. Now the endless chain takes over, imposing a uniform speed on its part of the process. Hanging on the conveyor, the carcass is opened at the chest and neck; the head is all but severed; the lymph glands are inspected by a veterinary; condemned animals are switched onto a separate line. The stomach is opened; intestines are removed, the entrails inspected, the liver and heart cut out, the spine is split in twain; the internal and external surfaces are again cleansed; the meat is inspected a second time, and stamped; finally the carcass is slowly conveyed into the cooler.

The second stage, as we have already seen,[55] is of significance from another standpoint. For it was through the whole method behind this process that the assembly line came about. In the packing industry, and in this particular phase, decades of assembly-line experience were gained. The automobile industry was able to work out its own assembly line with such astonishing speed because of the extensive practice gained here in working on the moving object.

More directly than a technical description, Upton Sinclair in *The Jungle* shows what happens in this phase:

> The carcass hog was then again strung up by machinery and sent upon another trolley ride; this time passing between two lines of men . . . upon a raised platform, each doing a certain single thing to the carcass as it came to him. One scraped the outside of a leg; another scraped the inside of the same leg. One with a swift stroke cut the throat. . . . Another made a slit down the body; a second opened the body wider; a third with a saw cut the breastbone; a fourth loosened the entrails; a fifth pulled them out. . . . There were men to scrape each side and men to scrape the back; there were men to clean the carcass inside, to trim it and wash it. Looking down this room one saw creeping slowly a line of dangling hogs . . . and for every yard there was a man working as if a demon were after him. At the end of this hog's progress every inch of the carcass had been gone over several times.[56]

Mechanization and Organic Substance

In the key period from the late 'sixties to the late 'seventies, the apparatus for mass slaughtering was built up. The number of animals processed at the packing center of Chicago was still comparable to that of a European metropolis like Paris. Yet, fundamentally, all was completely different: In 1867 the population of Paris with its suburbs was approaching the 2 million mark, while that of Chicago scarcely numbered 220,000. Chicago could not consume its quota. Even before the introduction of the refrigerator car, part of the Chicago production was sent into foreign channels; fresh meat in various forms was exported to England and Scotland by the late 'seventies.

---

[55] In the chapter Assembly Line.

[56] Upton Sinclair, *The Jungle*, New York, 1906, p.42.

115. Slaughtering Hogs in Chicago. 1886. *Hoisting by rope and pulley.* (Scientific American, 21 *August* 1886)

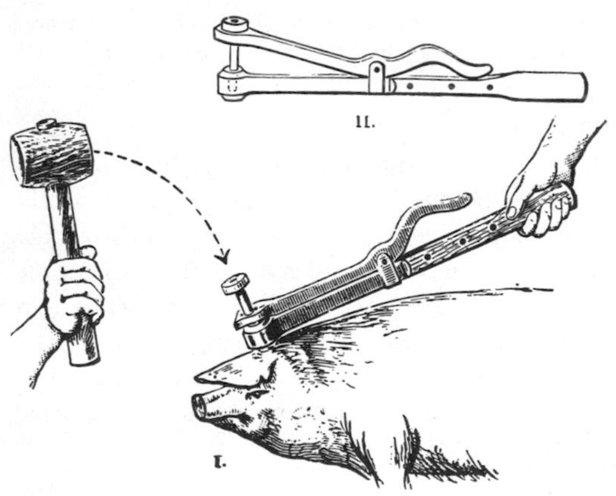

116. Koch's Pig-Killing Apparatus. (Douglas's Encyclopedia)

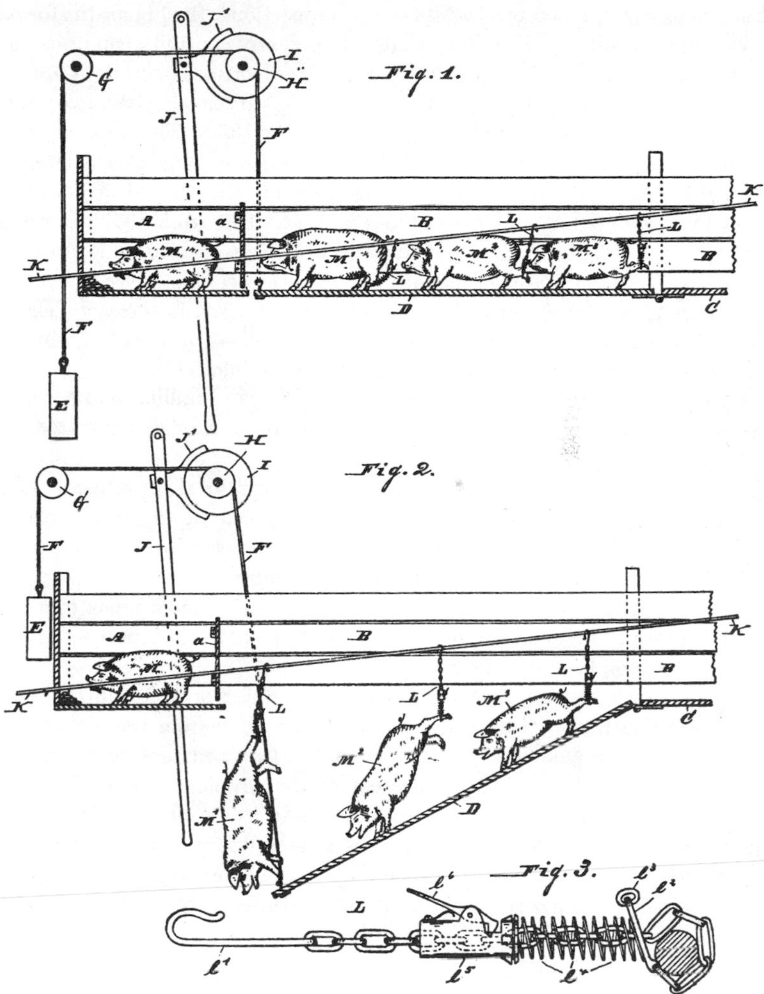

117. Apparatus for Catching and Suspending Hogs. 1882. *Here the living animal must be introduced into the 'disassembly' line.* From the 1870's *on when stunning was found too slow, devices were proposed to hoist the hog to the overhead rail without struggle: 'The hog M acts as a decoy for the others, and much time and labor are thus saved. The brake is manipulated to allow the trap D to slowly descend until the hogs are completely suspended, when they slide off on the bar K to the place where they are to be killed.'* (*U. S. Patent* 252,112, 10 *January* 1882)

Long before production reached its record proportions, the apparatus for mass processing was built up. The time of greatest inventive activity can quite easily be determined. A few patents for the mechanizing of various operations appeared after 1860. From the mid 'sixties through the 'seventies, they were constantly on the increase, continuing undiminished until after 1880. The basic mechanizing principles developed during that period remain unchanged even later. No less than six patents were granted for hog traps in 1872–3, and no fewer than twenty-four patents for various machines in 1874. But from 1877 on, we note a marked decrease, the majority of inventions having been developed between 1867 and 1877. Hog-scraping machines to clean the scalded carcass of its hairs and bristles are the exception. Most of these were devised in the early 'eighties. In 1881 four separate patents were granted for this class of machine, which has an important part to play in mechanized hog processing.

To varying degrees, spinning and weaving, baking and milling had been satisfactorily mechanized. Would it not be possible to mechanize meat production too?

Enterprising and inventive people tried their hand at this problem. Efforts were made to develop machines for almost every one of the time-consuming operations. Yet, as we indicated in discussing the development of the assembly line, a complex organic substance with its contingencies, its changing, easily vulnerable structure, is something other than a piece of amorphous iron. This was true also of the dead animal. Despite many attempts, processing of its carcass could not be fully mechanized.

This first clash between mechanization and complex organic substance is far more interesting from the historical point of view than from the technological. How are the unpredictable contingencies that nature produces to be overcome by mechanical devices? Such is the root of the problem. To anticipate the answer: The engineer did not emerge victorious in this contest.

It may be worth while to glance at this largely unexplored territory even if the patents occasionally concern somewhat devious proposals (figs. 116, 122) and in their early stages resemble medieval instruments of torture rather than highly developed machines.

CATCHING AND SUSPENDING THE LIVE HOG

No single invention for the mechanization of slaughtering drew so many efforts as the one that sought to incorporate the living hog into the production line. Here at the beginning of the operations it was most important to avoid bottlenecks that might hold up the entire factory.

In the 1870's, the time-consuming method of hitting the hogs on the head with a mallet, and transporting them in a stunned condition, was abandoned. When instead the living animals were suspended by one leg and allowed to slide to the killer by means of a conveyor, inventions for 'catching and suspending hogs' sharply increased.[57] Thanks to this method, the butcher was no longer compelled to drive the hog into a corner to deal it a frontal blow. Instead, catching and sticking were divided into two operations. One man caught the animal by its hind leg, fastening the chain around it. Now it was a matter of hoisting it to the rail as quickly as possible.

At first this was done in the simplest manner, as seen in the 1873 panorama of a Cincinnati slaughterhouse, which shows (fig. 109) the animal being hoisted by pulley. With increasing production, more rapid methods were needed in order to incorporate the hog in a continuous process and so far as possible at regular intervals. The task now consisted in 'catching, suspending, and conveying hogs to the place where they were to be killed.' [58] First it was proposed to drive the animals one after the other into a narrow pen and have a helper, unseen by them, quickly loop, around one hind leg, a chain already fastened to the conveyor rail, after which they were in one way or another lifted from the ground. This might be done, for instance, by an inclined plane at the end of a narrow passage. This descending plane turns out to be a rolling carpet set in motion as soon as the hog steps onto it. The horizontal top rail thus gradually lifts the animal into the desirable position.

But the animals are quite likely to become suspicious before stepping upon the inclined plane. Perhaps they will even resist being driven into the narrow passageway. A year later, one inventor proposed a slier method: 'It is a peculiarity of hogs that they are only to be driven with exceeding difficulty over any new and untried path; but when one has with apparent safety reached a point beyond it, especially if he appears to have found food thereby, others can be made to follow with much less trouble.' [59] At the end of the pen, he stationed a decoy hog before which food was placed. The floor upon which the decoy hog stood was solid; the rest was a movable trap section (fig. 117). The chain, already hooked to the overhead rail, having been attached to the hog, the floor was caused by a simple mechanism 'to slowly descend until the hogs are completely suspended, when they slide off. . . . When the hogs are all out of the

---

[57] Improvement in hog elevators, U.S. Patent 27,368; 6 Mar. 1860. Hog elevator, U.S. Patent 94,076; 24 Aug. 1869. Hog-lifting machine, U.S. Patent 120,946; 14 Nov. 1871.

[58] U.S. Patent 245,643; 16 Aug. 1881.

[59] U.S. Patent 252,112; 10 Jan. 1882.

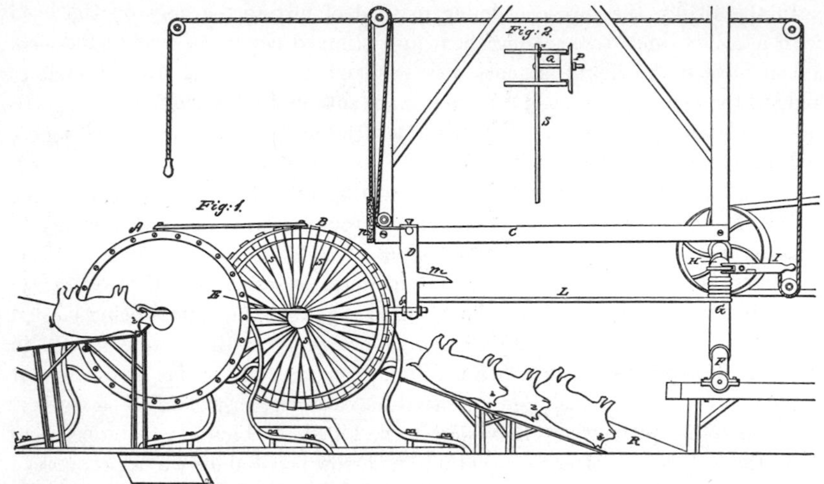

118. Hog-Cleaning Machine. 1864. *The flexibility of steel and rubber are used to operate upon an organic body mechanically. 'The capacity of this machine is from five to fifteen thousand per diem . . . The apparatus consisting, essentially, in the employment of substances of the requisite elasticity to yield to the irregularities of the body, while adhering thereto with the force necessary to remove the hair.'* (*U. S. Patent* 44021, 30 *August* 1864)

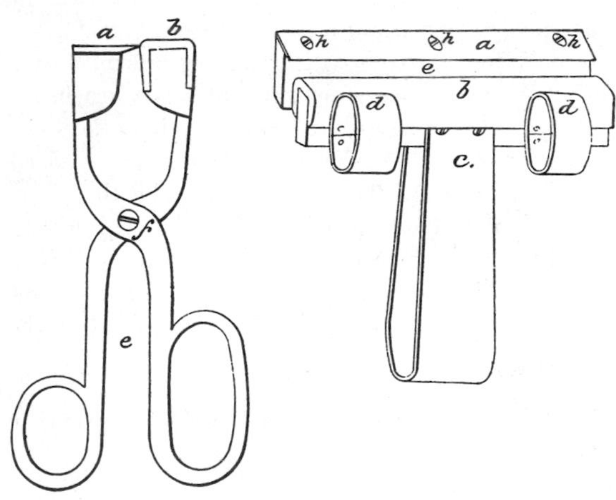

119. Instrument for Extracting Hair from Skins. 1837. *Imitation of the human hand. 'One of the jaws is designed to supply the place and office of the thumb as used in extracting hairs with the common knife, and is therefore covered or cushioned on the inside with leather, india rubber or other material . . .'* (*U. S. Patent* 244, 30 *June* 1837)

120. Pig-Scraping Machine. *c.*1900. *'An endless chain drags the pig through a series of little knives, attached to adjustable springs . . . They will fit themselves to the form of the pig without very much trouble. Capacity,* 8 *pigs per minute.' Mechanical scraping never became completely satisfactory.* (Douglas's Encyclopedia, *London.*)

way, the trap is drawn back to a horizontal position . . . another lot of hogs is then driven onto the track and the operation is repeated.'[60]

SPINE-CLEAVING MACHINES

Even today, when electrical handsaws are available, an axe is normally used to split the disemboweled hog down the backbone. Around 1870, when mass production was the aim, the inventor was not lacking who sought to adapt the circular saw — useful in so many other situations — to the mechanization of slaughtering.

It was deemed sufficient to slide the hogs automatically, lying on their backs, one after another down an inclined plane, to be sawed into halves by a rotary cutter. The hogs, the inventor claims, deliver themselves of their own accord to the cutter, and the backbone-splitting operation can proceed uninterruptedly.[61]

[60] U.S. Patent 252,112; 10 Jan. 1882.
[61] U.S. Patent 130,515; 13 Aug 1872.

MECHANICAL SKINNING

The earlier the time, the more boldly do the inventors attempt to replace complex hand-operations by mechanical devices. Skinning, too, was to be mechanically performed.[62] It would be done through a system of levers and pulleys, while the animals — cattle in this case — were moored to the floor by head and legs. The drawing of this invention (fig. 122), to which a certain artistic charm cannot be denied, shows a half-skinned cow with its hide drawn back; the skin of the head, already loosened by the knife, lies in the foreground. In the rear one sees the head and horns. This machinery must have been unsuccessful, for even today skinning is done by hand.

All machinery seems to be ruled out when it comes to skinning, the separation of the hide from the flesh. 'The head skinner, who skins the head and severs it from the body, handles his knife with so much skill that he can skin the head of the animal and sever it exactly at the junction of the skull and vertebra in the fraction of a minute.'

Sheep are skinned as they travel on a conveyor. This operation is nevertheless entirely hand-performed, and a whole team of workers divides the task into individual operations. The final stroke is given by back skinners who 'seize the pelts and pull them loose from the back of the lambs so as not to break the grain of the pelts or tear the tender fat of the rump and back.' This is done in one motion. It seems easy and simple as the fleece is torn with a sharp crash from the body, but it requires great skill. Above, the naked carcass moves on with the assembly line, trailing the fleece like a mantle through the crimson carpet of blood, which forms everywhere along the conveyor's path.

MECHANICAL HOG SCRAPING

Most attempts to handle organic substance by mechanical means failed. Only in one operation was the machine introduced with at least partial success. Characteristically, this operation was not on the inside of the body. It was the task of mechanically removing hair and bristle from the softened carcass as soon as it left the scalding vat. This is accomplished by a large shaving device designed to rid the whole body of hair thoroughly and in the shortest possible time.

Just as in mechanical dough mixers the kneading, beating, and pulling hand is replaced by metal pounders, screws, or other mechanisms, so in shaving the hog the knife-wielding hand, which so readily adapts itself to the contours of the body, gives way to a mechanical device.

The dough mixer was invented in Europe and was not used in America until

---

[62] U.S. Patent 63,910; 16 Apr. 1867.

121. Depilating Poultry by the Wax Process. *Wax depilation was applied to poultry too when they were killed in the continuous-production line, in the time of full mechanization. None of the mechanical scraping methods was altogether successful. Only the organic can adapt to the organic.* (*Photo courtesy of Berenice Abbott*)

after the Civil War. In Europe the idea of creating a hog-scraping machine had never arisen. For many reasons it would never have come into use.

The same effort to adapt mechanism to irregular, organically formed bodies appears in America in the late eighteenth century, when numerous devices were invented to remove the skin from the apple. Apple-paring machines of various models were kept in every farmhouse until well beyond mid-nineteenth century. Made of wood at first, later of cast iron, they are mainly based on the principle of rotating the apple against a paring blade carried on a resilient arm.[63]

From the 'thirties, when Americans began to change the form of tools, unchanged through the ages, more precisely to their function, we have a proposal 'for extracting hairs from skin' [64] (fig. 119). Instead of using the thumb to

[63] See 'Mechanization Encounters the Household,' p.554.

[64] U.S. Patent 244, 30 July 1837.

raise the hair about to be cut by the blade, a leather-covered jaw was provided; and instead of the knife, an interchangeable steel blade. These parts were connected by a spring arm or a scissors-type handle. The New York inventor gave his instrument, which resembled 'in form and size the common sugar-tong,' the name of 'clamp fur knife.' 'The pelt is confined upon a form or beam . . . it will be found much better if a beam be used as broad as the pelt and slightly rounded . . . cushioned and covered with Indian rubber.'

It is a broad step from this furriers' implement to the first proposal for the 'hog-cleaning machine,' as it was then called (fig. 118). The suggestion was put forward in 1864. The specification of this earliest attempt [65] to put the whole carcass through a machine that would shave off hair and bristles clearly states its objective: 'The nature of my invention consists in applying to the whole body of scalded hogs, disks, blades, or other devices . . . formed . . . to present *sufficient force or adhesion and yet be elastic enough* to yield to the irregularities of the body.' Firm pressure and a yielding adaptation — lest the skin be cut into and damaged — were the desiderata for which multifarious solutions were offered.

This inventor of 1864 raises in succession two iron hoops of 36-inch diameter, one behind the other, like the hoops through which circus dogs leap. The first hoop is filled by a rubber disk having a hole some 12 inches in diameter in its center. The second hoop consists of two rings of steel blades or scrapers. 'They will converge all to a common center yet leaving a hole of four inches': in other words they are arranged rather like the leaves of a diaphragm. The pig, hooked by the snout to an endless chain, was to be towed first through the rubber, then through the steel ring. The inventor holds great expectations for the machine's efficiency. 'It is calculated . . . the capacity of this machine is from five to fifteen thousand hogs per diem.' All this may sound fantastic and improbable. However, not only did it represent an early experimental use of rubber 'to yield to the irregularities of the body,' but this proposal for elastic steel scrapers, concentrically arrayed, is found again in practical models four decades later; now, however, they are arranged funnel-wise and claw at the carcass like the legs of a spider (fig. 120).

This idea of 1864 could expect little success in its primitive form. Ten years later the same inventor returns with a second proposal. Now he imagines a 'series of rollers, armed with spring scrapers, revolving simultaneously about their respective axes.' [66] The arrangement of the individual rollers made for

[65] U.S. Patent 44,021, 30 Aug. 1864, N. Silverthorn.

[66] U.S. Patent 153,183, 28 Jan. 1874, N. Silverthorn.

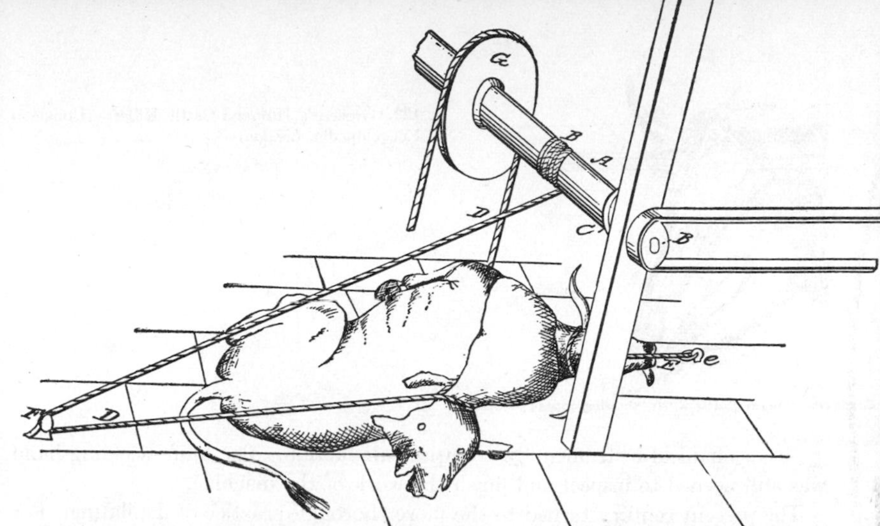

122. Skinning Cattle by Power. 1867. *Still impossible today, mechanized skinning was attempted at an early date. But the skin of animals is too delicate to handle otherwise than by knife and hand. This drawing, with its naïve means seeking to illustrate a mechanical device, forms an original piece of American folk art.* (*U. S. Patent* 63,910, 16 *April* 1867)

better adaptation to the animal shape. It is on this second attempt that the modern machines are based, which hourly scrape over 750 carcasses moving on the assembly line.

Toward the end of the 'seventies, and with all the refinement afforded by this time of rapidly improving techniques, even further approximation was made to the form of the animal. 'The machine should be entirely self-adjusting to the varying sizes of the carcasses passing through and also to the varying outlines. . . . My invention consists therefore in *a series of cylinders, each armed with sets of elastic scrapers* and distributed at different points. . . . Each of these cylinders . . . being independently movable and *free to advance and recede* to follow the contours of the carcass.'[67]

With expanding production in the early 'eighties and a yearly turnover in Chicago of some five million hogs, the demand for efficient machines of this sort became ever more urgent.[68] At a time when improvements of other machines in the meat-packing field were falling off, the number of hog-scraping patents was rising.[69]

[67] U.S. Patent 235,731, 21 Dec. 1880, J. Bouchard (filed 4 Dec. 1879).

[68] Neither was there a lack of proposals for machines 'for scraping hogs by passing them on an endless apron between rapidly moving scraping knives attached so as to be yielding and self-adjusting.' U.S. Patent 184,390, 6 Sept. 1876. Another time the 'profile of the scrapers' is made 'curvilinear' to permit more effective action. U.S. Patent 196,269, 29 Mar. 1877.

[69] 1881: four patents; 1882: two patents; 1886: three patents.

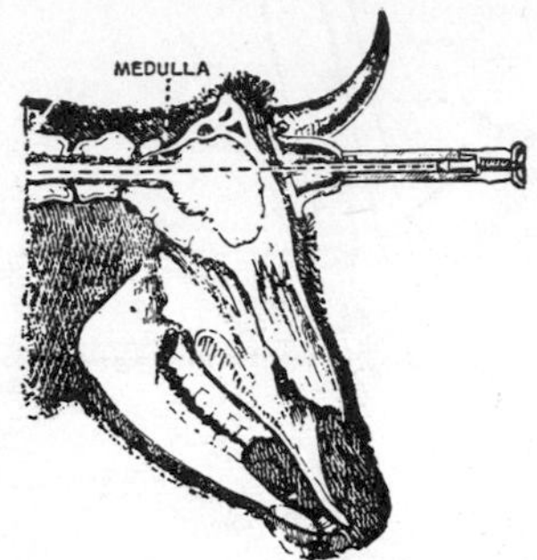

Greener's Humane Cattle Killer, showing course of bullet.

123. Greener's Humane Cattle Killer. (Douglas's Encyclopedia, *London*)

No mechanical instrument gave entire satisfaction. The knife-wielding hand was still needed to inspect and finish the work of the machine.

The present century turned to the more thorough practice of depilating. For this last cleaning, the carcass is plunged into a vat of molten wax, which when cold is torn off in strips, taking every trace of hair along with it.[70] Only the organic can conform to the organic (fig. 121).

The Mechanization of Death

The phenomenon of mechanized death will be regarded here neither from the sentimentalist's point of view nor from that of the food manufacturer. What interests us is solely the relation between mechanization and death; such is our present concern. Both are involved in the mass production of meat.

The development of this murder machinery can best be surveyed in the files of the Patent Office at Washington. There one can follow the manner in which hogs are slowly caught by their hind leg with the help of cunning devices; fed into the machinery, and, suspended in line, moved into the most favorable position for killing; the manner in which cattle are skinned by means of pulleys, ropes, and levers (fig. 122), and hogs scraped by revolving cutters and grippers.

The sole purpose of the drawings in the Patent Office is to illustrate the patent claim as clearly as possible. Yet freely viewed in their continuity, without regard to their technical interpretation and significance, they strike us as a *danse macabre* of our time. Their bare purposiveness is more direct, hence more impressive than the nineteenth-century portrayals of the relation of life to death. This schism is quite apparent in the famous woodcut series of the post-romantic

[70] When line production was applied to the processing of poultry in the 'thirties, similar methods were used: overhead conveyors, plucking machines — consisting of a drum strewn with elastic rubber fingers. We have seen this apparatus even in the smallest killing houses. Poultry packers also adopted the moulten-wax method for complete cleaning.

historical painter, Alfred Rethel (1816–59), about the mid-nineteenth century (fig. 126). He calls the series 'Another Danse Macabre' (1849). With sinister skill and in the noble woodcut tradition of Albrecht Dürer, death is abused for purposes of political propaganda. These woodcuts do not deal with the phenomenon of death. They represent a political satire against the revolution of 1848: Death masquerades as a demagogue. Moralizing stanzas warn against the slogans of republic, of liberty and fraternity.

> He lifts his coat, and as they look,
> Their hearts are terror-stricken.

Death has been degraded into a mere costume. An earlier cut, 'Death as a Strangler' (1847), pictures Death as fiddling on bones. The choice of the scene is significant. It uses Heinrich Heine's description of the outbreak of the cholera epidemic in 1831 at a Paris masquerade.

In the fifteenth century, the Last Judgment, inseparable from death, was a reality as threatening and perhaps more dreaded than death itself. In the nineteenth, only death in its biological nakedness remains, and even this is kept closeted. Hence all images of that time dealing with our relation to death,

124. Advertisement for a Chicago Packing House. 1890's. (*Courtesy J. Ryerson Collection, Chicago*)

Rethel's compositions among them, have become untrue. They use devaluated symbols unsupported by the living reality of belief.

The greater the degree of mechanization, the further does contact with death become banished from life. Death is merely viewed as an unavoidable accident at the end, as we shall point out in discussing why the medieval conception of comfort so differed from that of later periods. It is more honest to picture death in its crassness as the Spaniard, Louis Bunuel, in his motion picture *Le Chien Andalou* (1929), did symbolically (figs. 128, 129). There the symbolization of death is found in the play of irrational associations. Trivial everyday happenings and phantastic occurrences are interwoven into an artistic reality: A razor becomes a long-stretched cloud cutting through the full moon in the night sky, and turns into a murderer's knife slicing through a young woman's eye. The scenario runs:

A balcony in the night.

Near the balcony a man is sharpening his razor. The man looks at the sky through the window panes and sees . . .

A slight cloud moving towards the moon, which is full.

Then the head of a young woman open-eyed.

The slight cloud now passes before the moon.

The blade of the razor is drawn through the eye of the young woman, slashing it.[71]

---

[71] *La Révolution surréaliste*, Paris, 1930.

125. Killing Cattle. (Frank Leslie's Illustrated Newspaper, 12 *October* 1878)

126. Nineteenth-Century Relation to Death: Alfred Rethel, 'Another Dance of Death.' Woodcut, 1849. *In contrast to the fifteenth century, the mechanical age has no direct relation to the phenomenon of death; neither therefore does nineteenth-century art. If death is shown intervening, it appears in a literary, if not masquerade-like, guise.* (*Alfred Rethel,* Auch ein Totentanz, 1849)

All this is indifferently crass, cruel, and true. Its directness captures something of the eternal terror of death. The horror resides in the sudden, incalculable destruction of an organic creature.

The transition from life to death cannot be mechanized if death is to be brought about quickly and without damage to the meat. What mechanical tools were tried out proved useless. They were either too complex or outright harmful. Most of them hampered satisfactory bleeding. Our habit of eating meat only after it has been cleared of all blood must, it is asserted, be traced back to Jewish precepts, since both Greeks and Romans were anxious to keep the precious liquid in the carcass. They strangled the animals, or pierced them with heated spears, so as to prevent bleeding. Yet people would more likely abstain from meat than give up habits that have grown into instincts. Blood terrifies.

Only the knife, guided by the human hand (fig. 127), can perform the transition from life to death in the desired manner. For this operation craftsmen are needed who combine the precision and skill of a surgeon with the speed of a piece worker. It is established how far and how deep the throat of a hog should

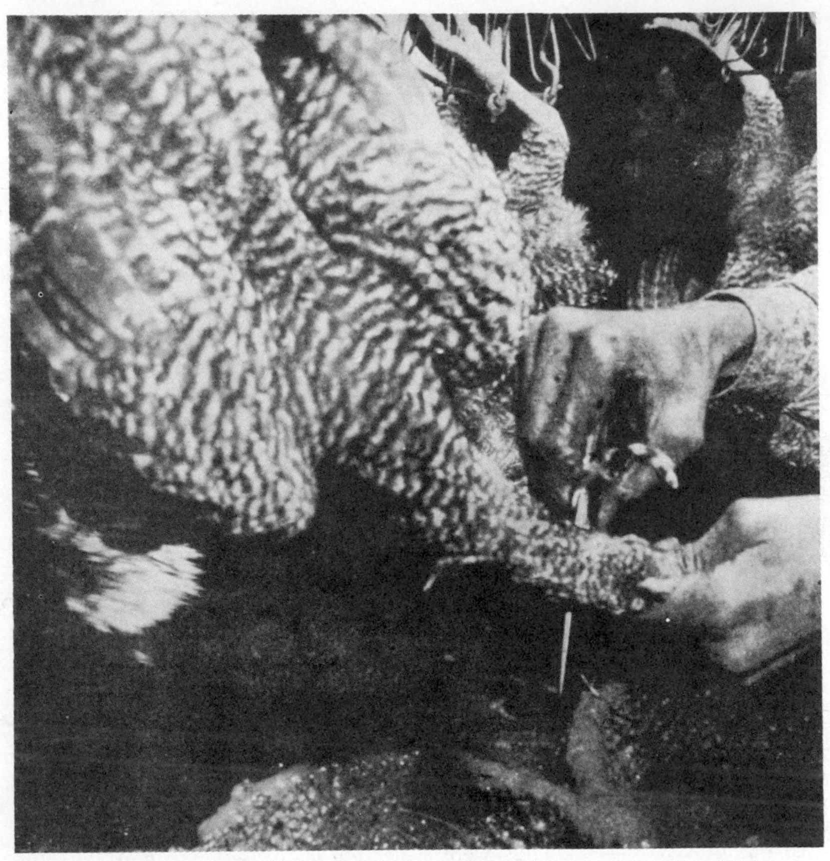

147. Killing Poultry by Hand in the Production Line. 1944. (*Photo courtesy Berenice Abbott*)

be pierced. A false stroke injures the meat product. And it must be done quickly — 500 hogs per hour.[72]

To sever the jugular vein, the sticker seizes the animal, suspended head downward by its forefoot, turns it properly, and pierces the throat about six inches. The same consummate skill and caution must be applied in butchering sheep; these less lively animals are hoisted to the rail in pairs. The stick is performed with a double-edged stiletto, just behind the ear.

[72] *Scientific American*, 21 Aug. 1866. The skill displayed in the then beginning large-scale production could hardly be improved upon subsequently. Even today a sticker cannot kill more than 500 to 600 animals per hour.

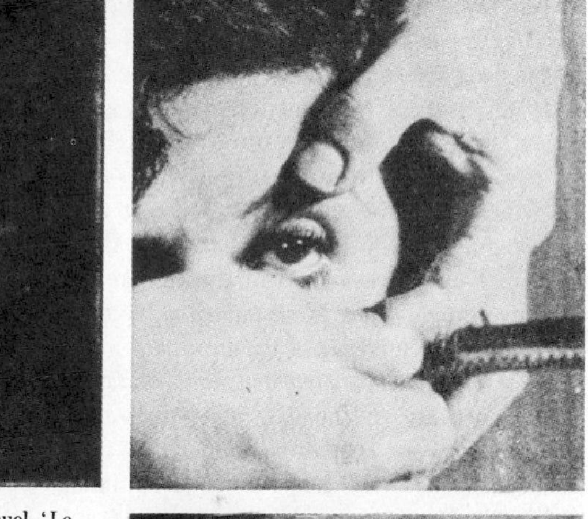

128. Death in Its Crassness: Luis Bunuel, 'Le Chien Andalou,' 1929. Cloud Passing the Moon, Eye of a Young Woman About To Be Cut by a Razor. *It is more honest to picture death in its crassness than to involve it in a masquerade. In the surrealistic film* 'Le Chien Andalou,' *Luis Bunuel communicates the idea of death by irrationally related symbols.* (*Courtesy Luis Bunuel*)

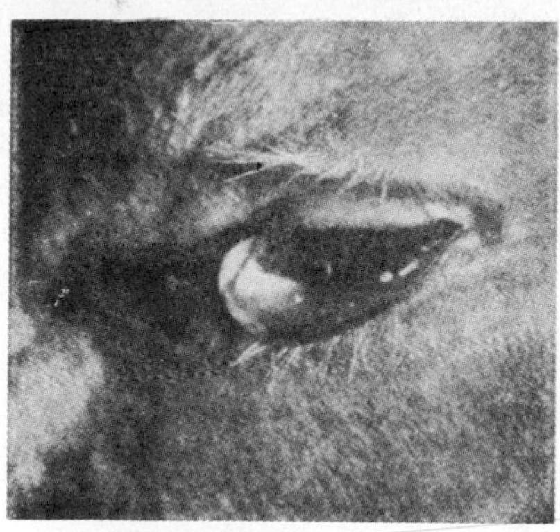

129. BUNUEL: 'Le Chien Andalou.' The Eye after the Cut. (*Courtesy Luis Bunuel*)

Cows are no longer taken to pens by the carload to be killed with a pointed spear. When they were, the sticker squatted on boards often placed crosswise over the pens awaiting the moment when he could best thrust the spear between the eyes of his victim. Today a four-pound hammer is used to smash in the skulls of the cattle in a narrow knocking pen; once hit, the animals collapse like wooden blocks. It is then that the workmen fasten the chain around the hind legs and hoist them to the rail, head downward. At the same time, the sticker thrusts a knife into the throat of the unconscious animal. The blood is usually gathered in special containers.

Killing itself then cannot be mechanized. It is upon organization that the burden falls. In one of the great packing plants, an average of two animals are killed every second — a daily quota of some 60,000 head. The death cries of the animals whose jugular veins have been opened are confused with the rumbling of the great drum, the whirring of gears, and the shrilling sound of steam. Death cries and mechanical noises are almost impossible to disentangle. Neither can the eye quite take in what it sees. On one side of the sticker are the living; on the other side, the slaughtered. Each animal hangs head downwards at the same regular interval, except that, from the creatures to his right, blood is spurting out of the neck-wound in the tempo of the heart beat. In twenty seconds, on the average, a hog is supposed to have bled to death. It happens so quickly, and is so smooth a part of the production process, that emotion is barely stirred.

What is truly startling in this mass transition from life to death is the complete neutrality of the act. One does not experience, one does not feel; one merely observes. It may be that nerves that we do not control rebel somewhere in the subconscious. Days later, the inhaled odor of blood suddenly rises from the walls of one's stomach, although no trace of it can have clung to the person.

How far the question is justified we do not know, nevertheless it may be asked: Has this neutrality toward death had any further effect upon us? This broader influence does not have to appear in the land that evolved mechanized killing, or even at the time the methods came about. This neutrality toward death may be lodged deep in the roots of our time. It did not bare itself on a large scale until the War, when whole populations, as defenseless as the animals hooked head downwards on the traveling chain, were obliterated with trained neutrality.

MECHANIZATION AND GROWTH

Around 1930 a new development begins and is now on the threshold of fuller realization. It points to a new epoch whose trend is away from the mechanical. It centers, as we have suggested, around man's intervention with organic substance. Animals and plants are to be changed in their structure and in their nature. The field of genetics, responsible for this radical intervention, is an offshoot of biology, with which it came into being.

From the beginning man has interfered with nature by domestication and breeding. He molded to his will the character of wild animals and wild plants. He domesticated them. He raised oxen and capons for his purposes. In Antiquity, he coupled the mare and the ass, creating the sterile mule. The Arabs of the thirteenth century are said to have artificially inseminated pedigree mares. For the hatching of eggs, the Chinese used baskets filled with warm rice and the Egyptians employed ovens. The American Indians bred corn with notable success.

The eighteenth century opened the field of genetics as it did that of mechanized agriculture, by scientific experiment and analysis. From the discovery that plants are sexual organisms (Camerarius, 1694), from the analytical hybridization of plants (Thomas Fairchild, 1717; Vilmorin Andrieux, 1727) [1] to the revolutionary experiments and discoveries of Gregor Mendel (1865),[2] interest in these experiments never fell off. The late eighteenth century extended genetics to the artificial insemination of mammals.

Thus the principles of genetics as such are not new. Genetics follow the usual path from handed-down experience to scientific experiment. The subject remained in this stage for a long while. What was to occur in the time of full mechanization is beyond all comparison with the earlier phases. It is a far deeper interference with organic growth. The structural alteration of plants and animals proceeds at a tempo that, compared to what existed before, almost eliminates the time factor. The dimensions grow to the gigantic.

This revolution bears some similarity to the revolutionizing of tools and implements a century earlier, when they were of a sudden reshaped or transformed into mechanisms. The impetuous tempo of the present development and the sensitiveness of the realms affected promise even more shaking consequences.

Seed

In the time of full mechanization, the plants that yield us food or clothing are restored to prominence. By special measures, particularly those intervening in their fertilization, we alter their structure and productivity. Wheat, oats, barley, sugar-cane, cotton, fruits, and vegetables are made more hardy and more resistant to drought and parasites. The soy bean, although introduced early in the last century, assumes a new significance. But most conspicuous of all are the results in corn breeding.

'Hybrid corn,' states the Bureau of Agriculture Economics, 'is as important among plants as the tractor is among machines.' [3]

---

[1] J. Oppenheimer, 'A Historical Introduction to the Study of Teleostian Development,' *Osiris*, vol. 2, 1936, pp.124–48, makes mention of the following eighteenth-century work in the field of genetics:

1761: Koelreuter performs the artificial fertilization of plants and obtains hybrids by this means.

1763: Jacobi reports on the fertilization of fish eggs (*Hanover Magazine*, 1763).

1785: M. E. Bloch, *Ichtyologie*, Berlin, 1785, with chapter 'On the Manner of Hatching [Fish] Eggs.'

[2] *Versuche ueber Pflanzenhybriden*, 1865.

[3] *Technology on the Farm*, U.S. Govt. Printing Office, Washington, August 1940, p.21.

By virtue of the American climate, corn forms the most important feed for livestock. Its improvement and rise in production within a few years border on the marvelous. The first attempts to raise hybrid corn commercially were in the 'twenties. It did not become available in quantity before the early 'thirties. Then, within four years, 1935 to 1939, a fivefold increase occurs. The area sown with hybrid corn is extended from about a half-million acres to twenty-four million acres. This represents over a quarter of the total production.[4]

Hybrid corn clusters around the cob in exceptional abundance and regularity. It is more prolific (15 to 30 per cent), more resistant, and more handsome.[5] A noteworthy fact was observed in the second generation of corn sown freely in the fields; it lost some of its desirable characteristics. The farmer must therefore purchase his seed from raisers, in whom seed-production tends to become increasingly centered.

The Egg

One instance at least may serve to show how the eighteenth century took analysis and experiment as its starting point in the mechanization of growth.

The Egyptians were masters in the use of incubators for chickens. Even in more recent times they had not quite forgotten their skill. In the eighteenth century, Berma, a village of the Nile Delta, still lived by artificial chicken raising, the secrets of which had been handed down from father to son. Thirty thousand fowl were hatched at a time, Réaumur reports, and sold by the bushel.

Just as exotic flowers were transplanted to northern climes, so a native of this Egyptian village was brought to Florence by the grand duke of Tuscany, that the court might enjoy young chicken in all seasons. In 1747 Antoine Ferchault de Réaumur, the great natural scientist, addressed the Paris Academy on the topic of chicken incubators, with sensational success, as his biographer tells us, for to have roast chicken on the table the year round was at that time a tempting dream.[6]

---

[4] In some parts of the corn belt, in Iowa, for instance, hybrid corn amounts to 77 per cent. Cf. *Technology on the Farm*, op.cit. p.136.

[5] To regulate the crossing and to develop the varieties as desired, the ears must be prevented from becoming accidentally fertilized and the female plants from fertilizing themselves. In normal circumstances the matured pollen grains would fall by the laws of chance from the corn tassels on the silk ear shoots and fertilize them. Male and female plants are therefore separated. Between every two or four feminine rows one masculine row is placed. The tassels of the female plants are pulled before they shed any pollen. This process is repeated at regular intervals, so that the whole field is fertilized exclusively by male plants of determined quality. At harvest time the male plants are eliminated, and only the grain on female cobs is used for further raising. This process — inbreeding — has to be continued for five to seven years. Described in further detail in *Technology on the Farm*, op.cit. ch. 21, and in more popular form in William R. Van Dersal, *The American Land, Its History and Its Uses*, New York, 1943, pp.54–7.

[6] Jean Torlay, op.cit. pp.303–14.

Two years later Réaumur published his handsomely engraved book, translated into English the following year.[7] In the foreword, he tells amusingly how this experiment began. A friend in the diplomatic service had given him a precise account of incubating as practiced in the Egyptian village. He soon knew that this was not going to be his method. He would engage no Egyptian experts, as princes might. His own thermometer would take the place of the Egyptian's secret. At first he used the natural warmth of a dung heap in which he sank a barrel containing the incubator (fig. 130). Then he experimented with the baking oven of a neighboring nunnery; and finally he built himself a wood-heated cylindrical 'stove' affording equable radiation. Even today American farmers state a preference for the coal-heated cylindrical brooder rather than the electrical type, which, they tell us, may be inadequate in cold weather.

One cannot read Réaumur's book without excitement, for in this banal matter the observation of the great savant is powerfully projected upon the slightest details. He knows precisely how the chicken breaks out of its shell, how the embryo forms; and he devises the 'artificial mother.'

In a half-darkened room of a St. Louis food factory, we have seen low wire cages, housing chicks that had emerged from the incubator a few days earlier. In the brooder was an inclined rubber cloth, electrically heated. The chicks crawled under this cloth, which took the place of their mother's wings in warming their lungs. Now, in mid-eighteenth century, Réaumur notes the same fact when he lines a box with lamb's fleece (fig. 130), inclines its ceiling like the rubber cloth in the twentieth-century brooder, similarly imitative of the hen's wings, and calls the whole device 'artificial mother.'

Around 1944, only 15 per cent of the chicks produced in the United States were brooded by hens. The other 85 per cent were incubated in some 10,000 hatcheries. In the electrically heated and thermostatically controlled incubators of today each unit contains some 52,000 eggs. They can be attended by one man. Réaumur's hatching device was immovable. The shelves of the modern incubators revolve on an axis, regularly changing the position of the eggs as the hen might, thus preventing the embryo from sticking to the shell. The average farm flock is of about 100 hens. Some hatcheries have a capacity of over a million eggs. Ten thousand chick factories produce some 1.6 billion chicks yearly.

[7] Réaumur, *L'Art de faire éclore des œufs et d'élever en toute saison des oiseaux domestiques par la chaleur du fumier et par celle du feu ordinaire*, Paris, 1749.

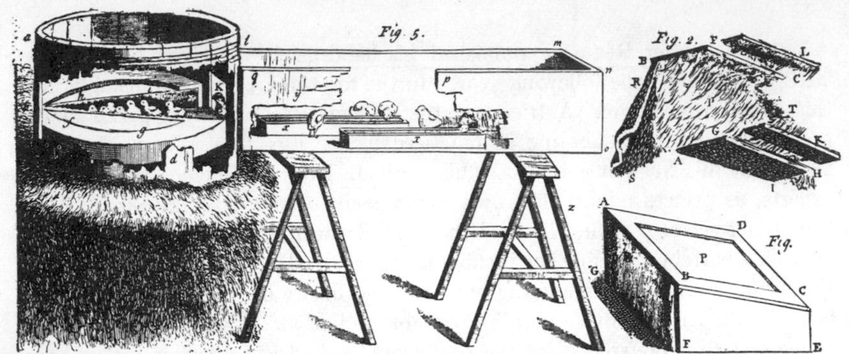

130. Intervention into Organic Substance: Réaumur, Artificial Mother. *c.*1750. *Réaumur's experiments were suggested by the Egyptian 'artificial mothers,' just as his century's effort to exploit steam and the atmospheric vacuum forms a parallel trend to Alexandrian technology. Perhaps oven hatching originated in the technically advanced Ptolemaic period; the practice was maintained until Réaumur's day in villages of the Nile delta.*

Left: *Artificial mother formed of barrel with fleece-lined chamber placed over a dung heap.* Right: *Artificial mother formed of 'a wooden frame against which a lambskin P is nailed, whose woolly side is within the mother; a loose curtain that falls almost quite to the bottom of the mother, and stops the whole front of it in such a manner that it takes not from the chicks the liberty of getting under the mother. They remove and lift it up easily.'* (*A. F. de Réaumur,* The Art of Hatching and Bringing Up Domestic Fowl at Any Time of the Year, *London,* 1750)

131. RÉAUMUR: Artificial Mother. *c.*1750. *'This plate exhibits the inside of a hot-room designed to bring up chicks in, and which may be as usefully employed to hatch them. A, marks the cover of a stove whose body is cylindrical. By taking off that cover one puts wood into the stove when it is wanted.'* (*Ibid.*)

132. Artificial Mother in the Time of Full Mechanization: Electrical Brooder, 1940. *Between 1918 and 1944 artificially hatched eggs in the United States increased from twenty per cent to eighty-five per cent of the total. The electrically heated incubator unit contains about* 52,000 *eggs.* (Hawkins Million Dollar Hen, *Mount Vernon, Illinois*)

The tremendous increase in artificial hatching comes with the time of full mechanization. From 1918 to 1944, artificially hatched eggs increase from 20 per cent to 85 per cent of the total. One reason given for this is that after 1918 young chicks could be sent through the mails. Actually, the rise is in keeping with the general trend. Mass production and rearing chicks from selected eggs are more profitable. One danger is the dissemination of disease; careful control is necessary. Another is that of unscrupulous dealers.

To keep production as regular as possible, artificial light is used in the laying houses on autumn and winter mornings, to stimulate the ovaries. Although this does not increase the total production, it equalizes it so far as possible throughout the year, and makes possible poultry processing in mechanized plants — introduced toward the 'thirties. The delicacy the Grand Duke of Tuscany was at pains to provide for his court is now available to all.

Before the advent of mass production in poultry raising, chicken used to cost about twice as much in winter as in summer. Now freshly killed poultry is available the year round. A mechanism is being sought that will mechanically separate the bones from the meat.

Mechanical Fertilization

How organic life is generated was of especial concern to the century that questioned everything to find an answer in everything. Skepticism and universality go hand in hand in the eighteenth century. Just as the period probes the life of plants and animals, of insects and mammals, so it seeks to explore microscopic life.

In one of the great scientific controversies of the century, the Jesuit Lazzaro Spallanzani, 1729–99, refuted the theory that *infusoria* are spontaneously generated by vegetative force, 'substantial power,' or 'occult virtue.' By obstinate experiment Spallanzani showed that bacteria enter nutritive solutions from the outside. He was interested in the generation of life, 'il gran problema della generatione,' from mammals and plants down to infusoria.

How do microbes breed? By copulation, it was affirmed. Horace Benedict de Saussure, the Genevan geologist, 1740–99, first man to climb the Mont Blanc, discovered in 1770 that infusoria multiply by cleavage. Spallanzani proved this through one of his genially planned experiments, and portrayed for the first time (1776) the stages of their growth, maturation, and division (fig. 133).

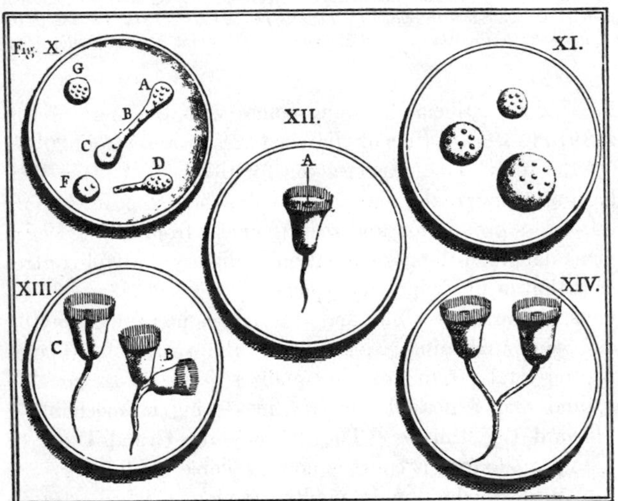

133. Mechanical Insemination: Lazzaro Spallanzani, First Visual Representation of the Partition of Infusoria. *Lazzaro Spallanzani and the Geneva scientists showed that microbes reproduced by fission, not by copulation. Scientific research into the creation of life dates from this time. Spallanzani traversed within a few years the cycle from one-cell organisms to the artificial insemination of a bitch.* (*L. Spallanzani,* Opusculi di Fisica Animali e Vegetabili, *Modena* 1776, *vol.* I)

From this point to experiments with spermatozoa and artificial fertilization was but a step. Spallanzani proceeded by degrees in his studies of generation. He experimented with toads, frogs, newts, and even with silkworms; finally he succeeded in artificially fertilizing a bitch.

The seed [Spallanzani reports] was injected into the matrix by means of a small syringe. . . . I had taken care to give the syringe the degree of heat which man and dogs are found to possess. . . . The bitch brought forth three lively whelps, two male and one female. . . . Thus did I succeed in fecundating this quadruped; and I can truly say that I never received greater pleasure upon any occasion since I cultivated experimental philosophy. I have no difficulty in believing that we shall be able to give birth to some large animals without the concurrence of the two sexes, provided we have recourse to the simple mechanical device employed by me.[8]

With more rigid standards, Spallanzani's experiment was soon repeated in England and applied by a large-scale dog breeder a century later.[9]

Within one generation the vast cycle was traversed from one-celled creatures to highly organized mammals. Since then the syringe has been technically refined, our knowledge of inherited characteristics and of how organs develop in the embryo has become vastly enlarged; but we have not penetrated much further the problems of the generation of life and of the effects of continued hybridization.

Russia and the United States have made the greatest advances in mechanical fertilization. Early, Russia's physiological experiments had bordered on the sensational. In 1907 a Russian physiologist wrote on the artificial fertilization of mammals.[10] In the time of full mechanization, what had formerly been laboratory experiments became tools of mass production. In the Soviet Union in 1936 over 15,000 ewes were fertilized from one ram; average conception: 96.6 per cent. In one district all the ewes — 45,000 — were fertilized by the semen of eight rams. In that year 6 million cows and ewes of the Soviet Union were mechanically impregnated [11] — a parallel to the introduction of hybrid corn in America.

In America around 1945, the introduction of artificial insemination on a large scale was still in process.[12] The apparatus is at hand and is adapted to cows, sheep, goats, dogs, foxes, rabbits, poultry.[13] Dummies with artificial vaginas and syringes for the injection of semen are ready. The immediate advantages and drawbacks are weighed. We do not know as yet within what limits or how long nature will submit to our mechanisms. It is idle to discuss the consequences. At all events a most delicate point is impinged upon when generation is treated as a mechanical process.

This sphere, above all others, demands that a position be taken relinquishing production for production's sake. In question here is not the fixed quality of iron or steel, of a motor or a refrigerator. It is a question of the quality of life

[8] *Dissertation Relative to the Natural History of Animals and Vegetables*, London, 1784, vol. 2, pp.197–9.

[9] Walter Heape, in Royal Society (London) *Proceedings*, 1897; 16, pp.52–63.

[10] Elie Ivanoff, 'De la fécondation artificielle chez les mammifères,' *Archives des Sciences Biologiques*, Leningrad, 1907, pp.377-511.

[11] W. V. Lambert, *Artificial Insemination in Livestock Breeding*, Circular no. 567, U.S. Dept. of Agriculture, Washington, D.C., 1940, pp.2–3.

[12] Ibid. p.6.

[13] Ibid. pp.20–61.

134. Crossing Varieties of Tomatoes by Pollination Method. H. J. Heinz Nursery. Bowling Green, Ohio. (*Courtesy H. J. Heinz Co.*)

— something which is transmitted from one generation to the next. A momentous responsibility is involved.

Seen in this perspective, the short-lived demands of the market take on a grotesque aspect. Before the Second World War, because of the competition of vegetable oils, pigs were bred for a minimum of fat; a few years later outside circumstances demanded a complete reversal of these characteristics. Instances like these show up the weakness of day-to-day expediency. A different attitude is necessary, as for instance that which guided the research center of Animal Industry at Beltsville, Md.,[14] in adapting pigs to the southern climate. Here the advantages of light-colored north European pigs — long pink bodies, good hams — were combined with the essential features of the American breed. The pink-skinned varieties were unable to withstand the sun of the southern states. In a few years, by cross-breeding, a darker-hued, red, black, or spotted pig was developed that satisfied all requirements.

[14] The Beltsville Research Center, attached to the U.S. Dept. of Agriculture, is located 13 miles from Washington, D.C. Beginning with 475 acres in 1910, it has expanded to 13,900 acres, with two thousand employees. It is mainly concerned with the improvement of plants and livestock, and the control of insect pests. Messrs. R. W. Phillips, John H. Zeller, and T. C. Byerly kindly allowed us access to the center and put their knowledge at our disposal.

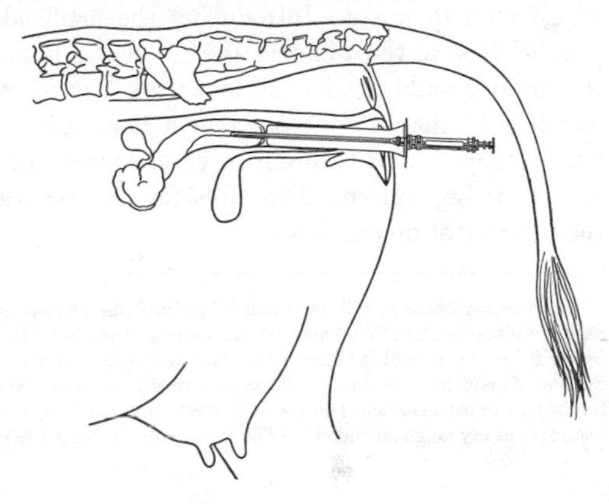

135. Mechanical Insemination. '*Median section of the cow showing the reproductive organs with nozzle of syringe inserted into the cervix.' The syringe, although technically refined, is still used for artificial insemination as it was by Spallanzani in the late eighteenth century. In the time of full mechanization, especially in the* 1930'*s, the Soviet Union experimented extensively. Six million cows and ewes were mechanically impregnated there in* 1936. *Without going so far in practice, the United States developed a great range of devices suited to the various species.* (U. S. Department of Agriculture Circular 567, *W. V. Lambert*)

Perhaps the most appealing side of this research appears in its deeper penetration into the habits of animals and the regulation of their living conditions accordingly. Given the opportunity, the pig expresses the same desire for cleanliness as the cat or man. What is surprising is the brief time needed to bring about a change in the breed. At Beltsville, in the space of a few years, turkey hens were so altered in size as to satisfy the requirements of a small family and fit into the modern oven.

These examples, drawn at random from many others, indicate that the postulates of experiment still waver between catering to a capricious market and thinking along more universal lines.

A cloud of question marks hovers over most of the procedures. Egg production doubtless increases when the maternal instinct of the hen is systematically repressed, and the chicks are hatched and raised without her, so as not to interfere with the egg-laying activity.

A steer is doubtless easier to control when its horns have been removed by caustics from the first, for he has been deprived of his natural weapons of combat. But may not this advantage tell upon the quality in the long run? Doubtless there is a more careful selecting of eggs in the great hatcheries; and the small farmer may obtain the semen of high-pedigree bulls such as he himself could never afford.

It is a noteworthy advance that makes possible the impregnation of 45,000 sheep by 8 rams. Yet the question remains whether nature is not in a sense ever bound to waste. Introducing the artificial insemination of mares to the Middle West in the 'nineties, the advocator himself raised the question whether the mare 'should not be "in love," as it were, with the horse.' [15] One thing is certain. Mechanization comes to a halt before living substance. A new outlook must prevail if nature is to be mastered rather than degraded. The utmost caution is imperative. This calls for an attitude turning radically away from the idolatry of production.

---

[15] 'The scientists may talk loud and long about the germ-plasms being unchangeable, but the writer's experience teaches him that when the contracting animals are in mental union the resulting foal is sure to be docile.' — 'On Breeding Mares,' *The Horseman*, Chicago, vol. XIV, 8 March 1894. Regarding the introduction of artificial insemination the same writer points out: 'When I first began to talk of it I was made fun of by almost everyone (that was in 1893) but today it is talked of almost as a necessity in many instances in my neighbourhood.' (*The Horseman*, 30 May 1895.)

PART V MECHANIZATION ENCOUNTERS HUMAN SURROUNDINGS

MEDIEVAL COMFORT

The Middle Ages and Mechanization

WHY, one may ask, do we begin with the medieval period? We are to study the growth of mechanization. Why not start rather with the Renaissance, whose rationalistic approach lies so much closer to the spirit of mechanization? There are many reasons.

We want to gain some understanding of the beginnings from which Western life has continuously developed. Beginnings offer the surest footholds. Looking at them, we see as in a mirror. What features have changed? Which are preserved? Which are lost? What are the new impulses?

The beginnings of this unbroken development were affirmed when, for the first time since Rome's collapse, living standards rose to a point making burgher life possible. For the first time since Rome, culture spread roots and prospered in urban society. The old European cities began to revive from the eleventh century on, and the thirteenth saw more towns founded than any later century.

The Renaissance, leaning on the Ancients, broadened our horizons. The Middle Ages embrace the roots of our very existence.

Not only do Gothic church spires dominate the town, but Gothic ways of life still survive, often beneath our consciousness. These modes of living have often retreated to the mountains or to other places inclined to steadfastness and tied to medieval methods of production. The tractor has no grip on steep mountain slopes. Peasant life, tenacious in its habits, in its houses, in its furniture, and even yet in its dress, lingers in the late Gothic. The peasant of central Switzerland or Appenzell draws the same 'shepherd's smock' over his head as the Amish and the Mennonites in Pennsylvania. Both garments have the same origin; they differ only in material; linen in Switzerland, corduroy in America.

More significant, but often less recognizable, are vestiges of the medieval attitude toward production. Guild ethics centered around one fundamental: maintenance of quality. The European countries whose sense of quality has remained vigorous alongside of mechanical production are those where Gothic modes of living have survived.

The survival of the baker, the butcher, the innkeeper, and many other craftsmen deeply influences the whole temper of life. If the complicated craft did

136. Egyptian Posture: Limestone Grave Stele. Middle of 2nd Millennium B.C. *From the present-day point of view, Egyptian seating habits are both Eastern and Western. The Egyptians equipped their houses with great skill. They developed benches, folding beds, and especially chairs and stools of various kinds. The chairs are adapted either to squatting in the Oriental manner — in which case the piece is lower than normal, and its seat deeper — or to sitting with one's legs hanging down in the western manner. The legs of the man to the left are resting forward, as in the Greek vase painting of the fifth century* B.C. (*Courtesy Metropolitan Museum, New York*)

not undergo mechanization as it did in America, this is not always due to incapacity or smallness of scale. Chain restaurants appeared in Paris, but it was in America that they expanded so as to affect everyday life. Resisting mechanization in a given sphere can often mean reluctance to sacrifice quality. Where such resistance will be set up, no fixed rule can decide. Industrialization marred the quality of cooking in England much more than in America. England's insistence on excellence in clothing, on the other hand, is a tradition inherited from centuries of handicraft. This is the demand for quality, having its roots in the guilds of the Gothic towns, a demand that is now at the point of re-awakening.

America had a farming economy. The settlers who came over in the seventeenth and eighteenth centuries scarcely differed from their medieval ancestors in their modes of living and working. Colonial America, as we shall see, sometimes preserved Gothic elements forgotten in the Old World. From the stage of primitive handicraft and a life of medieval austerity, America directly leaped into advanced mechanization.

The Changing Conception of Comfort

The word 'comfort' in its Latin origin meant 'to strengthen.' The West, after the eighteenth century, identified comfort with 'convenience': Man shall order and control his intimate surroundings so that they may yield him the utmost ease. This view would have us fashion our furniture, choose our carpets, contrive our lighting, and use all the technical aids that mechanization makes available.

The notion of comfort means different things to different civilizations. Comfort can be achieved in many directions. It amounts to whatever man holds necessary for his 'fortifying' his 'strengthening.'

The Oriental interpretation of comfort requires that man should at all times have control over his muscles. Thus the Orient has achieved postures that allow the body to find relaxation and comfort within itself. To enjoy such comfort, it is enough to take on one of these 'innate' postures, such as squatting with one's legs crossed beneath the body while allowing the muscular system to relax. No back or arm rests are needed; the body relaxes within and upon itself. Moreover, reclining is not used solely to induce sleep, but to favor bodily relaxation while taking meals or conversing.

The Oriental conception contrasts with the Western as represented by the unsurpassed subtlety and skill of the eighteenth century. Western comfort is based on the idea of sitting with one's legs hanging down. In this posture the body calls for outside support.

137. Roman Posture: Mural Painting, Boscoreale. 1st Century B.C. *The chair did not play a prominent role in the Roman interior. The heavy chair of the cither player connotes luxury more than it studies posture. Details like the purely decorative armrest and the richly treated legs are indications of this trend. After the decay of Roman civilization, a millennium elapsed before men again acquired the habit of sitting on individual chairs.* (Courtesy Metropolitan Museum, New York)

138. Medieval Posture: Pythagoras Writing. North Portal, Chartres Cathedral. 12th Century. *Seating and posture were improvised in the medieval period. People sat on the floor, on benches, window seats, cushions, small stools, or on a low cushion, as the Pythagoras of Chartres Cathedral may be sitting, supporting a portable writing desk on his knees.*

The framework of this support, the chair, records the notion of comfort as it has changed from period to period.

In this span, extending from *Periclean Athens* to Rococo France, there is a breach of continuity rarely to be observed by the historian. The Greek chairs, with their elegantly tapered legs, the slight backward tilt of their seat, and their broad, energetic shoulder curve, correspond in furniture to the sculpture of Phidias. In grace and sensitivity of form they have never been surpassed. After the decay of Rome, such refined seating was forgotten.

Not before the *eighteenth century* were the Greek standards of comfort surpassed, and then with another aim and direction. To earlier periods its softly upholstered seats would have seemed sections cut from a bed.

But now what science is brought to minister to the body and its support! The first care is to model and curve furniture with special solicitude for the sensitive regions of the body. The back rest molds the hollow of the spine; the outline of the seat is calculated to the length of the thigh and the sweep of the knees; the arm rests retreat in deference to feminine dress. The comfort of sitting, representative of our culture, here finds its most refined handling.

In a third step, the last half of the *nineteenth century* takes a new path to comfort: It introduces movability. It accomplishes this by dissecting the furniture into a series of mobile planes regulated by a mechanism. This furniture is not comparable in gracefulness to the Greek chairs, nor are its seats fashioned to the knees of conversing cavaliers. No precious material, no consummate form are found here. It is anonymous production stemming from anonymous inventors, serial production. This furniture is rooted in the habits and occupations of the nineteenth century. To the question whether the nineteenth century had an attitude of its own, or whether it was destined to flit from disguise to disguise, its furniture holds the key.

Posture in the Middle Ages

How did people sit in the Middle Ages?

Posture reflects the inner nature of a period. Medieval altars enthrone the madonnas in strong frontality before a golden background. On the Portals of Chartres, the figures stand in hierarchical array, as behind and above Biblical events are unfolded. At first glance, medieval posture would seem of ceremonial solemnity and these images projections of the ordered medieval society.

But beyond the too easy sociological interpretation, another prospect opens. The feudal lords and ladies of the thirteenth century could sit and walk with great dignity of carriage, as revealed in the Gothic statues. The Middle Ages were capable of supreme solemnity. But this bearing formed part and parcel of the worship. We have no faculty, perhaps, to feel the dignity and fervor that must have emanated from the medieval church service. No other furniture vied in splendor with the choir stalls for the ecclesiastics. The multitude knelt on the stone floor. Burgher life took quite another shape. Greece and the Middle Ages have this in common, for all their diversity: Monumentality is almost exclusively reserved for veneration of the divine.

Rome's collapse re-echoed in every sphere of life. Cultural values that a millennium and a half had consolidated lost their meaning or were mutilated beyond recognition. When the nomads plundered Rome, they found chairs that made no more sense to them than the statues, the thermae, the inlaid furniture, and all the instruments of a differentiated culture. Their habit was to squat on the ground, and so it remained.

The culture now taking shape pursued ends as different from those of the

139. High Court of France (Lit de Justice), 1458: Jean Fouquet's Frontispiece to the Munich Boccaccio. *The death sentence is being pronounced on the Duke of Alençon for conspiracy with the English. For three months prior to this moment, the dignitaries of the realm sat closely packed on benches having no backs. The justices — le parquet — sit on the floor in an astonishingly informal way.* (*P. Durrieu*, Le Boccace de Munich)

ancient world as Gothic skeleton construction, with its horror of the massive, from the heavy vaults of the thermae. Late medieval living standards could have allowed comfort in the sense of convenience. But this thought was foreign to the Gothic. The Gothic produced no furniture modeled to the shape of the body. In the fifteenth century, low three-legged stools were as much in use as in Romanesque times. Everything intimates that medieval people used to sit in improvised and informal fashion. They squatted more often than they sat. Seen in sideview, the arch-backed madonnas, sculpted in Romanesque times, tell how the woman was accustomed to squatting; she did not lean her body against the throne back. Only the sculptor sat her on this hierarchic seat. Thus too should be understood the richly worked draperies, hung on walls behind benches in the thirteenth century, and still seen in Italian Renaissance representations of the madonna.

People sat on the bare floor and on cushions. They sat on stairs and on the steps leading up to the high-posted beds. Romanesque chests — at least the few that have come down to us — were for sacred purposes and much too high to have been used as seats. As chests become lower, we will find them aligned along the walls. They filled the role of chairs and couches. Following this tradition, chairs and tables were made that were also containers, a custom still prevalent around 1500. The latter half of the fifteenth century closes the medieval period but is still penetrated with the medieval spirit. At the same time century-old habits are relaxed and new ones press forward.

How did people sit in the Middle Ages? A few examples drawn from divers countries and social strata of this transition period may give the most direct insight into its changing comfort.

High Court of France, Presided over by Charles VII, 1458

This miniature illumination by Jean Fouquet (fig. 139) depicts the sentencing to death of the Duke of Alençon, accused of conspiracy with the English against France — a solemn assembly and a solemn moment, as the three months' hearing reaches its conclusion. At the focal point, the king is on his raised seat; to his right and left, dignitaries of the realm, clergy, nobles, and justices are on rows of benches. Kneeling before the king is the proclaimer of the death sentence. The state proceedings observe the social hierarchy. An unmistakable solemnity pervades this audience, it fills the whole atmosphere: raiment, bearing, the tall Gobelin tapestries emblazoned to full height with heraldic figures.

But what comfort accompanies these proceedings? For three months, from August to October, the brilliant court sat closely packed — as always in the

140. Carnival in a Dutch Kitchen, *c.*1475. Dutch Engraving of 1567. *The entire social scale lies between Fouquet's supreme court and the company of revelers in this Dutch kitchen. Yet common to both places is the improvised manner of sitting. They use everything available: an overturned basket, stools of varying heights, or a chair with a stumpy back and turned legs, stemming from the Romanesque tradition.*

Middle Ages — on plain wooden benches without back rests, affording but little room for the legs — a striking contrast to the choir stall. The justices sit on the floor with astonishing informality, while six dignitaries on the steps of the royal throne are not much better off. There is no more comfort at this royal audience than in a circus tent.

Such renunciation of comfort of the flesh at the French court — known, with the Burgundian, as the most refined of its day — typifies the attitude the medieval period preserved to the last. In the seventeenth century such an assembly would be unthinkable without the seating appropriate to its authority.

***Carnival in a Dutch Kitchen,* c.1475**

The entire social scale lies between Fouquet's supreme court of France and the company of revelers in this Dutch engraving [1] (fig. 140), but similar practices

[1] It matters little in our connection if the design is not after Hieronymus Bosch as is indicated on the engraving, which rather follows the archaic trend of the late sixteenth century, imitating usages of the late fifteenth.

obtain in both places. Here is a motley group gathered around a hearth at which the woman in the foreground is making waffles. The man near by sprawls his mass over a small stool of the Romanesque tradition. Or is it a chair he is sitting on? With admirable directness, this engraving shows us how people used to sit: informally, at an angle, one arm thrown over the stumpy back rest.

The rest of the gathering sit on whatever is handy: overturned baskets, stools of various heights — all of which suggest that it was not their wont to gather around a table.

Here too everyone sits crowded together. The bodies touch. The often-heard explanation that people are crowded in medieval pictures because the artist wishes to portray as many as possible hardly seems plausible. Look into as many pictures as one will, all give the same account: Medieval society did not have chairs as we know them, and people took close seating for granted.

We are accustomed to sit on chairs that leave an unavoidable gap between persons, holding each sitter apart from his neighbor. This habit has become ingrained in our behavior. Unlike people in the Middle Ages, we feel it distasteful to touch or be touched by our neighbor, and back apologetically away.

141. Upper Rhenish Interior, *c.*1450: 'Mary Bathing the Child,' School of Konrad Witz. *The Virgin, whose rank is shown only by the cascading folds of her garment, may be seated on a low stool, or on the floor itself, or on a cushion such as those that lie on the plain chests lining the wall.*

142. Italian Bedroom and Study: Two Woodcuts from Francesco Colonna, 'Hypnerotomachia,' Venice, 1499. *Polyphilo's lady in her bedroom, reading his letter. Polyphilo writing to his lady. As in the Rhenish living room about four decades earlier, the main furniture consists of standard chests set end to end along the walls. The atmosphere is monastic in its simplicity. The purpose of each room is apparent in the furniture: the bed with its platform-like chests; the table near the wall with a portable desk on which Polyphilo writes.*

Upper Rhenish Interior, c.1450: Drawing of the School of Konrad Witz

Along the bare walls — paneling is not yet customary — a series of uniform chests are aligned (fig. 141). Mary, whose Child is gazing at His reflection in the hand basin, sits in a room that has no table.

In the statues of the saints of this period, our eye is drawn to the cascading robes surrounding their figures like the interlaced ornament around illuminated manuscripts. The broad folds of garments as seen in the Burgundian sculpture, so well mastered by Konrad Witz, are, in the whole interior, the only signs of Mary's rank. They hide from us whether she rests on cushions, on a low stool, or on the floor itself. The cushions lying upon the chests would suggest that she was using one of them.

Swiss Schoolroom, 1516

No less improvised was the posture when writing. This signboard, which Hans Holbein the Younger painted for a schoolmaster, shows a plain and simple installation (fig. 143). It differs but little from the haphazard seating in the Dutch kitchen some three decades earlier. One pupil, seated on a low stool, uses his neighbor's bench as a writing desk, while the other rests his exercise book on his knees. This is the habit of centuries, here carried on in a popular setting. On the north porch of Chartres Cathedral, Pythagoras occupies a low stool in a similar posture (fig. 138). With bowed back, he holds the narrow writing desk on his lap. In the fifteenth century, the desks of monastic painters or of secular scholars were carefully fashioned for convenience and adaptability (figs. 151, 152, 154).

In Holbein's schoolroom of 1516, with its stools and benches of varying heights, a woman, seated at a sloping lectern, is teaching a child. She now occupies a folding chair (Dante chair) as favored by the rising Renaissance.

***A King's Board: Salome Dancing before Herod. Catalan School, c.*1460**

In what posture did medieval people take their meals? The company is seated on benches with their backs to the wall (fig. 144). Here, as in the *Lit de Justice* of the French court, finely worked brocades and costly apparel set the tone. Here again we find not the slightest sign of refinement in furniture. The table consists of loose boards, which at mealtime are laid across roughly hewn trestles. As we shall see, the austerity of this furniture — which to later times would seem improvised — is not due to a technical inability to achieve comfort.

The Chair Makes Its Appearance, *c.*1490

We are nearing the time when the chair will be regarded as a standard article. A few forerunners (*c.*1490) [2] of present-day comfort have been preserved from the Palazzo Strozzi, Florence (fig. 145). In this chair the eye immediately recognizes traits of the earlier types, whose stamp it still bears: the three-legged stool, with roughly hewn peg-legs set directly into the slab, as in the stools of the Dutch kitchen or Holbein's schoolroom.

Then refinements set in. The seat becomes smooth, and a profiled molding conceals where the legs enter. The octagonal shape invites one to sit not only frontally, but diagonally, or at an angle, informally, like the people in the Dutch 'Carnival Scene.' The new style focuses in the narrow, stele-like back, topped by the carved arms of the Strozzi, in a *tondo* (circle).

It is hard to say whether this stiff, narrow board is meant as a back rest or whether it is a vestige of the Gothic backing intended as a symbol of rank. The chair's proportions reflect its lineage; the low and heavy understructure contradicts the finely elongated back shaped with early Renaissance delicacy. It is a beginning full of contradictions.

Most important of all is the fact that several uniform chairs have been preserved from the Strozzi Palace. This too suggests that around 1490 — in the

[2] Wilhelm Bode sets at *c.*1490 the date of the chair in the Figdor Collection. Cf. Wilhelm Bode, *Das Hausmoebel der Renaissance*, Berlin, 1921, p.21.

143. Swiss Schoolroom, 1516: 'Schoolmaster's Sign,' Hans Holbein the Younger. *This early sixteenth-century scene still shows the improvised mode of sitting: a boy seated on the bench rests his exercise book on his knees, while another sitting behind him on a sort of footstool, somewhat in the manner of Pythagoras at Chartres, uses the bench as a desk.* (*Courtesy Kunst Museum, Basel*)

south at any rate — the chair was losing its rare, honorific value, and is used in series.

In the sixteenth century this type is fitted with four peg-legs, instead of three, and the back rest is widened and curved. A sturdy type, it survives in Alpine peasant houses of today: one board for the back, another for the seat, and four pegs for the legs. This chair, which becomes increasingly adorned with florid carving, is primitively constructed. It points nevertheless to a changed mode of living. The table has become fixed and the seat movable. The chair is pushed up to the table, not the table to the fixed bench as before. The three-legged stools of the fifteenth century, whose legs were often turned as in Romanesque times, had been but occasional pieces. Now everyone has his chair at the table. The chair has ceased to be an honorary seat, a symbol of unusual distinction, and is placed in series around the table.

But as late as the first half of the sixteenth century, chairs are not the rule, even in the highest places. When Hans Holbein the Younger portrays Henry VIII and his privy council, in 1530, his woodcut shows the members of this exalted body as tightly packed on low-back benches as were the members of the *Lit de Justice* in 1458.

144. A King's Board, *c.*1450: 'Salome with the Head of St. John the Baptist,' Catalan School. *Clad in brocade and ermine, the king and his retinue are at table in a room with tiled floor and tapestry-hung walls. Yet they sit on benches backed to the wall. The same rudimentary comfort is observed in the primitive knives and the absence of plates. (Courtesy Metropolitan Museum, New York)*

The unpainted, primitively joined benches, tables, and chairs found in the Alps today, or among the American colonists well into the nineteenth century, represent the domestic tradition of the late Gothic carried through the ages. Such furniture was everywhere to be found at the turn of the fifteenth century, in the North as in the South. Its tradition took shape in the towns, and at the behest of burghers and patricians. It bears still the imprint of medieval austerity.

The scantness of the medieval household derived from a monastic conception of life, and from the insecurity of living conditions, which marked furniture with a nomadic stamp.

The Nomadic Furniture of the Middle Ages

Furniture numbers among the utensils most intimately bound up with man's existence. With it he lives day and night. It assists his work and his rest. It is the close witness of his life, his birth, and his death.

In French, the word *meuble* and the collective *mobilier* originally meant 'movables,' transportable goods. Non-transportable goods, 'immovables,' were *immeubles*, the term that even today designates houses and buildings. 'Movable' was not to be understood in its narrower present-day sense of articles capable of being taken from one room to another, or from one dwelling to another. These movables, it is generally agreed, were so called because they used to accompany the owner wherever he journeyed. Furniture, in the late fourteenth century, followed the master in his temporary changes of residence and followed him on his travels.[3]

[3] Henri Havard, *Dictionnaire de l'ameublement et de la décoration depuis le XIIIme siècle jusqu'à nos jours. Nouvelle édition augmentée*, Paris, 1890–94, vol. III, col. 851. 'Meubles sont appelés qu'on peut transporter d'un lieu en autre et qui suivent le corps de son seigneur et maître quand il change de résidence.' (Definition of 1380.)

←
145. The Chair Appears: Three-Legged Chair from the Palazzo Strozzi, Florence. *c.*1490. *This forerunner of the chair still shows close kinship with the stool, having three legs pegged directly into the slab, a construction still current in Alpine peasant houses today. Is the slender back a support against which to rest the body, or is it mere background, a vestige of the chair's ceremonial meaning in Gothic times?* (*Courtesy Metropolitan Museum, New York*)

↓ **146.** Peasant Chair, Valais, Switzerland. Early 19th Century. *Tradition continues the simple construction of the early individual chairs from Florence, without any change in principle through the centuries.* (*Courtesy Benedict Rast, Fribourg, Switzerland*)

By furniture — *mobilier* [4] — one meant all household movables, or 'the movable articles in a dwelling house,' to quote the *Oxford English Dictionary's* source of 1573 — silverware, jewelry, tapestries, kitchen utensils, horses.[5]

Taking along all the furniture and everything transportable, sometimes even prisoners, was a custom that did not die out with the Middle Ages. When Francis I, King of France, traveled from Paris to Nice in the south of his realm (1538), he took his household equipment with him, paying 1200 livres for the transportation of this 'furniture.' [6] Traveling with one's furniture seems to have persisted in some instances to the end of the *Ancien Régime.*

Neither did the puissant lords of earlier times take such precaution in vain. The Duc d'Orléans, arriving in Tarascon without household equipment in 1447, had to borrow furniture from the citizenry.[7] And so it goes, well into the seventeenth century. In 1649, the King's daughter slept on straw when the French court was forced to move at short notice. A bed was simply unobtainable.[8]

The castle of the high noble stood practically empty when its lord was not in residence. He would leave behind only miscellaneous fittings and whatever could not be taken away, such as the stone windowseats, the decorations of walls and ceilings, or the carefully sculpted chimney pieces.

Underlying all this was the profound insecurity of living conditions. Every class of society was menaced. Fortifications and weapons formed the chief expenditures of town budgets. The fortified towers of the noble families of Bologna, or of the Tuscans of Dante's day, show that these were fortresses within the fortress of the city. Even behind walls life was not secure. Jacob Burckhardt in his *Civilization of the Renaissance* reports impressive tales of assassination in the broad daylight of Perugia — all this toward the end of the fifteenth century as Perugino was painting his tranquil madonnas.

This profound insecurity, both social and economic, constrained merchants and the feudal lords to take their possessions with them whenever they could, for no one knew what havoc might be loosed once the gates were closed behind

[4] *Mobilier* is still, in many countries, the legal expression for everything movable, not forming a fixed part of the home.

[5] Havard, op.cit. vol. III, col. 851, after a French inventory of 1599.

So far as medieval furniture is concerned, what we are presenting here is but raw material. There is no typological history of furniture to which one might refer as, looking backwards from mechanization, we seek to establish the age, the origin, and the evolution of a type. One of the few available aids is the research of Henri Havard, 1838–1921, a scholar who has probed widely, often tackling problems on which there is no other literature. But, compiled in dictionary form, his researches cannot deal with the interrelations of types. They are, moreover, confined to French sources. Within those limits he offers a broad range of valuable material.

[6] Ibid. col. 854.

[7] Ibid. col. 853.

[8] Ibid. col. 855.

him. Thus deeply rooted in the word for furniture, *meuble*, is the idea of the movable, the transportable.

Easily transportable, the chest was the most common furniture of the Middle Ages. It formed the basic equipment and almost the main element of the medieval interior. It was the container for all movable belongings. No other medieval piece has come down to us in such numbers. Chests could at the same time be used as trunks. In them the household goods were ready packed. One was always prepared to take off.

People left only such things as were too bulky to move. Hence the creation of compact and, preferably, collapsible furniture. This transportable, collapsible furniture, as for instance the folding *X*-chairs, were used long before chairs in the modern sense. No lack of space produced these faldstools, collapsible and demountable tables, and trussing beds, but as the name indicates, the prospect of rapid folding, trussing, and loading.

The political chaos of the time is manifest in its nomadic furniture. Not only the traffic of merchants was imperiled, or the nobility whose feuds were never stilled; but whole states and their rulers were caught up in the general insecurity.

Six successive transfers of the French capital took place under the last Valois king. Charles VII, miraculously aided in his coronation by Joan of Arc, was kept ever on the move as he fled from the English in the final phase of the Hundred Years' War (1340–1453). He held temporary courts at Bourges, Poitiers, and Chinon.

The Chest as Universal Furniture

While the Romanesque churches were being raised in all their complexities of vaulting and tower construction, everyday life was still very primitive.

The mid-twelfth century might cover the Royal Portal of Chartres with figures great in force and conception, symbolizing the triumph and eternal reign of Jesus Christ. The glass paintings in the constructions of the roses and windows are unsurpassed in expression and in the intensity of their colors. Yet, at the same period, chests set up in the churches to collect money for the Crusades were mere tree trunks, roughly chopped, chiseled, and burned out. Their lids were coarse, heavy boards.

This return to the hollowed-tree container suggests how primitive was all the rest of the medieval interior. Hollowed-out tree trunks were often set on end for the storage of cereals, fruit, and other provisions. Fire-hollowed tree trunks were used for holding stores by the American colonists of the seventeenth century and even later. We can surely recognize them as descendants of the old type.

147. Romanesque Chest, Valère Castle Church, Switzerland, 12th Century. *Chests were the universal furniture of the Middle Ages. They stood in every room, sometimes against the wall, sometimes beside the bed or at its foot. Five chests, unique in their powerful cast, have been preserved in the Romanesque castle-church of Valère. They have high massive uprights, some of them chip-carved in deep arches.* (*Courtesy Schweiz. Landesmuseum, Zürich*)

Long, hollowed tree trunks still serve as drinking troughs in the Alpine valleys of Europe.

The chest formed the basic unit of the medieval interior. As a container it was used for storage in the widest sense: relics, weapons, documents, clothes, linen, spices, household ware, and whatever else was deemed worthy of preservation.

The chests that twelfth-century Popes ordered set up in the churches may be taken as representative of the normal type. The twelfth century could also fashion containers of compelling vigor and austerity. Five massive chests have been preserved in the Romanesque castle-church of Valère (near Sion, Valais, Switzerland), formerly the seat of a bishopric. Well warranting their ascription to the twelfth century [9] (figs. 147, 148), these larch and walnut chests are no belated peasant simplifications of Romanesque furniture. Through Valais, then a Burgundian dominion, passed the main road linking Italy with France and Flanders, the Great St. Bernard route. These chests, whose powerful cast makes them unique in their kind, have high, massive uprights, some of them chip-carved in deep arches. And the same arcade motif is countersunk over the entire face of the chest. For all the severity of effect, their construction

[9] Otto v. Falke and H. Schmitz, *Deutsche Moebel des Mittelalters und der Renaissance*, Stuttgart, 1924, pp.xv–xvii, reproduces all five of these chests.

148. Romanesque Chest, Valère Castle Church, Switzerland, 12th Century. *This ecclesiastical furniture was not used for seating purposes.* (*Courtesy Schweiz. Landesmuseum, Zürich*)

remains primitive: boxes of massive timbers secured by broad-headed nails.

Chests were developed in diverse shapes and sizes, and for many purposes. They were treated in a variety of ways: covered with leather, bound with iron bands or with wrought-iron scrollwork, painted, carved, inlaid with intarsia, or embellished with polychrome plaster reliefs.

Chests are the universal furniture of the Middle Ages. They stand in every room, sometimes to the wall, sometimes by the side or at the foot of the bed. Often chests of uniform size are arranged lengthwise, end to end along the walls. They are found in the North and in the South; they stand in the upper Rhenish interior, where Mary is bathing the Child (*c.*1450) (fig. 141), in the study where Polyphilo writes the letter to his beloved (1499) (fig. 142), and in the bedroom where his lady reads it. Normally chests were plain standardized containers without claim to individuality. Such easily transportable pieces were purchased as the need arose.

Well into the sixteenth century, clothes were not hung, but laid away horizontally. By the serial chests of the Middle Ages we may gauge the austerity of everyday life.

Chests arranged end to end along the walls were increasingly displaced around 1500 by the continuous bench skirting the whole circumference of the room. Albrecht Dürer's 'Jerome in His Cell' (1514) (fig. 167), where they are noted with great precision, and the Abbess's Room, Münster Nunnery, Grisons, Switzerland, built a few years earlier (1512) (fig. 166), show how rapidly continuous benches came into use.

No piece of the Italian Renaissance has reached us in such variety and number as the chest or *cassone*.[10] These are no serial articles. They are works of art, created for weddings and like occasions. Famous artists decorated *cassoni*. Florentines such as Paolo Uccello, Botticelli, Ghirlandajo, Andrea del Sarto; North Italians, such as Mantegna, Cossa, Carpaccio. The Florentine *cassoni* are especially precious for what they tell us of the private life and literary interest of the time. They are display pieces.

This medieval tradition runs to seed in the sixteenth century when sarcophagus shapes are enveloped in a pompous technique by the woodcarver's knife and treated in a way suited only to marble. Another factor hastened the end of this tradition: the growing stability of life. Increasingly stable types arose for the lay interior. They remained wed to the house, having to wander no more.

The Drawer

An element appears in the fifteenth century that is indissolubly linked with the later development of furniture, and largely takes over the containing duties of the chest: this device is the drawer. Henri Havard painstakingly attempts to lay open its origins.[11]

Our knowledge nevertheless remains fragmentary. One cannot be far mistaken in tracing the origin of the drawer to Flanders or Burgundy, centers that set the standard in the fifteenth century's growing concern with comfort.[12]

A notably early piece was preserved in the sacristy of the cathedral at Breslau[13] (fig. 149). It is a huge oaken cabinet for preserving records within the church. Well-known pieces of this kind, as that of Bayeux Cathedral, survive from an earlier period. They have rows of small doors. In the German document cup-

[10] Paul Schubrig, *Cassoni, Truhen und Truhenbilder der Ital. Renaissance*, Leipzig, 1924.

[11] Its history is a complicated one. The French word *tiroir*, according to Havard, entered the language in the seventeenth century. Prior to that time the drawer was termed *layette* or *liette*, and by 1471 we find designated, in an inventory of Hugers Castle 'une armoire a deux gichets et a une laiete, un pupitre paint a deux liettes qui se tirent.' Shortly afterwards, in 1483, mention is made of 'un petit coffre de bois plat a plusiers lietes.' Towards the end of the sixteenth century mentions of its uses become more numerous: in buffets, small tables, dressers, Havard, op.cit. vol. IV, col. 1329; vol. III, col. 287.

[12] The original meaning of the word *layette* confirms this. Havard (op.cit. vol. III, col. 290) points out that in Burgundy the word *laiete* designates 'la partie de la veine pierreuse entre la couche et le mur,' so that the original name of the drawer may have been taken from masonry.

[13] Later in the Diozesan Museum, Breslau. This cupboard bears 'an inscription in large minuscules, the capitals being reminiscent of the initials of the early printers: Anno dni mcccclv D[omin]us Joes Paschkowicz Canonicus p[rae]c[e]ntor ac m[a]g[iste]r fab[ri]c[a]e ecclie hac almaiar comparauit et constat 35 Flor. de pr[opr]iis.' Cf. also A. Lutsch, *Die Kunstdenkmäler der Stadt Breslau*, Breslau, 1886. Illustrated in Dr. H. Luchs, ed., *Schlesiens Vorzeit in Bild und Schrift*, Breslau, 1872, vol. II, p. 97. Professor E. Scheyer, Detroit, called our attention to this significant piece and kindly furnished the bibliographical indications.

149. The Drawer: German Document Cupboard or 'Almaiar,' Breslau. 1455. *In the fifteenth century there comes to the fore an element that will be indissolubly linked with later furniture: the drawer. Its development continued in the sixteenth and especially the seventeenth centuries. The record cabinet of oak, ten feet broad and six feet high, from Breslau Cathedral is a very early specimen. Rows of drawers, lettered from A to AZ, are built in behind its huge doors. Cathedral sacristies sometimes contain great record cabinets of earlier periods, but they had rows of small doors, here replaced by drawers.* (Schlesien's Vorzeit in Bild und Schrift, *Dr. H. Luchs, ed.*)

board, about 10 feet wide and 6 tall, marked with the date 1455, *drawers* lettered A–AZ lie behind two great doors. The inscription designates it as *Almaiar*, which at first seems a strange word: however, *almaiar* or *almarium* is a variant of the classical *armarium*,[14] and identical with the modern French *armoire*, all of which have the same meaning. The change 'r' to 'l' operates as a grammatical law in the passage from Middle High German to High German.

The drawer thus appears as a kind of small mobile chest, suitable for filing church documents. Whether this was its earliest form, or whether it was first adopted to store other things, such as medicinal herbs, has yet to be ascertained. It would be consonant with the origin of other differentiated types (the writing-desk, the *armoire*, the ribbed chair) if the drawer's first use was likewise ecclesiastical.

Early written sources — the first in 1471 — tell of the drawers being used in connection with the *armoire*, with the desk, and in a wooden casket 'with

[14] Du Cange, *Glossarium mediae et infimae latinitatis*, gives various Latin examples of the use of this word with the spelling 'l' instead of 'r.' Mr. F. M. Palmer, Reference Librarian, Harvard University, was kind enough to verify the sources.

several drawers.' [15] This is evidence turned up by chance. The development as a whole would suggest that the drawer first appeared in the standard furniture of the Middle Ages — the chest. We have chests from the sixteenth century whose front swung down to disclose two rows of drawers. When raised on feet, this is nothing other than the 'chest of drawers.' [16]

The drawer became an ever more important part of stable furniture: buffets, dressers, cabinets. From the seventeenth century its uses broaden and call for increasingly differentiated types until, in the late eighteenth century, the drawer becomes an inspiration to the English cabinetmakers, a vehicle for their highest virtuosity.

Gothic Joinery

The carvings of the grave, medieval church portals display, in their Biblical scenes, a perfect mastery over material and expression. The choir stall, most representative of furniture in the Gothic, is raised almost to the monumental. Consummate handicraft and sculptural vision combine to turn the bench ends, the high backs, the seat brackets, and the rows of openwork pinnacles crowning the whole, into a festival for the woodcarver's knife.

And in the waning Gothic, virtuosity of chisel and brace transforms the altar into a filigree, a seeming lacework of flexible threads. The flexibility attained by the woodcarvers' tools of the fifteenth century can be compared only to the wrought-iron grilles of the eighteenth.

Two woodworking tools are masterfully used by the Middle Ages: the woodcarver's knife and the adze.[17] These instruments are more nearly akin than one might suppose. In themselves they are rigid and unwieldy: everything depends on the hand that guides them. Skilfully used, they transmit with wonderful directness the motions guiding them over the wooden medium. That, it seems, is why the Middle Ages favored these instruments above all others. With them the medieval woodcarvers and carpenters developed their sovereign skill.

The heavy broad-bladed adze in the hands of the medieval carpenter takes on the sensitivity of a razor. Planks were frequently smoothed with the adze. The development of the timbered house, the roof skeleton of the Gothic hall without doubt bear witness to this. Here again, the craftsman pursued, rather than evaded, difficulties. This craftsmanship was not the possession of a few wealthy

[15] Havard, op.cit. vol. III, col. 287.

[16] 'The earliest chest of drawers that may be called the prototype of the commode dates from the last decade of the sixteenth century' and is of the Italian Renaissance. Cf. William M. Odom, *History of Italian Furniture*, New York, 1918, p.306.

[17] Use of the woodcarver's knife is not confined to the artisan; in the woodcuts of Dürer or Holbein it is at the service of great art.

150. Gothic Panel Construction, Lisieux. 14th Century. *In the 14th century the heavy uprights are reduced to lighter, grooved corner posts, leading finally to skeleton construction.* (*H. L. Magne*, Le Mobilier français, les sièges)

cities like Nuremberg or Augsburg; it was everywhere held in common, and is to be found even in the remotest Alpine valleys. In one valley, Davos, Grisons, Switzerland, the wooden spire (*c.*1500) rises above the church, tall and slender as an obelisk. But this apparently did not satisfy the carpenter's ambition. He twisted its ridges into an ascending spiral, which penetrates the sky like a screw.

The technique of the Gothic joiner is undeveloped. An altar of the late Gothic and a chair of the late Gothic seem the work of quite different periods; utmost refinement marks the one, clumsiness the other. The joiners for a long time formed no guild of their own. Furniture was made, almost offhandedly, one might say, by the carpenter. The reason was not lack of skill, but the attitude of the time. Concern with furniture and with comfort was foreign to medieval thought.

The saw, a basic tool of the joiner, was but sparingly used for medieval furniture. Although a more complicated tool than the adze and woodcarver's knife, the saw does not so readily convey to the wood each flexion of the hand. That, perhaps, is why the Middle Ages seem to have relied so little upon it. They were acquainted with the frame saw, inherited from the Romans and still current today. Frame saws with adjustable blades, as miniatures show, were in use by the fourteenth century. In keeping with the clear lack of interest in perfected joinery was the slow development of the sawmill, which was present for centuries before being put to wider use.[18]

Medieval furniture never frees itself from the massive wooden plank. The elements of construction were massive planks. No difference was made between the face of the chest and its uprights: 'The front face was formed ordinarily by a mighty piece of wood placed longitudinally. The uprights — styles — were made of other rough boards.' Measuring often 12 inches in width, they could easily be hewn out by adzes.[19]

When fixed tables other than the demountable trestle type appeared, in the fifteenth century, the table top rested on supports treated like boards along its entire width. If the Italian Renaissance treated these heavy boards in console manner and carved them over with exuberant ornament, it in no way altered the basic heaviness of the type. Nor was it otherwise with the bench, the chest, and the chair: They consisted of massive planks without framework.

The joinery was primitive: Boards were put roughly edge to edge and nailed. Notched grooves did not afford enough rigidity. Hence many chests were bound with iron ornamentation, while the strap hinges of the doors were much broadened and lengthened. The tall and narrow gable wardrobes [20] — the few pieces we possess — are strengthened with hinges such as these, and iron bands, for their wooden construction alone did not insure stability.

In the course of the fourteenth century, the upright boards, particularly in the chest, gradually shrink into corner posts — one step toward the wooden skeleton.[21] The boards are provided with tongues, and the uprights with grooves.

[18] In the famous sketchbook of the architect Villars de Honcourt (*c.*1245) one finds a sawmill driven by water power; the posts and supports consist of knotty branches; the whole presents a rather fantastic picture. The oldest accredited sawmill was in Augsburg in 1322. Its use seems to have been accepted with hesitation, for the next mention of a sawmill comes a hundred years later, in 1427, this time in Breslau. The *Chronique de Charlemagne* of 1460 (Musée National, Brussels) contains an illustration of siege in which the pitsaw operated by two men is seen at work. At this time wooden frame construction came into general use. These sources are illustrated in the excellent little book by Franz Maria Feldhaus, *Die Saege, Ein Rueckblick auf vier Jahrtausende*, Berlin, 1921.

[19] Fred Roe, *Ancient Church Chests and Chairs*, London, 1929, p.12.

[20] Falke and Schmitz, op.cit.

[21] The Romanesque benches and throne seats with their heavy turned posts barred any opportunity for technical development in their construction. Their technique belonged to another medium, stone.

Not until the end of the Gothic, when architecture had long been accustomed to hollow out interior space to the utmost and to make the pillars slender almost to breaking point, did the massive wooden wall begin to dissolve into a lighter framework. The fifteenth century carried the process further. Then furniture was treated as a skeleton, like the frame of a house. The massive plank walls broke down into a system of horizontal ties and vertical supports. Assembled according to carpenters' practice, their joints were carefully dovetailed. As in house construction, light, non-supporting panels were readily inserted into the frame in lieu of the wooden wall (fig. 150).

Late Gothic frame construction grew organically from the properties of wood. It allows for swelling and for shrinking. It is as vital to the development of later furniture types as is the sustained development of the cross-ribbed vault in architecture — a flight from massiveness toward refinement of form.

In detail, frame construction underwent many changes. New techniques appeared, but this late Gothic construction has remained until the present day as the method of building furniture. Not until recent decades was a new principle advanced, whose supporting element was the elastic slab of plywood or plastic.

Looking backwards, it would seem that time after time man forgets what he has once acquired. Frame construction, the drawer, and things for which the time was still to come — such as veneer or the gracefulness of Greek chairs — all these had formed part of everyday life in Antiquity. By arduous detours, the fifteenth century partially rediscovered them and used them in shaping intimate surroundings.

Movability in Gothic Furniture

Despite the crude execution and technique of medieval construction, efforts were not lacking to endow furniture with a degree of mobility.

Far from neglecting the mobility of furniture, the Middle Ages often build collapsible furniture such as faldstools, iron lecterns, or trussing beds. In the late Gothic, furniture is made mobile to assist special activities, such as reading, writing, or painting.

The simple mechanical means to these ends are the pivot and the hinge.

The Pivot

Before four-legged chairs came into use, the Middle Ages had movable chairs: collapsible seats or faldstools. These are simpler to make than the stable type, for essentially they consist of little beyond four members crossed *x*-wise, connected by a length of cloth or leather, while a pair of stretchers aid stability.

The camp stool, whose ancestry dates back to the Middle Empire of Egypt, is one of the commonest mass-production articles of today.

In the late Gothic, with its feeling for skilful wooden construction, these faldstools gained in refinement. The ribbed chairs of this period consist, as the name implies, of a series of thin ribs, crossed x-wise and pivoting around a common spindle. The ribs curve quite far outwards, much farther than is useful for the occupant's comfort: a non-adjustment to the body characteristic of the Middle Ages. Between the two rows of ribs slides a board forming the seat, a surprisingly narrow one, for it is situated near the crossing of the ribs. In Holbein's schoolroom of 1516, the woman whose proportions far exceed those of the chair (fig. 143) shows how it was used: on the narrow seat lies that panacea of comfort, the cushion. Where this type, termed 'Dante's chair,' originated, and how, we do not know.

On Roman coins there already appear camp stools with low backs, which are recognized as the ancestors of the 'Dante chair.'[22] Our earliest authenticated examples of the faldstool do not date further back than the Renaissance.[23] In nature and construction, the ribbed seats are late Gothic. They are ecclesiastical furniture, used in monasteries.

Faldstools of the x-pattern were commonly used in Antiquity. One of Sir Arthur Evans's most enchanting finds in the Palace of Knossos is the 'camp stool room,' so named from its fresco representing youths seated on faldstools with cushions.[24]

In Antiquity one sat — as do the youths of Minoan fresco — with legs over the stretchers connecting the cross-pieces.[25] This habit came from the Egyptians.

In the Middle Ages, this everyday furniture of the Ancients — a further instance — was kept for persons of high rank and unfolded only on ceremonial occasions. Such was the crimson-painted seat that the Bishop of Salzburg presented to an abbess around 1240.[26] Her chair, with its pressed-leather seat and its walrus-tusk inlay, consists of simple wooden members.

Tables of the earlier Middle Ages were also supported by x-crossed trestles.[27] From the fourteenth century we have reading desks composed of thin strips. Their x-shaped supports are of varying lengths, so that a book can be held at the angle desired, as in a music stand of today.[28]

[22] Gisela Richter, *The Oldest Furniture, A History of Greek Etruscan and Roman Furniture*, Oxford, 1926, p.126.

[23] Odom, op.cit. p.43.

[24] Evans, *The Palace of Minos at Knossos*, London, 1921–35, 4 vols., vol. IV, part II, pl. XXXI.

[25] Cf. also the *stamos*, illustrated in Richter, op.cit. fig. 112.

[26] Falke and Schmitz, op.cit.

[27] Viollet-le-Duc, *Dictionnaire raisonné du mobilier français de l'époque carlovingienne à la Renaissance*, Paris, 1855, vol. I, p.254.

[28] Havard, op.cit. vol. III, cols. 293–302.

151. Movability of Gothic Furniture: 'Boccaccio Writing,' Miniature by Jean Fouquet, 1458. *For their work the fifteenth-century humanists desired movable, pivoting, or adjustable furniture. The initial illumination of Book Four of* The Fall of Princes, *where Boccaccio announces that he still has a crowd of misfortunes to tell, shows him using a pivoting lectern of conical shape, but writing on a primitive board. (Boccaccio manuscript, Munich)*

152. Movability in Gothic Furniture: Pivoting and Adjustable Monastic Desk. *The fifteenth-century craftsman is astonishingly skilled in adjusting the writing desk with its sloping top to the positions of head and arm. The swing desk is mounted on a crank pivoting in a socket. (Macquoid and Tilling,* Dictionary of English Furniture)

Archaeologists now tend to agree that the oldest medieval folding chair, the gilded bronze armchair of the Merovingian King Dagobert, is of antique origin and formed part of the Merovingian treasure.[29] Folding chairs of metal (iron rods) are found in the Renaissance.

The fifteenth-century craftsman shows himself astonishingly adept at bringing mobility to writing and reading desks. From the first, medieval writing desks had sloping tops. They are better suited to the position of the head in reading or writing than are our horizontal-topped writing desks, whose whole construction follows English library tables of the late eighteenth century, roomy enough for the great folios of engravings then in fashion.

Medieval desks were small in size, just wide enough to hold an open book. People rested them on their knees, on a table, or mounted them on stands.[30] The desk tops gradually broaden in the late fifteenth century, and are endowed with a new mobility. The painting or writing desk developed in the cells of monks who used them diagonally. The swing desk (fig. 152) is asymmetrically mounted on a metal crank pivoting in a socket. Thus it can be moved at will. Also produced were various combinations — book rest, desk, and locker all in one.

The secular scholars of the late fifteenth century were no less interested in convenient instruments for study. We are in the age of Humanism, with its growing interest in the Bible, the ancient authors, and comparison of texts. Hence, revolving reading desks were developed, with polygonal or conic planes.

[29] Emile Molinier, *Les Meubles du Moyen Age et de la Renaissance*, Paris, 1897, p.4.

[30] The Middle Ages did not pedantically follow these rules. Boccaccio in the Munich miniature of 1458 is writing on a primitive bench (fig. 151), and Jerome in Carpaccio's painting of 1505 writes on a narrow table (fig. 158). Yet the strongly inclined plane is the rule. In Holbein's schoolmaster's sign (fig. 143) the steepness of the desk is more striking because it surmounts a massive body.

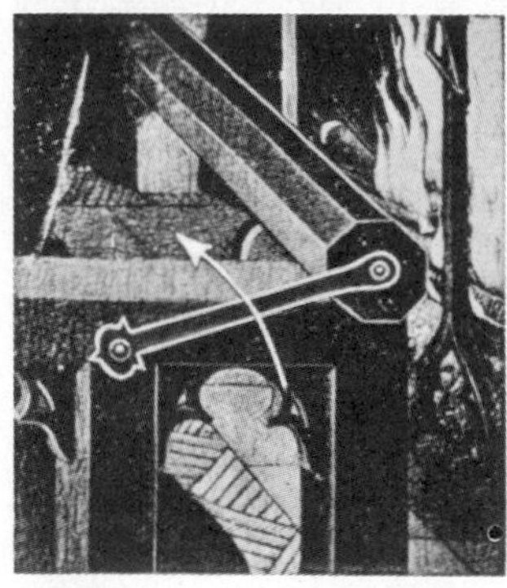

153a. Movability in Gothic Furniture: Gothic Swing-Back Bench, Detail of Werl Altar. 1438. *A remote forerunner of the American railway seat (fig. 271), where the swing back allows the passenger to face forward at all times. (Prado, Madrid; photo courtesy Fogg Museum)*

→

153b. Gothic Swing-Back Bench, St. Barbara Panel of Werl Altar, Master of Flemalle. 1438. *Saint Barbara is seated near the fireplace on a Gothic swing-back bench. The wooden bar serves as a backrest and is mobile, so that the user may turn her back to the fire or face it as she pleases. (Prado, Madrid; photo courtesy Fogg Museum)*

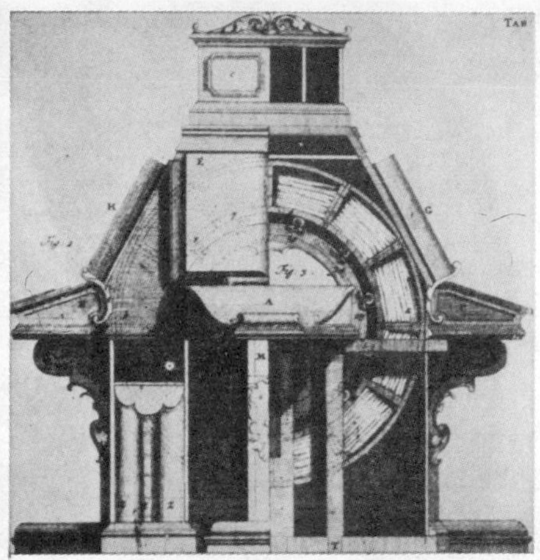

154. Reading-Desk Revolving on a Spiral Column. *c.*1485. *The height of the 'wheel desk' for reading is adjusted by means of a thick wooden screw around which it revolves.* (*Boccaccio manuscript, Munich. From Macquoid,* Dictionary of English Furniture)

155. Merchant's Combined Desk and Rotary File, Jacob Schuebler. 1730. *This polygonal desk for the use of merchants provided storage space for account books and the correspondence of an entire year.* The files are arranged around a wheel within the desk. (*Schuebler,* Nuetzliche Vorstellung, *Nürnberg,* 1730)

The stand would revolve at a touch of the reader's hand. An early example (1458) of the conical reading desk, with books lying upon it, stands by Boccaccio as he writes. The revolving bookstand of the American patent-furniture movement follows the same principle as Boccaccio's (fig. 151).

Reading desks around which several people could work at once (fig. 154) are found in the late fifteenth-century monastery and university libraries. Together the desks form an octagon, pierced by a massive wooden screw, which carries the entire desk and makes possible various heights, from sitting to standing. This desk, revolving on an axis, was called the wheel desk.[31] Occasionally flap seats were attached.

Fantasy worked further in this direction. In the sixteenth century, Agostino Ramelli, the Italian engineer who served the King of France and was famous for his hydraulic machinery,[32] devised 'a fine and artificious machine which is most useful and convenient to any person who takes delight in study. A man

[31] Percy Macquoid and Ralph Edwards, *Dictionary of English Furniture from the Middle Ages to the Late Georgian Period,* 3 vols. London, 1924–7, vol. II, p.209. fig. 1.

[32] Cf. fig. 43 in our chapter on the Assembly Line.

may read a great many books without moving from one place.'[33] (fig. 156). This is a true wheel. On its tilted planes, like those of a water wheel, the books were so placed that any desired volume might be carried to eye level. Around 1730 Jacob Schuebler designed an ambitious piece, a combination counting-table[34] for merchants, to house account books and the correspondence of a whole year besides. The single files were arranged around a wheel within the desk (fig. 155). Schuebler's idea of a rotating file for rapid reference reappears today in a wheel of steel tubes 'housing up to 15,000 reference cards within the convenient reach of the operator (fig. 157) while saving 40% operator personnel.'[35] And the production-planning department of an aviation plant has built, on an experimental basis, octagonal 'doughnut desks,' where the clerk sits in the central opening. The files radiate horizontally from the center. 'It has jumped clerical efficiency 850%.'[36]

The demand for adjustable and combinable furniture also makes itself felt in the late Gothic household. The swing-back bench has a movable back rest. It stood before the hearth, as in the Werl altar by the Master of Flémalle (1438) (fig. 153), and allowed the sitter either to face the fire or warm his back, at will.

---

[33] Ramelli, *Le diverse artificiose machine del Capitano Agostino Ramelli Dal Ponte della Tresia, Ingenere del Re di Francia*, Paris, 1588, p.317, plate CLXXXVIII.

[34] Schuebler, *Nuetzliche Vorstellung, wie man auf eine ueberaus vorteilhafte Weise Bequeme Repositoria, Compendiose Contoir und neu faconierte Medaillenschraenke ordinieren kann*, Nürnberg, 1730.

[35] *Time Magazine*, 9 Oct. 1944, advertisement.

[36] Ibid. 3 July 1944, p.76.

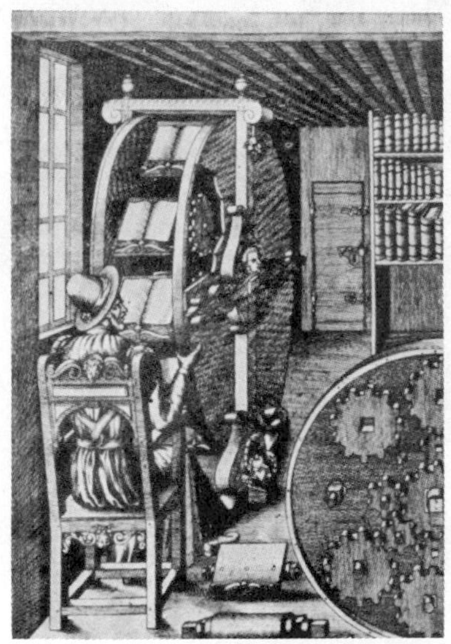

157. Rotary File, United States. 1944. *Schuebler's idea of a rotating file for rapid reference reappears in the office today as a tubular steel wheel housing up to fifteen thousand reference cards. (Courtesy Diebold Inc., Toledo, Ohio)*

156. Rotary Reading Desk, Agostino Ramelli. 1588. *Late Renaissance interest in mechanical devices produced a movable reading desk on the analogy of the water wheel. On its inclined planes the books were so placed that any desired volume would be conveyed to eye level by rotating the wheel.* (*Ramelli,* Le diverse artificiose machine, *Paris,* 1588)

159. CARPACCIO: 'St. Jerome in His Study.' Detail. The 'Revolving Chair.' c.1505. *Is this chair fixed or mobile? Since no revolving chair from the turn of the fifteenth century has come down to us, the question is not without interest. The legs probably contract to take the pivot on which the seat rotates. The two rows of bossed nails are hard to explain if the chair is not in two parts: the lower section with its stationary row of bossed nails, and the upper row revolving. In form this armchair is almost a precursor of the eighteenth-century gondola type.* (*Photo Alinari*)

←
158. CARPACCIO: 'St. Jerome in His Study.' Scuola Degli Schiavoni, Venice. *c.*1505. *Saint Jerome is shown as a high ecclesiastic official working in the worldly atmosphere of his oratory. The table at which he is writing rests on a tripod and folds to the wall. It is raised on a low podium, as was the table in Jean Fouquet's miniature of Boccaccio writing. In the background a comfortable chair and the praying desk are likewise raised on low platforms.* (*Photo Alinari*)

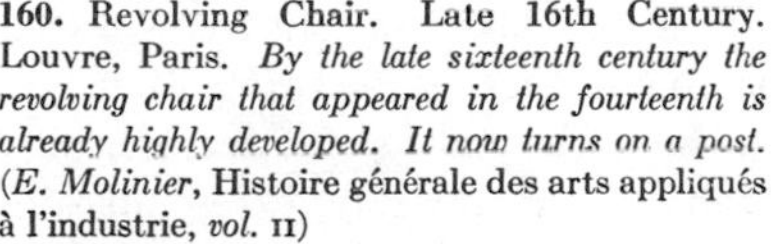

160. Revolving Chair. Late 16th Century. Louvre, Paris. *By the late sixteenth century the revolving chair that appeared in the fourteenth is already highly developed. It now turns on a post.* (*E. Molinier*, Histoire générale des arts appliqués à l'industrie, *vol.* II)

161. THOMAS JEFFERSON: First American Revolving Chair. *c.*1770. *With the late eighteenth-century's predilection for things mechanically movable, attention again turns to the revolving chair. Jefferson's chair is constructed much like that in Carpaccio's interior, its seat revolving on a circular base.* (*Courtesy P. B. Wallace, Philadelphia Philosophical Society*)

To this category also belongs the bench table (Tischbank, Pennsylvania Dutch *Dischbank*), a combination piece consisting of a settle whose high back swings around two pivots in the armrests. Lowered to the horizontal, the back becomes a table top, so that this chest furniture may form both a settle and, when necessary, a table. Doubtless late Gothic in type, our earliest examples date from the sixteenth century (fig. 259).

Another piece turning about an axis has a late-medieval origin: the revolving chair. Havard notes that the revolving chair with freely swiveling seat is mentioned toward the end of the fourteenth century, in an inventory of 1391.[37] We do not know what was the appearance of these early chairs; but like their fifteenth- and sixteenth-century successors, they were doubtless for honorific purposes.[38] Here, again, furniture appears in movable form before its modern, stable form prevails.

In the sixteenth century, the revolving chair appears largely developed, nearing in form the swivel office chair of the nineteenth. A late sixteenth-century revolving chair in the Louvre turns on a single post ending in three sprawls (fig. 160).[39]

Perhaps the chair shown by Carpaccio, behind the writing St. Jerome, may be taken as an early form of the revolving chair.[40] At any rate, it resembles in construction the most famous one of the period: the richly decorated cast-iron throne seat of later sixteenth-century Augsburg craftsmanship.

The late eighteenth century, with its predilection for things mechanically movable, brings a new interest to the revolving chair. Various elegant models appeared in the France of Louis XVI. In America, around 1776, Thomas Jefferson — this now seems certain [41] — had a revolving chair made. It is a writing chair (fig. 161), a Windsor type of colonial simplicity. As we suppose in the chair shown by Carpaccio, its seat rotates on a circular base.

Also belonging to the category of mobile furniture are the bed and cradle on rockers, appearing in the fifteenth century.[42] The early rocking chair, known as the 'nursing chair' in Lancashire, England, *c.*1750, further developed in America [43] during the late eighteenth century; the combined rocking chair and

[37] Havard, op.cit. vol. IV, col. 1403.

[38] 'Deux grandes chaises tournantes peintes et dorées' were made in 1484. Ibid.

[39] Molinier, op.cit. vol. II, p.170. St. Jerome in his study, Scuola degli Sciavoni, Venice.

[40] Carpaccio's biographer Molmenti does not describe it as a revolving chair. Cf. Pompeo Molmenti, *The Life and Works of Vittorio Carpaccio*, London, 1907, p.132.

[41] Fiske Kimball, 'Thomas Jefferson's Windsor Chair,' *Pennsylvania Museum Bulletin*, Philadelphia, 1925, vol. XXI, pp.58–60.

[42] Cf. the Altar of St. Stephan, Barcelona, Palacio Nacional de Monjuic. Illustr. in Grace Hardendorf Burr, *Hispanic Furniture*, New York, 1941, fig. 6.

[43] Cf. Julia W. Torrey, 'Some Early Variants of the Windsor Chair,' *Antiques*, vol. II, Sept. 1922, pp.106–10, figs. 9 and 10. We owe this and the following references to Miss B. Farwell, Dept. of Adult Education, Metropolitan Museum, New York.

cradle found in America c.1830;[44] the office chair of the 1850's — all are descendants of the late Gothic cradle.

The Hinge

Hinges are met with here and there, used in various ways, before the fourteenth century. The miserere seats of the choir stall turn up like the 'opera seats' that appeared in France around 1850. Choir stalls are actually seats of honor arrayed side by side for a privileged class, the clergy, in a privileged place, the choir. Their seats turn upon pin hinges so that the monk or ecclesiastic may kneel in performance of the holy office.

Furniture was designed to leave the room as unencumbered as possible. Carpaccio's St. Jerome (1505) writes at a table that will fold to the wall like an ironing board. It is but a step from this collapsible piece to the drop-leaf table, which has, besides the fixed top, movable sections that swing downwards. From the sixteenth century, we possess pieces already fashioned in rustic roughness, such as the drop-leaf table in the Folkwang Museum, Hagen[45] (fig. 163), whose hinged side leaves are sustained on pivoting supports.

The eighteenth century favored drop-leaf tables as it did the revolving chair. It further elaborated them (gate-leg table) and built them in ever-increasing sizes. But the late eighteenth century was especially drawn to more efficient methods of construction.

In America, as perhaps in Europe, rooms were divided by mobile wooden partitions hinged to the ceiling. The trace of these lowerable screens has been lost in Europe, but we may discover them in Connecticut, where stone houses of the first half of the seventeenth century had plank screens that were raised to the ceiling in summer and let down in winter to concentrate the warmth around the fireplace.

The Demountable Table

Medieval ways live on in our habits of speech. We 'turn the tables,' 'set the table,' 'clear the hall,' 'turn the table up.' To the Middle Ages, large tables standing permanently in the room were a thing unknown. Poems and inventories alike speak not of the table pure and simple, but of the board and trestle.[46] This usage persisted for a time even in the sixteenth century, when the four-legged frame table was still spoken of as a 'board and frame.' The usual Gothic table,

---

[44] Illustrated (fig. 4) in Esther Frazer, 'Painted Furniture in America,' part III, 1835–45, *Antiques*, New York, vol. VII, 1925.

[45] A. G. Meyer, *Geschichte der Moebelformen*, Leipzig, 1902–11, Serie IV, Tafel 2.

[46] Havard, op.cit., vol. IV, col. 1134–5.

also known from its monastic origin as the 'refectory table,' was long and narrow, the natural shape of the plank. Most often it was set up for the meal and taken down when the meal was over. The stone or wooden benches skirting the walls were fixed, while the table was mobile and drawn up to them. The Renaissance transformed these trestle tables into heavy display pieces of wood or marble, with richly treated supports, thus monumentalizing the simple, medieval type.

During the fifteenth century, the table, approaching a squarer form, tended to become permanently united with its supports. The old characteristic of demountability persisted in the new types — small tables on a single leg, which are assumed to have been collapsible.[47] Both the drop-leaf tables, already mentioned, and the extension tables, appearing in the sixteenth century, follow in the tradition of the movable type.

Demountability in tables and the collapsibility of the smaller type had their reason in medieval furniture's nomadic life. 'At a time when furniture followed its lord and master in all his peregrinations, it was only natural to make it as uncumbersome as possible.'[48]

The demountability of the table, we believe, has a further cause: the wish for free and unencumbered space. Large dining tables in the middle of the room were avoided so long as the need was felt to move within intact spatial surroundings.

The seventeenth century, especially in the north, was fond of heavy forms. In southern Germany and Switzerland, the great *armoires*, with their heavy profiles, are preserved in countless eighteenth-century examples. In the English mansion, there appeared long and ponderous tables, which transformed the medieval type into a stable and monumental one. They have heavy underframing and bulbous legs, as if to confirm that after so much turmoil a time of stable economy is coming in. The heavy *armoires* occupied not living chambers, however, but the vaulted passages of the burgher house, and the oaken tables of the English nobility were in scale with the spacious halls.

In the new palaces of eighteenth-century monarchs, one looks in vain for tables to seat all those who partook of the banquets. When needed, tables were set up for the feast and moved (as in the Middle Ages) at the end of the meal.

The term 'dining table,' Havard says, was unknown in France before the

---

[47] 'Tables resting on one foot with shaped ends suggested that they may have been collapsible.' Macquoid and Edwards, op.cit. vol. III.

[48] Havard, op.cit. vol. IV, col. 1130.

end of the eighteenth century. 'That variety of furniture formerly called "tables à l'anglaise" were generally of mahogany, of rounded shape, but provided with two drop leaves' so that they could be easily placed to the wall.[49]

Indeed, the development of large dining tables had begun in England about a century earlier, leading to manifold solutions.[50] In size these 'English tables' were midway between a dining table and the long trestle tables of the Middle Ages.

In keeping with the capricious and discriminating society of the eighteenth century, fancy freely plays with new forms and novel combinations. Now a square table becomes circular or oval, now a circular one grows into a square, or an oval. 'Horseshoe tables, seven feet long, using taper legs for the extension' also came into fashion.[51]

No less varied are the mechanisms for these transformations. The basic late-medieval transition types, such as the drop-leaf and the draw-leaf tables, are amplified and technically elaborated. Around 1800 a new type of extension was patented: 'detachable leaves carried on hinged diamond-shaped underframing.'[52] This type directly points toward the American patent-furniture movement in the first half of the nineteenth century (fig. 165).

Besides these drop-leaf and draw-leaf types, the medieval trestle table, long and narrow, lives on, but now is made in sections: an aligned series of small square tables, each resting on a turned column.[53]

Even the late eighteenth century prefers not to leave its tables permanently set up in the room. In Washington's larger dining room in Philadelphia, where the formal dinners were held, there was set up (1790) 'the sectional dining table on which the plateaus would be placed. But this room was also used for the Tuesday levees and for the reception of special delegations. Then the table would be separated into its units and placed against the walls.'[54]

Creation of Intimate Surroundings: Differentiation into Types

As the wanderings of furniture begin slowly to subside, the interior of the house grows more populated. New types arise, made for permanence and stability. Differentiation sets in.

For the Middle Ages, every piece of furniture was either a receptacle or an object outside the sphere of everyday life: a throne or a choir stall. Furniture,

[49] Ibid. vol. IV, col. 1125.

[50] Macquoid and Edwards, op.cit. 'Table, dining table, trestle table.'

[51] Cf. *The Cabinet Maker's London Book of Prices*, 1788, Pl. XIX, fig. 2.

[52] British Patent, no. 2396, 1 May 1800, Richard Gillow.

[53] Macquoid and Edwards, op.cit. vol. III, p.212.

[54] Stephen Decatur, 'George Washington and His Presidential Furniture,' *American Collector*, Feb. 1941, vol. X.

162. Italian Secretary Table. Second Quarter 16th Century. *When the demountable trestle table of the Middle Ages gave way to the fixed type, it was natural to use the space available within as a receptacle. This led to the hutch-table and the insertion of numerous doors and drawers. The Renaissance monumentalized the simple medieval type.* (*By courtesy of the Detroit Institute of Fine Arts*)

in the fifteenth century at least, was not given over solely to writing, sleeping, or dining; it served at the same time as a container. Hence the chest-bench or settle, the box-chair, and the hutch-table. These types started from the chest: the universal furniture and universal receptacle of the Middle Ages.

The objection that the chest cramps the legs would be completely foreign to the Middle Ages; or that the backpiece ill-supports the spine. The high backpieces, which came in with frame construction, were solemnly formal in tone; they laid no claim to functional relation with the lower part (fig. 150). Often the backpiece spreads into a canopy and forms a unit with the seat standing on a low plinth — features clearly carried over from the choir stall.

163. German Drop-Leaf Table, 16th Century. *As soon as the table becomes fixed and non-demountable, it is made into a receptacle, often with movable flaps.* (*Folkwang Museum, Hagen i.W. From A. G. Meyer*, Geschichte der Moebelformen)

164. Secretary, from the Augustinian Monastery, Basel. *c.*1500. Now in Basel Historical Museum. *A convertible piece that becomes a writing desk with small drawers when the top is opened. A lid in the writing top gives access to storage space in a way reminiscent of the chest. This is a forerunner of the fall-front secretaries of sixteenth-century Italy.* (*Courtesy Basel Historical Museum*)

The coffer-bench consists of a regular chest with a backpiece added. It was later reduced to the box-chair, an uncommon piece soon displaced by the chair.

The dresser or court cupboard is a chest raised upon styles. It makes its appearance early in the fifteenth century as a small square receptacle on slender legs — a companion piece, as it were, to the box-chair. It stood free within the room. Later in the fifteenth century it broadened into the dresser or sideboard with high backpiece.

Even the table unexpectedly turned into a receptacle. Often a whole array of caskets and drawers might be housed beneath it, the receptacle narrowing somewhat toward the base, since the sitter's feet could not be altogether ignored.

Patent Secured April 11, 1846.

PATENT CROSS-LEVER EXTENSION TABLES.

Lever of Wrought Iron,

Far surpassing every other invention of the kind now extant.—They can be extended from TEN to FIFTY FEET, and when closed, the leaves are all contained inside—an important feature. They are made to all

sizes & shapes, and are admirably adapted for Steam and Packet Ships, Steam boats, Hotels, Boarding Houses & large Private Families—forming when closed a complete Centre Table.

165. American Extension Table. 1846.
(*Collection Bella C. Landauer, New-York Historical Society*)

These fifteenth-century tables, a transition between the demountable trestle table and the four-legged, framed table of today, formed the starting point for this enclosure. They are seen in the studies of Polyphilo and St. Jerome, where the massive top is permanently fixed at each end to plank supports. Whether they are supported by x-crossed boards, recalling their direct ancestor, the trestle, or by carved slabs matters little.

The habit of utilizing the space within furniture must still have run strong in the early sixteenth century. The hutch-table was widespread in the North as in the South.[55] These were not used as dining tables, but as work tables, and the more elaborate ones (such as the Italian hutch-table of *c.*1530) (fig. 162), termed with good reason a 'secretary,'[56] may well have stood in some banker's or money-changer's office. In a writing desk from the Augustinian monastery, Basel (fig. 164), the table top is hinged and serves as a lid to the receptacle. It is a forerunner of the secretary with vertical fall front of sixteenth-century Italy.

Chairs in Romanesque Time

Chairs and benches undoubtedly existed in Romanesque time.[57] They were built of heavy lathe-turned posts, resembling in proportion the low-turned pillars of early Romanesque crypts and naves, connected by thinner turned members. Ecclesiastical pieces, they had nothing in common with the secular furniture of the fifteenth and sixteenth centuries. The primitive plugging of round into round was constructively inflexible and impossible of further development; it cannot be compared in flexibility to fifteenth-century frame construction.

Some have sought to recognize Nordic (Norwegian and Swedish) chairs and benches as the domestic types used in the French or German household during the eleventh or twelfth centuries.[58] Yet this Nordic furniture arose in recent centuries, when the use of chairs had become commonplace. At best it may have drawn upon sacral furniture for construction and ornament. It is unlikely that the primitive Romanesque interior should have possessed types that were not usual even in the Gothic.

[55] These hutch-tables are particularly common in Southern Germany, but seem also to have existed in sixteenth-century England. 'A table with a cupboard in it' is mentioned in the inventory of Henry VIII. Cf. Macquoid and Tipping, op.cit. vol. III, p.227. A German table is illustrated in A. G. Meyer, *Geschichte der Moebelformen*, Serie IV, Tafel q, fig. 10.

[56] Percy Rathbone, 'An Early Italian Writing Table,' *Bulletin of the Detroit Institute of Arts*, vol. XX, no. 6 (March 1941), pp.63–4.

[57] The surviving *Kirchenbank*, as it is called in the literature (ill. in Falke, op.cit.), is more probably an example of the Romanesque choir stall.

[58] Molinier, op.cit. p.8.

Charlemagne was found seated on a Roman throne of marble when the emperor's tomb was opened in Aachen Cathedral. And how strikingly primitive, even four centuries later, is the bishop's throne at Goslar,[59] with its seat of thick stone slabs: a coffer of stone that even the delicate woven work of its bronze superstructure cannot alleviate. The problem of differentiated furniture seems to have been quite foreign to the Romanesque centuries.[60]

Flanders and the Creation of Intimate Surroundings

The most favorable ground for the rise of stable furniture was in Flanders. Under Burgundian rule, Flanders had prudently stood aloof from the hundred-year feud between England and France, and had adopted a policy of good will toward the English. In industry and prosperity Flanders was a half-century ahead of any of her neighbors. Here the finest woolens were woven. From here came the Arras tapestry shot with gold or silver thread, the pride of the Dukes of Burgundy, who preserved them in special warehouses. The pictorial tapestry was loosely hung in the apartments of the great lords, and traveled as ducal presents to the courts of the Pope and of Europe. No later tapestry has equaled its power, its sureness of the use of material. The union of fertile Burgundy with industrial Brabant and Flanders lasted over a century and ended with the fall of Burgundy. The collapse of this productive state — a buffer between hostile France and Germany — proved nefarious for the later history of the Continent. But in the hundred years during which Flanders stood joined to Burgundy, a prolific culture sprang up, hothouse-like, around the two capitals, Dijon and Brussels: the softly draped Burgundian sculpture of the fifteenth century; the art of painting at the court of Dijon; and lastly, inventions closely linked to artistic expression — the oil painting of the brothers van Eyck; and the new luxury furniture that for the first time made use of late Gothic frame construction to create a secular comfort.

The earliest ornamental piece of the secular household, the dresser, it has been pointed out, first appears in one of the most beautiful of miniatures, the

---

[59] Ill. in Falke and Schmitz, op.cit.

[60] There is much uncertainty about the age of the low three-pegged stool. At any rate it must have been well suited to the uneven Romanesque floors. The type survives to this day as the milking stool. The three-peg stool is seen in miniatures and in fifteenth-century woodcuts before the four-legged chair was revived. In sixteenth-century England it takes the shape of a three-legged chair formed of three round posts, one of which is extended to form the back. It was also made into an armchair. A three-legged armchair from Savoy, with nearly semicircular seat, is illustrated in Falke and Schmitz, op.cit. fig. 140b.

'Heures de Turin,' which Hubert van Eyck painted for the brother of the Duke of Burgundy in 1416.[61]

A slender dresser on high legs stands amid this lying-in room where John is born. Its receptacle is small and seems less important than the advancing top shelf and the plinth close to the floor, and the bulging pewter and copper vessels of the late Gothic household. As the miniatures show, such dressers were found, like the chest, in the study and other rooms.

Far more common is the dresser backed to the wall and built around the chest of normal size. Chests had been raised on feet since Romanesque time. Now the broad-faced planks become slender styles; and the heavy lid, smaller doors.[62] The furniture is adorned in every way: back and canopy are added, and a web of enrichment and reliefs spreads over the whole piece. At the court of Burgundy, a superstructure of several shelves for the display of gold and crystal ware was usual. The number of these shelves increased with the rank of the owner. Only the Duke could claim to possess six shelves — for that 'one had to be a prince sovereign.'[63]

Ornamental pieces usually owe their form to a utilitarian past. (Thus the console tables beneath the tall eighteenth-century mirrors derive from the volute-supported wall desks upon which monks wrote in the sixteenth.) The dresser, a piece on which food was set out and displayed before serving, passed from the kitchen to the living room. It thus differs from the earlier types described, whose origin was monastic.

In the thirteenth century the kitchen of the burgher house became detached from the living room.[64] Cooking and living thus tended to become separated. How far the separate kitchen in the burgher house was linked to the new founding of cities lies open to enquiry. In the sixteenth century, too, the kitchen remained the room in which the burgher and, it is stated, the petty nobleman took his meals.[65]

---

[61] Ill., Falke and Schmitz, op.cit. p.xxvii, text p.xxxii. Havard (op.cit. vol. II, col. 199) reports in the Comptes des Ducs de Bourgogne for 1399 a *Drechoir fermant à clef*. The dresser may thus have been introduced toward the end of the fourteenth century. Even the sixteenth century does not accurately distinguish between the buffet, dresser, and cupboard.

[62] Often one chest was laid upon another with doors opening frontwards; but this trend is more in the direction of the wardrobe, which long preserved its division into two parts. For even the seventeenth century did not break with the custom of laying clothes horizontally away, as in the chest.

[63] Havard, op.cit. vol. II, col. 199.

[64] The great vaulted palace kitchens (Mont Saint Michel or the castle of Cintra in Portugal) are not considered here, for they were designed for large companies, which made detachment or separate housing unavoidable.

[65] Molinier, op.cit. p.25.

A surface for the preparation of food was needed in the kitchen. At first a table top was placed on trestles, like all other tables, *una mensa cum trecellis.* Horizontal boards above provided a ready means of storing kitchen ware. These were the elements from which the dresser developed into the display furniture of the fifteenth century, whose number of shelves was an index of social rank.

Research has centered largely around the history of styles, leaving much uncertainty as to where and how the types arose that now make up our intimate surroundings. Lacking is a typological history that would turn to account the facts piled up in the sixty years since Henri Havard compiled his *Dictionary.* What we need is not a dictionary of furniture, but a comparative history of types, which might order and evaluate the contributions of the various lands. In such a history, the place of Flanders would surely prove outstanding.

By creating these various types, the chair, the bench, the desk, and the dresser, and by giving the table its stable form, the fifteenth century laid down the beginnings of secular comfort.

These types may seem primitive beside the refinement of eighteenth-century artisanship, although this is far from true of their artistic expression. Neither can their artistic or their technical handling yield the full secret of their power. For they were not conceived as isolated pieces. They grew as integral parts of the late Gothic room, in which they were rooted as a plant is rooted in the soil.

Medieval Comfort, the Comfort of Space

From today's point of view the Middle Ages had no comfort at all.

The furniture was crude, the heating poor. Doubtless the sight of wood blazing in great piles will ever be an appealing one. The Middle Ages knew well how the hearth might be woven into domestic life and the fireside given a meaning far beyond its bare usefulness. But what a relapse into the primitive after the villas, with their evenly heated floors and walls, found wherever the Romans settled beyond the Alps!

It was cold in the medieval house. Time and again the miniatures show a small, round work table or dining table or bench drawn up close to the open flame, or, as it may be, a swing-back bench that allowed one alternately to face the fire and turn one's back to it (fig. 153).

The same relapse into the primitive runs through the whole medieval interior.

Was there no comfort at all? Rooms meagerly equipped with a series of chests, of rough-hewn trestle tables and clumsily joined bedsteads — could this be called comfort?

From the early Middle Ages until well into the thirteenth century, the monks were the agents and creators of cultural life. The nobles hunted and warred in the age of chivalry. From their warring and their loving, the great medieval epics arose. But in no broader sense were they the shapers of cultural life. In the Middle Ages, one has ever to fall back upon anonymous monasticism, which carried the whole burden of culture. Monasteries of various orders had become highly complex organisms during the early Middle Ages. Monasteries were the highest agents of civilization, the foci of social activity, of contact with other lands, the source of all education and learning, which preserved the ancient authors and wrote in Latin the chronicles of their own time. Their vast buildings afforded at once hostels for wayfarers, almshouses for the poor, hospitals for the sick. Over their abbey lands, which proved so attractive to the nobles of the Reformation, they ruled as powerful landowners and large-scale agrarians. In an age of lasting strife the monasteries alone offered a place of relative safety and stability.

In this milieu, medieval furniture took shape. Within monastic walls were developed the faldstools of bronze or wood and other ecclesiastical thrones of antique inheritance, the choir stalls, the lectern of chapel and sacristy, the writing desks of the cells, and the long, narrow trestle tables of the refectories. Piece after piece was later taken over by the secular household.

Even the washstands built into niches or corner cupboards reflect a monastic pattern in their narrow metal reservoir above a cock and hand basin. First having a conical reservoir, as in Dürer's 'Life of the Virgin,' and later built into the wash cupboard of tall Gothic proportions, they were finally fused into the dresser.

The monastic lavatoria of the thirteenth century (as for instance at St. Denis) were vaulted rooms near the refectory. Water usually flowed in thin streams from a central font, 'usually circular in shape and pierced with several openings.' [66] Here the monks carried out their prescribed light ablutions.

Of course there were always jugs for pouring water over the master's hands after meals. Some wooden or iron washstands of southern France had basins mounted on a metal or wooden pedestal.[67] But the lavatorium with reservoir tap and basin is quite different from these. It seems rather a section of the monumental lavatoria of the monks simplified and scaled to burgher life.

[66] Havard, op.cit. vol. II, col. 281.

[67] Ibid. vol. II, col. 797.

The monks were vowed to ascetic conduct and ascetic living. They little heeded such questions as how the body might best relax in a chair. No concern, this, for lives based on mortification of the flesh. Throughout its time, the medieval interior bore the mark of its austere origins.

In contrast to the primitive household was the raiment of its owners (fig. 144). The growing prosperity of the fourteenth century brought silk and brocades, and banquets lasting days, often consisting of six courses, each course a meal in itself.[68] Yet the ladies, with their costly damassé robes and long ermine-trimmed sleeves, ate at rough trestle tables, crowded on backless benches.

Not until the fifteenth century, and further in the sixteenth, did the bourgeoisie draw the consequences of their new power and bring to the interior and its furnishings a more easy or, if one will, a more secular note. Now benches with back rests are seen in the rooms, and sideboards for setting out foods, and the late Gothic dressers on their slender square uprights.

And yet there was a medieval comfort. But it must be sought in another dimension, for it cannot be measured on the material scale. The satisfaction and delight that were medieval comfort have their source in the configuration of space. Comfort is the atmosphere with which man surrounds himself and in which he lives. Like the medieval Kingdom of God, it is something that eludes the grasp of hands. Medieval comfort is the comfort of space.

A medieval room seems finished even when it contains no furniture. It is never bare. Whether a cathedral, a refectory, or a burgher chamber, it lives in its proportions, its materials, its form. This sense for the dignity of space did not end with the Middle Ages. It lasted until nineteenth-century industrialism blurred the feelings. Yet no later age so emphatically renounced bodily comfort. The ascetic ways of monasticism invisibly shaped the period to its own image.

One does not live for the day alone. Death is not regarded as an inescapable calamity; Death is bound up with life as man's steady companion. This needs no literary proof. The great cathedrals raised by the toil of surprisingly small communities show well enough how death, seen as the life beyond, was ever present in the world of the living. And the Dance of Death sequences repeat

---

[68] Several fourteenth-century menus have been preserved. Each course included the most diverse dishes and ended with a sweetmeat. These menus are from Flanders, the most productive region of Europe. Nevertheless their range is astonishingly varied: game and poultry of all kinds, fish, wine of every vintage, exotic desserts, pomegranates, almonds roasted in honey. (J. Henry Hachez, *La Cuisine à travers l'histoire*, Brussels, 1900, pp.138–46.)

166. The Abbess's Room. Muenster Convent, Grisons, Switzerland. 1512. *(Courtesy the Swiss National Museum)*

this burden: 'Death Dances through all Ranks and Callings of Men' as Holbein the Younger entitled his series toward the end of the epoch.

This otherworldly outlook had a deep influence on the shaping of medieval comfort. Quite other values come to the fore with the more material outlook of later time.

As against the insecurity of life without, there should be peace in man's intimate surroundings. And this is what one breathes in medieval chambers, quietude and contemplation. It is remarkable how often men were portrayed writing or painting, withdrawn into the silence of their study in the act of projecting their inner thought. Writing and painting meant not the common acts they have become today, but were a concentration upon the sublime. The early Middle Ages depict the evangelists with their parchment rolls, and espe-

167. ALBRECHT DUERER: 'St. Jerome in His Study,' Engraving. 1514.

cially St. Luke painting. Later, in the fifteenth century, the monks are shown in their cells. And toward the end of that century, in one of the most beautiful woodcut books, the secular writer appears: Polyphilo writing to his lady-love (fig. 142). Soon afterwards (1514) Albrecht Dürer portrays his St. Jerome in a burgher setting (fig. 167), in a room almost luxurious for the time. Soft cushions line the continuous windowseat and much household ware hangs on the flat wall in the background, near the broad hat of the Saint. But the intensity of the room is dominant: the oneness of rafters, ceiling, stone pillars, lattice windows, and the paneled wall in the background. The Saint, bending over his little desk as he renders the Biblical text into Latin, is, in Heinrich Woelfflin's words,[69] 'the learned contemplative man who must have a closed room and silence around

[69] Heinrich Woelfflin, *Die Kunst Albrecht Duerers*, München, 1905, p.196.

him.' Jerome's figure embodies in human form the seclusion of this atmosphere: quietude and contemplation. These are the fading echoes of the late Gothic, yet never was the warm security of the medieval chamber more powerfully conveyed. To the monastic atmosphere of concentration and quiet, the bourgeoisie, when it formed its own culture in the fifteenth century, added that of intimacy.

Jerome's room was perhaps richer than most. It nevertheless represents the atmosphere in which Dürer was accustomed to move. The contemporary abbess's room of a Swiss nunnery (1512) (fig. 166), preserved intact with its arched lattice windows, its bench seats, rafters, and wainscoting, exhales the same warmth and shows how unfeignedly Dürer recorded the late Gothic room.

The perfection of these chambers is the fruit of a development running through the entire Middle Ages. The unity of the medieval rooms was ensured at first by the vaulting in which it was gathered. Later, lightly painted ornament spread over walls and ceiling. In the fourteenth century, the more wealthy might hang their walls with pictorial tapestry from Flanders. But they were the exception. Flat, usually unplastered, walls remained the general rule. The sparse furnishings stood before plain walls. Dark rafters bridged the ceiling and took the place of the vault.

After mid-fifteenth century, a change sets in. Gothic framing forms not only the furniture but the room itself. The high wooden backs given to chests, beds, and dressers, as earlier to the choir stall, are but a transition stage. In their stead, and to about the same height, wainscoting now surrounds the room.

In the sixteenth century, the wainscoting grows up to the ceiling, enfolds the rafters and gives the room that sheltering fastness that re-echoes even today in the peasant houses of the Alps.

Not only does the shell of the room — walls, floor, ceiling — form a unit; even the doors are incorporated into the paneling and often one can hardly tell them from the wall. The benches are grafted into the wainscoting. The dresser reaching from floor to low ceiling envelops the washstand and is in truth an advancing section of the wall.

The late Gothic room marks at once the end of a development and the beginning of a new one. Forms will change in the course of the sixteenth, seventeenth, and eighteenth centuries. But this notion will remain: nothing should impair the unity of the room.

It is a living instinct in these periods that space shall be dominant, not furniture. To this everything else is unconsciously subordinated.

COMFORT IN THE EIGHTEENTH CENTURY

France: Rococo and Nature

A QUARTER MILLENNIUM elapses between the wane of the late Gothic and the full development of the Rococo in the fourth decade of the eighteenth century. Yet our leap is not an arbitrary one. The next truly inventive impulses in the sphere of comfort came only in the late Baroque, of which the Rococo is a phase.

Late periods sometimes have a privileged role. While standing distinct from earlier time, they possess a heritage of slowly gathered experience. They play with confident mastery upon the expression of their age. The idiom has become second nature, and tasks at which their forerunners had stopped they can now perform with ease.

The late Gothic of the fifteenth century and the late Baroque of the eighteenth are such periods. In the late Gothic, the atmosphere and values of monasticism were drawing to their end; in the late Baroque, worldliness of the Renaissance yielded its full consequences. These periods were enabled both to summarize the experience of many generations and to initiate a new development.

The Building of Receptacles

The Renaissance was less prolific of new impulses in the sphere of furniture than it was in painting or in architecture. It elaborated in detail what the late Gothic had broadly prepared. The trend to display pieces became increasingly pronounced in the course of the sixteenth century, recalling the drift from austerity to sumptuousness under the Roman Empire. Yet the Renaissance contribution was not an insignificant one.

Receptacle furniture and seating furniture, the two categories branching from the chest, move to further differentiation, the receptacles especially. The chair, toward mid-sixteenth century, was becoming an article of current use. In the various receptacles elaborated at this time, unusual care is given to that element, coming everywhere into demand, the drawer. Drawers of all sizes and proportions are built into secretaries and credenzas. There can never be too many of them. Framed by rich carvings and moldings, each one calls the eye to its presence. Italy was the leader, during the sixteenth century, in all matters of form and technique. Feudalistic city-states, each with its individual development, were dispersed over the whole peninsula. There, secretaries and credenzas were especially favored. Italian secretaries have come down to us from around 1500 and credenzas from the 1530's on.

THE WRITING TABLE

The Renaissance, with its lust for secular writing, took a strong interest in the writing table. The adjustable desk of the late Gothic monks, or the portable desk used even in 1499 by Polyphilo, now becomes the more ample secretary in two parts, the upper having all the drawers and doors for which there is room. This receptacle rests on a console — like the French buffets of the century — or on another cabinet with doors. The upper and the lower sections are often of independent design, suggesting that at first the secretary was conceived as two-part furniture — as a chest upon a frame.[1] The fall-front, which gives access to its interior, also serves as the writing surface. Soon the secretary is made in one piece, a type that endures through all stylistic changes well into the nineteenth century.

The bureau, having a fixed horizontal writing top above two or three narrow drawers, was an outgrowth of the monastic wall desk.[2] The consoles were later replaced by drawers often down to the floor.[3] This type, identical with that of today, is thought to have passed to France from Italy in the latter half of the seventeenth century.[4] The Rococo gave it a movable cylinder top. The secretary was made with growing lavishness, so much so that Louis XV, whose own sumptuous pieces set no example, issued a prohibition against desks of solid silver.[5] The time is near when it will be adapted to bourgeois use, and the older form, the tall secretary, will be preferred. In the American patent furniture era, the cylinder-top type, the display piece of the late Rococo, will become serially manufactured office equipment.

THE BUFFET

The Burgundian dresser of the fifteenth century, with its shelves for display vessels, was a piece of social distinction, which migrated from the kitchen into the banquet hall. The oblong Italian credenza, having two or three doors beneath a number of narrow drawers, was without this upper section. It had entered from the sacristy, becoming a utility piece much favored in the spacious mid-sixteenth century residences and palazzos of Italy.[6] Around the middle of

---

[1] Odom, William M., *History of Italian Furniture*, New York, 1918, vol. 1, p.302. 'It is quite evident that the upper sections were made to be placed on tablets of independent design.'

[2] Examples from various periods of the sixteenth century will be found in ibid. vol. 1, figs. 138, 306, 307.

[3] An early form, closely fused with the wall like the monastic console writing desks of the sixteenth century, is Schuebler's writing desk about 1730, with drawers down to the floor (fig. 239).

[4] Odom, op.cit. vol. 2, fig. 30.

[5] Havard, *Dictionnaire de l'ameublement et de la décoration depuis le XIIIme siècle jusqu'à nos jours.*

[6] Odom, op.cit. vol. 1, p.144: an early example, of 1535.

the sixteenth century, the secretary, the credenza, the chair, and the cupboard all grew into parts of the secular interior.

The English of the late eighteenth century gave careful attention to the dresser without shelves, the sideboard, and brought it to its present-day form. 'Sideboard' meant a table (board) standing against the wall (side), either on legs or leaning against the wall. The *Oxford English Dictionary* quotes such usage from the fourteenth century on down to Alexander Pope. The sideboard, which Sheraton and his time equipped with refined compartments, is of the credenza type, in which this shelfless form first appeared.

Another type of buffet, rooted in the late Gothic tradition, took shape beyond the Alps in the sixteenth century, especially in southern Germany and Switzerland. This was not independent furniture like the credenza, but, as we have noticed, an integral of the wainscoting; its body and superstructure form an unobtrusively advancing section of the wall. It can still be found in this form in inns and peasant houses of Switzerland today.

This was the type that nineteenth-century ruling taste molded to its wishes, isolating the buffet as an ornate monster which even invaded the not too large middle-class dining room. It was thus revived not in Germany in the 'eighties, but in France during the 'sixties.

THE COMMODE

The commode is a direct descendant of the chest. Yet, it was a latecomer to the house. It does not appear in Italy before the wane of the sixteenth century,[7] and in England it is first mentioned at about the same time.[8] Its initial form [9] consisted of three drawers, each of which, running the full width of the piece, was accentuated by heavily carved horizontal members. Above these was fitted a row of smaller drawers.

The size of its drawers is no doubt the reason for the late appearance of the commode. Small drawers present no great technical difficulty, but large ones are in every respect harder to handle. In addition to taxing the craftsman's skill, movable receptacles of unwonted size had tradition to overcome. If we take an early starting point, the archive *almaiar* of 1455 (fig. 149), a century and a half elapse before drawer-furniture reaches maturity.

Only with the Rococo did it enter into its brilliance. Havard thus seems jus-

---

[7] Ibid. vol. 1, p.306: 'The only Renaissance example we have dates from the last decade of the XVI century.' In the Victoria and Albert Museum, South Kensington, London.

[8] *The Oxford English Dictionary* reports, in the year 1599, mention of 'A great chest or standard with drawing chests or boxes in it.' Nothing, however, is said of its appearance.

[9] Odom, op.cit. vol. 1, fig. 250.

168. Eighteenth-Century Posture: 'Le Petit Jour.' *The eighteenth century brought back refined seating for the first time since the Greeks, developing it toward ease and flexibility of posture. The cavalier can turn freely to converse on either side. One leg rests aslant over the other. This* sans gêne *posture is characteristic of late eighteenth-century engravings.* (*Engraving by Nicolas de Launay after Freudenberger*)

tified in placing the emergence of the commode between the years 1705 and 1710.[10] Around 1720, it was in vigorous production. It became the furniture *par-excellence* of the eighteenth century. The late Baroque preferred lightly furnished rooms, and here the fantasy of this form-fascinated period took full flight. The side walls of the commode undulate in three-dimensional curves, as do the feet into which their sinuosity extends. The drawers, with their wavering fronts, are gathered into the general unification. Only a hair-thin crevice betrays their existence. This most elegant form on feet, with two deep, swelling drawers, was prized as a decorative piece. England, too, took over the French design in the second half of the eighteenth century. Chippendale and his school call almost every decorative piece with drawers a 'commode.'[11]

[10] Havard, op.cit. vol. 1, p.929.
[11] Macquoid and Edwards, *Dictionary of English Furniture*, op.cit. vol. 1, p.70.

169. Greek Posture: Palamedes before Persephone. Middle 5th Century B.C. *Posture and chair are one. The goddess, scepter in hand, is serenely seated on a cushionless chair in the fully relaxed pose acquired only by careful breeding and training of the body. The backrest enfolds body and shoulders in its sloping curve.* (*Attic red-figured mixing bowl, courtesy Metropolitan Museum, New York*)

The Renaissance form — the commode with drawers down to the floor — endured into later periods as the 'secretary.' The Empire, with its love for cubical forms, revived the heavy type, which kept its vogue throughout the nineteenth century. Moving into the bedroom around mid-nineteenth century, the commode was converted into a washstand (fig. 187). The marble top provided by the Rococo now carries the wash bowl and toilet jugs.

The Creation of a Sitting Comfort

POSTURE IN THE EIGHTEENTH CENTURY

Eighteenth-century France took up sitting comfort where it had been left by the Greeks of the fifth century B.C. The sociological context is radically different; the chairs and chaise longues of the Rococo are as far from the furniture

171. Nature and the Rococo: Tureen by Juste-Aurèle Meissonier. 1738. *Closely observing the forms of nature, the rocaille infuses objects with the free yet structural lines of living organisms.*

←
170. *Driftwood Root.* (*Photo Martin James*)

of the Greeks as the silks and laces of the ladies of the French court are from the austerity of the peplos. Typologically speaking, it was the return of a forgotten standard: To create a support for the body that would allow highly relaxed posture.

A red-figured bowl of the fifth century, on which Palamedes and Persephone are depicted, seats the goddess, scepter in hand, with that fully relaxed posture acquired by long breeding and training of the body (fig. 169). Posture and chair are one. The cushionless seat slopes gently backward and the broad back rest carries up to above shoulder height, enfolding the body in its curve. From the backward inclination of the trunk and the forward extension of the feet, at rest on the footstool — a custom acquired from the Egyptians — there emanates the same atmosphere of serenity and natural poise as from a Greek temple.

In the eighteenth century, this sitting comfort developed in the direction of ease, luxury, and flexibility in posture. The curved, upholstered backs introduced by the French are the last term of a slow development from the late Gothic on.

172. Candlestick, Juste-Aurèle Meissonier, 1728. *Meissonier transforms church façades (St. Sulpice, Paris) and interiors, tureens and candlesticks into a whirlwind of motion. To do this without loss of dignity demands, in art, an equipoise comparable to that of the tightrope walker.*

The cavalier of Louis XV's day sits somewhat informally. Here again chair and posture are one, the outcome of a long tradition. Here again the posture is relaxed — a prerequisite of all repose — but it is constantly modified by slight changes. It is not static repose. The cavalier turns toward this side or that. One leg is slantingly crossed over the other, the recurrent attitude in late eighteenth-century engravings (fig. 168).[12] We do not imply that the Rococo invented this informal posture. But it was then that such deportment became typical. Portraits around 1700 show one leg extended forward, the other drawn back: a transitional posture amid a transitional style. Rococo *fauteuils*, with their short armrests curving outwards in deference to ladies' fashion, were no less favorable to the *sans-gêne* posture of the masculine visitors.

---

[12] Representations of this sort only become prevalent in the later, genre-oriented decades. At the beginning of Louis XVI's period: the cavalier at his toilet, 'La petite toilette,' engraving after Moreau le jeune (1741–1814), by P. S. Martini; or 'Le petit jour,' after Freudenberger (1745–1801), engraving after Nicolas de Launay (1739–92).

173. Electrotype Candlestick, Birmingham. 1850. *The nineteenth century reduces an object to an anecdote. (Henry Cole,* Journal of Design, 1851.)

ROCAILLE

With the certainty and sureness of accumulated experience, seemingly improvised shapes are instilled with that unique fusion of discipline and flexibility which runs through the operas of Mozart.

For this union of discipline with flexibility, wherein objects are formed as if eternally in flux, the late Baroque invented a symbol in which all these qualities are gathered: the Rocaille.

The shell-form, with which a boneless organism surrounds itself and in which are joined the eternity of stone and the flux of living waters, seems as if created to express the will of this late period. The early phases, dating back to the Renaissance, are well known. Now a radical transformation takes place. The shell is transmuted to seaweed, lace, or other forms. It swells, becomes membrane-like, is broken up, or indentated, until the naturalistic form is changed into a sign or, as the modern painters say, transformed into an object. These signs appear singly or strung in *C* or *S* shapes, contrasting with or supporting other elements. Here fantasy freely plays amid the flexibility, finesse, and generosity of this late period.

The search for comprehensiveness appears everywhere, using the curve to embrace individual parts; in urbanism, in the layout and interrelation of squares and places, in the rounded corners of the interiors. This unique meeting of reason with the richness of organic form is nowhere more marked than in furniture, always so difficult of development. In furniture it is as if the store of experience accumulated since the late Gothic were suddenly bursting forth: the curved commodes, the mobile cylinder tops of the desks, and the finely modeled sitting or reclining furniture.

Just as the shell becomes an object infused with the most varied organic forms, so the legs of Rococo furniture approach the structure of the bough (fig. 170). Obedience to the lines of force of the wood gives it a natural similarity to the skeleton of the branch, whose softer parts the water has rotted away. The careers of the great naturalists (Buffon, Linnaeus) run parallel with the lifetime of Louis XVI. The generation that created the Rococo and sitting comfort probed more deeply than any before it the life of plants and animals.

The form-giving energy of this period may perhaps be measured in comparison to our own time, with our storehouse of new materials, and our inability to give them life. Had our age brought to human purposes a fraction of the inventiveness of the late Baroque, where might we stand today?

THE MODELING OF THE CHAIR

The Rococo tackled its seating forms in the most radical way. Little more than the skeletons of the seventeenth-century types is retained. They are thoroughly compounded. The curve intervenes. Often the original types are barely recognizable after their transformation. As its lines become fluid, the chair can adapt itself to the organic, to the body. The seventeenth-century armrests and upholstered seat are relaxed and fused into a continuous curve, a shell molded to the body. This is around 1725. The new form of chair, whose names and varieties are listed in numerous handbooks of the subject, was called *bergère.* One of the *bergère* types owes its name and shape to the gondola: the *bergère en gondole.* This wavy type with its semi-high back fully corresponds to the need of the century. In it, as the cabinetmaker Roubo points out, the occupant can 'rest his shoulder against the chairback while leaving the head entirely free to avoid disarranging the hair either of the ladies or the gentlemen.' One could hardly do more to accommodate a passing fashion.

Fashion merely supplied the impulse for something that far transcended fashion: adaptability of the chair to the human body. The curve, the three-dimensional curve, here appears, as in the late Baroque church vaults. It was intrinsically suitable to the human body. Under Louis XVI the form will be rationalized and simplified, but the gondola type will remain (fig. 168). It is noteworthy how often the semi-high backed chairs of Louis XVI will reappear in the fashion magazines of the Empire. It was in the shape of a *bergère en gondole* that a French upholsterer of the 1830's launched the first spiral spring *fauteuils*, producing their contour by means of a curved iron strip. The outline becomes blurred, the wood disappears, but the *bergère* type remains. For a while during the 1860's, it seemed that the upholsterer was finding a new foothold in this constituent type; but it soon became clear that, in his hand, furniture was being camouflaged as cushions.

The light, upholstered chairs, with or without armrests, accomplish the transformation. As in Rocaille, what occurs here in the shaping of furniture is an approach to organic form. In abstracted form, the double-*S* curve of the back rests follows the contour of human shoulders and trunk.

In this gondola line also belongs the two-seating marquise, which the Rococo develops from the settle. The marquise by Delanois, late 1760's, shows it fully developed (fig. 175). The marquise may be used by one or by two persons. In a Louis XVI engraving after Moreau le jeune,[13] a young married couple harmoniously occupy this enlarged *fauteuil;* and in 'Le Mari confesseur,' an engraving of the 'nineties after Henri Fragonard (1732–1806), the lady is sitting

[13] 'J'en accepte l'heureux présage,' engraving of Philippe C. Trière after Moreau le jeune (designed 1776).

174. The Marquise (Easy Chair for Two). 'Le Mari confesseur,' Engraving by N. F. Regnault after Fragonard. 1795. *This consciously archaic print after Fragonard's illustration to a fable by La Fontaine is treated in the playfully anecdotic and superficial manner that forms a starting point for the ruling taste in nineteenth-century painting.*

alone, the cavaliers around her, as the husband arrives unexpectedly on the scene [14] (fig. 174).

He who would know the spirit of the Rococo must not trust too far the late engravings of the 'seventies, and even less the erotic subjects of later date. The erotic scenes are backward-looking witnesses, artificially prolonging a bygone period. In the late lifetime of Fragonard, this atmosphere degenerates into one of superficial playfulness. This lapse into genre treatment forms one of the starting points of nineteenth-century ruling taste: Rococo for bourgeois consumption.

The meaning of the Rococo appears — as is so often the case — in painting, at a time when neither Rococo furniture nor Rococo interior yet existed. Early in the eighteenth century, Watteau (1684–1721) anticipates the fusion of organic form with spiritual alertness that was later to become a reality.

---

[14] 'Le Mari confesseur,' engraving of N. F. Regnault, after J. H. Fragonard, from his series illustrating the *Fables of La Fontaine*.

175. Marquise by L. Delanois. Late 1760's. *The gondola type, which Delanois' marquise represents at its height, molds the body like a shell. The simplified curves, vigorous lines, and delicate profile show how discipline and flexibility are fused in this late period. By the end of the Rococo the cushions rise to a noticeable height.* (*Louvre, Paris, Archives Photographiques*)

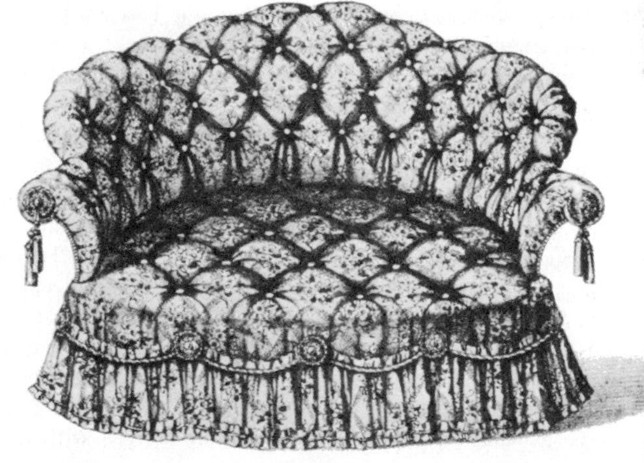

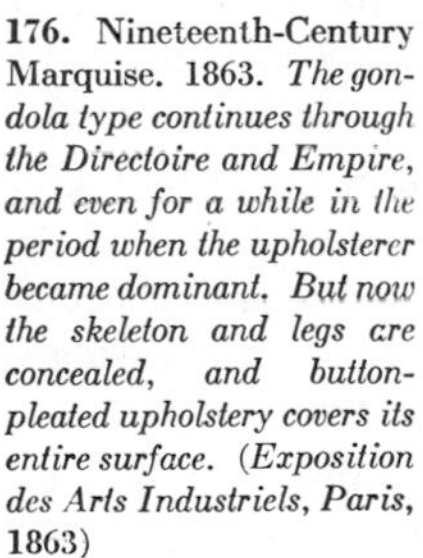

176. Nineteenth-Century Marquise. 1863. *The gondola type continues through the Directoire and Empire, and even for a while in the period when the upholsterer became dominant. But now the skeleton and legs are concealed, and button-pleated upholstery covers its entire surface.* (*Exposition des Arts Industriels, Paris,* 1863)

RECLINING FURNITURE

The modern types of rest furniture were likewise formed in the late eighteenth century. They were for brief transitory relaxation, and gave a comfort quite different from the static repose of a bed.

The chaise longue is, as its name indicates, a lengthened form of the chair. It has a headpiece, like the bed, but more emphatic. From the settle, there developed in France and England, in the first decades of the seventeenth century, a reclining chair, day bed (*lit de repos*), the head section of which was adjusted by gears or chains. In the chaise longue, the curved gondola form replaced this adjustable plane. If before a *bergère* is placed an upholstered bench or stool (tabouret), a 'long chair,' or chaise longue is produced. Made in one piece — of this too there were many varieties — it was called a *duchesse* (fig. 177). This furniture, as its names indicate — *marquise, duchesse* — was intended for the ladies of the nobility, who occupied it while receiving in light attire.

Once fantasy began to create reclining furniture, the most diverse combinations appeared. The top section of the chaise longue being made to open up, a shallow bathtub was inserted in the frame, as sometimes seen in erotic plates of the late eighteenth century. Or with a tabouret, a high-backed and a low-backed *bergère* might be placed on either side; this combination was called *duchesse brisée*, divided *duchesse.*

Around 1800, the *duchesse* became the *psyche*, in imitation of Pompeiian furniture. Later we shall encounter its American derivative around 1830 (fig. 322), whose surface undulates in a free form at best suited to brief intervals of relaxation. We shall then look into its link with recent developments, LeCorbusier's tubular steel recliner, the 'chaise longue basculante' (fig. 323). LeCorbusier's austere, unupholstered recliner adheres in mood to the starting point, the seventeenth-century day bed; but its adaptation to the body incorporates the experience of later centuries.

The patent-furniture era, especially the 'sixties and 'seventies, mechanized the chaise longue. Various ways of transforming it into twin beds now come to hand (fig. 264). The upholsterer, meanwhile, destroying its structure as he destroys the *fauteuil's*, turns it into an invertebrate piece. Now the chaise longue is mainly to be found near the bed in the bedroom, a usage that first appears in the erotic scenes around mid-eighteenth century.

The sofa continues the settle, the upholstered bench with back and armrests. Its shaping advances parallel with that of the chair, of which it is increasingly conceived as a companion. It is essentially a salon piece (fig. 178).

Rocaille reflects the will of the period to render things flexible. Impelled by the demand for expression indissolubly merged with function, it produced far

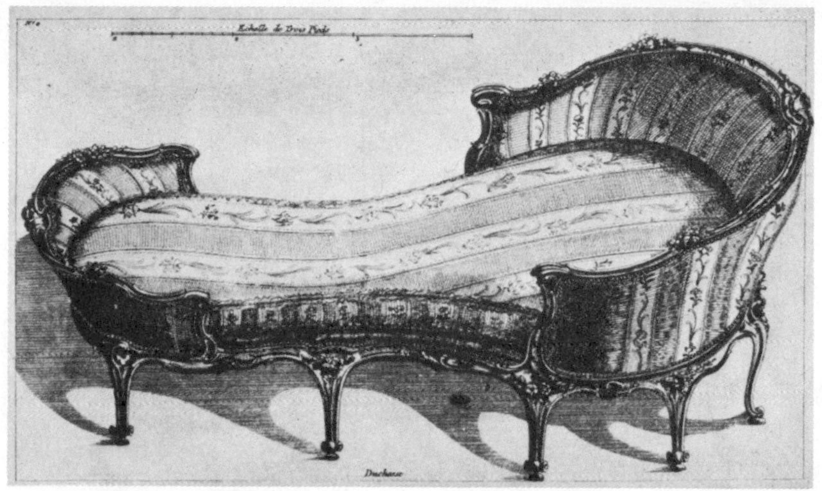

177. One-Piece Duchesse, Mathieu Liard. 1762. *The modern furniture types for temporary relaxation were also shaped in the eighteenth century. The gondola type, encompassing the body in a single curve, is adapted to rest purposes. The duchesse was at first in three parts: two gondola-type easy chairs of different depth and height, with a tabouret between them. The later Rococo merged these into a single piece.* (*Mathieu Liard,* Recueil des petits meubles, *Paris,* 1762)

more than a *style pittoresque* or a *goût nouveau*, as the French then called this new trend.

The masterful perspective drawings and the complicated sections drawn up by the cabinetmakers reveal, beneath seemingly purposeless curves, a fantasy ruled by analysis and precise observation of human posture. The furniture of the Rococo expressed no grandiose pretensions. It sought merely to yield comfort and to fulfil what was required. So doing, it created modern comfort.

One does not have to consult the late eighteenth-century engravings to sense the erotic atmosphere of the apartments. This atmosphere settled down under Louis XVI into a bourgeois one, which the Revolution no more than passingly disturbed. The Rococo in France had its home from the start in the intimate setting. The sense of scale so apparent in the French development recognized the Rococo as most productively suited to the interior.

Louis XV waited until Cardinal Fleury's death at ninety before assuming in earnest the duties of government. As Molinier points out, he liked small gatherings, intimate suppers. Otherwise the court remained passive to the new trend down to 1738. The Rococo — a point recently stressed by Fiske Kimball [15] —

[15] E. Fiske Kimball, *The Growth of the Rococo*, Philadelphia, 1943, p.152.

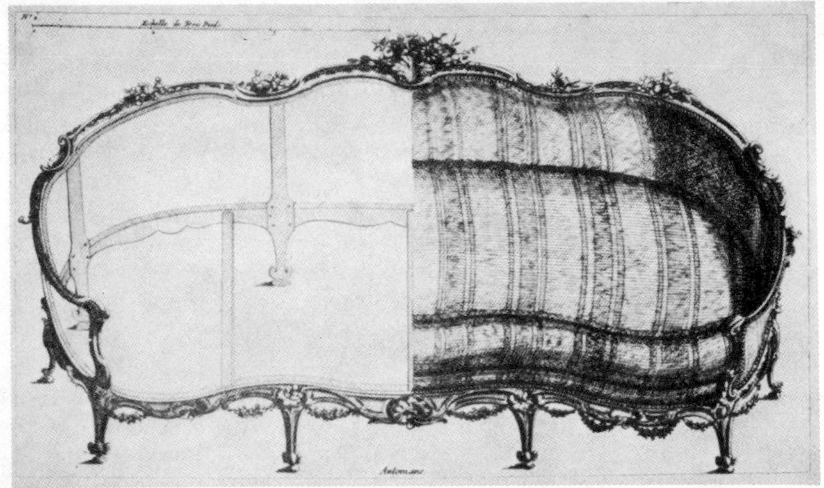

178. Automane by Mathieu Liard. 1762. *The greatest mastery and finesse in woodcarving developed as Louis XVI classicism was beginning to spread. Through knowledge of lines of force, the skeleton is reduced to astonishing slenderness, and shaped with the elegance of organic forms.* (Recueil des petits meubles, *Paris,* 1762)

arose far from Versailles in the palaces of the French nobles. Its scope was the interior. A refined, *spirituel* society, enjoying life to the point of corruptness, created this furniture.

Just as works of art imply more than they were intended to convey, so does this furniture perpetuate the inventiveness it appealingly embodied. The Gothic wrested from stone and the Rococo from wood their last resources of flexibility and lightness. The purposes for which they were developed afford an index to the outlook of their periods. Never did France display more brilliant inventiveness in the realm of comfort.

England: Form and Mechanism

The first half of the eighteenth century in England and the latter half are so dissimilar that we might almost be speaking of distinct countries.

The first decades are fraught with the rough habits of the preceding century. In the second half, a surprising differentiation imposes its mark upon almost every domain of life. Even the Englishman, at least that type regarded as the ideal, is radically altered after 1750.

In the 'thirties, when William Hogarth became the chronicler of contemporary England, the Falstaff type still prevailed: A man, heavy of bulk, like the furniture of his time, a hearty eater, lusty in all appetites. Hogarth did not mince matters. He showed great inventiveness in his engravings when it came to portraying tares and vices, animals being refinedly tortured, or women spitting gin into one another's eyes. The portrait is but a few steps removed from the sadistic.

Not many decades later, the favored male type is slender, immature, ephemeral, and his feminine counterpart is the mild, dreamy maiden, innocent of passion. The late eighteenth century, at first in literature, then in painting, brings the forerunners of those sentimental types[16] that were to hold the public taste throughout the following century.

Just as England had first assimilated Flemish painting before developing it further, so it adapted the industrial methods that the Huguenot refugees of the seventeenth century brought with them from Holland. An immense entrepreneurial energy develops, leading to the mechanization of motive power, of spinning and weaving, to a rapid building up of transportation — canals, bridges, and highways and to the revival of farming, the 'new husbandry.'

---

[16] These remarks are based on earlier unpublished studies by the author on the beginnings of ruling taste in painting. These types have their roots not in the French circle around Greuze, but in a circle of English painters and archeologists in Rome of the late 1760's.

179. Grand French Settee Chair. England, 1775. *When the English wished to be à la mode they followed French examples. This heavily carved piece is still concieved in the rigid seventeenth-century manner; it cannot be compared in ease with the French pieces of the time. The comfort that England developed in the late eighteenth century was quite different in nature and purpose.* (*R. Manwaring*, The Cabinet and Chair Maker's Real Friend and Companion, *London*, 1775)

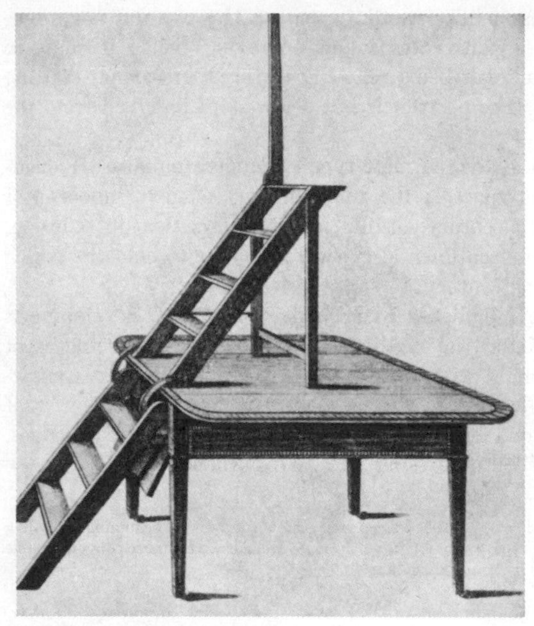

180. THOMAS SHERATON: Table Convertible into Library Steps. 1793. *In the last decades of the eighteenth century, England influenced the tastes and habits of all Europe. England shaped the dining room, the library, and later the bathroom. From Chippendale on, even the library steps were carefully thought out and treated as convertible furniture.*

England similarly took the lead in comfort in the last decades of the eighteenth century. This too was a *novum*.

A quiet and confident line also runs through certain English furniture types in the first half of the century, such as the winged armchairs with their high upholstered backs and armrests. This is the line that, starting from the Italian Renaissance, was further developed in France and in England. The comfortable English types, which took shape around 1700, have remained popular to the present day. But it was France that created the new comfort in the Rococo. This was not without effect upon England. Throughout, France remains hovering in the background. Even in the 'sixties, design books[17] are published with parallel texts in French. Brackets for busts and candles, candlestands, girandoles, illuminaries, chandeliers, seem to draw greater interest than the chairs. Even in the 'sixties, the successful cabinetmakers[18] turn, in their uncertainty, to naturalistic detail: garden chairs with backs carved in imitation of rocks and

[17] Ince and Mayhew, *The Universal System of Household Furniture*, London, 1762. (Dedicated to the Duke of Marlborough.)

[18] Manwaring, *The Cabinet and Chair Maker's Real Friend and Companion, or the Whole System of Chair Making Made Plain and Easy*, 2 vols., London, 1765, 1st ed.

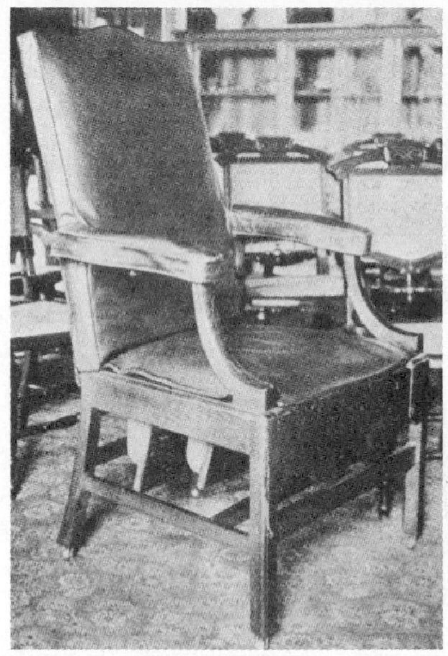

181a. BENJAMIN FRANKLIN: Chair Convertible into Library Steps. *c.1780. Franklin designed this chair for his library, just as he devised grippers to select books from the higher shelves.* (*Courtesy Philosophical Society, Philadelphia*)
181b. Benjamin Franklin's Chair Converted into Steps.

trees,[19] or a large uncomfortable piece with heavily carved back called a 'French Settee Chair,' still helplessly conceived in the seventeenth-century manner, but at great pains to keep up with French taste [20] (fig. 179).

The Gentleman Sets the Style

The last decades bring a quite different situation. In the brief period before the influx of the French Empire style, the English interior and English cabinet-making attain an almost timeless maturity, which sums up and enlarges upon the experience of centuries. It is the same restrained mastery that laid out the contemporary squares of Bloomsbury or the curved crescents of Bath.

It is a man's society, and an austere note prevails in England in the waning eighteenth century. The great club buildings of London, built in the first decades of the nineteenth century and equipped with the most up-to-date interior comforts of the time, attest the continuation of this man-centered society. Woman,

[19] Ibid. ed. 1775, plate 27: 'Rural chairs for summerhouses; they are the only ones of the kind that ever were published.'

[20] Ibid. pl. 19.

182. WILLIAM MORRIS: Sideboard. *c.*1880. *Morris made several such sideboards. The elegantly curved front shows his close ties with the eighteenth century. Without the elaborate display of china, the bond would be even more apparent.* (*Courtesy Mr. Marillier, Morris & Co. Art Workers Ltd., London*)

in contrast to France of the Rococo, loses influence. The gentleman sets the tone. He is not limited to the ranks of nobility; he does not have to be born into a title; he belongs to no closed social class; increasingly, he becomes identified with a moral concept.

By 1710 Steele was thus defining him in *The Tatler:* 'The appelation of Gentleman is never to be affixed to a Man's circumstances, but to his behaviour in them.' And Chippendale entitles his famous catalogue (1754) *The Gentleman and Cabinetmaker's Guide.* Besides the nobility, the great cabinetmakers numbered among their clients the middle class, artists, actors. And the designs in Hepplewhite's, Shearer's, and Sheraton's books show that their wares are intended for the newly rising classes.[21]

As the gentleman passes from the feudal into the middle-class atmosphere, certain rooms of the mansion pass into the middle-class dwelling.

[21] It has been pointed out that the foreword to George Hepplewhite's *Cabinet-Maker's and Upholsterer's Guide* (1787) makes no appeal to the nobility and gentry, but addresses itself to 'the residents of London.' Cf. Herbert Cescinski, *English Furniture from Gothic to Sheraton*, Grand Rapids, Michigan, 1929, p.353.

183. English Sideboard. *c.*1780. *The English dining room received its carefully designed table, chairs, and sideboard in the second half of the eighteenth century. It was then that the light sideboard on slender legs became standard.* (*H. Cescinski,* English Furniture of the Eighteenth Century)

The Library

Only the greater noblemen had libraries, usually in connection with medal and curio-cabinets. The eighteenth century read. Voltaire, Goethe, Hume, Jefferson, all were great readers. The demand for universality called for source material from everywhere. It is striking how, from Chippendale on, glassed library cases come to the fore, and in what variety of size and execution. Often this leads to a piece in which the secretary and bookcase are combined; that is, a glassed-in bookcase replaces the many drawered upper section of the Renaissance secretary. The care with which Chippendale furnished the library of the actor Garrick is well known.

For the large folios with their engravings and aquatints, then favored in all branches, from natural science to Greek temples, broad, flat surfaces were needed — library tables such as are already found in Chippendale by mid-century. From this generous furniture, there developed the large desk of today, with its flat top and the two drawer sections beneath it on either side. For writing, the eighteenth century was content with small surfaces.

Steps were needed to reach the higher shelves. They should remain out of sight until needed for use. Thomas Chippendale, in one of his most brilliant commissions, Hardwood House, 1770–75, built a case in which the steps folded away.[22]

Benjamin Franklin solved the same problem in his own manner by placing the stepladder on the underside of the seat of his *fauteuil,* which would turn out on hinges (fig. 181). For the upper shelves, as is known, he had a forceps at the end of a pole, which he would gladly demonstrate to visitors. Sheraton concealed his ladder in a table (fig. 180).

The Dining Room

The dining room too, as it became separate, was provided with special furniture: chairs, draw-leaf tables, buffets.

The chairs of the great cabinetmakers are known in every detail of their legs, seats, and heart-shaped or interlaced backs. They are graceful, but no more. Their constituent content is not in proportion to the esteem in which they are held. These chairs were mainly designed for parlor purposes.

More interesting are the English sideboards of the late part of the century (fig. 183). Their light, frequently curved body is raised on slender legs. Robert Adam gave them heavy sidepieces, pedestals capped by urns (a motive to be found in every English garden) to hold cutlery; but these soon disappeared and there remained the light and elegant form, whence a line leads to William Morris (fig. 182).

As we have seen, dining tables were at first called by the French *tables à l'anglaise.* Great care was used to give them skilful mechanism, ensuring lightness of aspect and yet the faculty of drawing out to almost unbelievable lengths. Even horseshoe-shaped dining tables were made to be extensible (1788).[23]

The Rediscovery of Cleanliness

Cautiously, the late eighteenth century discovers that cleanliness and hygiene have a place in life. The interest is there and leads to the most interesting furniture of the time. Sheraton designs a variety of simple washstands to fill corners or to stand against the wall.

Free-standing washstands, as preferred in France (*lavabo*), were also used.[24]

Shearer elaborately equips the dressing stand of a gentleman (1788)[25] with

---

[22] Illustrated in Oliver Brackett, *Thomas Chippendale,* London, 1924, p.277.

[23] *Cabinet Maker's London Book of Prices,* London, 1788, compiled by Thomas Shearer, pl. 19, fig. 2.

[24] In the Empire they were pompously disguised as antique tripods. Cf. Havard, op.cit. vol. III, p.271, 'Lavabo: petit meuble en vogue pendant le consulat et l'Empire . . . jusqu'à la fin de la restauration on continue d'en faire usage.' In the 'thirties the English turned to broad washstands with marble tops (fig. 187).

[25] *London Book of Prices,* op.cit. pl. 9.

a hinged, flat top, having a mirror inside, drawers, and a tambour-front opening to the right and to the left (fig. 184). In the feminine counterpart — Lady's Dressing Stand — the small eighteenth-century washbowl pulls out like a drawer to the front and the bidet to the side (fig. 185). A cistern to take the used water is also built in.[26]

Elegance of form, reduction to the essential, are combined with extreme movability in Rudd's Table or 'Reflecting Dressing Table.'[27] The center drawer 'slides by itself' — and the two side drawers 'swing horizontally on a center pin' so that the lady may see herself from all angles. This is the same period that solves the complicated problems of spinning machines.

Movability

The Rococo contributed suppleness of form and lightness of construction. Movability, in which the Rococo and Louis XVI were to some degree interested — from the invention of the roll-top desk and revival of the swivel chair to card tables and collapsible furniture — now enters the foreground. The designers seem to take especial pleasure in drawing their pieces with all pigeon holes, mirrors, fall- or tambour-fronts open, one might almost say, in motion. Mastery of form is natural to them. They do not need to stress it. They wish only to show of what their furniture is capable.

Interest turns anew to the movable receptacle, the drawer. Its construction is basically improved. It slides freely on runners. Often, series of sliding shelves are arrayed, one above another, so that on opening the buffet or the commode all its contents may easily be surveyed. Secret drawers released by springs form a seemingly indispensable part of the desk. Drawers suspended from their top rim, as in Rudd's table, are also favored. Tambour-fronts made of numerous wooden strips (beads) glued to strong canvas are much in vogue and built into the most diverse pieces. Replacing the solid cylinder top, they push back into much less space. 'Pullover' writing tables were a familiar article between 1780 and 1790.[28]

Spiral springs, later built into upholstered furniture, were used at an early date by Sheraton in a form of 'chamber horse' (fig. 224).

This furniture, even to the manner of its representation, has direct links with the constituent furniture of the nineteenth century.

---

[26] Sheraton gives various models of night-stools and traveling bidets, which recall the Englishman's custom in the following century, of traveling with a portable bathtub.

[27] Hepplewhite, pl. 79.

[28] Herbert Cescinski, *English Furniture of the Eighteenth Century*, 3 vols., London, 1911–12, vol. II, p.147.

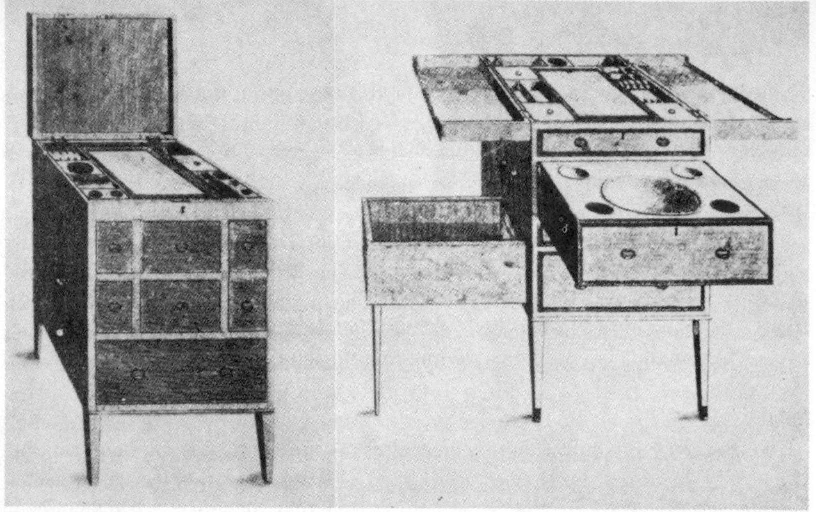

184. SHEARER: Gentleman's Dressing Stand. 1788. *The interior fittings of dressing tables and wash-stands form one of the starting points of modern hygiene facilities. 'Four real drawers and three sham ditto; a flat top; a glass inside the top; a cup-board under the drawer with a tambour-front to run right or left.'* (The Cabinet Maker's London Book of Prices, 1788)

185. SHEARER: Lady's Dressing Stand. 1788. *Again interest turns to the mobile receptacle, the drawer, whose construction is fundamentally improved. Drawers, pigeonholes, and tambour-fronts express the delight in elegant mechanical solutions. Shearer's description reads: 'Two drawers and two sham drawers in front of square bidet, supported by two drop feet; a glass-frame hinged to a sliding piece, and four cups; a flap to cover the basin hinged to the back of the drawer;* a cistern behind to receive the water from the basin drawer; a sweep bidet.'

186. Collapsible Barber Chair and Stool. U. S. Patent, 1865. *From the late eighteenth-century cabinetmakers, one line leads to William Morris and another to the American patent furniture. This portable barber chair has receptacles for hot and cold water, implements of trade, money drawer, etc. 'The legs are hinged so that they can be folded up.'* (*U. S. Patent* 50,032, 19 *September* 1865)

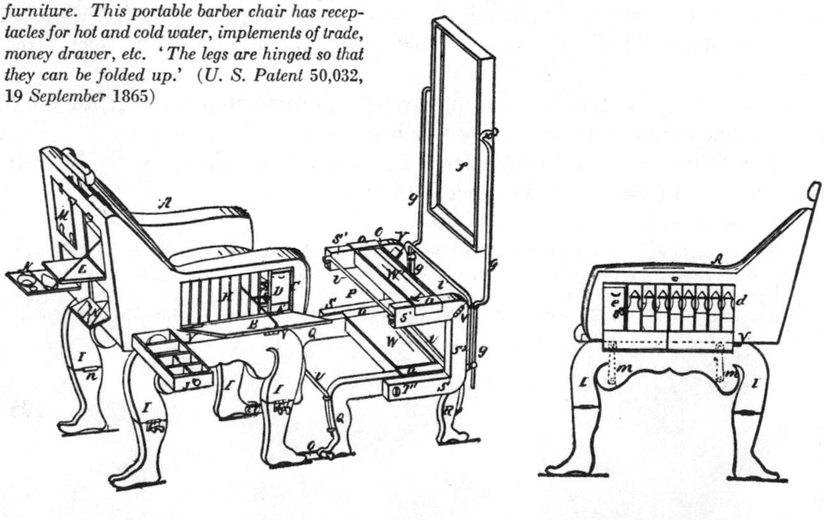

187. English Washstand. ***c.*****1835.** *Early example of the washstand as enlarged by the nineteenth century. Its marble top is mounted on a table of the first Rococo revival. In the middle of the nineteenth century the table was replaced by the marble-topped commode with drawers.* (*English catalogue, watermarked* 1835. *Courtesy Metropolitan Museum, New York*)

188. Reflecting Dressing Table, or Rudd's Table. 1788. *'This is the most complete dressing table made.' The English cabinetmakers love to show their ingenious pieces with movable parts — doors, sliding mirrors, or drawers on runners — opened up or swung out. A similar eagerness to display the mechanism appears in the American patent furniture drawings.*

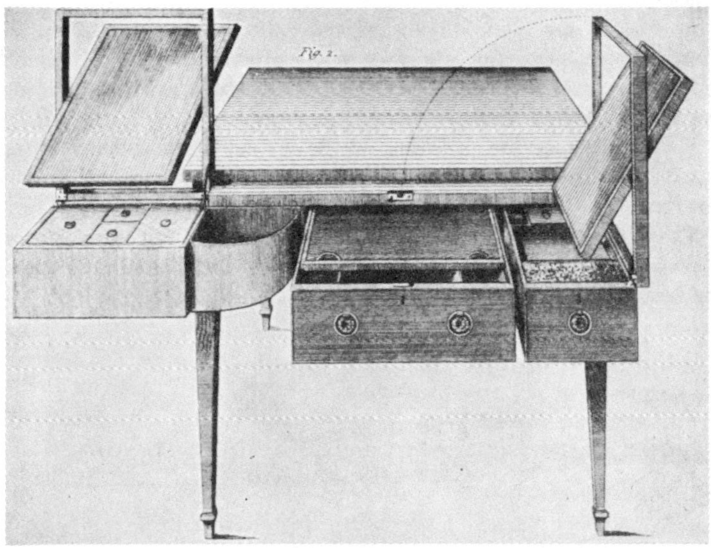

Mechanism and form — thinking and feeling — are embodied as an indivisible unity in the English furniture, the most intense phase of which falls within barely two decades. The nineteenth century seemed predestined to grow into the most brilliant epoch of urbanism and, backed by all the knowledge of the eighteenth century, to develop its intimate setting to hitherto unknown perfection.

In addition, the power of mechanization was at hand, which, as Henri de Saint-Simon could believe, would forever do away with human drudgery.

But history, like nature, follows no simple logic. It seems senseless to us that, for unknown cosmic reasons, fruit blossoms must be killed by frost or wheat destroyed by hail. We cannot understand why suddenly and without apparent cause, developments full of promise are cut short and their constituent elements forgotten until a similar psychical constellation is ready to gather them up again.

The unity of form and mechanism becomes split in the nineteenth century. The circle around William Morris strives for morally pure forms; and the anonymous American patent-furniture movement pursues motion problems. Both move side by side in the latter half of the nineteenth century, and the roots of both go back to England of the late eighteenth.

It is on the tragic side of the nineteenth century that thinking and feeling go separate ways, or, as T. S. Eliot expresses it, 'the substantial unity of soul' is destroyed.

It was not merely an outside influence, the Empire style, that sterilized the English movement. The late work of Sheraton, and especially the posthumous publication from studies for an encyclopedia, which never got beyond the first few letters, already show the flame extinguished.

A human change was occurring, on the one side of the channel as on the other; but it crystallized more palpably in the figure of Napoleon and of the formers of the Empire style.

They introduce what we call the ruling taste: the transitory phenomena that absorb the feeling of the masses as, in artificial fertilization, dummies intercept the seed of the bull.

THE NINETEENTH CENTURY: MECHANIZATION AND RULING TASTE

The Beginnings of Ruling Taste: Empire Style

Napoleon and the Devaluation of Symbols

STRICTLY SPEAKING, the Empire style falls within the ten years of Napoleon's imperial reign, starting in 1804 and ending in 1814. With better reason it can be dated by the years during which its founders, Percier and Fontaine, kept up their close collaboration: from 1794 to 1814. The influence of *Style empire* spread throughout the civilized world, from Russia to America. In democratized form it long survived Napoleon's death.

Napoleon's rise to empire gave sociological meaning to elements that lay at hand. The idea of a return to Classicism — thought of as 'simplicity' — had already been toyed with. But when the revival finally came it proved far different from that intended by the purist worshipers of the classical (Louis David, the painter, for instance, who chose the 'Etruscan Style' for his own house).

Napoleon grew up in the eighteenth century. It was firmly rooted in his mind that every specific station in life had a corresponding environment. His own setting, then, had to be created anew down to the last piece of furniture and the last ornament. This setting forms the backdrop to all his activity, yielding an intangible but ever-present resonance. The Empire 'style' is a portrait of Napoleon, an inseparable part of the Napoleonic figure.

Is the *Style empire*, as so often claimed, the last of the great historic styles? Is it of the same order as that of Louis XV? Or is it a signal for all that will emerge in the nineteenth century? Is it a beginning or an end?

One might equally well ask: Was Napoleon an emperor in the sense that Louis XIV — to compare him with a man of like calibre — was a king? Was his rule the legitimate expression, the culmination of a social group?

The difference is beyond question. Napoleon typifies the figure that later dominated and shaped the nineteenth century: the self-made man. Only in time of great revolution can such men of boundless energy reach the top. Normal times, routine, and conservatism break them before they have started; it matters little in what domain the revolution takes place, whether in politics or in production. In the age of guilds the self-made man could be only the exception, never the rule. The self-made men later arising in the economic realm cannot be compared to Napoleon's giant proportions. But the sociological conditions that opened the way for their rise were in both cases the same. And — this is significant in our context — they face the world on similar terms.

189. The Devaluation of Symbols: Percier and Fontaine, Armchair with Swan Vases, *c.*1800. *This theatrically conceived piece is not a throne but an armchair designed for a wealthy client.* (Recueil de décorations intérieures, 1801)

Napoleon was brought to power by the French Revolution. The ideas of the Revolution, invisible aids, stood over his conquests. True he turned vanquished lands into tools for his war machine. He bled them white; he plundered the Italian galleries; whatever art objects he could lay hands on he carried across the Alps. And in 1798, during the first Industrial Exhibition held in Paris, he led the masterpieces forth on triumphal chariots, as hostages were once displayed to the Roman people.

But Napoleon was not merely the conqueror. He at the same time swept Austrian despotism out of Italy, confined the Pope within boundaries, and set up a democratic constitution for the newly founded Italian republics. This was in the beginning.

190. The Devaluation of Symbols: Max Ernst, 'Le Lion de Belfort.' *Several of Max Ernst's picture-novels, some of them without words, expose the false façades as well as the eerie side of nineteenth-century feeling. The* collage *was an appropriate medium: fragments of nineteenth-century engravings pasted in irrational associations reveal new complexes of meaning.*

The first collage in Max Ernst's Lion de Belfort *grafts upon an overstuffed uniform a lion's head from some chair or monument. Napoleon looms in a shabby picture on the wall. A stone lioness is springing at the uniform.* (Une Semaine de bonté, *Paris,* 1934)

Later, as Emperor, he limited political freedom increasingly. Yet his troops carried with them a breath of the Revolution and its basic ideas, social equality and religious toleration. No reaction could wholly erase their passage.

In Poland and Prussia, he bettered the state of the peasantry. On the principle of religious tolerance, he dissolved the German ghettos, granting the Jews equal citizenship. During his brief occupation of Switzerland, he ended the disproportionate power of the patrician families who had dominated the land. By simplifying the map of Germany, he made way for national union.

Behind him lay the finest work of his youth, the Civil Code, completed at the end of his Consulate in 1804. This concise and lucid collection of civil law, first of the modern codes, vested the Rights of Man with juridical form and severed the Church and the State.

Napoleon's tragedy was that he failed to cast a new, a vital social form from the favorable opportunities the Revolution had opened; failed, perhaps, to create a new Europe. This was not merely Napoleon's fate, but the fate of the whole nineteenth century. Instead of forging new and lasting forms, he did an about face. He tried to imitate the old ruling dynasties of Europe. To become their equal he adopted their titles, their ceremonies, their forms of government. To become one of them he mingled his blood with theirs in marriage, miscalculating so far as to believe that a new dynasty might be founded in the nineteenth century. Beside him the monarchs of his time are without stature. Yet as soon as he seeks to be their equal, they tower over him. In other terms, it is as if a modern painter were craving admission to the French Academy.

That is the split running through the Napoleonic figure. He lost the eighteenth-century feeling for totality. He became unsure of himself. He needed something to lean on, for the problems of life could not be brought into meaningful shape. His immense appetite for power and craving for conquest, found no social channel that it might have constructively filled. At all events, his imperium, patterned on obsolete models, neither feudal nor democratic, proved wholly inadequate.

Napoleon lost himself in the social sphere, like the self-made man of the later industrial era whose taste failed him when he leaned on it to scale social heights. Still within the shadow of the eighteenth century, Napoleon's dimensions never allowed him to deal in half measures. He willed a style worthy of the Caesars and of himself, and did not hesitate to make this setting his own. It bears his imprint through and through.

The Founders of Empire Style, Percier and Fontaine

The elements of Napoleon's style lay ready at hand. The early manifestations were visible before Napoleon came to rely on the two architects who, more closely than any others, paralleled his own desires.

Like Napoleon, Percier and Fontaine had lived through the same austere youth of the Revolutionary years. Percier's father was a concièrge in the Tuileries; Fontaine came to Paris as the son of a small provincial contractor. When Napoleon first knew them they were beginning their careers. They developed with him, and he, throughout his rule, never changed his architects. As long as their connection lasted he kept them from private work. Napoleon was without writers and without painters marching in the same direction as himself. Louis David, the painter of an earlier generation, had already passed his peak. But Percier and Fontaine, the architects, were well suited to clothe Empire feeling with tangible form.

Pierre François Louis Fontaine (1762–1853) had the executive ability for dealing with clients and artisans. Of the two, Fontaine was the engineer, and even in his later period he constructed within the Palais-Royal the glass-vaulted Galerie d'Orléans, one of the starting points of nineteenth-century glass and iron construction.

Charles Percier (1764–1838) [1] was the designer, whose gift for drawing attracted early notice; his sure and distinguished stroke may be felt in their common work. Percier remains in the studio, producing new designs for the French jewelers, the Sèvres manufactories, the textile weavers and cabinetmakers. The outside world holds no great interest for him, and shortly before the end of the Empire he retires to his quarters in the Louvre, devoting himself to his pupils as earlier in his career.

Percier and Fontaine's collaboration from 1794 to 1814 (1812 is the date sometimes given) meant at once the forming and the unfolding of Empire style. Although their collaboration rested on a financial basis, it was the outcome of friendship and common ideals. They were brought together in the studio of a Paris architect, and again in Rome as Academy scholars. Their common studies centered less around Antiquity than one might expect, and more around the Renaissance, the period to predominate over all others in nineteenth-century architecture. Percier and Fontaine's early discovery of the Renaissance is set forth in the two engraved volumes they later published in Paris.[2] They remained four years in Rome, the Revolution causing Fontaine to return. In Paris Fontaine found but temporary work as an architect's copyist; he designed hangings and textiles but could not make a livelihood. No one was building. After some adventures he fled to London without a passport. There the same experience awaited him: textile design, wallpaper, ornaments, and snuff-box painting. In London of the early 'nineties the cabinetmaker flourished as never before. Robert Adam's influence can doubtless be traced in Empire style. But the ornament and plane surfaces influenced Fontaine more than did the efficiency of English furniture. By then Fontaine was already moving in another direction. A letter from his father seems to have cut short his stay in London, for the Convention was to dispossess all families having members illegally abroad.

Percier, who had remained in Paris, had just been offered the position of scenic designer to the Opéra (1794). He asked that Fontaine should be called with him. This was the turning point.

The task that brought them to Napoleon's notice was that of renovating, in 1798, the Paris mansion of M. de Chauvelin, once ambassador to England.

[1] The life and work of Percier and Fontaine have not yet received any adequate evaluation. Although there exist fragments of an autobiography by Fontaine, statements concerning dates often widely disagree. Mr. Fouché's biography of Percier and Fontaine in *Les Grandes Artistes* is not sufficiently informative.

[2] Percier and Fontaine, *Choix des plus célèbres maisons de plaisance de Rome*, Paris, 1809; *Palais, maisons et autres édifices modernes à Rome*, Paris, 1798; 2nd ed., Paris, 1830.

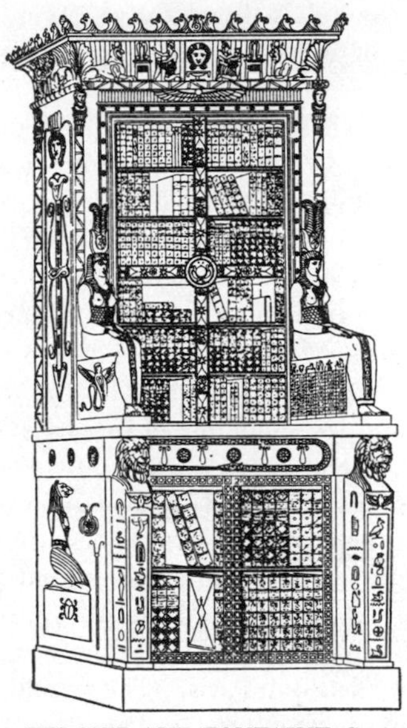

191. PERCIER AND FONTAINE: Secretary-Bookcase. 1801. *The secretary-bookcase favored by the English cabinetmakers is hardly recognizable under the fashionable ornament it received in Percier's hands. Nineteenth-century ruling taste was in full swing before the impact of mechanization.* (Recueil de décorations intérieures)

192. Secretary-Bookcase, English-American, 1790's. *The glass-fronted bookcase of the English cabinetmakers is modest in appearance. Conveniently fitted and simple, it never asserts itself at the expense of its surroundings.* (*Courtesy Metropolitan Museum, New York*)

Chauvelin's neighbor, Joséphine Beauharnais, the First Consul's wife, having bought the old castle of Malmaison (1798), became dissatisfied with the architects who were to remodel it. She saw Percier and Fontaine's near-by renovation; Isabey, the society painter, introduced them. She appears to have been delighted by their work and entrusted Malmaison to their care. Another circumstance may have moved her to do so. Madame Récamier, the society beauty, had just furnished a bedroom in the antique style (1798), showing how well its delicateness might grace a woman's beauty (fig. 195).

Louis Marie Berthault, a pupil of Percier's, carried out the design, but under the direction of the two architects. Indeed, every detail of ornament, the painted drapery with fringes, betrays Percier's hand. Josephine's bed, like Madame Récamier's, was ornamented head and foot with swans. Josephine preferred Malmaison above all other places, lived there to the end (1814), and died there in the swan-bed that Percier had designed for her.

By the time of Napoleon's coronation, the Empire style was well under way. In 1801, in the Collected Interior Decorations issued by Percier and Fontaine, the signs of Empire style are fully developed.

To what works did Napoleon apply his architects?

There was no respite for building. Napoleon's projects were many, but those executed were disappointingly few. Hoping to found a new dynasty, he had a tremendous palace designed for his son, the King of Rome (1810). It is as well that Percier and Fontaine's plans remained unexecuted. They were as dead as the problem to be solved.

The one large-scale architectural project they carried out was the building of the Rue de Rivoli, open on one side to the Tuileries.[3] Minds disciplined enough for such tasks of city planning, which became the spring-stones for Haussmann's later transformation of Paris, were no mere decorators.

Napoleon applied his architects to remodeling, to festival decorations, and to the numerous knickknacks that were the fashion under the Empire. The stress laid on festivals and ceremonies serving Napoleon's prestige appears in the two albums issued by Percier and Fontaine to commemorate Napoleon's coronation by the Pope (1804) and his marriage to Marie Louise of Habsburg (1810).[4]

Percier and Fontaine's greatest influence was upon the interior. 'Percier was the inspirer of everything produced to make a setting worthy of the Emperor. And the activity of these two artists enabled them to leave their hallmark on the slightest object of the imperial household.' [5] There were also the luxury objects that Napoleon liked to have around him: vases, services, bronze candelabra (*lustres*), as well as the jewelry that played so important a role. A special Service de Cadeaux provided gifts to foreign sovereigns. Percier's hand is everywhere to be found.

This combination of the entrepreneur, or engineer type, Fontaine, with the artist, Percier, is often repeated in the course of the nineteenth century. The abolishing of the guilds, the tearing down of barriers between the various crafts, was the postulate for enterprises such as were undertaken so early by the firm of Percier and Fontaine.

Percier and Fontaine, and the Empire style they created in all its ramifications, yield the key to an understanding of the nineteenth century. They are

---

[3] Giedion, *Space, Time and Architecture*, Cambridge, 1941.

[4] Percier, Fontaine, and Isabey, *Sacre et couronnement de Napoléon, empereur des français et roi d'Italie*, Paris, 1807; Percier and Fontaine, *Le Mariage de S. Majesté l'Empereur avec S.A.I l'archiduchesse Marie Louise d'Autriche*, Paris, 1810.

[5] E. Hessling, *Dessins d'orfèvrerie de Percier conservés à la Bibliothèque de l'Union centrale des Arts Décoratifs de Paris*, n.d.

193. The Devaluation of Space: Percier and Fontaine, Flower Stand. 1801. *The tremendous* jardinière *commissioned by a Swedish count anticipates anything the nineteenth century later used to annihilate space. It was for the middle of a salon. It was in three parts: one section accommodated a goldfish bowl, another the flowers, and the last a bird cage. Flowers grew out of the sphinxes' heads.* (Recueil de décorations intérieures)

the first representatives of the ruling taste, which pushed isolated forms into prominence and shrank from the underlying reality of a thing. But Percier and Fontaine work on a plane that one can no more compare to the decorators who swamped the nineteenth century with their products than one can compare the figure of Napoleon to the self-made man in the industrial domain.

What Happens in Empire Style?

As we once sought to point out, Classicism is not a style; Classicism is a coloring.[6] Behind the shield of antique forms, two great conceptions clash: Baroque

[6] S. Giedion, *Spaetbarocker und romantischer Klassizismus*, München, 1922.

194. The Devaluation of Space: Léon Feuchère, 'Large Flower Stand Surrounded by Divans.' 1842. *In comparison with Percier and Fontaine's flower stand, this piece by an influential theatre architect and scenic designer shows how far the ruling taste had pervaded life by the 1840's. The* jardinière *with its ring of seats seems to announce the great round sofa or borne that will be placed in the middle of the room.* (*See figs.* 212–14.) (L'Art industriel, *Paris*, 1842)

universalism (the English school; Louis XVI) and nineteenth-century specialization, with its trend to increasingly isolated forms.

To grasp the nature of the Empire style, we must begin with the single form, with Ornament. In the furniture of the English cabinetmakers, ornament gradually became a delicate accompaniment subordinated to technical solutions and to efficiency. In *Interior Decorations*,[7] as Percier and Fontaine entitled their first published designs, the cabinetmaker is not even mentioned. No new types, no opened drawers as in Sheraton's design books: everything is rendered in

[7] Percier and Fontaine, *Recueil de décorations intérieures*, Paris, 1801; 2nd ed. 1812; 3rd ed. 1827. This publication was used as a design book and was immeasurably significant for the diffusion of the Empire style. It went through three editions within thirty years.

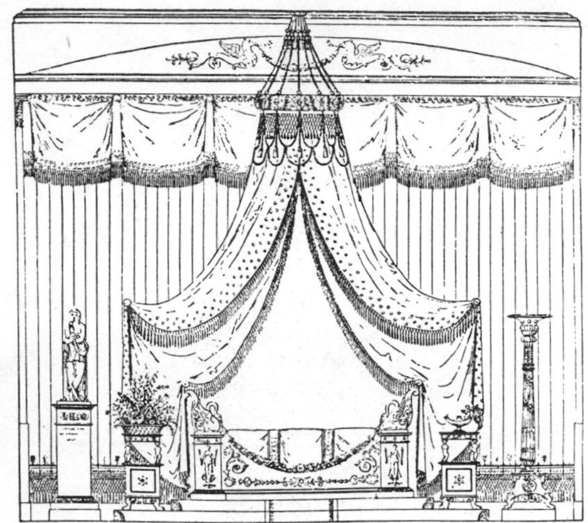

195. Madame Récamier's Bedroom by L. M. Berthault. 1798. *The drapes painted on the wall, the real drapery with double row of fringes, the décor of candelabras, statuette, bed table, and flower stand provide a foretaste of things to come.*

thin outline as first done by John Flaxman, who, we may note, went to Rome the same year as Percier and Fontaine. Fontaine's plates are not easy to read; in them the spatial dissolves into the decorative, which overruns everything.

Sheraton would cut lock shields out of plain metal or leave them entirely undecorated. Now they become the pretext for bright, gilded bronze, in strong contrast with the red mahogany. The gilded metal is affixed not on the locks only, but in all possible places. Other periods have seen ornament pass from the delicate to the florid; but now ornament dazzles the eye; and, proclaiming the difference of its material, strikes a jarring note.

THE DEVALUATION OF SYMBOLS

Behind all this is the reminiscence of imperial Rome. From the Renaissance on, the Classical panoply had served time and again: arabesques, trophies, torches, the horn of plenty, palms as used by Robert Adam, the Roman eagle with thunderbolts, the Roman fasces, the swan, the genii, the winged victory bearing laurels in her outstretched hand, Pegasus and griffons, sphinxes, Hermes, lion heads, helmed warrior heads or Olympian scenes, symbols of power and fame. Singly or in groups, this treasury of emblems is spread upon the walls or, in miniature form, nailed to furniture.

The variety of emblems on the power and fame motif is almost impossible to digest. That Percier and Fontaine handled them with great elegance becomes clear by contrast with what was created elsewhere in imitation of the French.

196. Influence of the Upholsterer: Drapery. Two Croisées. 1810. *The rule of the upholsterer is foreshadowed in Napoleon's time. Agitated movement seizes the curtains, the upper part of which is draped and slung over the rod in picturesque manner. Eagle heads carry the lambrequins in their beaks. A contemporary remarks in* 1804: '*When I see a golden eagle bearing in his talons the curtains of a financier I cannot help smiling with pity. Your beds with lances are nonsense: fit, at best, for generals; they believe themselves under a tent. But I don't see what this military outfit can signify to a* petite maîtresse, *who knows only the arrows of love . . . Elegance and taste . . . cannot consist in puny columns . . . and least of all in those heads and claws of fabulous animals which one sees sculpted on house doors and furniture.*' — Voyage à la Chaussée d'Antin, 1804. (*Osmand, Cahiers de Draperies, Paris,* 1810)

Even Thomas Sheraton, who during his later period could not escape the French influence, seems remarkably heavy when he attempts such decoration.

The ornament is chosen and assembled from various conventional motifs. Its elegance of line cannot be denied, but it no longer flows freely from the springs of invention. Perhaps it has been too naturalistically torn out of the frame within which it once had meaning. Indeed, it is not internally assimilated, as in the Renaissance when originality ran stronger than the borrowed forms of Antiquity.

The motifs multiply. But do they ever reach the threshold of feeling? Are they not rather like advertisements that one carelessly passes by, having seen them too many times? Do not the eagles, lion heads, torches, and griffons too insistently stress the envied Roman ancestry? And the trophies, the genii with palms, the spears and swords, encrusted on furniture and walls, do they not speak too often of victories?

What takes place in the Empire style is nothing other than a devaluation of symbols. As Napoleon devaluated nobility, so he devaluated ornament.

This devaluation of symbols is seen time after time in the Empire style. The laurel wreath, which the Romans used sparingly because of its significance,

197. Draped Bed. France, 1832. *What the Empire began, the following decades developed further.* (*La Mesangère*, Meubles et objets de goût, *no.* 737)

198. Drapery Croisée. 1860's. *The croisées become heavier and more and more complicated, until in the latter half of the century the whole interior is filled with a gloomy, oppressive atmosphere.* (*Jules Verdellet*, Manuel Géometrique du tapissier, *Paris*, 1859)

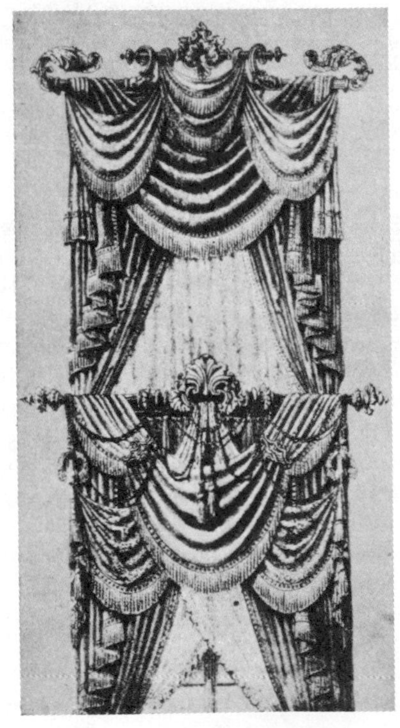

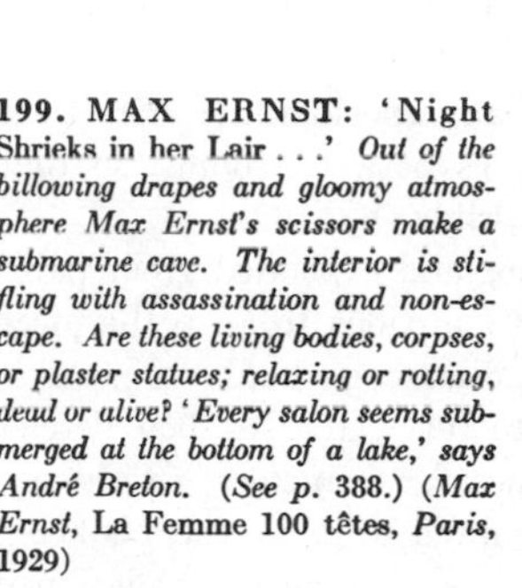

199. MAX ERNST: 'Night Shrieks in her Lair . . .' *Out of the billowing drapes and gloomy atmosphere Max Ernst's scissors make a submarine cave. The interior is stifling with assassination and non-escape. Are these living bodies, corpses, or plaster statues; relaxing or rotting, dead or alive? 'Every salon seems submerged at the bottom of a lake,' says André Breton.* (*See p.* 388.) (*Max Ernst,* La Femme 100 têtes, *Paris,* 1929)

forms almost the trademark of the Empire style. Beginning in the Directoire, it appears singly, but now it spreads like ivy over entire pilasters, or is stamped upon the walls of the Tuileries throne room, which Percier and Fontaine decorated for Napoleon. And is it not telling that one felt no incongruity in using friezes of crowning victories with palms even on teapots? [8] Or that the thyrsos staff, carried in Antiquity by the worshipers of Dionysus only at the most solemn festivals, now serves as a curtain rod (fig. 196)?

In the enormous flower stand they sent to Sweden (before 1801) (fig. 193), Percier and Fontaine used sphinx heads as supports for flower baskets with real plants. The motif was not new. Sphinxes were painted in light color on the panels of Marie Antoinette's boudoir in Fontainebleau.[9] They too carry slender flower baskets on their heads. But all this is a gentle unreal play of dream elements that the eye delights to follow — as irrational as the sphinxes' tails, curling into arabesques that sprout a thin stem balancing a vase. In Napoleon's time, the sphinxes become solid metal beasts and real flowers are supposed to

[8] Hessling, op.cit. pl. 3.

[9] L. Dimier, *Fontainebleau, les appartements de Napoléon I et de Marie Antoinette,* Paris, 1911, pl. 74.

grow out of real vases. Dreams lose their fascination when frozen into naturalistic terms. And it is also significant for the devaluation of symbols that the Empire architects enthrone a god on an almost ceiling-high pylon in the midst of a room, and call it a wardrobe.[10]

FURNITURE BECOMES DOMINANT

The decisive step toward the nineteenth century in Empire style was the beginning of spatial disintegration.

Furniture is treated in the spirit of self-sufficient architecture. Pieces are often conceived as isolated entities, and furniture loses its relatedness to the surrounding space.

When the eighteenth century designed pieces of any considerable size, it set them as far as possible flush to the wall, sometimes between rooms, so that their volumes should remain as inconspicuous as possible (fig. 192).

The cabinetmakers of late eighteenth-century England expended great pains on the glass-fronted bookcase. They were especially anxious to keep the piece modest in appearance, of such proportions as to hold as many books as possible in the least space. They set the container close to the wall. In 1800 Percier and Fontaine designed a similarly modest bookcase for Napoleon's residence in Malmaison. But, at the same time, they are tempted to make the bookcase into a display piece (fig. 191), such as the 'secretary used as a bookcase' designed for an Amsterdam client. In its parts, it takes after the English bookcases. But the meaning has changed. Access to books is no longer the guiding motive. More urgent, it seems, is that the furniture should be shaped like an Egyptian temple door, and covered with hieroglyphs. Percier and Fontaine comment, 'The Egyptian form adopted by us had been requested to set forth a series of various rare woods and to afford the motives for various incrustations. The two sitting figures with Osiris heads are in bronze.' [11] Exotic appeal and decorativeness are here the yardstick.

Space cannot hold its own against the gigantic flower stands flanked by four plant-bearing sphinxes, where three tiers accommodate a goldfish bowl, flowers, and a birdcage. By 1800 this stand, commissioned by a Swedish Count, has anticipated whatever the nineteenth century will contrive in this way (fig. 193).

THE INFLUENCE OF THE UPHOLSTERER

And finally the trend of Empire style appears in an adjunct that is far from the genius of serious design and which seems purely accessory at first glance: This is the great role played by drapery. It reaches its peak toward the end of

[10] Percier and Fontaine, *Recueil de décorations intérieures*, Paris, 1801.

[11] Ibid.

the Empire and, as much as anything in Napoleon's time, forms a premonition of things to come.

Here the upholsterer, the decorator, announces his claim to leadership. Within a strong architectonic framework, hangings with various valances and side-pieces were introduced under Louis XIV. Jean Marot helped to give them a clear shape, such as might merge with the architectural space. Under the Directoire began the replacing of panels by drapery painted on the wall in allusion to Antiquity, as in Madame Récamier's bedroom. This, together with the treatment of furniture as self-sufficient architecture, did much to further spatial disintegration. Napoleon seems at first to have resisted the fashion. Back from his campaigns, he deprecated the hall at Malmaison, which Percier and Fontaine had draped in tent shape: it 'resembled a cage for wild beasts.' [12] After drapery painted on the wall, real fabric soon wrapped space in its garments, muffling all boundaries.

Drapery is elected to play a quite special role. The Directoire attempted to give calico curtains a somewhat informal air by hanging them from large rings, loosely held on a rod. Agitated movement takes hold of the curtains under the Empire; 'What has left us a particularly forceful memory of this period is the mode of execution of this drapery, so dense, and so daring in its effect.' [13] This is what made the greatest impression on an upholsterer of the 'seventies. The upper part of the curtain (*lambrequin*) is picturesquely draped, and slung, toga-like, over the curtain rod, to which motion is also communicated. Eagle heads hold the *lambrequins* in their great open beaks (fig. 196). Fringes, double or threefold, give additional weight. The calico curtains, asymmetrically crossing, are gathered in generous folds. In the same way, windows, doors, and alcoves are abandoned to the upholsterer's fancy.

This florid drapery was of well calculated carelessness. Skilled workers knew how to cut and sew these difficult pieces, and to cast them with casual effect over their curtain rods — the spear or the thyrsos staff. The draperies are still made of light calico. Under Louis Philippe the picturesque grouping of the Empire will be combined with heavy, Louis XIV fabrics.

---

[12] G. Rayssal, *Château de Malmaison, texte historique et descriptif*, Paris, 1908? p.13.
[13] Deville, *Dictionnaire du tapissier*, Paris, 1878, p.197.

The Mechanization of Adornment

How far were man's intimate surroundings permeated and transmuted by mechanization? The question escapes any simple answer and still eludes full clarification. It opens upon the sphere of feeling, where things cannot be narrowed to a single interpretation.

The attack of mechanization was a total one, pouring in from all sides. We shall trace its impact upon the intimate surroundings along three lines:

Obvious symptoms will often show how mechanization confused the human environment — symptoms such as the industrial reproduction of art objects, the counterfeiting and adulteration of handicraft methods, and a decaying sense for materials. From the 'forties on, reformer followed reformer in decrying the persistent evil, but mechanization proved the stronger.

Other symptoms lie hidden and unexplored. They were at work beneath the surface and cannot be directly apprehended. But they show how mechanization is linked to the utensils closest to man's daily life, furniture. In the section on the *Reign of the Upholsterer*, we deal with the coming about of this mechanization.

And lastly, we shall trace the influence of mechanization where it was not hampered by fashion, where it proceeded boldly and undeterred: in the types of furniture created by needs inherent to the century. These possess a vitality of their own. In 'The Constituent Furniture of the Nineteenth Century: *The Furniture of the Engineer*,' we shall attempt to point out their significance.

The guilds produced wares of a consistently high standard. The guild system meant a controlled economy. Prices were fixed, and were very high in comparison with the hourly wage. Goods were not easily acquired. They embodied human as well as material values, and strong personal bonds attached a man to his favorite possessions.

This was the situation when the Industrial Revolution set in. Mechanization transformed the objects of everyday use, as well as those serving emotional and representational needs. The wish for adornment is innate in man and proves ineradicable, like hunger or love.

All depends on how these wishes are satisfied. We are dealing with intangibles, which cannot be proved by dates and figures; yet, the whole nineteenth-century development shows how the devaluating of symbols recoils on man.

The machines began to pour forth statuary, pictures, vases, flower bowls, and carpets in mass. Simultaneously, furniture became bloated and its forms dulled. There followed a further packing of the room with all sorts of objects called forth by the growing demand for adornment. The less costly it became to produce, the more this adornment flourished.

Lost, it would seem, was man's instinct for quiet surroundings and for the dignity of space. The same temper pervaded all classes of society. Only the materials and execution vary. The statuary may be in chiseled bronze, or, for the less wealthy, cast iron; marble or plaster; china or papier mâché; hand-wrought silver or pressed tin. The process moves on to attack wall and floor surfaces; the carpets may be oriental or machine-made, the pictures originals or chromolithographs.

At no other time in history did man allow the instinct for the goodly ordering of his surroundings to suffer such decay. Before then, cramming would have been unthinkable on economic grounds alone. One wonders how men came to such lack of restraint. What led them to this abandon? Was mechanization alone responsible?

The initial urge is easy to understand. Men born into the first decades of the nineteenth century grew up in the firmly rooted belief that all products embodied high labor values and were to be won only by long toil. But now the machines began cutting to a fraction of their former cost not only cotton goods, but almost every product used in art and adornment. Did not the vases, statuettes, and rugs resemble handmade objects? Were they not as miraculous in their own way as the railroads then beginning to sweep the breadth of the land?

Mechanization, which made possible this profusion of objects, cannot be the ultimate cause; neither can the mere cheapening of manufactured goods.

The urge would soon have spent itself were there no deeper forces behind it. Mechanization is neutral. What matters is how one uses mechanization. The marks of ruling taste were already visible in the Empire style; that is, at a time when mass production in this sphere did not exist. Mechanization merely enlarged these symptoms to undreamed of proportions. The elements lay ready in the man of 1800. It was not mechanization that devaluated symbols, but the manner in which mechanization was employed. When did this start?

Substitute Materials and Imitation Handicraft, 1820–50

With bewildering speed in the space of the 'thirties and early 'forties, industry asserted itself in the many provinces of adornment. This expansion had only been made possible by an intensive technological preparation, which, within fifty years, achieved the complicated mechanization of spinning and weaving. Such tasks, with their breakdown of the work process and their differentiated machines, showed how the problems of mechanization were to be tackled. It proved easier to imitate handmade household articles mechanically than to create the mechanisms to spin the tenuous fibers of cotton.

It began with the carpets. Spreading carpets were in demand after 1820, bestrewn with figures, landscapes, and giant flowers. The invention of the self-actor had brought textile machinery to a peak. An English patent is announced in 1827: 'an improvement in the manufacture of Venetian carpet.' [14] The flowers are made much wider and longer and may extend quite across a four-quarter carpet or a still wider carpet if necessary. . . .[15]

'The Royal Damask Carpet,' the inventor proudly named his multicolored textile, whose expanse and breadth of pattern had never before been achieved. The Jacquard loom, by increasing the number of cards and needles, freed the designer from the limitations of handicraft and enabled him to realize his every caprice, reasonable or absurd.

But when did mechanization of adornment take full effect? When did mass production begin to proliferate statuettes, vases, vessels, and tableware?

It was assumed from the start that these objects should appear to have been made by hand. To simulate this, machines and devices had to be invented for ornamenting, embossing, counter-sinking, or raising surfaces.

Indeed the British patents of 1830 and 1850 show that industry never tired of inventing new means to simulate handicraft with imitation materials and imitation forms. In less than ten years, from 1837 to 1846, the Office granted thirty-five patents for 'the coating and covering of non-metallic bodies,' 'coating surfaces of articles made of wrought iron which may be used *in substitution* of japanning and other modes now [1843] in use,' and 'mastic or cement which may be also applied as an artificial stone and for covering metals.' [16]

Then galvanizing began to thrive — the 'dipping process' whereby castings or sheet-metal objects were dropped into molten zinc. The dull edges and loss of definition did not affect their popularity.

As the century advanced, reproduction by electroplating (invented by the Russian Professor Jacobi, of Dorpat, 1837) grew on a large scale. This made it possible to cover plaster with a hair-thin layer of metal so as to give the appearance of bronze.

The abuse of mechanization led, by around 1840, to a decay or at least a weakening of the sense for materials.

It went beyond the hiding of inferior materials in more valuable coatings. Devices were invented to manufacture the objects that filled the rooms. This meant stamping, pressing, punching, and making matrices or dies. Patented in 1838 were 'means of producing figured surfaces, sunk and in relief, and of printing therefrom and also of moulding, stamping and embossing'; [17] in 1844, there is concern with the manufacture 'of blocks for stamping, embossing and mould-

[14] British Patent No.5501, 1827.

[15] Ibid.

[16] British Patent, No.9841, 1843.

[17] British Patent, No.7552, 25 Jan. 1838.

200. Stamping Machine. 1832. *The machines began to mass-produce statuettes, pictures, vases, and common articles imitating the appearance of handmade objects. The rapid, mechanical stamping of coins forms one of the starting points of mechanized adornment.* (*Charles Babbage,* On the Economy of Machinery and Manufacture, *Cambridge,* 1832)

ing';[18] and, finally, in 1846, with 'obtaining and applying motive power for working stamping machines.'[19] In one year, 1846, three patents dealt with mechanical processes for this method of reproduction.

The call for machine-made adornment was reaching a peak. Between 1830 and 1850 a whole arsenal of substitute materials was created, whose indelible effect is still at work today.

Against Misuse of Mechanization: The English Reformers of 1850

When was protest first raised against this abuse of mechanization?

By 1850, industrialization in England, for good as well as for evil, was ahead of that in other countries. Here a few men of foresight had become alarmed at the state of man amid mechanization. The organizing force of the movement was Henry Cole (1808–82),[20] an English civil servant, first noted for his preservation of medieval chronicles.

[18] British Patent, No.10377, 1844.

[19] British Patent, No.11077, 11 Feb. 1846.

[20] The compass of this book does not allow us to become further acquainted with this interesting figure. We have dealt with the reforming movement of 1850 in an unpublished study *Industrialisierung und Gefühl* (Industrialization and Feeling), based on Cole's manuscripts and diaries preserved in the Victoria and Albert Museum, London. Here we can but fragmentarily touch upon the movement, and only in so far as Cole's activity impinges upon the mechanization of adornment. His important role in the mid-century has been almost wholly forgotten. His writings, edited after his death by his daughter, yield much information concerning his efforts: *Fifty Years of Public Work,* 2 vols., London, 1884; also the 40 volumes of his Miscellanies and Diaries.

The group attempted to restrain the recklessness of industrial production. Thus, within two decades, the evil of wrongly used mechanization was recognized at its roots. Cole's group of reformers included several of England's noted painters and sculptors. Its ideas differed from those of Ruskin, who was then beginning to arouse interest, and from the ideas of the Morris circle of 1860. The reformers of 1850 did not preach a return to the handicrafts. They did not seek to escape from industry, but to cut clearly through to the core of the problem: To refute mechanization is not to cope with it.

Machines running unchecked flooded the land. The answer of Henry Cole and his circle was an attempt to bridge the gaps between the artist, the manufacturer, and the designer. He set out to 'show the union of fine art with manufacture.' Hence he invented the term 'Art Manufactures.' The thought had come to him by 1845: 'I believe I originated in 1845 the term art manufactures, meaning fine arts or beauty applied to mechanical production.' [21]

Hoping thus to strike at the root of the evil, he wanted to form and reform production. As he expressed it: 'An alliance between art and manufacturer would promote public taste.' [22] Within a few years he won over leading industrialists of long standing: the famous Coalbrookdale Iron Works, first large-scale iron producers and builders of the first cast-iron bridge (1775–9); the Wedgwood Potteries; Hollands in furniture; and Christie's in glass.

For the furthering of his plan, Henry Cole needed a social foothold. The 'Society of Arts' ('Society for the Encouragement of Arts, Manufactures and Commerce' was its full name) had sponsored competitions since its foundation by the painter William Shipley in 1754.[23] In 1845 the Society of Arts offered a prize for the 'production of a tea service and beer jugs for *common use*.'

The award went to Felix Summerly, the artistic and literary pseudonym of Henry Cole. His tea service (fig. 202) met with tremendous popularity, and — the Secretary of the Society tells me — is manufactured to this day by its original makers, Minton and Company. This tea service offers nothing unusual to the modern eye, but viewed historically it commemorates the start of nineteenth-century reform. To Henry Cole it supplied the stimulus for new and far-reaching plans.

HENRY COLE'S JOURNAL OF DESIGN, 1849–52

Each year now, in the handsome building designed for the Society of Arts by the Adam brothers, Cole holds modest exhibitions of industrial products,

[21] Cole, *Fifty Years of Public Work*, vol. I, p.107.

[22] Ibid. p.103.

[23] This was the select society which, as we have seen, offered the first 'premium' for 'a machine to answer the purpose of reaping corn.'

the 'Felix Summerly Series.' By criticism and praise he would win industry to his views. His desk is laden with patterns of fabric sent in by manufacturers throughout Britain. His small but fighting *Journal of Design* yields immediate insight into Cole's thought and into his campaign. 'Novelty, give us novelty, seems to be the cry,' he writes of the patterns lying before him, 'heaven and earth and the wide sea cannot obtain the forms and fancies that are here displayed . . . like the whimsies of madness.' [24]

At the same time, he shows that considerable profits may be earned by acceptable patterns, thus proving the 'commercial value of the ornamental design.'

The six small volumes of the monthly *Journal of Design*, its first number dated 1849 and the last February 1852, deal with almost every branch of manufacture, wherever industry is concerned with adornment or with 'the familiar things of everyday use.' Here as scarcely anywhere else are displayed the fears and preoccupations of the period. Problems of child education are boldly and thoroughly discussed within its pages. Patterns of fabric are criticized and pasted in the *Journal* like plants in a herbarium. Preserved in their original colors, they afford rare insight to the modern observer. Side by side with criticism of textile patterns or of match boxes made to resemble a Gothic tomb (fig. 201), Cole takes his stand toward the most important new books. Young Ruskin and his escapism promptly drew a scathing attack. It is the *Esprit nouveau* of 1850, except that it would embrace the whole of industry, the entire world, and was not confined like its counterpart around 1920 to a small magazine of the *avant-garde*. But the great disadvantage of Henry Cole and his circle in comparison with the movement of 1920 was their inability to proffer a new artistic vision. This denied them lasting influence.

MATCH-BOX: *Crusaders' Tomb*, in Parian, manufactured by Mintons. This fanciful trifle presents a curious history of prices worth noting. It was first produced in or-molu, in London, and sold for four guineas. It was then made by Messengers, at Birmingham, in bronze, and sold for thirty shillings; and now it is brought out, in parian, at four shillings! Lights were constantly burnt over tombs in old times, so we presume the designer thought the present an allowable adaptation of the idea. We do not agree with him.

201. Match Box in Shape of Crusader's Tomb. *c.*1850. *Henry Cole's wry comment shows an awareness of the growing danger of devaluated materials and symbols.* (*Henry Cole,* Journal of Design)

[24] Cole, *Journal of Design*, vol. I, p.74.

Of every object exhibited, Henry Cole demanded that it should serve its purpose, or, as he prescribed: 'produce in each article superior utility, select pure forms.' From 1847 to 1848, backed by the exclusive Society of Arts, he organized his small but increasingly successful exhibitions. Under his influence the Society awakened from its decades of somnolence and again became a living force. In 1848 he suggested to the Prince Consort Albert, president of the Society, that a national exhibition of British industry be held. 'The answer was discouraging,'[25] Cole reports, but he did not give up. The success of the Industrial Exhibition held in Paris in 1849 came to his rescue, and Cole pushed his aims even farther. Cautiously and by tactful queries in an interview at Buckingham Palace, he led the Prince Consort to decide that there should be held in London a Great Exhibition of the Industries of All Countries, the first truly international one.[26]

THE MECHANIZATION OF ADORNMENT AND THE GREAT EXHIBITION OF 1851

As is well known, the Great Exhibition was planned by the Society of Arts, or rather by the driving force of Prince Consort Albert and Henry Cole, who steered it through obstacles and hazards that might have discouraged less determined men.

The 'First Exhibition of All Nations' would allow the comparison of human efforts throughout the world, a gigantic balance sheet. Cole's aim was clear: to enact in large what his *Journal of Design* had urged in small: Learning to See: Seeing by Comparing. How was the art industry faring elsewhere? Was industrial production holding its own with the handicrafts as practiced in the East?

Cole's first speech to the public (October 1849) made this point: 'We may expect to have at our exhibition some of those Indian manufactures which are now almost unknown to us.'[27]

Comparison of the European with the non-European products, as Cole meant to show, proved damning to mechanization. Here were the serene Indian patterns, conceived on the two-dimensional plane; the Cashmere shawls; or the thin muslins, with their abstract, light blue ornament. Next to these stood the dazzling machine-made carpets, proudly blooming, thanks to their 30,000 cards, in all shades and colors.[28]

---

[25] Henry Cole, *Fifty Years of Public Work*, vol. I, p.121.

[26] Ibid. pp.124–5.

[27] Ibid.

[28] Matthew Digby Wyatt, *The Industrial Arts of the Nineteenth Century. Illustrations of the choicest specimens of the Exhibition of* 1851, 2 vols., London, 1851. Here large chromolithographs show Chinese, African, and Indian adornment side by side with machine-made carpets (Axminster), genre statuettes ('The First Step'), or fantastic crystal fountain made in Birmingham, and sumptuous objects such as state beds and overdecorated pianos.

Spectators were shocked by the contrast.

'At the exhibition the visitor will see flowers and leaves and fruit of a size such as was never seen in this world before. He will find his eyes dazzled and perplexed by moss-roses that give him a headache with their brightness.' Then follows the question, what are carpets for? 'The uses of a carpet are no mystery. In the first place make your carpet a background for setting your furniture appropriately and well. Now is that to be done by broad and startling contrasts of color, which are constantly drawing the eye downwards instead of allowing it to rest agreeably upon other objects?'[29]

On one hand was mechanization, implemented by the most highly differentiated means; on the other, primitive, labor-consuming handicrafts. The question imposed itself: 'Does the process of civilization and the increased value of knowledge and labor destroy principles of taste?' For the first time it

202. HENRY COLE: Society of Arts Competition, 1845. Tea Service 'For Common Use.' *This popular tea service represents one of the early endeavors to improve public taste: 'A model of plain and cheap earthen ware. The aim has been to obtain as much beauty and ornament as is commensurate with cheapness. Ornaments on the handles are so designed as not to interfere with the simplicity of the outlines. The cup, being much deeper than wide, offers least scope for the radiation of heat.'* — Fifty Years of Public Life. *(Courtesy the Society of Arts, London)*

became clear that the degree of industrialization is no measure of culture or of our ability to shape life. Since then it has become ever more apparent that intensive mechanization rarely coincides with the mastery of living.

With the exhibits so closely juxtaposed, no one could deny that the so-called primitives knew dignity and had contact with the material. The Europeans, as soon as they left the safe ground of neutral fabric, betrayed insecurity in their mixture of ornament and naturalism no less than in their use and abuse of materials. As an article in *The Times* on 'Universal Infidelity in Principles of Design' expressed it, 'The absence of any fixed principles in ornamental

[29] The whole attitude of the article, which appeared in the London *Times*, reflects the circle around Henry Cole; Cole reprinted it in the *Journal of Design*, vol. v (1851), pp.158–9.

design is apparent in the Exhibition . . . it seems to us that the art manufacturers of the whole of Europe are thoroughly demoralized.' [30]

'The systematic transgression of every principle of design,' another verdict ran, 'an abuse of modern scientific progress. Man has become a servant of the machine.' [31] Henry Cole expresses this awareness in his unassuming way: 'It was from the East that the most impressive lesson was to be learned . . . here was revealed a fresh well of art. . . .' And swiftly reaching from Eastern handicraft to the second creative center of the Exhibition: 'I venture to submit whether our American cousins did not, in their reaping and other machines, *adapted to new wants* and infant periods of society, teach us next the most valuable lessons.' [32] The instinct that led Cole to grasp these two poles simultaneously, primitive expression on one hand and products of high mechanization on the other, the two wellsprings of modern art, shows him far ahead of his own time.

Only five men made up the Exhibition's executive committee: first and foremost, Henry Cole; a great civil engineer, Robert Stephenson, who had just completed the tubular bridge across the Menai Strait; Digby Wyatt, the architect and reformer; and another Society of Arts member, noted for his reorganization of the *Daily News*, who brought his experience to the catalogue. This team was to see through the most uncompromising task of the whole Exhibition — a building 'adapted to new wants.' Here Henry Cole could put into practice what he had been preaching to the art industry: he offered to Joseph Paxton the opportunity of constructing a crystal palace, a great proof that in mechanization too a vision lies concealed, in which 'all traces of materiality dissolve.' [33]

Completed by a near miracle, the project, in more timid hands, would never have become a reality.[34] A pseudo-monumental building would have been decreed; and, had further obstacles arisen, the whole idea would have been dropped.

In creating a building, an exhibition, anything of artistic value, the patrons are nearly as important as the designer.

So not Paxton alone was to be thanked for this building, but the London of 1851, whose atmosphere made it possible. Is it not strange that a short while later, for the New York World's Fair of 1853, Paxton designed a late-romantic Gothic structure which fell wide of any genial solution? [35]

---

[30] Reprinted in the *Journal of Design*, vol. v (1851), p.158.

[31] Nicolette Gray, 'Prophets of the Modern Movement,' *Architectural Review*, London, Feb. 1937.

[32] Cole, *Journal of Design*, vol. vi, p.252.

[33] Lothar Bucher, *Kulturhistorische Skizzen aus der Industrieausstellung aller Voelker*, Frankfurt a.M., 1851, pp.10–11.

[34] Henry Cole himself narrates in a few pages the exciting events that led to the building of the Crystal Palace. Cf. Cole, *Fifty Years of Public Work*, vol. i, pp.163f.

[35] Illustrated in B. Silliman Jr. and C. R. Goodrich, *The World of Science, Art and Industry*, New York, 1854, pp.1–3.

'WE HAVE NO GUIDING PRINCIPLES'

The lesson of the Exhibition was widely discussed by contemporaries,[36] who asked what conclusions it held for time to come. Henry Cole tried to save for the future the guiding principle: Learning to see, Seeing by comparing. He transplanted them into educational practice.[37]

Industry itself could not be held in check; production would go its way. But the spirit of reform did not die out in England, as could be seen at international exhibitions when English furniture, painted a simple white, appeared next to the sumptuous display pieces of the Continent. In France and other Continental countries, no forces were yet alive to give industry a direction.

As Owen Jones, the designer in Henry Cole's group (fig. 203), frankly declared: 'We have no guiding principles.' [38]

Behind these words appears the shape of things of 1850. There is no doubt that the mechanization of adornment moved in step with the ruling taste of the public. Genre scenes and coyly posed nudes seem as if painted by the tongue. Today every museum has relegated such canvases to its cellar, almost as if they outraged decency. Yet they dominated the market and the customers' taste from 1850 to 1890, crowding out all other works. They show the same sickly and debased sense of material as do the punched ornaments or flowery carpets of the art industry.

THE SEARCH FOR BASIC PRINCIPLES OF DESIGN

What counter-proposals did Henry Cole's circle have to offer? The attitudes of the reformers were shaped in the late Romantic background of their youth. They had always believed that contact with good examples was in itself edifying. When Felix Summerly (Henry Cole) published a series of children's books in the 'forties, he illustrated them with woodcuts from Dürer and Holbein.

These men are contemporaries of Victor Hugo. Like Delacroix, Owen Jones went on tour to the East in the 1830's, where he greatly admired Arabian forms and ornament. A few years prior to the Great Exhibition, he published a lavish book on the Alhambra.[39]

England's artists around 1850 were competent craftsmen. They trod an honorable middle path. Their art could yield no deeper impulses. Yet, the

---

[36] William Whewell, *Lectures on the Result of the Exhibition*, London, 1852.

[37] The unexpectedly large earnings of the Exhibition were used to purchase objects from which Henry Cole gradually assembled the first museum of decorative art, The Victoria and Albert Museum, South Kensington. After this, with the help of his fellow workers he realized his plans for a School of Design.

[38] Owen Jones (1853), quoted in Gray, op.cit.

[39] Jones, *Elevations and Sections of the Alhambra*, London, 1847–8.

insight and freedom of their declared principles proved better guides than their executed work.

Although this may not strike one at first sight, they sought to establish basic and elemental principles. Owen Jones' *Grammar of Ornament* (1856) [40] clearly states this aim. It carefully assembled ornament of widely separated peoples and periods, from China and the Near East to Celtic enlacement and the Baroque. Jones lifts the ornament from its material — silk, linen, wood, stone, or pottery — and flattens it out in color upon the plane surface. His aim was the reverse of what it might seem.

'I have ventured to hope that in thus bringing into immediate juxtaposition the many forms of beauty . . . I might aid in arresting that unfortunate tendency of our time to be content with copying, whilst the fashion lasts, the forms peculiar to any bygone age.' [41] These pattern pictures should directly stimulate perception, just as do the Dürer woodcuts in Cole's books for the young. Owen Jones makes this clear in the last chapter, where he offers examples of his own. Here he does not succumb to the 'fatal facility of manufacturing ornaments.' He does not try to invent new ones. He does not go to nature for a photographic or plastic copy, or choose to follow his own advice of 'engrafting on the experience of the past the knowledge we may obtain by a return to nature for fresh inspiration.' He wishes only to 'detect the laws which are to be found in nature . . . we may gather this from a single leaf.' [42] Across the whole page, without light or shadow, he draws the large and small leaves of the horse chestnut, pressed onto a flat surface, like a Chinese print (fig. 203). As in a herbarium, he gathers the scarlet oak, the passion flower, the onion, the daffodil, the dogrose, or the iris. He confines himself to a few elements; but when one observes how the chestnut leaves are organized within the white page, and how the iris is simplified in form and color and its flowers represented in plan and elevation, 'from which it will be seen that the basis of all form is geometry,' one realizes that guiding principles of *Art nouveau* at the turn of the century will be closer to his outlook than the sumptuously flowered carpets of his own time.

His attitude to color is also wholly unimpressionistic. He visualizes color as components of planes, not as coloring for illusionistic purposes. He seeks a return to elementary colors: 'Use primary colors' — pure blue, red, yellow, and use them in architecture for inherent spatial interaction; forms and planes for their advancing or receding value. It is much as if LeCorbusier were taking one through a building to make clear the function of color. Against strong opposition, Owen Jones painted color into the skeleton of the Crystal Palace

[40] Reprinted, London, 1910.

[41] Jones, *Grammar of Ornament*, Preface.

[42] Ibid. p.157.

203. OWEN JONES: Horse-Chestnut Leaves Pressed onto a Flat Surface. 1856. *The reformers of the 'fifties tried to escape eclecticism and 'arrest that unfortunate tendency of our time to be content with copying, while the fashion lasts, the forms peculiar to any bygone age.' Owen Jones arranges the leaves of the horse-chestnut tree over the whole page, without light and shade, in pure lines and contours. He is moving in the direction of the late nineteenth-century's 'Art nouveau.'* (*Owen Jones*, Grammar of Ornament, *London*, 1856)

following Semper's method. He seems to have been successful, for to quote a critic of the time, 'I had the impression — and the longer I stayed, the stronger it became — that the coarse matter with which architecture works was completely dissolved in color. The building is not decorated with color, but built of it.' [43]

Blue recedes, yellow advances, red is suited to the middle distance, and white is recommended for the vertical 'neutral' planes. He frames the basic laws of color in architecture.[44]

STANDARD OBJECTS AS MODELS

The *Journal of Design* is sparing of large illustrated supplements. In the first volume (1849) Henry Cole indulges in only one, to trace in outline on dark brown background the plain objects of everyday use: augers, keys, saws, pans, cups. All are shown in the flat, without perspective. A second sheet, whose white outlines stand on the brown background, is devoted to 'sketching objects in which perspective is gradually introduced.' Here, too, they are the regular objects of common use: 'Cups, bottles, shoes, boots, hats, coal-scuttles, boxes, simple chairs.'

Design, Cole believed, should be introduced in all elementary schools. In these plates, he reports experiments successfully made in a small school in Kent 'with the view of promoting habits of correct observation.' Cole rejects the pencil; the children shall work with unsharpened chalk 'because it enforces a bold style and precludes small drawings.' The blackboard is recommended, and where this is unobtainable, a slate or blackened cardboard.[45]

To awaken observation and feeling, to cultivate the children's taste, he uses the precise outlines of non-sentimental objects, elements of the child's constant surroundings: the simple, serial objects of anonymous industrial production (fig. 205). This method shows that Henry Cole and his fellow workers no longer looked down upon useful objects as poor in content and barren of feeling. How far the reformers were themselves conscious of this is not altogether ascertainable. Certain it is that this 'learning to see' in anonymous industrial production grew from the roots of the era no less than did that unexpected creation, the Crystal Palace.

LIMITATIONS OF THE REFORM

The three main figures of the reform circle, Henry Cole, Owen Jones, and Richard Redgrave, were all civil servants. Cole and Redgrave were high officials

[43] Bucher, op.cit.

[44] *Journal of Design* (1850), vol. IV, pp.131–3.

[45] Ibid. (1849), vol. I.

of the full Victorian era. Henry Cole (1808–82), as 'sole secretary of the department of design,' controlled, among other things, the English drawing schools, the number of which by 1864 had grown to 91. Owen Jones (1809–74), an interior designer of wide activity,[46] became 'Superintendent of the Works of the Great Exhibition.' Richard Redgrave (1804–88), a genre painter tending to social implications in the later part of his career, was at the same time 'Inspector-General for Art and Surveyor of the Crown.'

Henry Cole was the tireless propagandist and organizer. Owen Jones was more active on the artistic side and became influential through his *Grammar of Ornament,* which went through repeated printings down to 1910. Richard Redgrave was the best thinker of the circle. To follow Redgrave in his thinking, one must turn to his official reports and to the addresses he made when presenting medals and prizes in the school.[47] A rare thing it is, in the nineteenth century, to discover a historical source within the pages of official orations.

No member of the circle attempted to make a final summary of its thinking. Its significance lies in the manifesto, in the fragment, in the unexpected advance. Presenting prizes at the Society of Art in 1850, Redgrave discusses the meaning of 'utility':

> Do not misunderstand me: I do not refer to that common and obvious sense of utility, by which we know that the use of a carpet is to cover a floor, a glass to contain a liquid . . . which, whilst it requires more studies and thought to arrive at, is no less real, and would save us from many errors both of choice and taste. A carpet, whilst it covers the floor, is also the ground from which all the furniture and the various objects in the apartment are to arise: it should therefore be treated as a flat surface . . . but these utilities are violated.[48]

The intellectual outlook of the circle is more or less in keeping with Utilitarianism as expounded in its philosophical and economic aspects by John Stuart Mill (1806–73). Henry Cole, moreover, early came in contact with Mill. The two met twice a week during the early thirties, for discussion at a friend's house.

Only Gottfried Semper, the German architect (1803–79), attempted to mold the experience and principles of this London of the Great Exhibition into a broad system. Living in England as an emigré at the time, he worked close to Cole's circle, collaborated on the Great Exhibition, and became an instructor in Architecture, Metalwork, and Decorative Art at the newly founded School

[46] He also built shop fronts having windows where the binders of cast iron or bronze were left visible: 'Shop front for Mr. Chapper in New Bond Street, London,' was still standing before the Second World War. Illustrated in *Journal of Design,* vol. VI, p.13.

[47] The compilation of Redgrave's writings by his son is none too satisfactory, for it fails to distinguish the words of the author from those of the compiler. Cf. Gilbert R. Redgrave, *Manual of Design,* compiled from the writings and addresses of Richard Redgrave, London, 1876.

[48] Cole quotes this speech, *Journal of Design,* vol. I, p.101.

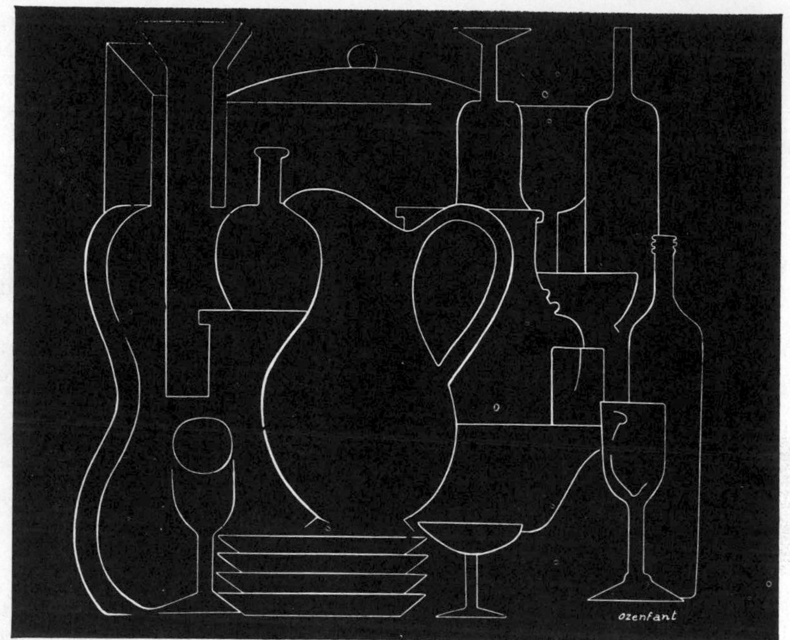

204. OZENFANT: Drawing, 1925. *The things we use daily become part and parcel of our life. Like the Cubists, the Purists of the* 1920's *pointed to the objects purified and standardized by long use, with plain and simple outlines leading to 'mariages de contours.'*

of Design. Henry Cole, who scarcely ever makes personal recommendations in his *Journal of Design*, calls to the attention of English manufacturers that Semper's 'knowledge both of architecture and of general decoration is profound, and his taste excellent.' And that Semper is the man 'from whom our manufacturers would be likely to obtain great help.'[49] When later, in 1855, Semper was appointed professor to the newly founded Technische Hochschule in Zürich, he systematized the expressions and experiences of London in his *Style in the Technical and Tectonic Arts, or a Practical Aesthetic.*[50] The first two volumes appeared in 1860 and 1863; the third, which was to have shown the bearing of art on social development, was never printed. For decades, Semper's stand influenced art theory. As late as 1910, the German reform movement in the decorative arts, which took fitness to purpose as its final criterion, regarded

[49] *Journal of Design*, vol. VI, p.113.

[50] *Der Stil in den technischen und tektonischen Künsten*, 1860–63, 2nd ed., 2 vols., München, 1878–9.

205. HENRY COLE: Drawings of Simple Objects for Child Education. *For teaching school children, Cole recommends drawing with thick chalk on a blackboard, omitting detail. Their observation will be trained by rendering serial-produced articles of daily life: bottles, jugs, glasses, etc.* (Journal of Design, *vol.* I, 1849)

him as a basic authority. To the utilitarianism that guided the English reformers, he owed his starting point: that practical art existed before architecture, as he set forth in an essay written in London in 1853. Utilitarianism colored his interpretation of historical epochs. Semper ranks among the few significant architects of his time, and he was gifted enough to systematize the intellectual views of the 'fifties. It is questionable, however, whether these attitudes were comprehensive enough to be forged into a system. An insurmountable barrier of feeling kept this generation from perceiving the pure forms latent in machine-made objects.

Only through fragmentary utterances did one glimpse the abstract forms inherent in industrial production. *The Times* article, which clearly bears the mark of Cole's circle, says of the Great Exhibition: 'Some sections, especially that of machinery, feeling their preeminence secure and undoubted, have been content to be plain and unpretending. The only beauty attempted is that which the stringent of mechanical science to the material world can supply . . . there is developed a style of art, at once national and grand.' [51]

PURISM AND STANDARD OBJECTS AS SYMBOLS

All unnoticed, the articles of everyday use act upon man. How they become part and parcel of his life, the Cubist painters revealed around 1910. The simple objects recommended to train the eye of the child in 1849 are now a starting point for artistic expression. And the quiet outlines of jugs, bottles, glasses flow through the paintings of the Purists of the 1920's, Ozenfant and Jeanneret (LeCorbusier) (fig. 204).

To render the livingness of their forms, the contours are made to flow, are set in motion, interrupted, rent asunder, repeated, or conjoined. Their shape fades away and reappears. They are concrete and intangible, transparent and opaque, hovering and at rest, thin as air and massive in turn. In the early still lives of Juan Gris, the wooden structure of a wall or of a violin infuses an area, asserting itself as insistently as a tree picked out by a projector against the night.

The same is done with the color: brown, black, blue, neutral shades, or green. They, too, shed their descriptive function, meeting in planes or penetrating one another in obedience to their own laws: a development that the following decades constantly carry further.

All this is made possible only by a spatial vision that has broken with copying and with perspective; an approach that allows structure, color, and form to be gathered into planetary systems; that changes bottles, glasses, plates, pipes, tables, musical instruments, into objects that lay bare the very essence of their meaning.

SURREALISM AND MECHANIZED ADORNMENT

It is otherwise with the products of mechanized adornment. The seething surfaces and tormented lines cannot join in unifying curves, in *mariage de contours;* no transparency or structural statement lays bare their meaning. Taken one by one, the statues, pictures, vases, carpets, are harmless and insignificant. Among them one may even find delightful pieces (fig. 206) whose raw-boned naturalism recalls the woodcuts of a Granville (1803–47). But viewed in their totality, accumulated museum-fashion, as the custom was, their bastardized forms and materials react upon the spectator and corrode his emotional life.

---

[51] Quoted in *Journal of Design* (1851), vol. v, p.158.

What took place was a sort of reciprocating action, an inducted current. Industry engendered its wares according to the rule stated by Redgrave in 1853: 'The industrialists consider pure and perfect taste antagonistic to commerce, and sum up their views in the axiom: "That is best what sells best."' [52] These scrap piles of mechanically reproduced historical mementoes acted upon whoever dwelt among them. The innate sense for form and material decayed; the disciplined handling of space perished.

It mattered little that all this had been known since mid-century, and that criticism was exercised to the point of superfluity. The objects proved stronger than judgment.

What emanated from this chaotic setting, what repercussions shook our moral constitution cannot be conveyed in rational terms. No logic, no sociological account, can portray the situation. Artistic symbols alone are adequate. It was among the Surrealists' functions to reveal this. They captured the sense and nonsense of the nineteenth century and showed how this inextricable mixture of the banal and the eerie had penetrated our being.

No one did so more pungently than Max Ernst. Drops of the nineteenth century still seemed to flow in his veins. We are thinking of his picture-novels, and especially *La Femme 100 têtes* [53] — 'The Woman with a Hundred No-Heads.' What can this be but a symbolic name for the nineteenth century and its restless meanderings? Here irrational images unmask the devaluation of symbols

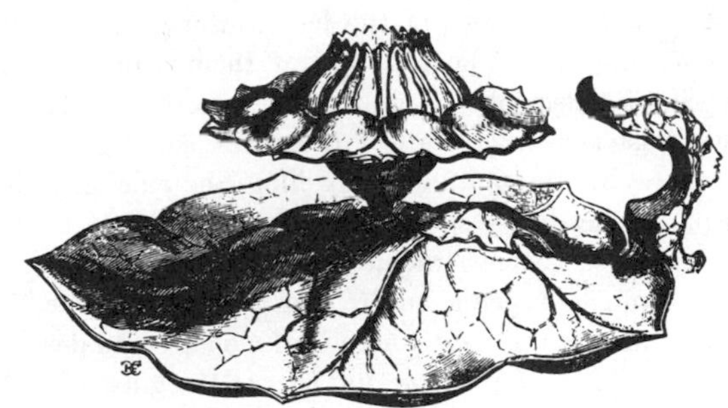

206. Leaf-Shaped Candlestick, Electro-process. *c.*1850. (*Henry Cole*, Journal of Design)

one of the most graceful adaptations which the "natural" school has produced. It is delicately light and a beautiful specimen of the electro-process, shewing how it may perfectly realise all the effects of fine beaten metal-work, and much more cheaply.

---

[52] Redgrave, *On the Necessity of Principles in Teaching Design*, London, 1853, p.8.

[53] *La Femme 100 têtes*, Paris, 1929, and *Une Semaine de bonté ou les sept éléments*, Paris, 1934, are perhaps the most apt to our purpose. See also *Misfortunes of the Immortals*, New York, 1942, and *Rêves d'une petite fille qui voulut entrer au Carmel*, Paris, 1930.

207. 'Sabrina' Porcelain Figure. England, 1850.

at work. Following one another without regard to external logic, the picture cycles are not to be read for their naturalistic meaning. What matters is their psychic comment. They are *collages*, fragments culled and pasted from the long-forgotten woodcut books of the last century. Max Ernst raised them to the status of 'objects.' The scissors cut them asunder, and the artist's fantasy, taking up the elements, combines them anew (fig. 208).

The plaster-of-Paris statues roam abroad. The woman with a hundred no-heads walks through everyday life. She rules it. She and her companions, their plaster heads transplanted onto contemporary necks, flit along the façades, or, 'her uncle no sooner strangled,' she takes off in all her plaster nudity: 'L'oncle à peine étranglé, la jeune adulte sans pareille s'envole.' [54]

Almost always the atmosphere is of violence and death. From a glassed book-case of the 'fifties, *La Femme 100 têtes* in the guise of a plaster bust will perhaps fall out onto a learned bystander, while the stamped lion heads of the chairs come to life grimacingly changed into a giant ape, which the caption designates with Dadaistic impudence as 'the monkey who will be a policeman, catholic, or stock-broker' (fig. 230).

These pages of Max Ernst show how a mechanized environment has affected our subconscious. I once asked Ernst about the origin of his novels, and he

[54] *La Femme 100 têtes*, ch. III.

208. MAX ERNST: The Plaster Statues Roam Abroad. (La Femme 100 têtes, 1929)

L'oncle à peine étranglé, la jeune adulte sans pareille s'envole.

replied: 'They are reminiscences of my first books, a resurgence of childhood memories.'

The artist fuses these childhood memories into a mirror to morality. But there are many people for whom nineteenth-century ruling taste still forms the well of feeling, and in whose souls, as T. S. Eliot once put it, the nineteenth century lingers on into the twentieth. Still among these are most of our contemporaries, in particular the men whose taste determines public buildings and monuments. For most of these, the origin of their esthetic faith has never come to consciousness.

Do not Carlyle's lines written toward mid-century in his restive *Latter-Day Pamphlets* seem to echo a caption for Max Ernst?

> The fact is . . . the Fine Arts, divorced entirely from truth this long while, and wedded almost professedly to falsehood, fiction and such-like, are got what we must call, an insane condition: they walk abroad without keepers, nobody suspecting their bad state, and do fantastic tricks.[55]

---

[55] Cole cites this passage in the *Journal of Design* (1850), vol. III, p.91.

The Reign of the Upholsterer

The Upholsterer

The upholsterer (*tapissier*) is a man whose concern is with fabrics and their arrangement. For a long time in France, the word *tapissier* was used in two senses: 'Sometimes one means thereby a workman who makes carpets, sometimes a tradesman who sells or lays them,' and in the fifteenth century the tapissier was a man 'who hung and took down tapestry.' The statutes of his guild go back to the middle of the thirteenth century. 'Today,' continues this definition of 1875, 'an upholsterer is a furniture-seller who undertakes to decorate apartments.' [56]

In the nineteenth century, the upholsterer becomes identical with the decorator who, from the days of the Empire style on, debased the cabinetmaker's craft. As we have seen, his peculiar function began around 1800 with profuse curtains, crossdraped at the windows (*croisée*) and hanging on the walls. Later, under the Restoration, he also took possession of the furniture. At his hands chair and sofa become bulky pieces of upholstery.

The great designer of furniture, the 'cabinetmaker,' formerly present in all countries, is lacking in the nineteenth century. True, the routine cabinetmakers included more highly skilled ones, who made imitations for the antique dealers. Others produced models of their own design, which a contemporary aptly calls 'a microcosm of all the styles of the world.' These artisans produced nothing of constituent value, for their skill was not imbued with creative power. One dominating influence is felt in the furniture and interiors of the ruling taste: the upholsterer increasingly controls the situation. His attention was directed toward a theatrical type of adornment, not to original creation. In addition to upholstering furniture he draped hangings and arranged the articles of mechanized adornment with picturesque effect. He set up still lives in drawing rooms and, by the last decades of the century, he grouped figures, helmets, vases, drapery, in compositions of pleasing disorder.

The transitory currents cannot be fully surveyed. They ruled the day, together with parallel productions in painting and architecture. We cannot grasp the dual soul of the nineteenth century so long as we overlook the springs of feeling among the broad masses. Picturesque disorder fascinated people, for it was a reflection of the chaotic state of feeling. The upholsterer, by embellishment of furniture and artistic hangings, sets up a fairyland to enchant the drabness of the industrial day.

---

[56] L. Douet-D'Arq, 'Recueil de documents et statuts relatifs à la corporation des tapissiers, de 1258 à 1879,' in *Extraits de la Bibliothèque des Chartes*, Paris, 1875, tome XXXIII, p.6.

As France had set the fashion under the First Empire, so it did under the Second. There many of the transitory furniture types of the epoch were first seen. But the structure of society had changed much since the day of Napoleon I. His successor to the imperial throne achieved no style appropriate to his way of life. The new types, like the whole interior, answered to the taste of an anonymous rising class, the self-made man, of which Napoleon I was an early representative. The work of the upholsterer and the taste of the rising class seemed to be marked out for one another.

This class, owing its wealth mainly to the mechanized means of production, grew up wherever industrialization succeeded. It was international: in France, in England during the Victorian era, in America at the time of the railroad boom of the early 'seventies, and finally in Germany, which suddenly entered upon a hitherto unknown prosperity. Germany's late, almost hectic industrialization after 1870 went hand in hand with the extreme development of the ruling taste. Nothing seemed able to withstand the devaluation of symbols.[57]

Counter-Currents: The Engineer and the Reformer

As so often in the nineteenth century, the most contradictory tendencies arise simultaneously and side by side. In America during the 'fifties and 'sixties inventive fantasy and the instinct for mechanization were the common property of the people. There, the furniture of the engineer was created in glorious unconcern. It is the absolute opposite of the ruling taste. We shall pay considerable attention to this furniture of the engineer, which developed parallel in time with the furniture of the upholsterer, for despite its mechanization it was created without reflection, like products of popular art. The anonymous inventors were concerned only with the solution of specific problems.

In England the situation was quite different. Henry Cole and the reformers of 1850 directed their struggle against the false mechanization of adornment. The next generation, led by William Morris and John Ruskin, stressed the leveling and dehumanizing side of mechanization, and condemned the machine on principle. The basic aim of the Morris circle, which made itself heard around 1860, proved impossible of fulfilment: a revival of handicraft together with a return to the late Gothic. At first the circle produced dressers, beloved of the

---

[57] How influential the ruling taste became strongly appears in Georg Hirth's repeatedly printed collection of examples: *Das Deutsche Zimmer, Anregungen zu haüslicher Kunstpflege*, 3. stark verm. aufl., München, 1886. Here Hirth, founder of the periodical *Jugend* (whence the 'Jugendstil' or *Art Nouveau* drew its name), reproduced still lives of helmets, daggers, and vases that an upholsterer or decorator had designed for an upper-middle-class dwelling.

late Gothic,[58] which William Morris painted with scenes from medieval legends. The whole was a work of care and good taste. The Pre-Raphaelites Dante Gabriel Rossetti and Burne-Jones, who were closely linked with Morris, were superior artists to the circle of painters and sculptors that had gathered around Henry Cole. Yet their talent too lay rather in the literary domain than in their own, the optical. It was not otherwise with the furniture. Lacking was the power of fresh vision. It little availed to build late Gothic dressers in the full of the nineteenth century. Necessarily most of the types produced by the Morris circle were more akin to eighteenth-century cabinetmaking than to the Gothic ideal.

Yet we, perhaps better than the preceding generation, can see how Ruskin and Morris were attracted to the Middle Ages. For them it formed the greatest possible contrast to the mechanization of their own time. But there was no direct contact, no continuity, for more than a dozen generations lay between. The strength of William Morris and his circle lies in their moral orientation.

The Furniture of the Upholsterer

The easy furniture of the upholsterer no longer owns any decided shape. It has lost its clarity of structure and has become boneless.

The skeleton of the chairs and sofas has retreated deep into the cushions: a process that the French have called *La victoire de la garniture sur le bois* [59] — 'the victory of the trimmings over the wood.' Every and any means are used to make the armchairs, sofas, divans, ottomans, as heavy and as bulky as possible. Foot-long fringes sometimes veil even the stumps, all that remain of the legs. The furniture increasingly tends to suggest bloated cushions. The statuary loses its constituent form beneath the machine-like smoothening, and so it is with the surfaces of the furniture, overspread at first with dull red plush, later by fabrics of dazzling orientalism.

Beneath these furry textures, which clothe cushions flat or cylindrical, the woodwork decays like fallen trees obliterated beneath blankets of moss. Heavy and unwieldy furniture dominated the situation throughout the second half of the century. The Second Empire brought to full maturity a trend that had been germinating under the Restoration during the 'thirties. When Honoré de Balzac describes an interior of the period in *Une Fille d'Eve* (1838), he notes the strong

---

[58] Victoria and Albert Museum, South Kensington, Catalogue of *An Exhibition in Celebration of the Centenary of William Morris*, London, 1934. Cabinet designed by Philip Webb in 1861 and painted by William Morris with scenes from the legend of St. George, pl. XI.

[59] Havard, *Dictionnaire de l'ameublement*, vol. IV, col. 623.

209. The Oriental Influence. Léon Feuchère: Smoking Room in the Oriental Style. 1842. *The 1830's considered it anachronistic to smoke in medieval and Renaissance interiors. As the medieval revivalist Pugin declared: 'The style of a building should so correspond with its use that the spectator may at once perceive the purpose for which it was erected.' The pipe rack allows a conspicuous object to be placed in the center of the room, in the same manner as the Empire 'flower stand' (fig.* 194) *and the later* borne (*fig.* 212).

210. Smoking Room in the Oriental Style. 1879. *The oriental influence was felt directly and indirectly throughout the nineteenth century and helped to increase the gloominess of the interiors in the last decades.*

penchant for cashmere and soft carpets: 'Underfoot, one feels the mellow pile of a Belgian carpet, thick as a lawn.'

THE ORIENTAL INFLUENCE

Ponderous armchairs and sofas followed in the wake of orientalizing romanticism. In literature, Victor Hugo's much acclaimed poems, *Les Orientales* (1829), voiced the growing interest of the age in a legendary and dreamlike East.

The influence took firmer root when *le goût du pittoresque oriental* was interpreted by the painters. At the Salon of 1831, the public spiritedly welcomed Decamps' large canvas 'Ronde de Smyrne'[60] and his other Oriental scenes. They were the fruit of his travels through Asia Minor in search of picturesque impressions (1828–9).[61] And three years later, when Delacroix exhibited his 'Femmes d'Algérie' at the Salon of 1834, this painting, despite its austerity,[62] enjoyed a no less immediate success.

Delacroix's keen eye for movement was mainly attracted to the noble and serene deportment of the Berbers. He found in their relaxed poise a living vestige of the ancient world. Baudelaire, one of Delacroix's earliest admirers, sought to convey this to contemporaries. The East is reflected in various media and by diverse talents. The vision of these masters was a far thing from the outlook of the Oriental motif seekers, and Delacroix's conception is but distantly related to the upholsterer's Orient. But the influence as a whole forms an integral part of the century.

Oriental motifs soon made their appearance in the art industry. Two years after Delacroix had shown his 'Femmes d'Algérie,' the *Album Ornemaniste*[63] of Aimé Chenavard (1798–1838) was suggesting Arabian and Persian patterns for the 'tentures' so dear to the Directoire; it also included a Persian carpet.[64] Persian designs became fashionable for industrial imitation only after mid-century.

Oriental motifs formed but a fraction of Chenavard's *Album*. They marched amid the long procession of historical styles that France of the 'thirties was marshaling into readiness for the art industry. Aimé Chenavard filled the strategic position of councilor to the royal manufactories of porcelain and tapestry, Sèvres and Beauvais. Beauvais executed several of his tapestries and

---

[60] Metropolitan Museum, New York.

[61] Jean Alasard, *L'Orient et la peinture française au XIXme siècle, d'Eugène Delacroix à Auguste Renoir*, Paris, 1930, traces in detail the successive phases of the Oriental influence.

[62] This canvas was straightway purchased by the Government. Although neither artist repeated his journey, Decamps' impressions of Asia Minor (1828) and Delacroix's memories of his visit to Algeria and Morocco in 1832 remained vivid to the end of their lives.

[63] *Album Ornemaniste*, Paris, 1836.

[64] Ibid. p.64. Motifs Persans, pl. 44; Bordures Arabes, pl. 15, 5a; Tentures, pl. 44.

211. The Filling of Space: The Borne under Louis Philippe. 'Soirée at the Duc d'Orléans'.' 1843. *Under Louis Philippe a sort of double-bed with a rudimentary arm or back rest occupied the center of the room. Its central position typifies the century's growing* horror vacui. *The graceful print shows that ingenuous posture was accepted in high society.* (*Jules Janin*, Un Hiver à Paris, *Paris*, 1843)

screens,[65] and Sèvres his Renaissance vases and painted glass, which in Chenavard's own words were 'imitations of sixteenth-century paintings.' [66] This work, although privately commissioned, already has that derivative lifeless tone that mass production was soon to spread through the whole interior. What we have said of the Empire style must also be said here: The signs of ruling taste were present before mechanization took effect.

While England shaped the workshop of mechanized adornment (stamping, pressing, substitute materials), France made ready the intellectual molds in which the ruling taste was to run. Chenavard, who was most certainly an innovator in this sphere, influenced taste through his albums rather than through the art objects which he designed for the court of Louis Philippe.

[65] Chenavard's designs are collected in his *Recueil de dessins de tapis, tapisseries, et autres objets d'ameublement executés dans la manufacture de M. Chenavard à Paris*, Paris, 1833–5. Also included is an 'intérieur Turque,' pl. 117; but it is a theatre decoration. Chenavard was accustomed to this type of work and renovated several Parisian theatres. No account of the rise of ruling taste is available.

[66] Painted glass, ibid. pl. 24. Tapestries and screens, pl. 31 and 35.

Perceptive men immediately sensed the temper of their day, an atmosphere that was to prevail throughout the century: 'We have left no imprint of our age either on our dwellings, on our gardens, or on anything else,' was Alfred de Musset's comment in 1836, 'we have culled something from every century but our own . . . we live off fragments.' Our interest here, however, is only in the rising tide of orientalism as it appeared in the pattern collections of the industrial-art trade. The rule of the upholsterer was to reach its full extent in the 'seventies.

The Orient, to the nineteenth century, meant at once color and adventure, romance and legend, and was somehow felt to reflect that wisdom of life the period seemed to have lost.

Everywhere the Oriental influence appears: in countless genre paintings for the ruling taste; or again in the Odalisques, or reposing nudes which Ingres painted around 1800, down to the Odalisques of Henri Matisse. It is seen in attempts to introduce the Turkish bath in industrial England (*c.*1850); in the Moorish-style villas; or in the borrowing of 'Persian' carpets, genuine or machine-made. Mechanized man in the nineteenth century yearned for an atmosphere other than that of his own surroundings. In the East everyone, rich and poor alike, has time and leisure. In the West no one has. Western life tends toward strain; Eastern life toward relaxation.

The Oriental influence must be counted as one of the many strivings for escape that darkened the emotional life of the last century and gave it a tragic note. Man was not content to live in his own skin. This could lead to nothing but the grotesque. The chambers of the Orient were spacious and serene; their couches closely skirt the wall. Now, as these are transformed by the upholsterer into cushion furniture with springs, the divans jut forth in sudden and conspicuous isolation.

As banal as the East became in the upholsterer's hands, the Oriental influence proved far more persistent than most revivals. Medievalism, brought so lovingly to the fore in the Romantic era, left no lasting traces upon the dwelling. More influential were the several Louis revivals. Yet their role was a more superficial one than their recurrent popularity would suggest.

The Oriental influence is often found at work beneath the surface, and not recognizable at first. With it may be connected the latter half-century's penchant for dimly lighted interiors. What this influence did to furniture we shall have occasion to observe in the following pages.

TYPES OF CUSHION FURNITURE

France was the first country to voice the Oriental influence, and here cushion-furniture first became fashionable. Thus France became the center for the rep-

213. English Ottoman Seat, *c.*1835. *The English equivalent of the* borne *had a more modest and clear-cut outline, and no fringe.* (*Thomas King,* Cabinet Maker's Sketchbook, *2nd edition*)

212. Parisian Borne with Jardinière for the Center of a Salon. 1863. *The large circular or quatrefoil sofa, in French called* borne, *was normally destined 'pour le milieu du salon.' The* borne *can be traced back to Percier and Fontaine's flower stand of* 1800, *and the jardinière of* 1842 *with its surrounding polygon of seats (see figs.* 193–4). (*A. Sanguineti,* L'Ameublement au XIXe siècle, *Paris,* 1863)

CIRCULAR SOFAS

214. French Borne, Early 1880's. *The typical* borne *with truncated conical back rest is found in hotel lounges, railway stations, or picture galleries late in the century. The palm, natural or artificial, is a vestigial flower stand, surviving like the vermiform appendix in man.* (*Havard,* Dictionnaire de l'ameublement)

resentative furniture of nineteenth-century ruling taste. This occurred in the late 'thirties following the success of Delacroix's and Decamps' painting.

The Divan: Needless to say, the Oriental influence was not native to the 'thirties. The Louis XV cabinetmakers, for instance, created the elegant *turquoise*, with its three-cushion seat and other loose cushions against the wall.

Again Thomas Sheraton designed a 'Turkish sofa,' fronted by two columns, suggesting an alcove. U-shaped, it modestly skirts the end of the room, quite unlike the nineteenth-century types, which seek to display their bulk.

The nineteenth century opens a new chapter. The devaluation of symbols went hand in hand with the devaluation of space. Furniture became a means of filling the room; to inflate its bulk was the first step.

In 1834, the year of Delacroix's 'Femmes d'Algérie,' Balzac's description of a boudoir in *La Fille aux yeux d'or* conveys this softened atmosphere, which developed with the century; his fancy turns around an enormous Turkish divan. 'One half of the boudoir made a *softly* graceful curve in contrast with the perfectly square half of the room. The horseshoe contained a *Turkish* divan that is, a mattress laid on the floor, but a mattress as large as a bed, a white cashmere divan fifty feet around. The head of this tremendous bed rose several feet above abundant cushions.' Fondness for cushions is also reflected in Bonington's 'Reclining Woman' of 1826 (fig. 233).

Divans penetrated public places, too, although in the more austere shape of upholstered benches. This furniture gave its name to the locale, then called *café divan.* They first appeared in Parisian literary cafés. 'The first divan opened in Paris around 1838. For years the café-divan of the rue Pelletier was familiar to artists.' [67] The Romanticists, Gerard de Nerval and Balzac himself, were frequent visitors. This café disappeared around 1859, when Haussmann began his transformation of Paris.[68]

In the Paris of 1850, divan-benches sprang forth everywhere, even in public arcades. They remain in Parisian restaurants to this day, and determine the arrangement of the tables parallel to the walls.

Fancy Chairs — Sièges de fantaisie: It was a point of honor with the French upholsterers to launch endlessly new types with new names, just as at a later time American ranges or refrigerators were redesigned every year, rousing envy afresh. These *sièges de fantaisie*, or fancy chairs, as the French aptly called them, were a furniture of fashion, and models lived their short season like modish hats.

[67] Larousse, *Dictionnaire du XIXme siècle*, Paris, 1870, art. 'Divan.'

[68] Ibid.

FANCY CHAIRS

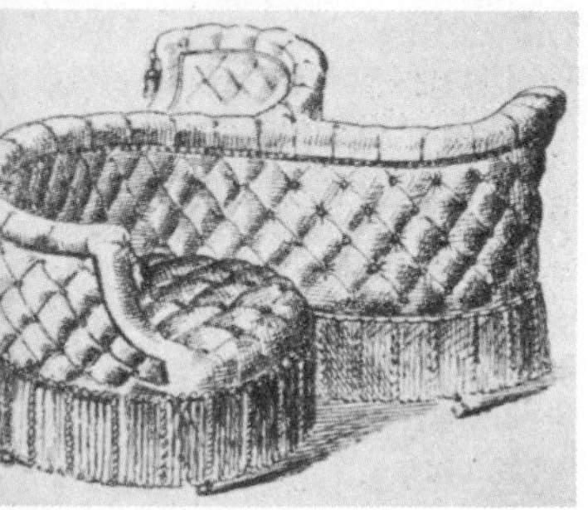

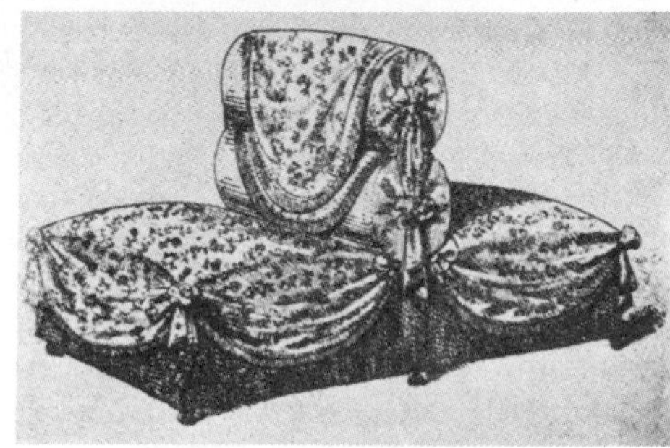

215. French Three-Seat 'Confidante,' Late 1870's. *The French upholsterer was continually launching 'fancy chairs' with new names. The* confidante *was an intimate type of seating, formed of two or more chairs on an S-plan.* (*Havard,* Dictionnaire de l'ameublement)

216. French Boudeuse, *c.*1880. *The* boudeuse *is a twin chair for the drawing room, arranged so that the sitters have their backs to one another. It is entirely draped.* (*Havard,* Dictionnaire de l'ameublement)

217. Pouf, *c.*1880. *The pouf, a favorite piece of the ruling taste, is described as a 'large tabouret, cylindrical and upholstered, with a long and thick fringe, always without visible woodwork.'* (*Havard,* Dictionnaire de l'ameublement)

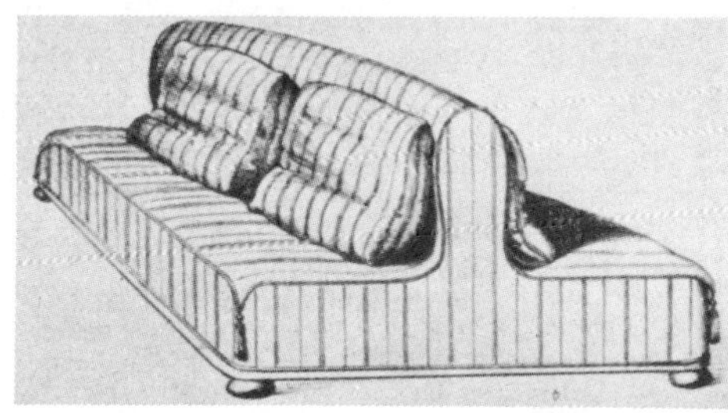

218. French 'Fauteuil Bébé,' 1863. *A fauteuil with low back rest, combining features of the pouf and the gondola type.* (*A. Sanguineti,* L'Ameublement au XIXe siècle)

219. English Back-to-Back Seat, *c.*1835. *Like the English version of the* borne, *its form is more concise than that of the French models. France was the birthplace of the ruling taste.* (*Thomas King,* Cabinet Maker's Sketchbook)

There were combinations of chairs, which the upholsterer garnished. Two chairs coupled on an s-plan were named a *confidante*. *Confidantes* were also made of three chairs, joined like the spokes of a wheel (fig. 215). There were combinations for sitting face-to-face (*vis-à-vis*), or back-to-back (*dos-à-dos*); whence the *petite boudeuse* (fig. 216) (*bouder*, to sulk), a twin drawing-room chair with a common back so that the sitters have their backs to one another. 'This type is very modern,' Havard tells us in his *Dictionary*, 'and is as a rule entirely draped.' [69] The back of the *petite boudeuse* consists of two stacked cylindrical cushions with a drapery casually tossed over, while other festoons fringe its twofold seat. These are but a few random examples.

Cushion Tabourets, the Pouf. Circular Sofas, the Borne: In 1845 the *pouf* made its entrance into French salons. 'Large tabourets, cylindrical and upholstered, the whole trimmed with a long and thick fringe, always without visible woodwork.' [70] The dainty tabouret, on which high nobility was once privileged to sit at royal levées, is here transformed in the nineteenth-century manner, orientalized. A charming sight, Théophile Gautier recalls, were pretty women seated on *poufs* in a salon: like sculptures, they could be admired from every side. These *poufs* already indicate what kind of posture the nineteenth century liked. On the rounded cushion seats, one spontaneously assumes a changing and half-slumped position. In the 'sixties, a low-humped back is sometimes added (*fauteuil bébé*) (fig. 218). They become ever more squat and cushion-like. Contemporaries blame the upholsterer for exploiting the tabouret so playfully. Indeed, by 1880, it seems to have drawn closer to the birthday cake than to furniture (fig. 217).

Related to the *pouf* is one of the period's most voluminous pieces. It filled the center of a salon, or stood at either end of a ballroom: the immense circular seat or sofa, called in French *borne* (boundary stone).[71] Often exceeding two metres in diameter, it sold in the most diverse patterns and forms: as a square, a polygon, segments of a circle, clover leaf, or (later the standard shape) circular. A *borne*, having no back rest and resembling a gigantic pouf, stood in Napoleon III's Salle de Conseil in the Tuileries.[72]

But the typical *borne* was a circular seat around an upholstered back rest in the shape of a truncated cone. Whether the *borne* in its mid-century form dates

---

[69] Havard, op.cit. vol. I, col. 357.

[70] Ibid. vol. IV, col. 623.

[71] 'Dans les galeries ou dans les très grands salons on plaçait un de ces sièges à chaque extrémité, de là son nom de borne.' Jules Deville, *Dictionnaire du Tapissier*, Paris, 1878–80, p. 43.

[72] 'Salle de Conseil de Napoléon III,' Watercolor by F. D. Fournier. Collection Firmin Rambaux, reproduced in Henri Clouzot, *Des Tuileries à St. Cloud*, Paris, 1925.

back to the First Empire, we could not ascertain. A lineage striking us as plausible might rather attach the standard circular *borne* — from whose cone shrubs, vases, statues, lamps, must ever sprout — to the many-tiered flower stand (fig. 193) that Percier and Fontaine placed in mid-room around 1800. In his steel-engraved *l'Art industriel* (1842), Léon Feuchère (1804–57), one of the anemic late-Romantic designers who greatly influenced ruling taste, shows a *grande jardinière entourée de divans* (fig. 194). A ring of seats encircles the whole piece. Its plastic ambition has outstripped the amplitude of Percier and Fontaine's piece. During the *borne's* development in the 'eighties, when objects sprouted from the center, its palm trees, real and artificial, seem survivals of the flower stand — vestiges, like our vermiform appendix, of an earlier function. More significant than its exact lineage is the inner kinship of this enormous circular seat of the 'eighties with the flower stand designed for the center of a Swedish salon by Percier and Fontaine. Both betray a weakening sense of space. 'Today [1878] people are so keen on these seats that a circular borne, 2 metres in diameter often stands in a small middle-class drawing room 4 metres long.' [73] This period, driven by its horror of the void, fills the central space of a room, which the medieval and Baroque had always respected (figs. 212, 214).

In the 'forties the central sofa became fashionable. In the brilliant salon of the Duc d'Orléans (1843), this sort of double bed (without framework, naturally, but with a rudimentary arm or back rest) held the middle of the room [74] (fig. 211). It enjoyed its greatest popularity during and after the Second Empire. These sofas spread rapidly, and soon appeared in the most unexpected settings. In 1850 A. I. Downing, the well known American landscape gardener, whose career falls into the first half of the century and who explicitly calls for good taste, asking that the country house be furnished 'with more chasteness and simplicity than the town house,' [75] recommends 'the octagonal ottoman.' 'Perhaps the most pleasant form is the octagonal ottoman stuffed seat placed in the middle of a large room. . . .' [76] At its peak in the 'sixties, the central sofa is button-pleated, covered in damask or cretonne (later in red plush, which becomes nearly standard), and has a *frange royale* hanging to the floor. Contemporary England favored this central piece in its various forms, but kept it more modest and clearer in outline. No fringes (fig. 213). Later these imposing sofas found their way into hotel lounges, art galleries, and waiting-rooms. In the private dwelling it was replaced toward 1900 by the corner sofa.

---

[73] Deville, op.cit. p.43.
[74] Jules Janin, *Un Hiver à Paris*, Paris, 1843, p.141.
[75] A. I. Downing, *The Architecture of Country Houses*, New York, 1850, p.409.
[76] Ibid. p.427.

220. Apparel of the Ruling Taste: The New Ideal Bustle, 1880's. (*Trade card, courtesy Bella C. Landauer Collection, New-York Historical Society*)

Upholstered Easy Chairs — Confortables: These examples should suffice to indicate the trend. Most of the models appearing on the market rapidly passed away. Some stayed with an undeniable longevity. Such were the upholstered easy chairs known as *confortables* (fig. 223). Their characteristics are a skeleton entirely cloaked and enveloped in fabric, and voluminous cushions, usually built around spiral springs. The origin of the widespread category can be traced to Louis Philippe's time. We even know the name of the Parisian upholsterer who first covered the entire chair with fabric, and for what reason he did so.

'From 1838 we can attest the existence of those arm-chairs known as *confortables*. It was *Dervilliers*, an upholsterer of that time, who replaced the *bergères* with chairs upholstered over springs.' [77] This was the signal for a line of chairs and sofas so long and varied as to defy enumeration. All are built around spiral springs. 'Confortable' was the name that Dervilliers gave to his new 'elastic arm-chair' first exhibited in 1834.[78] Its woodwork was still visible and not yet cloaked in fabric. Its feet stood free.

---

[77] Deville, op.cit. p.21. Havard, op.cit. vol. I, col. 581, accepts this indication.

[78] The report on the Paris exposition of 1834 contains this remark: 'Les fauteuils élastiques de M. Dervillé [Havard and Deville spell the name otherwise], à Paris, qu'il qualifie de *confortables*, nous ont paru élegants tout à la fois et très commodes, sans que leur prix soit à beaucoup près aussi élevé que celui des *meubles du même genre* qui nous avaient été envoyés d'abord d'Angleterre et de l'Allemagne. C'est à se rendre de tels que s'en étudiait longtemps cet ébéniste-tapissier.' *Musée Industriel, description complète de l'exposition des produits de l'industrie française faits en* 1834, Paris, 1834, vol. 3, p.159.

221. Painting of the Ruling Taste: 'La Grande Tza,' Bukovac (School of Cabanel, 1890's).

In the 'thirties came the first of the several Rococo waves that were to follow one another during the century. And so the type of a century earlier was revived, the *bergère en gondole* with its shell-like cradling of the body. The models that Dervilliers put on the market in 1838 were completely covered with material. The reason was that iron could more easily be bent into the gondola form.[79] This armature had to be concealed from view. Soon (1840) the iron frame, found to bend out of shape, was replaced by glued beech, which afforded greater rigidity. The habit of enveloping the entire chair nevertheless persisted.

In the next two decades the *bergère*, the chair of elegant posture, goes out of fashion. The armchairs gain bulk and weight. Their contours become softened, as for instance in the *confortable senateur* (1863).[80] The mound-like treatment of their surfaces stresses the cushion and mattress-like quality. Their button-pleated finish is not hard to explain: the upholsterers had found a use for the short-staple cotton and wool combings, by-products of mechanized spinning. Tasseling and fringes did not lessen the blubbery aspect that charmed the 'sixties. Dimensions grow and mobility decreases. The armrests become two cylindrical cushions, similar to those we noticed in the back of the *boudeuse*. The seat and the whole chair appear to the naïve eye as a complex of cushions somehow mirac-

[79] Deville, op.cit. p.21.

[80] A. Sanguineti, *Ameublement au XIXe siècle*, exécuté par les principaux fabricants et décorateurs de Paris d'après les dessins de A. Sanguineti, Paris, 1863, p.26.

222. View of a 'Fauteuil Confortable,' Surrealist Interpretation, Max Ernst, 1934. *In the semidarkness a* confortable *stands supreme, its* frange royale *sweeping to the floor. A nude has descended from her gold frame . . .* (*Max Ernst,* Une semaine de bonté, *Paris,* 1934)

ulously held together (fig. 223). This orientalizing influence became tyrannical. Headrests disappear — the proportions had to be low and squat. Cylindrical cushions on either side walled the sitter in a frontal posture. This is the model found from about 1880 on in almost every home. Ordinarily a set of this ponderous cushion furniture formed companion pieces to a sofa, spiral-sprung, also having cylindrical cushions at both ends, possessing no legs, but a high superstructure with shelves for knickknacks. These heavy, cushioned pieces have almost become the symbols for nineteenth-century ruling taste. In their own way they expressed the feelings that fascinated the masses. They would surely have become popular in any case, but one circumstance favored their spread: mechanization to which their manufacture was so closely linked and which made them available to the broader public.

MECHANIZATION AND CUSHION FURNITURE

Spiral Springs: To eighteenth-century eyes, the upholstered furniture would seem artificially swollen. For resiliency, spiral springs require a greater depth

223. Fauteuil-Coussin Confortable, *c.*1880. *The* confortable *at its peak. The skeleton is entirely cloaked in fabric and the armrests have grown into cylindrical cushions. The whole seems an agglomeration of cushions held together by some miraculous means.* (*Havard,* Dictionnaire de l'ameublement)

than horsehair or feather stuffing. These springs consisted of iron wire coiled into two inverted cones. One base was fastened to straps, on top of which a thin layer of horsehair was spread. Thus furniture turned into agglomerated slices of mattress.

The *confortables* brought the first extensive use of springs in furniture. At this time, mechanical manufacture considerably reduced the cost of their coils.

The first use of spiral springs has not been exactly dated. Some say that a German blacksmith of the early nineteenth century was the pioneer,[81] but everything would suggest that they were invented earlier.

The eighteenth century attained consummate skill in the use of springs for all imaginable purposes: to power its cunningly conceived automata or to lend resiliency to its elastic chairbacks.

English patents for springs date back to the early eighteenth century. Patented in 1706, without detailed specifications, was a 'mathematical instrument con-

[81] Deville, op.cit. p.179, anecdotally mentions this and other forerunners.

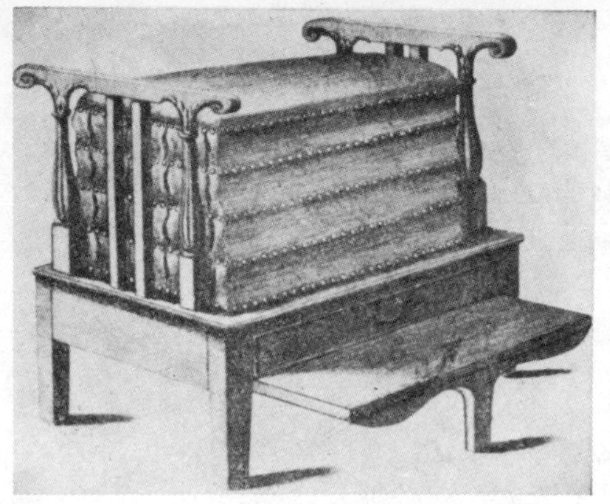

224. Springs Used for Exercise: Thomas Sheraton, Chamber Horse. 1793. *The great cabinetmaker designed this 'chamber horse' for the gentleman who wished his riding exercise regardless of the weather. Since Sheraton could only obtain springs of very limited travel, he used several layers separated by thin boards.* (*Thomas Sheraton,* Appendix to the Cabinet Maker and Upholsterer's Drawing Book)

sisting of several springs, for the ease of persons riding in coaches, chairs and other conveyances.' [82] Patents were also taken out for carriage springs [83] and even for a machine to manufacture them.[84]

The 'spiral spring' is mentioned in 1769, here again as a 'method for better construction of wheel carriages by the application of united spiral springs.' [85]

The phases of this development are not fully known. So far as we could establish, the first English patent to use spiral springs in furniture was not

[82] British Patent No.376, 1706.
[83] British Patent No.470, 1724.
[84] British Patent No.768, 1762.
[85] British Patent No.932, 1769.

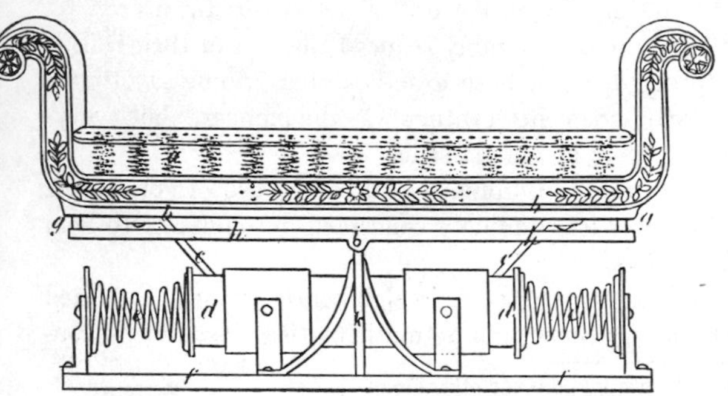

225. Springs to Prevent Seasickness: Elastic and Swinging Seat. 1826. *This first spring-upholstered chair, patented by an English inventor, was in the form of a swinging apparatus 'to be used on shipboard for the purpose of preventing the unpleasant effects of seasickness.'* (*British Patent* 5418)

applied for until 1826. But several intermediate stages were never put into the shape of patent specifications.

Chippendale is said to have invented gymnastic chairs consisting of spiral springs in several layers. Thomas Sheraton gives a thorough description and drawings of a 'chamber horse' (1793) (fig. 224), designed for the gentleman who, eager to take riding exercise in all weathers, might do so gymnastically in his own room. The inside of this chamber horse consisted of 'five wainscoat inch boards clamped at the ends; to which are fixed strong wire twisted around a block in regular gradation, so that when the wire is compressed by those who exercise each turn of it may clear itself and fall within each other.' [86]

Thomas Sheraton describes the springs in great detail, as one announcing a new invention.

Also vouching for the novelty of the method is the fact that Sheraton was able to construct springs of but very limited extension. The only way he could prevent his springs from buckling was to use them in distinct layers separated by thin boards. At this point further developments enter the picture.

---

[86] Thomas Sheraton. *Appendix to the Cabinet Maker and Upholsterer's Drawing Book*, London, 1793, pl. 22, p.43.

226. Spring Fauteuil, Caricature of Martin Gropius, c.1850. *A Berlin humorous paper imagined the following adventure: 'A visitor comes in and is asked to sit down. He admires the chair's resiliency, but will not believe that it contains 24 springs. They cut open the upholstery, and the visitor pays for his distrust by a sudden and not altogether agreeable movement.'* (Kladderadatsch, *Berlin*)

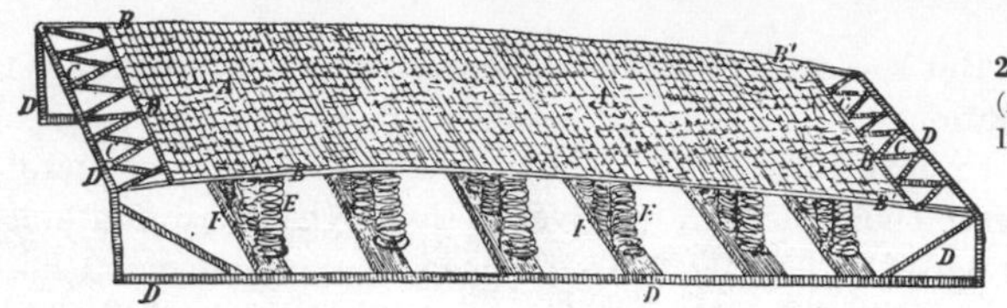

227. Early Wire Mattress. (*British Patent* 99, 12 *January* 1865)

Eighteenth-century endeavor, early and late, used spiral springs for purely technical purposes, either to take up and buffer impact (carriage springs), or to reciprocate impact (chamber horse). The owner of the chamber horse rode a hard leather-covered board and did not use the springs' resiliency to further his comfort.

In 1826 Samuel Pratt[87] took out a patent for a spring chair; now the seat, fabric covered and with spiral springs, is used as a cushion and aims to promote comfort. But even here the resiliency mainly serves as a shock-absorber: the first spring-upholstered chair was invented for seasick persons. 'Conceived as a swinging apparatus,' says Pratt, 'the object of my invention is to construct an *elastic and swinging seat*, to be used on shipboard for the purpose of preventing the unpleasant effects of seasickness' (fig. 225).[88]

The 'cushion,' which spiral springs make elastic, is for this inventor a mere accessory. We may note that the cushion has a 'swinging frame, made of wrought iron, upon which the seat is secured.' (This may explain why Dervilliers built his first spring-upholstered *fauteuils* around a frame of iron.)

A foundation of canvas upon which are placed a convenient number of spiral springs made by twisting steel wire into the form of an *hour-glass.* The lower parts of these

[87] Samuel Pratt: British Patent No.5418, 1826. 'The patent,' he adds, 'was partly communicated to me by a foreigner resident abroad and partly my own discovery.'

[88] Ibid.

228. American Woven-Wire Mattress, 1871. (The Manufacturer and Builder, *vol.* III, *no.* 5, *May* 1871)

229. The Wire Mattress in the Home. English Children's Beds. 1878. (*Lady Barker,* The Bedroom and Boudoir, *London,* 1878)

springs are to be sewn to the canvas or webbing, their upper part secured in their erect position by small cords tied or braced from one to the other, crossing like a net.[89]

The principal aim of the inventor was to neutralize the tossings of the ship, so he balanced his seat in flexible suspension on four large springs: 'lateral springs are applied below a swinging frame to meet resistance. . . .'

This complex construction shows how in England toward 1830 mechanization affected furniture in extravagant, sometimes fantastic ways. The time was shortly before America developed its patent furniture. The French, on the other hand, made use of the new process by manufacturing cushions of wire, and fashioned the *confortable,* furniture of the ruling taste.

At the same time, in the 'twenties, beds and chairs were being made of metal tubes,[90] the beginnings of a development that was not carried to fulfilment until

[89] Ibid.

[90] Robert Walter Wingfield, British Patent No.5573, 4 Dec. 1827. Tubes or rods for furniture. The same, British Patent No.6206, 20 Dec. 1831; Bedsteads from hollow tubes. The same, British Patent No.8891, 22 Mar. 1841; Metallic bedsteads.

more than a century later. But the emotional climate then prevailing and the technical temper of the times followed entirely divergent paths. This explains why the new potentialities of the nineteenth century found no inner contact with the objects whose structure they formed. Here in the sphere of comfort, the same phenomenon can be seen as later on in architecture, when stylistic fancies cloaked skeleton construction.

The adoption of springs for non-technical purposes spread rather slowly. Even in 1851 it seems not to have been usual for easy chairs to be fitted with coil springs. Early in the 'fifties the well-known architect Martin Gropius [91] constructed elastic easy chairs in this way. The humorous Berlin paper *Kladderadatsch*, made fun of it, in a page devoted to 'Latest Inventions,' showing how a skeptical visitor was lifted to the ceiling for having tried to discover whether there were really twenty-four of these coil springs (fig. 226).

After a number of preliminaries (fig. 227),[92] springs in the form of woven-wire mattresses were invented around 1870. 'The discovery was recently made that a long spiral spring of small wire, when interlocked in a certain way and put to a certain degree of tension, formed a [flexible] fabric of great strength and durability' (fig. 228).[93]

In the novelty of the find, quite understandably, the virtues of the wire mattress were somewhat exaggerated: '. . . strange as it may appear, it can be used as an excellent sleeping arrangement with only a folded blanket above the wire. The surface of the wire . . . mattress is in fact as sensitive as water, yielding to every pressure and resuming its shape as soon as it is removed.' [94]

When iron bedsteads were introduced around 1830, they were used in hospitals and prisons, not in the household. Now in the 'seventies the elastic mattress is used in the new means of transportation: '. . . intended for steamer berths, sleeping cars . . . for any place where a clean and cool sleeping arrangement is desired.' [95]

A use for it was nevertheless seen in upholstered furniture: 'this device appears to be also destined to fill a place in the upholstery line, and already lounges, car-seats, etc., are being made of it. The company [96] hopes before next summer to

[91] Martin Gropius (1824–80) ranks as one of the few distinguished architects of the third quarter of the nineteenth century and was later especially noted for his functional hospital buildings and for his Berliner Kunstgewerbemuseum with its large glass-roofed inner court. He is the great-uncle of Walter Gropius.

[92] British Patent No.99, 12 Jan. 1865.

[93] *The Manufacturer and Builder*, vol. III, no. 5, May 1871, p.97.

[94] Ibid.

[95] Ibid.

[96] Woven Wire Mattress Company, Hartford, Connecticut.

put on the market a neat and very comfortable settee for country piazzas, which shall be as easy as the hammock to lie on . . .' [97]

The airy wire mattress soon became a favorite. In 'Art and Home,' one of the handy popular series of the time, which directed the English public toward sensibly hygienic furnishing, one reads (1878): 'I would recommend a new sort of elastic mattress; it resembles a coat of mail and possesses the triple merit in these travelling days, of being cool, clean and portable.' [98] Lady Barker recommends the wire mattress for low iron cribs for children (fig. 229).

What Happens to Man's Surroundings in the Nineteenth Century?

The history of nineteenth-century ruling taste, with the sociological and emotive documentation it would need, is still waiting to be written. Here we have merely drawn out fragments indicating the power of mechanization over man.

For the mechanization of adornment we have confined ourselves to England. Here, around 1850, mechanization was running ahead of other countries. Here, the first dangerous symptoms appeared. Here, the first warners and reformers were heard. Which is not to say that France played a minor part. From the time of Colbert, who fostered the luxury industries and brought them to the fore in the seventeenth century, France had been the arbiter of fashion. And she performed brilliantly, from the standpoint of ruling taste, at the great international exhibitions of the nineteenth century. The exhibition catalogues and those of the large Parisian firms, mass producers of statues and balustrades, fancy railing and clocks of gilded zinc, are conclusive enough. In 1867 the jury of the Parisian International Exhibition computed at 150,000 [99] the number of gilded zinc clocks that French industry had delivered throughout the world.

The specially commissioned cutlery of Christoffle metal for Napoleon III and the hand-chased, silver gondola that the Empress Eugénie presented to Fernand de Lesseps when opening the Suez Canal have as definitely lapsed into insignificance as the names of the artisans who designed them. But the anonymous products of mass fabrication are of leading interest in this period, because of their influence on the emotional formation of the masses. The multiplication and development of this mechanized adornment is by no means explored.

For furniture, we confined ourselves to a few examples from France. More plastically than the English, the French development shows what inroads the nineteenth century made into the organism of furniture. Side by side with

---

[97] *The Manufacturer and Builder*, May 1871.

[98] Lady Barker, *The Bedroom and Boudoir*, in *Art and Home Series*, London, 1878.

[99] Cf. Henri Clouzot, *Des Tuileries à St. Cloud*, Paris, 1925, p.104.

230. Surrealist Interpretation of the 19th-Century Interior, Max Ernst, 1929. *Peering from a glassed bookcase, the woman with a hundred no-heads in the guise of a plaster bust startles a pensive bystander. The stamped lion heads of the chairs are changed into a giant ape.* (*Max Ernst,* La Femme 100 têtes, *Paris,* 1929)

France's orientalizing cushion furniture, England developed a plainer style, connected with the habits of club life. These black leather easy chairs and sofas were destined for groups of pipe-smoking men. From this furniture, direct lines lead to the reforms of William Morris and his followers and thence to the present day. The English also did not allow the upholsterer so free a hand in their comfortable seating for the drawing room or the bedroom. But our knowledge of this development is fragmentary.

For a time it seemed that the Rococo wave that gripped France in the 'thirties promised more than a stylistic revival. The chairs of the Rococo, molded to the human form were elaborated in the 'sixties with an originality that cannot be wholly ignored. The seats become broader, lower, and deeper. Various hybrid forms arise, designed for what is neither sitting nor lying. They have one point in common: the invitation to informal posture. We shall see how truly this non-static, changing posture corresponds to the character of the century.

Describing this furniture, a writer in whom the *Ancien Régime* still lives on, as in so many Frenchmen, cannot repress the comment as he surveys the various species of *confortables,* 'On entering our *salons* these days (1878) one involuntarily asks oneself whether these women, these men, so *nonchalantly* reclining and sprawled, can be the descendants of that French société once outstanding for its brilliancy, its deportment and its savoir-vivre.' [100]

[100] Deville, op.cit. p.21.

231. Sarah Bernhardt's Studio. 1890. (The Decorator and Furnisher, *New York*, 1891)

Toward 1880, as the confusion of feeling on the Continent is reaching its high mark, the interiors of ruling taste dissolve into endless details and nuances, the sense and nonsense of which is a closed book to later generations.[101] This is also the time when the *confortable* becomes a drift of cushions.

Thus in the last decades, the authority of the upholsterer was ever increasing. He was the man to gather superficially loose ends. He provided oil paintings and their gold frames for a middle class unable to afford originals. He arranged still lives from the bric-à-brac of a mechanized past. *Décorations mobiles*, the French of 1880 called these strange compositions that were set up with an air of casualness on tables or chairs.[102] Cushions and heavy draperies completed the effect.

Here too the Surrealists tell what was taking place within. In one of his ghoulish *collages* of the 'Lion de Belfort,' [103] Max Ernst portrays the process by which furniture was attacked. There, in semidarkness, a *confortable* stands supreme, with its *frange royale* sweeping to the floor; in it is posed one of those unambiguous nudes which hung in the fashionable salons of the period. The beauty

---

[101] Cf. chapter 'Grammaire de l'Ameublement' in Henri Havard, *L'Art dans la maison*, nouv. ed., Paris, 1884.

[102] How deeply such custom was rooted in the times may be gauged from its treatment by that eminent scholar Henri Havard, to whose authority we have so often referred. His book on the interior decoration of his day, *L'Art dans la maison*, contains a full-page reproduction of a *fauteuil* garnished with such a *décoration mobile*.

[103] Max Ernst, *Une Semaine de bonté ou les sept éléments capitaux;* Cahier: Le Lion de Belfort, Paris, 1934.

has descended from her gilt frame into the *confortable* amid exuberant cushions and drapery. Prowling around her nakedness are the head and paws of the lion from the Belfort War Memorial. What the ending may be is suggested by the amputated hand that hangs from a lion's jaws instead of a tassel (fig. 222).

The phantasmagoria of the upholsterer is stamped everywhere. André Breton conveys this in his manner at the close of his introduction to *La Femme 100 Têtes* (1929).

The woman with 100 no-heads will become the picture book par excellence of this time, when it will appear more and more clearly that each salon is bottomed in a lake, and it deservedly should be stressed with its scaly lights, its astral gilt, its weed dances, its floor of mud, its toiletary scintillations.

Of the billowing drapes, of the murky atmosphere, Ernst's scissors make a submarine cave [104] (fig. 199). Are these living creatures, plaster statues or models of the academic brush found reclining here, or rotting? To this question no answer can or should be given. The room, as nearly always, is oppressive with assassination and non-escape.

Night shrieks in her lair and advances upon our eyes like quick flesh.

Such is the demonic side of nineteenth century, ever scented behind the banal forms. Here it has been overcome and, at a safe distance, may be evoked through the Dadaistic *collage*. The pathos of a decadent society that has made its house an operatic setting is not to be taken in earnest. But what the Surrealists mockingly portray is at bottom the same phenomenon that Henrik Ibsen, living within the period, attacked in deadly earnest and incarnated in his personages — the ceaseless roaming in search of one's soul: Nora's longing to escape from her domestic prison, the millstream débâcle in *Rosmersholm*, Oswald's madness in *Ghosts*. There, as here, it is the nineteenth century, never finding the way to its true self, devaluating symbols without shaping new ones.

---

[104] Man Ray, at a later Surrealist Exhibition, Paris, 1935, showed *in natura* a 'Taxi Pluvieux' (Rainy Taxi), a cab in which lifesize manikins are seated; onto them, water trickles from the moss-hung roof. Salvador Dali, who set the Surrealist stage for the public audience, placed this 'Taxi Pluvieux' in his dark Pavilion of Venus, next to his aquarium, in which, through glass windows one watched live mermaids swimming under water with inflated rubber tails, New York World's Fair, 1939.

THE CONSTITUENT FURNITURE OF THE NINETEENTH CENTURY

As outlined in *Space, Time and Architecture* we distinguish two categories of historical facts. One category we call constituent, the other we call transitory. The distinction becomes necessary if the historian is seen as not exclusively concerned with individual styles and periods and with the comparison of their similarities and differences: if one sees history, like biology, as concerned with the problem of growth and development — not to be confused with progress.

Certain tools of analysis must be granted to the historian, and he must use them with care and discernment. Thus he draws a line around the short-lived facts, those performances that lack creative force and invention. They are the transitory facts. For contemporaries they may hold the fascination of a fireworks display and succeed in taking over the center of the stage, as did the ruling taste in painting, architecture, or furniture during the nineteenth century.

The constituent facts, on the other hand, are marked by creative force and invention; by accumulation and accretion they form the core of historical growth. Surveying the nineteenth century, the historian who has accepted history as a problem of growth is inevitably led to find patent furniture the constituent furniture of its period.

Patent Furniture and Ruling Taste

The furniture of the ruling taste, like the painting of the ruling taste, is an outgrowth of fashion. Every period shapes life to its own image and drapes it in forms peculiar to itself. By a historical necessity, each fashion — indeed every style — is bounded within its own limited time. But across and beyond this circumscribed period there enters another factor, of fluctuating intensity: This is the quantum of constituent elements, of fresh impulses generated within the period. In them lies the historical import of an era. They can wither from memory perhaps for centuries, as did the antique heritage. But at a certain time they come up again in man's consciousness, reaffirm their reality, and form the solid ground for new departures. So, for instance, the Renaissance used Antiquity as its springboard, and so in recent decades, the study of primitive man furthered insight into repressed instincts.

It was the ill fortune of the nineteenth century that the art and furniture of its ruling taste seldom found access to the absolute, the genuinely inventive. In the course of time, artistic and historical journeys may reveal other aspects, as the surrealist painters have already discovered. The mixture of banality and *haut goût*, naturalism and eeriness, which pervades the nineteenth century can arouse a certain nostalgia. The interiors of this age, with their gloomy light, their heavy curtains and carpets, their dark wood, and their horror of the void, breathe a peculiar warmth and disquiet. All in all, they reflect the profound pessimism that hangs over the whole realm of feeling in this period. That is one face of the century, a direction opposite to that of practical life, to the aggressiveness and optimism of industry.

The realm of feeling remained under the spell of that somber, chaotically splintered, often mendacious side. Taste was robbed of its emotional security, and gyrated in circles from period to period. Thus, in the 'thirties, the 'sixties, and the 'nineties, the Rococo manner was adopted again and again in various ways.

There is no difference between the pseudo-monumentality of the buildings and that of the furniture. Both belong to the transitory phenomena, unquickened by the blood of true inventiveness. Yet they dominate the feeling of their day and mercilessly stifle every impulse that springs from the deeper sources of the period.

The unexplored complex of patent furniture stands apart from the ruling taste. It called forth nearly all the constituent powers of the century. It revealed the century as it liked to relax when wearing none of its masks. This patent furniture tackled problems in a manner completely new to the century.

How did it come about?

A unifying trend runs through the abundance of still unreckoned solutions. Furniture was dissected into separate elements, into separate planes. These movable elements, which a governing mechanism linked and regulated, enabled the furniture to change in adaptation to the body and various postures. The furniture was thus endowed with a flexibility unknown before, and ceased to be a rigid, static implement. Not by accident did the problem of mechanically operated artificial limbs draw so strong an interest at this time (fig. 232). Patent furniture could perform alternate functions. What interests us more, it could take on any desired position of the human body, change from this position, and return to the normal. Comfort actively wrested by adaptation to the body, as against comfort passively derived from sinking back into cushions — here is the whole difference between the constituent furniture and the transitory furniture of the last century.

The basic problem of patent furniture was above all a problem of motion. The Americans of about 1850 to 1893 drew upon an almost inexhaustible fantasy to solve the motion problem for furniture. Often they were completely disinterested in the special use their chair was to serve; they simply wished to contrive a new mechanism, such as a seat that would incline and be fixed backward or forward. And so the American Patent Office would introduce a new category, such as 'tilting chairs.' Abundant as the solutions were, this problem of motion was by no means simple. European furniture about 1920 likewise sought to adapt to the contours of the human body. But there dissection into separate planes fell short in almost every attempt. The sitter stays anchored in the unvarying position of the frame of these pieces; he is not carried back — as in the American office chair or barber's chair — from the reclining position to the normal, which permits him to rise without effort.

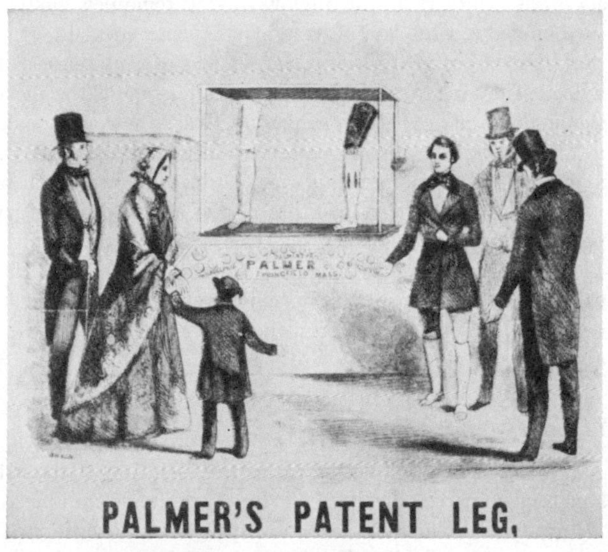

232. Interest in Mechanical Mobility: Artificial Limb, 1850's. '*Lifelike elasticity, flexibility and likeness.*' *Parallel with the improved flexibility of artificial limbs, furniture developed a mobility unknown before, being made adaptable to every change in posture.* (American Portrait Gallery, *vol.* III, *New York*, 1855)

In the four decades from 1850 to 1890 no activity of everyday life was taken for granted. An unbridled inventive urge shaped everything anew. Furniture, like other things, underwent transformation. This called for an independence of feeling and a courage to see with new and untried eyes. These very qualities made the nation's vigor at that stage. No conventions cramp the combinatory faculties, whether the anonymous inventors develop types for new purposes or whether they endow existing types with an undreamed of convertibility and mobility.

The America that exhibited at the international expositions between 1851 and 1889 was not ashamed of its non-'artistic' furniture, which, seen beside the pompous European display pieces, no more caught the eye than did the simple revolver of the American Samuel Colt, beside the hand-chased pistols of the French smiths.[1] A page from the catalogue of the Paris International Exposition of 1878 [2] tells us in what lay the American's pride at that time: perforated veneer seats, office desks, adjustable book supports, an automatic sofa spring-bed and lounge, a combined rocking chair and cradle.

A glance over the publications of the United States Patent Office shows what ramified subdivisions had become necessary in every category. Some 70 different subdivisions were added in the 'seventies solely for chairs of different purposes. The Patent Office in Washington is the only place where this movement can be surveyed. Until 1926, the original models remained sheltered there. As a whole they offered a rare vista of American inventiveness in a most original field, and they seemed destined to form the nucleus of a museum of the American way of living. They might have stood witness for one of the most vital periods in the shaping of America. The prosperous 1920's, however, could spare neither room nor money for the further preservation of these models. They were sold as so many odds and ends: a baffling lack of historical consciousness.

That this constituent furniture of the nineteenth century should so far have passed unnoticed in history one can understand; it slips through the meshes of an approach confined to purely formal and stylistic criteria. It was created as the functional answer to specific problems — functional, it is true, but the veritable meaning of the problems has roots deep in the fundamental nature and habits of man.

Furniture and Mechanization

How mechanization is related to the furniture of the ruling taste on the one hand and to patent furniture on the other should no longer be hard to explain.

Furniture also mirrors the dual ways of mechanization we have already noticed in several other fields. The first, the easy way, seeks cheaper substitutes for handicraft work. By stamping, stenciling, turning, or other means of low-price production, machines could inexpensively turn out the profiling, the ornamentation, and every form of earlier periods. The mechanical dexterity, and sometimes a certain ornamental bent, cannot be denied. But all in all it was a trampling of the same ground, incapable of creating new types. The mechanization of

---

[1] At least from the aesthetic point of view. The *Illustrated London News* of 1851 does not mention the Colt revolver, but describes and illustrates each ornament of these other objects, worthless today from any point of view whatsoever.

[2] Official catalogue of the United States exhibitors, Exposition Universelle, Paris, 1878.

upholstered furniture and the mechanization of adornment during the first half century has shown us how this easy way was condemned to linger in the transitory.

The second way of mechanization in furniture led to solutions hitherto unknown. Here the mechanical was used to aid and support the human organism. The furniture was constructed by engineers, not designed by upholsterers. Its inventors are practically unknown and uncounted. Now they create a completely new type; now they devise a new and simple means of movability. They belong to the anonymous history of the century. The inventor's name heads each patent specification. But it is only a name among other names, drifting past one's eyes like the names and numbers of a telephone directory. In the agglomerate, they form a storehouse of ideas largely unused and of experience lost.

***The Decades of Patent Furniture*, 1850–90**

The patent furniture of the nineteenth century has its distinct place in the history of comfort. It forms a link joining the ingenious French and English furniture of the eighteenth century with the attempts of our own time to adapt furniture to posture in simple ways.

The development from Sheraton to 1850 is but fragmentarily known. We lack detailed research into the constituent trends. Certain it is that in France and England during the first half of the century the development continues, if only as a lesser stream. Its keynote is a stronger emphasis on the mobile and the technical.

From 1850 on, America takes the lead and raises patent furniture to a stature never approached in Europe. The preparatory phase, from 1830 to 1850, is still tentative. Toward 1860, in pace with the growing activity of invention, an overwhelming rush sets in that culminates, within a decade, in a high degree of technical proficiency. The knack of solving the motion problems of furniture grows so rapidly that during the 'eighties — here again in step with other fields — it reaches a maturity to which little could be added.

In the 'nineties an influx of European ruling taste flooded America. Well known as the turning point is the Chicago World's Fair of 1893. The attitude that it enthroned — a surrender to copied Classical architecture in direct supply from the French Academy — rejected the flat machine-made surfaces of American equipment as too meager, and the patent furniture as ridiculously out of place. Mechanized furniture disappeared from living quarters. People began to be ashamed of it. From then on, the whole movement gathered around furniture for special, technical purposes. Patent furniture was banished from the house, and the countless attempts to create a truly nineteenth-century comfort went to waste. This happened at a time when Europe was beginning to realize into what plight it had been drawn by the ruling taste.

Possibly the concentration of financial power into fewer hands — 1893 is a noteworthy date — decreased the small inventor's chances. Decisive, however, was the taste that possessed the country as a whole, the broad masses of the people. The year 1893 also marks a rift in the proud and independent skyscraper construction of the Chicago School, a break that after four decades is only beginning slowly to heal.

An Approach to the Furniture of the Nineteenth Century

The furniture of the nineteenth century is difficult of approach. Not for lack of material, which abounds at every turn. The difficulty lies rather in the psychological domain. We have not simply to judge the furniture of the period according to what it claims to be. We have first to resolve a seeming paradox.

The furniture of the ruling taste assumes to liberate a wealth of feeling and fantasy. But its pieces were not created in the most direct way. They were reflectively created. It is thus that we may understand the recurrent imitation of styles. T. S. Eliot calls the poets of the Victorian taste 'reflective.' 'They think, but they do not feel their thoughts as immediately as the odour of a rose.' No less than the poetry of the ruling taste, intimate surroundings were created reflectively. Lacking was the leap into the unknown, the inventive. A powerful side of the nineteenth century is here revealed: the mask-like. Its view of real life is as deceptive as that of a wax museum.

Over and against this, stands patent furniture. Here there is no room for reflection. All derivative feeling has fallen away as the skin from a skeleton. Sometimes patent furniture strikes the grotesque: often it is congenial and startlingly direct. In this furniture, whose sole aim is to serve needs previously without claim or without solution, and whose construction rules out everything but bare formulation and inventive fantasy, the creative urge succeeds in piercing through.

This would suggest that the paradox is inherent in the century.

We can aim here only at a survey, not a detailed knowledge, of the true furniture of the nineteenth century. To catalogue patent specifications and examples would scarcely further historical understanding. It would leave us hopelessly stranded in the technical. Purely formal and stylistic enquiry, on the other hand, glances off the surface.

To understand its true nature we must choose another approach. As Brancusi, the sculptor, once said, stroking the marble planes of his 'Fish' in his studio in

Paris, 'The sculptor must allow himself to be led by the material; the material will tell him what he should do.' This is even truer of the historian's task.

In the present case a problem arose: What does the patent furniture imply? It soon became clear that we had to broaden our basis of approach and again raise the question: How does man's posture in the nineteenth century differ from that of earlier periods? If a new manner of sitting developed, we shall have to decide whether patent furniture, the furniture of the engineer, offered better solutions than did the furniture of the ruling taste. This complexity will be found to center around adaptability.

The second problem of patent furniture will center around convertibility. Multiple functions are performed by each piece. Hence are found combinations of the most heterogeneous elements, sometimes even a naive mimicry.

The development of the *sleeping car* will warrant our special attention, as a rare case of convertible furniture coming down in unbroken tradition to our own day. And we shall not overlook the *hammock*, which may seem to lie at the most distant pole of aesthetic interest: its handling by the Americans of the early 'eighties reveals that hovering and informal posture to which the nineteenth century is unconsciously drawn.

Furniture for the Middle Classes

Here the transitory types of the ruling taste and the constituent types of the engineer meet face-to-face.

In architecture, the nineteenth century meant the rule of pseudo-monumentality. Monumental forms were indiscriminately used everywhere and anywhere, from public edifices to the lowest tenement. This same orientation was responsible for the furniture of the ruling taste, with its excess of decoration and ornamentation. Things that only the topmost classes had been able to purchase, mechanization now made available to everyone. True, in the long run, this palatial style could not continue to thrive in three rooms. But the insignia of wealth and panoply wield a fascination that, for a considerable while, may inhibit healthier instincts.

The other side of the nineteenth century is embodied in the structures of the engineer, in the furniture of the engineer. Patent furniture consists of types evolved by the middle brackets for their own urgent needs. Wealthy people had no call for a lounge convertible into a cradle, or a bed convertible into a wardrobe. They owned both the space and the means to satisfy their needs in other ways. The patent furniture arose, in America at least, from the demands of an intermediate class that wished, without over-crowding, to bring a modicum of comfort into a minimum of space. The chair that converts into a lounge, the bed that converts into a wardrobe, the bedroom that converts into a living room, were more naturally and more thoughtfully suited to the two or three rooms of the rising middle-class than was the heavy furniture of the ruling taste. Patent furniture indeed arose in the limited quarters of a growing urban middle class. But it did not stop at economy of space. As soon as the human spirit seeks to vivify a given field, unexpected solutions are wont to appear that often branch into quite new directions: in this case, solutions for the best adaptability to posture.

Posture in the Nineteenth Century

Improvised and informal as in the medieval period, frontal as in the Renaissance, relaxed as in the eighteenth century — all these postures are found again, reappearing like the various styles, in the furniture of the nineteenth century. When the nineteenth century builds its heavy chairs of cylindrical cushions and spiral springs, it gives them the stiff upholstery and the formal aspect of seventeenth-century armchairs. It also used the curved and attenuated forms of the eighteenth century, and under Oriental influence went even further than did the medieval period in cultivating informality of posture.

Almost impatiently one asks: Was the century without distinct needs of its own? Did it never find the key to its own character?

The nineteenth century did evolve a posture of its own and possibly laid the basis for a development that we cannot as yet perceive. But this posture cannot be traced in the furniture of the ruling taste, whose show place was the salon. As so often, the nineteenth century bares its genius in its places of work, where it has shed all pose and dares to be self-reliant. Then it can hold its own with other centuries; and where one might expect it least: in the province of furniture.

The posture of the nineteenth century — this too, in full contrast to the ruling taste — is based on relaxation. This relaxation is found in a free, unposed attitude that can be called neither sitting nor lying. Once again the painters are first to voice the unconscious inclinations of their time by surprising and capturing the model in this indefinite posture. In a rippling water-color of 1826, Richard Bonington paints his 'Reclining Woman' (fig. 233), relaxedly using an upholstered sofa as if it were a reclining chair. She leans lightly back, half-sitting, half-lying, her feet at rest on the floor.

This posture was unfamiliar to earlier periods. When Boucher in the middle of the eighteenth century, and Fragonard in the second half, portray their beauties in carefree pose, these were sure to be nudes, studies for a 'Toilet of Venus' or similar subject. Cupid or a spectator stood in the picture or was understood to be not far away.

233. Nineteenth-Century Posture: Richard Bonington, 'Reclining Woman.' Water Color, 1826. *The true posture of the nineteenth century is found in a free, unposed attitude that is neither sitting nor lying. Once again it is the painter who first voices the unconscious inclination by catching his model in this indefinite posture before chairs corresponding to it existed. (Andrew Shirley,* Bonington, *London,* 1941)

Bonington shows the woman fully clothed and relaxing, her head framed in a shawl. Unconstrained posture seems to have developed in an Empire society that felt drawn to Court without having been born into it. The furniture it created was stiff outwardly, but seems to have been used in quite a different manner. Among Bonington's earlier works is a copy after the court-painter Gérard, showing a lady, said to be Joséphine, seated on an Empire sofa, sharply rectangular in outline (fig. 242). She uses it diagonally, her feet on the floor, legs aslant to the seat, trunk resting backwards in the angle. It is significant that Bonington copied this picture of the otherwise tediously conventional Gérard.

Richard Bonington died of consumption in 1826 at the age of twenty-five. He knew what sitting and lying meant. In a letter to a French friend he tells of the reclining chair existing only in his invalid's dream.

Bonington's study of the 'Reclining Woman' with its easy, flowing treatment is a portrait of nineteenth-century posture. The line of chairs adjustable to the body stretches countlessly from the 1830's down to LeCorbusier.

Mobility

Just as exploring the mobile and exploiting its practical uses form one of the basic trends of our period, so in furniture the key word was mobility.

The nomadic furniture of the Middle Ages that could follow its owner wherever he journeyed was primitive. Demountable, collapsible pieces were customary before stable ones. The table consisted of loose planks set on trestles, and was placed to the wall after meals. The table with four legs and a fixed frame comes in later, contemporaneously with the Renaissance chair, having arm and back rests. The faldstool, an inheritance of Antiquity, was standard long before the four-legged framed chair. Desks were movable and well differentiated according to purpose — writing or reading.

The demand for mobility, although weakened by the advent of more stable conditions, never became quite extinct. In the stable household of the late fifteenth to the late eighteenth centuries, quite other values matured, tending toward form and convenience.

Already the late eighteenth century, an age that had begun to invent not only cunning automata but spinning machines, delighted in ingenious, mechanically contrived comfort; and this less in the concealed secret drawers than in small, compact furniture devised for new ends and often serving multiple purposes. In England, and especially in France, the mid-eighteenth century produced 'portable beds' or 'traveling beds' that with a few motions would pack away into a bag. America as well as England has preserved beds that could be converted into reclining chairs.

The nineteenth century turned mobility into a specific channel. Life was more stable, while living quarters were often cramped, particularly in America. This frequently led to highly inventive types and combinations, sometimes fringing on the grotesque. It produced much that was new: the sleeping car, for instance, based on the principle of convertibility.

The new tasks, demanding near-absolute solutions, are those in which mobility is made to serve our physiological requirements. A mode of sitting develops that aims at complete bodily relaxation. As we shall see, it is often achieved through conscious interplay of the body with the mechanism of the chair. Lying too, and the many positions between sitting and lying — arm support, relaxation of the head — are met in a wide variety of constructional solutions.

Posture Physiologically Considered

The architectural movement around 1920 sought artistic forms to express our physiological requirements: for sitting, a hovering posture; for lying, a posture

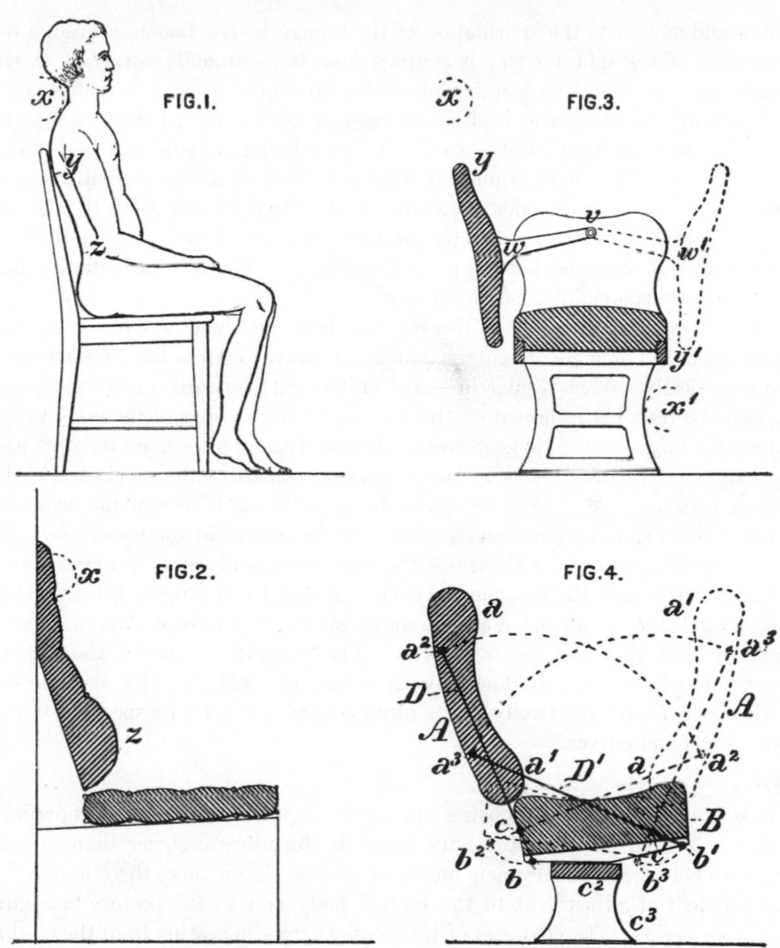

234 a, b, c, d. Posture Physiologically Considered: Car Seat, 1885. *In the heyday of the ruling taste in Europe, American engineers took pains to curve the seat and back rest organically. The inventor begins by explaining the relation between seating and anatomy, and shows in diagrams the points at which support is needed.*

(a) *Relation of the rear outline of the human body to an ordinary chair.*

(b) *Ordinary American car seat.*

(c) *English railway seat.*

(d) *'My invention is designed to afford suitable supports . . . Its upper portion acts as a head rest, and its lower as a support for the lumbar region of the back of the occupant, the seat being also rearwardly inclined, as is desirable for comfort.'*

(*U. S. Patent* 324,825, 25 *August* 1885)

that would answer to the articulation of the human body. Looking through the magazines of the mid-nineteenth century, one is continually surprised at the insight and care spent on meeting physiological requirements. 'Comfort, convenience and adaptation to health,' we read in 1869, 'are the chief ends to be secured in the construction of a seat.'[3] In introducing a metal lounge destined to become one of the most popular models (fig. 256), 70 different positions were claimed; physiological considerations came first: 'Physiologists tell us that nearly three hundred muscles are directly or indirectly connected with motions of which the small of the back is the pivotal center. . . . People of sedentary habits are constantly complaining of the back.'[4]

The railway seat, from the 'fifties onward, becomes the object of a searching experimentation, and the inventors take great pains to curve the back rest and seat organically. When a later inventor (1885) puts forward a new 'reversible car seat' he rests his argument on the fact that 'the portions of the body which require the most exertion to keep erect, when in sitting posture, are the neck and the loins. . . . In these the only bony supports consist of the cervical and the lumbar vertebrae. . . .'[5] And he shapes his seat (fig. 234) so that the neck and lumbar region shall be particularly cushioned by curves in the upholstery. To make clear his purpose, he illustrates his words with a diagram of a man seated in an ordinary chair, the point in the neck line that lacks support being marked with a circled *x*. A second diagram shows an English railway seat and the *x* indicates that the head can rest back. The patentee diagnoses the regular American railway seat's weakness by an *x* drawn in mid-air. His own solution carries no *x*, for it successfully meets physiological needs by its specially traced proportions and curves.

Sitting

It is not hard to bring a chair's appearance up to date by a few superficial touches. Yet no greater complexity faces the furniture designer than to construct a chair demanded by new habits of sitting. Each time, there is raised a new problem of adjustment to the human body and to the posture emerging in a given period. The centuries of toilsome progress in seating from the Gothic to the Baroque show how inelastic is our imagination in this sphere.

How does the nineteenth century like to sit?

We already know how its posture differs from earlier centuries. Sitting is an instance. Its chairs will aim at greater ease and fuller relaxation. But the question that interests us is how this special type of ease and relaxation was attained.

[3] *Manufacturer and Builder*, New York, 1869, vol. 1, p.9.
[4] The Wilson Adjustable Chair Mfg. Co., 592 Broadway, New York, 1876, advertisement.
[5] U.S. Patent 324,825, 25 Aug. 1885.

To anticipate the answer: in a resilient mode of seating, by interplay of the body and the chair mechanism.

We do not know of any research into the effect on the blood stream of small shifts in posture, minor changes of equilibrium. That they somehow influence relaxation and may often take the place of upholstery is suggested by the rocking chair, never so thoroughly developed as in America during the late eighteenth century (fig. 235).

The rocking chair owes its comfort to nicety of fashioning. It derives from the Windsor type. Its slender hickory spindles, well suited to cradle the spine, and its curved saddle seat reflect the quality of colonial life: medieval austerity tempered by sensitive workmanship. The rocking chair, like clapboard, is one of the constants of American life. The American farmer, at the end of the day, will instinctively move to the rocker on his porch. The European peasant sits immovable through the twilight as if nailed to the bench before his cottage. These simple differences must be understood, for more profoundly than one might think, they change the course of inventive fantasy. They underlie the divergence of American and European comfort in the nineteenth century. As soon as mechanization became a decisive power in furniture, these differences began to show.

How is this resilient mode of sitting achieved?

In 1853 — the time of experimentation with movable railroad seats — the first chair of this type appears. It solves at first blow the problem of seating made resilient by a knitting together of the mechanism and the sitter's body.

It will later be refined and elaborated, but its basic principle will remain unchanged.

The crossing of two types, fertilized by a potent mechanical fantasy, yields a new and improved variety. What Americans were later to perform so well in the hybridization of plants appears here in the mechanical domain. The two types to be combined are the rocking chair and the revolving chair (figs. 235, 236, 237, 238). But now the rotary motion of the revolving chair is combined with the oscillating motion of the rocking chair. This is where inventive fantasy comes in. The body of the rocking chair is raised and mounted on a base. Everything else is a matter of mechanics.

In the early 'thirties, Americans attempted to make the rocking chair more resilient by placing wagon springs between the rockers and the seat (fig. 236). The handwritten letter patent of 1831[6] terms it 'health vehicle . . . a combina-

[6] U.S. Patent, 23 Apr. 1831.

235. Windsor Chair, *c.*1800. *The Windsor type of rocking chair has been standard in the American home for* 150 *years. Whether the rocking chair originated in Lancashire around* 1750, *or whether Benjamin Franklin used iron rockers around* 1760, *are questions that preoccupy us far less than the fact that the rocking chair is predestined for flexible and resilient seating.* (*Courtesy* Antiques)

236. Mechanization: Improved Rocking Chair, 1831. *Efforts were made in the 'thirties to heighten the elasticity of the rocking chair by inserting wagon springs between the rockers and the seat.* (*U. S. Patent,* 23 *April* 1831. *D. Harrington*)

tion of certain parts of machinery attached together at their middle . . . three elliptic springs of steel are used.'

Here again, springs form the starting point for a nineteenth-century product, but their use differs distinctly from their use in upholstery. This time they are not cheaper substitutes for feather stuffing or a means of artificially bloating the chair. Rather, they represent progress within the program of the English inventor who conceived the first chair having spiral springs 'as a swinging apparatus' (fig. 225).

The chair of 1853 (fig. 237) [7] that makes possible the new mode of sitting clearly shows its derivation from the rocking chair. The curved steel segments mounted directly beneath the seat still have the original rocker shape. 'The top and seat shall rock upon the bottom part, while the legs remain stationary.' In other words, it is a rocking chair lifted from the floor, a hovering rocking chair. It oscillates through a wider sweep than the chair whose rockers are on the ground, calling for an accurate mechanism if the sitter is to be spared

[7] U.S. Patent 9620, 15 Mar. 1853.

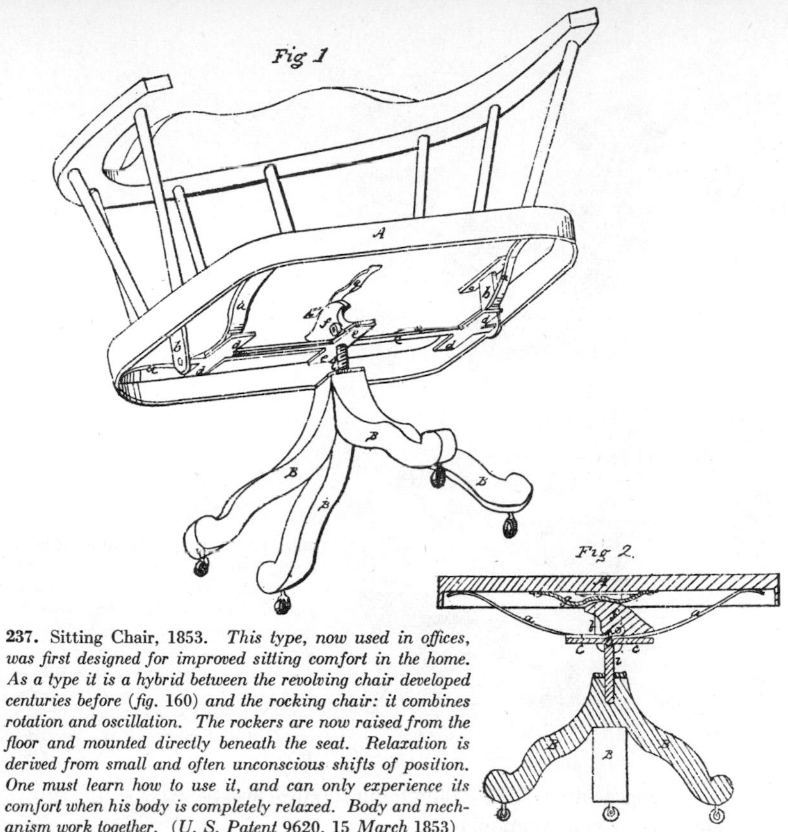

237. Sitting Chair, 1853. *This type, now used in offices, was first designed for improved sitting comfort in the home. As a type it is a hybrid between the revolving chair developed centuries before (fig.* 160) *and the rocking chair: it combines rotation and oscillation. The rockers are now raised from the floor and mounted directly beneath the seat. Relaxation is derived from small and often unconscious shifts of position. One must learn how to use it, and can only experience its comfort when his body is completely relaxed. Body and mechanism work together.* (*U. S. Patent* 9620, 15 *March* 1853)

unpleasant surprises. Safety devices are needed, springs to arrest any too violent motion, a safety guard is used to prevent the chair from going back suddenly or going back too far. Both rockers sway on two extended arms, as the inventor makes quite clear in his underside view. In his first model, already the whole upper part rests on a pivot, enabling one to swing both backwards and forwards or to either side.

The chair of 1853 was meant for relaxation. Its inventor, Peter Ten Eyck, a name as unknown as those in a telephone book, had nothing in mind beyond an improved rocking chair, or, as he calls it, a 'sitting chair.' No one thought of its one-sided use in the office. The 'fifties used chairs of this type in the home.

The advertisements and catalogues of this time (fig. 238) list them as 'piano-stools,' 'library chairs,' upholstered, high-backed 'easy chairs,' and sometimes under the blanket name of 'spring revolving chairs.' Their forms overlap with

238. Rocking and Rotating Chairs, 1855. *The so-called office chair was originally intended for the home, for 'invalids, parlor, drawing-room, library, counting house, office or garden.' In the following decades it was reduced to a desk chair. Unfortunately this means of perfect relaxation has so far been neglected by furniture designers and architects.* (American Portrait Gallery, *vol.* III, *New York,* 1855)

those of the ruling taste. Their voluminous bodies are belied by the subtle thought behind their construction.

A person accustomed to a rigid type of chair has first to learn this mode of sitting in which body and mechanism collaborate, for in contrast with rigid sitting, the body must do its share. A first condition is to sit fully relaxed. The knees, ankles, and toe joints form part and parcel of the chair's mechanism; it is they that regulate the position of the body backwards, forwards, or sideways, so far as circumstances or relaxation require. The pivots of the movement are the toes and balls of the feet. They are the fulcra. They are the constant regulators of the movement, never losing their activity. In a humble way they act as the ankles of a ballet-dancer in the heel-toe.

Relaxation of the body is not induced by stuffing, but is achieved by a method of seating, both resilient and oscillating; by movement forwards, backwards, or sideways, in reaching, or in any other spontaneous motion. Such unconscious shifts of position avoid the cramps that easily trouble the sitter in rigid seating.

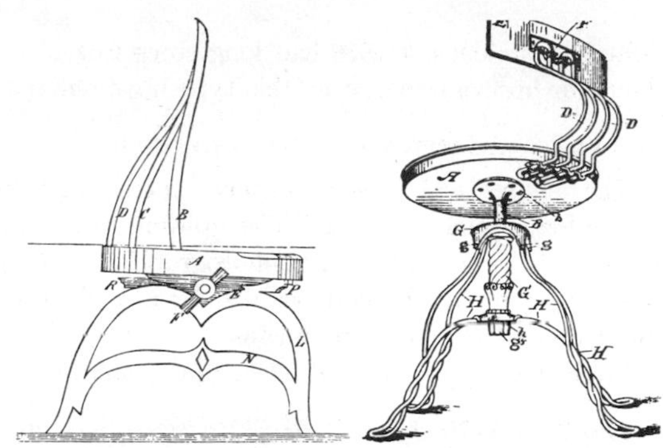

239. J. J. SCHUEBLER: French Chair for Writing Table, *c.*1730. *A forerunner of the typewriter chair giving flexible support to the back. 'The back is padded to the hollow of a man's spine and provided with a resilient spring so as to yield backwards without breaking.'* (*Schuebler,* Nuetzliche Vorstellung, *Nuernberg,* 1730)

240. Sewing-Machine Chair, 1871. *'Constructed on scientific principles to prevent many of the diseases peculiar to those operating sewing machines. The spindles DC form a deep recess at the lower part of the back. By this means the muscles of the thighs are relieved from pressure whilst the back just below the shoulders receives a suitable support.' Seating was differentiated for every activity, from flexible reaper seats to sewing-machine or barber chairs.* (*U. S. Patent* 114,532, 9 *May* 1871)

241. 'The Typewriter's Chair,' 1896. *The typewriter chair is a late comer. Backward oscillating movement would be wrong for the typist, who needs only resilient support for her back and freedom to turn to the right and left.* (*U. S. Patent* 552,502, 7 *January* 1896)

In the 'sixties, as the type approached a standard form, it began to be listed as an office chair.[8] The mechanism, its adjustability, the regulating of springs, are later solved in many ways, without anything really new being added.

To know how the American would sit if the ruling taste were not master in his house, we must watch him at the office; how the desk-chair behaves beneath him with almost organic flexibility, and how he unconsciously varies his posture without end. The American seems to have become one creature with his chair, as the Arab with his horse.

No other period knew this mobility, this adjustability to the body. The informal, resilient method of sitting, formed of the spirit of the epoch, could have been pushed further in admirable fashion. But ruling taste barred the way, for it demanded heavy, circumstantial, furniture. The period failed to understand its opportunities, to capture and infuse with artistic blood the organic so strongly embodied in this chair.

The architectural movement around 1920 that made resilient sitting so much its concern was based on an altogether different tradition in furniture, while in

[8] 'Office Chair,' U.S. Patent 67,034, 23 July 1867. Here the chair pivots like the arms of a balance.

America the ideas of 1850 had long since frozen around purely technical aims. Thus the horizons opened by this type have remained unexplored to this day.

THE CHAIR ADAPTED TO SPECIALIZED NEEDS

The 'sixties and 'seventies move increasingly toward the construction of chairs for special activities. The guiding principles are the same throughout, whether in school furniture, photographer's posing chairs, railroad seats, or operating tables. The best posture for any given moment is the constant aim; differentiated mobility, the means.

From these types we shall select but a handful.

The Sewing-Machine Chair: The 'seventies construct sewing-machine chairs (fig. 240) 'on scientific principles so as to prevent many of the diseases peculiar to those operating sewing machines. . . .' The effort focuses on 'relieving the muscles of the thighs from constant contact with the front edge of the seat and suitably supporting the back of the operator, thus promoting ease and comfort.' As the patentee does not forget to stress: 'much more labor can be accomplished in a given time.'[9] He relieves the sitter's thighs by 'arranging the seat of the chair to incline forward.' The back rest, too, is given a forward tilt, corresponding to that of the sewer's body.

The Typewriter Chair: The Americans come to differentiate chairs for the writer and chairs for the typist. A typists' chair built on the rocking principle of the office chair would be quite unfit for typewriting. More to the point is a resilient back rest that will at all times bolster the trunk, allow the shoulder muscles to relax, and relieve the hands from exhaustion.

The difference between the desk chair and the typewriter chair corresponds to the two different activities. Desk writing is a type of handicraft, with all its freedom and alternatives; it is not tied to any fixed posture, and much depends on the personal habits and preferences of the writer. Thus we may understand the freedom of the desk chair to oscillate, whether in leaning backward for occasional relaxation or when turning in this reclined position to face a visitor.

Typewriting, like any mechanical activity, breaks down to specific movements, continually repeated. Any oscillating seat is out of the question. All one needs is resilient support for one's spine and the freedom to reach right or left. The typewriter chair therefore revolves but does not tilt.

The typewriter chair is a late-comer in the development. It does not appear before the 'nineties — that is, nearly two decades after the typewriter had reached its standard form, and over four decades after the office chair appeared.

---

[9] U.S. Patent 114,532, 9 May 1871. Improvement in Sewing Machine Chairs.

By now the movement has lost its former keenness. This shows up in the way the back rest of the early models is made mobile. Tilting panels branch from the framework of the chair;[10] they seem excrescences rather than a mechanical device. The solution of 1896[11] (apparently the first patented), with its four sickle-shaped springs joining seat to back rest, does not appear any too satisfactory (fig. 241).[12]

Springing the back rest was an idea put forward around 1730 by the Nuremberg furniture designer, Johann Jacob Schuebler (fig. 239). He calls it a 'French comfortable chair in which the back rest is padded to the hollow of a man's back and is provided with a spring so that the backrest will flex backwards, bending but not breaking.'

This chair, with its sprung back rest, was for use at a writing desk, but it undoubtedly involves the principle of the later typewriter chair.

Gradually a form of support was developed that would automatically seek contact with the typist's shoulders; it has a forward tilt as in the sewing machine chair of 1871. But this time the whole back rest is mobile, being pressed to the spine by a spring beneath the seat. These are called 'posture chairs.' The sitter must first push back the forward-tilted back rest, which will then cling to his body and constantly follow his movements.

Thus, around 1900, the back rest becomes a 'back-supporting arm hinged to the seat,' like the beam of a balance. The short arm projects downward beneath the seat, where it is connected in one of many ways with a spring that maintains the back rest in constant forward pressure.[13]

During the metal shortage of the Second World War, wooden models were put on the market, in which the occupant's weight was used as a substitute for springs. Gravity supplied the constant leverage necessary to spring the back rest.

Lying

With the same lack of constraint that marked its sitting, the nineteenth century explored the possible manners of lying. Prolonged rest, night-time sleep, was not its object here. It sought a furniture for passing relaxation. For such pieces to have been admitted within the house, social convention must have sanctioned the informal posture that Bonington so keenly sensed in his 'Reclining Woman' of 1826, before the corresponding chairs existed (fig. 233).

[10] U.S. Patent 574,602, 5 Jan. 1897, Franklin Chichester.

[11] U.S. Patent 552,502, 7 Jan. 1896, H. L. Andrews.

[12] The inventor did not give up, and later arrived at a form approximating that standard today.

[13] U.S. Patent 647,178, 10 Apr. 1900.

In sitting, the problem was to maintain the body as relaxed as possible, while performing its tasks — to insinuate rest into the midst of activity.

But lying, and the postures between sitting and lying that now steadily gain favor, call for relaxation in a passive state — from the simple adjustable lounges, railroad seats, barbers' chairs, to complicated operating tables.

The starting point is found in circumstances where the body requires special care: among the sick and the bedridden.

As is so often the case, the trail leads back to an English patent of the early seventeenth century. All we have to go on is a rather incomplete description: 'A Backframe or Back-Screene for Bedridden Invalids . . . for the Ease and Reliefe of such sick Persons . . . as are troubled with Heate on their Backes through continuing lying on their Beddes.' [14]

In the late eighteenth century, bed machines were constructed in which the mattress was divided into three mobile sections corresponding to the legs, thighs, and back. At first, cumbersome wooden constructions held these sections; heavy iron worm-and-gear drive was used later [15] (fig. 243), as in the first decades of the nineteenth century.

Chairs convertible into beds — a few are preserved [16] — existed in the eighteenth century. The nineteenth sets itself an altogether different task: to develop what is neither bed nor chair, but hybrid furniture that will fluctuate between the chair and the couch without sudden transformation.

The early phases take place in England and in France. They are still uninvestigated but do not seem a very promising field.[17]

America — starting in the late 'thirties, and at a growing pace from 1850 — clearly takes the lead. Among the earliest of this type, 'the Variety-Couch or Invalid-Chair' of 1838 [18] (fig. 245) contains the nucleus of the future development: 'The basis is formed by a stool with legs and casters. The back of the couch may be placed at any desired degree of inclination, even vertically or horizontally, by means of a spring-bolt and circular segments.' Provision is

---

[14] British Patent No.16, A.D. 1620.

[15] As for instance: British Patent No.3744, 1 Nov. 1813: 'Sofa or machine for the care of invalids.'

[16] Cf. Macquoid and Edwards, *Dictionary of English Furniture from the Middle Ages to the late Georgian Period*, vol. II, op.cit. p.164: a reclining bed 'to be converted into a winged arm chair.' The date attributed, 1730, seems rather too early. American examples of the same type, furniture 'which may serve either as a Queen Ann winged chair or a cushion day-bed' is shown in Wallace, 'Double purpose furniture,' *Antiques*, vol. 38, no.4 (1940), p.160.

[17] For example, 'Minter's Reclining Chair,' British Patent No.6034, A.D. 1830, with 'self-adjusting leverage of the back and seat.' Or 'Chairs or machines calculated to increase ease and comfort,' British Patent 5490, 28 Aug. 1827. Here the back rest is already equipped with two hinges for adjustability. In France even more complicated machines were built at this time: 'Surgical Chair Bed,' British Patent No.5605, A.D. 1828; the French inventor's patent specification extends to ten pages.

[18] U.S. Patent 775, 12 June 1838.

made, as well, for flexibly suspending the chair by metal rods from the ceiling. Similar but less complex 'invalid couches' are not unusual at this time. Thomas Webster's popular 'Encyclopedia of Domestic Economy'[19] feels justified in depicting and fully describing such a couch, after a London design (fig. 244).

A broad and comprehensive category, of which we can barely touch the surface here, regulates passive postures and conveniently offers the body to manipulations — from shaving to surgery. At first the barber's chair, the surgeon's, and the dentist's are identical, just as barber, surgeon, and dentist were gathered in the same person. Proposals of this type are found even in the 'sixties.

In the mid-'fifties came those experiments so urgently striving for the democratic railroad seat, convertible without loss of space into a couch. (We shall deal with this in its place.) The search for the adjustable railroad seat stimulates other categories of chair.

During the 'sixties, differentiation sets in between the barber's and the dentist's chairs. In the dentist's chair, headrest, back rest, and footrest become ever more adjustable and independent. At the same time its driving mechanism becomes more complicated.[20] By the end of the 'sixties, hydraulic pressure pumped by pedal levers is used to raise and lower the dentist's chair. Particular care goes into constructing the headrest to relieve the neck of strain. A decade later the dentist's chair approaches its standard form[21] (fig. 253), and the operator can 'readily . . . raise and lower the chair body without shock and jar.'

The decade between the Paris Exhibition of 1878 and that of 1889 saw the problem of vaulting by means of iron construction solved no less daringly than rapidly. This is the decade in which American patent furniture rises to technical maturity. In medicine, during the same period, the nineteenth century's specific talent, the technical, develops at a growing pace. Surgery becomes increasingly ambitious in scope, and calls for more accurately adjustable operating tables. One can appreciate the technical perfection required in these surgical chairs or tables — which categories are no longer distinguished. An inventor sets forth the program:

> Surgical chairs are required to be adjusted to a great variety of positions, so as to bring the patient to a sitting, reaching or lying position, to raise and lower the head or the feet simultaneously or independently, to tip or turn the patient to either side, and, generally, to secure any position necessary for convenient treatment or manipulation by the surgeon.[22]

[19] Thomas Webster, *Encyclopedia of Domestic Economy*, New York, 1845.

[20] U.S. Patent 55,368, 5 June 1866.

[21] U.S. Patent 222,092, 25 Nov. 1879.

[22] U.S. Patent 360,279, 29 Mar. 1887; lines 29–37. 'Surgical Chair,' Frank E. Case.

242. Posture in the Early Nineteenth Century: Portrait of Empress Josephine, Water color by Bonington after Gérard. *Even before 1810 there is a noticeable gap between posture and furniture. The lady is sitting diagonally on the rigid Empire piece. Informality is the keynote.* (*Andrew Shirley*, Bonington, *London*, 1941)

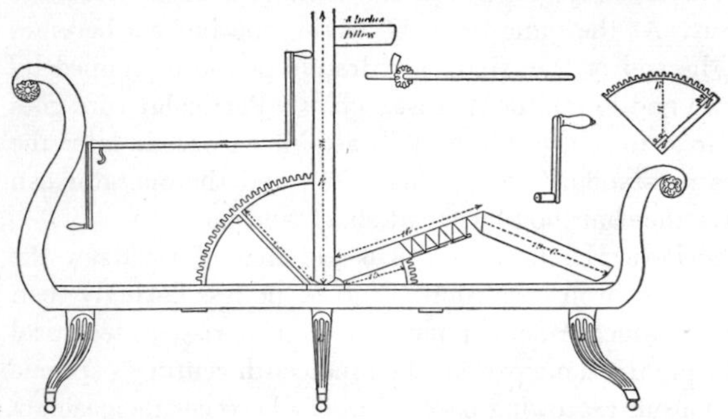

243. Sofa or Machine for the Care of Invalids, 1813. *Furniture suitable to the informal posture between sitting and lying was first used by the sick. Hence its adaptability. The late eighteenth century devised 'bed-machines' with the mattress segmented into three planes, which in the first decades of the nineteenth century were raised at various angles by means of a cumbersome system of winches, worms, and gears.* (*British Patent* 3744, 1 *November* 1813)

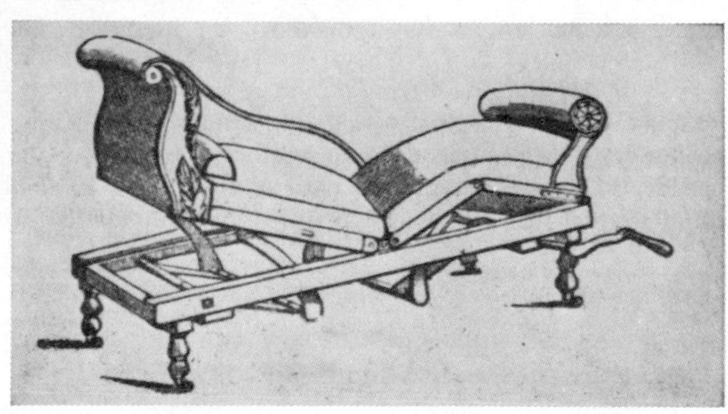

244. Invalid Couch, London, after 1840. *'An invalid couch, contrived to raise the back to any angle, and to conform to the situation of the legs by elevating part of the frame by means of a winch.' Even the popular Encyclopedias gave consideration to adjustable couches at this period.* (*Thomas Webster*, Encyclopedia of Domestic Economy, *New York*, 1845)

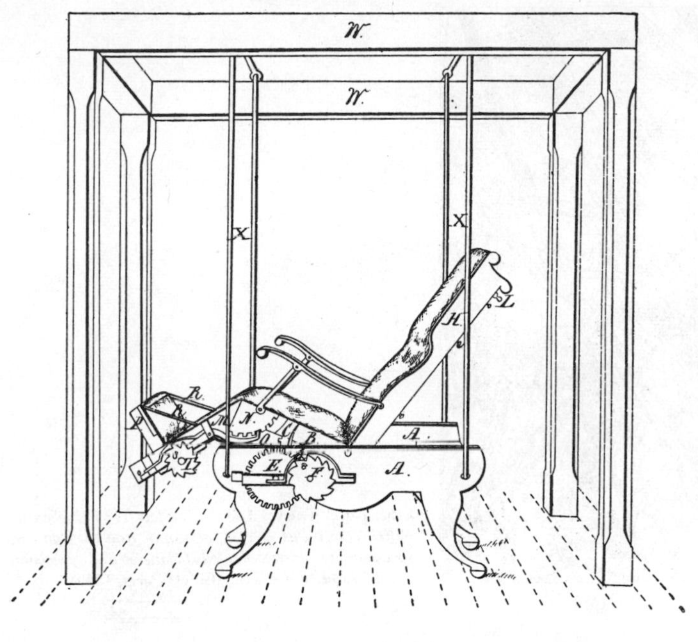

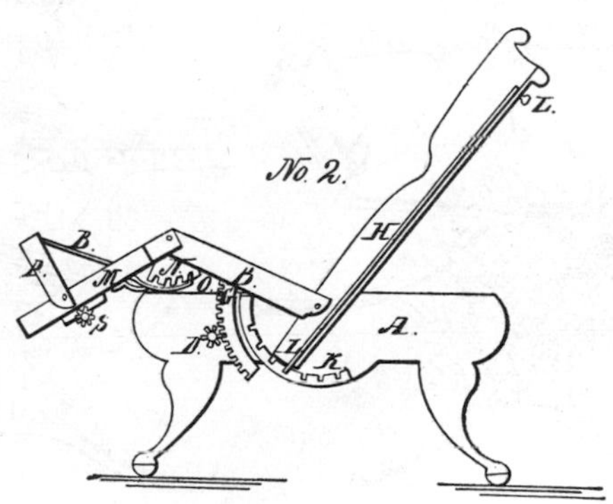

245. Variety Couch or Invalid Chair, 1838. *Unwieldy as it is, this invalid chair nevertheless announces the extreme adjustability and movability patent furniture was to attain in later decades. 'The basis is formed by a stool with legs and castors. The back of the couch may be placed at any desired degree of inclination, even vertically or horizontally.' The apparatus swings when suspended by rods from the ceiling.* (*U. S. Patent* 775, 12 *June* 1838)

246. Eiffel Tower, 1889. *The late 1880's, when the Eiffel Tower was erected, developed iron skeleton construction to unprecedented boldness and precision.* (*G. Tissandier,* La Tour Eiffel, *Paris,* 1889)

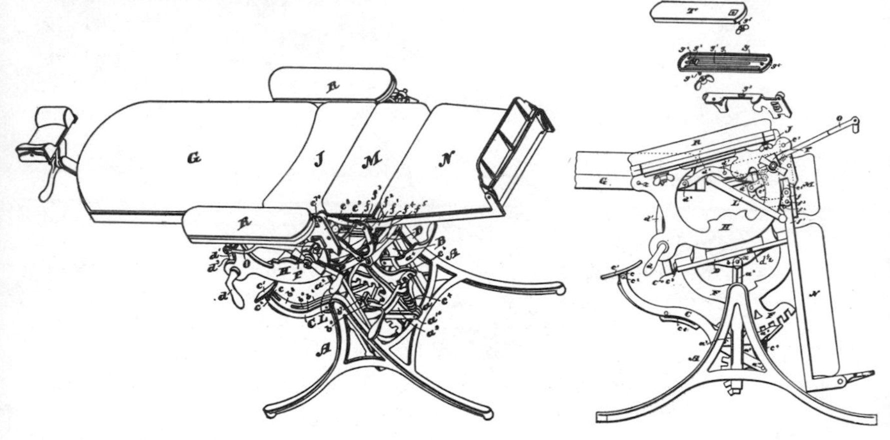

247 a. Surgical Chair, 1889. *The engineer developed precision and skill simultaneously with the surgeon. The operating table reached a hitherto unknown degree of adaptability. Here the supporting plane is articulated into seven planes moved by levers and pedals, and fixable in any inclination. It has elaborated the elements already present in the 'variety couch' of* 1838. (*U. S. Patent* 397,077, *29 January* 1889)

247 b. *'Means for raising or lowering vertically, or to rotate or rock the body of the chair on the supporting base' have produced a complex mechanism which here is left open, but soon will be enclosed in white enamel and operated by hydraulic devices.*

These are quite new challenges to the engineer. To gauge the achievement, let us select from the long line an example of 1889 — the year the Eiffel Tower (fig. 246) was raised. The body-supporting surfaces have by now broken up into seven different sections (fig. 247): headrest and footrest, two mobile armrests, and a body rest subdivided into four panels. The base becomes a receptacle for the machinery, with its interlocking system of rods, levers for adjusting the position as desired. 'Means of raising vertically or lowering the body of the chair or to rotate the body of the chair on the supporting base' [23] are provided as a matter of course. The iron framework of the base with its machinery is still open to view. Later it will be concealed and the mechanism hygienically housed in a white enamel case. But near the end of the 'eighties the essential solution — machinery for more differentiated control — is already reached.

MECHANIZATION OF THE BARBER CHAIR

Does the barber chair belong in the line of adjustable lounges or among ordinary chairs? The answer depends upon whether we have in mind the European or the American barber chair.

In Europe the lordship of ruling taste left the barber chair an unwieldy thing, as stiff and static as the railroad seat, the lounge, or the sofa. In 1901, when Henry van de Velde installed a long row of barber chairs in the glistening interior of Haby's — Berlin's fashionable hair-dresser,[24] one of the first shops to be decorated by an artist — these chairs had the tenuous *Art nouveau* curves; but rudimentary headrests aside, they remain perfectly rigid and immovable, in striking contrast to the lines sinuously playing throughout the shop itself. Even in 1940 in Europe, the static barber chair was almost universal. As in the eighteenth century, a barber has to peer beneath the chin of the customer he is shaving and only by a characteristic upward tilt of the elbow is he able to see what he is doing.

In America around mid-century — as the patent furniture movement gets under way — the barber chair begins to throw off its century-old stiffness. At this period, we have recalled, the barber was, at the same time, dentist and, often, surgeon. He performed simple operations such as extracting teeth and bloodletting, and for centuries the two professions were united in that of the 'barber-surgeon.'

Various as are the dentists', the barbers', and the surgeons' needs, they have one common requirement: to bring the patient's head or body into the position of greatest accessibility.

[23] U.S. Patent 397,077, 29 Jan. 1889. [24] Karl Ernst Osthaus, *Van de Velde*, Hagen i W., 1920, p.29.

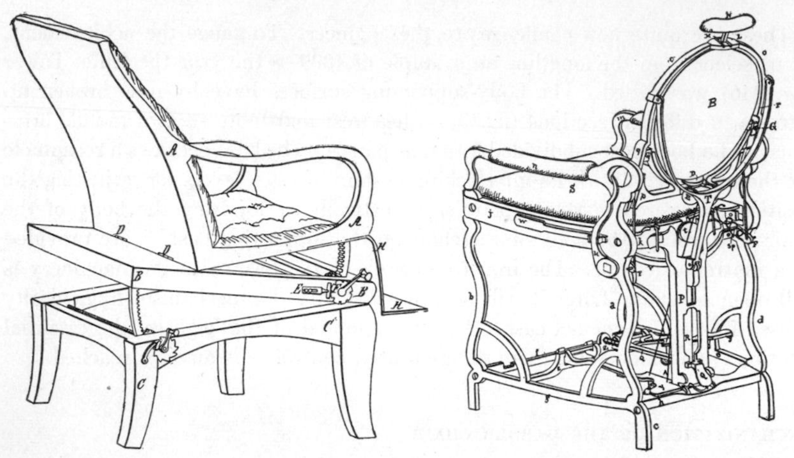

The American barber chair, like the American railway seat, differs fundamentally from its European counterpart. The one is rigid, the other mobile. The problem was to make the seat and back mobile and capable of being fixed in variable positions.

248. Dental and Surgical Chair, 1850. *This is one of the earlier and fumbling solutions for the barber chair. In three parts, it is elevated at front and back by rack and gear. 'By means of these two movements the seated person can be raised to any convenient height and placed at any angle of inclination desired.'* (*U. S. Patent* 7224, 26 *March* 1850)

249. Barber Chair, 1873. *Long and patient labor finally gave the chair mobility. The peak of the patent-furniture movement produced very complicated devices interconnecting the elements, and enabling the seat and back rest to be reversed in one motion.* (*U. S. Patent* 135,986, 19 *February* 1875)

The barber's problem is simple. The customer should either sit upright or lie almost horizontally. Hair-cutting cannot do with foreshortened perspective; there is but one correct position, the vertical, which requires a normal seat. For shaving, the customer is in the most favorable position when swung so far into the horizontal that both cheeks and the underside of the chin present almost vertical surfaces. Then the barber may work most efficiently. Moreover, the customer lies in a helpless position, which discourages unforeseen movements. This posture calls for surface on which to lie at full length. Readily to combine the two activities, shaving and hair-cutting, the chair should be movable and adjustable. This careful breakdown of the functions to be fulfilled by the barber's chair reflects the whole difference between the developments in America and in Europe.

Long and patient labor ultimately gives the chair differentiated movability and the power of locking in any desired position. In 1850 no better way of

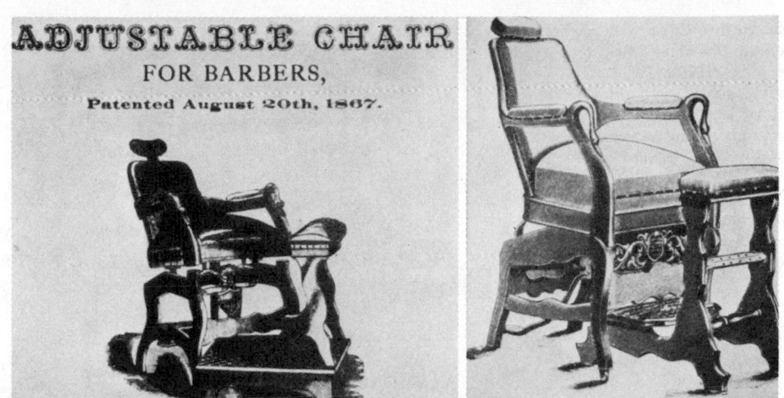

250. Adjustable Barber Chair, 1867. *Such simple, tilting barber chairs remained most common down to the late 1880's. The movable chair section can be set at either of two angles on the tilted planes of the base, the customer resting his feet on a footstool often as high as a praying desk.* (*Advertisement*)

251. Barber Chair, 1880. *The tilting-chair principle still prevails; separate foot rest.* (*Catalogue Theo. A. Kochs, Chicago*)

tilting was known than by dividing the chair into three elements, the chair, the base, and between them a middle plane.[25] (fig. 248). The body of the chair would tilt backwards by means of rack and gear, and forwards by raising the middle plane.

Soon tilting is more simply achieved: the chair comprises two parts, the chair proper and the base on which it pivots. The rear of the base offers an inclined plane; the inclination of the chair is fixed by the plane on which it rests. Cited to the advantage of this chair in 1867 is that it 'causes the person to sit up straight while having the hair dressed, or lean back while being shaved' [26] (fig. 250). For decades these 'tilting chairs,' for whose mobility devices of every sort were proposed, formed a category of their own in the American patent lists.

In the 'seventies there was no lack of complex devices that enabled the seat and the back rest to be reversed in one motion before the next customer took place in the chair. Throughout the patent-furniture movement the aim was greater adjustability and mobility, and the parts came to be ever more flexibly interconnected. As complicated as the barber chair becomes in the course of its development, the main problem always remains the same: easy transition

[25] U.S. Patent 7224, 26 Mar. 1850. 'Dental and Surgical Chair.'

[26] Advertisement, 20 Aug. 1867; U.S. Patent 83,644, 3 Nov. 1868; cf. U.S. Patent 224,604, 17 Feb. 1880 (fig. 251). This chair enjoyed wide favor and is still listed in the catalogues of the 'nineties.

252. Barber Chair with Vibrassage Machines, 1906. *By the early 1890's the barber chair, mounted on a column, was both reclining and revolving. Raising and lowering by means of fluid operated mechanisms within the column became standard in the United States around 1900.* (*Catalogue Theo. A. Kochs, Chicago,* 1906–7)

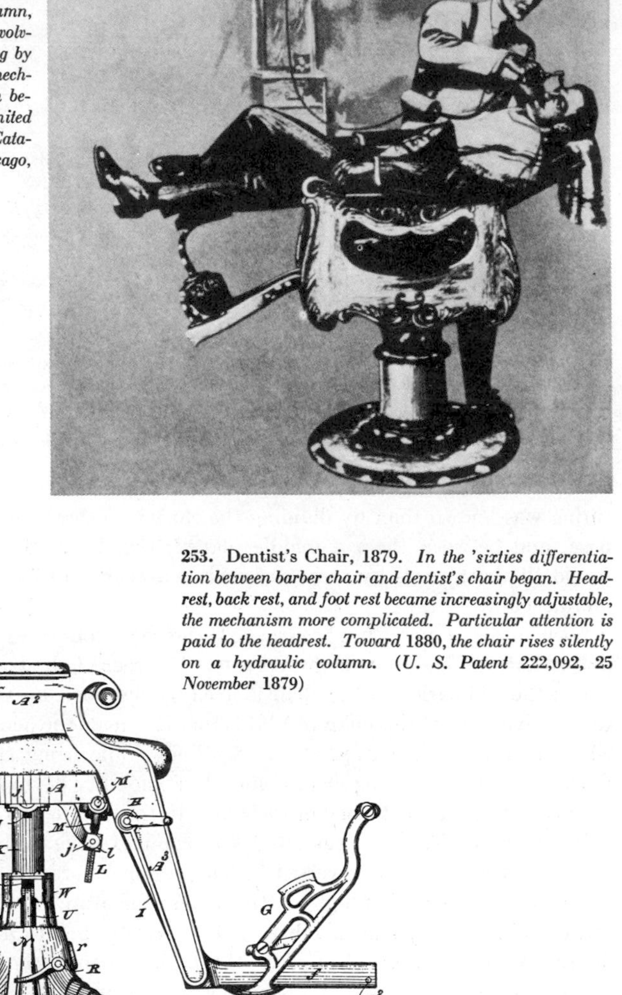

253. Dentist's Chair, 1879. *In the 'sixties differentiation between barber chair and dentist's chair began. Headrest, back rest, and foot rest became increasingly adjustable, the mechanism more complicated. Particular attention is paid to the headrest. Toward* 1880, *the chair rises silently on a hydraulic column.* (*U. S. Patent* 222,092, 25 *November* 1879)

254. Barber Chair, 1894. *Revolving and mounted on a column like the desk-chair.* (Catalogue Theo. A. Kochs, Chicago, 1894)

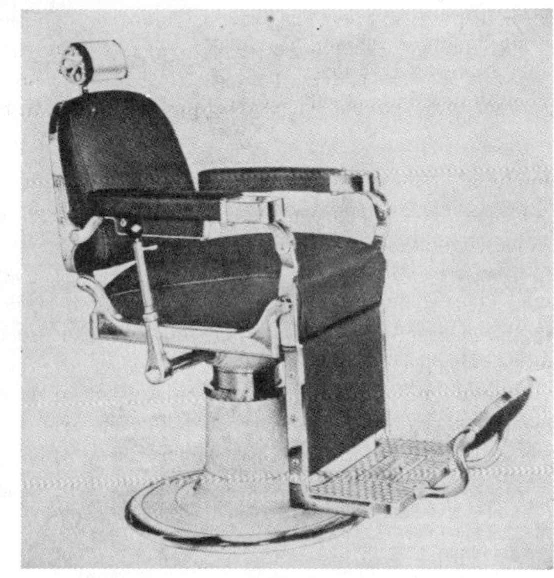

255. Barber Chair, 1939. *Around 1910 the barber chair reached its present-day form, with white enamel frame and armrests, and mounted on a broad smooth base.* (Catalogue Theo. A. Kochs, Chicago, 1939)

from the sitting position to the lying. By the early 'seventies there had reached the market simple models in which a common mechanism interconnects the foot, the body, and the head rests.[27] But these are rather the exception. The separation of the chair and the foot rest persists until late in the 'eighties. The chair is four-legged and its separate footstool sometimes attains the size of a praying-desk (fig. 251). Then comes the demand for a chair that will revolve.[28] And so it is mounted on a column similar to that of the office chair, radiating four short legs (fig. 254). By the early 'nineties, the barber's chair has become both reclining and revolving. Now raising and lowering are added, so that the chair may stand 'low enough for the short barber and high enough for the tall barber.' By 1900 [29] raising and lowering are carried out by fluid-operated mechanisms (fig. 252). Hydraulic drive, as we have seen, had already appeared during the 'sixties in the dentist's chair. Only the rising American living standard around the turn of the century made possible this expensive mechanism, which almost doubled the price of the barber chair.[30] By about 1900, then, the chair is capable of four movements: revolving and reclining; raising and lowering. Around 1910 it reaches the standard, present-day form: smooth, white-enameled frame and armrests, and a smooth base displace the writhing cast-iron ornamentation, now confined to the iron leg and foot rests (fig. 255). A light squeeze of the trigger will release the tilting mechanism and the chair automatically locks in position when the finger is removed. The moving parts — more than 200 in number — remain out of sight in the white enamel base so that the customer is lowered without noise or jolt into the horizontal, to await massage and hot towels: a moment of relaxation amid the rush.

MECHANIZATION OF THE RECLINING CHAIR

Barber's chairs, railroad seats, and operating tables are not part of our constant surroundings. They do not belong to the home. But they made excellent task-masters when it came to opening up the unknown sphere of movable furniture. The vigor of this patent furniture suited it, in simplified form, to enter the intimacy of the home. For a long time the Americans successfully accomplished this acclimatization.

It would be a mistake to focus our attention on mechanization alone. We must look beyond. These chairs express the true nineteenth-century posture, whose keynote is informality. Lounges and sofas, expressing such posture,

[27] Catalogue of the Theo. A. Kochs Company, Chicago, 1873. Cf. also fig. 279.

[28] U.S. Patent 335,594, 9 Feb. 1886 and 374,840, 13 Dec. 1887.

[29] U.S. Patent 598,877, 8 Feb. 1898.

[30] $85 in 1904.

appeared before the chair was turned into a mobile, organic system. So pressing is the demand for relaxed posture that furniture is built that unconsciously seeks the answer without drawing on mechanical means.

In America during the 'thirties and 'forties, there appeared on the market a couch known for its uncommon proportions as the 'Kangaroo.' It had the form of an ocean wave inviting the body to nestle in its curve. As men sometimes set their feet up on the mantle or the table-edge at this time, the end of this couch freely rose to the convenient height in a steep curve (fig. 322): 'The back is delightfully supported,' a contemporary exclaims, 'and when the feet rest upon the other end the ease and comfort of the position can hardly be described.' [31]

Tradition bars the way only when creative power runs weak. When creative power comes to life, objects that centuries of use have left unchanged — plows, hammers, saws, or furniture — take on a new aspect. Thus a slight variation on the classical faldstool, formed of two x elements, produces a reclining chair (1869) whose curves are admirably suited to the human body [32] (fig. 258). Unassisted by complex mechanisms, it is virtually a sleight-of-hand. Having grasped the spirit in which this patent furniture germinated, we may easily understand its separate products. An inventor who can thus transform a camp utensil into a comfortable reclining chair by a single motion must surely be accustomed to regard a chair as a system of planes: planes not rigidly fixed in relation to one another, but transmutable and able to serve several functions.

In traditional fashion, the chair folds around central pivots. Both back rest and seat are upholstered. The back rest does not end at the seat, but prolongs its upholstered plane below seat-level. At first sight this would seem rather aimless. But if one unhooks the seat and spreads the folding legs to their widest angle, the dead plane will come into play. The oversize back rest joins with the seat, folded over and out to form a new combination: a long-curved easy chair.

As for its mechanical equipment — a few hinges — this chair could well have been invented in the fifteenth century. But altogether different methods of thinking lie behind it: the notion of the chair as a utensil composed of planes transmutable according to purpose. Behind it lies the constructive urge of the 'sixties, succeeding here with genial simplicity.

The Americans tend to become dissatisfied in the late 'sixties with one or two positions as obtainable from this folding chair of 1869. They wished for everyday household use the multiple combinations that had become familiar in invalid chairs. But this involved more or less complicated apparatus.

---

[31] Quoted in Esther Singleton, *The Furniture of Our Forefathers*, London, 1901, vol. 2, p.649.

[32] Folding Chair, U.S. Patent 92,133, 29 June 1869.

Again we shall limit ourselves to a single example. Slowly, over a decade, from 1870 to 1878, the mechanized reclining chair takes shape. The phases are not hard to follow.[33] The Wilson chair — so named after its inventor — was among the earlier models to carry over the movability of the invalid chair into furniture for everyday use (fig. 256). It enjoyed wide popularity in its day; the sales of the Wilson Adjustable Chair Company, founded for the sole purpose of its manufacture, ran into tens of thousands.

At first sight such a chair seems overwhelmingly complicated, but by breaking its system of catches, pivots, and braces into basic components, we reach the simple postulates from which it was built. Following the universal practice of the time, this collapsible chair is dissected into simple planes articulated one to

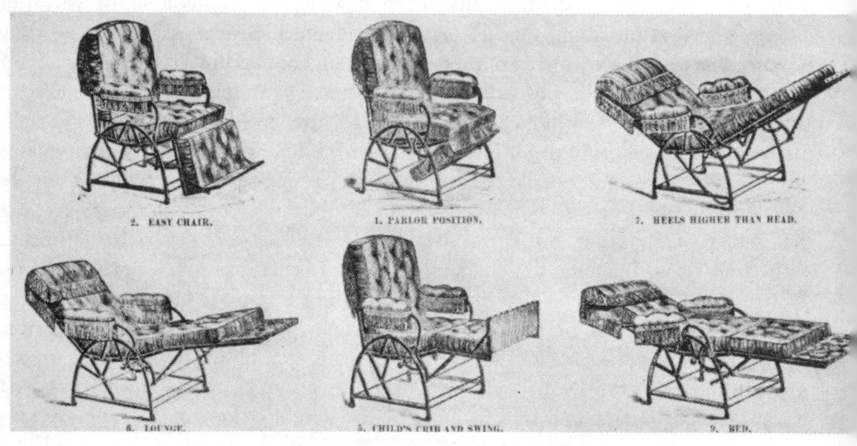

256 a. Adjustable Chair, 1876. *When the ruling taste was not master, the nineteenth century drew its mobile seating from the technics of the engineer. This late and simplified model (see figs.* **256** *b and c) illustrates the convertibility and movability that the reclining chair had acquired by the 'seventies. Motion problems, so difficult for designers of the twentieth century, were solved with natural mechanical facility.* (*Catalogue, Wilson Adjustable Chair Mfg. Co., New York*)

another. They may be adjusted either in combination or individually, and locked in almost any desired position. Thus various combinations are possible, ranging from an easy chair with lowered foot rest, through a reading chair with narrow desk, to a lounge with inclined back (yielding, if one wishes, a 'heels

[33] Three patents: U.S. Patent 107,581, 20 Sept. 1870, still very primitive; Patent 116,784, 4 July 1871 — mobility attained by a complicated construction; Patent 210,733, 9 May 1878 — simplifies the form and construction.

256 b. G. WILSON: Iron Folding Chair, 1871. *This working model, delicately constructed of bronze strips, was bought by the author at one of the public auctions of the U. S. Patent Office originals. These documents of the American spirit have been passed from hand to hand since their dispersal.* (*Photo by Soichi Sunami, Museum of Modern Art, of original patent model in the possession of the author*)

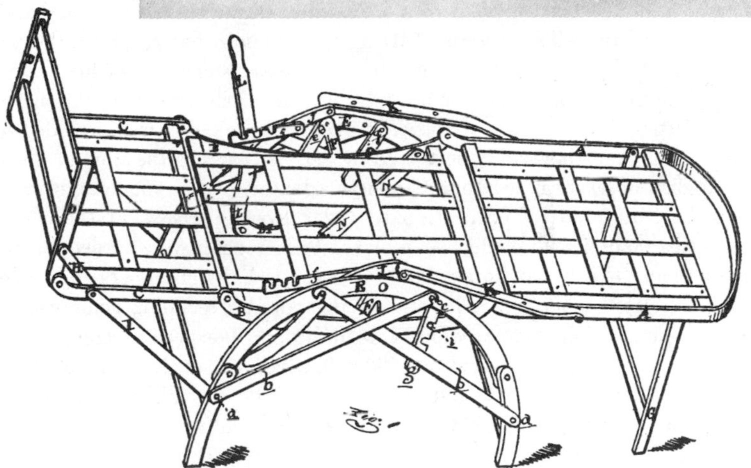

256 c. G. WILSON: Iron Folding Chair, 1871. *The legs have become a pair of iron arches, at the crest of which the seat is suspended like a balance. The occupant can control the mechanism without rising by means of a single lever* (*L*). *Back rest, seat, leg rest, and foot rest are divided into four articulated planes that can be adjusted to practically any position.* (*U. S. Patent* 116,784, 4 *July* 1871)

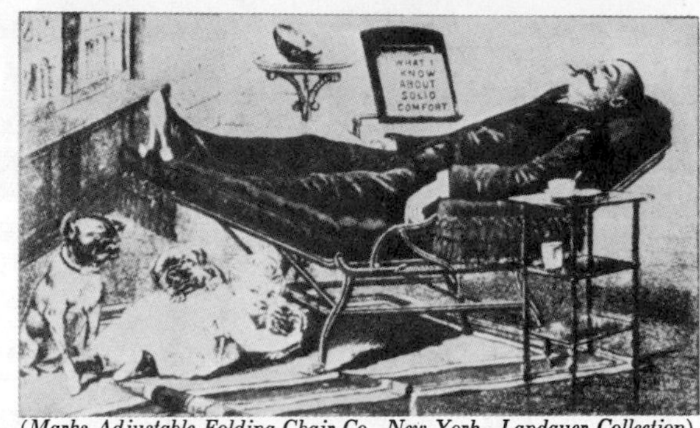

257. Adjustable Chair, Chicago, 1893. *'It is the best chair in the wide world. It combines in one a Parlor, Library, Smoking and Reclining Chair, a Lounge or a full size bed adjustable to any position. More than* 80,000 *now in use.' The mechanized reclining chair, although made in simple, inexpensive models, was soon discarded from the home. It could not satisfy the values that the Chicago World's Fair of* 1893 *enthroned for the new period.*

(*Marks Adjustable Folding Chair Co., New York. Landauer Collection*)

higher than head' posture), to a bed, and finally, when suspended, to a child's crib and swing: a very paradise for this period so enamored of combinations and informality (fig. 256, a, b, c).

Another continuous trend is represented in Wilson's chair; like the surfaces of the operating table and the barber's chair, its supporting planes are distinct from the base. The four legs of the regular chair have turned into two arches of a bridge. Between these arches of the base swing the seat, back, and foot panels, freely suspended on pivots. This makes for easy movability and convertibility of the whole system. Sitting in the chair, one regulates the position from a central point as a puppeteer moves the arms and legs of his puppets.

The 'seventies and 'eighties brought in variations and elaborations of this type. Often, as in the case of the Wilson chair, companies were founded to produce a single but thoroughly perfected model. As early as the start of the 'fifties, an English observer noted that Cincinnati factories were manufacturing chairs on a scale quite out of proportion to the European. Now, at the end of the 'seventies, complicated models such as the Wilson chair were turned out in mass production. This is something new, for invalid chairs and operating tables had a more restricted market. The aim of the popular reclining chair was typical of the time: to join ample comfort with simple, inexpensive construction. A late model, whose sales totaled over 80,000, according to the boast of the manufacturer, attains simplicity and cheapness at the sacrifice of movability and adjustability. The year is 1893, close to the movement's end, year of the Chicago World's Fair, which marks the turning point (fig. 257).

People began to look down upon this kind of furniture. It failed to voice the notions of wealth and splendor to which everyone now seemed born. At any rate it disappeared.

Convertibility

Metamorphosis in Mechanics

Just as in the myths of antiquity, a man is changed to a stone or to a tree, and nature is peopled with creatures half horse, half man; half fish, half man; half snake, half man; so that there is no telling where the animal ends and the human begins, likewise in the singular creations known as patent-furniture it is almost impossible to tell where one category ends and where the next begins. They dissolve into one another. Multiformity and metamorphosis are part and parcel of their being. An armchair that changes into a couch, a couch that changes into a cradle, can justly be termed combination furniture, as can a bed that turns into a sofa, into a chair, into a table, into a railway seat.

Everything is collapsible, folding, revolving, telescopic, recombinable. Where does this part end and that part begin? No sooner have we reached a clean-cut verdict than all is shuffled afresh, leading to no end. The reason lies in the nature of this furniture. Part merges with part as, in the mermaid, fish and woman. They fuse into a new entity.

When the medieval period used a piece for multiple purposes, there was reason enough in the scarcity of furniture and the primitiveness of the entire household. No mechanism was necessary to make chests into potential containers for every kind of object, serving as benches, as sleeping accommodation, or as steps rising to the high bedside. Only in the fifteenth century were chests provided with backs. The sixteenth century enlarged the back rest so that when swung up and over it served as a table top.

This type commemorates the old usage of moving away the table after meals. Colonists took this bench-table with them to Pennsylvania (fig. 259).[34] Peasant use simplified the richly ornamented Renaissance type into one so practical that it lived on well into the nineteenth century.

Chairs combined with writing facilities date even further back. The medieval practice of resting a small desk on one's knee, as Pythagoras is seen to do in the twelfth-century reliefs of Chartres Cathedral (fig. 138), develops during the fifteenth century into the combination of seat with adjustable writing board. Later on, this leads to the broadening of one arm of the Windsor chair so as to afford a writing surface, as in Thomas Jefferson's revolving chair of around 1776 (fig. 161), and as in the chairs of almost any American lecture hall today.

For its convertible furniture the nineteenth century drew upon the same saturation with the mechanical that created adjustable furniture for sitting

[34] Kindly communicated to us by Dr. F. Reichman, Librarian of the Carl Schurz Foundation, Philadelphia.

and lying. Convertible furniture and adjustable furniture developed simultaneously: initial attempts before 1850, strongest impulses in the 'sixties, 'seventies, and 'eighties.

In Europe this convertible furniture never found itself altogether at home. The early nineteenth century, in continuation of an eighteenth century trend, paid it some attention, both in France and in England. As one writer observes:

> The [Paris] expositions of 1834, 1844 and even of 1849 . . . stood out . . . by their quantity of divan-beds, invalid's chairs, etc. . . . By patient study the inventors have indeed produced endless manners of containing a bed ready made up . . . whether in the chest or in the swing-down backrest, or lastly by mechanical means of ascent and descent; and in addition, toilet utensils and clothes-drawers. It is nonetheless certain that for comfortable sleep a divan-bed is still not what one needs. . . . If of a bedroom you wish to make a drawing room, or of a drawing room you wish to make a bedroom, take a divan bed that has won prizes at every exhibition, supplement it with a bed-table-washstand, a wardrobe-desk, or easy chair-lounge . . . and you will easily become the protector of the inventors who are on such interesting terms with the fair commissions.[35]

These words were written in retrospect from the late 'seventies by the author of a *Dictionary of the Upholsterer*, which aimed mainly at being a guide to the most decorative arrangements of drapery. The author voices the ruling taste of the period, hostile in basic outlook to the new types of furniture. English opinion of patent furniture was not very different.[36]

In America, it was quite otherwise. Furniture could not be allowed to take up room; there was a shortage of space in the dwellings of an expanding economy. America around 1850, in contrast to Europe, had but a thin stratum of well-to-do who might set the fashion for the masses. Besides, a piece that combined two or more functions called for smaller outlay. All this encouraged the old American predilection for coupling the most dissimilar objects, such as the bowie knife-pistol of 1837.[37] 'The nature of my invention,' runs the patent specification, 'consists in combining the pistol and Bowie knife, in such manner that it can be used with as much ease and facility as either the pistol or knife could be if separate.'

The Americans had humor enough to make fun of the itch for combination and its lapses into the grotesque. A 'comicality' of *Harper's Weekly* (1857)[38] imagines a traveling-case packed with pistols, dagger, hatchet, shoe-horn, loaf of bread, plates, and live baby (fig. 266).

[35] Jules Deville, *Dictionnaire du tapissier. Critique et historique de l'ameublement français depuis les temps anciens jusqu'à nos jours*, Paris, 1878–80, text-vol., p.47.

[36] John C. Loudon, *An Encyclopedia of Cottage-Farm and Villa Architecture and Furniture*, new ed., London, 1836, in the chapter 'Furniture for Cottage Dwelling' mentions folding beds, but only for the sake of completeness, with the reservation that such furniture was not needed in the English household.

[37] U.S. Patent 254, 5 July 1837.

[38] P.544.

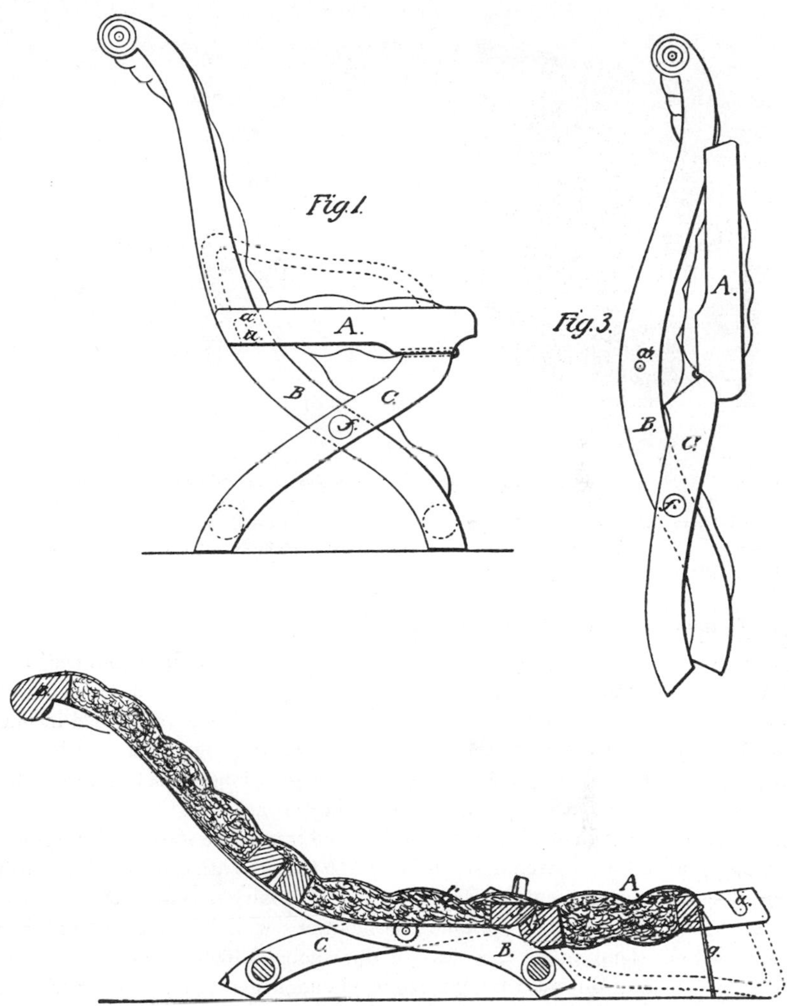

258. Folding Chair, 1869. *A slight variation on the classical X-shaped faldstool gives a reclining chair whose curves admirably fit the human body. Convertibility through the transmutation of plane surfaces is achieved here without complex mechanisms. The inventor describes it thus: 'Somewhat similar to the ordinary campstool. The legs BB, extending with a slight forward inclination above the seat, serve to form the back of the chair. The space between said combined leg and backpieces is cushioned along its entire length. The seat A, cushioned on its underside also, is hinged, at its front edge, to the upper ends of the legs C. The chair may be folded into a compact form for transportation or storage.'* (*U.S. Patent* 92,133, 29 *June* 1869)

259. Bench-Table, Pennsylvania Dutch 'Dischbank.' *The conversion of the chest or bench to a table is connected with late Gothic and Renaissance habits, transplanted to America. 'A bench seat with side arms on which sits a table top fastened by four pins. When the forward pins are removed, the top can be raised and converted into a back for the bench.'* (*Photo and description courtesy the Curator, Landis Valley Museum, Lancaster County, Pennsylvania*)

The Transmutability of Plane Surfaces

The sometimes grotesque effect of things promiscuously combined is a by-product. Worthy of interest is the aggressive plowing into inherited objects and the changing of them down to their very roots. This is performed in multiple-function furniture with the same thoroughgoing vigor that mechanized the doorlock and tools as simple as the hammer and plane, recasting forms that had stiffly preserved their identity through the centuries.

Our folding armchair of 1869, which one motion transforms into a reclining chair (fig. 258), called for no mechanism unknown to the fifteenth century. The furniture of the nineteenth century (table, sofa, bed, chair) is composed of various mobile planes entering into variable combinations with one another and even changing their significance. The seat of this chair of 1869 becomes a foot rest simply by folding downwards; the same phenomenon can be observed in a swivel chair of 1875, where the back rest changes into a horizontal plane (fig. 261), or again in an armchair of 1874 (fig. 262), where the seat becomes the head-rest of a sofa. This process we call the transmutability of plane surfaces. In certain medieval types we can speak of the transmutability of planes. The late Gothic settle, which became the *Dischbank* of the Pennsylvania colonists

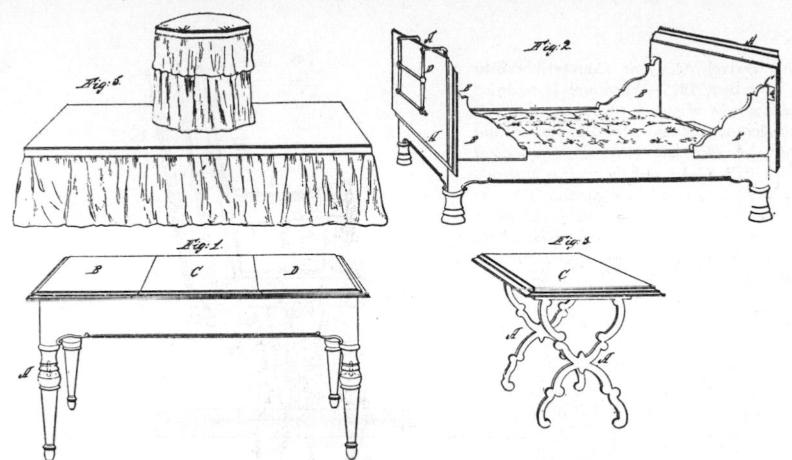

260. Table-Bedstead, 1849. *Table converted into a bed by folding up two leaves and unscrewing the high legs in the middle (fig. 1). The third leaf forms another table (fig. 3). 'I have invented the 'Table-Bedstead' or Grand Ottoman with its small ottoman, so as to include a dining table and other different useful articles. The side of the small ottoman [pouf] will slide up to get to the toilet utensils.' (U.S. Patent* 6884, *20 November* 1849)

(fig. 259), had a movable back rest that became a table top when swung 90° into the horizontal. But this treatment of planes never before formed the constituent starting point it became in the nineteenth century, nor was it played upon with such freedom of fancy, which often incorporated quite complex mechanisms.

Again, we choose to illustrate the coming about of this law by a few examples that might equally well have been constructed in the medieval period.

The Shakers, with their highly skilled handicraft, produced various types of combination furniture in the first half of the nineteenth century. Toward the middle of the period, some examples of patent furniture clearly foreshadow the future development; such was a table-bed of 1849 (fig. 260).[38]

A table is to be converted into a bed. The starting point is a dining table. With its three leaves, it looks like an extension table. Only in this case — another token of the independent tackling of problems — the leaves fold up into the vertical, being secured by hinged corner flaps. When the middle leaf is removed, folding legs drop down beneath it, and an occasional table is formed. 'The four legs of the dining table are made movable in the middle and are fastened by means of a dowel.' What follows is easy to guess; the high legs of

[38] U.S. Patent 6884, 20 Nov. 1849. Combined table and bedstead. The combination of table, bed, and chairs was subsequently solved by complicated mechanisms, e.g. combined wardrobes, bedsteads, chairs and tables, U.S. Patent 142,387, 2 Sept. 1873. A particular favorite was the combination of bed and desk, e.g. U.S. Patent 241,173, 10 May 1881.

261. Swivel Armchair Convertible into a Day Bed, 1875. *Furniture is regarded as composed of mobile planes entering into various combinations with one another, and changing their significance. The patent states: 'The back rest of the chair is hinged to the seat. To convert the chair into a lounge one has only to fold down the back rest; a folding-leg concealed in the backside of the frame serves as support.' (U.S. Patent* 169,752, 9 *November* 1875)

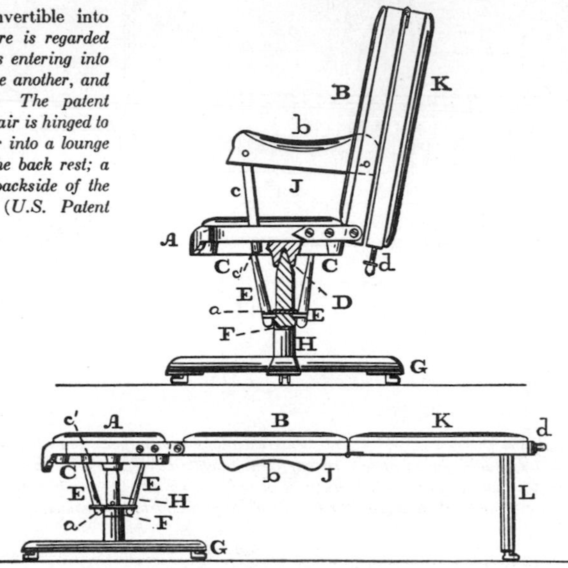

the table are unscrewed in the middle and the bedstead rests on the floor. The table frame has become a bed frame, and the end leaves, folded upright, have become the bed ends. The separate stool is quickly converted into a washstand with all necessary 'chamber utensils.'

The following period steadily broadens this tendency to form variable combinations by variable arrangements of the planes. A proposal of 1875 offers at first glance a swivel armchair.[39] On closer examination, we notice that 'the back rest of the chair is hinged to the seat . . . and the armrests are jointed to the back.' The back is upholstered on both sides. In reality it consists of two frames that are themselves connected by hinges. To convert the chair into a couch, one has only to release a catch 'which holds the frame (*K*) to the back (*B*), so that said frame may be unfolded.' Within the frame is concealed a folding leg that carries the horizontal back rest. The arms disappear into the frame and the swivel chair has become a day-bed (fig. 261).

An armchair of 1874 [40] (fig. 262) shows this same supple imagination always ready to change the significance of the planes in unconventional ways. In type, this armchair of metal strips belongs to the family of folding chairs as used

[39] U.S. Patent 169,752, 9 Nov. 1875. Improvement in convertible chairs.

[40] U.S. Patent 157,042, 17 Nov. 1874. Combined chair and lounge.

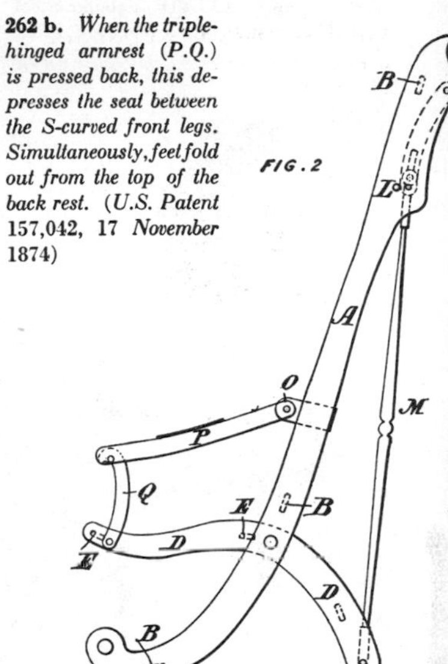

262 b. *When the triple-hinged armrest (P.Q.) is pressed back, this depresses the seat between the S-curved front legs. Simultaneously, feet fold out from the top of the back rest.* (*U.S. Patent* 157,042, 17 *November* 1874)

262 a. Easy Chair Convertible into Lounge. *A further example of planes changing their significance in an unconventional way.* (*U.S. Patent* 157,042, 17 *November* 1874)

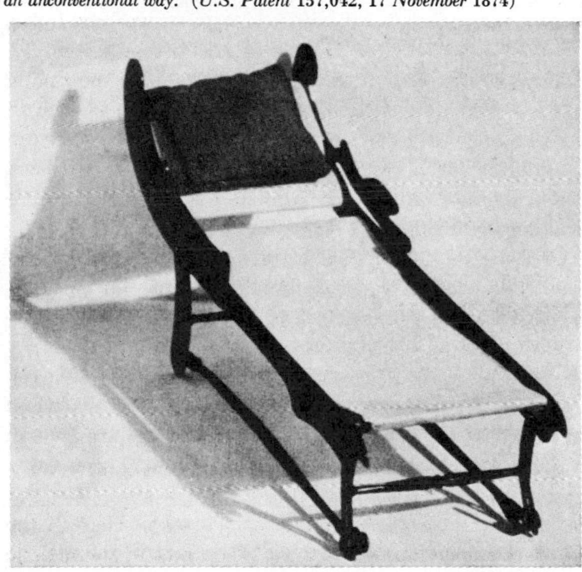

262 c. *To become a lounge, the chair is dropped backwards 90°. What was formerly the seat becomes a headrest, while the high back rest becomes a mattress. 'When changed to a chair, the parts before forming the head become the seat.'* (*Photo by Soichi Sunami, Museum of Modern Art, of the original model in possession of the author*)

263. ALVAR AALTO: Tubular Steel Sofa Convertible into a Bedstead, 1932.

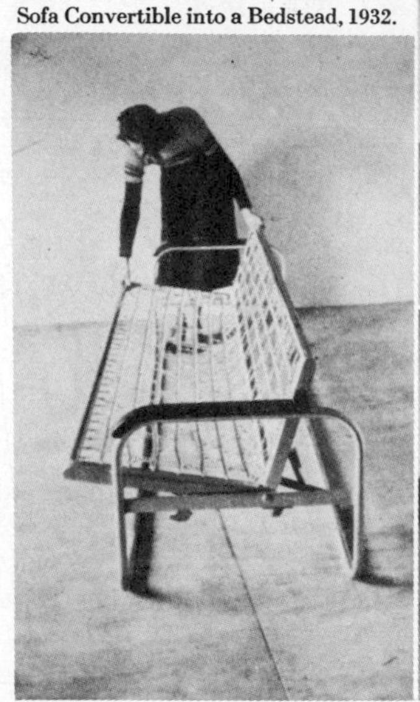

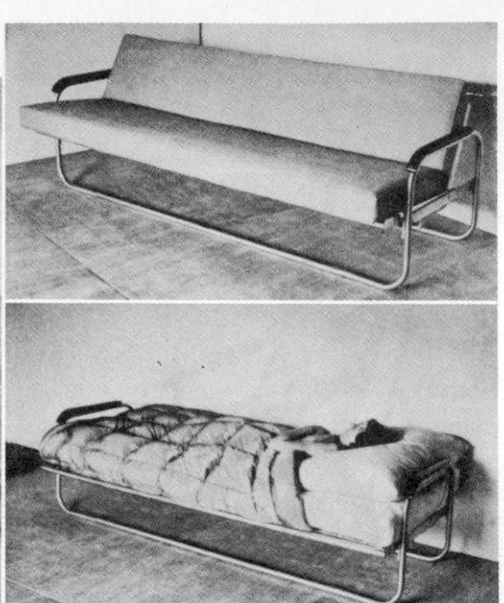

One of the few pieces of our time to tackle problems of movability. Left: *The inclinations of both back rest and seat are adjustable to various angles.* Upper right: *Normal position.* Lower right: *When fully lowered, back rest merges with the seat to form a bed.* (*Wohnbedarf, Zürich*)

since Antiquity. All its parts are in flexible interconnection. Like the timing gear of a steam engine, the motion of one member sets the whole system in motion. Press back the triple-hinged armrests and the seat sinks down between the *S*-curved front legs; simultaneously, two feet appear at the top of the back rest, where rods have carried the movement. The armchair is now a sofa standing on end. It is finally righted by dropping it 90°.

What has happened? Pressure on the armrests, the simultaneous sinking of the seat, and dropping the whole piece have made the former seat into a headrest while the high back has taken on the function of a mattress. The conversion was achieved by a transmuting of the planes.

In the folding chairs of Antiquity, the legs cross at a point halfway between the seat and the floor. Here the crossing point is at seat level; the scroll-shaped front legs extend into an unexpectedly high back and the rear legs are bent in boomerang shape. Their short arms rest on the floor, while the long arms carry into the horizontal seat.

Unwonted proportions have been adopted for efficiency's sake. Here in the field of mechanized furniture we encounter something often met in the artistic

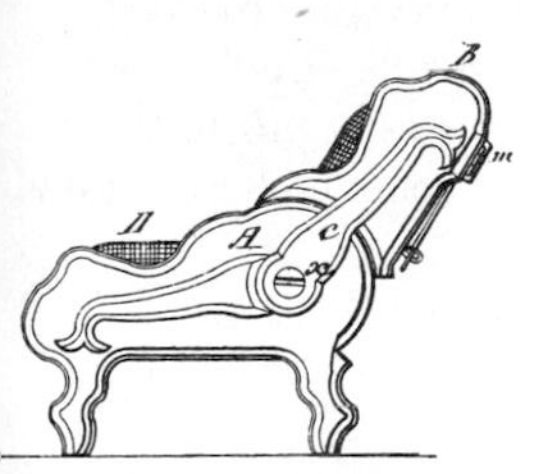

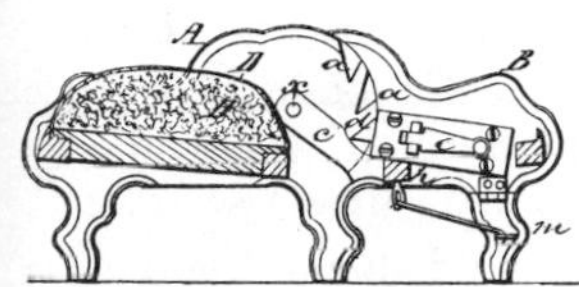

264 d. Sofa Bedstead, 1868. (*Photo by Soichi Sunami, Museum of Modern Art, of the original model in the possession of the author*)

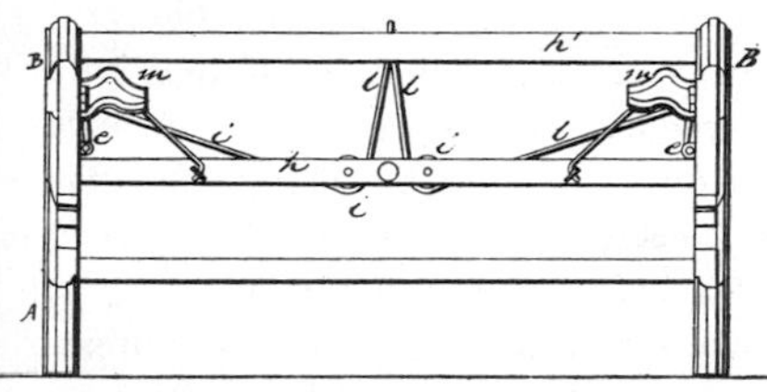

264 a, b, c. Sofa Bedstead, 1868. '*When it is desired to change the inclination of the back of the sopha, or to form a bedstead, all that is necessary is to pull the cords* l l (*fig.* 264 c), *thus withdrawing the bolts* d *from notches* a *in which they may be fitting. To the rear of the end frames* B *of the back are hinged legs* m m *for the support of the back when turned so as to form a bedstead. These legs, when not in use, are folded against the rear of the back.*' (*U.S. Patent* 77,872, 12 *May* 1868)

domain: disturbance of normal proportions. The Gothic, the sixteenth-century Mannerists, and the painters around 1910 used distortion to achieve new modes of expression.

To make a sofa convertible into a bed, in fact, a twin bed (1872), one proceeded more or less as follows [41] (fig. 265).

In a sofa that is convertible into a twin bed, one mattress will conceivably lie on top of the other. Less obvious is the scheme used here, where the elements of the future mattress lie back to back — a principle already seen in the swivel

[41] U.S. Patent, 127,741, 11 June 1872. Bed-Lounge.

chair of 1875. This time the two sections are joined along their length by sliding hinges. The twin bed is produced in one movement for, quite unexpectedly, the lower mattress begins to revolve on two pivots at the middle of either end. One has merely to pull the seat outwards and the lower mattress begins to turn. The upper section moves with it until both come to rest in a common horizontal plane.

American solutions of the 'sixties and 'seventies approach certain problems along lines parallel to those of today. Form and materials differ, but the methods are often the same.

In 1932 Alvar Aalto brought out a tubular steel sofa, which soon became known in Europe as the 'Aalto sofa' (fig. 263). It represents one of the few contemporary pieces to have tackled problems of movability: this time it is a matter of adjusting the back rest of the sofa to the occupant's comfort. When fully lowered, it joins with the seat to form a bed. Aalto's piece was good so far as form went, but its governing mechanism was rather rudimentary. Attempting to smooth out this difficulty in a Swiss factory, we could think of nothing better than a device borrowed from the adjustable back rest of hospital beds.

How is this same problem of motion met by an American 'adjustable sofa' of 1868 [42] (fig. 264)? So that the back rest may be adjustable at will and fully lowerable, the lower frame has curved rear ends; the upper frame can slide through this curve to the horizontal. An arm on either side connects the movable frame with the fixed one. To sustain the back at various angles, the curved segments are ingeniously notched to admit a bolt held in position by springs. Both bolts are released by the simple device of a cord passing through the upper frame. This simple construction yields a solution that is not without elegance, contrasting with the furniture of our own time in its evident familiarity with problems of motion.

Combinations and Mimicry

Beds that swing vertically or horizontally away, beds folding upward or upon themselves — the most variegated methods have been tried for saving daytime space in dwellings. We are thus led into the domain of convertible beds that may assume the shape of other furniture by day or may disappear into the wall and even into the ceiling. In the earlier stages the process involved no more than folding the bed to the wall and sometimes sheathing it in a case. These

---

[42] U.S. Patent 77,872, 12 May 1868.

265 a. Bed Lounge, 1872. (*Photo by Soichi Sunami, Museum of Modern Art, of the original model in the possession of the author. U.S. Patent* 127,741, 11 *June* 1872)

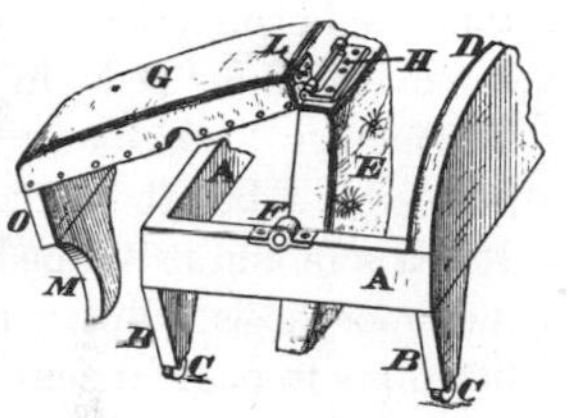

265 b. Bed Lounge, 1872. Detail of Patent Drawing.

practices go back in part to the seventeenth and eighteenth centuries.[43] Improvements in the technical sense came about during the 1830's. Simple devices 'protect the bedclothes, bolster and pillows from falling out when turned up.' [44] The patent-furniture era spent much care on the construction of these wardrobe beds, which replaced a separate bedroom in many American dwellings. In the

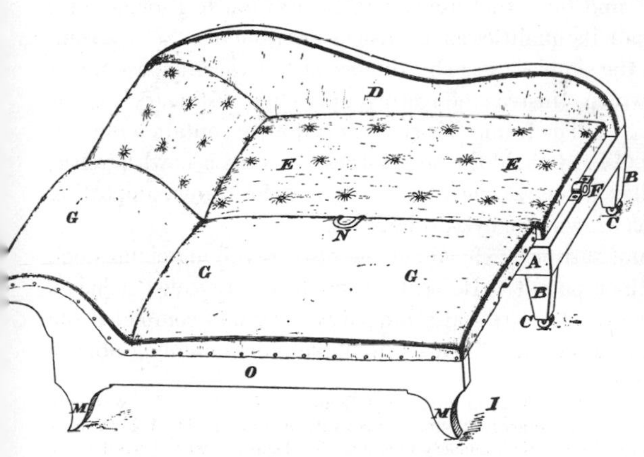

265 c. Bed Lounge, 1872. '*In the normal or closed condition the two mattresses are folded back to back. To open, the operator grasps the loop* N, *and by pulling the same, causes the outer mattress to fold outward and the lower mattress to half revolve on its pivots, and the rigid legs* M *find their place upon the floor. The outer mattress is brought into exact coincidence by the sliding hinge* II.' (*U.S. Patent* 127,741)

[43] See Havard, *Dictionnaire de l'ameublement et de la décoration depuis le XIIIe siècle jusqu'à nos jours*, Paris, 1890–94, vol. I, cols. 241–2. Wallace Nutting, writing in October 1940 on 'Double-Purpose Furniture,' in *Antiques* (vol. XXXVIII, p.160) mentions the fact that 'in 1770 Oliver Goldsmith wrote of a piece of furniture that was a bed at night and a chest of drawers by day.'

[44] U.S. Patent 668, Wardrobe Bedstead, 2 Apr. 1838. Cf. also U.S. Patent 23,604, Improved Wardrobe-Bed (fig. 267), 12 Apr. 1859.

'eighties they found their standard form, and toward the end of the period they were made as real display pieces, such as the bed of 1891 (fig. 269), which, when folded, became a mirrored wardrobe of 'richly figured mahogany.' These beds were also called 'parlor bedsteads,' for they were to stand in a parlor, not in a bedchamber. In later years they became quite rare in private houses, although frequently used in hotel rooms, until even there they slowly disappeared. These beds folding on one end were not revived until many years later, when the Pullman Company, in 1937, brought out its roomette cars (fig. 270).

Few pieces so preoccupied the inventors between 1850 and 1890 as the bed that would convert into some other object. Furniture was used dummy fashion, as envelopes for beds, in numerous ways. It is a widely ramified but none too satisfactory field, for in most cases it means not metamorphosis so much as mimicry. A bed that becomes a sofa for day use justly serves its double purpose: It is a sofa and it is a bed. It changes not merely its appearance but its nature: metamorphosis. But a bed that assumes, for instance, the guise of a piano, attempts to pass for something that it is not. This is mimicry.[45] Here the ruling taste and the constituent furniture of the nineteenth century met, leading to a cleavage that sometimes bordered on the ludicrous. Here historians who like the grotesque will find abundance of rich material.

At the outstart, problems of convertibility were tackled in full earnest. New, almost incredible, combinations were contrived. Thus one inventor (1866) constructed a piano combined with an almost complete bedroom set (fig. 268), and he stated: 'It has been found by actual use that this addition to a piano-forte does not in the least impair its qualities as a musical instrument.'[46] This combination was achieved in the simplest way, by the use of the vacant space under the body of the piano, which, 'instead of resting upon the customary legs, is supported by a frame, B. . . . The frame B is so arranged as to contain a bureau, E, and two closets, F and G . . . to hold the bed-clothes . . . a wash-bowl, pitcher, towels, &c.' The bed filled a sort of gigantic drawer in the frame supporting the combination, and was drawn out by two handles.

Still the inventor was not satisfied. He added thereto a revolving piano stool, 'also reserved for a distinct patent.' Its seat, when lifted, revealed a lady's workbox and a toilet mirror. Drawers and a hinged writing flap completed the roster of diverse equipment which it offered. The naïveté of combining objects

[45] U.S. Patent 97,101, Combined Bed and Musical-Instrument Board, 23 Nov. 1869. There is quite an early drift toward this dubious field of dummy furniture. Yet constituent problems still hold the foreground. Occasionally, in the wane of the period, mimicry falls into the absurd, as with the bed whose daytime envelope is a chimney: U.S. Patent 334,504, Combined Bedstead and Fire-place, 19 Jan. 1886.

[46] U.S. Patent 56,413, Improved Combined Piano, Couch, and Bureau, 17 July 1866.

266. Patent Traveling Case, Caricature, 1857. *The Americans of the patent-furniture era ridiculed their fondness of combinability, just as those of the* 1940's *made fun of the many gadgets in the kitchen* (*fig.* 408). (*Harper's Weekly*, 1857)

that hardly gain by acquaintance is obvious. The inventor apparently sensed this as he commented on the limited usefulness of his piece: 'The convertible piano has been designed principally for the benefit of hotels, boarding-schools, &c., containing apartments which are used for parlors, &c. in day-time and yet required for sleeping-rooms at night.' This procedure reminds us of the hat from which the conjuror extracts objects in unexpected number.

What interests us here is not the object — one of hundreds — but the method behind it. The economy of space that appeared naïvely in the piano-bed forms part of a tradition that, although momentarily crushed by the ruling taste, has never been wholly forsaken in the United States. It reappeared in due time in the equipment of the trailer or of the roomette.

The roomette is an enclosed Pullman compartment with broad upholstered seats on either side. 'To lower the bed you simply turn the handle located above the seatback, pulling it down, and holding it in that position. The bed will then lower on balanced springs, until it rests. . . .' [47] In the morning, when the traveler wishes to wash and dress, he releases a catch and the bed folds back. Now he

[47] Leaflet of the Pullman Company.

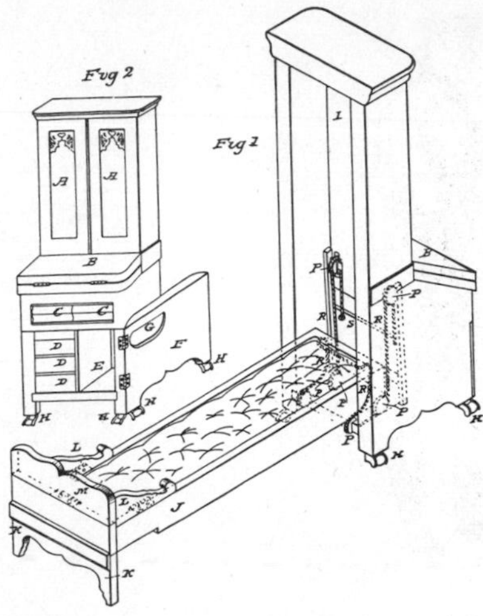

267. Mimicry and Convertibility: Wardrobe Bed, 1859. *One of many variations, it possesses 'the combined advantage of a secretary, wardrobe, and toilet accommodations.'* (*U. S. Patent* 23604, 12 *April* 1859)

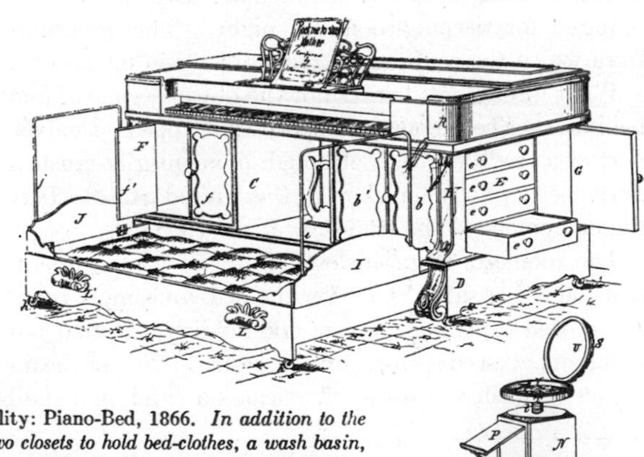

268. Mimicry and Convertibility: Piano-Bed, 1866. *In addition to the bed, it contains a bureau and two closets to hold bed-clothes, a wash basin, pitcher, towel, etc. Space economy, naively manifested in the piano-bed, is an American tradition, which, although temporarily stifled by the ruling taste, was never altogether forsaken. The trend reappears in the trailer and even more strongly in the Pullman roomette,* 1937. (*U. S. Patent* 56,413, 17 *July* 1866)

269. Parlor Bed, 1891. *Wardrobe beds, already known to the seventeenth and eighteenth centuries, were made to substitute for a separate bedroom in many American dwellings of the patent-furniture era. They eventually succumbed to the ruling taste and became almost extinct, until revived in the roomette.* (Decorator and Furnisher. *New York*, 1891)

270. Sleeping Car: Pullman Roomette, 1937. *The roomette is not actually a room. It is combination furniture inside which the passenger can move. The bed, lowering on balanced springs, absorbs almost the entire floor space. Walls and upholstery will reveal closets, wash basin, and toilet facilities. One of the few convertible pieces in which the tradition of the* 1850's *has lived on.* (*Courtesy the Pullman Company*)

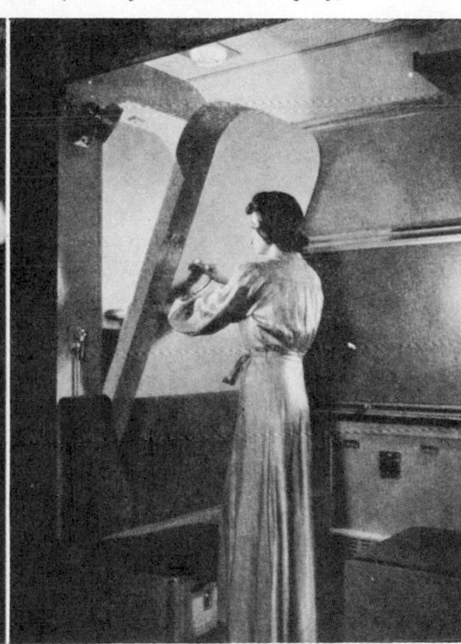

has room enough to open the washstand, the clothes closet, and the toilet closet in the opposite wall. 'By raising the cushion top of the seat, toilet facilities are afforded.' The roomette is not an actual room. It is combination furniture inside which a traveler can move. When unfolded, the bed absorbs the seat areas and the entire floor space.

This bed, which when folded away becomes part wall and part upholstered back rest, follows from the same principle as the wardrobe bedstead of 1859 (fig. 267). Operating in both cases is the law of the transmutability of plane surfaces.

The roomette is one of the few convertible pieces in which the tradition of the 'fifties has survived to the present day. The reason lies in its belonging to an institution that from its earliest phase has developed without break — the sleeping car.

Railroads and Patent Furniture

The French report on the Centennial Exposition of 1876 at Philadelphia is a thorough guide to the tools, machines, furniture, and other implements there displayed.[48] The reporter, looking for an adequate term to explain their peculiarity to the French public, could find no other expression than 'Pullman car style.' He was alluding to simple outlines and plane surfaces, free of ornamental overgrowth. These are the characteristics that naturally emerge in the course of mechanized production. To the European of 1870 or 1880, who used mechanization to simulate handwork, plain furniture must have appeared as something out of ken, as something not yet named, that most suitably was to be labeled after the most popular product of the American development: the Pullman car.

Instinctively the right word was chosen. The sleeping car associated with Pullman's name is almost the sole survivor of the immense group of patent furniture. The sleeping car alone has continued to develop without break to this day. All the other categories — excepting purely technical furniture — suffered a setback around 1893 from which they never recovered.

To the contemporary of 1855 all these ventures in building barbers', dentists', and invalids' chairs that would be comfortable, suited to function and to physiological demands, ranked on a par with the patent reclining railroad chairs. Even the now forgotten models of convertible sofas and folding beds were regarded as important as the earliest, trail-breaking patents for the upper berth.

If we probe the now commonplace notion of the 'sleeping car' and ask: Of what elements does it really consist? we find two widespread types of furniture — the convertible seat for the lower berth and the folding bed for the upper. And if we put the same question for the ordinary American coach, it too proves to be based on a particular type of patent furniture that was elaborately developed, the reclining chair. Sleeping car and coach, parlor car and dining car, are typical products of the American movement. They sprang from patent furniture, from the aspiration to create a new type of comfort.

Even today a wide gap separates the American conceptions of the traveler's comfort from the European.

The Traveler's Comfort

The extraordinary comfort that has slowly developed in American travel undoubtedly had something to do with the great distances. Overproduction — private lines competing against one another — also was a contributing factor. But the basic reasons must be sought in another sphere; they are to be found in

[48] Quoted in Giedion, *Space, Time and Architecture*, p.263.

sociological ground. The explanation lies in the divergent political attitudes that prevailed in Europe and in America in the 'thirties, when railroads came into being.

Distance was not the decisive factor. As early as 1836, six years after the opening of the first American passenger and freight line, a thirteen-mile stretch between Baltimore and Ellicott, a rudimentary sleeping car was rigged up for a night journey of a few hours on the Cumberland Valley Railroad, today a section of the Pennsylvania. A passenger coach was divided into compartments, each containing three simple bunks, one above the other.[49] It was not, as one might think, competition that decisively stimulated this development. Rather, it was the attitude toward comfort that so sharply differentiated the American from the European trends.

The way each country met the question of comfort and of segregation into classes around 1830 mirrors the attitude of the ruling groups to the people as a whole. Over France and Germany at this period, the Restoration reigned, giving absolute privilege to its ruling classes. The railroad cars were built on the principle that the masses deserved little consideration. More than 80 per cent of those who traveled sat huddled together on rough wooden seats, and countries with four classes also used cattle cars for passengers. Only the upper strata of society could afford any degree of comfort.

In these things, the birthmarks often linger on long after their original causes have vanished. On the Continent to this day the 'wooden' class has survived. True, the space allotted to the individual has tripled since the 'forties, the wooden benches have been somewhat fitted to the shape of the body — but they remain stiff and immovable, as at the outset.

America had one travel class only (except for Negroes and later for immigrants). European observers between 1830 and 1860 are constantly surprised that the United States had not two, three, or four passenger classes, but only one. Although it had certainly no superfluous window space and was simple and even primitive, the American coach of the 'forties revealed a regard for human dignity and, in the upholstered benches, a rudimentary attempt at comfort (fig. 271). For all its simplicity it reflected the democratic ways of the time, for everyone knew: 'No other shall have any better than I.' And this democratic conception lived on into the mid 'sixties, until Pullman became one of the first to arouse an inclination for luxury in the American public. The notion endures, even today, that every person who travels is entitled to a minimum of comfort. This standard — a coach class with fully adjustable seats — no other country has rivaled.

---

[49] *Pullman News*, Chicago, October 1940, p.43.

271. Men's Compartment of an American Railroad Coach, 1847. *The upholstered seats are separated from one another by rails over which the back rest, a simple iron bar, can be swung backward and forward. Open gangway to the next coach. The windows are scanty, or as Charles Dickens dryly commented, there is 'a great deal of wall.'* (L'Illustration, *Paris*, 1848)

As the cause that had greater weight than all the others in developing comfort in American travel, we may point to the fact that the energetic construction of American railroads in the second half of the 'fifties coincided in time with the efflorescence of patent furniture. It was a fortunate era, eager with the spirit of pioneering and enterprise, when men did not fear to take chances or to answer with their own person.

The Coach and the Adjustable Seat

The American coach of the 'forties was simple; yet it started with a dignified conception of man and in the quest for comfort. Technically described, seat and back rest became independent of one another. True, the back consisted of no more than a bar, a prop for one's spine, but a mobile bar that the passenger could swing over so that he might always sit facing the direction of travel. In pattern this swing bar was nothing new. Placed before the hearth, the Gothic

272. Reclining and Self-Adjusting Car Seat, 1855. *The swing back becomes a starting point for comfort. The convex side of the curved back rest bolsters the spine for day travel; the concave side supports the head and shoulders at night.* (*Courtesy Bella C. Landauer Collection, New-York Historical Society*)

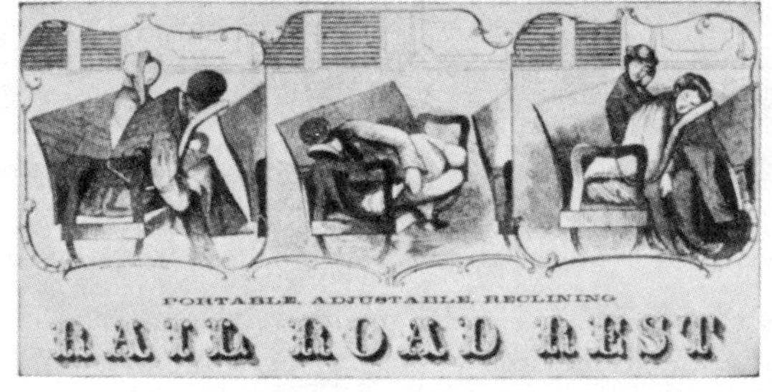

273. Portable, Adjustable, Reclining 'Railroad Rest,' 1857. *The passenger fixed the 'railroad rest' to his seat at a convenient angle.* (*Courtesy Bella C. Landauer Collection, New-York Historical Society*)

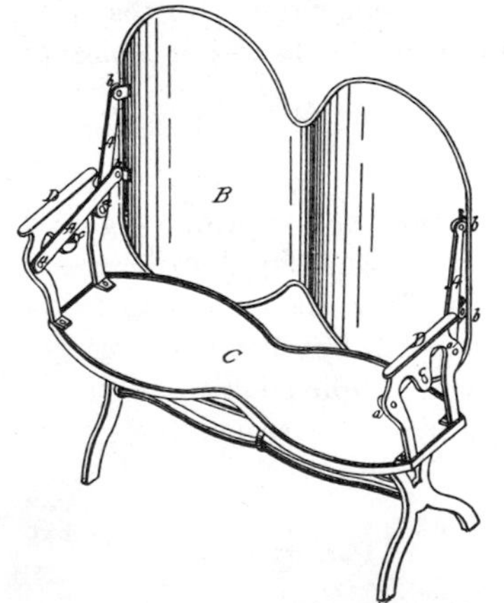

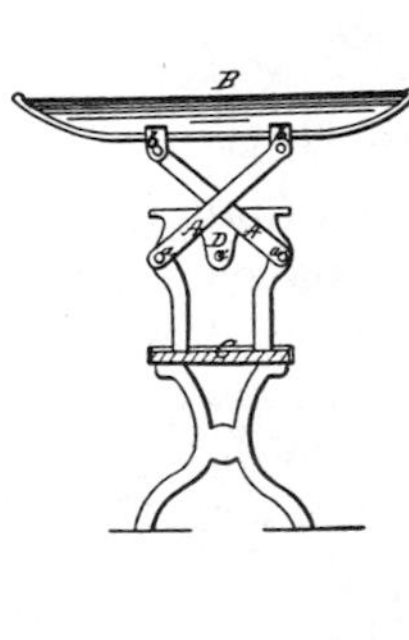

274. Adjustable, Reversible Railroad Seat, 1851. *The second United States patent for an adjustable railroad seat. Back rest adjusted by an 'arrangement of two levers . . . so that any required height of back may be carried and reversed from and to either side of the seat' and secured 'firmly in its position at any required angle.'* (*U. S. Patent* 8508, 11 *November* 1851)

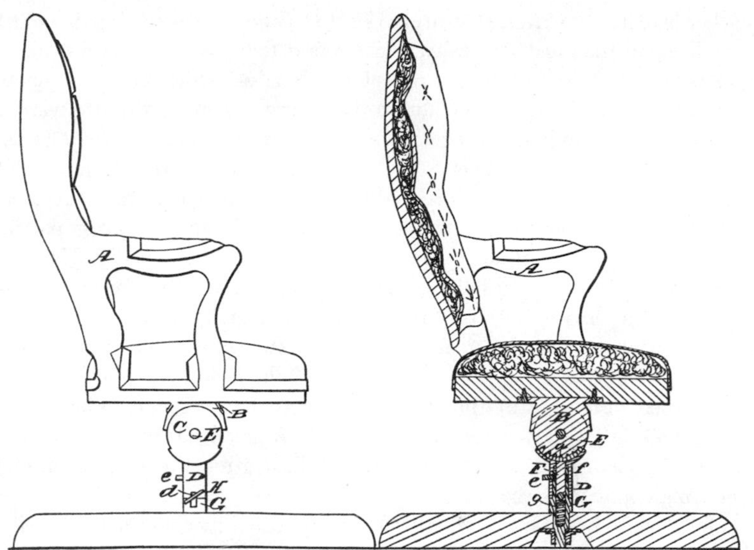

275. Recumbent Seat for Railway Carriages, 1855. *Mounted on a metal disk clamped between two plates, tilting backward and forward, and swiveling.* (*U. S. Patent* 13,464, 21 *August* 1855)

276. Adjustable Railroad Seat, 1858. *Mobility is achieved by a system of slotted hemicircles and thumbscrews. The leg rest slides out telescopically.* (*U. S. Patent* 21,052, 27 *July* 1858)

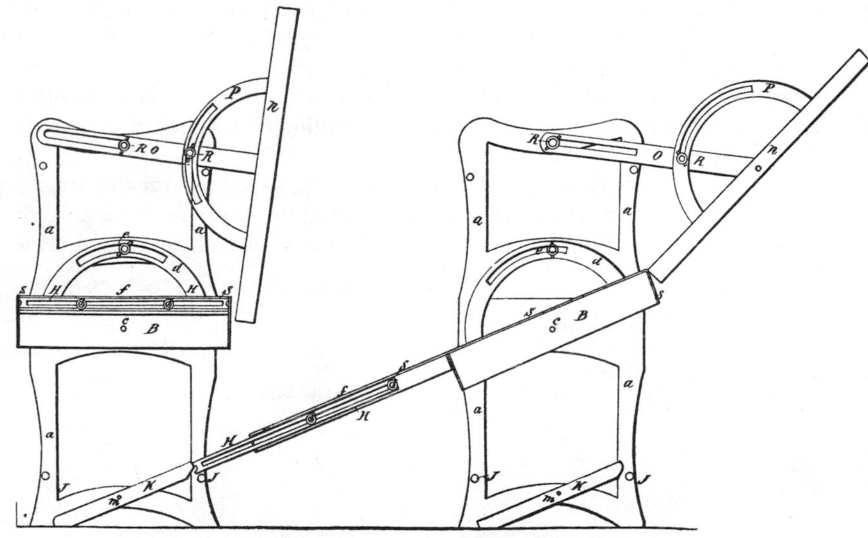

swing-bar bench of the fifteenth century (fig. 153), allowed the sitter to have either face or back to the fire. The swing backs found today on American trains and streetcars derive from this simple rail of the 'forties, which at the same time opened the way for the future mobility of the railroad seat. Soon afterward, the 'fifties were to develop in rapid sequence whole series of solutions, often fantastic.

Starting from the swing back, the earliest patents (1851) [50] contemplated means of setting the back rest for height as well as for inclination. It became adjustable, for example by 'an arrangement of two levers in a cross position,' and was secured 'firmly in its position at any required angle' [51] (fig. 274).

Thence grew the desire to build seats that could be adapted for day or night traveling by the device of a back rest whose front and rear followed different curves. In its normal position, for day travel, the convex side supported the spine, while at night the concave side supported the head and shoulders — 'the outside turned inside . . . at the same time raised high enough to support the head and body equally well for nightriding.' [52] A small advertisement for this patent has by chance been preserved, clearly illustrating the adaptation of the day and night positions (fig. 272).

Comfort was to be attained, whether by complicated mechanisms or by simple devices like the 'railroad rest' (1857) that the passenger brought with him and hooked on (fig. 273). Soon another problem moved rapidly to the fore, and attention turned to the convertible armchair. What had originally been invented for invalid chairs was now to be transplanted to every railroad seat.

Toward the close of the 'fifties, inventors seemed possessed with the idea that the railroad seat, within its narrow space, must be made as comfortable, as adjustable, as convertible as was humanly possible. Not satisfied 'to adjust the seat to any position required,' [53] they were ambitious to make 'the seats . . . adjustable for night travel so as to form a comfortable berth,' [54] that is, to transform seats into beds with no loss in numbers. It was like squaring the circle, and proved insoluble. But there is something appealing in these often freakish ideas: a desire to find the democratic solution that will allow everybody to enjoy an equal share of comfort.

Everyone was entitled to a bed. One inventor proposed a 'swinging frame,' which would be upright and reach the ceiling during the day, and which at night could be lowered like a drawbridge to offer the traveler a slightly inclined plane

---

[50] Three United States patents were issued in the year 1851: No. 8,059, 22 Apr.; No. 8,508, 11 Nov.; No. 8,583, 9 Dec.

[51] U.S. Patent 8,508, 11 Nov. 1851.

[52] U.S. Patent 13,471, 24 Aug. 1855. Compare also U.S. Patent 12,644, 3 Apr. 1855, which, however, did not use the differentiated curving.

[53] U.S. Patent 21,178, 17 Aug. 1858.

[54] U.S. Patent 21,052, 27 July 1858.

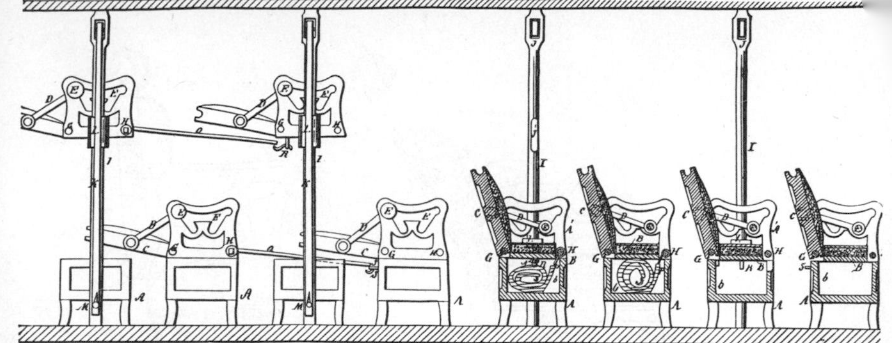

277. Railroad Seats Convertible into Couches, 1858. *This composite sketch, comprising two of the inventor's patent drawings, shows an effort in 1858 to transform the railroad seat into a couch without pre-empting extra space. The inventor's plan was to hoist every second bench ceilingward, after which both benches would unfold to form beds.* (*U. S. Patent* 21,985, 2 *November* 1858)

on which he might stretch out.[55] Another suggested 'constructing every alternate seat in two distinct parts' — one, the frame, remaining fixed; the other being raised on guiding columns or posts. 'In this manner the seats are enabled to be converted into comfortable double sleeping couches situated upon horizontal planes at different elevations, the backs of the several seats being thrown back and sustained . . . to effect this result.' Thus the passengers would sleep in two tiers, which overlapped like the tiles on a roof [56] (fig. 277).

A whole string of inventors, mainly around 1858,[57] tried to devise railroad seats as, later on, barbers' chairs or dentists' chairs came to be designed: with adjustable headrests, hinged backs, and swing footrests. One — as early as 1855 — mounted his swivel seat on a clamping disk carried by a post. It could tilt backward and forward like a bicycle seat [58] (fig. 275). A second inventor aimed at mobility by a system of slotted hemicircles and thumbscrews, while he slid out the leg rest telescopically [54] (fig. 276). A third balanced his seat on an 'oscillating pedestal.' [53] A fourth constructed his with swinging footrests, adjustable back, and headrest regulated by helical springs [59] (fig. 278). These complicated devices also were adapted to barbers' chairs, but not until decades later (fig. 279). A simplified form of this type of armchair with extensible footrests appeared in the 'eighties in the parlor car, destined for wealthier passengers (fig. 281). It was then in current use: An advertisement shows a gentleman travel-

---

[55] U.S. Patent 21,870, 26 Oct. 1858.

[56] U.S. Patent 21,985, 2 Nov. 1858.

[57] In 1858, thirteen patents were issued for improvements in car seats, and eight for improvements in car seats and berths (or couches).

[58] U.S. Patent 13,464, 21 Aug. 1855.

[59] U.S. Patent 19,910, 13 Apr. 1858.

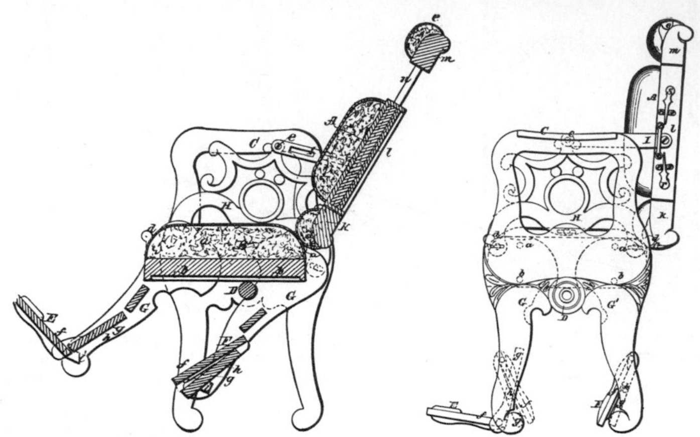

278. Adjustable Railroad Seat, 1858. *Swinging footrest, adjustable back, headrest regulated by helical springs. To support the human body as completely as possible, the inventor dissects his chair in articulated limbs, imitating the human anatomy. The railroad seat takes on the aspect of a jointed doll. The design has an undeniable originality, which later periods unfortunately failed to develop.* (*U. S. Patent*, 19,910, 13 *April* 1858)

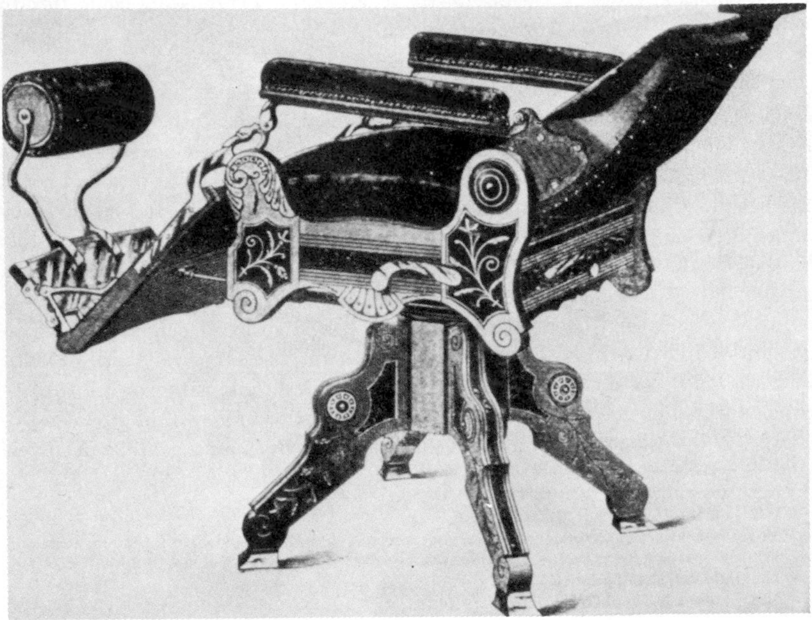

279. Barber Chair, 1888. *The barber chair of the 'eighties is a simplified form of the adjustable railroad seat three decades earlier.* (*Catalogue of Theo. A. Kochs, Chicago*)

280. Napoleon III's Salon Car, 1857. *Presented to Napoleon III by the Chemin de Fer de l'Est. In Europe of the 'fifties comfort in travel was regarded as an emperor's privilege. The monarch is seated in his 'place d'honneur.' A 'salon' on rails with rigid furniture, it is not at all adapted to the needs of travelers.* (L'Illustration, *Paris,* 1857)

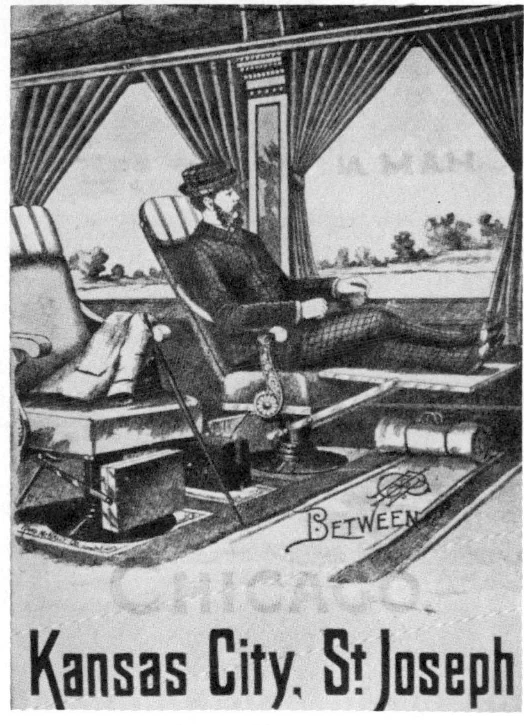

281. Parlor-car, Chicago-Kansas City, 1888. *Comfort in travel became a privilege of the well-to-do in America after the late 'sixties. The swivel chair with high back rest and extending footrest was originally conceived in America as appropriate for everybody.* (*Trade card, Bella C. Landauer Collection, New-York Historical Society*)

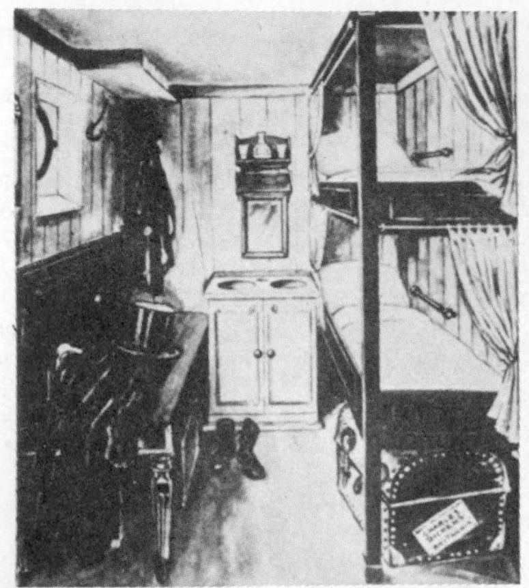

282. Steamship Cabin in the 'Forties. *Charles Dickens' 'stateroom,' S.S. Britannia,* 1842; *even on the ocean liners of the time comfort was primitive. Dickens, in his* American Notes, *humorously complains of 'a very flat quilt, covering a very thin mattress, spread like a surgical plaster on a most inaccessible shelf. And I sat down upon a kind of horsehair slab, or perch, of which there were two.'* (*Science Museum, South Kensington, London*)

283. Sleeping Car in the 'Forties. *Sleeping car for ladies on the Baltimore and Ohio Railroad,* 1847. *'Divided into several apartments or sleeping rooms each holding six beds or rather couches placed in three tiers along the sides. Three perpendicular straps guarantee the sleepers from falling . . .'* (L'Illustration, *Paris,* 1848)

ing at ease between Chicago and Kansas City in 1888. The patents of the 'fifties intended the comfort of their seats to be shared by everybody.

The attempts pile up, too numerous to list. The inventors were determined to conquer comfort for travel, to let each passenger be free to shift his position at will. Many of these types were found unfit for practical use, yet they were alive with an original, savage, mechanical fantasy that disdained the hard and fast, the clinched and riveted, that aspired to realize anything, even the impossible. These railroad seats are the Jules Verniads of furniture. As a totality they bear within them the seed of a future development.

The Sleeping Car: Convertible Seat and Folding Bed

The creation of the sleeping car as we know it today followed soon after construction of the reversible and adjustable railroad seat was attempted. The first American patent is usually taken to be one issued in 1854. This patent did not yet speak, as later ones were to, of a sleeping car. Its aim was to convert a seat into a couch; it belonged among the many experiments in the same direction.

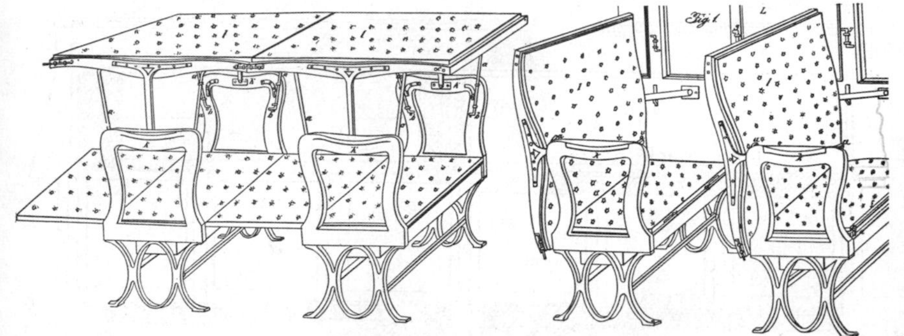

284. 'Car Seat and Couch,' 1854, 'First' American Sleeping-Car Patent. *Horizontal sleeping surfaces are obtained by folding over the seats and the seat backs. The sleeping car evolved from the reversible and convertible car-seat: early inventors did not use the word 'sleeping car,' but, like the inventors of railway seats, spoke of 'couches' or 'seat improvements.' As there are no sharp transitions, there is some arbitrariness in calling this solution of* 1854 *the 'first' American sleeping-car patent.* (*U. S. Patent* 11,699, 19 *September* 1854)

On the threshold of the great railroad panic in 1873, a record trackage was built: almost 7500 miles in 1871, or more than the total construction of the first twenty years. Closely connected with this expansion was the rise of the luxury car in its various types. But — it should always be stressed — a demand for heightened comfort in American travel was already finding its response at a time when train runs on European and American lines were nearly comparable in length. The luxury types were in use on the regular routes several years before the transcontinental lines were opened. In 1869 the Union Pacific, building from the East, made junction with the Central Pacific, building from San Francisco. And in 1870, when George M. Pullman invited the Boston Board of Trade on the first through-journey across the continent, made in seven days, he had only to pool the cars in his depots.

The luxury types entered service in this sequence: 1865, the palace sleeping car *Pioneer;* 1867–8, hotel car and dining car; [60] 1867, drawing-room car of Webster Wagner, Pullman's competitor, who succeeded in running his cars on the Vanderbilt lines, where they continued in operation until after Pullman's death in 1897; 1875, Pullman's drawing-room car, at first called 'reclining-chair

[60] The hotel car combined the sleeping and dining cars; the dining car pointed to the present-day type. Pullman's patents for these types were granted the following year, 1869 (U.S. Patents 89,537 and 89,538, 27 Apr. 1869).

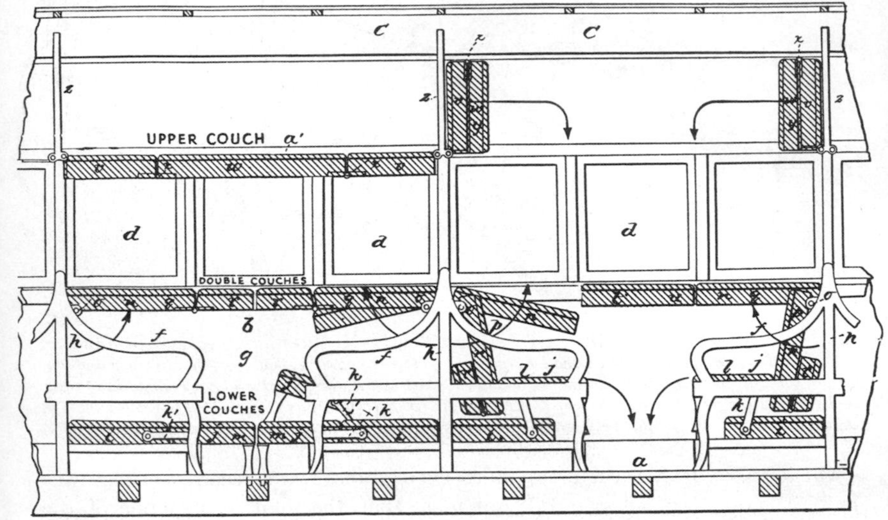

285 a, b. Woodruff's 'Seat and Couch for Railway Cars': Basic Solution for the Upper Berth, 1856. *Second of the basic sleeping-car patents, the 'Seat and Couch for Railway Car' (above) and 'Improvement in Railroad Car Seats and Couches' (below) of Theodore T. Woodruff, most fertile inventor in this field, offered the principle that has not been abandoned in America. Anyone curious for the details may peruse Woodruff's lucid specifications. The main principle of patent furniture consists in extending the law of transmutability of plane surfaces. Seats, backs, wall surfaces, all are articulated; nothing is hard and fast. Like his predecessors, Woodruff folds the seats down to floor level. The topmost bed — the fifth — embodies the decisive solution: when not in use it swings up, bridging the angle of roof and wall. This idea was taken over by Pullman in the famous 'Pioneer' of* 1865 *(fig.* 286). *The difference between these two patents of Woodruff's, both submitted on the same day, is that the one (above) dissects the upper bed into four parts articulated in pairs, whereas the other (below) swings the bed up bodily, as is still done in the Pullman car.* (*U. S. Patents* 16,159 and 16,160, 2 *December* 1856)

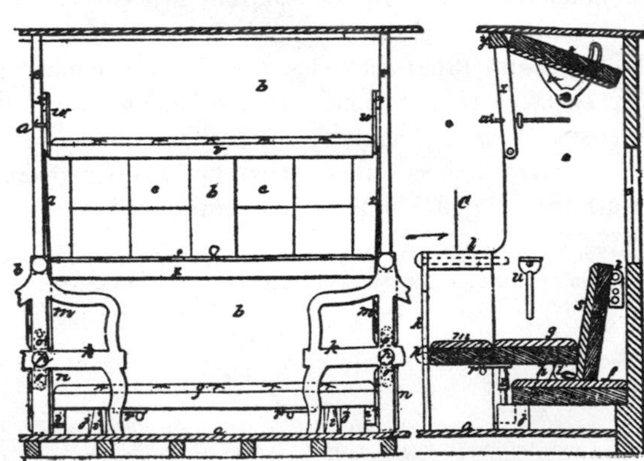

286. Pullman's 'Pioneer, 1865. Interior. *The 'Pioneer' provided the comfort of a good hotel. Every detail was given careful thought. (Courtesy of the Pullman Company)*

car' after its type of adjustable armchair, and later called 'parlor car.' It has run since this date.

In short, today's types were established by the end of the 'sixties. In 1886, nearly twenty years later, came the vestibule, by which the entire train was brought under one roof like the different rooms of a house. From the technical angle this important safety device, continually improved, is perhaps the most original contrivance to have left Pullman's workshop. No other fitting found such rapid and enthusiastic acceptance.[61] Here as in many other spheres, the future development had already taken shape in its basic features by 1890. The sleeping car exhibited at the Chicago World's Fair of 1893 and reproduced in a great colored folder [62] established a standard that endured for decades.

[61] First train to be equipped with it, 1886; patented, 1887. For its reception by contemporaries, see Horace Porter, 'Railway Passenger Travel,' *Scribner's Magazine*, vol. IV, pp.296–319 (September 1888). About a half-century later (1934) the streamline train came in. But this innovation, like the streamlining movement as a whole, is more a matter of formal design.

[62] *The Story of Pullman*, 1893.

287. Pullman's 'Pioneer,' 1865. Exterior. *The long car, which makes for smooth travel, becomes possible by the flexible mounting on bogies; this, like movable seats and couches, is a characteristic of American travel. (Courtesy of the Pullman Company)*

This is the period when the patent-furniture movement neared its end. Like the fashionable interiors of the period, the sleeping cars and the dining cars succumbed in the 'nineties to superficial luxury. They were overfestooned with Rococo ornamentation, and their high curved ceiling — known as 'full empire' — masqueraded as a stone vault. In one of his articles, Edward Bok, editor of the *Ladies' Home Journal*, sharply attacked this 'veritable riot of the worst conceivable ideas.' He learned that 'women whose husbands had recently acquired means' were ordering of their furnishers 'certain styles of decoration and hangings which they had seen in the Pullman parlor-cars. . . . Every foot of wood-panelling was carved and ornamented . . . gilt was recklessly laid on everywhere. . . . Mirrors with bronzed and red-plushed frames were the order of the day.' [63]

George W. Pullman and Luxury in Travel

If George M. Pullman be measured by his technical inventions, he loses in stature. On that score, any of the anonymous constructors of patent furniture can lay equal claim. In the early, the decisive days, he was less keen for technical innovations than for the use of them in combinations.

When at length, in 1864, he entered his first patent together with another inventor, he was following some hundred predecessors in the field of the sleeping car. And even this patent was relatively old fashioned; it still followed the principle of mooring the upper berth flush with the ceiling.[64] Only in his second patent, of September in the following year,[65] did the upper berth appear as a flap that swings down on hinges above the window and folds away to the ceiling in an inclined position. This original construction, in which the bed folds away to an inclined position, he derived from one of his predecessors. He adopted it in his famous *Pioneer* of 1865, and it has remained standard in America to this day. We shall return to it in discussing the convertibility of sleeping-car furniture.

Pullman's strength, then, was not in mechanical devices: Here he availed himself of anything appropriate to his purposes. His strength lay in quite another sphere, not the technical but the sociological. His invention was luxury in travel. This was his domain. Here he showed his creative capacity, outstripping all others in foresight, strategy, and boldness. Here he was able to work out and enlarge his idea to the utmost. Here he gained overwhelming and lasting success.

---

[63] *The Americanization of Edward Bok*, New York, 1921, p.251.
[64] U.S. Patent 42,182, Field and Pullman, 5 Apr. 1864.
[65] U.S. Patent 49,992, Field and Pullman, Sleeping Car, 19 Sept. 1865.

George Mortimer Pullman (1831–97) began as a joiner in his brother's business. He was not a wagonmaker by trade as were his two most important competitors.[66] Organization, enterprise, rather than joinery, was his field. When the Erie Canal was widened, he transported houses from the old bank to the new, and when Chicago began to raise its houses several feet above the swampy ground, he found a similar outlet for his talent. His feat there, it seems, was, in 1855, raising a hotel bodily with its sidewalk while custom continued. Pullman was then 24. Toward the end of the 'fifties, the sleeping car began to arouse general interest; in 1857, Theodore T. Woodruff, the leader in this field of invention, built his new sleeping cars and started them in operation. In 1858, Pullman purchased two old cars, which he remodeled as sleeping cars for $1,000 apiece. Then the Civil War broke out. Pullman removed to Colorado and temporarily turned to mining enterprise. By furnishing materials to the mines he realized $20,000 and returned to Chicago; he was 34 when he carried off the great coup.

The 'sixties, on the European as well as on the American continent, fostered a middle class growing in wealth and numbers. In Europe at this time arose the luxury hotels on the Lake of Lucerne and the Riviera; in America, the luxury sleeping car. Pullman's strength lay in his early recognition of this swelling demand for luxury. He staked his $20,000 on one card and in 1865 built the *Pioneer* (figs. 286, 287) at four times the cost of any other sleeping car.

It seemed unbelievable at the time that so heavy an investment would ever yield a return. Besides, Pullman's sleeping car could not be used in normal traffic, as it was too wide for the bridges and fouled the platform roofs. However, things happened as Pullman foresaw: The bridges were widened, and the platform roofs were adjusted to the size of car he believed necessary for comfort, which has remained unaltered to this day. He was one of the first entrepreneurs to master the effective use of publicity. Just as in 1870 he was to invite American industrialists on his first continental crossing, he found in the unusual events of 1865 a means of bringing celebrity to the *Pioneer* and of getting the platforms cut down to admit his cars. The luxury sleeping car *Pioneer* made its first journey as a hearse. It carried the body of Abraham Lincoln to its resting place in his home town.

Pullman found no trouble persuading the public to pay $2.00 for a night's journey, instead of the former $1.50. Once again he had guessed right. 'The

---

[66] Theodore T. Woodruff, the leading inventor of convertible furniture for the sleeping car, and Webster Wagner (1817–82), who worked under Vanderbilt's patronage and is credited with the introduction of the drawing-room car and the invention of the oval car-roof.

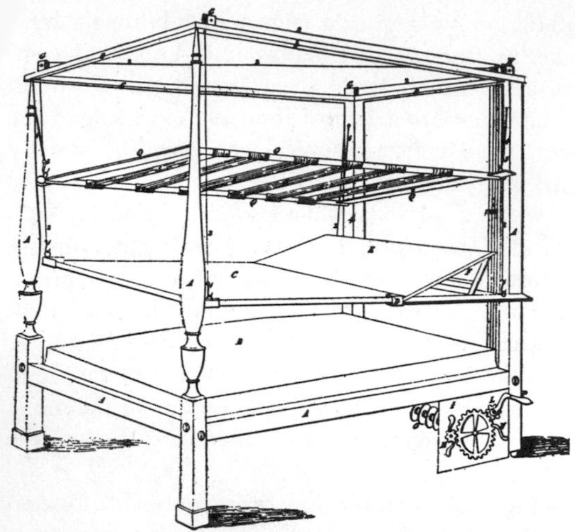

288. English Invalid Bed, 1794. *The bed is raised by a complicated mechanism of lines, winch, gears, posts, and flywheel.* (*British Patent* 2005, 7 *August* 1794)

289. Hoisted Railroad Bed, 1858. '*The upper bed is neatly fitted into the roof of the car, and when out of use is drawn up into its place. The bed is easily drawn down by the loop with pillow and blanket upon it, ready for use for two passengers.*' *The principle of this patent, as of Woodruff's two years before, was foreshadowed in the eighteenth century.* (*U. S. Patent* 21,352, 31 *August* 1858)

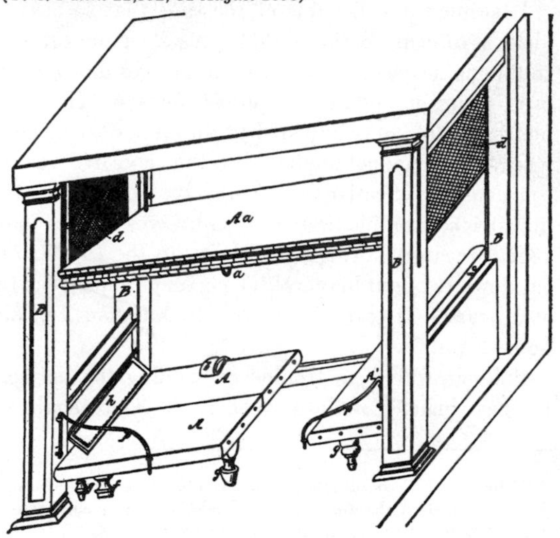

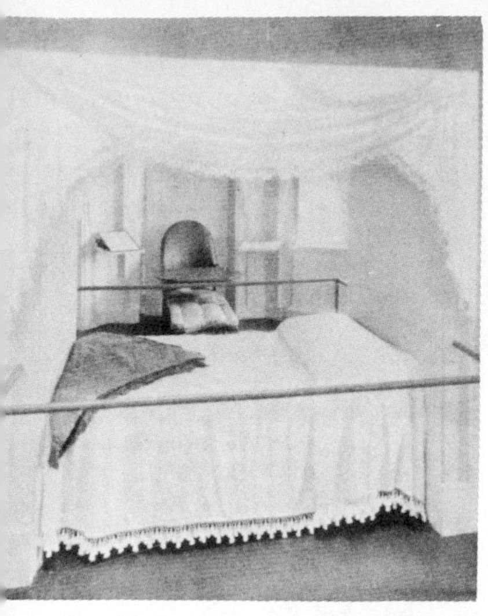

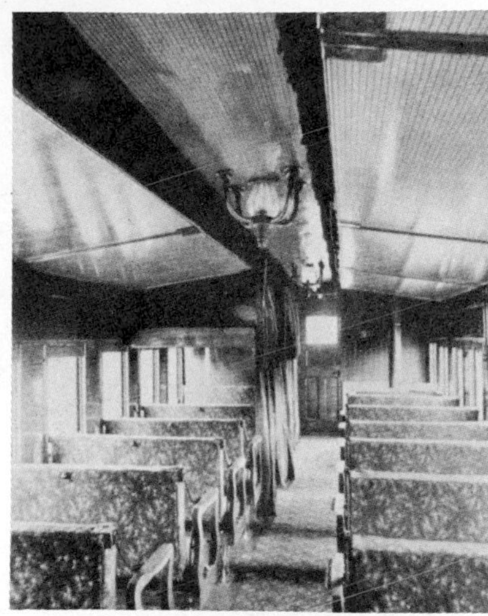

290. Thomas Jefferson's Bed, Monticello, around 1793. *It filled the passageway between Jefferson's study and his dressing room. An early tradition, that it could be hauled ceilingward by ropes during the daytime, is now denied. Yet it is difficult to understand his building it across an open passageway if it did not disappear when not in use.* (*Courtesy of the Thomas Jefferson Memorial Foundation*)

291. 'No. 9,' One of the Two Coaches Remodeled by Pullman in 1859. *In the daytime the upper berths were pulled up to the almost flat ceiling by ropes and pulleys. Mattresses, blankets, and pillows (no linen) were stored in vacant section during the day.* (*Courtesy of the Pullman Company*)

public flocked into the Pullmans and the old cheaper cars were taken off.' [67] The other companies had to fall in line. The *Pioneer* afforded the comfort of a good hotel. It had interior appointments of 'black walnut woodwork' and 'richest Brussels carpeting.' Every detail was the object of careful thought. Instead of plain candlelight, 'several beautiful chandeliers' hung from the ceiling, and 'French plate mirrors [were] suspended from the walls' [68] (fig. 286).

Luxurious travel in Europe was for none but the elect. It may well be that Pullman, when he projected his first palace car, had in mind the imperial trains that the French railroad companies presented to Napoleon III (figs. 292–4, 296). Pullman, who kept a watchful eye wherever novelty was stirring in his sphere, certainly did not overlook the 'train impérial' with which the Compagnie de Chemin de Fer de Paris à Orléans honored Napoleon III in 1857. A widely circulated and impressive publication,[69] in details running to color reproduction,

[67] *A Pioneer's Centennial*, Chicago, 1931, p.9.

[68] The *Illinois Journal*, 30 May 1865, quoted *in extenso* in Joseph Husband, *The Story of the Pullman Car*, Chicago, 1917, pp.45–6.

[69] Compagnie de Chemin de Fer de Paris à Orléans, *Wagons composant le train impérial offert à Ll. Maj. l'Empereur et l'Impératrice*, Paris, 1857.

292. 'Train Impérial' Presented to Napoleon III by the Compagnie de Chemin de Fer de l'Est, 1857. *Interior of the imperial couple's bedroom, showing the fixed beds.* (L'Illustration, *Paris*, 1857)

293. 'Train Impérial' Presented to Napoleon III by the Compagnie de Chemin de Fer de Paris à Orléans, 1857. *The sofa-like imperial seat in the* wagon d'honneur *was designed by the distinguished architect, Viollet-le-Duc, who decorated the whole train.*

294. 'Train Impérial' Presented to Napoleon III by the Compagnie de Chemin de Fer de l'Est, 1857. *View of the observation car, dining car, and 'drawing-room car.'* (L'Illustration, *Paris*, 1857)

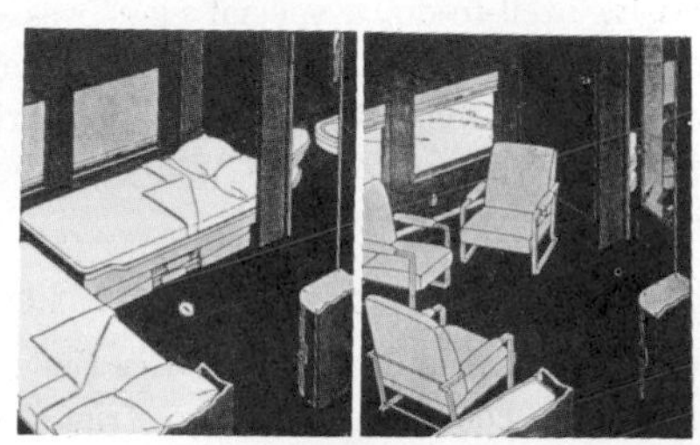

295. 'Master Room,' Pullman Company, 1939. *Convertible room for day and night use. Comfort equal to a two-room apartment is achieved by folding beds and a number of folding chairs. Comfort here is based on convertibility, in contrast to Napoleon III's rigid room and fixtures. (Courtesy of the Pullman Company)*

acquainted the world with this masterpiece of French taste and French construction. Camille Polonceau, the great engineer — still remembered for the iron roof construction bearing his name — constructed the train, connecting the cars by deftly contrived platforms. Viollet-le-Duc designed the interior with its studied ceiling decorations, its heavy hangings and carpets. As with Pullman's *Pioneer*, the dimensions of this train were wider and higher than the normal. The imperial train with its brilliantly polished lattices and wheels, with its *wagon d'honneur*, its dining car, its splendrous sleeping car for the imperial couple, its open, glassless observation car in the middle, kindled in every prince of Europe the desire to emulate Napoleon III in this as in his transformation of Paris.

Eight years later, in 1865, Pullman's sleeping car, the *Pioneer*, began to democratize aristocratic luxury. Pullman possessed the same instinct as Henry Ford half a century later, for stirring the dormant fancies of the public until they grew into demands. Both careers centered around the same problem: How might the instruments of comfort, that in Europe were unquestioningly reserved to the financially privileged classes, become democratized?

Yet the word 'democratization' cannot here be used without reserve, for with Pullman's innovation America gave up its single-class system. In the 'forties and 'fifties European travelers repeatedly mentioned their differentiated travel classes, for which the Americans of that time had no use. 'There are no first and second-class carriages as with us; but there is a gentlemen's car and a ladies' car: the main distinction between which is that in the first, everybody smokes; and in the second, nobody does. . . . The cars are like shabby omnibusses, but larger.' Such are Charles Dickens' impressions on first acquaintance with the American railroads in 1842. And somewhat dryly he comments on the sparing allotment of windows: 'There is a great deal of wall.'[70] Even in the late 'fifties, the French noticed with surprise: 'Il n'y a pas sur les chemins de fer américains, comme en France et comme en Angleterre, différentes catégories de places. . . .'[71]

With Pullman's introduction of the palace-car *Pioneer*, the situation changed. For the rapidly increasing well-to-do, a special class was created in America, and in the course of time it came to be identified with the name 'Pullman.' Like Napoleon III, but with greater comfort, American industrialists were to have their private coaches that compressed into one car the luxury for which Napoleon III needed a whole train.

***Precursors of the Sleeping Car* (1836–65)**

The problem of the sleeping car is foreshadowed in the ship's cabin. As conveyances, both ship and train command a very restricted space. Yet railroad cars must be even more parsimonious with their space than must the larger ships. This immediately poses the problem overshadowing all others: economy of space, how to secure adequate comfort for the traveler without pre-empting extra space.

It is not possible to construct for everyone an apartment like that of Napoleon III. It is not possible to put on wheels a bedroom with fixed beds, a reception room, a dining room, and an open veranda. Nevertheless, in America from 1865 to the year of the first vestibule train, 1886, the train became more and more a traveling hotel. Only one item of the imperial train had to be foregone: the bedroom with fixed beds.

A car now had several functions to fulfil: It must be convertible — living quarters by day and sleeping quarters by night. Even the dining cars at first turned into sleeping cars at night, being called 'hotel cars.' The beds, in which the travelers enjoyed as much comfort as Napoleon in his, had to disappear at daytime. Hence the problem of the sleeping car focuses around its convertibility: how to dissect the seat into elements that a couple of motions — twisting, pulling, or unfolding — will recombine into a bed.

In 1836, improvised bunks had been in use on the Cumberland Valley Railroad. In the 'fifties, up to five berths were stacked in tiers and side by side. But once the railroad seat is considered as a couch, the whole problem of the sleeping car falls into place and becomes part of the long line of patent furniture: the convertible seat and the folding bed. In the 'fifties, patents were not taken out

[70] Charles Dickens, *American Notes for General Circulation*, ch. iv.

[71] *L'Illustration*, vol. XXXI, p.215 (3 Apr. 1858).

for sleeping cars but for 'improvements for railway car seat and couch.' The emergence of today's standard types followed in the period 1854 to 1865, alongside the most effervescent period of inventiveness in American patent furniture.

The convertible cars offered only the barest comfort. Traveling in them was hardly a pleasure. In the topmost berth the passenger lay so close to the ceiling that he could not sit upright; and in the bottommost, so close to the floor that he could look out on the soles of passing feet. But transportation in those early days was not an everyday matter, and one sacrificed convenience as when sheltering in a mountain hut. The cabin, denominated 'stateroom,' which Charles Dickens occupied on his crossing to America in 1842 (fig. 282) was almost as austere as the American sleeping car of 1847 [72] (fig. 283). This sleeping car of the Baltimore and Ohio, with its lath frame that folded to the wall at daytime, might do, but only as a makeshift. 'To tell you that these beds are perfectly comfortable would be a lie, but one is thankful to find them such as they are and to be able to pass a pretty tolerable night.' [73]

This sleeping car of 1847 had close ties with the sleeping accommodations on American canal boats of the time. Nathaniel Hawthorne suggests, with the grace of his language, what life was like in a canal boat's cabin — living quarters, dining room, and dormitory in one. 'The crimson curtain being let down between the ladies and gentlemen' — as he calls it, 'the sexual division of the boat' — 'the cabin became a bedchamber for twenty persons, who were laid on shelves one above another. . . . Forgetting that my berth was hardly so wide as a coffin, I turned suddenly over, and fell like an avalanche on the floor. . . .' [74]

In 1854, three years after the appearance of the convertible railroad seat, the United States Patent Office granted the first American sleeping-car patent [75] (fig. 284). An English patent (1852) [76] mentioned in the literature of the subject has nothing to do with the sleeping car. It attempted — in scarcely satisfactory fashion — to double the seating capacity of the car at the expense of headroom: a double-decker. A glance at the sketch made by the Buffalo inventor of 1854 shows that he took the reversible seat as his point of departure. Instead of swinging the back rest through the customary 180 degrees, he swung it only through 90 degrees, up to a horizontal position in mid air, where it was made fast. He carried his back rests higher than the usual, 'so arranging the backs of contiguous seats that they may meet and remain in the same horizontal

---

[72] L. Xavier Eyma, 'Souvenirs d'un voyage aux Etats-Unis en 1847,' *L'Illustration*, vol. xi, pp.316f. (22 July 1848).

[73] Ibid.

[74] In 'Sketches from Memory' from *Mosses from an Old Manse*, New York, 1846.

[75] U.S. Patent 11,699, Henry B. Myer, 19 Sept. 1854.

[76] British Patent No. 587, 30 Oct. 1852.

plane.' A second bed was formed from the seats proper; in the words of the inventor, 'I open and extend these cushions of the seats, . . . which are upholstered on two sides, and fitted with hinges . . . by raising them up and turning out the lower half.' Beds, these boardlike affairs? The inventor did not call them such. He saw himself as converting seats into couches. Indeed, between bed and couch no sharp line can be drawn.

Economy of space is the mother of convertibility. 'As many seats by day, so many beds by night' went the rule of the early days. Often more beds would be conjured up than there were seats in the same place. This sleight could be achieved only if one of the beds were caused to disappear into the ceiling. It would reappear when needed, like the magic 'set-thyself' table at the wedding feast of Marie de Médicis in Florence.

A Detroit inventor for instance proposed in 1858:

> The upper bed . . is neatly and compactly fitted into the roof of the car, and when out of use is drawn up into its place by four counter-weights and cords from its corners, and no one would suspect anything but the roof to be there. . . . The bed is easily drawn down to the stops by the loop, with pillow and blanket upon it, ready for use for two passengers[77] (fig. 289).

Thomas Jefferson had a strong predilection for mechanically actuated furniture, automatic folding doors, and so on — consider the wine-bottle elevator between his cellar and dining room. The beds in his home at Monticello were built into sleeping alcoves in the usual way. Alone Thomas Jefferson's own bed stood in a peculiar place (fig. 290). It filled the passage between his study and his dressing room. That it could be hauled ceilingward by ropes during the daytime, as an early tradition maintains, is now denied. On the other hand, one can hardly understand his building it across an open passageway if he did not intend to make it disappear by day. The idea of an ascending bed is to be found in an English patent for an invalid's bed[78] (fig. 288), granted at the time when Jefferson was remodeling Monticello. In this patent a complicated mechanism of lines, winch, gears, and retarding flywheel was provided to raise and lower the mattress frame between four sliding posts.

The upper berth of the sleeping car is the real space-saving factor. But beds let down at the end of ropes no longer afforded a convincing solution. Even before the Detroit inventor's proposal, the present-day construction of the upper berth in the American sleeping car had been found. This happened toward the end of 1856, when the second patent was taken out.

To lay bare at the first stroke a principle on which a whole later development

[77] U.S. Patent 21,352, 31 Aug. 1858.

[78] British Patent No. 2005, 7 Aug. 1794.

will be based is not exceptional at this period. In the mechanization of the household we can see how, at the outset, some devices — from so modest a utensil as the rotary egg beater (1856) to the vacuum cleaner (1859), the dish-washing machine (1865), the washing machine with gyrator (1869) — were straightway laid down in the principles that were to guide their future development.

It was Pullman's rival of his early days, Theodore T. Woodruff (1811–92), who worked out the decisive solution for the folding bed in the sleeping car [79] (fig. 285). His was true inventor's blood. From the standpoint of 1850 he belonged to the modern type of wagon builder. To make a bed disappear into the ceiling by hauling on ropes was too awkward for him. To him furniture meant a series of mobile planes to be combined in various ways. It is a pleasure to observe how skilfully he uses hinges for his purposes, swinging up the back rest of his seat through 90 degrees to a horizontal position, so obtaining two middle berths. The seat bottom folds down to a lower position, where a horizontal plane is waiting to join with it; this gives him two more berths near floor level. Decisive is the idea of hinging the upper bed above the window. By day it forms a connecting surface between the ceiling and the wall of the car. Woodruff phrases it in simple words: 'Hinged . . . frames are arranged in such a manner that they can be converted into a couch above the car windows.' Woodruff conceived the folding bed with its hinges as others before him had conceived the folding chair. This was new.

Nevertheless, Woodruff's patents still did not speak of the sleeping car but only of a 'car seat and couch.' The space available for each person was indeed limited. One realizes that Woodruff could accommodate five people in this manner, four in the two lower berths and one in the topmost.[80] Today one recognizes the guiding role played by Woodruff's proposal to fold the upper berth between the wall and the ceiling.

It presented for the first time the idea of a folding upper berth, it was a radical departure from the arrangements in use before. . . . While the invention of the sleeping-car is commonly associated with other names, the credit for the original idea and for priority of patent, and for having constructed under his patents the first practical sleeping-car, belongs to Theodore T. Woodruff.[81]

---

[79] U.S. Patents 16,159 and 16,160, 2 Dec. 1856. Today's solution is embodied in the second of these.

[80] In subsequent patents, Woodruff retained the idea of the folding bed — cf. U.S. Patent 24,257, 31 May 1859. He even complicated it into a double-folding 'elevated couch' for two sleepers.

[81] Charles S. Sweet, 'Sketch of the Evolution of the Pullman Car' (1923), in manuscript, p.116. Through the courtesy of the Pullman Company, Chicago, we had access to this manuscript, the most objective and solidly documented record of the subject. It considers the sleeping-car bed but not the convertible seat. It is especially concerned with all technical details of the Pullman car: brakes, wheels, heating, water, lighting, and so on.

Theodore T. Woodruff was a wagon builder who, like so many of his contemporaries, designed all manner of machines: steam plows, reapers, locomotives, and ships' propellers. To promote his sleeping cars he formed a company of two million dollars' capital (1857). His cars ran successfully on many lines. Then, in the early 'seventies, he brought action for infringement of patent against Pullman, who had adopted the sideways and inclined disposition of the folding bed for his palace cars. The decision went in Woodruff's favor, but Pullman was already the stronger. 'No part of the judgement was ever collected and by a strange miscarriage of justice the Pullman Company continued to use the Woodruff patents and prospered, while Woodruff's company was practically ruined and the rightful inventor's name became almost entirely forgotten.' [82]

Pullman's Expansion

A few years after his litigation with Theodore T. Woodruff, George M. Pullman lost his franchise over the very line on which the *Pioneer* had first run. Not even Pullman could always escape humiliation: In those merciless years, that man would come out on top who fought with financial power on his side. To Cornelius Vanderbilt fell the satisfaction of opening this line to the sleeping cars of a company financed by himself. This was Webster Wagner's Palace Car Company.[83]

Structural resemblances link the careers of George M. Pullman and of the great packers, Philip Armour and Gustavus Swift. They all belonged to a generation born in the 'thirties. They all left the eastern states for Chicago, to find there the field for unlimited enterprise. Pullman and his idea of comfort in travel, Swift with his successful operation of the refrigerator car, conquered the dimensions of the land.

In both lived the same urge to expand in breadth as in depth: horizontally toward monopoly and vertically by expansion into anything that might be linked with their basic concern. The great meat packers processed the cattle, assured transportation in their own cars, created a nation-wide marketing organization, and built up industries to exploit the by-products. In the same way Pullman ran his cars wherever he could force an opening. He bought out every competitor but one, the company controlled by Vanderbilt. Two years after Pullman's death, however, the New York Central System, on which Vanderbilt had run the Wagner cars, was also brought in; the Pullman monopoly of first-class service was complete. Vertically, Pullman expanded by constantly length-

[82] Sweet, op. cit., pp.123–4.

[83] For insight into the financial manipulations involved, see the Chicago *Tribune*, 22 Sept. 1875, quoted in Edward Hungerford, *Men and Iron; the History of New York Central*, New York, 1938, p.274.

ening his list of manufactures. He built not only his own types but also anything connected with rolling stock.

The Sleeping Car in Europe

It is easy to understand that the democratic form of sleeping car had to be transplanted to Europe. The transplantation took place in England, as well as on the Continent, eight years after the *Pioneer* had first entered regular service. Pullman's shipment in 1873 of eighteen sleeping cars to the mother country of railroads shows how relatively early American influence was felt in this branch.

The same year, another American entrepreneur ran the first sleeping cars over the Vienna-Munich route. The types used for this purpose are still current in the European service. Known as 'boudoir-trains,' they have their berths walled off into separate compartments. In contrast to the American berths, which run lengthwise, these are placed transversely. This arrangement comes from deeply rooted habits. In America, even in the nineteenth century, the rooms of a house flowed into one another and the doors were left open. In Europe a hedge surrounds the house, the rooms are as far as possible isolated from one another, and the doors are kept carefully closed. The same custom is found in the preferential travel classes of Europe: Cars are subdivided into numerous small compartments.

In Europe the sleeping car — and travel comfort in general — made but indifferent progress; it is still considered a luxury. In America the Pullman fare is set no higher than a night's stay in the average hotel.

The Extension of Travel Comfort: Dining Car and Parlor Car

In the late 'fifties, dining cars were for potentates only. Napoleon III and his imperial staff banqueted at a large central table, which was attended by liveried servants (fig. 296).

The dining car began as an old baggage car into which had been moved a lunch counter, together with some high stools. 'The diner of 1862 was a baggage car . . . and bare as to the interior except that it was furnished in the middle with an oblong counter around the four sides of which the patrons ate while sitting on high stools. . . . From the inside of this oblong the viands were served by colored waiters in white jackets.' [84] Pullman's touch changed the dining car as it had changed the sleeping car; he opened it to comfort.

When Pullman secured his dining-car patents in 1869,[85] he was not especially

[84] Edward P. Mitchell, *Memoirs of an Editor*, New York, 1924, quoted *in extenso* in the *Pullman News*, vol. XIII, no. 4 (Apr. 1935).

[85] U.S. Patents 89,537 and 89,538, 27 Apr. 1869.

296. 'Train Impérial' Presented to Napoleon III by the Compagnie de Chemin de Fer de l'Est, 1857. '*Dining-room car.*' *In the 'fifties, dining cars were for none but potentates. The Emperor is presiding over a large table placed in the center. Around it, liveried attendants serve the ruler and his suite.* (L'Illustration, *Paris*, 1857)

keen for new inventions. What he claimed was a particular arrangement and combination. Still uncertain of the trend, he patented two distinct combinations. Could he risk a dining car having no sleeping accommodation, or was it advisable to unite both facilities into a single type? The 'hotel-car' of 1869 (fig. 297) is still a sleeping car, with a small kitchen built in at one end. The details are not specified. It was the type, the combination, that Pullman was anxious to protect. This hotel car was interesting for a further reason: 'My improvements are designed to provide a convenient car in which passengers, and especially families, may ride, eat, and sleep.' The other end of the car held the privileged, segregated cabins. These Pullman described in detail and referred to as 'state-rooms.' Only a narrow passageway led around them; the common aisle was done away with. They were for the traveler who desired privacy. It was the first appearance in America of a preferred section set apart within the car. It meant further differentiation in favor of a class system.

His other combination (fig. 297), the 'improved dining-car . . . intended to be used as a travelling dining-saloon and restaurant,' forewent sleeping accommodations altogether, but the sleeping car still dominated its pattern, as Pullman himself allowed: 'The seats are arranged transversely, and so as to face each other, as in the sections of a sleeping-car.' Still lacking were the chairs that Napoleon had in his dining car of 1857. The table was moved to the seats, not the seats to the table, 'one end of which is supported by a leg . . . while the

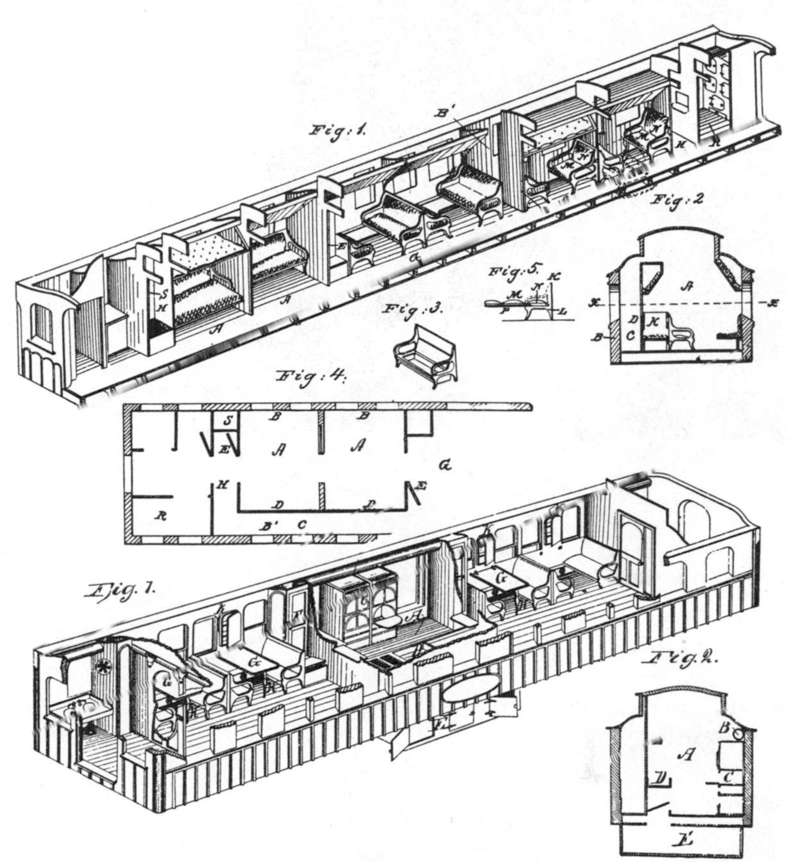

297. Pullman's Dining-Car Patents, 1869. *Could Pullman risk a car with dining service only, or should he unite dining and sleeping accommodation in the same car? Still uncertain of the trend, he patented both alternatives. Top: Pullman's 'hotel-car,' where 'passengers and especially families, may ride, eat and sleep' carries at one end a small kitchen* R. *To our knowledge, the first appearance in America of privileged sections, or 'state-rooms'* A, *which are by-passed by a narrow passageway* C. *The chairs* K *are 'free to move about the room.'*

Below: *Pullman's 'Improved dining-car' is already without sleeping accommodation. 'The seats are arranged transversely as in the sections of a sleeping car.' Unlike the individual seats of Napoleon's 'dining-room' of* 1857, *the seats here are fixed and the table is movable. The kitchen occupies the centre of the car; it is still reminiscent of the domestic type, having its provision room and icebox below floor level, like a cellar.* D *is the sink,* C *the range,* B *the water tank.* (*U. S. Patents* 89,537 and 89,538, 27 *April* 1869)

298. The First Pullman Drawing (Parlor) Car, 1875. *The revolving and adjustable armchairs with their simple outlines are as far from the exuberant forms of the 'nineties as from the overstuffed streamliners of the* 1930'*s.* (*Courtesy of the Pullman Company*)

299. Adjustable Folding Chair Used in Airplanes, 1936. *Although well-designed from the point of view of light materials and in the best tradition of patent furniture, it suggests a trend to artificially heavy appearance — the outcome, it would seem, of 'streamlining,' which perpetuates the showiness of nineteenth-century ruling taste in so many areas.* (*Courtesy Douglas Aircraft Company, Inc.*)

other end is hooked into sockets . . . so as to be readily detachable.' The dwelling house was still at the back of Pullman's mind. He sank the provision room like a cellar beneath the floor of the car; there were china closets between the windows and a large water tank above the kitchen.

Napoleon III had his *wagon d'honneur* in which to hold receptions. Divans lined its walls as in fashionable drawing rooms of the Second Empire. For the ruler there was reserved a seat of honor, sofa-like, and set apart (fig. 293). Viollet-le-Duc, who designed the train for the Paris and Orléans Railway Company, imparted to this seat something of his delicate romanticism. These *wagons d'honneur* became drawing-room cars for everyone in America, ten years later (1867), when Vanderbilt's protégé Wagner gave them to the public. George M. Pullman's first drawing-room car dates from 1875. In it were no divans along the wall, no stiff and upright seat of honor; instead, there were a number of equally comfortable swivel chairs with adjustable backs in which one could pivot with ease. Comfort was rapidly growing. Soon the movable footrests already projected in the 'fifties came into use, together with the various amenities of the patent-furniture movement, then reaching its fullest extent. The simple, concise lines of the adjustable swivel armchairs of 1875 were the logical result of obedience to function. No William Morris was needed to purify their design. As we have mentioned, from 1893 [86] onward the appointments and the ceiling became increasingly exuberant, and one realizes what detours had to be threaded before there could be any return to forms better suited to purpose. The parlor-car chairs of 1875 were as far from the exuberant ornamentation of the 'nineties as from our own 'streamline' designs.

Retrospect

American society of the railroad-building era was democratic in tone at a time when reaction governed European society. In Europe, that is to say, the upper classes walked amid every deference, while the common people had to put up with anything. This democratic outlook of the early years of American railroad building has been passed down to the modern European traveler in the continual perfecting of his comfort. Item by item, as they appeared, the improvements in travel comfort were taken over from America: in 1873, the sleeping car; in 1879, the 'dining-room carriage,' as the English called it; in 1889, the vestibule train.

---

[86] Charles S. Sweet, in his 'Sketch of the Evolution of the Pullman Car' (op.cit.), distinguishes two nineteenth-century styles: 'the plain type ceiling of 1865–1892' and 'the semi- and full-empire ceiling about 1893' — the heavily ornamented and vaulted ceiling.

Nowhere does this American democratic impulse show forth more clearly than in the strivings of the 'fifties, in the efforts to make the common railroad seat adjustable to posture at all moments and even to make it transformable into a reclining chair or a couch. The stimulus came from the principle that each passenger is entitled to an equal place and an equal comfort. For this reason the period admitted but one travel class, a tradition still alive in the American coach class.

After the Civil War a change set in, with the appearance of Pullman and luxury in travel. It was still a democratization of comfort; yet, silently and without labels, it introduced a multiclass system in America. As time went on, increasing differentiation tended further and further in the direction of luxury.

The second source behind the comfort of American travel is the mechanization of furniture. Its elements are the convertible seat and the folding bed. They make possible the conversion of day quarters into night quarters, of living room into bedroom. The convertible seat and the folding bed belong to the family of patent furniture — to that furniture which is adjustable to posture by virtue of its mobility and to multiple function by its powers of mechanical metamorphosis.

The Nomadic Furniture of the Nineteenth Century

Light Camp Furniture

Collapsible, transportable camp furniture opens a wonderful playground to fantasy. All must be encompassed within slight bulk and any combination of different utensils must be packed into the smallest space with the barest reliance on mechanical impedimenta. Everything must be simple. Every idea must find its most direct expression.

The germ of collapsible furniture is the *x*-chair, whether folding or, as sometimes in Antiquity, fixed. What had been a household piece in the classical world became, we recall, a kingly throne in the early Middle Ages (King Dagobert's seat from the Merovingian treasure). In Gothic times we found an abbess's chair of this shape. The Renaissance elaborated the pattern as a series of ribs, *x*-shaped or hip-jointed (fig. 143). In the nineteenth century the folding camp stool becomes one of the common articles of the mass market.

This collapsible camp stool is not left unaltered. Problems arise: How can it be made more comfortable to sit on? How can it be equipped with a back rest and still fold compactly?

Manifold ideas come to light. One of them consists in movably binding the legs at mid-point (by means of a metal ring, for instance). When collapsed, the chair forms a bundle of four struts. One motion will open them like an umbrella, so that their four ends extend a taut fabric. This action simultaneously raises a pair of arms linked by a strip of canvas forming the back rest.[87]

To compress a bed into narrow compass is somewhat harder. In Gothic times, trussing beds appear, often carried in the field. Charles the Bold of Burgundy seems to have been first to use a camp bed (1472).[88] In the field everyone apparently slept on the ground; Burgundy was then the most refined court of Europe. The seventeenth century carried the appointment of these beds beyond the threshold of luxury. Schübler's collapsible bed of about 1730, already mentioned (fig. 300), likewise falls into the category of demountable camp furniture.

In mid-eighteenth-century France (1756), we hear of 'carpenter-mechanics' (*menuisier-machiniste*) — combinations comprising 'bed, canopy, cover, stool,

---

[87] U.S. Patent 40,208, 6 Oct. 1863. Portable stool. The Museum of Modern Art, New York, saved the original model from the Patent auction of May 1943. The Museum also owns the model of a 'Pocket-Chair' (U.S. Patent 163,623, 25 May 1875), whose case serves as a seating surface, and which is constructed on a similar but less ingenious principle.

[88] Havard, op.cit. vol. III, col. 464.

300. JACOB SCHUEBLER: Collapsible Bed, *c.*1730. '*Newly invented French beds. The frame is in two sections made fast by screws,* A, B; *each leg is pushed up into two iron brackets,* C. *The narrow head and foot boards are movable on hinges, as at D. At the head end is a hinged pole pierced by a hole. When one wishes to uncover the bed one pulls the cord until the curtain is folded together.*' (Neu inventierte franzoesische Feldbetten *Nuernberg* 1730)

table,' capable of being set up in two minutes and taken down for storage in a bag.[89] The price, fifteen to twenty golden Louis, indicates a luxury article.

Collapsible iron beds have been preserved that are associated with great names. Napoleon I's camp bed is still shown in Malmaison, with its delicately shaped legs and narrow sheath.

Nineteenth-century progress was not rapid either in England or in France. Napoleon III on his Italian expedition (1859) preferred to use the equipment that had journeyed with the first Emperor. Only his elegant three-room tent of tubular iron (fig. 301) was really new.[90]

In America it was quite the other way. The steadily retreating frontier, especially after mid-century, and the opening of the West and of the Great Plains created a natural demand for highly transportable furniture. The development of American camp furniture sets in rather early: in the beginning of the 'sixties. It starts with rudimentary utensils, such as a camp chest that unfolds

[89] Havard, ibid. col. 1465–67, reports this advertisement, as well as advertisements of the years 1765, 1773, 1783, indicating that there was a continuous demand for camp furniture of this type.

[90] It was by Gandillot, who, as far as we know, was first to make chairs of iron tubes, *c.*1844 (fig. 312).

to become a table and in which both work tools and kitchenware are carried;[91] or a proposal to 'connect two camp stools together by means of rods between which is extended a piece of sacking.'[92] The development proceeds parallel with that of the sleeping car. It matures with surprising rapidity and draws to an early close.[93]

Comparison of Napoleon III's three-room tent (1859) with an American combination camp utensil of 1864[94] reveals the extraordinary rate of progress. This too is a camp chest (fig. 302). Its size is that of the regular portmanteau, 2′ square by 2′4″ high. It is made up entirely of combination furniture — a full set. Opened, it becomes an easy chair or a lounge. Within its coffer-like base there is room for a drawer that contains not only washing gear, but also 'cooking and table utensils' and 'an army cooking stove such as is in use.' Moreover, a collapsible frame may be annexed, forming a second chair or bed. This can continue in serial fashion. The armrests are extensible, allowing a table leaf to be laid across them. To one side of the lounge a table surface is at hand.

Beside these American field chests with their cleverly compressed housekeeping, the European camp furniture of the period takes on a primitive aspect; as markedly as — by the standards of the ruling taste — American furniture for the drawing room seemed primitive beside the luxury appointments of the Continent. Like the sleeping car in its initial phase, this American camp furniture was directed not to the few but to the many.

The Hammock

Even so simple an article as the hammock is drawn into the American patent furniture movement and completely transformed. To recline in this hovering, suspended network, made fast only at each end, comes close to the idea of mobility as realized in the adjustable seating of the period. We shall not be surprised to find variations on the hammock arousing greatest interest just as the patent furniture reaches its peak, during the 'eighties. Suddenly a whole series of hammock patents are entered each year: 6 in 1881; 8 in 1882; 11 in

---

[91] U.S. Patent 32,643, 25 June 1861. The earliest American patent covering camp furniture. Seven patents for camp furniture were granted in that year.

[92] U.S. Patent 33,362, 24 Sept. 1861.

[93] Mainly from 1861 to 1864. We have no exact survey, for camp furniture often lurks among the innumerable other headings of the patent records.

[94] U.S. Patent 44,578, 4 Oct. 1864. Described and illustrated in the *American Artisan and Patent Record,* vol. I, no. 31, New York, 7 Dec. 1864.

301. Camp Tent of Napoleon III, 1855. *Made in 1855 for the Crimean War, but used by the Emperor in Italy, 1859. Consisting of a salon, bedroom, dressing room. The iron bed as well as the folding seats and other utensils belonged to the first Emperor.* (Harper's Weekly, 1859)

1883. During the whole period down to 1873, America had only two such patents [95] — one of which was English in origin.

THE HAMMOCK: INDIAN FURNITURE

The hammock, with its airy network and continuous ventilation, arose in a tropical climate. It belongs among the rare furniture whose home is America, or, more exactly, the Caribbean region.

Christopher Columbus saw it in 1492 on his first voyage to the Bahamas. The careful account that Las Casas copied from Columbus' manuscript clearly reflects the novelty of this first impression.[96]

The watering party visited several native houses, and reported that 'their beds and furnishings were like nets of cotton.' 'These,' comments Las Casas,

> are in Hispaniola called *hamacas*, which are in the form of slings, not woven like nets with the threads going zig-zag, but the lengthwise threads are so loose that you can insert the hand and fingers, and at a hand's breadth more or less they are crossed with other

---

[95] U.S. Patent 33,678, 5 Nov. 1861, Improved Hammock. This patent merely covers a conventional hammock in connection with a 'portable folding frame.' The second patent (U.S. Patent 68,927, 17 Sept. 1867), of English origin, would replace the net by collapsible boards.

[96] We follow the quotation in Samuel Eliot Morison's *Admiral of the South Sea, A Life of Christopher Columbus*, Boston, 1942, p.245.

302. American Combined Camp-Chest, Lounge, Table, 1864. '*This invention is for officers and soldiers, and designed to combine in one compact mass, easily transportable, such matters as are necessary in camp life. Figure* 1 *shows it packed, excepting that the drawer is open and the strap unbuckled. Figure* 2 *shows it spread for use. The Box A has a drawer for papers and linen. Above the drawer there is room for the cooking and table utensils, and for a small army cooking stove. Above this is a folding frame, with canvas upon it, which may be set as a chair or as a lounge, or as a bed. Leaves to serve as tables may be attached. The whole when packed, measures two feet square by two feet four inches.*' (American Artisan and Patent Record, *vol.* 1, *no.* 31, *New York*, 1864)

close-woven threads like well-made lace trimmings, in the manner of sieves which in Seville are made of Esparto grass.

These hammocks are . . . finished off in many loops. . . . And at the head all these loops are joined together as in a sword hilt, which at each end is attached to the posts of the houses, and thus *the hammocks are off the ground and swinging in the air*. . . . It is very restful to sleep in.

Every successive navigator in the West Indies, S. E. Morison adds, noted and admired the hammock. The Spaniards, first to experience its convenience in a hot climate, were first to introduce it aboard ship.[97]

According to the *Oxford English Dictionary* also, the hammock is of Caribbean origin.[98] It has never lost favor in the tropics. Soldiers as well as sailors

[97] Ibid. p.245.

[98] The O.E.D.'s sources go back to the middle of the sixteenth century. Thus Sir Walter Raleigh's words are quoted: 'They lay in hammocks, which we call Brazil beds.'

303. The Hammock in Tropical Warfare: Nicaraguan Filibusters at Rest, 1855. *The hammock is among the very few furniture types that are native to the American continent. When Columbus and his crew landed in the Bahamas in 1492 they found entire families sleeping in enormous hammocks or 'Brazil Beds,' as the English called them. Their use has never ceased in this tropical area.* (Frank Leslie's Illustrated Newspaper, 9 May 1855)

knew its practical value, and carried it with them. Frank Leslie's *Illustrated Newspaper* of 9 May 1855, reporting the Nicaraguan Rebellion of that year, takes us into a camp of filibusters at rest (fig. 303). At that stage the hammock had not yet become fashionable garden furniture for languid relaxation. The natural way these soldiers used theirs, having fastened them to ceiling and walls, may indicate that the hammock was then still their constant companion.

MECHANIZATION OF THE HAMMOCK

Now, in the 'eighties, attempts are made to broaden the use of this Indian furniture and to extract from it new combinations. The first danger for the inventor to meet was that the body might become enmeshed in the net like a snared animal, or that it might fall out if the hammock were not cautiously used. Cross-bracing was to hold the net always at the right tension and, connected with it, a simple device to shelter the reclining lady from sun or rain [99] (fig. 306).

[99] U.S. Patent 495,532, 18 Apr. 1893.

Others, for sanctuary from mosquitoes, envelop the hammock in a cylindrical net carried on sliding hoops (fig. 304).[100] To one inventor comes the bizarre inspiration for a hammock that instead of swinging between two boughs hangs on an overturned tricycle.[101] At the same time ropes fold the body at its joints so that it will occupy less than its normal length. Finally, a waterproof cloth is stretched over this tricycle of the 'eighties 'to convert the vehicle into a sleeping apartment' (fig. 305).

We do not hesitate to present examples of such grotesque flavor. Taking a broader view, it matters little whether or not these particular proposals were successful in practice. What matters here is to show the imagination, impetuous and even bordering on the ludicrous, that was at work to release furniture from its rigidity. But this urge, even in the limited field of the hammock, is not confined to the grotesque.

Elaboration of the hammock into a kind of combination furniture is not astonishing for this period. One of the most appealing solutions, of the early 'eighties, is preserved in an advertising leaflet (fig. 307).[102] Taken over from the hammock is its light suspension beneath a bough, or from a hook. The light frame, capable of assuming many positions of balance, becomes by a mere shift of the body now a kind of hammock and easy chair, now a swinging seat.

304. Hammock Combined with Mosquito Net, 1885. *The cylindrical mosquito net is carried on hoops, which slide apart to admit the occupant.* (*U.S. Patent* 329,763, 3 *November* 1885)

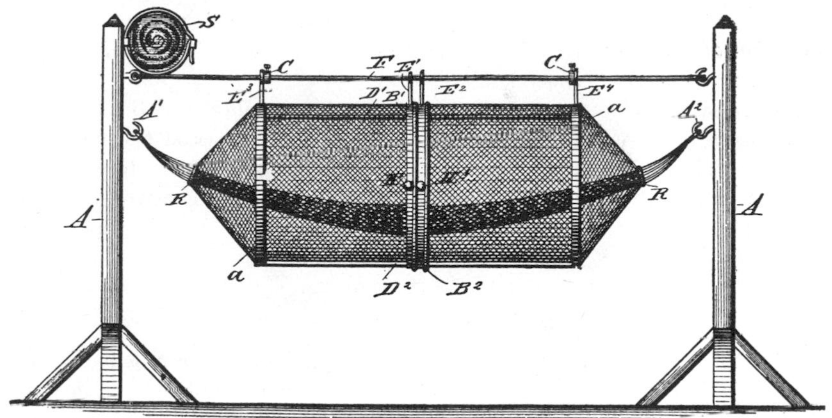

[100] U.S. Patent 329,763, 3 Nov. 1885.

[101] U.S. Patent 278,431, 29 May 1883.

[102] In the Collection at Worcester Historical Society, Worcester, Mass.

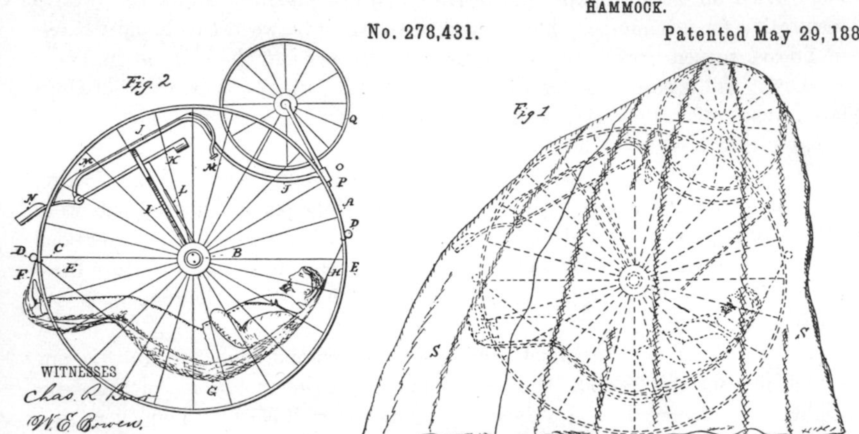

305. Hammock Combined with Tricycle, 1883. *Somewhat grotesque ideas reached the Patent Office. The hammock swings from an overturned tricycle. A waterproof cover spread over the whole allows one to 'convert the vehicle into a sleeping apartment.'* (*U.S. Patent* 278,431, 29 *May* 1883)

The whole construction is aerial and hovering as the nest of an insect. Everything here is based on mobility, on a system of interlocking parts 'composed of a number of jointed links or boughs and legs and suitable cross-rounds. . . . The footrest is not connected rigidly with the framework of the chair, but is sustained by a flexible connection.' [103]

This is not the place to quote from the detailed specification. But whoever would see for himself with what ease and competence the period had mastered motion problems may peruse the actual wording of the patent. He will need no further explanation why we stress the carefree manner, the originality with which the Americans of the period exorcised the spell that the ruling taste had cast over furniture.

The Hammock and Alexander Calder

From this hovering system, ever ready to change its poise, there is but a step to the art of the American sculptor, Alexander Calder. Both are intimately rooted in the American environment. Indeed, Calder's art — and herein lies its strength — is deeply at one with the broad stream of modern evolution.

[103] U.S. Patent 236,630, 11 Jan. 1881.

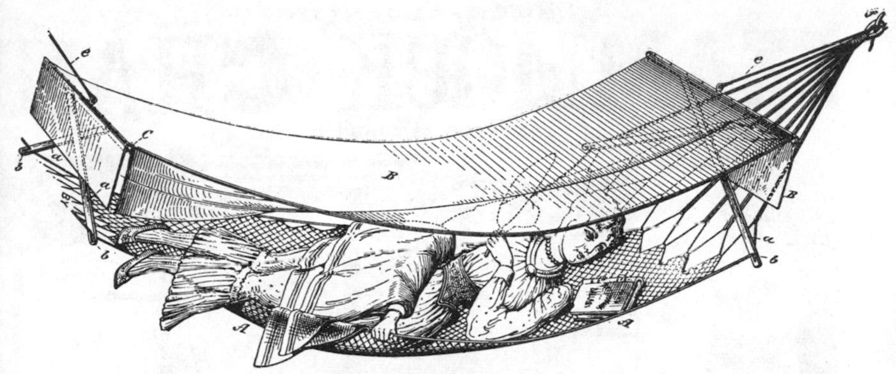

306. The Fashionable Mechanized Hammock of the 'Nineties. *Patent-furniture influence: cross-bracing is to hold the net always at the proper tension. A simple sheltering device protects the lady relaxing with her fan and poems à la mode.* (*U. S. Patent* 495,532, 18 *April* 1893)

It was Calder's instinct that led him to spend year after year in Paris, steadily growing. There he experienced the only creative schooling for the man of our day: living week in, week out, in contact with the men who had created our new means of expression. There his eyes were opened to the bounds of naturalistic representation. Along this path, he clearly saw, whatever stirred within him would never find its artistic outlet. Nor was it one artist or another: It was the plane upon which artistic problems were to be met that carried Calder to the creative sources within himself. This self was rooted in the nature of American experience. America had produced a tremendous body of inventions strongly affecting everyday life. But artistically, on the emotional side, they had not spoken. The inventions were at hand. They were useful. They yielded returns. But no one had pointed to them. No one had hit upon the symbolic content underlying their everyday usefulness.

None other in contemporary art was born into this American experience, which lies, as we often stress here, in a particular relation, a gearing of the American man with the machine, with mechanism, with the mobile. No other people is in such close touch with these abstract structures. Calder absorbed the modern means of expression, slowly amalgamating them with his own background until, by 1931, he had attained a sensitivity to states of equilibrium that he stressed in his 'mobiles' (fig. 308). He was carrying on the tradition of his artistic forerunners, now blended with the American consciousness.

A motor, a draft of air, or a push of the hand, will change the state of equilibrium and the interrelations of his suspended elements, connected in a mobile

307. The Hammock and Convertibility: Hammock Chair, 1881. *This multi-functional Hammock Chair dispenses with the net, being 'made of strong canvas, fitting perfectly the entire length, without drawing the clothing so tightly around the body, thus making it just as cool, while the annoyance of catching buttons, tearing down the lady's hair, and the double somerset in the air is avoided.' A highly movable and convertible piece produced at the height of the patent-furniture movement: a small shift of the body varies the equilibrium within this suspended system.* (*Advertising leaflet in Worcester Historical Society, Worcester, Mass.*)

wire system, forming unpredictable, ever-changing constellations and so imparting to them the aspect of space-time.

The solution of motion problems never loses its fascination over the American mind. This urge takes the form of an obsession — no matter how bluntly the inventor's reason may tell him to work on for the sole purpose of making money. In Alexander Calder's mobiles, this urge for the first time found its artistic reality.

308. ALEXANDER CALDER: Mobile, 'Black Dots,' 1941, Sheet Metal and String. *It is but a step from the suspended hammock, ever ready to change equilibrium, to the art of the American sculptor Alexander Calder. A draft of air, a push of the hand will change the poise of the mobile's hanging elements connected in a mobile wire system, whose interrelations form ever-varied, unpredictable complexes seen in a space-time aspect. (From a photo by Herbert Matter, courtesy Museum of Modern Art. Collection of Mrs. Charles B. Goodspeed, Chicago)*

The Constituent Furniture and Its Significance

Just as samples are taken from an abandoned mine to indicate that some material is buried there, we have taken a few samples representing that almost unknown complex: the nineteenth century's constituent furniture. The presentation, we know, is incomplete; but a start had to be made in claiming its historical birthright and appraising its true worth. That the movement will gain its rightful place in the history of human comfort we may no longer doubt. The history of furniture and of comfort, from the standpoint of movability and combinability, is not yet written, and whoever cares to dig deeper will find rich, unworked material, of which these are the first bare hints.

In English furniture of the late eighteenth century, the ingenious shaving tables, the refinedly compartmented washstands, the cylinder top desks with concealed mechanism, technique is of one cast with form. Their spirit is not split between form and construction. The late eighteenth century's innate sensibility enabled it instinctively to fuse its technical with its esthetic experience. For behind it lay centuries of tradition and superior craftsmanship. The nineteenth century, owing to its split between thinking and feeling, can equal the performance only when function tightly holds the reins. But inventiveness was not lacking, and it is in this that the constituent furniture of the nineteenth century excels that of former periods.

The Americans of the second half of the century were virtuosos in solving motion problems. What makes this material so exciting for the historian are the new and unexpected solutions he encounters at every turn: not only the historian, but also architects and designers, looking back at these forgotten solutions for mobility incorporated within the organism of furniture, may find aid and stimulus. Motion problems are among the most difficult of their field. One must live with these problems and constantly exercise upon them like a juggler; then they become second nature. But for this a specific atmosphere is needed, just as an atmosphere is necessary for the creation of stained-glass windows. When such atmosphere fails, the skill and experience die out. This happened in the present case. When nineteenth-century ruling taste stifled patent furniture, furniture again lapsed into its rigidity.

Against Mechanization in Furniture

It is often asserted that furniture should contain no moving parts: they are complicated and unnecessary.

All that we can say is that our yes or our no must depend on the conception of comfort at any given period. From an absolute standpoint, perhaps, the oriental conception may be considered the more organic, for the posture it evolved is independent of all outside agency. Western culture, we noted earlier, has from the fifteenth century moved toward an increasingly differentiated posture. The West sits with downward hanging feet. The most advanced step along this direction was taken when the last century engineered interplay between the mechanism and the body, a state of hovering equilibrium.

Some may condemn this mechanical intervention. Mechanized furniture may be rejected together with the mechanized household. For both answer to the same mode of living. Perhaps the direction followed by the furniture of the engineer will prove more interesting than the mechanization of the household in one respect. Constituent furniture frequently tackles the problem of relaxation, and not — as in the vacuum cleaner or the automatic washing machine — that of labor-saving alone.

Patent Furniture and the 1920's

The architects around 1920 were becoming ever more aware of the interrelation between the new methods of construction (iron and ferro-concrete) and new demands (lightness, transparency, and spacial penetration). Furniture too was drawn into this process: But the anonymous American patent furniture had long ago fallen into abandon. Purely technical solutions, when unsupported by feeling, perish all too easily. The solutions of the engineer found no real response in the emotional temper of the time.

An alliance of the anonymous inventors of the 1860's with the European architects of the 1920's might be imagined; a pooling of resources, that would have added to the power of making furniture mobile and adjustable its endowment with corresponding esthetic values. For the two movements have undeniable points of resemblance. The nineteenth-century Americans and the architects around 1920 did not design single pieces to a customer's personal whim. They created types. And on the creation of types the movement of the 'twenties was based.

Whenever our moderns and the Americans of the 'sixties tackle similar problems, the circles touch. This occurs surprisingly often. But the gap of half a century lies between; and thus the modern movement was robbed of its naturally appropriate soil. All that the Americans had devised and developed, before their surrender to ruling taste, was wholly unknown to the Europeans then taking the lead. They lacked the long American experience that delighted in motion problems. They had to start from scratch. History is part of nature, and nature does not operate without waste.

THE CONSTITUENT FURNITURE OF THE TWENTIETH CENTURY

Furniture and Its Shapers

UNTIL around the end of the fifteenth century, carpenters fitted the woodwork of the house. They were succeeded by the joiners, and in the seventeenth century, by the cabinetmakers — men skilled in the working of fine woods, dextrous handlers of inlay and veneer.

The nineteenth century put the decorator in charge. The Empire setting, elaborated by Napoleon's designers, Percier and Fontaine, opened the way for the upholsterer. Increasingly the upholsterer became master of the ruling taste. Only in American patent furniture did the engineer and the mechanic exert their influence.

Thus from medieval times, the artisans have followed one another as creators of furniture: carpenter, joiner, cabinetmaker, decorator-upholsterer, mechanic-engineer.

The 'Craftsman'

In England, parallel in time with the American patent-furniture movement, a revolt was growing against the machine. This revolt had nothing in common with the patent-furniture movement. It was a protest against the first stages of mechanization, of which England was feeling the effect by 1850. The circle around William Morris, with John Ruskin in its background, gained an influence that ultimately spread to the Continent and to America. This was at the turn of the century. With the arts and crafts movement, as carried on by William Morris's British followers, who demanded furniture and interiors 'intended to be the expression of an individuality,' a new figure came to the fore: the craftsman.

The movement, spreading to the Continent and to America around 1900, did not bring identical results everywhere. On both sides of the Atlantic, it looked to Ruskin and William Morris as patrons, and was of marked literary bent. In America it advocated 'the simplification of daily life and a more reasonable way of living.' It advocated country houses, often sound in detail. It advocated self-sufficiency: 'a pleasant comfortable dwelling situated on a piece of ground large enough to yield a great part of the food for the family.' [1] Self-sufficiency, as a reaction against mass production, was to be urged again later by Frank Lloyd Wright.

[1] Gustave Stickley, *Craftsman Homes*, New York, 1909, p.202.

This movement, as against the English arts and crafts, was simply called 'Craftsman': Craftsman houses, craftsman furniture, craftsman farms.[2] It did not seek individuality in furniture. Back to the ways of our pioneer forefathers! A spokesman argues that it 'represents the fundamental sturdiness of the American point of view . . . seeking the inspiration of the same law of direct answer to need that animated the craftsman of earlier days.'[3]

The movement shares many points of agreement with the Europeans: It condemns the 'black walnut parlour suites' mass produced in Grand Rapids. It wishes flat, unpainted, unornamented wood. It is against heavy draperies and artificial coating, and has a good feeling for well-lighted, sun-flooded rooms, with the kitchen table placed beneath the window. It leans, as in Europe, to chairs or sofas of well-made wicker. Its forms are kept deliberately stiff and severe. Many of the wooden chairs, particularly the spindle chair with slender wooden members, might have stood in an interior by Frank Lloyd Wright.

Most of its furniture was rough and heavy. Visible pegging and dovetailing seemed an asset. Later, the whole movement gained the name of 'mission style.' But primitiveness of fashion was all that the style had in common with the late eighteenth-century furniture of California monasteries.

The American craftsman movement lacked inventive artists. It had its own mouthpiece, *The Craftsman*, still read in the second decade of the century. But from the start it had no chance of survival. Even if seconded by real genius, such attempts must have been abortive in an environment growing ever closer to full mechanization.

From time to time, *The Craftsman* would carry designs of benches, bookshelves, tables or chests, 'solely for the purpose of the home-worker.' One 25-cent booklet of the *Popular Mechanics* series addresses the amateur on 'Mission Furniture, How to Make It.'[4] The movement was to end in a hobby.

The Architect, Former of Types

On Continental soil, the Morris movement had a different outcome. Its influence took two divergent paths. In one direction, it gave status to the decorative artist, who is a professionally reformistic designer. His changing of superficial form for playful effect was a peril from the start. The moral purity of Morris's teaching was lost as it became reconciled to the ruling taste. This

---

[2] The movement had its own periodical, *The Craftsman*, published from 1901 to 1916.

[3] Stickley, op.cit. p.159.

[4] Henry H. Windsor, *Mission Furniture, How to Make It*, Chicago, *c.*1909–12.

was most clearly demonstrated at the Parisian Exposition Internationale des Arts Décoratifs (1925), which marks the final merging of the movement with the transitory. About this time the modern movement in architecture began to gain ascendancy.

In the other direction William Morris had moved consciences and had set many minds thinking. Led by the German Werkbund, from around 1907, the narrow movement broadened out, moved closer to industry, and encompassed architecture within its sphere: Peter Behrens and later (1914) Walter Gropius.

Around 1920 the architect superseded the decorative artist as the author of new furniture types. Architects who also designed furniture have existed at all times — among them names such as Ducerceau. It is easy to understand why this displacement occurred. The movement of the 'twenties started from new artistic premises, from a new visual orientation. Here reform was not enough.

It was not a matter of designing single pieces or even complete suites of furniture. Now, for the first time since the eighteenth century, the room and its contents were felt as a single entity.

By the new standards, the decorative artist, superficially changing forms, had failed. The initiative passed into the hands of architects. Architect and designer merged into one person. And many who began as designers later revealed themselves as architects.

'Looking at present-day trends' we commented in 1931, 'one sees that the decorator has lost all prestige as a designer of furniture. Almost every important inspiration comes from architects now setting standards for the future. Today the slightest item of furniture must participate in the new architectural spirit — a fusion that the architect takes quite for granted.' [5]

The art and architecture of our day show many facets. A movement may represent but one segment, a single trend within our time. But different as the trends may be in themselves, each works with means of its own to clarify reality. As a whole they constitute the vision of our time. And when a movement ends or flows into another, it still remains a living parcel of our consciousness. No single country, no one person, has created our furniture or the equipment of the house. Each land contributed its atmosphere, its talents, whenever an idea was being worked out. This co-operation guarantees the validity of the whole development.

---

[5] *Die Bauwelt*, Berlin, 1933, no. 33.

No sooner has a new idea appeared — the tubular chair for instance — than its implications are worked out by new creative talents, only to return to the inventor who resolves them into standard form. As in all periods, there is continual give and take, an unconscious but active collaboration.

Yet the manner of invention is different from in the patent-furniture era. Invention of form now takes precedence. Inventors are no longer anonymous like the subscribers in the telephone directory. Their names and personalities are all sharply defined; and often behind an abstract form we may perceive the contribution of a country or of an individual.

The Shaping of the Types

G. Rietveld, the Precursor

The Dutch were the first to project the new artistic vision into furniture. Among them G. Rietveld of Utrecht had already pointed the way before 1920. Rietveld did not stand alone. He was linked with the Dutch *avant-garde*, with Theo van Doesburg, with Piet Mondrian, with J. J. P. Oud, all of whom, from 1917 on, had been voicing their esthetic in the periodical *De Stijl*. 'Our chairs, tables, cupboards . . . will become the abstract-real artifacts of future interiors,' Rietveld proclaims as he publishes his early chair designs in 1919.[6]

As in painting and architecture, it was necessary temporarily to forget everything and begin afresh, as if no chair had ever before been built. There should be no dovetailing. The framework of the chair is composed of square members simply screwed together. They cross one another but do not penetrate, and their overlapping distinctness is emphasized. As Rietveld puts it, the separate elements shall be 'visibly connected' (fig. 309). Line likewise crosses line in Piet Mondrian's colorless paintings and drawings of the same period, often called the 'plus and minus' pictures (fig. 310). Seat and back in the chair of 1918 consist of smooth, unbent plywood planes kept at a deliberate distance from one another.

It is easy to see what was going on: Furniture was being dissected into its elements, into a system of struts and planes. The effect should be as light, as transparent, as hovering as possible, almost like an iron skeleton.

This becomes even clearer in Rietveld's buffet of 1917[7] (fig. 311). Here, furniture resolves into vertical and horizontal elements. The dresser top, a plain board,

---

[6] *De Stijl*, Jahrg. 2, Leyden, 1918–19, no. 11.

[7] Reproduced in *10 Jaaren Stijl*, Jubilee series, 1927, p.47.

309. RIETVELD: Chair, 1919. *Under the influence of the new artistic vision, furniture is broken down into its basic elements. Space flows between the parts, and where they must touch, the members are 'visibly connected.'* (*Courtesy G. Rietveld, Utrecht*)

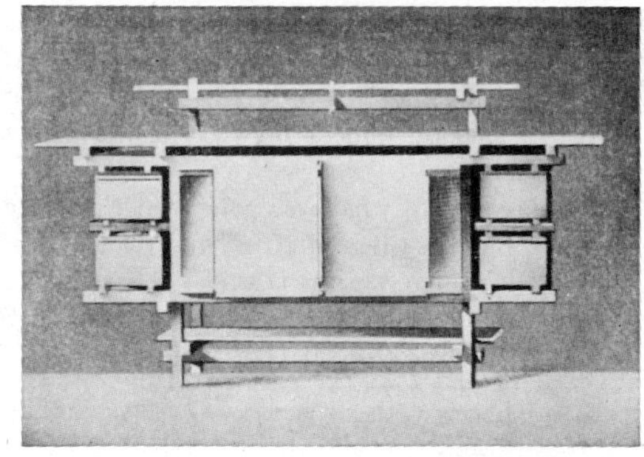

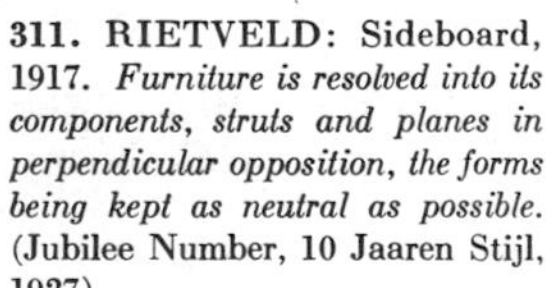

311. RIETVELD: Sideboard, 1917. *Furniture is resolved into its components, struts and planes in perpendicular opposition, the forms being kept as neutral as possible.* (Jubilee Number, 10 Jaaren Stijl, 1927)

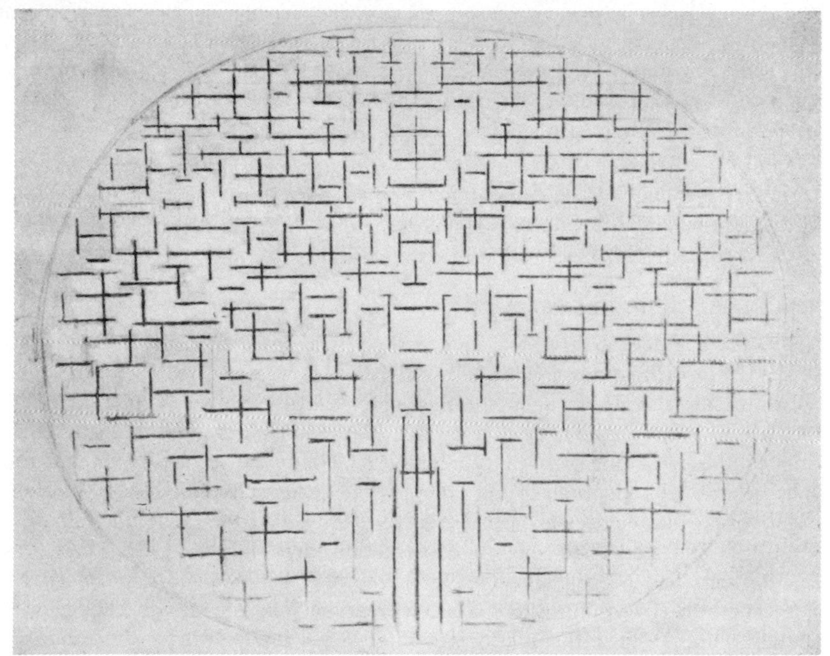

310. PIET MONDRIAN: 'Pier and Ocean,' *c.*1914. *The painter Mondrian collaborated with the architects and urbanists of the* De Stijl *group. Around* 1914, *forms are liberated from the natural or conventional aspects and reduced to the utmost in his so-called 'plus and minus' drawings.* (*Collection the Museum of Modern Art, New York*)

cantilevers out at either end — as will so often occur in architecture — giving a sense of weight dematerialized. Air flows between all its parts, even between the drawers. Its doors are sliding planes.

Specialists can easily object: The plain wood screws of the chairs are inadequate; or the buffet of 1917, a master stroke in the way it anticipates later expression, will collect dust in its recesses. But these pieces must be judged from another point of view. One cannot accurately gauge the effect of political manifestoes; yet such utterances form real turning points and guides for the future. These Rietveldian pieces are manifestoes. They guide the direction of an entire development. No assembly line, no routineer can supply the fantasy they embody. As furniture is broken down to make a fresh start possible, its elements resolve into a system of struts and planes. Its form is as neutral as possible.

The painters around 1910, or a ferro-concrete engineer like Robert Maillart, use these same elements in their quest for new potentialities and new expressions.[8] One of the few hopeful signs of our time, parallel methods, appears in furniture too. Soon the mid-twenties will bridge the gap between the manifesto and the standard piece. Then, with startling speed, the diffusion begins.

Again we limit ourselves to a type of sitting accommodation formed in this period: the tubular steel chair. We shall see how this piece, seemingly the product of dry mathematical invention, was worked upon by men of various countries, each one bringing his own distinctive contribution.

The Shaping of the Tubular Type

The tubular steel chair is as truly a part of the heroic period of the new architecture as are the transparent shells of glass that replace bearing-walls. The tubular chair also draws upon the new potentialities evolved in our period — media that were accessible to all eyes, but that remained useless so long as their implications were not grasped. Behind this blindness, as we know, lay the split between thinking and feeling; a split that made it impossible to translate construction into emotional terms. Architecture called forth the latent potentialities of iron and ferro-concrete construction, and simultaneously there was reborn what had been languishing for a century: a new conception of space. It was not otherwise in furniture. Its new creations were nurtured in the renewed spatial feeling. And so the interior decorator began to give way to the architect.

The tubular chair has many antecedents. In England around 1830, as we noticed, iron tubes were used for beds, and various attempts were made to solve the ever awkward joining of horizontal and vertical tubes.[9] From England, experience in the welding of iron tubes came to France.[10] Soon we find Parisian chairs having bent tubular legs, such as the model of 1844, shown here (fig. 312). The tubes are reinforced by a core of glue or plaster. These tubular iron chairs were meant not for the garden but for the drawing room; a fact of some interest in a period so fond of showiness as was the Second Empire. If we read a water-color of the period correctly, chairs of this type stood in the Empress Eugénie's apartment.[11] Yet the ruling taste could not stand the plain material even attenuated by a covering of paint; and the tubular form was altogether discarded.

[8] Cf. ch. 'Construction and Aesthetics: Slab and Plane' in Giedion, *Space, Time, and Architecture.*

[9] English patents for iron bedstead, 1827–41. Cf. our section, Mechanization and Cushion-furniture, p.383.

[10] Charles Dupin, *Les Artisans Célèbres*, Paris, 1841, pp.499–502.

[11] In the Château of Saint Cloud, which later burned down.

312. Hollow Tubular Chair by Gandillot, France, 1844. *Gandillot introduced the new welding method for the manufacture of tubes six years earlier, in* 1838, *from England. Instead of lead or copper, welded iron tubes were used for gas, water, and steam mains. In this way tubular chairs came into fashion in France. Gandillot's chair was patterned on the form of the wooden chair, the metal being painted over to imitate wood and inlays. (Musée des arts décoratifs, Paris)*

313. MARCEL BREUER: Tubular Chair, 1926. *In contrast to the metal chair of the ruling taste in* 1844, *Breuer's chair is conceived according to the laws of bent and welded tubular steel.* (*Marcel Breuer*)

These antecedents do not help to explain the rise of the modern type. The modern type is wholly a new one. Behind it was the urge to create a light and semi-hovering structure. It grew up in the atmosphere of the Bauhaus, the one center in the 'twenties where educational training ventured into the unknown. Marcel Breuer, who invented the type, came to the Bauhaus as a youth of eighteen, in 1920. In 1925 he constructed his first tubular armchair. These seamless steel tubes, also known as Manesmann tubes, had the advantage of compactness. The lines of the first steel-tube chair, as well as the suspension of its seat, herald tendencies that will soon be further developed: the seat, back, and arm surfaces use the membrane-like resilience of taut cloth. Marcel Breuer was of the generation following Rietveld's. Breuer's wooden chair of 1923 [12] had shared with Rietveld's models a similar wish for dissection into elements, for lightness and simplicity of joining. But it already announced new tendencies, with its free span of canvas, forming seat and resilient back rest, its greater reliance on cantilever elements, and its use of standardized wooden sections, with a view to serial production.

The basic principles of the tubular chair were already present. Walter Gropius' building of the Dessau Bauhaus in 1926 gave the opportunity of furnishing the auditorium with tubular chairs. The type was brought to public notice by a postcard issued for the opening of the New Bauhaus and showing Breuer's chair. The same year, 1926, Breuer created his stacking stools, also used as tables. Their first formulation proved definitive. These stools clearly show how the new type was to be understood. Here, as later, both in Breuer's

314. MICHAEL THONET: Bentwood Veneer Chair, 1836–40. *All parts, including the top rail, were heat-pressed in molds. The flat side-members form a 'solidary unit' with the front and rear legs. In some ways this first model is more advanced than the later ones: the first curved veneer strips employed here form the beginning of a development that, after a sporadic appearance in America about* 1870, *was successfully carried forward by the modern movement.* (Michael Thonet, *Vienna,* 1896)

315. MICHAEL THONET: Bentwood Chair, London Exhibition, 1851. (Michael Thonet, 1896)

316. MICHAEL THONET: Bentwood Chair, Vienna Exhibition, 1850. *The components are joined by metal screws and shipped in unassembled state. In* 1891 *seven million chairs of this type had been produced, with only minor changes in the design.* (Michael Thonet, 1896)

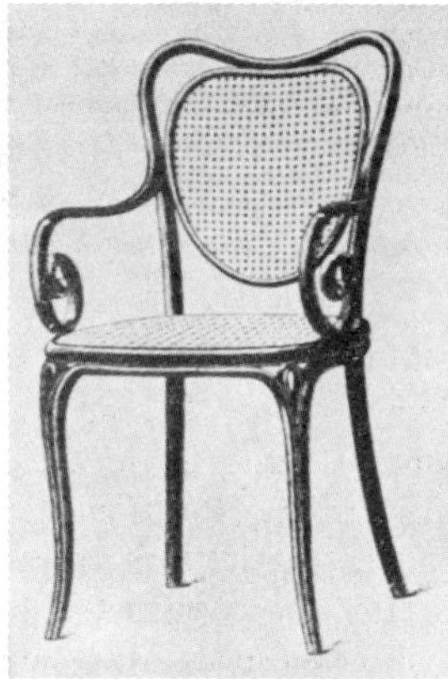

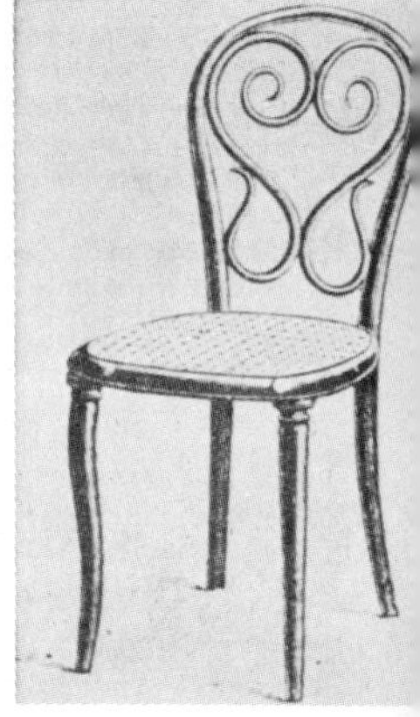

[12] First illustrated in *Staatliches Bauhaus Weimar*, 1919–23, Weimar, 1923, p.83.

317. LeCORBUSIER AND PIERRE JEANNERET: Pavillon de l'Esprit Nouveau, 1925. Interior. *Bentwood Thonet chairs, model B–9. 'These chairs bear titles of nobility.' Table with tubular frame. Paintings by Léger and LeCorbusier.*

tables (1928) and in the cantilever tubular chair, the elements are not joined. The tubing flows in an endless line, as in Irish interlacement work. And instead of the two-dimensional structure, we have a spatial one, stressing transparency, expressing the new spatial conception of our time.[13]

For three years Marcel Breuer's chairs, conceived in terms of mass production, were put out by a single craftsman, until, in 1928, the Thonet firm took over their manufacture.

The exact stages leading to an invention cannot be reconstructed. The glistening handle bars of a bicycle may have led Marcel Breuer to use the same material for chairs. The tubular steel chair may perhaps have links with the earlier bentwood chair. Michael Thonet [14] (1796–1871) experimented at Boppard, Germany, with chairs of which all parts, top rail included, were composed of four to five layers of veneer shaped by heat in molds (1836–40) (fig. 314). Standardization

[13] The fullest treatment of Marcel Breuer's work, especially of his architecture, is H. R. Hitchcock, Jr., *Exhibition by Marcel Breuer*, Harvard University, Dept. of Architecture, Cambridge, 1938, mimeographed catalogue.

[14] His biography was printed for private circulation by his sons and grandchildren: Michael Thonet, Vienna, 1896. We owe this rare document to the kindness of Dr. W. Eitner, Director of the General Electric Corp. Cf. also W. F. Exner, *Das Biegen des Holzes*, 3rd ed., Vienna, 1893.

318. Pavillon de l'Esprit Nouveau, Paris, 1925. Interior. *Square cupboards and cabinets raised on steel legs. They are intended as separations between two living areas.*

and mass production began in the early 'fifties (figs. 315, 316) and were never discontinued. When the architect around 1920 could no longer endure the *art décoratif* furniture, these simple beechwood chairs offered what they were seeking: form purified by serial production.

Almost as manifestoes, LeCorbusier showed these standardized chairs in his Pavillon de l'Esprit Nouveau at the 1925 Exposition des Arts Décoratifs in Paris (fig. 317). LeCorbusier himself tells us the reason for his choice: 'We have introduced the humble Thonet chair of steamed wood, certainly the most common as well as the least costly of chairs. And we believe that this chair, whose millions of representatives are used on the Continent and in the two Americas, possess nobility.'[15] In the Pavillon de l'Esprit Nouveau, LeCorbusier raised his cabinets on tubular steel legs and set his table tops on welded tubular frames (fig. 318). Above all, he was proud of his staircase of bent and curved tubes: 'We have made a staircase like a bicycle frame' (fig. 319).[16] The chair, always the most delicate problem, he did not venture to touch. To work it out was reserved for Marcel Breuer, who constructed his first model that same year, 1925.

Its seat was neither cantilevered nor resilient, although here already the elasticity of the steel tubing worked with the taut canvas to spring the seat, and

[15] LeCorbusier, *Almanach d'Architecture Moderne*, Paris, 1925, p.145.
[16] Ibid. p.195.

the back and arm rests.[17] Unlike the American patent furniture with its mechanical mobility, this type uses the resilience, the springiness, of materials to provide a modicum of elasticity. Soon the tubular chair loses all resemblance to the earlier wooden chair: part merges into part, flowing in an endless circuit.

Diverse but familiar elements pass into the inventor's mind, and are fused into a new whole. It was not only tne bicycle handle bars or the steamed-wood chair that entered into the new type, but a new optical vision. The emphasis on structure and the desire for transparency are signs first discerned in painting. The Russian painters and sculptors around 1920, Suprematists and Constructivists, may have furnished certain esthetic impulses. Constructivist wire sculpture, with its aerial lightness and transparency, truly fit Marcel Breuer's description of his tubular chairs, 'They do not encumber space with their mass.'[18]

The Cantilever Tubular Chair

The development of the tubular chair was completed in the space of a few years, from 1925 to 1929. In 1927, under the leadership of Mies van der Rohe, the German Werkbund built a settlement near Stuttgart, an undertaking as bold as it was unique. Architects of the various European countries in which the new movement stirred were invited to build houses where they might translate their ideas into reality without censorship of any kind. Besides LeCorbusier, Walter Gropius, J. J. P. Oud, Peter Behrens, and others, the younger growth was also given its opportunity. For many of these younger men, this was their first chance to see their plans put into practice. Among them was the Dutchman, Mart Stam; in one of his houses tubular steel chairs were seen, having not four legs but two. The front legs ended in 'runners,' which gave the seat a hovering aspect. These were the first cantilever chairs.[19] Mart Stam's black-painted chairs were neither elegant nor resilient. The tubes were connected by woven canvas strips (fig. 329), and only in the seat and back rest of his armchair did he aim at elasticity, by stretching broad rubber strips. Nevertheless these chairs, with their compact rectangular outline, announced the form that was to become standard.

A few weeks later, Mies van der Rohe exhibited cantilever tubular chairs[20] in his own flat at the Weissenhof settlement at Stuttgart. These chairs were

[17] Canvas stretched by the sitter's weight was familiar in camp and deck-chairs. Now the elasticity of the steel tubing is brought into play to keep the material permanently taut. 'The taut cloth forming the back rests and seats are of a material so far used for tropical belts and boot-laces . . . The traditional materials thus take on a new meaning, with unknown and so far overlooked potentialities. . . .' Marcel Breuer, *Berliner Tageblatt*, 19 Oct. 1929.

[18] Ibid.

[19] Illustrations of Stam's interiors in the Werkbund settlement at Stuttgart will be found in *Innenraeume* by Werner Graff for the German Werkbund, Stuttgart, 1928, Abb.98; chairs: Abb.51–2.

[20] Ibid. Mies van der Rohe's Interiors; chairs: Abb.53.

319. Pavillon de l'Esprit Nouveau, Paris, 1925. Tubular Staircase. '*We have made a staircase like a bicycle frame.*'

resilient and their skeleton was spanned by leather or elegant caning. Mies van der Rohe claims to have been the first to recognize and exploit the springiness of the steel tubing. This resilience he obtained by curving the legs in a semicircle (fig. 328) such as one might observe on the exuberantly curved Thonet rockers of the 'nineties (fig. 326). The idea of the cantilever chair was in the air. Mies van der Rohe developed it independently. Mart Stam had but once mentioned to van der Rohe a first model that he experimentally designed for his wife. It consisted of heavy gas pipe connected by L-shaped elbows. Stam in turn says that he found his hint in the auxiliary seat of American automobiles, a collapsible cantilever that sank into the floor when not in use.[21]

[21] Adolf G. Schneck's *Der Stuhl* (Stuttgart, 1928) gives insight into the various models at this stage and illustrates those which Schneck assembled for the Stuttgart Exhibition of the German Werkbund in 1928, the year after the Weissenhof Settlement. The esthetic rediscovery of earlier serial types such as the Windsor chair and the American office chair is stressed.

320. Pavillon de l'Esprit Nouveau, Paris, 1925. Exterior. *The Pavillon represented a two-story flat, one cell of the apartment houses that LeCorbusier planned for the Paris area. The open space to the left is intended as a hanging garden.*

From Mart Stam and Mies van der Rohe, the cantilever chair returned to Marcel Breuer. He took over Mart Stam's more compact formulation with its upright supports, improved the construction, and gave to the tubular chair the shape that has spread far and wide.

During this period, from 1925 to 1929, England was slumbering as if its reformers had never existed; while America had given itself over heart and mind to the cult of antiques and to their imitators. Frank Lloyd Wright meant no more to the public than did the Modern Movement as a whole. The houses and interiors for which the struggle was being so bitterly waged on the Continent were non-existent so far as England and America cared. In the 'thirties, the Americans manufactured cantilever tubular chairs in Breuer's definitive formulation, mass-producing them on a great scale and at a fraction of the European cost. Like other contemporary furniture, they were not allowed to enter the drawing room. They were used in barber shops and mainly as kitchen equipment.

And yet the idea of the cantilever chair has closer ties with America than with any other country. But one has to go back to the patent-furniture movement.

The resilient cantilever seat that Europe created in 1927 to satisfy an inner need had appeared in America in the 'eighties. We first find it in unexpected whereabouts: in agricultural machines. In the 'sixties already the seats of sulky plows, mowers, and reapers were being bracketed to the frame by a single support that projected diagonally into the air. In the early 'eighties, the manufacturers set out to discard all wooden parts and to make their machines — plows, harrows, and reapers — of iron alone. Tubular frames were widely used for the sake of lightness. At this moment, support of the driver's seat became a resilient steel strip that would take up the jarring of rough ground (fig. 324). Cast or stamped, the seat with its large ventilation holes admirably fits the body and is in direct line of the saddle seats of early nineteenth-century American Windsor chairs (fig. 235).

Had a fraction of the thought devoted to the comfort of the reaper seat been extended to domestic utensils, how much further we would be today!

The idea of the free-hovering and resilient seat seems to have moved the American inventors at the peak of the patent-furniture movement. One of them imagined, in 1889, a curious device for sea-going vessels (fig. 325). To a large round dining table, rotary to facilitate the serving of meals, the chairs were adjustably fastened by 'suspensory rods,' while a weight beneath the seat helped the passenger 'preserve as near a vertical position independent of the motion of the table.' [22]

These examples are merely indicative of the fact that the problems of American patent-furniture and the later European movement often tend in the same direction. In the case of the cantilever chair this overlapping is even more obvious.

Washington refused to grant Mies van der Rohe's patent for his tubular cantilever chair. He was referred to specifications drawn up a few years earlier for a chair likewise resilient, and having curved supports (fig. 327).[23] True to the American tradition, it was equipped with adjustable gadgets and derived its springiness from a spiral winding. This American chair, applied for in 1922, was conceived not as tubular, but as being made of solid steel rods. In other words it did not touch upon the most difficult and pivotal problem of European tubular furniture: how to secure resiliency without mechanism; moreover it was intended not for the living room but as a 'lawn-chair.'

This chair seems never to have been executed. Nevertheless, Mies van der Rohe told us he was obliged to build a model on the American's specifications

[22] U.S. Patent 396,089, 15 Jan. 1889. Rotary dining table.

[23] U.S. Patent 1,491,918, 29 Apr. 1924 (Application 1922). 'The primary object is to provide a novel lawn-chair . . . which is *of resilient nature*. . . . The main body portion thereof is formed from a single strand of steel rod and bent into such a form as to provide a support for a flexible back seat rest.'

321. LeCORBUSIER AND CHARLOTTE PERRIAND: Armchair with Pivoting Backrest, 'Fauteuil à Dossier Basculant,' 1928.

as tangible proof of the impracticality of the resilient spiral. This done, his patent was granted.

The Mobile Tubular Chair

A material so abstract as steel tubing might seem refractory to personal handling. Yet in practice the different countries developed different forms of expression. France too made its contribution between 1925 and 1929.

Superficially viewed, from the time of Napoleon I on, France is full of inner contradictions. On the one hand it is the country of obstinate academism in all artistic matters. On the other, the course of painting and construction in the nineteenth century is inconceivable without France. Whatever creative impulses came into the open did so against the will of the majority and in direct conflict with the ruling taste. That they were expressed at all was owing to the vigor of a way of life that France never allowed to be overwhelmed by mechanization.

Around 1920 France ranked as a land altogether bogged in routine in everything pertaining to the house. The extent of the void may be measured by the Paris Exposition Internationale des Arts Décoratifs of 1925.[24] The only display that has not fallen through the historical sieve was the Pavillon de l'Esprit Nouveau, erected by LeCorbusier and Pierre Jeanneret. It was relegated to the outskirts of the exhibition and, as LeCorbusier himself remarked, 'it was the poorest and the most hidden away.' At the Parisian International Exposition of 1867, Edouard Manet had to build a plank hut outside the grounds in order to show his outlawed canvases. One thing was common to both cases: the authorities were ashamed of their artists.

The Pavillon de l'Esprit Nouveau of 1925 was not merely LeCorbusier's protest: 'Nous ne croyons pas à l'art décoratif' (We do not believe in interior decoration). The Pavillon showed what was ready to take the decorator's place. Its creators had a surfeit of problems to set before the public, but little space to display them. The Pavillon was to fulfil the spirited writing of the review *L'Esprit Nouveau*, put out by Ozenfant and LeCorbusier in collaboration with Paul Dermée from 1920 to 1925. It was to speak for the new dwellings with their *plan libre*, for the new painting and the new urbanism. It was designed as a two-story cell of the large apartment houses that LeCorbusier had planned for Paris. How these houses would stand in the city as a whole was shown by a great diorama of Paris, the *Plan Voisin.*

---

[24] Numerous publications and periodicals served to spread the influence of French interior decoration effectively among the greater public in France as well as in America — e.g. the *Larousse, Arts décoratifs modernes, France*, par Gaston Quenioux, Inspecteur Général de l'Enseignement de Dessein, Paris, 1925. The American furniture industry was strongly affected by these publications, and behind most of the bloated and streamlined objects of the 'thirties there lurks the Paris Exhibition of 1925.

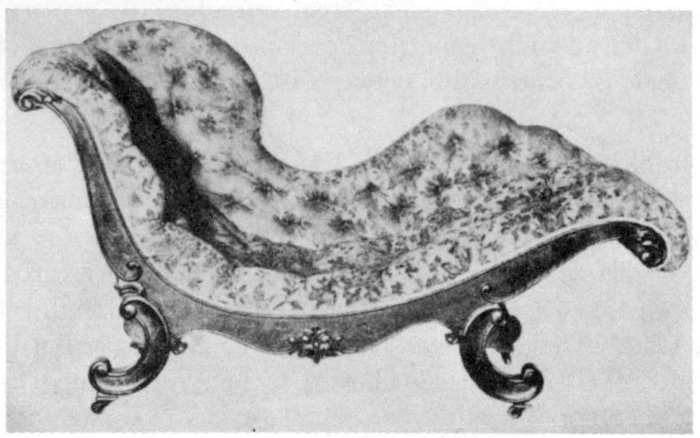

322. American Kangaroo Sofa, Virginia, 1830's. *The Psyche or Kangaroo possesses unconventional curves to conform with the relaxing body.* (*Courtesy Doubleday and Co.*)

The whole interior laid down the new standard. Instead of 'designed' vases of glass or ceramics, there were laboratory jars, forms purified by use and function. Instead of elaborate cut-crystal, there were the simple wine glasses of any French café, objects whose form never ceased to refresh the fantasy of the Cubist painters. Instead of the carpets of interior decoration were the vigorously woven Berber carpets from North Africa, with their simple abstract patterns. Instead of tear-drop chandeliers were stage floodlights or store-window illumination. Instead of the knickknacks of arts and crafts were the mother of pearl spirals of a sea-shell; and on the balustrade of the upper floor, a free-standing sculpture by Jacques Lipchitz.

In the same spirit and as a final touch, the colored walls were hung with paintings by Juan Gris, Fernand Léger, Picasso, Ozenfant, and LeCorbusier. Throughout was the search for a pure, more direct form wherever it might be found: in nature, in laboratories, in Bedouin carpets, in industrial manufacture purified by serial production. This union of seemingly unrelated elements did away with the idea that all the objects of an interior should be designed by one hand. A room is not an incubator to be sterilized of all foreign germs. The forms of life, past and present, shall be given an opportunity to interact.

The atmosphere that can arise from the free interplay of heterogeneous elements is familiar to all those who have set foot in later interiors of our period. It was at the Pavillon de l'Esprit Nouveau, in 1925, that one first saw this so clearly and consistently expressed.

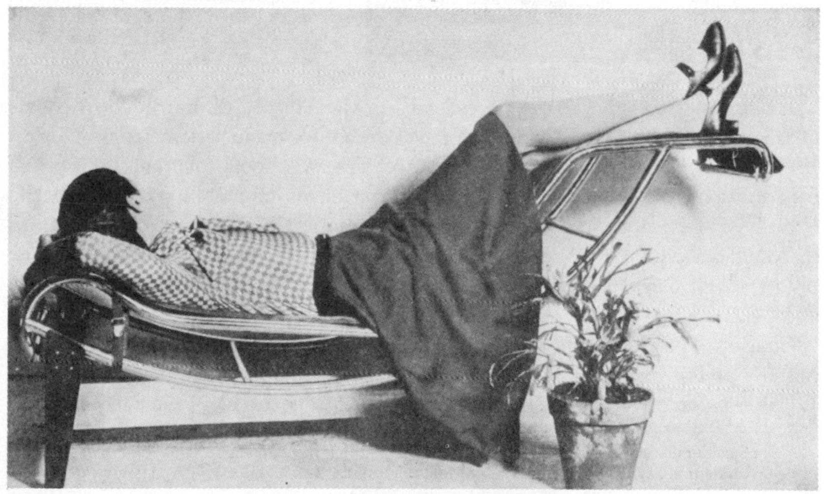

323. LeCORBUSIER AND CHARLOTTE PERRIAND: Lounge, 'Chaise-longue Basculante,' 1929. *This sofa by the distinguished French architects shows an adaptation to the body similar to that of the American 'Kangaroo' sofas a hundred years earlier.*

324. Elastic Cantilever Seat on a Reaper. *To absorb the jolting of rough terrain, the pierced metal reaper seat is resiliently mounted on a steel strip. Its comfortable shape follows the American tradition of wooden saddle seats found on Windsor chairs and rockers. The metal seat and its springy mounting was formed in the* 1880's, *when metal skeleton or tubular construction replaced the clumsy wooden reaper frame.* (*Photo Martin James*)

LeCorbusier recognized the pure forms in the Thonet chairs; his own efforts at this time did not go beyond a reformed design for cushion armchairs. Marcel Breuer's pioneering impulse in tubular chairs was soon followed by French contributions. It is significant how often problems of mobility appear in the French models; not virtuosity in conveying motion by mechanical systems as in American patent furniture; but the use of simple means such as hinges or pivots. Well marked, however, was the effort to bring European furniture out of its rigidity.[25]

Charlotte Perriand, the young French architect, began her work in LeCorbusier's atelier in 1927. She sought to adapt revolving chairs of tubular steel to the boudoir without straying into the merely decorative. She succeeded by

[25] The first tubular steel armchair by Marcel Breuer (1925) was collapsible. Alvar Aalto was also concerned with motion problems. Compare his adjustable tubular lounge (1935) with an American mechanism of 1868, in our section on 'Convertibility' (figs. 263–4).

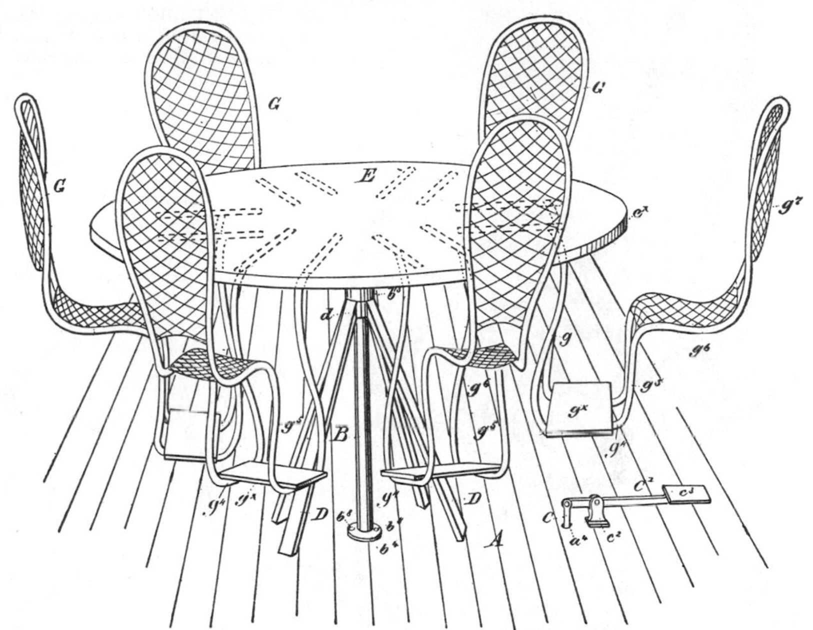

325. Elastic Cantilever Seats for Seagoing Ship Saloons, 1889. *Seats for steamship passengers cantilevered out on rods from the table top. Further independence is given the seat by mounting it on a pivot on which it is free to vibrate, suitably counterbalanced by a weight beneath. The patent is to facilitate the task of serving meals in rough weather. By a pedal* C *the table, chairs, and all are rotated on an axis, bringing the passenger to the waiter.* (*U. S. Patent* 396,089, 15 *January* 1889)

simply wrapping a leather cushion of caterpillar shape around the backrest, a horizontal tube. In type, this chair derives from the traditional Thonet model such as LeCorbusier had shown in his pavillon: but it has by now evolved as a creature in its own right. Its mobility, as in all European furniture, was primitive and its technical devices hardly went beyond the sixteenth century. It is said that LeCorbusier and Charlotte Perriand also planned to lighten the office chair, with its sensitive balance, and adapt it to the living room. But events of recent years interfered.

Most of the standard models resulted from LeCorbusier's collaboration with Pierre Jeanneret and Charlotte Perriand. Such was the 'fauteuil à dossier basculant,' 1928, with pivoted back rest (fig. 321).

The adjustable recliner, or lounge, *chaiselongue basculante* (fig. 323), shows the same freedom from tradition as did the Kangaroo sofa (fig. 322) of the Ameri-

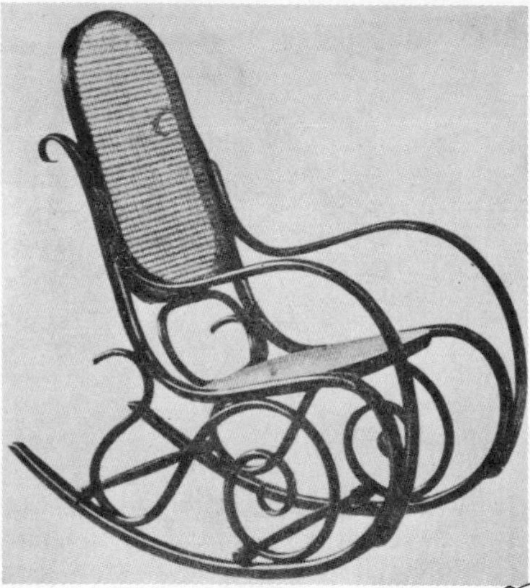

326. THONET BROS.: Rocking Chair No. 1, 1878. Model of 1860. (*Courtesy the Museum of Modern Art, New York*)

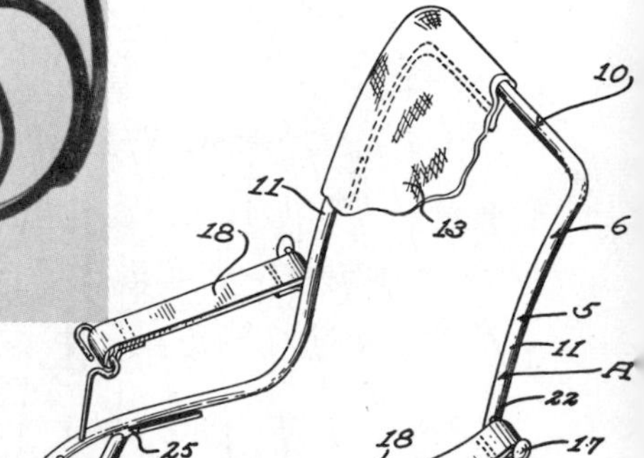

327. American Elastic and Adjustable Cantilever Chair, 1928. '*A lawn chair formed from a single strand of steel* rod . . . *with a shock absorbing or resilient portion.*' *Mies van der Rohe was required to demonstrate the impracticability of this scheme before being granted a patent on his simple-curved tubular chair for domestic use.* (*U.S. Patent* 1,491,918, *filed* 1922; 29 *April* 1924)

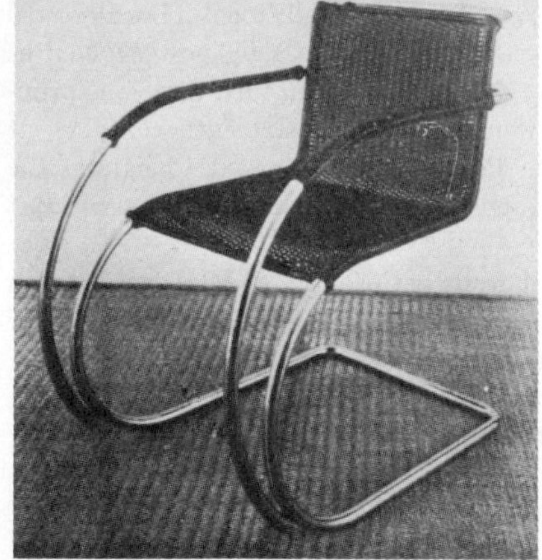

328. MIES VAN DER ROHE: Elastic Cantilever Chair, Tubular Steel, 1927.

cans a century before, which boldly molded to the human body the lines of the rigid Empire sofa or 'psyche.' The *chaiselongue basculante* is adjustable. Its immediate ancestor is the invalid chair formed of two separate parts — an independent base on which is mounted a sitting or lying surface. Such invalid chairs were everywhere to be found in the nineteenth century.

On the broad, black base of the adjustable recliner rests the chromium-tubed upper part, secured at any desired angle by its adherence to two rubber pads on the underframe. Unlike the mobile planes of the invalid chair, the supporting surfaces of the *chaiselongue basculante* are bound in a rigid curve. This means that the sitter must rise to his feet whenever he wishes to alter the slope. And as in much of the furniture of this time, rising is not too easy. Adjustable chairs — the barber's, the office chair, or the adjustable lounge — restore the sitter to the normal position as he rises.

Not the least appeal of the adjustable recliner is its contrast of vigorously curved planes above the single span of the base. Reservations apart, one must admit that a century of effort to make lounges adjustable to the body is here condensed in classical form. It should be mentioned that France did not further develop the cantilever chair.

329. MART STAM: The First Modern Cantilever Chair, Jointed Piping, 1926. (*Adolf G. Schneck,* Der Stuhl, *Stuttgart,* 1928)

330. MARCEL BREUER: Elastic Cantilever Chair, Closed Steel Tube, 1929. *The idea of the resilient cantilever chair was in the air during the 'twenties. Mies van der Rohe's formulation stresses resilience, while Mart Stam's achieves the cantilever form. The idea then returned to Breuer, who, synthesizing the two features, reached the form that has become standard today.* (*Courtesy the Museum of Modern Art, New York*)

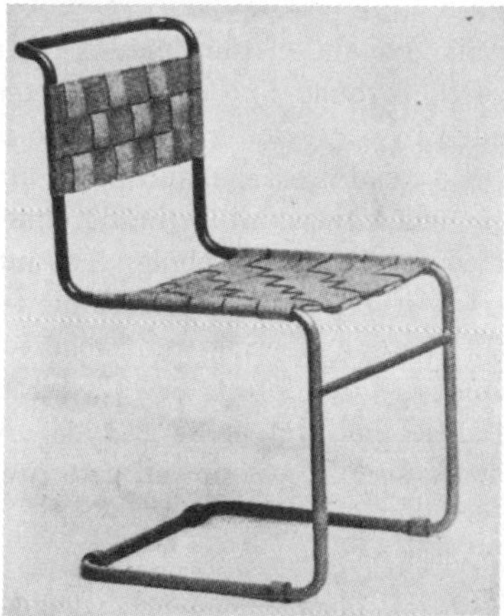

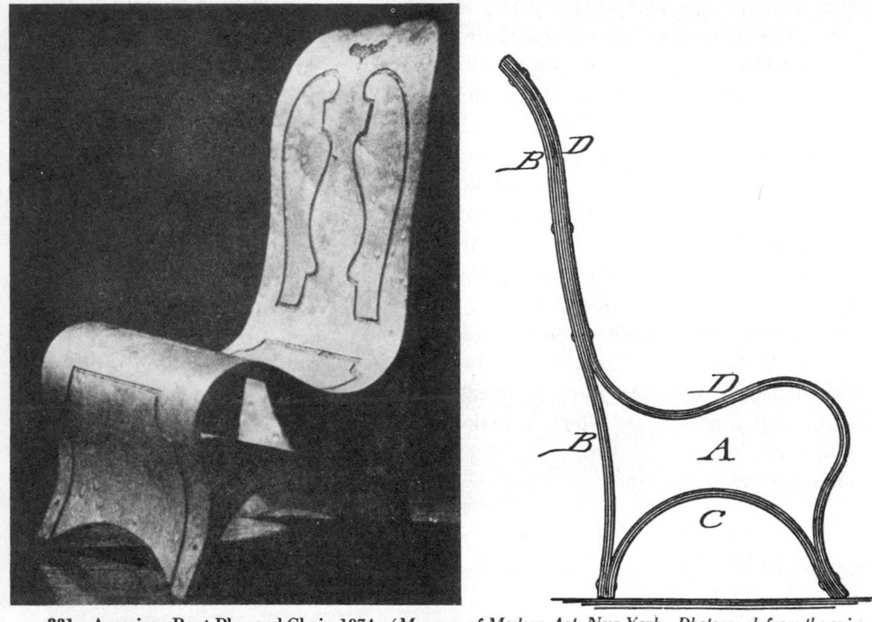

331. American Bent Plywood Chair, 1874. (*Museum of Modern Art, New York. Photograph from the original U.S. Patent Office model*)

332. American Bent Plywood Chair, 1874. Cross Section. *The chair is made of three sections of laminated wood. 'Obtained by pressing several layers of veneer into forms of corresponding shape. If three layers of veneer are used, the grain of the middle one runs crosswise to that of the outer layers. The elasticity and strength of the veneers are thereby considerably increased.'* (*U.S. Patent* 148,350, 10 *March* 1874)

The Cantilever Plywood Chair

The cantilever chair is rooted in a specific demand of the time. A chair was sought that would seem to hover above the ground like cantilever concrete slabs or houses on stilts, houses surrounded by air. One was drawn to things that seemed to defeat gravitation. This emotional need is as innate to our own time as the buttress to the Gothic and the undulating wall to the Baroque.

In material, cantilever chairs were not confined to steel tubing. The interest in new techniques led to cantilever chairs of wood. The impulse came from a borderland of our civilization, Finland. There lumbering and woodworking form the very basis of life. Finland abounds in birch forest, and the birch tree yields a soft pliable wood whose potentialities had yet to be grasped. Many are the lands endowed with a generous wood supply, yet not all give rise to a

333. ALVAR AALTO: Cantilever Chair of Laminated Plywood, c.1937. *It was the Finnish architect Alvar Aalto who first dared to use laminated wood in a cantilever-chair construction. The wood is curved by machine and steam process, then sawed into narrower sections. The slab forms its constituent principle. (Photo Herbert Matter, courtesy Museum of Modern Art)*

new artistic impulse. It required a stimulus that does not derive from the soil alone. The man who brought to life an age-old, primitive tradition in Finland was the architect Alvar Aalto. He never lived outside Finland for long. After his first appearance at the International Congress for Modern Architecture, in 1929, nearly every year saw him in some part of Europe and later in America. He needed to settle nowhere, for his tentacles were feeling everywhere. He knows what is being built and painted. Like the sculptor, Calder, but in the field of architecture and furniture, Aalto mastered the expression of our time and fused it with the things of his native surroundings. This alliance of the regional with the language born of a period has been fruitful in every age.

Aalto's starting point was the cantilever chair of tubular steel. His first model (1931) has a steel-tube frame on which is screwed a curved plywood slab forming the seat and back. The frame recalls Breuer's stacking stool of 1926, but stood on end. The original feature of this chair is its curved plywood slab, used as an element of construction — for the back, part of this single slab was laminated and unsupported.

This resilient plywood slab foreshadows Aalto's next step: the cantilever chair made of wood. Here he utilized the elasticity peculiar to birchwood, a springiness that the Northern countries had formerly used only in skis. For its bearing elements, Aalto chose laminated wood of suitable thickness (fig. 333). In outline it is identical with the tubular cantilever chair. These laminated strips, forming in one continuous line the 'runners,' legs, arms, and frame to carry the back rest, are first bent by steam and machinery into broad curved slabs, then sawed up into narrower sections. Two of these sections are bridged by a pad seat or one of curved plywood.

The bearing elements of the Aalto chair are not of an unambiguous skeleton construction, as the tubular chairs; the supporting sections by origin, and perhaps by mechanical function, are to be regarded as slabs.

Bent plywood chairs, where a single curved slab forms the back, seat, and leg sections, are found in America during the 'seventies. The Museum of Modern Art, New York, owns an inventor's model of 1874, saved from the riddance-auction of the American Patent Office[20] (figs. 331, 332). 'The chair is made of several parts which are obtained by pressing several layers of veneer of suitable size and thickness into forms of corresponding shape. If three layers of veneer are used, the grain of the middle one runs crosswise to that of the outer layers . . . the elasticity and strength of the veneers are thereby increased considerably . . . The chair is made of three parts . . . and the front part . . . extends up over the upper part of the back.'[21]

Directions for the bending of plywood sheets to the human body and for sawing them appear long before Aalto's chairs in many American woodworker's handbooks. In Holland also, G. Rietveld curved slabs of plywood or fiber and fixed them between iron rods. But no one exploited the resiliency that Aalto drew from the Finnish birch. No one dared to use laminated wood in cantilever construction. Which was decisive here, form or technique?

None of the moderns knew what tremendous pioneer work America had accomplished in this field; work that lay buried and forgotten in its own land.

It is the problem of resilient seating that appears again in the wooden chair. But only in its later European form, for the early American models such as that

[20] U.S. Patent 148,350, 10 Mar. 1874.

[21] Ibid. Patent Specification.

334. JENS RISOM: Dining Chair, 1940. *All joints are machined for mass production.* (*Courtesy H. G. Knoll Associates, New York*)

335. Chicago School of Design: Z-Chair Based on the Wood Spring, *c.*1940. *A specially treated, laminated plywood in connection with the Z-spring permits double rocking action. The introduction of materials and processes from the new industries such as aviation opens the way to new possibilities.* (*Courtesy Institute of Design, Chicago*)

of 1874 were non-resilient. Resilient seating — as we noted in the American patent movement — means relaxation through slight variations of posture.

The attempt was made in the Bauhaus at Dessau to bend plywood for seats and back rests, to utilize its resilient qualities when mounted on regular four-legged chair frames (1928).[22]

Meanwhile, the aviation industry found new methods of bonding the plywood lamina, as by resin glue. Aalto still had to steam-curve his plywood. Resin glue permits dry bonding, by electrical means with hydraulic pressure. This opens fresh possibilities to the constructor. From 1939 on, the Institute of Design in Chicago, under the leadership of L. Moholy-Nagy, made extensive trials, seeking to raise the elasticity and resilience of plywood, and at the same time to inject a degree of mobility into the system as a whole. Experiments

[22] *Bauhaus* 1919–28, edited by H. Bayer, W. Gropius, I. Gropius, New York, The Museum of Modern Art, 1938, p.133.

with plywood chairs were methodologically knit into the program of studies. Flat sheets of various materials are to be given a three-dimensional structure. By such manipulations as bending, embossing, etc., the structural properties of the material can be changed. In this way Charles Niedringhaus and others produced models such as one on 'runners,' having a sharp *Z* profile (fig. 335), whose plywood seat permits slight variations in posture. The younger generation of American architects, such as Eero Saarinen and Charles Eames, combine production-line methods with sensitive designs.

In closing, we should not pass over the question: Was it only the demand for new techniques that gave fresh life to the wooden material and set free its hidden potentialities? The causes go deeper than that; to the trend toward the organic that asserted itself in the early 'thirties and gained strength in following years. We want around us objects that bear the trace of life. Bark, grotesque roots, shells, fossils. Things that have passed through time and tide. Painting again gives objective confirmation when, in the early 'thirties, the work of Joan Miro or Hans Arp betrays a growing drift to the organic. Joan Miro wins freedom of expression by the use of organic forms, sometimes rounded and fishlike, sometimes snakelike, often calligraphic symbols, but always freely floating in space without naturalistic moorings. And Hans Arp cuts his wooden forms on the bandsaw, placing them by the rule of chance — 'objets placés à la loi du hazard.'

The Diffusion

We have but roughly outlined the beginnings of the movement that sought to bridge the split of a century between expression and construction. The development, in pace with the new architecture, matured rapidly, the tubular chair appearing from 1925 to 1929 and the cantilever plywood chair directly afterwards.

It is distinctly a furniture of types. The chairs, tables, cupboards, beds, desks, bookshelves, and combination furniture — of which we shall say nothing here — all had to be formulated afresh. Unlike the true furniture of the nineteenth century, the furniture of the engineer, these new types no longer stood in an alien setting. The architects first created the surrounding spaces, and then, from the same spatial feeling, their furniture. The types are conceived in functional terms. They may call new materials into use, or use traditional materials in new ways, but their vigor is above all one of esthetic invention, one rooted in feeling. They rapidly spread through Europe during the 'thirties. We must unfortunately pass over the details of their progress.[23]

With the mid-'thirties came a lull in the invention of new types. A not inconsiderable factor was that the architects whose names we associate with the new types were called to more urgent tasks: greater buildings, urbanism, and large-scale planning in which interest was growing. To the field they left, this was a loss, but from a broader point of view, a favorable portent — architects at the same time formulating chairs and shaping cities: A sign that the architect's vocation is one of the first in our time to transcend specialization and to approach problems in a universal way.

At a time when the Continental countries, from Spain to Sweden, were awakening to their self-inflicted surroundings, the two great lands of nineteenth-century enterprise fell into inactivity. Following the death of William Morris and the wane of Arts and Crafts, England began to slumber in architecture and in furniture. The last manifestation of international scope was McIntosh and the Scottish school. In America at this time the late Louis Sullivan and Frank Lloyd Wright were non-existent to the public mind. The center of gravity shifted to the Continent, and here the new architecture and the new interior were formulated.

America, which in the nineteenth century made such pioneering attempts in the field of furniture, is altogether missing from the decisive phases of the 'twenties. In the whole movement and its direction we believe America's absence can be felt. America not only lost all enthusiasm for the furniture of the engineer, its combinability and its mobility; there was also a falling away of interest in the rooms in which we eat and relax.

At a time when Europe was beginning to take stock of her architecture and interiors, America gave way to a growing penchant for 'antiques.' Industry

---

[23] Thus Sweden, guided by men such as Gregor Paulsen, the historian, and Asplund, the architect, began to take leave of its sugary and popular arts and crafts. This occurred when the Swedish Werkbund (arts and crafts society) held its bold exposition in Stockholm in 1930.

The Swiss, whose architectural campaigns started in the 'twenties, took the decisive step with the Neubühl Settlement (1932) of the Zurich Werkbund. This settlement was founded under the auspices of the Swiss Werkbund through the collective efforts of the Swiss members of International Congresses for Modern Architecture (CIAM) — M. E. Haefeli, W. M. Moser, E. Roth, R. Steiger, H. Schmidt, and others. At the same time, 'Wohnbedarf' (standards for the interior) was established in Zürich to test and put into production the furniture designs of leading Swiss and European architects. Its furniture was intended for the middle class and great care was taken to turn out 'popular' models (*Volksmodelle*).

From 1921 on, the Italians held their Triennial Expositions, seeking time and again to give currency to the ideas of the modern movement. But in contrast to results in Sweden and Switzerland, the Italians never succeeded in reaching the greater public. In Spain the organizing talent of J. L. Sert brought Barcelona to the forefront. And finally the British joined the movement in 1937 with the Burlington Gallery Exhibition. The initiative was taken by architects of the MARS (Modern Architectural Research) — British section of the CIAM.

produced the same types, in various guises, over and again. The shapes became dulled; forms lost their original vitality, became vague and indefinite, as when colors run into one another on the palette.

America in this time of full mechanization looked away from the living rooms and turned toward mechanization of the household. Now the rooms in which one dwelt, the things of one's surroundings, were for the most part left out of discussion. The kitchen, the bathroom, and labor-saving devices roused the imagination. And inventiveness, formerly embodied in patent furniture, flows into mechanization of the household, where America takes the unchallenged lead.

PART VI MECHANIZATION ENCOUNTERS THE HOUSEHOLD

MECHANIZATION ENCOUNTERS THE HOUSEHOLD

Mechanization in industry meant the change from handicraft to machine work. But machines were not enough. They had to be integrated one with another, calling for organization of the work processes in the shape of the assembly line and scientific management.

So it was with the mechanization of the household. America had outstripped all other countries in mechanizing the complicated craft. Cooking and housekeeping are likewise complicated crafts. And if, turning to household mechanization, we ask how it has progressed and what were its defects, the United States again will yield us the most adequate insight, even if many impulses and inventions came from England and the Continent.

The house and the factory are not in every way comparable. One can hardly speak of household 'production.' The factory and the household have only one factor in common, but a crucial one. Both must improve organization and curtail waste labor. This is the goal to which the whole development tends.

The curtailing of household labor is achieved through the mechanization of work processes once performed by hand, mainly cleaning operations: laundering, ironing, dishwashing, carpet sweeping, furniture cleaning. To these must be added mechanized heating and refrigerating processes.

Improvements in organization are achieved by closely reviewing old established work processes and ordering them in a more rational way.

From what we have seen so far, it would not be strange if mechanization of the household work process came about during the 'sixties of the last century. Which is indeed the case.

The Feminist Movement and the Rational Household

The Status of Woman

Curtailed household drudgery and improved organization lead to greater independence, that is, to the enfranchisement of the housewife and ultimately to the family-serviced home, the servantless household.

The mechanization of the household had its starting point in social problems: the status of American women and the status of domestic servants. The Feminist

Movement, Abolitionism, and the servant problem all are rooted in the notion that a democracy can suffer no disfranchised class, no privileged sex.

All these problems agitated America at the time of the Civil War, while Europe, having put down all its revolutions, clung to a pseudo-feudalistic class system.

American women held aloof, nevertheless, from such radical projects as the Saint-Simonians in France of the 'thirties put forward and practiced, or from Fourier's plan of a society in which *la loi de l'attraction* was to govern relations between the sexes.

American women are less open to such views. They seek their rights within the family framework, an attitude harking back to the Puritan way of life. Woman shall rule in the household. She shall be educated for this, and to this she shall educate her children. Marriage forms one fulcrum of her power, education the other. Ruling both, her power automatically expands.

American women opposed radical solutions, but they wanted political responsibility. They fought for it stubbornly between 1848 and 1918. And if educating women for marriage as a vocation is rooted in Puritan conceptions of the family, the quest for political equality stems from Quaker views. The Quakers have always regarded women as the equals of men.

American women 'hold that the natural head of the conjugal association is man,' the conservative Alexis de Tocqueville told Europe in his famous *De la Démocratie en Amérique* (1835). This contrasts curiously today with the Declaration of Sentiments agreed upon by the Quakers in 1848 at one of their yearly meetings: 'The history of mankind is a history of repeated injuries and usurpations on the part of man toward woman, having as direct object the establishment of a direct tyranny over her.'[1] In the Quaker's view, 'it is the duty of women to secure to themselves their sacred right to the elective franchise.'[2]

Female Education and the Feminist Question

One side of feminism, the wresting of political responsibility, lies beyond our present scope. The other side, the assuming of domestic responsibility, leads us straight to our problem, the rational household.

This rationalization was guided by spiritual motives. And its goals were seen before the practical means of attaining them were at hand.

Such goals do not arise in the void. Usually they are announced by a prophetic

---

[1] E. C. Stanton, S. B. Anthony, and M. J. Gage, *History of Woman Suffrage*, New York, 1881, vol. I, p.70.

[2] Ibid. p.72.

personality. Here the main lines were traced by Catherine Esther Beecher (1800–1878). Like so many reformers, Catherine Beecher came from a New England minister's family. She approached the household as Emerson his *Essays*, or their contemporary Sylvester Graham the art of breadmaking. Housekeeping for her was not an isolated problem, but one that grew out of the feminine question as a whole. The generation born around 1800 came to its tasks with something of that eighteenth-century universalism which often lasted into the first half of the nineteenth.

In 1841 Catherine Beecher published a *Treatise on Domestic Economy*. Although intended as a 'text-book for female schools,' it met with extraordinary success. The work does not start with cooking recipes. It opens with a chapter on 'The Peculiar Responsibilities of the American Woman.'

She raises her questions in the very preface: 'In what respects are women subordinate? Wherein are they superior and equal in influence?' This woman, who at the age of twenty-one already taught domestic economy in an institution of her own founding, blamed her sex's many disappointments on the fact that 'women are not trained for their profession.'

Her *Domestic Economy* carefully weighs the problems facing the women of 1840. Before coming to her subject, she could not help discussing human physiology. Without such an understanding, it seemed to her, practical rules were bound to be mere patchwork.

She treated in detail practical household tasks — how to cook, wash, clean, how to furnish the home, or choose vegetables and trees for the garden. As for kitchen recipes, there were none. They were published later, separately. Her every word shows that efficient housekeeping was not an end in itself. It was but an instrument to be properly mastered; and above all it was the medium through which she hoped to guide American women to their responsibilities.

In a speech to American women in the 1840's, Catherine Beecher pointed to the 'evils suffered by American women and American children.'[3] She dealt with the female lot among all classes of society. She told of '10,000 women in New York living by needle work, who by working twelve to fourteen hours can earn only twelve-and-half cents.' She has seen a 'New York office opened to aid domestics in finding places' where in 'a large room so crowded that she could think of nothing but a slave market,' servants were selected like chickens on a counter. She investigated living conditions among the workers at the Lowell textile mills (regarded as a model factory settlement in her time) and differed in her conclusions from Charles Dickens, who had visited them some

[3] *The Education of the Rising Generation*, Address to the Women of Cincinnati, 1846.

years earlier. The fourteen-hour day, she found, was toil beyond the girls' endurance: 'At five the bells called for labor. . . . Work prosecuted without remission till twelve . . . then half an hour allowed for dinner and work till seven o'clock.' And finally she came to 'another class of evils endured by a large class of well-educated, unmarried women of the more wealthy classes. . . . It is the suffering which results from inactivity.'

Catherine Beecher's aim was not the achievement of outward power. She was thoroughly opposed to feminism in the political field. Her goal was to give women self-assurance and confidence in their profession. That is why all her life she demanded that 'domestic economy' be taught in the schools as a science no less than physics and mathematics. Only properly trained women could rise to the status for which they were destined.

The Servant Problem

With the same forthrightness, Catherine E. Beecher faced the servant problem. She saw here a social issue almost beyond solution in America. She was sensitive to the basic paradox of 'domestic service' within a democratic state.

'There is no point where the women of this country need more wisdom than in relation to those whom they employ in their services,' she wrote in 1841 in her chapter 'On the Care of Domestics.' 'The subject is attended with many difficulties. The peculiar trials which American women suffer from this source are the necessary evils connected with our most valuable civil blessings.' [4]

With her sister, Harriet Beecher Stowe, author of *Uncle Tom's Cabin*, she completely rewrote her textbook on domestic economy. The new version, dedicated to the 'American woman' and entitled *The American Woman's Home*, appeared in 1869. Here the earlier fragmentary hints were elaborated: 'Every human being stands (according to the Declaration of Independence) on the same level. . . . There are no hereditary titles, no monopolies, no privileged classes. . . . All are to be free to rise and to fall as the waves of the sea. . . . The condition of domestic service, however, still retains about it something of the influence from feudal times.' [5]

The pseudo-feudalistic conditions then prevalent in Europe are brought out by comparison of America with England: 'In England the class who go to service *are* a class and service is a profession. . . . In America domestic service is a spring-stone to something higher.' [6]

---

[4] *A Treatise on Domestic Economy*, p.204.

[5] Catherine E. Beecher and Harriet Beecher Stowe, *The American Woman's Home*, New York, 1869, p.318.

[6] Ibid. p.321.

The authors did not avoid the issue: 'Now, what is the matter with domestic service? . . . We cannot in this country maintain to any great extent large retinues of servants. . . . Every mistress of a family knows that her cares increase, with every additional servant.' Their verdict is unequivocal: 'A moderate style of housekeeping, small, compact and simple domestic establishments must necessarily be the general order of life in America.'[7] And finally they point to the solution: 'This being the case, it should be an object in America to exclude from the labors of the family all that can be . . . excluded out of it by combined labor.'[8]

Even today, one could hardly state the problem more trenchantly. By force of circumstance, reality is gradually moving toward this state. Sampling at random the views expressed around 1910, we learn that the servant problem is to be solved' 'on the same plane as in other employments,' and as a direct result, 'we are gradually coming to the abolishment of a permanent serving class in our homes.'[9] Meanwhile the problem increasingly shifted into the psychological sphere. 'There is a very strong case against the presence of the permanent worker in the home. . . .' She forces 'psychological adjustment . . . on the homemaker and on the entire family. . . . In many cases the standard of the home is consciously or unconsciously made less simple or adapted to the expectation and demands of the worker.'[10] All this points back to Miss Beecher's proposal of 1869, that housework should be divided up so far as possible among the members of the family. In 1915 more pressing reasons are given: 'The servantless household (by servantless is meant without resident workers) offers the only opportunity for a family to follow *the exact standards* . . . and enables a family cooperation and a chance for training the children.'[11] The prerequisites for such a solution were supplied only when mechanization made it possible to reduce manual drudgery to a minimum.

Organization of the Work Process

One must not confuse organization of the work process with the use of mechanized tools. Organization of the work process, it should be stressed, was underway before mechanized tools became available. These were not universal even in households of 1940. Household planning, then, began before household

[7] Catherine E. Beecher and Harriet Beecher Stowe, *The American Woman's Home*, New York, 1869, p.333.

[8] Ibid. p.334.

[9] Christine Frederick, 'The New Housekeeping,' *Ladies Home Journal*, 1912, vol. 29, no. 12, p.16.

[10] Frederick, *Household Engineering; Scientific Management in the Home*, Chicago, 1919; first issued in 1915.

[11] Ibid. p.380.

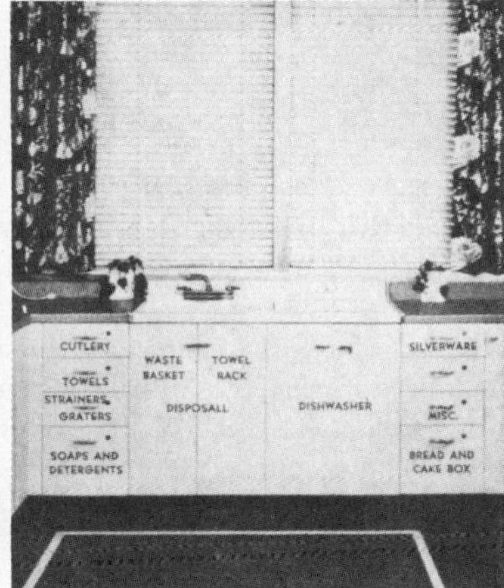

336. Continuous Working Surfaces: Preparation and Cleaning Center of Kitchen, by Catherine Beecher, 1869. *The tendency to view the housewife's work as a craft or a vocation arose in the New England Puritan environment.*

Well-lighted surfaces of minimal size at waist height, with storage center beneath. Drawers for rye and coarse Graham flour used in breadmaking. Lid of flour barrel fits flush with other surfaces. The molding board turns over to form a preparation surface over the sink. (Catherine Beecher, The American Woman's Home, *New York,* 1869)

337. Continuous Working Surfaces: Preparation and Cleaning Center of Electric Kitchen, 1942. *In the mechanized kitchen of today, three working centers are acknowledged: storage and preservation; cleaning and preparation; cooking and serving. Two of these centers, storage-preservation and cooking-serving were clearly distinguished by Catherine Beecher in 1869, and treated as units. (Courtesy General Electric Corp., Schenectady, N. Y.)*

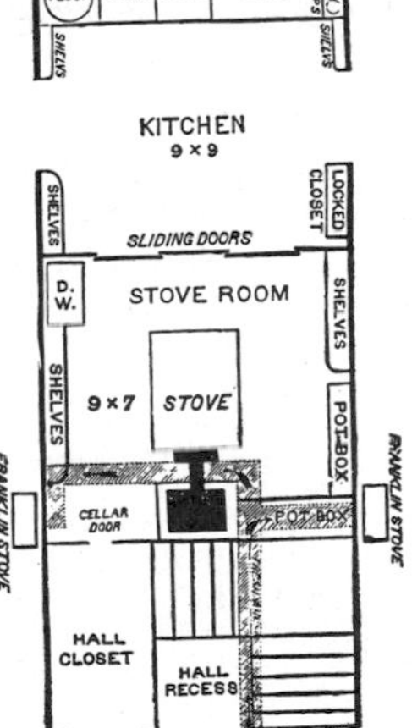

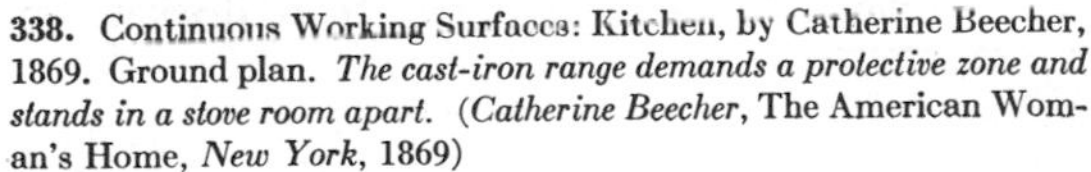

338. Continuous Working Surfaces: Kitchen, by Catherine Beecher, 1869. Ground plan. *The cast-iron range demands a protective zone and stands in a stove room apart. (Catherine Beecher,* The American Woman's Home, *New York,* 1869)

mechanization. As they arose the mechanical aids found a ready place within the science of housekeeping.

Organization of the work process emerged toward the end of the 'sixties.

Organization of the Work Process, 1869

Catherine E. Beecher had grasped the essentials of the trend (1869): 'The cook's galley in the steamship has every article and utensil used in cooking for 200 persons in a space . . . so arranged that with one or two steps the cook can reach all he uses.' [12]

When the modern architects in their turn recognized the importance of the well-planned kitchen after 1920, they took the dining-car galley as a prototype; but this did not exist when Catherine Beecher wrote her book. As we have seen, George Pullman applied for a patent covering his rudimentary dining car in the same year, 1869.

'In contrast to this,' she continues, 'the cooking materials and utensils, the sink and the eating room are at such distances apart that half the time and strength is employed in walking back and forth to collect and return the articles used.' [13] How to her mind the organization of the work process might be tackled, she shows in careful drawings and descriptions (figs. 336, 338).

The large table and the isolated dresser, one first notices, have disappeared from her kitchen. Instead of the table, more compact working surfaces extend beneath the windows. Instead of the dresser, there are shelves, drawers, and receptacles beneath the working surfaces.

In the mechanized kitchen of today, three working centers are acknowledged (fig. 337): storage and preservation; cleaning and preparation; cooking and serving. Two of these centers, preservation-storage and cooking-serving were clearly distinguished by Catherine Beecher in 1869, and treated as units. The cooking range, however, still had to stand apart within a protective zone.

At the same time she brings together the implement and its working place.

Her working surfaces are well lighted and no larger than necessary. On the left the cover of the large flour bin stands flush with the working surface, continuous with it at waist-height. The housewife has only to raise the lid and sprinkle flour on the adjacent 'board for molding bread.' We are still in the time when the American housewife — as against the European — baked her bread at home. 'The true housewife,' Catherine Beecher says elsewhere, 'makes her bread the sovereign of the kitchen.' [14] Understandably, then, drawers for

[12] Beecher and Stowe, op.cit. p.33.

[13] Ibid.

[14] Ibid. p.35.

barley and coarse wheat flour, used in Graham or barley bread, slide beneath the working surfaces. Beneath these, but not so handily located, are further ingredient drawers.

The board 'for molding bread' may turn over for the preparation of meat or vegetables. And the surface next to it, the 'dish drainer,' is on hinges so that it may either 'rest on the preparation surface ('cook-form,' as Miss Beecher calls it) 'or be turned over and cover the sink.'

This is 1869, the pre-plumbing period. So Catherine Beecher devises her own running water; near the sink are 'two pumps for well and for rain water.'

'The width of the sink matches the cook-form,' she expressly says. Thus storage and preparation-cleaning are gathered around a single center. In these respects she goes beyond the stage of 1910, which conceived the table, dresser and range as self-contained elements to be placed side by side.

To avoid discomfort in summer and to cut down kitchen odors, Catherine Beecher places the range in a room apart, which glazed sliding-doors divide from the preparation room.

Organization of the Work Process after 1910

Anonymous phases link the development of the 'sixties with the next decisive moves made around 1910. These sound steps of the 'seventies and 'eighties toward kitchen planning in line with American needs are as yet uninvestigated.[15] To enquire into them would be a rewarding task.

Now, over four decades after Catherine Beecher's clear framing of the problem, there took place a further elaboration down to the most minute details.

The American woman had meanwhile won all that Catherine Beecher had claimed and perhaps more. The influence of woman in American life had become stronger than in other countries, and more than in any other land became responsible for the sound as well as for the doubtful trends.

This reorganization of the household undertook, it is true, to set free the 'all tired out woman with no energy left.'[16] But the impulse had its roots elsewhere: in scientific management. Surveying the growth of the assembly line, we spoke of scientific management and its analysis of the work process, research that around 1910 was yielding impressive results. It brought people to observe afresh age-old domestic tasks, especially in the kitchen; it suggested motion studies of single appliances and analysis of overall kitchen planning.

---

[15] See *Space, Time and Architecture*, pp.288–9, for a few examples of the 'seventies and 'eighties, showing how America gave expression to the cook's and housewife's problems in the plan and arrangement of the kitchen.

[16] Frederick, *The New Housekeeping, Efficiency Studies in Home Management*, New York, 1913, preface.

339. Industry Becomes Interested: The Organized Cupboard, 1923. *American industry began to organize the working process in the kitchen after a long succession of reformers had explored the question. The manufacturers of kitchen furniture began the trend that gas and electricity companies took up more systematically in the 'thirties. The early effort is toward space-saving, compression. Note the breakfast nook. A single subdivided cabinet holds utensils, staples, cleaning equipment.* (*Courtesy* Kitchen Maid, *catalogue* 1923)

When Frederick W. Taylor raised the efficiency of coal-shoveling by analyzing each of the worker's movements and improving them accordingly; or when Frank B. Gilbreth raised the efficiency of bricklaying by the reduction of stooping and a rational arrangement of the tools, American housewives questioned the efficiency of their own work, began to observe their movements, to count their steps as they went about their daily routine. Doubtless, a household could not be managed like a factory; but clearly too the only escape from drudgery was through precise analysis.

The idea was in the air. Farmers' wives were thinking about it. And quite early, in 1909, a farm woman gave her 'plan of a small house designed particularly to insure the saving of steps in housework.' [17] When in the autumn of 1912 Christine Frederick, one of the first women to concern herself with 'bringing the science of efficiency to the home,' published her series on 'The New House-

[17] *The Journal of Home Economics*, vol. I, no. 3, p.313, Baltimore, June 1909.

340 a, b. Continuous Working Surfaces: Kitchen of Haus am Horn, Bauhaus, Weimar, 1923. *One of the first kitchens designed by the architect, as an integrated unit within the modern house. On the long wall are a plain kitchen sink, and a sideboard separated into base cabinet and wall cabinet. The broad working surface beneath the swing window is continued by the gas-range top, which is extended in turn by a working surface. The working surfaces total those of a kitchen two or three times greater. The fully utilized window area recalls the American Craftsman kitchens around* 1910.

keeping' in the *Ladies Home Journal*, widespread interest was aroused. The editors headed each installment with a reference to scientific management. The following year Christine Frederick expanded her articles into a book; its chatty preface tells how her husband's casual conversation with one of the new efficiency engineers had suggested the applying of scientific management to her daily household routine.

'Didn't I with hundreds of women stoop unnecessarily over kitchen tables, sinks and ironing boards, as well as bricklayers stoop over bricks?' [18]

She had already given the answer in her articles beginning with dishwashing: 'For years I never realized that I actually made 80 wrong motions in the washing alone, not counting others in the sorting, wiping, and laying away.[19]

'Do we not waste time by walking in poorly arranged kitchens? . . . Could

[18] Frederick, *Housekeeping with Efficiency*, New York, 1913, preface.

[19] Frederick, 'The New Housekeeping,' *The Ladies Home Journal*, vol. 29, no. 9, Philadelphia, Sept. 1912.

not the housework train be despatched from station to station, from task to task?'[20] One easily follows in this readable book how she took over the principles one by one from the factory and applied them to the household. And elaborating her point of view, a few years later she chose a title in itself revealing: *Household Engineering, Scientific Management in the Home.* Now the word 'household engineering' enters instead of 'domestic science' or 'home economics.'[21]

Organization of the Work Process in Europe around 1927

Cautiously and belatedly in Europe, factories ventured into scientific management. Often the smaller scale allowed but little scope for these methods: few European manufacturers had a mass market. The inquiry into home management, pushed so vigorously in America around 1912, passed almost unnoticed or tucked away in lesser European publications.[22]

Household organization in Europe found its starting point elsewhere: within the new architectural movement. In the nineteenth-century kitchen and bath, the plan of the house, its very organization, had bowed before decorative ambitions. Cutting away the false-front economy, the young architectural movement based itself upon the functional. This limitation proved a most beneficial cure.

The Continental trend, then, stemmed neither from industry nor from scientific management. Its mover was the architect. The architect re-stated the whole problem of the house, and reconquered the position he had lost in the nineteenth century. He became once more the specialist to build a framework for living. He opened up the house, re-shaped its interior space, created its furniture types, and found his own social awareness. No longer isolated, the

---

[20] Frederick, *Housekeeping with Efficiency*, preface.

[21] The initiative in household reform, the 'home economics movement,' proceeded from the Women's Congress called at the Chicago Exhibition of 1893. This Congress resolved that 'matters pertaining to the household had not kept up with the procession of progress,' and to remedy matters founded the National Household Economic Association. Together with numerous women's clubs, this Association, predecessor of the American Home Economics Association, aided the reform mainly by founding schools of domestic science and urging the introduction of such studies into public schools. Cf. *The Journal of Home Economics*, Baltimore, April 1909, vol. 1, no. 2, p.185. A short sketch of this movement in America will be found in J. Bévier and S. Usher, *The Home Economics Movement*, Part 1, Boston, 1906. The main goals of the movement were then stated by its leader, Mrs. Ellen H. Richards: 'The utilization of all the resources of modern science to improve the home life' (ibid. p.21).

The idea of 'household engineering' also originated, among others, with the classical investigator of movement, Frank B. Gilbreth, who in 1912 expressed the hope 'that teachers of home economics and housekeepers may be able to apply [the principles of scientific management] in some measure to the solution of their problems' (*Principles of Scientific Management*, p.4, 1938 edition).

[22] Irene Witte, *Heim und Technik in Amerika*, Berlin, 1928.

kitchen grows out of the organism of the house. This outlook led very early to an organization of the work process.

In 1923 the Bauhaus at Weimar invited the public to a first view of its efforts in a display of work by masters and students, dramatic performances and festivals. A one-family house, Das Haus am Horn, was erected for this occasion.[23] The Haus am Horn had a kitchen conceived as an L-shaped unit and designed with architectonic consistency (figs. 340). Its starting point was the storage center: A plain kitchen sink and sideboard were placed to the long wall, the sideboard being already split up into two elements, the base cabinet and the wall cabinet. The window space is fully utilized, recalling the American Craftsman kitchens around 1910. A broad working surface runs beneath the swing window and flush with this extends the top of the gas range, extended in turn by a surface such as was to appear on American ranges in the early 'thirties.

What strikes one looking at this, perhaps the earliest example of the kitchen in which organization is joined to form, is the close co-ordination of the storage, the cleaning-preparation, and the cooking centers, favored by surfaces and appliances at equal heights. Neither should one overlook the free-hanging wall cabinets that turn the corners.

Germany in the 'twenties enjoyed a woefully brief time of cultural creativeness. Talent from everywhere was attracted and put to work. In architecture, too, Germany proved hospitable to the new movement. From 1919 on, in keeping with the Dutch example, housing projects went up for the working and middle classes. At Frankfurt in the large-scale housing development headed by Ernst May in the later 'twenties, Dutch, Swiss, and Austrian architects were called in to assist and speed the development.

Good will toward the new movement was nowhere better expressed than when the German Workbund decided on its settlement at Weissenhof, near Stuttgart, and Mies van der Rohe called upon young foreign architects to build by the side of their German colleagues. Among these was the Dutchman J. J. P. Oud, who will long be remembered as the first to regard workers' dwellings as an artistic concern, a problem to be met not by columns and ornament, but by a carefully worked-out plan providing low-cost rooms with dignity and a maximum of comfort (1919). Oud built a row of houses at the Weissenhof settlement, and there were created the kitchens that, despite their simplicity, found the solution taken for granted today (fig. 341). At first glance the elementary boards and planks suggest few links with the chromium plate, the shining enamel, and highly mechanized kitchen of 1940. Yet in their organization they already held

[23] Adolf Meyer, *Ein Versuchshaus des Bauhauses in Weimar* (*Bauhausbücher #3 hersg. von W. Gropius und L. Moholy-Nagy*, München, 1924, pp.52–3.

341. Continuous Working Surfaces: J. J. P. Oud, L-Shaped Kitchen, Weissenhof Settlement, Stuttgart, 1927. *J. J. P. Oud, who carefully planned large flats for workers in Holland before* 1920, *brought his skill to the L-shaped kitchen of row houses at the Weissenhof experimental settlement. Although this low-cost kitchen seems to have little in common with the white-enameled, mechanized kitchen of* 1940, *its organization embodied almost everything the manufacturers were later to offer in luxurious versions.*

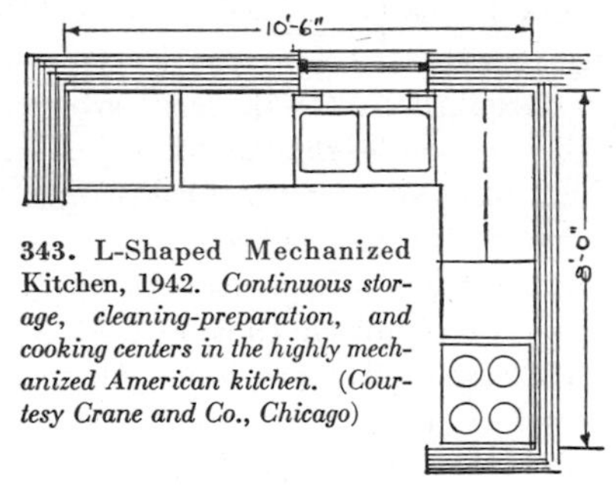

343. L-Shaped Mechanized Kitchen, 1942. *Continuous storage, cleaning-preparation, and cooking centers in the highly mechanized American kitchen.* (*Courtesy Crane and Co., Chicago*)

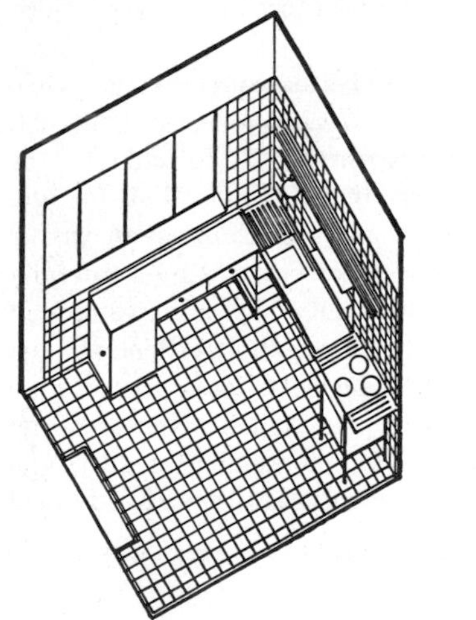

342. J. J. P. OUD: L-Shaped Kitchen, Weissenhof Settlement, 1927. Ground Plan. *Continuous storage, cleaning-preparation, and cooking center.*

344. Partially Continuous Working Surfaces: The Black Kitchen, 1930. *Early use by the industry of wall-cabinets, base cabinets beneath working surfaces, and built-in sink. But they are still treated as isolated pieces of kitchen-furniture. The range does not fit into the surrounding units, nor is it integrated in the work process.* (*Courtesy* Kitchen Maid)

345. Heterogeneous Equipment. Experimental Kitchen Used by Lillian Gilbreth, Brooklyn Gas Co., 1930. *One of American industry's first attempts to rationalize kitchen work by studying movement and charting steps, and to arrange the miscellaneous equipment in a more compact way. Faced with the chaos then prevailing, the production engineer Lillian Gilbreth comments: 'The manufacturer must realize that he has little knowledge of what the housewife needs.'* (*Courtesy* Architectural Forum)

almost everything that industry was later to put out in more luxurious versions.

Beneath the ample windows the storage center consists of a plain food chest ventilated from the courtyard, over which the working surfaces run. Oud treated the food chest as Catherine Beecher had arranged the flour barrel in 1869. The cleaning and preparation center consisted of smooth working surfaces and a plain sink — instead of the 'electric sink' advocated around 1940. A built-in refuse can is serviced from the court. At a right angle is the cooking center, which directly communicates with the dining room through a hatch.

The year before, 1926, a book had appeared in Germany bearing a title not unlike Christine Frederick's book of 1915. *The New Household, A Guide to Scientific Housekeeping* [24] proved most timely and was read by architects, manufacturers, and housewives. Unlike the American literature of its kind around 1910, this work did not draw its immediate inspiration from scientific management. Germany too lacked the long American tradition that viewed housekeeping as a profession, and for that very reason Dr. Erna Meyer's book stirred the public. Within a year it went through thirty printings, and ultimately forty. The American reader would be taken aback by the primitive devices it so eagerly prescribes for the lightening of household drudgery.

The authoress had discussed with Oud the organization of the work process, and to him the book owes its clear and formal simplicity. It shows that even when he takes the kitchen board in hand, the true artist may apprehend and trace the lines of a future development.

J. J. P. Oud was not alone. Mies van der Rohe, Walter Gropius, Josef Frank's electric kitchen, and LeCorbusier's long tiled working surfaces all show the same decision to deal with the kitchen as a unit.[25] The Weissenhof settlement not only gave the signal for the spreading of the new architecture and to some extent of the constituent furniture of our century, but it also solved the organization of the kitchen.[26] The trend was rapidly taken up all over the Continent.[27] By 1930 it had won acceptance.

In the mid-'thirties America took the lead. Meanwhile all the machinery basic to kitchen mechanization had been evolved. It was to find room in the

---

[24] Dr. Erna Meyer, *Der Neue Haushalt, Ein Wegweiser zur Wissenschaftlichen Hausfuehrung*, Stuttgart, 1926.

[25] Werner Graef, 'Innenraeume,' *Hersg. im Auftrage des Deutschen Werkbunds*, Stuttgart, 1928, Kuechen, figs. 164–76. S. Giedion, 'La Cité-Jardin du Weissenhof à Stuttgart,' *L'Architecture vivante*, Printemps-été, 1928.

[26] Then began the standardizing of the kitchen and the tendency to compress it to the extreme, as at the Berlin Exhibition of 1929, *Die Neue Kueche*.

[27] For Sweden, cf. O. Almquist, 'Koekets Standardisering nagra synpunkter vid pagaende utredningsarbete,' in *Byggmaestaren*, heft 9, 1927. For Switzerland, cf. Gewerbemuseum, Basel, Ausstellung, 'Die Praktische Küche,' Feb.-Mar. 1930.

vacant space beneath J. J. P. Oud's working surfaces. Before we pass on to the organization of the work process around 1935 and to the development that ensued, we shall seek typological insight into the appliances prevailing in the mechanized kitchen.

Mechanization of the Hearth

The Range: Concentration of the Heat Source

The history of the kitchen as we know it today is largely bound up with the growing concentration of its heat sources. The open flame of the hearth, coal within the cast-iron range, gas, and finally electricity followed one another as the heating agents. Their eras were of unequal length. For ages, the open flame reigned supreme. During a half century between 1830 and 1880, the cast-iron range became prevalent. Between 1880 and 1930, the gas range won acceptance. Then, in ever rising tempo, began the era of the electric range. We are speaking here of things in flux, not of rigid dates. The different forms compete side by side, and before a heating agent triumphs it must usually pass through a prolonged incubation period.

The open fire, the flame in the hearth, ran through the ages. Until late in the seventeenth century it was often the sole heating agent in the cold season. The chimneys of colonial times, whose stone blocks formed the heavy backbone of the house, are some measure of the tradition's vigor. In the large Gothic households, at the Burgundian court, or in the lordly castles, several fireplaces might be united in a kitchen building, as at Dijon or the royal palace of Cintra in Portugal. Their flues, meeting in a conical vault, formed the dominant of the architectural complex.

Only in the fifteenth century, with the awakening of a burgher consciousness, did the kitchen become a separate room of the house. But even into the seventeenth century it often served as the burgher dining room, 'often as the bedroom too,' and occasionally as a social chamber.[28] It was a neatly kept place and its rows of coppers became the display pieces that so often glow in the Dutch little-masters of the seventeenth century. A drawing ascribed to Jerome

[28] Havard, *Dictionnaire de l'ameublement et de la décoration depuis le XIIIe siècle jusqu'à nos jours*, vol. I, col. 1132.

Bosch (fig. 140) bears witness to the feasting and merrymaking enjoyed in the fifteenth-century burgher house around the tall fireplace of the kitchen.

In the seventeenth century the kitchen ceased to be one of the main dwelling rooms. It became solely 'a service utility.' [29] In the nineteenth century, with its speculative building and ceaselessly growing city populations, the kitchen lost every vestige of charm.

The Cast-Iron Range

The fireplace runs through the centuries. The cast-iron range, heated by wood or coal, prevails in the nineteenth. The steam boiler and the iron range

346. Cast-Iron Plate of Pennsylvania Dutch Stove, 1748. *From the stove of iron plates used by German and Swiss colonists the basic heat source of nineteenth-century America was to develop. This plate is inscribed:* W B [*William Bransen*]; K T F [*Koven Tree (Coventry) Furnace*]; *Gotes Brynlein hat Waser die Fyle* [*God's Well has Water in Plenty*]. (*Courtesy Landis Valley Museum, Lancaster County, Pa.*)

are as characteristic of the nineteenth century as hydraulic power and electricity are of ours. No country produced iron stoves and ranges in such profuse variety as America. The English observers note this, from Charles Dickens's comment on 'red-hot monsters' in the 'forties to Oscar Wilde's complaint some four decades later against heat-radiating decorations often seen in the center of the room. The cast-iron stove and range were identified with America much as the automobile was later. From America the most diverse models reached the Continent and even England. But the tile range with its even store of heat was still favored in the European kitchen, despite the fact that specialists were required to build it tile by tile. Catherine Beecher, if not on the esthetic grounds of the English observers, voiced practical objections to the cast-iron range, which in the 'sixties was already supreme. 'We cannot but regret that our old

---

[29] Havard, *Dictionnaire de l'ameublement et de la décoration depuis le XIIIe siècle jusqu'à nos jours,* vol. I, col. 1133.

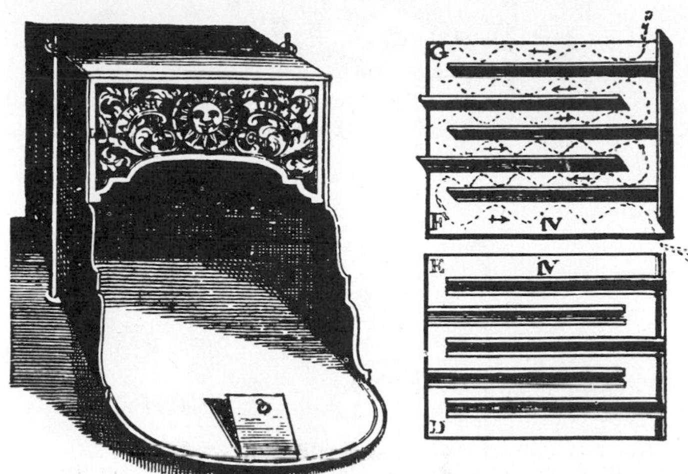

347. Toward Concentration of the Heat Source: The Franklin Stove, *c.*1740. *A further step toward the cast-iron stove of the* 19*th century. Thermal efficiency is improved by passing the combustion gases through flues. Franklin notes that his stove is based on earlier French experiments.*

steady brick ovens have been almost completely superseded by those ranges which are infinite in their capacities and forbid all general rules.' [30]

The range is based on the concentrating of the heat source within a reduced space, and all the skills of a scientific century were needed to channel the heat effectively and overcome the range's drawbacks. Thermal efficiency lay beyond the craftsman's scope. It was a matter for the physicist. The steam boiler and the cast-iron range have a common prerequisite: the efficient utilization of heat by the correct channeling of combustion gases. Understandably then, the men who guided the development of the range were rarely stove makers by training.

Benjamin Franklin built no kitchen range, but had designed before mid-eighteenth century a stove to be placed in the fireplace, for utilization of the unexhausted combustion gases. In France especially, as Franklin himself admits,[31] attempts had already been made to improve the thermal efficiency of fireplaces. Franklin's 'Pennsylvania Fireplace' of 1742 (fig. 347),[32] although it met with no favor in its own day, has remained the most famous of such efforts. Franklin also found suggestions in the 'Dutch Stove,' which was wide-

[30] Beecher and Stowe, op.cit. (1869) p.175.

[31] Nicolas Gaucher.

[32] In his Biography of Franklin, Van Doren gives the date as 1740.

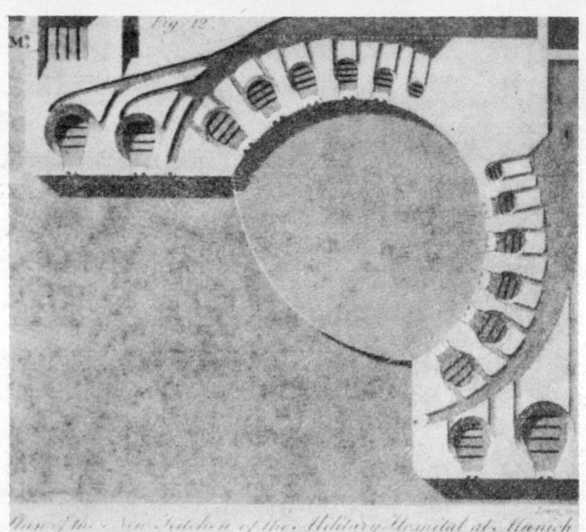

348. RUMFORD: Oval Range for Military Hospital at Munich, Late 18th Century. *The formation of the modern kitchen stove is connected with the growth of soup kitchens and other mass-feeding facilities. Rumford hollows his ranges in semi-circular or oval form, like rococo* maisons de plaisance. *The cook does not have to move around the range, but can watch his pots while standing in the center.* (*Count Rumford,* Complete Works, *Boston,* 1870–75, *vol.* III)

spread in Pennsylvania (he also calls it 'Holland Stove'). It was made of cast-iron plates. Using the same material, he formed an air box with cast-iron walls in which 'the smoke ascends and descends and heats the plates' (fig. 347). By this and other improvements he more fully used the escaping heat, and allowed it to radiate more equally through the room.[33]

Benjamin Thompson, Count von Rumford (1753–1814), raised in colonial America, was a British officer, Bavarian statesman and general in chief, and, which is to the point here, one of the great late eighteenth-century physicists. We have already mentioned [34] Rumford's indirectly heated oven, designed for the kitchen of a workhouse that he founded in Munich, where the heat and smoke passed through a ramification of flues around the sunk-in saucepans.

Investigator of latent heat, inventor of the soups that still bear his name, author of an essay 'Of the Excellent Qualities of Coffee and the Art of Making It in the Highest Perfection' [35] (giving recipes and several designs of percolators

[33] It is rewarding to read Franklin's own description and the six methods he lists for artificial heating in his time; and interesting to note that he mentions to the disadvantage of the Dutch Stove that 'There is no sight of the fire which is in itself a pleasant thing.' And of the 'German Stove,' where the heat is piped in from another room, he remarks 'People have not even so much sight of the fire as in the Holland Stove.' Cf. Jared Sparks, *The Works of Benjamin Franklin,* London, 1882, vol. 6, pp.33, 43, 44.

[34] Referred to in 'The Mechanization of Baking,' above.

[35] Sir Benjamin Thompson, (Count) Rumford, *Complete Works,* 4 vols., Boston, 1870–75, vol. 4.

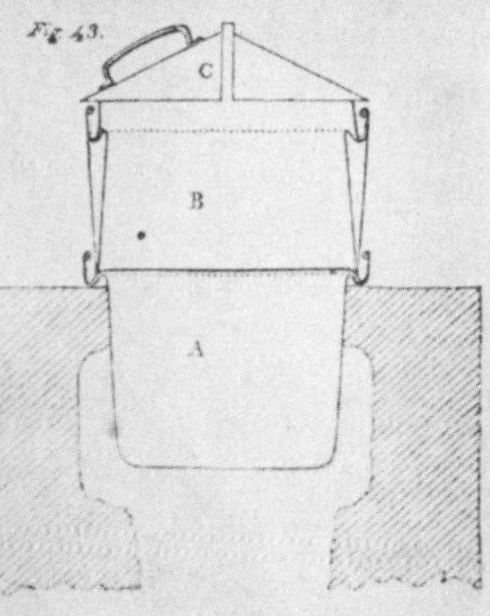
Of Cooking in Steam.

The following figure, which repreſents a vertical ſection of the apparatus, will ſhow this contrivance in a clear and diſtinct manner:

Fig 43.

C

B

A

A. is the boiler, which is ſeen ſet in brick-work.
B. is the ſteam-diſh; and
C. is the cover of the boiler, which is here made to ſerve as a cover for the ſteam-diſh.

The ſides of the ſteam-diſh (which is made of tin) are double, for the purpoſe of confining the heat more effectually.

350. RUMFORD: Sunken Steam-Saucepan.

349 a. Cross Section of Rumford's Range for a Bavarian Nobleman. *Concentration of the heat source: sunken saucepans; with complex flue system heating the whole outer wall of the pans.*

349 b. Top View of Rumford's Range for a Bavarian Nobleman. *Same arrangement: the cook stands in the center.*

still used today, and voicing the idea that coffee should become the beverage of the masses) Rumford, with his scientific experience, was indeed the man to perfect the range.

The social experiment of cooking for a thousand people daily in his Munich workhouse offered an excellent opportunity. Rumford also built large ranges for Bavarian aristocrats (fig. 349), for military academies (fig. 348), and for hospitals in Italy. All were shaped along similar lines: The cook did not walk around his pots but watched them from the center. For the range was hollowed in the same semicircular or oval shape as the small *maisons de plaisance* in the Park of Nymphenburg, where Rumford was a frequent guest. In form, these ranges were infused with the eighteenth-century spirit, and bore no resemblance to the towering monsters created by the nineteenth century. They are described

351. Electric Range with Sunken Pans, 1943. Libbey-Owens-Ford Glass Co. Wartime Dummy, Designed by H. Creston Dohner. *Sunken saucepans, waffle-iron, and food mixer. Panels are lowered over working units to convert the kitchen into playroom or study room (fig. 439). Glass-enclosed oven (left) and refrigerator (right).*

and precisely shown in one of Rumford's most perspicacious essays, the tenth. These 300 pages 'On the Construction of Kitchen Fireplaces and Kitchen Utensils, Together with Remarks and Observations Relating to the Various Processes of Cooking and Proposals for Improving that most Useful Art' [36] are a store of experience and suggestions based on exhaustive theory and a gift for technical solutions. It is almost the outline of what was to follow.

How was the kitchen equipped in Rumford's time? There were then no kitchen appliances in the present-day sense. All were yet to be invented. 'The kitchen fireplace of a family in easy circumstances in this country,' he wrote on his return to England, 'consists almost uniformly of a long grate for burning coal placed in a wide and open chimney.' [37] In its stead he proposed the range he had evolved in Munich, but went a step further. The heat source, he repeatedly stresses, should be contained within the smallest possible compass. He shows the 'usefulness of small iron ovens and the best methods of constructing them,' [38] and, before 1800, had designed 'small ovens for poor families.' [39] Most interesting

[36] Sir Benjamin Thompson, (Count) Rumford, *Complete Works*, 4 vols., Boston, 1870–75, vol. 3. Cf. another essay in the same volume, 'Of the Management of Fire and the Economy of Fuel.'

[37] Ibid., vol. 3, p.227. [38] Ibid. ch. VI. [39] Ibid. vol. 3, p.321.

perhaps, in this connection, is a 'very simple and useful portable kitchen furnace' with Rumford's sunken stewpan, around which the combustion gases may pass (fig. 354). The conically tapered fire chamber is suspended like a bird's nest. This confining of the heat, as well as the suspension allowing ready access of air, laid down the pattern for the rational range of a later time.

He painstakingly argues to the public the advantages of the roasting oven in even radiation and greater juiciness of the meat, and proposes roasting ovens made of 'a hollow cylinder of sheet iron, closed at one end and set in brickwork, so that the flame of a small fire may play directly beneath'[40] (fig. 352).

He pays special care to the design of the cooking vessels to be placed on a compact heat source. And here we see the iron adapter rings later used to make the range take pans of varying size. The utilization of steam for cooking and the economy of heat by stacked pans are outlined in strikingly adequate constructions. The sides of the steam dish are double 'for the purpose of confining the heat more effectually.' There is even an elegant proposal for a self-contained kitchenette shut off by doors, which he recesses, cupboard-like, into the wall. Rumford calls it a 'concealed kitchen.'[41] Rumford often moves along paths that were not later traveled. But, he points out, his suggestions, although based on wide practice, are tentative. He is delving into an unknown sphere, and as a creative scientist he often anticipates things later to be laboriously wrested from the trial and error of everyday experience.

The successive American improvements of the cast-iron range were largely elaborations of the Pennsylvania Dutch oven. Over three decades passed before the stove of cast-iron plates entered upon its expansion. It was given a special grate such as had long been usual in fireplaces. An ash chest was added, and on one side a roasting oven heated above and below by the combustion gases[42] (fig. 353).

The third name directly linked with the shaping of the range is that of the man who comes closest to the description of a stovemaker, for he later engaged in their manufacture. He was Philo Penfield Stewart (1798–1868), who began as a missionary and teacher, riding two thousand miles on horseback to preach before an Indian tribe. He was instrumental in the founding of Oberlin College, and possessed the inventive gift, as widespread in the America of his day as the gift of painting in the Renaissance. Philo Stewart hoped to combine study in his college 'with such economy that the students may defray all their expenses.' The school opened in 1833, and the next year Stewart took out a patent for a

[40] Ibid. vol. 3, p.257. [41] Ibid. vol. III, pp.460–67.

[42] For particulars of this development, see William J. Keep, 'Early American Cooking Stoves,' *Old Time New England*, vol. XXII, Oct. 1931, which includes a list of the American patents down to 1836.

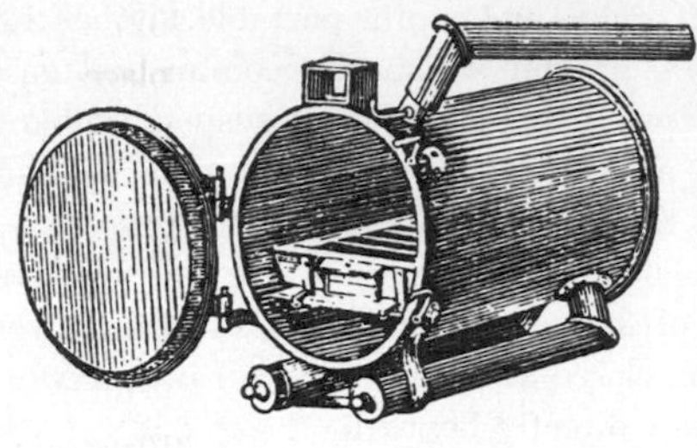

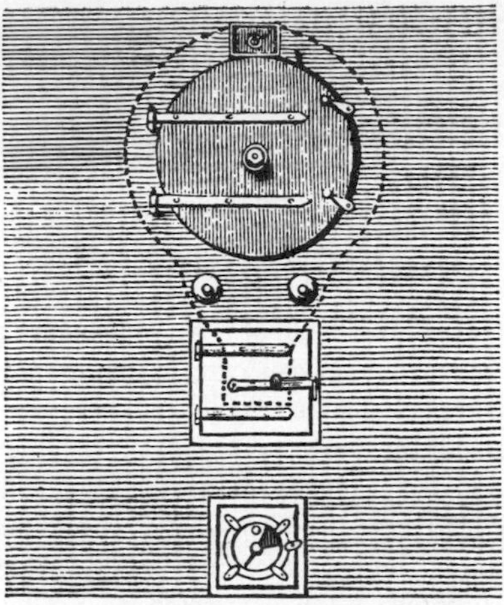

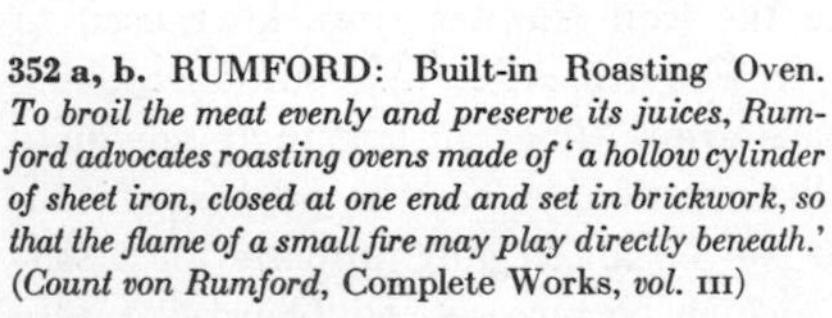

352 a, b. RUMFORD: Built-in Roasting Oven. *To broil the meat evenly and preserve its juices, Rumford advocates roasting ovens made of 'a hollow cylinder of sheet iron, closed at one end and set in brickwork, so that the flame of a small fire may play directly beneath.' (Count von Rumford,* Complete Works, *vol.* III)

cast-iron stove, which he named Oberlin, after his institution. When he registered a last patent a few years before his death, the mechanism had been thoroughly thought out and proved in use. A glance at the sketch reveals the features he had intended from the first: utmost concentration of the heat source (which burnt the fuel then usual, wood); free suspension of the fire chamber

353. Cast-Iron Cooking Stove, American, 1858. *The cast-iron range, which developed from the Pennsylvania stove, gave rise to many ingenious variations mostly based on more efficient arrangement of grates and flues. (Courtesy Edison Institute, Dearborn, Mich.)*

Of Portable Furnaces, &c.

A very ſimple and uſeful portable kitchen furnace, with its ſtew-pan in its place, are repreſented by the following figure :

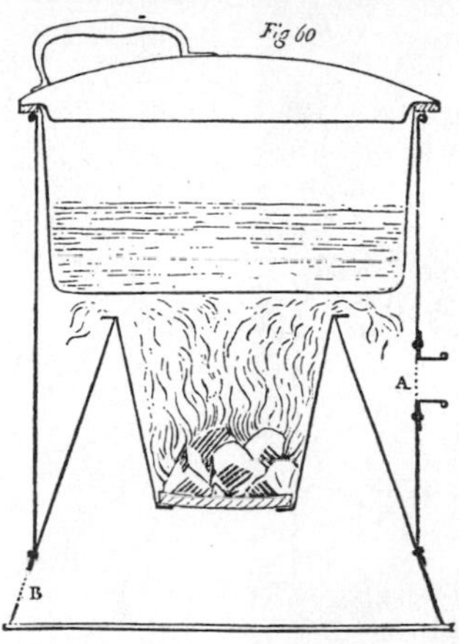

This furnace is made of common ſheet-iron, and it may be afforded at a very low price. It is compoſed

354. RUMFORD: Portable Sheet-Iron Stove with Tapering Firebox, *c.*1800. *Rumford, who introduced soup kitchens for the poor, later proposed this cooking range to conserve fuel for the working classes. Note the sunken saucepan with cleverly designed handle. The heat source is concentrated in a perforated conical fire chamber.*

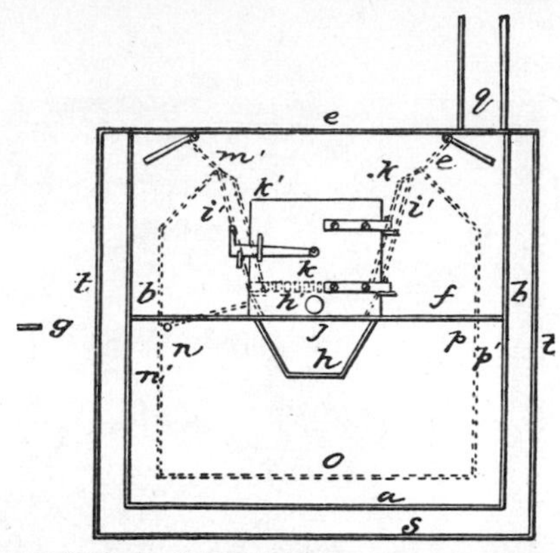

355. PHILO P. STEWART: Summer and Winter Cooking Stove, 1838. *Economical cooking equipment was developed within a century, mainly by men who were not professional stove builders, such as Franklin, Rumford, or the missionary and educator Philo P. Stewart.*

Utmost concentration of the heat source, freely suspended fire chamber as in Rumford's range, perforation of the chamber walls which taper toward the bottom. (*U.S. Patent* 915, 12 *September* 1838)

like a bird's nest, as in Rumford's range; the surrounding of this chamber by air; perforation of the chamber walls, which as in Rumford's model taper toward the bottom.[43] We may take it that a man of Stewart's type must have been acquainted with Rumford's writings, which enjoyed an extraordinary wide public. He nevertheless went his own way, for he had to join his theoretical knowledge of heat with the stove as developed in America from 1800 on.

When he patented his first stove in 1834, Stewart, thinking that the royalties might yield some income, made over the patent rights to his college. These are

356. Range with Rotary Plate, 1845. *Hundreds of mid-century patents express the interest in cast-iron stoves and ranges. Unconventional ideas occur, such as this labor-saving device of a rotary plate to move the pans. 'The heat can be made to act either upon the rotary plate or the stationary boiler or both at pleasure, by merely changing the dampers.'* (*U.S. Patent* 4248, 1 *November* 1845)

[43] Philo Stewart's patents: 19 June 1834, 12 Sept. 1838 (fig. 355), 18 Jan. 1859 (No. 22,681), 28 Apr. 1863 (No. 39,022).

357. Table-Top Gas Range, 1941. *The 'table-top' range entered production during the early 'thirties. The standard form, resulting from a long development, is a combination of white-enameled range, cupboard, and work-table. It has become fully integrated with the working process.* (*Courtesy Tappan Co., Don Hadley, designer*)

clear indications that we are in the pre-business period. But Stewart soon left Oberlin and moved to Troy, where in thirty years he manufactured some 90,000 stoves.

Philo Stewart's Oberlin Stove, it is generally recognized, formed the starting-point for the technified range. Then begins the time of specialists and technical improvements. By around 1840 the cast-iron cooking stove was a vigorously plastic type, having a base and superstructure. It drew the same interest in its time as the streamline-kitchen a century later. As in other fields, the most active period of invention was from the middle 'fifties down to the 'seventies. An advertisement of 1848 charmingly shows the manifold possibilities then available: combined coal and wood firing, movable grates, storage space (fig. 358).

The uninsulated vertical copper boiler combined with the range came into use during the 'seventies (fig. 360).

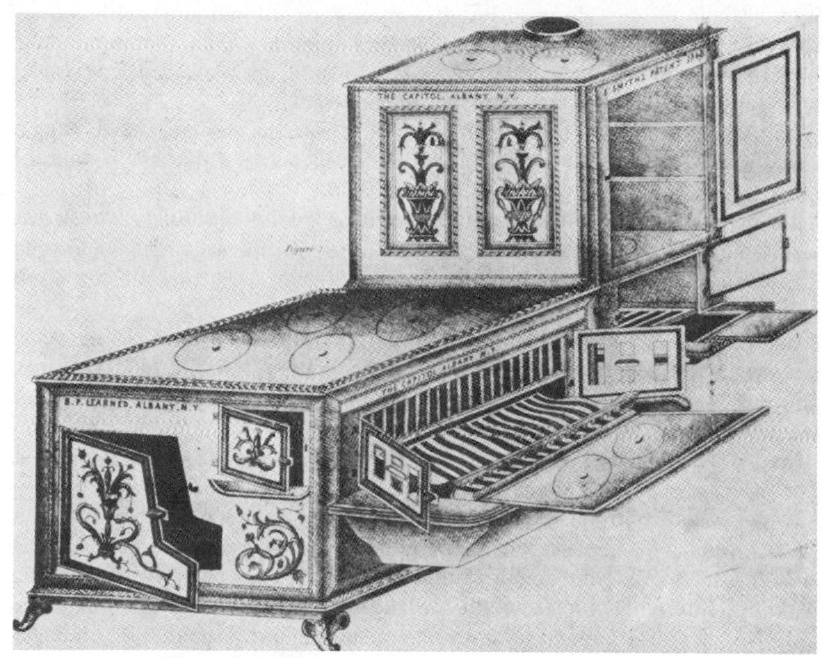

358. American Cast-Iron Range, 1848: 'Two Stoves in One.' *This vigorous advertisement indicates how rapidly after Stewart's patent of* 1838 *the range was made movable, combining many purposes, as in the patent furniture of the period. The drawings often show all doors open, as in the eighteenth-century cabinetmakers' designs. (Courtesy Bella C. Landauer Collection)*

The Time of the Gas Range, 1880–1930

The advent of coal gas made possible a further concentration of the heat source. Although the open flame is still used, it is now confined within the narrow bounds of a burner ring.

Just as England led the seventeenth century in the utilization of coal for industrial or household purposes, so it led in the manufacture and use of coal gas during the nineteenth.

Compared with its rapid popularity for illumination purposes, gas established itself surprisingly slowly and belatedly as a heating agent.[44] True, several starts

[44] F. N. Morton, 'The Evolution of the Gas Stove,' *Public Service*, Chicago, July 1908, vol. xv. According to Morton the first English patent on gas appliances for heating purposes was taken out at the beginning of the nineteenth century by F. A. Windsor. Other patents and proposals, in 1825, 1830, and 1832. Illustrations of these in Morton.

were made in the first decades, but it was only toward mid-nineteenth century that interest began to awaken among the English public. Demonstration kitchens were put on view where a wide variety of gas-cooked dishes proved how well this tenuous fuel could serve the household.

Well in the direction of the future standard was the gas range with a plain cast-iron top and spiral burners (fig. 361), constructed by a Glasgow restaurant owner and shown at the Great Exhibition of 1851.

But even then the general public failed to patronize the range, which was mainly purchased for hotel kitchens. 'The history of the use of gas for heating and for cooking' during the three decades from 1850 to 1880 'was one of exceedingly slow development.'

In 1879 an English firm exhibited 'over three hundred appliances in which gas was to be used for other purposes than lighting' [45] — for ranges, ovens, flat-irons, and other laundry appliances. This is supposed to have given considerable impetus to the new fuel.

Around 1880 the time slowly sets in during which the public loses its distrust of the gas range. But one must not suppose that people at large were quickly or easily won away from wood and coal to the imponderable fuel. In 1889 [46] a Chicago catalogue stresses: 'For eight years we have been manufacturing the Jewel (fig. 362). We were among the first to appreciate that gas was to be the fuel of the future. Is the use of gas for cooking purposes an extraordinary luxury? No, it is an economical necessity. The popular prejudice is gradually giving way.' [47]

As late as 1910 'combined coal and gas cooking ranges' are listed.[48] And even around 1915 the catalogues appeal in verse with the ever-returning refrain 'Save the Wife her Time and Care: Cook with Gas.' [49] Nevertheless in 1910 half the volume of gas used for illumination was already being consumed for burning purposes.

Deviously, the pure forms of the gas range emerge around 1930 — that is, at a time when gas cooking already had to reckon with a new rival, the electric range. There seemed to be no breaking loose from its prototype, the coal range; in the larger models the baking oven and broiler were still placed above the cooking top. In the smaller ones this led to somewhat giraffish proportions.

[45] This, and the material above, from Morton, op.cit.

[46] Prior to this time, from around 1880 on, America, with its abundant petroleum, had specialized in the gasoline stove, later perfected and still in use (kerosene stove) throughout the country.

[47] George M. Clark & Co., 179 N. Michigan Ave., Chicago, Jewel Gas Stove Catalogue; a copy in the Edison Institute, Dearborn, Michigan.

[48] Catalogue of the Fuller and Warren Company, Troy, N. Y.; copy in the New York Public Library.

[49] Catalogue of the Standard Lighting Company, Division of the American Stove Company, Cleveland, Ohio: 'New Process Gas Ranges'; copy in the New York Public Library.

359. Combined Fireplace, Boiler, and Cast-Iron Oven, 1806. *A friend of Oliver Evans, inventor of the assembly line, offers this very early scheme combining a hot-water boiler and oven with an open fireplace. 'By drawing a damper either of them will heat by the fire that is used in common. The boiler should have a tube with brass cock which projecting into the kitchen gives hot water whenever wanted.'* (*S. W. Johnson,* Rural Economy, 1806)

360. Improved Range with Boiler, 1871. *In this period the free-standing, uninsulated vertical boiler, still found in American farm houses, came into use.* (Manufacturer and Builder, *New York, November* 1871)

All that at first glance distinguishes them from the coal range is the table-like frame on which they stand, whose curved and highly ornamented cast-iron legs seem to have emigrated from some Regency salon. These models had their day from the 'nineties into the second decade of our century. With their exuberant ornamentation of their silvery metal, they betray the inner insecurity and helplessness of that prosperous era.

But these diversions are secondary. Of greater consequence was the fact that, bogged in the pattern of the coal range, the gas range was segregated within an insulating zone. This delayed its merging into the kitchen work-process.

Side by side with this, however, ran another form more in keeping with the nature of the gas cooker. Here the flat range top, cut by circular burners, prevailed, as in the model seen at the Great Exhibition of 1851. The broiler and oven occupy the space beneath, while to either side perforated stacking surfaces extend the range top.

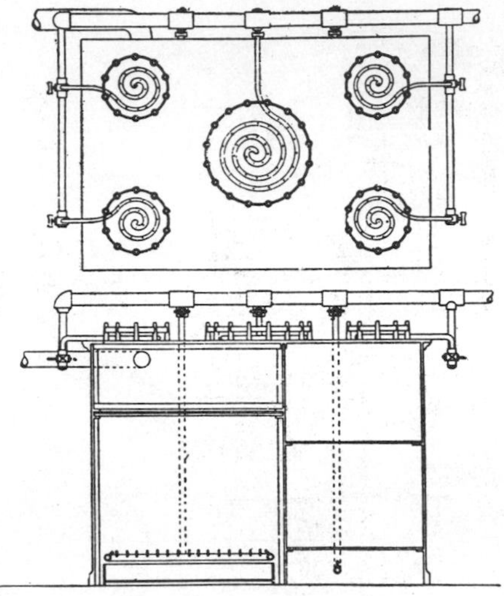

361. Gas Range, Glasgow, 1851. *Gas appliances for heating purposes were patented from the early nineteenth century. But the introduction of gas as a cooking fuel was very slow. This gas range with spiral burners and plain cast-iron top is in the direction of the later standard. Hotels were almost the only users of gas for cooking.*

362. Gas Range, 1889. *Toward* 1880 *'the popular prejudice is gradually giving way.' This type with the broiler at the base was developed in England from the start (fig.* 361) *and was adopted by American production in the 'eighties. Later the coal range with broiler above (fig.* 353) *was imitated by the gas range as well as the early electrical range (fig.* 367). *(George M. Clark and Co., Chicago. Jewel Gas Stove Catalogue in collection of Edison Institute, Dearborn, Mich.)*

The white areas of porcelain enamel, which were later to cover the range and radically change the aspect of the kitchen, were in use by 1910, although confined at that period to the range top and splashback.[50]

From the flat-topped English type with its stacking surfaces, where oven and often a broiler occupy the base, the Americans after 1930 developed their 'table-top range.' Now the black top has become a working surface of white enamel, cut only by the burner openings to the left. Under the name of 'compact table-top range [51] (fig. 363) — although they have no true working or

[50] Catalogue of the Reliable Stove Company, Division of the American Stove Company, Cleveland, Ohio: 'Reliable Gas Stoves and Ranges,' 1914; copy in the New York Public Library. Cf. p.10: 'Some years ago we introduced the beautiful . . . porcelain enameled idea which has proven a decided success. . . . We are now operating one of the most complete enameling plants.'

[51] Catalogue of the Standard Gas Equipment Corporation, 18 East 41st Street, New York, N.Y.: 'Gas Ranges for Apartments, Residences and Housing Developments,' p.9; copy in New York Public Library.

363. Compact Table-Top Gas Range, 1931. '*Latest Table-Top Style, Hinged Cover.*' *Beginning of the range's integration with the other working surfaces.* (*Catalogue of the Standard Gas Equipment Corp., New York*)

stacking surface — the earlier models appear around 1931. The catalogues advise that the new range 'makes smaller kitchens possible, makes kitchen planning easier.' The influence of household planning is taking effect.

That the gas industry supplied the leadership at this time is not strange. It had long practice in setting up demonstration kitchens equipped with household aids. Beginning in the early 'thirties, trailer demonstration kitchens traveled the land. As we shall see in the work process around 1935, the gas industry was first in the commercial field thoroughly to investigate scientific management in the kitchen.

The automatization of the range, so carefully perfected in America during the time of full mechanization, began with the gas cooker. In 1915 appeared the oven regulator, a thermostat adapted to this purpose, the first notable invention since mid-century.[52] This begins the mechanical regulating of time and temperature, later an American specialty, particularly in the electric range.

The table-top range fits the height of other working surfaces, and, the makers stress,[53] is proportioned so as to merge with the base cabinets continuous along the wall. Soon the abbreviated legs altogether disappear. The table-top range, with its drawers for accessories, has found its standard form. It is furniture

---

[52] 'The first major development was the Lorrain oven regulator by an engineer of the American Stove Company.' Cf. American Gas Journal, vol. 140, N.Y., May 1934, p.110.

[53] Standard Gas Equipment Corp. op.cit.: 'Table top height 36″ fits in well with cabinet work.'

among furniture. The concentration of the heat source has been carried to its logical conclusion.

The Electrical Heat Source

Electrification shrinks the heat source to a mere spiral of wire, a thin resistance, which the current causes to glow and radiate heat. From the first, the main task was to bring this radiation in close contact with the object to be heated. The problem was technically solved in several ways, no change of principle being involved. Now heat is instantaneously produced without so much as the striking of a match.

The creation of heat without visible source went counter to the age-old association of heat with flame. Yet gas fuel had opened the public mind to new and unfamiliar methods. The gas range had taken eight decades to be introduced; the electric range no more than half that span. Now around 1930, household mechanization, previously a cause of hesitation and distrust, became the strongest of sales' inducements.

Obstacles there were. But they lay rather in the nature of things. The electrical network was sporadic, current too expensive, the apparatus too highly priced and too delicate for the household.

For a long time, a tinge of the wondrous seemed to pervade all things electric. There was in truth something to marvel at when the seventy-year-old Michael Faraday toured the English lighthouses in 1862 and first beheld the practical application of his light, or 'magnetic spark' as he called it, which had arisen in his hands three decades earlier.

When, late in the 'eighties, the idea of using the current for culinary purposes was toyed with, its portrayal was more suggestive of witchcraft than of useful invention. One of the popular scientific booklets,[54] then so numerous, reports a Canadian invention 'answering to this fantastic desideratum,' cooking by electricity (fig. 364). The description is the more fantastic in that the inventor claims to have baked cakes with his apparatus, and these are supposed to have an indefinable 'electrical flavor.'

Yet electrical cooking caught on quickly enough. Practical experiments were first made in England around 1890. An electrical fair held at the Crystal Palace, London, in 1891, is said to have brought the new cooking agent before the public.[55]

---

[54] Max de Nansouty, *L'Année industrielle*, Paris, 1887, p.14.

[55] Society for Electric Development, Inc., N.Y. *The Electric Range Handbook*, New York, 1919, p.48.

364. Imaginary Electric Kitchen, 1887. *Toward the end of the 'eighties electricity came closer to the household. Among fantastic 'Canadian inventions' is a kind of electric saucepan, heated by current from a battery, the walls of the utensil serving as conductors. Food cooked in it is said to have an 'electrical flavor.' The portrayal is suggestive of an alchemist's kitchen.* (*Max de Nansouty,* L'Année industrielle, *Paris* 1887)

The Chicago World's Fair of 1893 outdid in one respect the Eiffel Tower and Halle des Machines of its immediate Parisian forerunner: It gave a display of electrical illumination such as had never before been witnessed. A number of industrialists had spiritedly begun electrical experimentation in various directions. Included in the exhibition was a 'Model Electric Kitchen' (fig. 365), having a small electrified range, electric broiler, and electric kettles.

Just as demonstration kitchens had been set up to bolster confidence in the gas range of 1850, the same strategy was used four decades later to popularize electrical cooking. The Algonquin Club in Boston is recorded as having set up a demonstration restaurant for twenty persons, where a full dinner was cooked (from the bread to fish, sirloin roast, and coffee), the 'cost of fuel' amounting to barely over a cent per person.[56] But this dinner seems to have proved no more persuasive than the electrically cooked banquet held in 1895 in honor of the Lord Mayor of London. There followed an incubation period (1890–1910). The electrified ranges that then made their appearance had the same giraffish aspect as the contemporary gas stoves. 'Between 1909 and 1919,' a

[56] *Electricity at the Columbian Exposition*, Chicago, 1894, p.402.

365. Electric Kitchen, Columbian Exhibition, Chicago, 1893. *The Columbian exhibition of* 1893 *put on an unprecedented display of electrical illumination. The application of electricity to household appliances was demonstrated in the first electric kitchen. Each saucepan, water heater, broiler, or boiler was connected to an individual outlet, a principle that was revived in the kitchen of the* 1940'*s* (*fig.* 436a, b).

contemporary handbook states, 'electric range manufacturers had developed the most perfect cooking device in the world.' [57]

Various producers of electricity were now delivering current for cooking at a low price, and the network was spreading. The electric range was recognized as a large consumer of current, and modern sales organizations grew up in America to apply the necessary stimulus. They were later imitated in most electricity-producing countries.

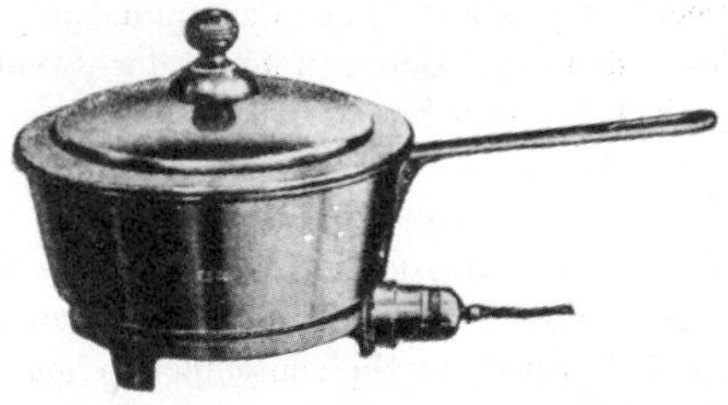

366. Electric Saucepan, Columbian Exhibition, Chicago 1893.

[57] Society for Electrical Development, op.cit.

367. General Electric Range, 1905. *During its incubation period* (1890–1910), *the electric range took its pattern from the gas range with oven or broiler above the cooking surface. Electrical heat was still handled with experimental precaution.* (*Courtesy General Electric Corp., Schenectady, N. Y.*)

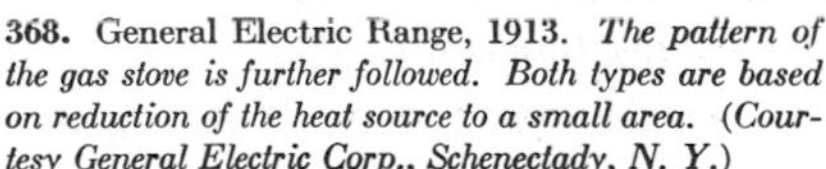

368. General Electric Range, 1913. *The pattern of the gas stove is further followed. Both types are based on reduction of the heat source to a small area.* (*Courtesy General Electric Corp., Schenectady, N. Y.*)

369. The Electric Range Popularized: Mail-Order Catalogue, 1930. *The pattern of the cast-iron cooking stove is still evident. The mail-order catalogue forms a yearly index to American civilization. Any article in its pages has entered large-scale production.* (*Montgomery Ward and Co. catalogue,* 1930)

Yet for 1919 this optimism was perhaps too rosy. Indeed, five years later a long series of articles on the electric kitchen for private houses tells us that disappointments were not unknown. 'Some people who tried electric cooking gave it up again on account of the excessive repair bills and the inconvenience connected with the burning out of elements. This shows that there must be many defects still connected with electric cooking appliances and room for considerable improvement.' [58]

About the development of the electric types, there is little more to be said than for the gas range. They were patterned on the gas range of the type already mentioned, the console raised on legs, with oven and broiler above the cooking top. Until 1930, when the electric range's popularity began, the gas range held the lead, and was apparently first to attain the 'table-top' form, standard today. From then on, as the larger electrical firms take to selling entire kitchen units and undertake their own investigation of the work process, the electrical range comes to the fore. This is in the mid 'thirties. Now it has a gleaming white enamel casing, and the oven cannot be distinguished from the utensil drawers. It has merged with the kitchen. And even more clearly than where there is a visible flame, one can see how the kitchen of today developed from the serving pantry, the room with continuous working surfaces where, in large middle-class households, domestics added finishing touches.

[58] H. Bohle, 'The Electrical Kitchen for Private Houses,' *Electricity*, vol. 38 (New York, July–Aug. 1924).

370. Electric Range, 1932. *The electric range still stands on legs, like the gas range in fig.* 363. *The table-top form, in which it immediately followed the gas range, is still imperfect.* (*Courtesy General Electric Corp.*)

371. Electric Table-Top Range, 1942. *The white-enameled electric range with automatic regulation of time and degree of heat has become the established standard.* (*Courtesy General Electric Corp., Schenectady, N. Y.*)

MECHANICAL COMFORT IN THE HOUSEHOLD

As we noted at the start of the chapter, the lightening of household burdens by the mechanization of work processes was most conspicuous among the cleaning tasks: laundering, ironing, dishwashing, carpet sweeping, and furniture cleaning. Parallel with this ran the automatization of heating and refrigeration.

When did the methods that led to mechanization of the various processes first make their appearance?

Here the answer is, as so often: in the 'fifties and 'sixties. To gain a perspective of the whole, we shall list the various categories in the order of time. We shall mention in order of their appearance the types that will be taken up again in the course of later development.

The succession begins in 1858 with carpet cleaning.[59] The aim is to dispense with back bending and with the to-and-fro motion of the broom-wielding hand. This end is achieved by means of rotating mechanisms used at the end of a handle. The principle of the domestic vacuum cleaner based purely on suction, which after many vicissitudes prevailed six decades later, was invented and clearly formulated by 1859 [60] (figs. 372–3).

This patent of 1859, earliest in the long line of pure suction types, aims, as the inventor states, at avoiding the 'detrimental' effect of rotating brushes. 'The carpet sweepers heretofore contrived have operated by means of a cylindrical brush in contact with the surface of the carpet. . . . My present invention . . . consists in the employment of a revolving fan (*F*) in lieu of the brush.'

This fan consists of four metal blades carried on a spindle. It is highly geared to a wheel, which runs over the carpet so that 'by the motion of the fan the dust is blown into the pan and the carpet is cleaned even more perfectly than can be effected by a revolving brush.' The inventor is careful to stress that the fan 'is adjusted so as not to come in direct contact with the carpet.'

The mechanical dishwashing machine came most surprisingly close to what six decades after was to prove its solution. Like Yale's lock, it was subsequently improved in detail while remaining unchanged in principle. The mechanical solution of the dishwashing process consists in driving water against the objects to be cleaned. This is done by metal blades rotating in the bottom of the tub and forcing the water upwards. In order to gain the benefit of its full force, the plates are stacked in a fixed wire frame at such an angle that the water impinges tangentially against them. It is a sort of turbine in reverse. This solution was offered by 1865 (fig. 375) [61]. The inventor may describe it more

[59] In the year 1858 there were 5 patents awarded, and 9 in 1859.

[60] U.S. Patent 22,488, 4 Jan. 1859, Carpet Fan Sweeper. [61] U.S. Patent 51,000, 21 Nov. 1865.

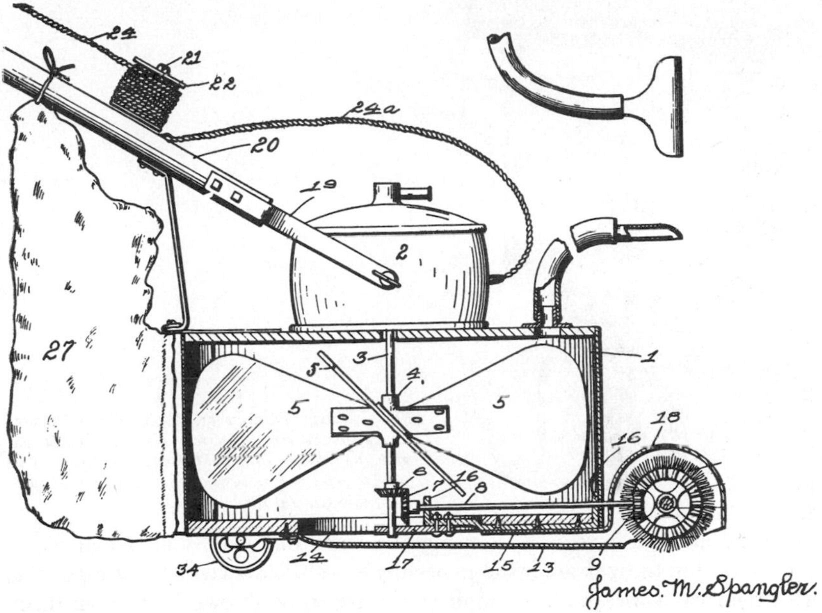

James M. Spangler.

372. Electrical Vacuum Carpet Sweeper, 1908. *The principle of the first carpet sweeper using suction alone* (1859) *is that which was to prevail when the light electric power unit finally made it practical six decades later. Today motor, dust intake, suction, beating mechanism, and bag are mounted on a compact trolley.* (*U.S. Patent* 889,823, 2 *June* 1908)

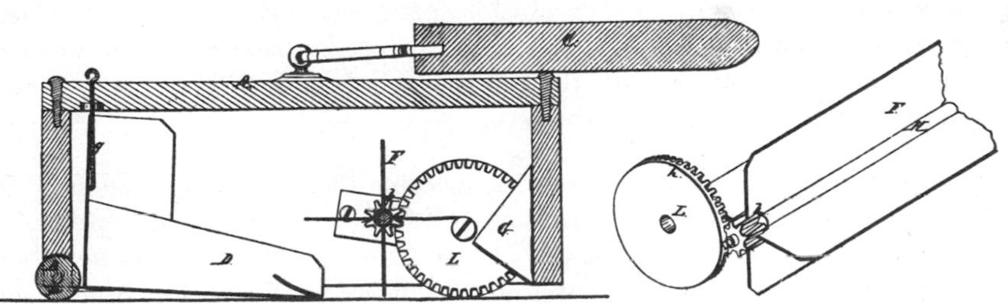

373. Formulation of the Type: Carpet Fan-Sweeper, 1859. *Earliest cleaner to use pneumatic action alone, although the dust is not sucked up, but blown. 'The carpet sweepers heretofore contrived have operated by means of a cylindrical brush in contact with the surface of the carpet . . . To avoid the objection of wear upon the carpet is the object of my present invention. By the motion of the fan the dust is blown into the pan and the carpet is cleaned even more perfectly than by the brush.'* (*U.S. Patent* 22,488, 4 *January* 1859)

374. Electric Dishwasher, 1942. Cross Section. *Except for the small electric motor that made it possible, the modern dishwashing machine differs in no fundamental way from the turbine principle of* 1865. (*Courtesy General Electric Corp.*)

clearly in his own words: 'By curving the wires the plates and similar dishes when placed in the rack are made to occupy a position tangential, corresponding with the curved wires . . . to permit the water to be thrown in between them, impinging both upon their front and rear surfaces and thus washing them effectually.' With great thoroughness and forethought other details are provided, including even the metal ring fixed to the rim of the tub 'for the purpose of preventing the water from dashing against the underside of the cover and working out around the edges of the tub.' This detail, in somewhat refined form, is still in use today. The dishwashing machine likewise remained a 'shelved invention' until the advent of the electric motor; for hand propulsion was too arduous. In comparison with the refrigerator, the dishwashing machine still has a quite small number of users.

The first appearance of the washing machine that was later successfully to mechanize the most toilsome of the housewife's tasks is harder to date precisely. In few fields — the revolver or the cast-iron stove — was American invention more prolific than in the mechanization of laundering. By 1873 we count some two thousand patents in this category.

Actually it is a matter of what question we raise. If we ask when the method was first invented that forced hot soapy water through the fabrics, instead of scrubbing and rubbing in imitation of the washerwoman, we are brought to

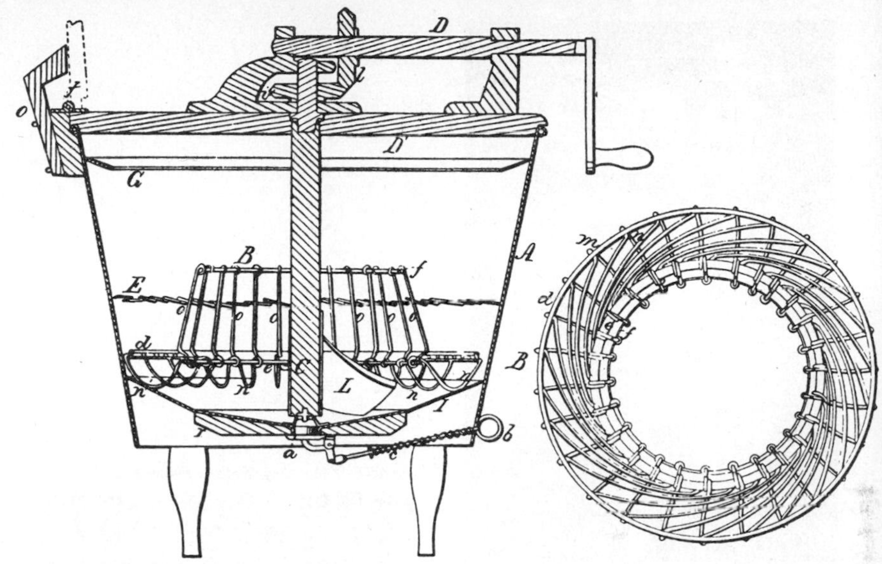

375. Formulation of the Type: Dishwasher, 1865. '*After the water has been thrown outward among the dishes it will flow back again to the center. The plates are made to occupy a position tangential to permit the water to be thrown in between them.*' (*U.S. Patent* 51,000, 21 *November* 1865)

the start of our chronological list: the year 1850. This machine with rotary inner drum was mainly used in large-scale laundering, and is so used today.

But if we seek a date for the type that, with the coming of electrical propulsion, was to prevail in household use, we are taken to the end of our chronological list: the year 1869.[62] The body of this type is cylindrical, tapering slightly upwards. A four-bladed rotor at the bottom of the tub drives a current of water through the fabrics. This rotor, agitator, or gyrator is driven by a shaft that passes down through the tub bottom (fig. 377).

Anyone who has a feeling for elegant and precise construction will see in the compact moving parts of its drive — crank, connecting bar, and bevel gear — a well-thought-out model seemingly earmarked for success. But it had a long while to wait. Six decades after this hand-driven model, the great rush to mechanize the household set in. The year 1929 alone saw fifteen patents for this gyrator type, which was improved in many points without departure from the principle. Whether the machine is hand-driven and equipped with primitive blades, as in 1869; whether it is electrically driven, while the blades, carefuly modeled and broadened, are made of aluminum or plastic; whether the simple rotary movement is made reversible — all these are details added by successors. Later

[62] Improved Washing-Machine, U.S. Patent 94,005, 24 Aug. 1869.

Handles 7 Lbs. Dry Clothes Every 3 to 10 Minutes

$37.95 Cash Electric Model
$3 Down, $4 a Month

This Standard Water Witch turns out your laundry in no time at all. Equipped with countless work-saving and safety features.

Anti-Splash Seamless Steel Tub, 7-sheet size, holds 23 gallons water to top, 16½ gallons to load-line. Easy cleaning white porcelain enamel finish inside and out. Tub cover, chassis and legs finished in White Baked-on Enamel.

$57.95 Cash Gasoline Model
$3 Down, $4 a Month

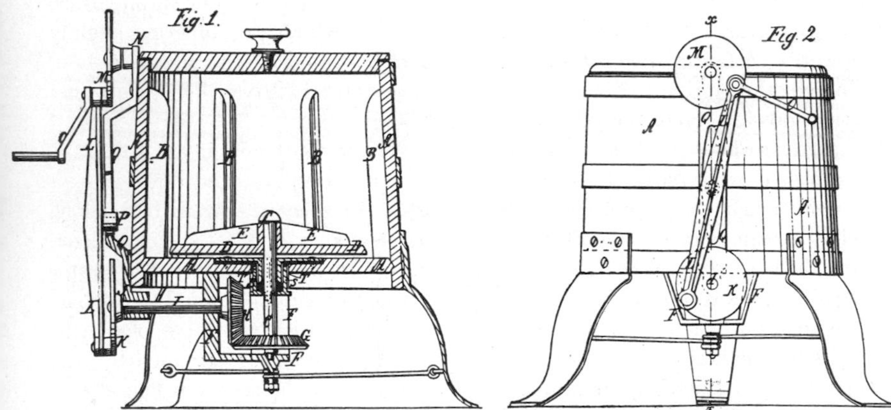

377. Formulation of the Type: Washing Machine, 1869. *Gyrator type. A small four-bladed rotor at the bottom of the tub drives the water through the fabrics. 'Cylindrical in its general form. To the inner surface is attached a number of upright ribs. A shaft passing down vertically through the center of the bottom' carries 'a number of radial ribs of flanges . . . A handcrank O.'* (*U.S. Patent* 94,005, 24 *August* 1869)

generations are privileged to succeed where earlier inventors fall short of perfection.

There is no doubt that the modern washer, the machine for use in the small household, is typologically rooted in the year 1869. It belonged to those shelved inventions whose release awaited the coming of the small electric motor.

To sum up, we find the types making their first appearance at these dates:

1859 The vacuum cleaner
1865 The dishwashing machine
1869 The modern type of washing machine

Mechanization of the Smaller Tools Around 1860

We cannot survey here the minor labor-saving devices that mechanize and take over various motions of the human hand. Yet these direct products of the American environment should not pass unnoticed. The apple-paring machines, meat choppers and egg beaters could, like patent furniture, have been invented in the fifteenth century so far as their mechanical equipment is concerned; yet they came about only with the general American recasting of work tools. Their principle, like that of all mechanization, consists in replacing the to-and-fro action of the hand by continuous rotary movement.

Eli Whitney, inventor of the cotton gin, is said to have begun his career by devising a mechanical apple parer at the age of thirteen, in the 1770's. This seems a very early date, for the first authenticized paring inventions begin with the nineteenth century. They are substantially improved in the 'thirties: a single machine claims to quarter and core the apple besides [63] (fig. 378). The fruit is impaled on a fork. The right hand rotates the shaft by means of a crank, while the left hand guides the blade, 'until the apple is pared from one end to another in a *continuous* paring.' The fruit is then forced through a four-bladed quartering knife and cored. The principle is apparent at first glance: the action of the lathe has been extended to fruit. In the following decades, an iron frame will replace the wooden one and the blade will be guided automatically by a spring arm (fig. 379). In the 'sixties the mechanism reaches its standard form. Invention of domestic coring, slicing, paring, and dividing appliances was still in full swing during the 'nineties. The canning industry was then gradually coming to the fore, and here — a rare exception to the normal trend of mechanization — the small household device gave rise to large industrial paring-machines. This factory equipment still has the rotating prongs, the paring knife, and the

[63] U.S. Patent 686, 13 Apr. 1838.

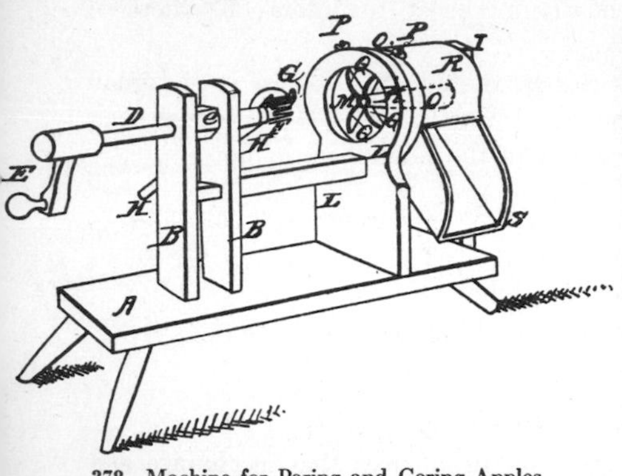

378. Machine for Paring and Coring Apples, 1838. *After impaling the apple on a fork, the operator rotates a crank with his right hand while guiding the knife with his left. The fruit is then forced through a four-bladed quartering knife and cored. The frame is of wood.* (*U.S. Patent* 686, 13 *April* 1838)

379. Combined Paring, Coring, and Slicing Machine for Apples, 1869. *The apple parer reaches its standard form in the 'sixties. It is now made of iron and has an automatically guided blade arm. 'The factory has a capacity of* 2000 *machines per week.'* (*Webb's* N.E. Railway and Manufacturers' Statistical Gazetteer, 1869)

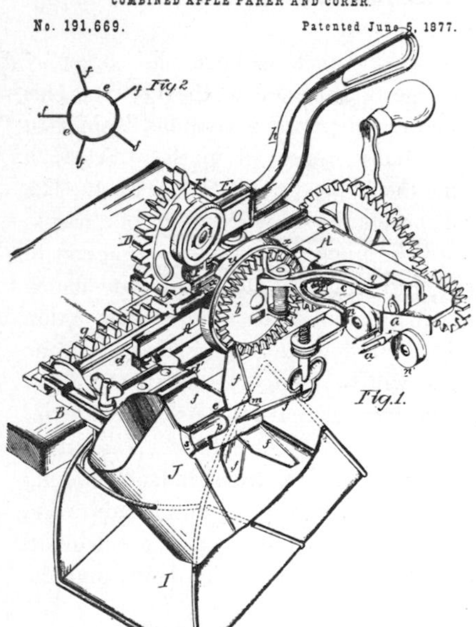

MECHANIZATION OF THE SMALLER TOOLS

The time of the apple parer was from the early nineteenth century almost to its end. These machines were in demand so long as apple trees grew around every American farmhouse. The apple-paring machine applies to fruit the principle of the lathe.

←

380. Combined Apple Parer and Corer, 1877. *The apple parer becomes an over-elaborate precision instrument. There is a 'supplemental paring-knife' to remove the skin near the stalk. Cheeks* n,n′ *support the apple at its base to prevent breaking. This is the period of great mechanical facility which invented the mechanical sheaf-knotter.* (*U.S. Patent* 191,669, 5 *June* 1877)

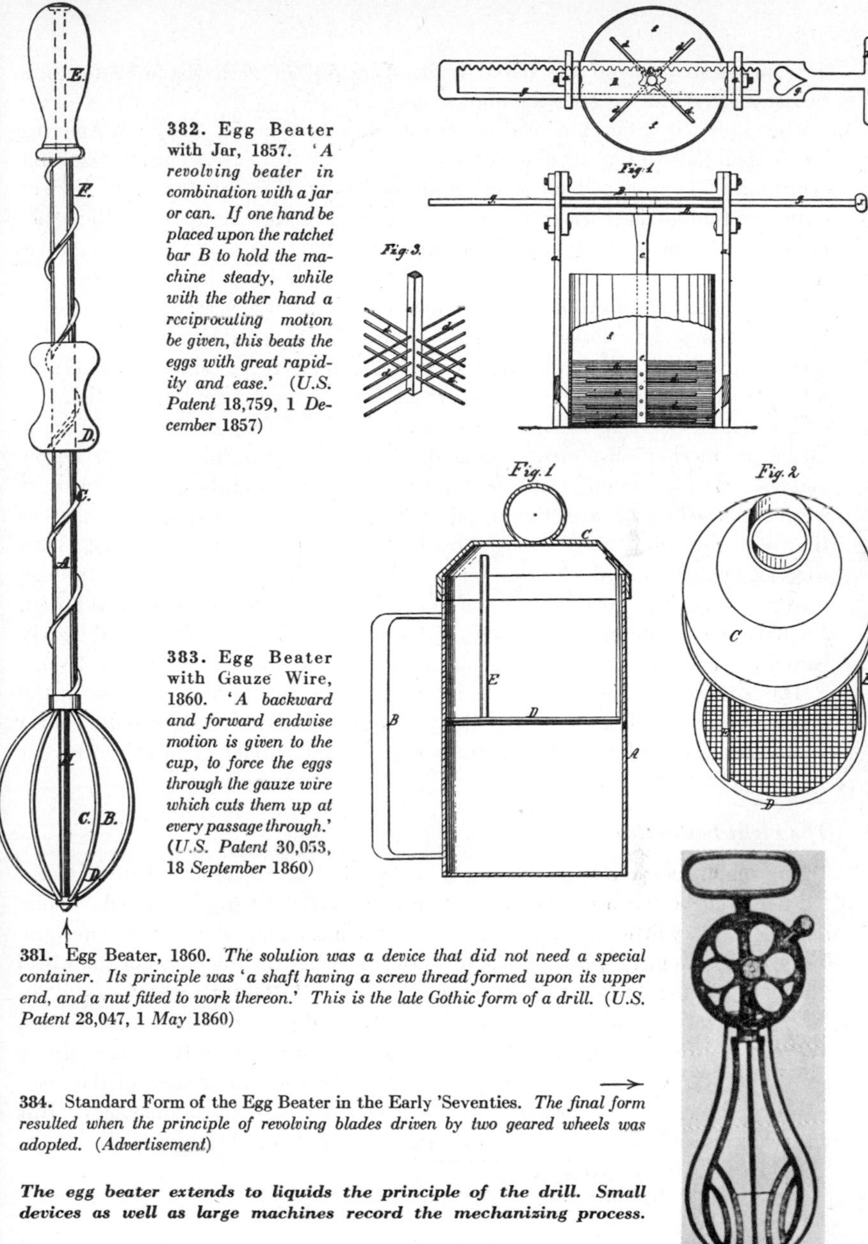

382. Egg Beater with Jar, 1857. *'A revolving beater in combination with a jar or can. If one hand be placed upon the ratchet bar B to hold the machine steady, while with the other hand a reciprocating motion be given, this beats the eggs with great rapidity and ease.' (U.S. Patent* 18,759, 1 *December* 1857)

383. Egg Beater with Gauze Wire, 1860. *'A backward and forward endwise motion is given to the cup, to force the eggs through the gauze wire which cuts them up at every passage through.'* (*U.S. Patent* 30,053, 18 *September* 1860)

381. Egg Beater, 1860. *The solution was a device that did not need a special container. Its principle was 'a shaft having a screw thread formed upon its upper end, and a nut fitted to work thereon.' This is the late Gothic form of a drill.* (*U.S. Patent* 28,047, 1 *May* 1860)

384. Standard Form of the Egg Beater in the Early 'Seventies. *The final form resulted when the principle of revolving blades driven by two geared wheels was adopted.* (*Advertisement*)

The egg beater extends to liquids the principle of the drill. Small devices as well as large machines record the mechanizing process.

mechanism to push off the pared fruit. But replacing the hand, a rotating carrier mechanically pushes the apples onto the fork.[64]

The apple-paring machine was never introduced in Europe. Even in America its life span falls within the nineteenth century, when fruit trees clustered around every farm. As soon as fruit growing became a specialized industry, with trees in tens of thousands of the same variety, the devices were relegated to the attic. Even in 1945 the old trees may continue to bear when it pays no one to gather their fruit.

The mechanization of chopping or mincing might be traced in like manner. Diverse means were found to ensure continuous up-and-down movement of the knife. Machines for mincing meat or chopping vegetables had devices to rotate the foodstuff constantly beneath the blade's regular guillotine action.

The Patent Office files egg beaters in the same category as other rotating or oscillating mechanisms, such as cement mixers, kneading machines, or butter makers. Mechanization of the butter churn was accomplished in a variety of ways after 1850. A few of the proposals for 'breaking up and mixing together the yolks and whites of eggs' may show in what roundabout way (figs. 382, 383), the egg beater reached its final form. The mechanical prototype of the egg beater is the drill. Indeed the beater's principle is that of 'boring into' a liquid. Its drive was accordingly patterned on that of the drill [65] (fig. 381). In the early 'seventies it was given its now standard drive by two geared wheels (fig. 384).

The 'sixties took the same lively interest in the smaller hand tools as in the major cleaning appliances. These light appliances reached their standard form within the period, while the heavier ones were shelved, having to await the advent of the electric power unit.

The Light Power Unit

The small electric motor, ranging from the size of a billiard ball to that of a football, can be inconspicuously built in and moved wherever needed. While demanding very little care and upkeep, it is the most adaptable of prime movers. It meant to the mechanization of the household what the invention of the wheel meant to moving loads. It set everything rolling. Without it, mechanical comfort in the house could have advanced little beyond its condition in the 'sixties.

From mid-century on, labor-saving tools were designed with a surprisingly sure hand. As we have seen, the principles of the vacuum cleaner, of the dishwasher, of the washing machine, were discovered almost instantaneously. But their success and assimilation had to await the mechanical mover.

[64] U.S. Patent 1,455,997, 20 Feb. 1923.

[65] U.S. Patent 28,047, 1 May 1860.

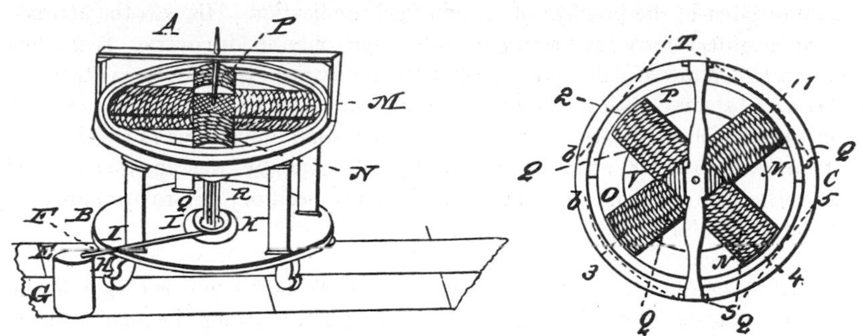

385. First American Electric Motor, 1837. *Powered from a copper and zinc plate battery. The patent is entitled 'Application of Magnetism and Electro-Magnetism to Propelling Machinery.' Faraday invented his motor shortly after discovering inducted currents* (1831). *Several electric motors were designed in England during the following year.* (*U.S. Patent* 132, 25 *February* 1837)

The electric motor likewise went through a long incubation period. To trace its hopeful beginnings, its fumblings and false starts, more numerous than for any other mover, would lead us away from our topic. We shall merely give a few co-ordinates by which to locate it in time. The first electric motor was built by Michael Faraday after his discovery of inducted currents (1831). It consisted of a copper disk rotating between the poles of a powerful magnet. The galvanic current arising in the disk could easily be canalized. But Faraday was

386. Small Motor with Three-Blade Fan, by Nicola Tesla, 1889. *The electric power unit entered the household fifty years after the electro-magnetic principle was used to drive a motor. Nicola Tesla's 1/6 horsepower A.C. motor was probably the first of the commercially produced small power units that later punctuated the house.* (*Archives of Westinghouse Company, Pittsburgh*)

not interested in the problem of its practical application. His was the attitude of the eighteenth-century scientist, interested only in discovery. Regarding himself as a natural philosopher, he left the industrial exploitation to others.

Many obstacles stood in the way of immediate solution. Over half a century had to pass before the electric motor, from the small dimensions in which Faraday had conceived it, after passing through the gigantic, was again condensed into the small and reliable instrument; and almost a century before its ubiquitous use was taken for granted.

The coming onto the market of the small electric power unit is closely linked with the name of Nicola Tesla, although it was far from being the main achievement of this master of high-frequency currents and of the multiple-phase motor that first made possible the economical transmission of energy. In the spring of 1889, almost immediately after his pioneer patent for the multiple-phase motor, Nicola Tesla, together with the Westinghouse Company, put on the market a $\frac{1}{6}$ horsepower alternating current motor directly driving a three-blade fan (fig. 386). This motor could not be regulated in speed or direction. But the simple appliance, easily portable from one room to another, marks the starting point of innumerable moves to punctuate the house with local power units. The year 1889 saw many other patents drawn up for fans driven by electric motors.[66] But Tesla's simple apparatus owes its significance to the fact that it did not remain a mere idea, but was commercially manufactured and put on the market.

The hot and damp American summer inevitably brought attempts to substitute mechanical devices for the hand fan — something, at any rate, that should free the hand of its waving to-and-fro motion. Such mechanisms 'operated by means of a single lever and cord' [67] might be pedal-driven or harnessed to a rocking chair. 'When a person is sitting in the chair and rocks it . . .' the fan placed overhead 'is vibrated by the slightest motion of the chair.' [68] If in the 'sixties one wanted a truly automatic fan, it would have to be a clockwork one. 'The case containing the works is attached to the ceiling and provided with revolving wings.' [69] There were also at this time clockwork fans for tabletop use, adjustable in speed.[70]

Nicola Tesla's electric fan of 1889 led the development by about a quarter century. Electric current in the 'nineties in Europe as in America, was a luxury.

[66] For instance, U.S. Patent 414,758, 12 Nov. 1889; or 417,474, 17 Dec. 1889.

[67] U.S. Patent 133,164, 19 Nov. 1872.

[68] Ibid. As is well known, Franklin's visitors admired such a device on his easy chair around 1780.

[69] U.S. Patent 76,175, 31 May 1868.

[70] U.S. Patent 81,539, 25 Aug. 1868.

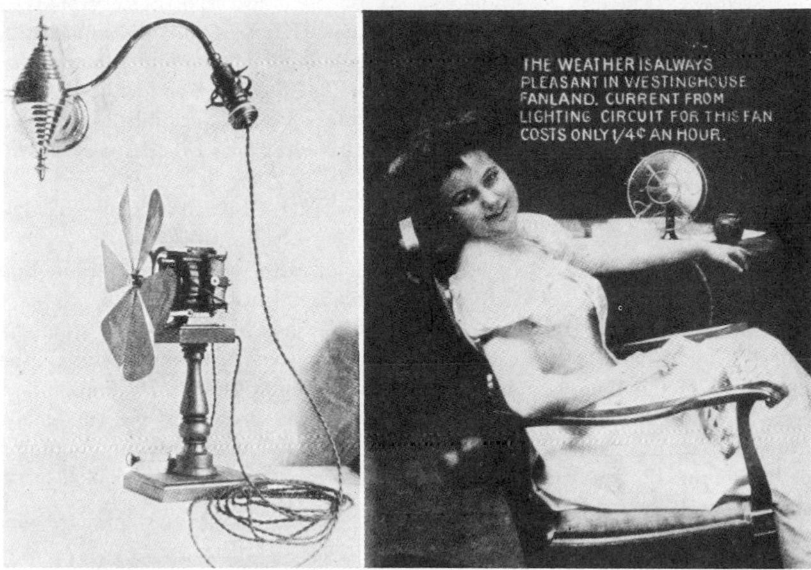

387. First Universal Fan Motor, 1891. *This motor could be regulated in speed, unlike the first motor of 1889.* (*Archives of Westinghouse Company, Pittsburgh*)

388. Electric Fan, 1910. (*Archives of Westinghouse Company, Pittsburgh*)

There were no electrical networks.[71] The first large-scale generating plant was projected in 1891, but did not begin operation until 1896. Erected by the Westinghouse Company near Niagara Falls to supply the near-by city of Buffalo with current, it consisted of three Tesla A.C. dynamos, each of 5000 H.P.[72] Theaters such as the Paris Opera, department stores, factories, generated their own current. Most of the power then consumed was for propelling electrical streetcars. There were devices by which current for dental offices might be tapped directly from the 500-volt streetcar lines 'without the least danger for the operator and the patient.'[73]

The question whether electricity should be made available to the masses was

[71] The first long-distance transmission of electric current was realized by Marcel Deprez for the International Electricity Exhibition held at Munich in 1882.

[72] Other large installations were projected at this time for the American West: one of 4000 H.P. for Sacramento and another of 12,000 for Portland, Oregon. Cf. *Electric Review*, London, 1895, vol. 36, p.762.

[73] J. P. Barrett, *Electricity at the Columbian Exposition*, Chicago, 1894, p.446.

discussed everywhere in the 'nineties. At London's exclusive Society of Arts, which, we recall, sponsored the first International Exhibition in 1851, a lecturer, Crompton, concluded that electric current was 'too expensive to become general.' Wherever the question was raised, in Philadelphia [74] or in London, the experts were dubious. Only the great inventors saw its possibilities. Nicola Tesla, at the start of the 'nineties, foretold that electricity would soon be used as casually as water.

Even around 1900 people were wondering whether electricity would ever displace gas.

The cheapening of current went hand in hand with the gradual introduction of the small electric motor. Toward 1910 this trend made itself more strongly felt. But the motor was still seen as an outside body, a unit distinct from the object to be driven. More usual was the water motor. Leafing through the catalogues of the time, one immediately notices that the electric motor is a rarity. Should a housewife wish an electric motor, instead of the customary water motor, the manufacturer warns: 'I can't quote you a price on an electric motor to run the washer until I have the information what kind of electric current you have and the voltage.' [75]

The Mechanization of Cleaning: Laundering

IMITATION OF THE HAND

Eighteenth-Century England: The Americans ever take the lead in mechanically overcoming the difficulties of a complicated craft. This does not mean that other countries failed to show an early interest in the problem. Late eighteenth-century England turned a slight stream of its tremendous inventive current into the modest sphere of washing machines. With the exception of a solitary forerunner of 1691,[76] whose mechanism is rather hard to picture from the letters patent, invention in this field begins in 1780, bringing new patents almost each year, five in 1790.[77]

By and large, they are cumbrous constructions moved by cranks, wheels, levers, and balances. Like the early steam engines they employ a mighty apparatus to little effect, amid great agitation of pistons, hammers, or sliding trays. Even when it claimed domesticity — and the inventor hopefully entitles his

---

[74] J. Chester Wilson, 'Electric Heating,' Engineering Club, Philadelphia, *Proceedings*, 1895, vol. 12, no. 2.

[75] 'Motor Self-working Washer,' catalogue *c.*1906.

[76] British Patent No. 271, 27 Aug. 1691.

[77] British Patents Nos. 1744, 1759, 1770, 1772, 1786. This period demands more detailed investigation.

drawing 'Washerwoman's assistant or Housewives' Economist'[78] — such machinery was out of question for the household.

No more than a minimum of skepticism is needed to tell one that these contrivances could neither assist the washerwoman nor bring economy to the household. It is a time of groping, in which the guiding principles were not to be discovered. It was too early.

***America before* 1850:** By its very nature America was moved more than any other country to invent compact and handy washing machines for household use.

Both eighteenth-century England and America until 1850 started from the idea of directly imitating the to-and-fro movement of the hand.

What the washerwoman accomplished with her fist, vigorously rubbing the fabrics against the ribbed washboard, the machine should now perform. Taking over her drudgery, the machine should, like her, scrub and wash the clothes piece by piece.

In the first half of the nineteenth century, even in America where the mechanisms were more simple, the eagerness for a direct solution often led to quite grotesque contraptions. To take one whose lineage dates back to the eighteenth century, and which had a surprisingly long life, a model of 1846[79] (fig. 389): Here the to-and-fro motion of the human hand is imitated by causing a curved receptacle to slide over a similarly curved bed of rollers, thus pressing and rubbing the linen caught between these two mechanisms.[80] A threefold crank simultaneously swings the bed of rollers and the receptacle in opposite directions. The 'swinging box for holding the clothes,' which also presses them against the washboard, is directly abstracted from the human hand. Despite its rather grotesque design, this type with the curved, mobile washboard and the container passing over it in an opposite direction has remained in use until well into this century, and is found, for instance, in Montgomery Ward's catalogue for 1927 as 'Our Famous Old Faithful' (fig. 390).

The inventor of 1846 readily admits that the idea of using a bed of rollers is not new. He asks credit only for its curved form, also given to the box. Actually this awkward arrangement, which travels like a swing through the tub, goes back to English forerunners. There the idea already appears of replacing the hand by a swinging and curved grating of boards, which rubs the linen and presses it against the bottom of the tub.

[78] British Patent No. 1882, 21 May 1792. Washmachine by John Harrison.

[79] U.S. Patent 4891, 15 Dec. 1846.

[80] It had its beginnings in England. British Patent No. 1772, 18 Aug. 1790.

Likewise imitative of the human hand was the 'wringing out' before rollers or centrifugal force were used. Such a proposal appears in the first washing-machine patent of 1780 [81] 'In the machine over the trough are fixed two hooks, over which wet linen is hung, and by giving a circular movement to one of the hooks, presses the water out of the linen.' Ten years later, in 1790, the washing is already laid in a 'wringing cloth of netting' [82] which is a slit sack fastened at either end, to receive the wet clothes. The sack and its contents are twisted by means of a crank much as if it were being wrung by hand. The American patent of 1847 [83] (fig. 391) improves the fastenings but in other respects it follows in the track of the eighteenth-century types.

THE TWO WAYS OF MECHANIZATION

Technically considered, washing machines fall into several types. Four is the number usually given. Whoever cares to look further will find them often described in special literature.[84] But methodological enquiry is more in our line of interest. Considered from this standpoint, two ways of mechanizing the laundry process have so far appeared. Both are closely bound up with the developments of the period.

The first method is mainly of service in the larger *commercial laundries*. Here automatic operation is based on the use of steam. This method has remained supreme in the large-scale establishments from mid-century down to the present. Here too the system that has prevailed is that of the first industrially produced model. The model of 1851 (fig. 396) immediately proved its worth. Exploiting the natural circulation of steam and boiling water, it reinforces this action by a rotary movement. The mechanical parts consist of a pair of concentric cylinders of which the inner one is mobile. Fire plays beneath the outer, fixed cylinder. They are to be half filled. 'As soon as steam begins to escape from the boiler, put in sufficient soap, give the boiler a few turns . . . then put in your clothes . . . and let them stay in from 3 to 20 minutes turning the boiler occasionally.' [85]

In a now rare catalogue preserved by the Library of Congress, the inventor explains what truly takes place in the washing process with the same careful detail as his contemporaries argue the advantages of the bath. 'Dirt is a compound held together and fastened to the fabric by oily glutinous or vegetable

[81] British Patent No. 1269, 5 Dec. 1780.

[82] British Patent No. 1772, 18 Aug. 1790.

[83] U.S. Patent 5106, 8 May 1847.

[84] Edna B. Snyder, *A Study of Washing Machines*, Nebraska, 1931. The types distinguished are: The Dolly, the Gyrator, the Cylinder, and the Vacuum.

[85] U.S. Patent 8446, 21 Oct. 1851, James T. King, Washing Apparatus.

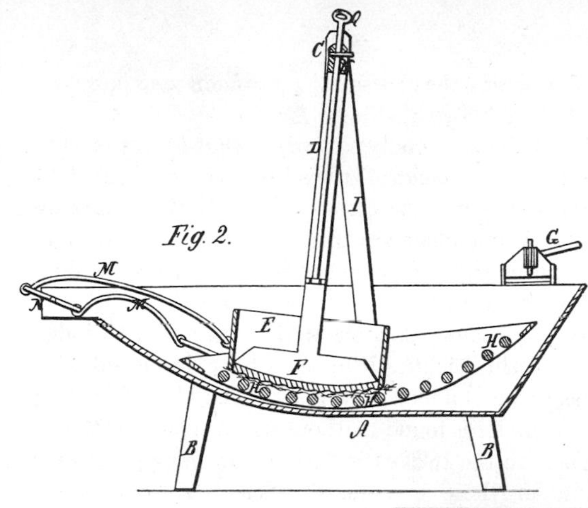

389. Washing Machine, 1846. *Imitation of the to-and-fro movement of the human hand by a curved receptacle sliding over a bed of rollers. 'Cranked at* N, *the rollers and the cradle slide against one another in opposite directions, squeezing the clothes between them.'* (*U.S. Patent* 4891, 15 *December* 1846)

Our Famous "OLD FAITHFUL"

THE OLD FAITHFUL SELF WORKING WASHER

$17.98

390. Hand-Power Washer, 1927. *The lineage of this curved washboard goes back to late eighteenth-century England. It is a hardy type, appearing even in our century, in the mail-order-house catalogues, where it is still carefully described: 'At every stroke of the hand lever, two curved corrugated washboards, moving in opposite directions, rub the clothes in much the same manner as on a washboard.'* (*Montgomery Ward Catalogue*, 1927)

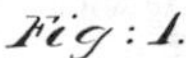

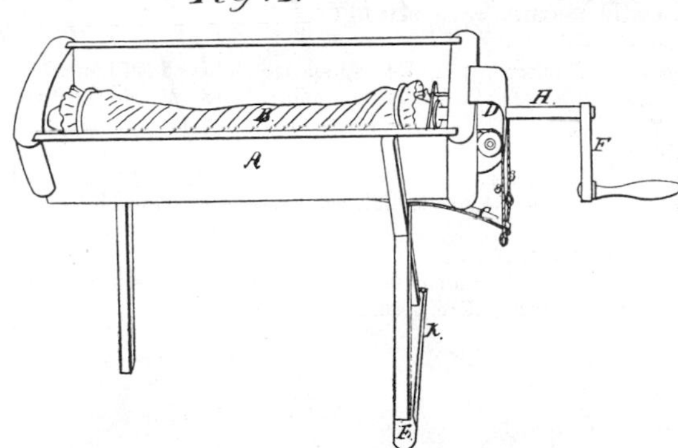

391. Wringer, 1847. *Imitates the hand by twisting of a slit sack, before continuous rotation was achieved by rollers or centrifugal spinning.* (*U.S. Patent* 5106, 8 *May* 1847)

particles . . . washing means neutralizing the cohesion . . . common soap possesses these neutralizing properties '[86] (fig. 395).

After this the inventor, James T. King, proudly announces that he has mechanized the process without imitating the hand. 'Other inventors have tried to succeed by imitating as nearly as possible the common process of washing by rubbing, pressure or friction . . . in our machines the clothes are alternately in steam and in suds; the former opens the fibres and the latter removes the dirt. Therefore no rubbing, pounders, or dashers.'

This cylinder type became the most popular one of the 'seventies, to judge by the number of patents, and in the 'eighties it appears fully developed with an inside cylinder made of sheet iron stamped with holes. The idea of putting washables in a rotating cage or cylinder is found (without use of steam) in 1782[87] (fig. 393). It was used in England in the 1820's (fig. 394) for washing potatoes.[88]

What were the antecedents of these inventions? Scientifically designed apparatus, which use the circulation of steam and boiling water for cleaning, had appeared in France in the 'thirties. Significantly enough, they were not conceived for laundries, but for bleacheries of the textile industry, where yarn and fabrics were made ready for dyeing.[89]

An apparatus popular in his day is shown by the great French chemist Jean-Baptiste Dumas, in the plates to his *Traité de chimie appliquée aux arts* (Paris, 1847).[90] Steam is formed in a boiler. This steam drives hot water through an ascension pipe into a double-bottomed vat where it scatters evenly over the fabrics. A valve opens and closes at regular intervals, alternately filling and emptying the vat (fig. 392). The pattern is almost identical with that of a coffee percolator.[91]

England's striking interest in washing machines during the last twenty years of the eighteenth century is confined as in France to the industrial processing of textiles, with only an occasional 'Machine called a laundry for washing and pressing apparel.'[92] English interest in mechanical laundering rather weakened in the nineteenth century, while the American quest for a device to lighten the laundering burden of the housewife became ever stronger.

---

[86] American Steam Washing Co., New York, Catalogue, 1855, 'Description and philosophy of James T. King's Patent: Washing and Drying Apparatus, adapted for the use of families, Hotels, Public Institutions, and large laundries.'

[87] British Patent No.1331, 1 June 1782.

[88] *Mechanic's Magazine*, London, 1823–4, vol. I, p. 301.

[89] Even in the 1780's the *Grande Encyclopédie* gives its detailed information on washing machines in the article 'Bleaching.'

[90] Planche 136. Duvoir's apparatus, invented in 1837.

[91] Rotating wash-drums are also constructed, but these are quite primitive apparatus used only for rinsing.

[92] British Patent No.1269, 5 Dec. 1780.

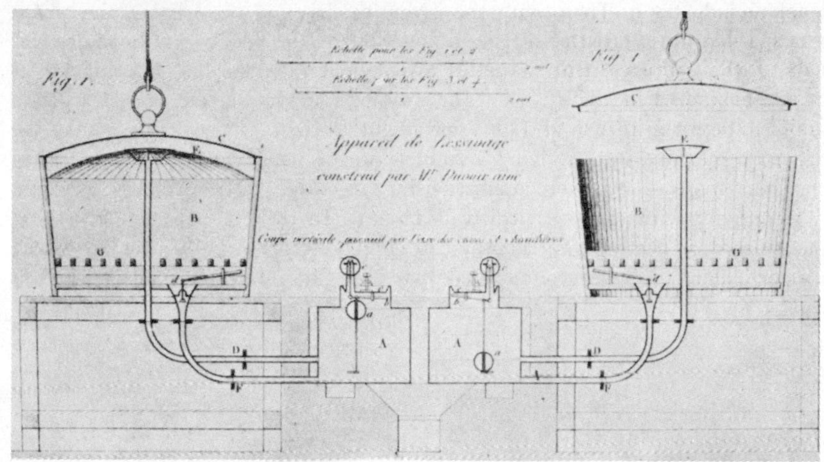

392. French Automatic Washing Machine by Duvoir, 1837. *Washing machines employing the natural circulation of steam and boiling water were first made for industrial use in French textile bleacheries of the 1830's. 'Steam is formed in the boiler and, pressing upon the liquid, causes it to mount through the ascender tube which projects it uniformly over the surface of the linen.' In the* 1940*'s fully automatic washers for the home employ the same principle, spurting 'geysers' of water through the fabric (fig.* 404). (*J. B. Dumas,* Traité de chimie appliquée aux arts, *Paris,* 1847)

James T. King's cylinder washing machine of 1851 marks the inauguration of automatic laundering. But, it should not be overlooked, such ideas had long been in the air. An American patent of 1831,[93] which has survived the Patent Office fire in the shape of a handwritten specification, shows the inventor already working with two concentric cylinders. The water is admitted to 'an outer cylinder . . . constructed so as to be water tight,' while 'the open cylinder is made to revolve upon iron gudgeons.' Here too steam was used in the cleaning, but was generated in a separate cauldron.

FALTERING INTRODUCTION

The first American washing-machine patent dates from the year 1805. From then on efforts to perfect it into a practical appliance were almost unceasing. Its introduction came about falteringly. Over a hundred years elapsed before the mechanization of laundering took effect in the average household. Despite the many patents, it is only from around 1860 that we can speak of a washing-

[93] U.S. Patent 6711–X (old numbering), 10 Aug. 1831. John Shull, Washing Machine.

machine industry.[94] Then, with the inventive drive of the 'sixties, the tempo was speeded up. Statistics register a small but rising production in the second half of the century. But statistics often yield only surface information of events behind them. Thus, when the washing-machine output is seen to have doubled between 1870 and 1890, one might at first glance assume that the domestic machine was enjoying a sudden run of popularity. Actually it was the sharp increase of power laundries using large and costly machines.[95]

Here living witnesses will yield truer insight. In 1869, as patents for washing machines were nearing two thousand in number, Catherine Beecher advocated no particular one, but recommended that every dozen families should share a

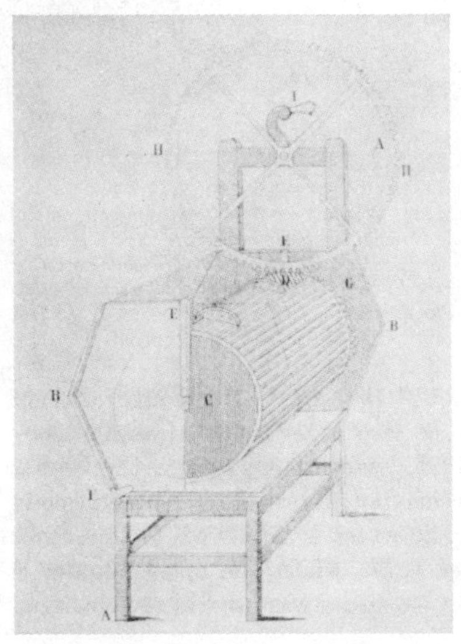

393. English Washing Machine, 1782. *The idea of rotating a cylinder so as to bring the clothes in intimate contact with suds and water goes back to the first great wave of invention in the late eighteenth century.* (*British Patent*, 1331, 1782)

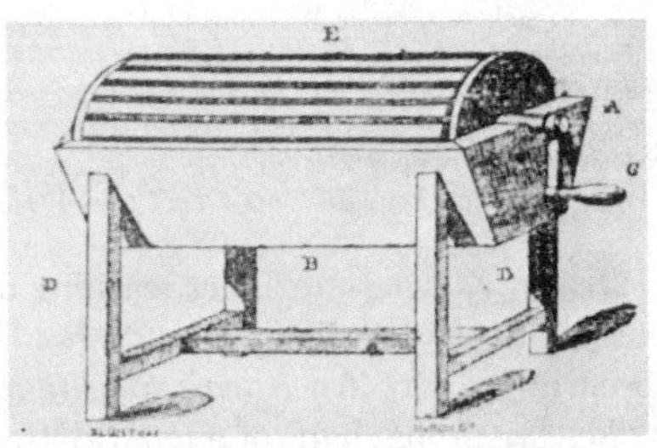

394. Potato Washer, 1823–24. *The revolving motion of a cylinder so fashioned that the liquid can stream in and out was also adopted for cleaning potatoes.* (Mechanics Magazine, *vol.* I, *London*, 1823–4)

[94] We follow the data given in one of the few researches into this field, Jacob A. Swisher, 'The Evolution of Wash Day,' *The Iowa Journal of History and Politics* (Iowa City, Jan. 1940), vol. 38, no. 1.

Annual product value of washing machines in the U.S.:

Year	*Dollars (Millions)*
1860	.08
1870	1.00
1880	1.182
1890	2.4
1900	3.7
1910	5.0

[95] This may be gathered from the number of factories entering into production of the commercial type machine as well as from the catalogues. The census figures are available only from 1900 on.

395. Washing Apparatus for a Large Laundry, by James T. King, 1855. *Reinforces the natural action of steam by a rotary movement. The mechanical parts consist of a pair of cylinders of which the inner is perforated and revolving. This first industrially produced type is the one that has proved successful down to the present.* (*American Steam Washing Co., New York. Catalogue,* 1855. *Library of Congress*)

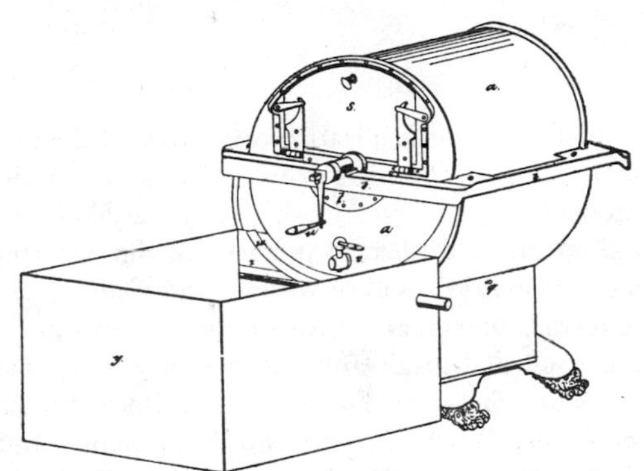

396. Washing Machine by James T. King, 1851. (*U.S. Patent* 8446, 21 *October* 1851)

communal laundry as successfully provided for the working class of England and France in the mid-'fifties.

'How it would simplify the burdens of the American housekeeper to have washing and ironing day expunged from her calendar. . . . Whoever sets *neighborhood laundries* on foot will do much to solve the American housekeeper's hardest problem.' [96]

---

[96] Beecher and Stowe, op.cit. p.334.

Around 1900 the hand-cranked washing machine began to replace the back-breaking washboard, as a pamphlet of 1924 retrospectively records.

In 1912 Christine Frederick, who was in close touch with the situation, wrote in the *Ladies Home Journal*, 'Washing is done in most houses without washing machines and with only a common boiler.'

HOME LAUNDERING FULLY MECHANIZED

Washing machines and vacuum cleaners are an index of mechanization in household cleaning. Their use expands as their cost is lowered. In 1926, refrigerators had an average retail price of $400, and 200,000 units were sold; by 1935 their price had sunk to $170 and sales reached 1.5 million units. The identical thing occurs in washing machine sales. 'From 1926 to 1935 washer demand rose from 900,000 units to 1.4 million units, while the average retail price was more than halved — from $150 to $60.[97] A large mail-order house cut the washer price to a record of $29.95 in 1936. This is the time of the democratization of comfort.

Just as full mechanization concentrated the grain production line from reaping to bagging in the small baby combine, so in this period home laundering was brought to the verge of being fully mechanized. The idea of an automaton, a self-operating washer, to perform all the operations from soiled linen to washed and damp-dried clothes without interference of the human hand, preoccupied numerous inventors. Intricate mechanisms are necessary in order to eliminate the hand and attain full automaticity — mechanisms to time each operation, introduce the water into the tub, release the washing water, introduce rinsing water, expell it and re-circulate it by pump, and finally damp-dry the clothes. Two distinct operations have to be combined within the same receptacle: washing and drying.

The fully mechanized washing automaton follows two basic designs. One is the *horizontal* 'cylinder type' originating in the 1850's, where a perforated inner cylinder rotates on a horizontal axis (fig. 396).[98]

The second type is on a *vertical* axis, the clothes being cleansed by an agitator

---

[97] We are indebted for this data to Mr. Tom J. Smith, Jr., Cleveland, Ohio.

[98] U.S. Patent 8446, 21 Oct. 1851. The automatic machines manufactured by Bendix (1939), Westinghouse, and several other firms are of the horizontal cylinder type.

within a perforated metal basket. The vertical type with agitator became the usual nonautomatic home washer. It originated in the 'sixties [99] (fig. 377).

The final operation is the centrifugal drying of the clothes. Here one of the greatest difficulties arose. Washing has to be performed by slow rotary or oscillatory movements, while the drying or expelling of water requires high-speed spinning. Thus speed-change and timing mechanisms are prerequisites of the automatic washer.

The automatic washer, whether on a horizontal or a vertical axis, typically consists of a single receptacle or tub, inside which there rotates a perforated basket. The single-tub and drier type, which expells the water from the basket by centrifugal force, also goes back to the wave of invention of the late 'sixties.[100]

The 'seventies disclosed the broad idea of extracting an amount of the washing and rinsing liquid from the basket by centrifugal force and recirculating by pump from the tub back to the basket.[101] A patent was filed in 1878 for a power-driven, single-tub washer and dryer having two speeds, low for washing, high for drying.[102] The speed change was of course accomplished by hand.

The idea of full automatic laundering was pursued time and again down to the period of full mechanization. The early 'twenties saw the manufacture of various single-tub washing and drying machines, where slow-speed washing and high-speed spinning were used for successive washings and rinsings. After 1900 the problem of the self-operating washer became largely narrowed down to finding the means of *automatic control*. A clock or electric-motor timer sets off electro-magnets or operates a hydraulic mechanism to open and close the valves, connect and disconnect the power from the cylinder.[103]

A further problem hindered the rapid solution of the washing automaton: the mechanical speed change from washing to drying action. This was not difficult to deal with as soon as the means came to hand, the two-speed electric

[99] U.S. Patent 94,005, 24 Aug. 1869. The vertical type was pioneered by machines such as the Laundryette (1917), whose production was discontinued in 1923. In the whole period down to 1939 no single-tub washer and drier type was on the market. The principal patents for the automatic vertical type are those of James B. Kelly, designer of the Laundryette, filed between 1924 and 1928. They form the basis for licenses for the vertical cylinder type.

[100] Our remarks on the automatic washer are based on a patent investigation made in Dec. 1944 by the patent department of the Apex Electrical Manufacturing Co., Cleveland, Ohio, 'On the History of the Automatic Washing Machine Prior to Wales Patent' (typewritten), and on personal letters from Mr. Frantz, President of Apex. We are glad to be able for once to refer to comprehensive research made by the industry itself; indeed we are not aware of any writings on the subject other than current advertisements and magazine articles.

[101] Centrifugal Machine, U.S. Patent 139,108, 20 May 1873.

[102] Centrifugal Machine, U.S. Patent 215,428, 20 May 1879. In 1883 application was made for a patent (U.S. Patent 420,742, issued 2 Feb. 1890) which outlined the principle of a modern automatic washer (Bendix), in so far as it provided a two-speed, *horizontal* cylinder.

[103] Automatic Controlling Means for Washing Machines, U.S. Patent 1,005,093, 3 Oct. 1911.

motor with automatic speed-changing device. Besides the American Patents, French and English ones[104] also moved in this direction.

The long line of experimentation striving from semi-automatic to fully automatic laundering did not yield practical results until about 1939. It is as difficult to say who invented the first automatic washer as it is to name the inventor of the vacuum cleaner. Both are based on collective efforts and slow cumulative experience. Moreover they are compounds of inventions in various fields.[105]

Another trend comes to the fore in 1946. The agitator whose arms may still be a vestige of the rubbing hand is done away with. The automaton cleanses by virtue of a continuous and forceful penetration of the clothes by sudsy water. The basket does not revolve in the usual manner, but bounces vigorously. The floating clothes are patted and slapped at the rate of 600 times a minute, and penetrated by 'geysers' of water spurting from the bottom (fig. 404).

This procedure, which demands a refined mechanism, goes back to the first scientific approach to laundering. Energetic spurts of water, we have seen, were used for treating textiles in French bleacheries of the 1840's (fig. 392). A liquid is driven by steam pressure up a tube terminating in a conic spray so as to circulate evenly and continuously through the fabrics.[106]

Washing, normally a rough business, is now entrusted to an automaton as sensitive as the radio, which receives waves from the air — if not actually more sensitive. As always in mechanization from the first spinning automatons onward, release from drudgery is paid for in highly complex machinery.

The mechanized washing machine is as typical and natural a product of America and full mechanization as the precision watch is of Switzerland and highly skilled handicraft. If any organic inter-exchange of commodities is to be brought about, their production will be concentrated more or less in the countries most suited to create them — a fact that no artificial barriers can alter.

The automatic washing machine made its appearance on the market toward the end of full mechanization. Then began the race among competing firms to eliminate the draw-back of automatons, their high cost. Most manufacturers, however, will probably continue for some years to struggle with the problem of perfecting a now very intricate mechanism into a trouble-free, simple one, and to improve results through newer methods. A contest sponsored by a well-known woman's magazine reports, concerning the post-war market:

---

[104] French Patent 586,163, 16 Mar. 1925. British Patent 168,294, 4 June 1922.

[105] The claim of, among others, the Wales Reissue Patent 21,020, 28 Feb. 1939, to have been the first adaptation of automatic control to a single-tub washer has been sharply disputed.

[106] In the 'seventies in France this method was adapted in simplified form to home use and is still popular.

Most of the women who voted cherished the idea of owning an automatic washing machine. This vote of approval is five times as high as for either spinner or wringer types. However, unless the price gap between automatics and other styles is narrowed, spirits may be considerably dashed when the price tag is examined.[107]

The Mechanization of Cleaning: Ironing

The problem was raised from mid-century on: How can one do away with re-heating the flat-iron every ten minutes? It is no pleasant task to heat a piece of metal repeatedly in the fire until it glows, before transferring it to the hollow iron, or to array a battery of heavy irons with their bottoms to the stove.

How can the cooling be delayed? How can ironing be made a continuous process?

The answer is clear: only by a continuous heat source within the iron itself. In the 'fifties gas was the only continuous heat source available. In the experimentation with other heat sources at least one suggestion hard to take seriously was that of the iron 'fastened by a tube to a tea kettle and heated . . . by steam.' [108]

An advertising leaflet in the Edison Institute, Dearborn, shows how the early 'fifties attempted to use gas as a constant heat source. A gutta percha tube directly connected this 'gas-iron' to the outlet in the ceiling (fig. 397).

We need not judge here the advisability of using a gas tube in the manner of an electric cord. What is striking is the directness with which the problem was tackled: 'Ironing Simplified and Systematized.' For, it was now proclaimed, 'the process of ironing can be continued unceasingly.'

When it is recalled that the gas range was not introduced until after 1880, the earliness of this attempt to do by gas what electricity alone could achieve is apparent. The gas iron is here portrayed in almost the same inviting words as, in our century, the electric iron: 'Pleasant — the oppressive heat of a stove is dispensed with; convenient — for the iron may be used in any room or chamber where there is gas.'

In 1906, when the Westinghouse Company felt that a series of newspaper advertisements was called for to familiarize the public with the advantages of the electric iron, it particularly stressed the point that the housewife may now do her ironing in the open air on the veranda. And it did not seem superfluous to remind the husband of what it means to stand by a hot range on a summer's

---

[107] Mary Davis Gillies, *What Women want in their Kitchens of Tomorrow, a report on the Kitchen of Tomorrow Contest conducted by McCall's Magazine*, New York, 1944, p.155.

[108] Swisher, op.cit. p.32.

Ironing Simplified and Systematized.

100 PER CENT. SAVED IN LABOR AND FUEL.

LITHGOW'S PATENT

GAS-HEATING

SMOOTHING IRON,

FOR

TAILORS, HATTERS,

AND

FAMILY USE.

397. Gas-Heated Smoothing Iron, c.1850. *A gutta percha tube is attached to the overhead gas jet in this early effort to achieve continuous ironing. 'A saving of time and labor, for when once the iron is heated the process of ironing can be continued indefinitely. Time alone must bring it into universal use.' (Advertisement, courtesy the Edison Institute, Dearborn, Mich.)*

Put a Stove in Your Office

and build a good rousing fire in it. It will give you some idea of the heat your wife has to endure every time she irons.

You think it's hot, do you? Then what does your wife think while ironing to the accompaniment of a hot stove?

Why not kick that stove out and get her a Westinghouse Electric Iron? Don't you think she would be grateful for it? If you have any doubt about it, you can have an iron on free trial.

393. Introduction of the Electric Iron, 1909. *Even in 1909 strong persuasion was needed to convince the public of the advantages of electric ironing. A series of advertisements by the Westinghouse Company appealed to the men's compassion, and the women were told: 'Why iron in the laundry? Why not iron out on the cool porch where you can get fresh air?' (Advertisement, Westinghouse, Inc.)*

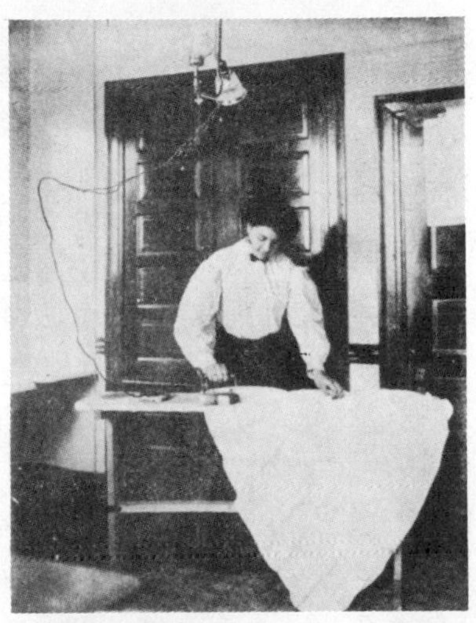

399. Electric Ironing, 1911. *Electricity has made continuous ironing possible. In the early days of domestic current, the iron was plugged to the chandeliers, like the gas iron of the 'fifties. The side-by-side use of gaslight and electric light, and the rigging of the cord suggest the improvised use of the whole appliance. (Archives of Westinghouse Company, Pittsburgh)*

day — the hardship to which he was submitting his wife: 'You think it is hot, do you? Put a stove in your office' (fig. 398).[109]

The next step is the attack on the small iron itself. In 1922, Christine Frederick turns to the American housewife: 'You may say you do not use the old type of flat iron, that you use an electric iron; that indeed is one step in advance. Even that is inefficient.' And she who, ten years earlier had begun her New Housekeeping Series with a reckoning of wasted motions in dishwashing, argues once again: 'Now isn't it foolish to iron a tablecloth, an area of about 18,000 square inches, with a heated tool measuring only 24 inches?'[110] The new household tool was the ironer. In this instrument the ironing board has become a padded roll and the iron has taken on the aspect of a curved and gleaming brake-shoe extending the whole width of the cylinder and electrically heated (fig. 402). One may easily remove it from contact with the roller or cause it to press the roller's surface. The thickly padded cylinder, in the later models at least, has 'two roll-speeds, slow for heavy, faster for light articles.' The heating elements within the shoe are controlled by thermostats. As so often in mechanization, the to-and-fro motion of the hand has been transformed into continuous rotation. The whole instrument in the form now quite widespread in the American household is a product of electrification. It first appears in mail-order

[109] In an advertising pamphlet, *You and Your Laundry*, Chicago, 1922.
[110] Ibid.

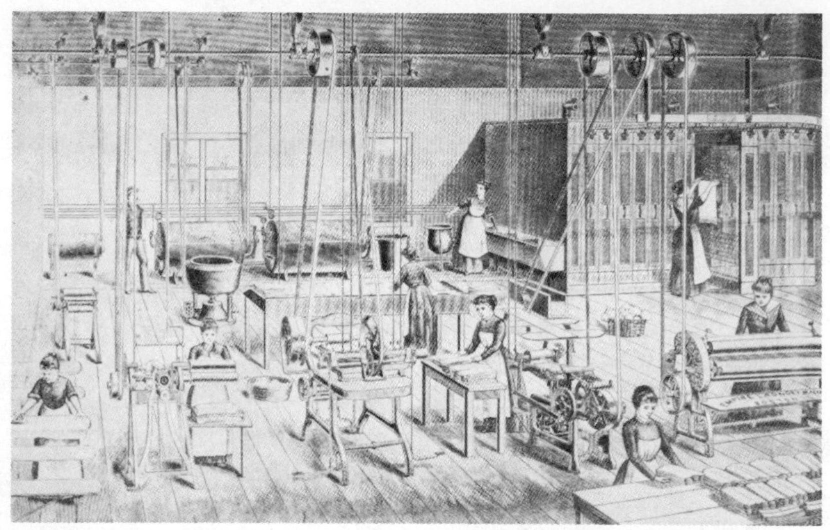

400. Commercial Laundry Equipment, 1883. *Reversing rotary washers and a centrifugal extractor are shown (rear). Steam-heated mangles for the blankets (right). Rotary ironers with steam-heated cylinder are forerunners of the electric ironer, introduced in the American home about 1922. The ironers in this establish ment of the 1880's were specialized for collars, shirts, etc.* (*Empire Laundry Machinery Co., Boston Mass.*)

401. Great Western Ducoudun Ironer, c.1900. *This heavy laundering equipment consists of a hot, polished metal bed and a heavy roller, the whole mounted in a cast-iron frame. The ponderous metal bed later became the curved electric 'shoe' of portable domestic ironers.* (Laundry Management, *London,* 1902)

catalogues in 1926. Trollied from place to place, it is as portable as the vacuum cleaner and takes up but little room. The motor is housed out of sight in a white enamel casing, and closed in its enamel cover the machine can form a transportable working surface in the kitchen. One cannot deny the esthetic appeal of this clean-cut instrument.

Handy ironing appliances such as these are the direct descendants of the heavy cast-iron machines that came into use in the commercial laundries during the early 'eighties. Called 'rotary ironers,' they were specialized to take various

LADIES, PLEASE BE SEATED!

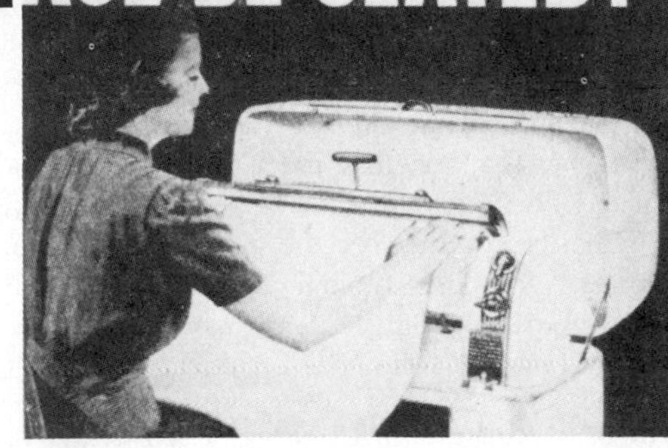

402. Electric Ironer Democratized. *The domestic ironer reaches standard form in the time of full mechanization. Machines sheathed in white enamel and with everything for the housewife's comfort are offered at a low price by the mail-order houses from* 1926 *on.* (*Sears Roebuck Catalogue*, 1941–2)

403. Folding Ironer, 1946. *The ironer, like the vacuum cleaner, evolves from a large machine to an extremely handy tool. This machine 'folds up to occupy just* 1¾ *feet of floor space and rolls easily on wheels when folded up. The ironing mechanism is counterbalanced on its tubular steel stand so it opens easily to ironing position.'* (*Courtesy Earle Ludgin and Co., Chicago*)

types of articles, collars, shirts, or towels (fig. 400). Usually one roller was heated and the other covered with felt. But the modern instruments' immediate ancestor was the Ducoudun ironer (fig. 401), so named after its French inventor. The Ducoudun ironer, like the later electric models, had a 'polished, concave and heated metal bed and a heavy roller, fitted in a strong cast-iron frame.' [111]

This mechanical aid soon became democratized too, and in their 1941–2 catalogues the large mail-order firms offer it at a price ranging from $20 to $60. The caption reads: 'Ladies, please be seated!' (fig. 402).

Thus ironing has become almost a pleasure: 'Relax, sit down, and enjoy ironing.' A resilient tubular chair, whose elasticity favors relaxation, is included.

Away with the flat iron! Or, as the catalogue puts it:

'Free yourself from back breaking drudgery.'

The Mechanization of Cleaning: The Dishwashing Machine

As we have mentioned, the solution for mechanical dishwashing that became general in the era of full mechanization was already proposed in the 'sixties. Ideas of various kinds had preceded it. At first the rotating blades are housed in a chamber separate from the things to be washed. Then an inventor places the agitator 'within the chamber that contains all the dishes and the washing water.' [112] The principle has been clearly grasped: a bladed wheel shall 'throw the water against the plates and other articles.' The crockery, held in wire racks, is situated tangentially to the whirling of the water.

One cannot but think of the water turbine. Indeed this is the birth time of the Francis turbine. James B. Francis (1815–92) based the turbine that bears his name on an exact insight into the laws of the flow of water. Francis, who started in locomotive building in England, became hydraulic engineer of Lowell, Massachusetts, building canals and waterworks. His first theoretical research into the little-known field of hydrodynamics was published in 1855. The Francis turbine is still used to handle large volumes of water in low head installations. In the shaping of its blades and its whole construction, it is a plastic expression of the behavior of smoothly flowing water.

The dishwashing machine is a modest offshoot of this thinking. Here, however, the process is reversed, just as the motor reverses the dynamo. In the turbine the water is speeded through vanes to move the blades, while in the dishwasher

[111] *Laundry Management, A Handbook for Use in Private and Public Laundries*, 4th ed., London, 1902, p.160. Ironing machines, particularly for tailors, were patented in America during the 'fifties and 'sixties. Unlike other household appliances of the time, these cannot be regarded as true forerunners. U.S. Patent 21,450, 7 Sept. 1857. Hollow cylinder with rollers, operated by a crank. U.S. Patent 72,773, 12 Mar. 1867. Hollow revolving or rotating heated iron.

[112] U.S. Patent 40,280, 13 Oct. 1863.

404. Laundering Fully Mechanized: American Washing Machine, 1946. *The broad idea of automatic laundering dates from the early 1870's, and in that decade the basic principle was patented; low-speed washing action followed by high-speed expelling action in the same tub. Although automatic washers appeared in the 1920's, their permanent success begins about 1939. In 1946 the agitator, last vestige of the hand, was eliminated in this machine, the clothes being penetrated by geysers of sudsy water spurting from the bottom of the vigorously bouncing basket.* (*Courtesy Apex Rotarex Corp., Cleveland Ohio*)

405. Automatic Dishwasher and Washing Machine Combined, 1946. *Even before the automatic washing machine reached the broad mass of consumers, it was given a second function, dishwashing, in the American tradition of combinability. 'Converting from a clothes washer to a dishwasher takes less than a minute and a half. It's an easy matter to lift out the clothes washer parts and replace them with the dishwasher attachments. All parts are light-weight.'* (*Courtesy Earle Ludgin and Co., Chicago*)

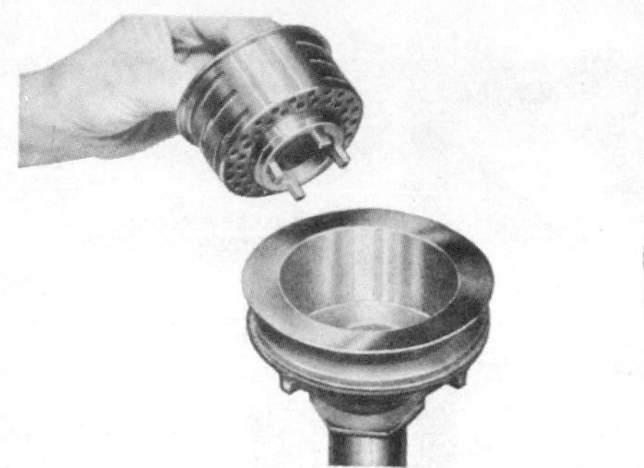

406. Basket Strainer, 1942. *In the U.S.A. even the form and efficiency of the sink outlet are carefully studied. Basket strainers in two movable parts are as unusual as the tabletop range in European production of the* 1940's. (*Courtesy the Schaible Co., Cincinnati*)

the blades of the rotor dash the water against the dishes disposed in their racks.

The manner in which the inventor of the dishwashing machine of 1865 [113] (fig. 375) gives shape to his thought tells us how soon the reasonings and experiments of the great theoreticians and inventors were reflected in household appliances.

A long incubation then began. Not until the New York State Fair of 1910 did a manufacturer [114] exhibit a mechanical dishwasher. It was still hand-cranked as in the 'sixties. Certainly this firm persevered with the problem and did not slacken until the present-day electric dishwasher had taken shape. In 1930 the company was purchased by General Electric, who began to build their own machines. The first square-tub and single-knob-control models were then brought out (1932), which, combined with the sink, formed a unit ready to merge with the mechanized kitchen — a parallel with the table-top range. New combinations are still in the making.

In contrast to the mechanical refrigerator, the electrified dishwashing machine, which made its appearance in the 1930's, has had a relatively limited market. It now becomes a precision instrument with a variety of automatic devices (fig. 374). It had not yet made its way into the catalogues of the large mail-order houses, which usually show when an invention has reached the larger public. In the contest conducted by *McCall's Magazine* in 1943–4, of 11,446 women answering, only 115 possessed an electric dishwasher.[115]

[113] U.S. Patent 51,000, 21 Nov. 1865.

[114] The Walker Co., Syracuse, N.Y. Information by General Electric Co. Whether this was the first manufactured dishwasher is to be further ascertained.

[115] Mary Davis Gillies, *What Women Want in Their Kitchens of Tomorrow: A Report of the Kitchens of Tomorrow Contest conducted by McCall's Magazine*, New York, 1944.

Around 1945 the electric dishwasher in a sense still belonged among the shelved inventions. Its production for the mass market will doubtless have to await such time as the servantless household becomes universal.

The Mechanization of Cleaning: The Mechanical Garbage Disposer

Latest in the line of cleaning appliances is the automatic garbage disposer, or electric sink. It is mounted directly beneath the strainer in the drain outlet. A dishwasher and an electric sink may be joined side by side in a single unit (fig. 407).

The purpose of the electric sink is 'the sanitary elimination of food waste where it originates, by flushing it directly through the outlet of the kitchen sink and into the sewer systems to be carried away by the magic of water transportation." [116]

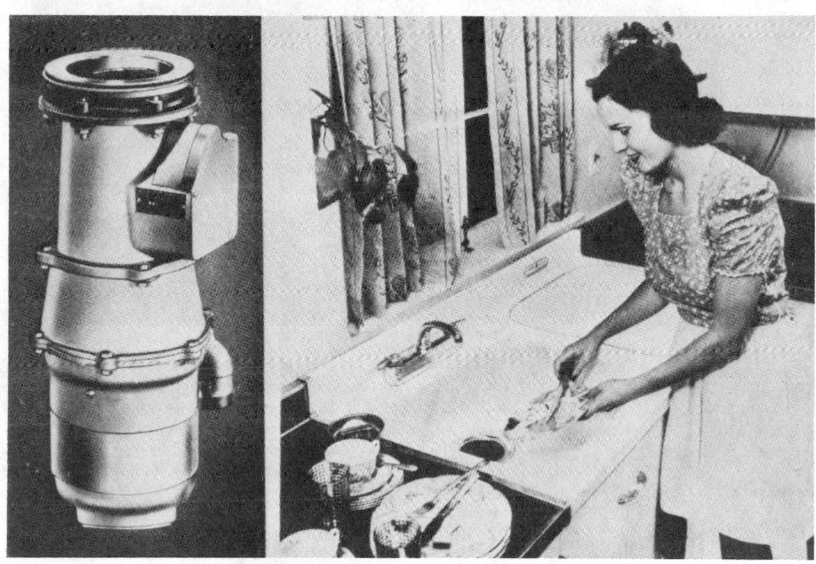

407. 'Electric Sink' with Built-in Garbage Disposer, 1939. *The mechanical garbage disposer is mounted directly beneath the sink. By means of electrically driven shredding machinery it eliminates food waste as it occurs. A large corporation began to experiment with the idea in* 1929, *bringing it to standard form and factory production in* 1935. (*Courtesy General Electric Co., Schenectady*)

---

[116] J. H. Powers, 'The Disposal,' *General Electric Review*, March 1943, vol. 46, no. 3, pp.175–7. This article explains the appliance in detail. J. H. Powers developed the machine from 1935 on.

408. Manufacturer's Satire on the Overgadgeted Kitchen. *It is a healthy sign that a critique of overmechanization starts from within industry itself. This leaflet, widely circulated by an American plumbing-equipment manufacturer, satirizes the public's willingness to be sold any mechanical gadget whatsoever: 'In the kitchen of tomorrow (whenever that is) everything is automatically run by electronic control. Everything in easy reach of a giant whirling faucet . . . Self-rocking rocket cradle for streamlined baby of tomorrow . . . Packaged dust for a year's supply of food . . . Flowers of tomorrow show influence of streamlining.'* (*Courtesy the Schaible Co., Cincinnati*)

In 1929 the idea was taken up as a development problem by the General Electric Company; preliminary model in 1930; standard form and factory production, 1935: Its bulk was reduced, the shredding mechanism improved, but the principle retained.[117]

This appliance, shaped like an elongated milk can, has a rotating disk at the bottom of its conical receiving chamber, which feeds the waste to the shredding

[117] Information of the General Electric Co., Bridgeport, Conn.

elements. Mixed with water so as to form a flowable mixture, the waste is pumped away down the drain.

The electric sink is symptomatic in one respect. The washing machine, the ironer, the vacuum cleaner, the electric motor, and the refrigerator were originally conceived for commercial use. The electric sink, devised at a time when the mechanized kitchen and its appliances had penetrated the household, entered in reverse order. It was the domestic model that later had to be adapted to hotels, ships, and public establishments. In the Second World War they were used by the United States Army and Navy. The small units are also retained in commercial use, but placed in the food-preparation and dish-cleaning counters.

The Mechanization of Cleaning: The Vacuum Cleaner

The word 'vacuum cleaner' did not come into use before the beginning of our century, probably in 1903.[118] The nineteenth century speaks only of 'carpet sweepers.'

At the turn of the century, heterogeneously named firms appeared in America, claiming to have solved by air suction the problems of mechanical cleaning. 'Air Cleaning Company,' one enterprise called itself, after the medium used. Another's title, 'Sanitary Devices Company,' stresses the hygienic aspect (elimination of flying dust). Finally a firm that acquired all the then basic patents [119] assumed the name that was later to stand for the whole category: 'Vacuum Cleaner Company.'

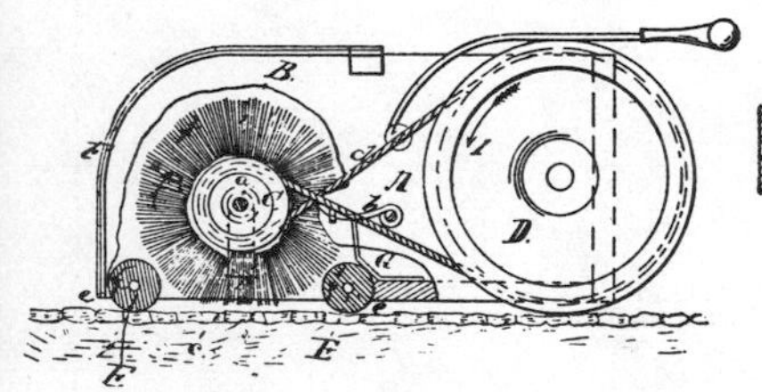

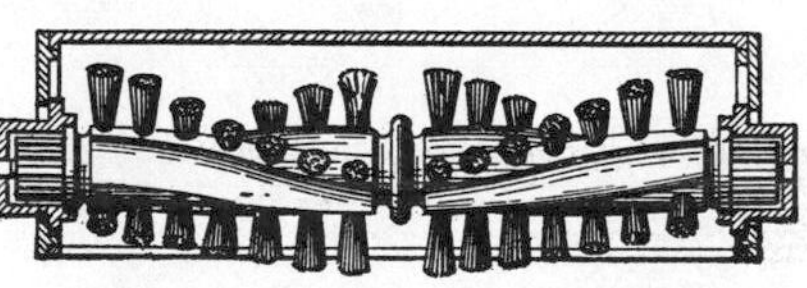

409. Revolving-Brush Carpet Sweeper, 1859. *Revolving-brush sweepers were patented several times in the late* 1850'*s.* '*The brush rotates in the opposite direction to the rollers . . . By means of the springs*, b, *the brush bears down on the floor at all times with the proper force.*' (*U.S. Patent* 24,103, 24 *May* 1859)

410. Revolving Brush of Hoover Vacuum Cleaner, 1915. *Today's bag-type of vacuum cleaner uses revolving brushes in basically the same way as the early patents of the 'fifties.* (*U.S. Patent* 1,151,731, 31 *August* 1915)

THE EARLY PORTABLE MACHINES *c.* 1860

Toward the end of the 'fifties proposals were made to relieve back-bending by means of devices to be rolled over the carpet at the end of a handle. Five carpet-sweeping patents were granted in 1858, nine in 1859. These patents laid down the basic types. The solutions center around the idea of a cylindrical revolving

[118] The *Oxford English Dictionary* quotes from the *Westminster Gazette* of 30 May 1903, showing how unfamiliar was the idea of cleaning by a void: 'There is a machine at work, called the vacuum cleaner.' The French speak at that time of a 'nettoyage sanitaire par le vide' (*La Nature*, Paris 1903, p.576).

[119] David T. Kenney, U.S. Patent 739,263, 15 Sept. 1903, and U.S. Patent 781,532, 31 January 1905. These patents do not mention a 'vacuum cleaner.' They speak of an 'apparatus for removing dust.'

brush[120] caused to turn within a small chassis mounted on wheels or rollers. Neither the drive nor the form of the device has undergone any change of principle since the 'fifties[121] (figs. 409, 410).

THE STREET AND THE CARPET

Revolving brushes were first used to clean the streets. We must discount statements in the specialized literature to the effect that the street sweeper with revolving brushes appeared almost at the same time as 'its counterpart the carpet-sweeper.'[122] Indeed the modern street-sweeping machine was invented by the great English tool designer, Joseph Whitworth, as early as the 1840's.[123] Its forerunners of the 'twenties[124] are extremely primitive. In one of these

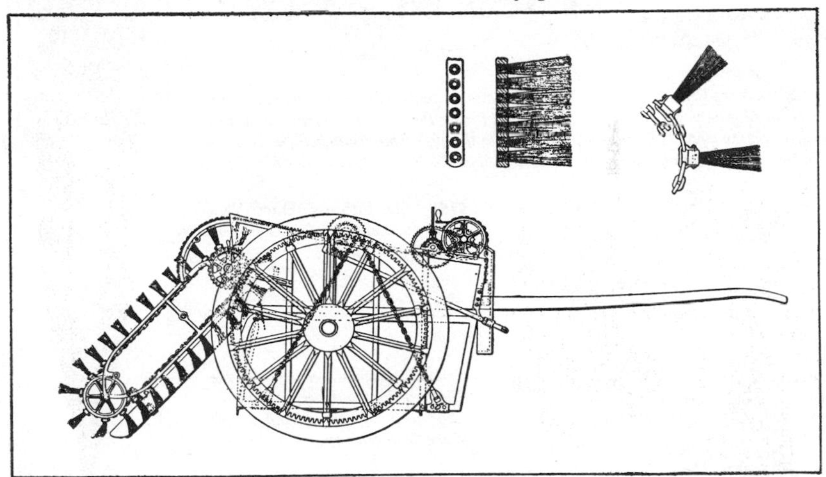

411. JOSEPH WHITWORTH: 'Street Sweeper,' British Patent, 1842. *In this first mechanical device for street sweeping, an endless belt of brushes carries the dirt up an inclined plane. The design of the chain betrays the accomplished engineer. 'I claim the mode of forming the broom or scrapers into endless chains by means of open and closed links.'*

[120] The first patent for mechanical carpet-cleaners, U.S. Patent 21,233, 17 Aug. 1858, is based on 'a revolving brush connected with driving wheels.' As we shall see presently, the rotary brush first appears in the street-cleaning machines (1840). The second, U.S. Patent 21,451, 7 Sept. 1858, represents 'a combination of a brush with a traction roller.'

[121] Cf. U.S. Patent 24,103, 24 May 1859.

[122] M. S. Cooley, *Vacuum Cleaning Systems*, New York, 1913, p.3.

[123] There are two patents. The first: 15 Apr. 1840, British Patent No. 8475, 'Machinery for cleaning and repairing roads and ways,' the second: 2 Aug. 1842, British Patent 9433, 'Apparatus for cleaning roads.' This is also the first American patent for street-cleaning machinery: U.S. Patent 3124, 1 June 1843. The Patent of 1840 includes, among other features, an early (perhaps the first) use of the large rotary brush, which Whitworth calls a 'circular broom.' It was driven by a crossed sprocket chain.

[124] British Patent No. 5275, 1 Nov. 1825.

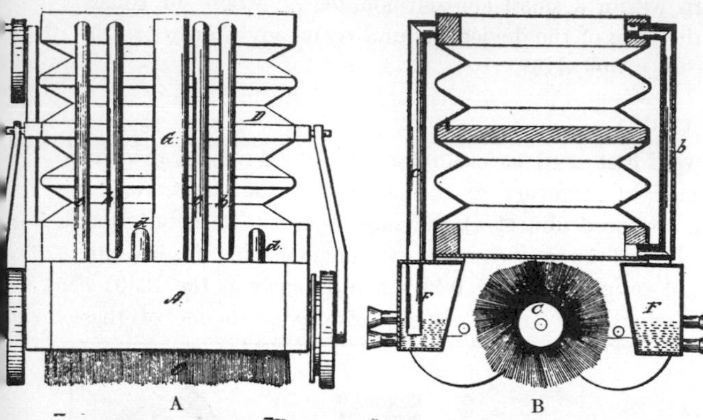

412. Bellows Carpet Sweeper, 1860. *Bellows driven by the wheels form another method of producing a suction draught. This is the earliest sweeper in which suction is constant. The dust-laden air passes through water chambers, as in some of the later stationary apparatus.* (*U. S. Patent* 29,077, 10 *July* 1860)

413. 'The Success' Hand Vacuum Cleaner, *c.*1912. (*Collection Tom J. Smith, Jr.*)

Bellows cleaners, driven by the wheels or by hand, were manufactured well into the second decade of the 20th century.

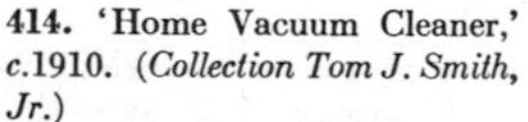

414. 'Home Vacuum Cleaner,' *c.*1910. (*Collection Tom J. Smith, Jr.*)

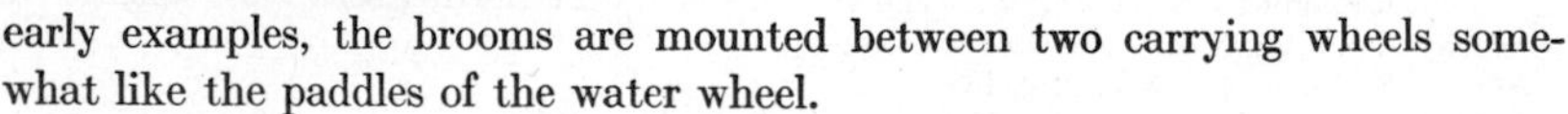

early examples, the brooms are mounted between two carrying wheels somewhat like the paddles of the water wheel.

But in Joseph Whitworth's apparatus (fig. 411) we are dealing with precision machinery. He uses an endless chain of brooms, driven by the axle of the cart.[125] A master hand is seen in the way that Whitworth, breaking with traditional

[125] Cf. in our chapter on the Assembly Line the introduction of the traveling grate for steam boilers by Johann Georg Bodmer in 1834.

notions of the chain, forms it of open links and closed ones, which carry the brooms. Carried on the endless chain, the brushes raise the dirt up the inclined carrier plate, and dump it into the container. Whitworth's street sweeper, the first to perform the task mechanically on a broad scale, reveals in all its details the touch of one skilled in the improvement of complex spinning apparatus, the engineer who around mid-century had brought machine building to a high level of precision.[126]

EARLY STAGES OF THE VACUUM CLEANER

When we listed the cleaning appliances chronologically and by type at the start of this section, we found the vacuum cleaner based on pure suction appearing in 1859. It was no chance occurrence. This was a time of many projects,[127] often fantastic ones, exploiting the gases, air-pressure, or atmospheric vacuum, and ranging from the injection of carbonic acid into dough to the Bessemer process's blasting of air through molten iron, or to primitive proposals using air suction to clean carpets. Only a few months after the first mechanical (brush) carpet sweepers (1859), there appeared the vacuum appliances already mentioned, whose wheels drove a four-bladed fan (fig. 373). Also formulated at this time (1860) was the second type of vacuum cleaner, which combined revolving brushes with a continuous draft.[128] The brushes sweep the dust into the draft produced by bellows driven by a connecting rod attached to the wheels[129] (fig. 412).

Let us anticipate and glance at what was to follow. These two appliances, that of 1859 and that of 1860, created the basic types, in which the principles underlying the whole development down to the present day were embodied.

The bolder principle, that of 1859, which carried the dust away by suction alone, was used on a magnified scale in the fixed American installations after 1900, as well as in the mobile apparatus of England and France.

The second type, that of 1860, which used air draft together with rotating brushes, was continually improved in its hand-driven form during the nineteenth century and the beginning of the twentieth. Successfully electrified after 1910, it then began to displace the fixed installations.

The type of 1859, using suction alone, also flourishes today in the portable field. Both types number among the shelved inventions of the nineteenth

[126] He built planers accurate to the millionth of an inch.

[127] Cf. the section on 'Bread and Gas' in our chapter on 'Bread.'

[128] U.S. Patent 29,077, 10 July 1860.

[129] 'The nature of my invention consists in drawing fine dust and dirt through the machine by means of a draft of air and [this suggestion is interesting at so early a date] forcing the same into water or . . . anything else which will retain the dust.' Why not then into an airtight bag, as later became the rule?

century. They are flashes of the inventive mind, which slipped unnoticed into oblivion until the electric motor suddenly raised them to prominence. It is nevertheless a task of the historian to ensure the shedding of their anonymity.

THE VACUUM CLEANER *c.* 1900

The portable machines were arrived at by a wide detour. Just as the electric motor had to pass through the gigantic before giving rise to a reliable small motor, so time was needed before the automatically driven vacuum cleaner could be reduced to an implement of convenient size. As the vacuum cleaner gradually took shape, shortly before 1900, it was a considerable plant, an installation suitable only to hotels, department stores, or railroad terminals.

Three phases can be distinguished before the vacuum cleaner was finally introduced.

At first carpets were sent to special centers, often connected with laundries, for cleaning. There bulky carpet-beating machines were used. These carpet beaters, like the washing machines of the first half of the century, imitated human motions — in this case the arm swinging a carpet beater. The first patents appear around 1860.[130] Even after 1900 an English handbook on *Laundry Management* surveys the diverse systems without any mention of the vacuum cleaner.

Stationary installations within the building formed the second phase. Pipelines connected the suction machines in the basements of large establishments with outlets throughout the edifice. This explains why around 1900 vacuum apparatus might be made by the central-heating manufacturers.[131] America was first to develop installations of this sort.

In the third phase, frequently co-existent with the second, mobile plants on wheels were used. By hand, by horse, or by motor, they were moved from house to house. A long flexible hose was taken into the apartment from the street or court where the cleaning unit was stationed. At least two men were needed to run this outfit, one to look after the machinery, another to do the cleaning.

Such mobile plants were developed by the French and especially by the English. H. C. Booth, inventor of what the English claim to be the first satisfactory vacuum cleaner, recalls his experiences in the early days, between 1901 and 1903: 'It was assumed by the police authorities that the machine [the

[130] Three patents for carpet-beating machines were taken out in 1860: U.S. Patent 27,730, 28,389, and 30,590.

[131] *Laundry Management*, a Handbook for Use in Private and Public Laundries, 4th vol. London, 1902, ch. 23: 'Carpet Beating.'

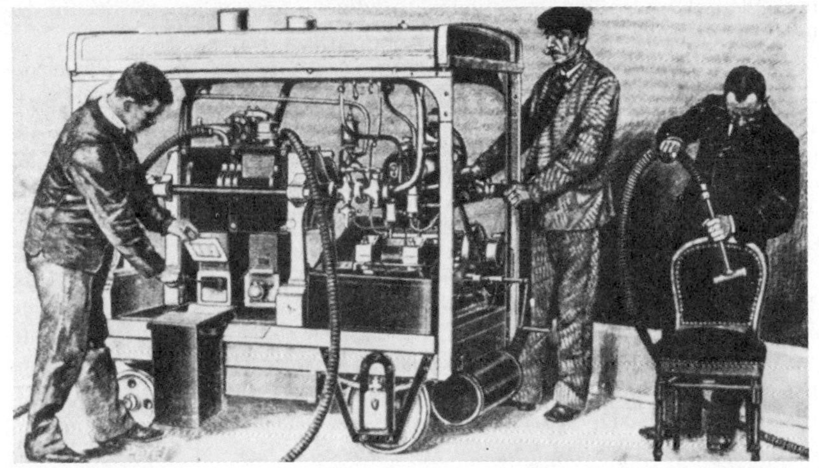

415. French Vacuum Cleaner Mounted on Truck, 1903. *Operated from the street, these vacuum plants on wheels required a crew of two. The semi-mobile machines were soon reduced in size, although portable domestic machines in the U.S.A. around* 1905 *were closer to the type shown above than to today's light appliance.* (La Nature, 1903)

vacuum cleaner] had no right to work on a public thoroughfare. . . . The Vacuum Cleaner Company was frequently sued for damages for alleged frightening of cab horses in the street.' [132] The mobile units were soon reduced in size. The French had such moderate sized machines in operation at an early date (fig. 415). They represent a transition phase prior to introduction of the portable type in the private home.

THE QUESTION OF ORIGINS

The closer we are to our own time, the less accurate is our historical information. In the present state of research, there is little certainty where the modern type of cleaner with mechanically-created suction first appeared. Hesitation is noticeable in the experiments around 1900, which waver between the use of suction and compressed air, between sucking up the dust and blowing it away. Occasionally, this led to a dual method, a complex fusion of compressed air and vacuum methods. The forerunner of the vacuum cleaner was the 'compressed air cleaner used in foundries to blow dust from castings.' The first use in clean-

[132] Booth, 'The Origin of the Vacuum Cleaner,' *Newcomen Society Transactions*, London, 1935, vol. 15, p.93.

ing buildings, we are told, 'was undoubtedly in the form of an open jet for dislodging dust from carvings.' [133]

American machines that blew compressed air into the carpet were also demonstrated to the public of other countries. In one of his few references to himself, the Englishman Booth recalls: 'My attention was first directed to the mechanical removal of dust from carpets in 1901 through a demonstration of an American machine by its inventor. . . . The machine consisted of a box to which compressed air was supplied, the air was blown down in the carpet from two opposite directions.' [134]

As we see, it is hard to ascertain where a satisfactory vacuum cleaner first came into being. The English name Booth as the inventor of the first machine operating exclusively by suction. His device was patented in 1901 [135] and successfully introduced. The inventor claims as his own the idea of using suction by itself, having been stimulated by demonstrations of those American machines that blew air into the carpet. Booth suggested that the American try blowing in the opposite way, and he attempted 'the experiment of sucking with my mouth against the back of a plush seat in a restaurant in Victoria Street with the result that I was almost choked. . . .[136] There is no doubt that Booth made his invention independently, not finding out until later that a long series of nineteenth-century patents had traveled the same path. In his reminiscences upon 'the origin of the vacuum cleaner,' he gives an interesting enumeration of early patents. Booth's machine of 1901 was a mobile one, mounted on a pushcart.[137]

Shortly after 1900 the French too, as the illustration shows, were building compact machines driven by electric motors and mounted on wheelcarts. They claim the invention of a nozzle (which Booth claims as his) for use in cleaning their furniture. Booth claims moreover to have been the earliest to introduce this combination of hose and handle. In France such machines seem to have been originally used for cleaning theater seats. Two hundred and seventeen

---

[133] Cooley, op.cit. p.4. Mr. Joseph H. Young, the superintendent for the Union Pacific at Salt Lake City, and David Patterson, master mechanic, attempted in 1892–3 to clean car interiors by coupling together a number of air-brake pumps so as to blow away the dust. As this proved impracticable, they worked out a syphon method, whereby air was sucked up and blown out of the window, with such success that it was generally adopted by the Union Pacific for cleaning coaches and Pullman cars at its passenger terminals. They also developed a nozzle to spray paint on freight cars and wooden buildings, a procedure that was adopted for painting ships. A patent was denied, however, on the ground that the principle was covered by patents that blew oil from a tank by compressed air to kindle fires in locomotive fire boxes. We owe this information to Mr. Young, now vice-president of the Westinghouse Brake Co.

[134] Booth, op.cit. p.85.

[135] British Patent No.17,433, 30 Aug. 1901.

[136] Booth, op.cit. p.86.

[137] Illustrations, ibid. pl. XI.

kilograms of dust are said to have been sucked from the chairs of a single theater.[138]

Taking over an English model in 1905, the Germans performed experiments to test its efficiency.[139] Wet gelatine plates should allow a comparison of the dust that settled in ordinary beating and sweeping with that raised by the new vacuum cleaner. The machine is described as if it were some newly discovered variety of plant life. Favorable tests notwithstanding, the hygienists concluded that vacuum cleaning failed to save either time or labor.

In keeping with the general trend of household mechanization, the initiative then passed into American hands. The Americans support the candidacy of David T. Kenney, who 'installed the first mechanical cleaning system in which the vacuum alone was used as a cleaning agent'[140] in the Frick Building, New York (1902). Kenney's pioneering patent was granted by 1903 and is said to have been lying in the Patent Office for years before. Here the chronological trail becomes rather blurred, particularly as the English inventor mentions his forerunners, but remains silent concerning his successful foreign contemporaries. We can roughly decide as follows. America pioneered in the stationary models while England and France developed the early mobile ones.

One thing is certain in all this. The American vacuum-cleaner industry — whether manufacturers of portable or of stationary types — became licensees of the Kenney patents, the validity of which was upheld in official inquests into the state of the vacuum-cleaner industry. 'The Kenney patents (fig. 416) are the basic vacuum-cleaner patents that have been litigated and upheld by the courts.'[141]

THE VACUUM BECOMES A HOUSEHOLD TOOL

The circle closes some six decades after the advent of the first portable machines in which suction was tried out.

In the interval it was especially the type with bellows and revolving brush that received most attention. We find it in 1917, the year a large mail-order firm introduced the portable electric machine. The type, one is assured, 'accomplishes practically as much as an electric cleaner at much less cost.'[142]

---

[138] G. Richou, 'Nettoyage sanitaire par le vide,' *La Nature*, Paris, 1903, p.577.

[139] Dr. Berghaus, 'Der Vacuumreiniger, ein Apparat zur staubfreien Reinigung der Wohnraeume,' *Archiv fuer Hygiene*, vol. 52 (München, 1905).

[140] Cooley, op.cit. p.13.

[141] Report of the Federal Trade Commission on the House Furnishing Industry, 6 Oct., p.6 (Washington, 1925).

[142] Catalogue of the Montgomery Ward Co., 1917, p.703.

The standard types were created within a few years after this lapse of several decades. The years 1901 and 1902 brought the first satisfactory fixed vacuums in America and in England. The first portable vacuum cleaner is said to have materialized in 1905.[143] But this American machine with large turbine fan and motor mounted on a chassis was still rather voluminous and closer to the French machines on wheels than to the later and lighter instruments. Two years later, 1907, the patent was submitted for a more portable machine tending toward the now standard form.[144] (fig. 372). Now the fan revolves around a vertical spindle directly coupled to the motor, just as in Tesla's electric fan of 1889. The carefully shaped motor-casing is made to carry a swivel handle. In brief, the carpet sweeper has been mechanized. The main trend is now toward simplifying and reducing the number of parts. The inventor formulates this in his next patent (1915) (fig. 421): 'The object of this invention is to provide a construction which will be composed of few simple parts, put together in a practical mechanical manner.'[145]

In short, hardly more than five years elapsed from the advent of the cumbersome fixed vacuum to the creation of the portable standard form in which the vacuum became an everyday household tool.

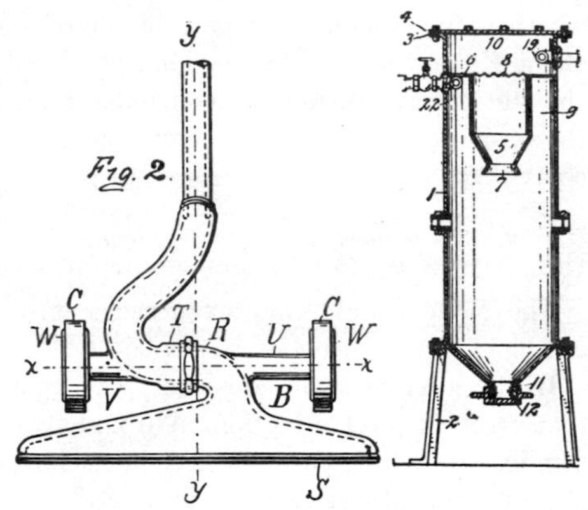

416. The Basic American Vacuum-Cleaner Patent, 1903. *From 1902 on, stationary plants, whose pipes ran through the structure like central heating, were installed in the larger American buildings — Astor Hotel, Frick Building* (1902). Right: *The first and basic patent for both fixed and portable vacuum cleaners was that of D. T. Kenney: 'Separator for apparatus for removing dust,'* 1903. *Here the handle and the hose are still distinct.* Left: *The vacuum cleaner approaches standard form: a few years after his first patent Kenney ran the suction through a tubular handle with a dust inlet slot at its end, mounting the whole flexibly on wheels. From this the bag type of today was apparently derived.* (*U.S. Patent* 781,532, 31 *January* 1905)

---

143 Illustrations by Cooley, op.cit. p.16. Inventor: Dr. William Noe, San Francisco.

144 U.S. Patent 889,823, 2 June 1908. James M. Spangler. He already shows the dust bag.

145 U.S. Patent 1,151,731, 1915, 31Aug. This is the machine that was made over to the Hoover Suction-Sweeper Company, a corporation of Ohio. In a sequence of further improvements the present standard type was developed.

417. Residential Vacuum System, *c.*1910. *Electric motor, flywheel, and airpump in the cellar. This apparatus existed only in the houses of the well-to-do. (Leaflet, collection Tom J. Smith, Jr.)*

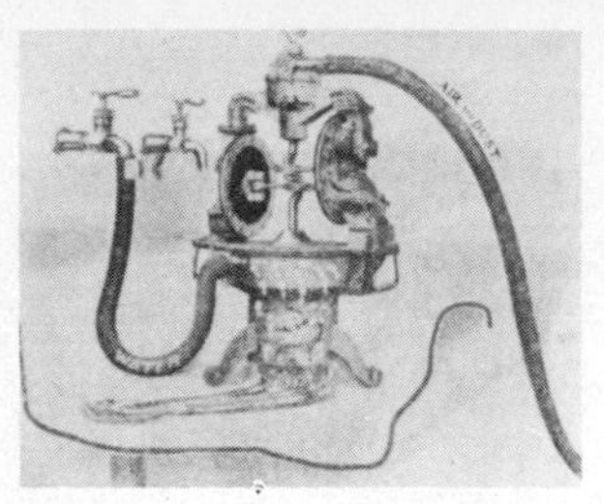

418. 'Water Witch' Motor, *c.*1910. *'Set temporarily in the kitchen sink, bathtub, or wherever a water faucet and drain are convenient. Operated by ordinary water pressure; weighs less than 23 pounds; dust and germs automatically mixed with water and carried away; absolutely safe; sells for $75.00. All other efficient portable cleaners require electricity for operation.'* (*Leaflet, Collection Tom J. Smith, Jr.*)

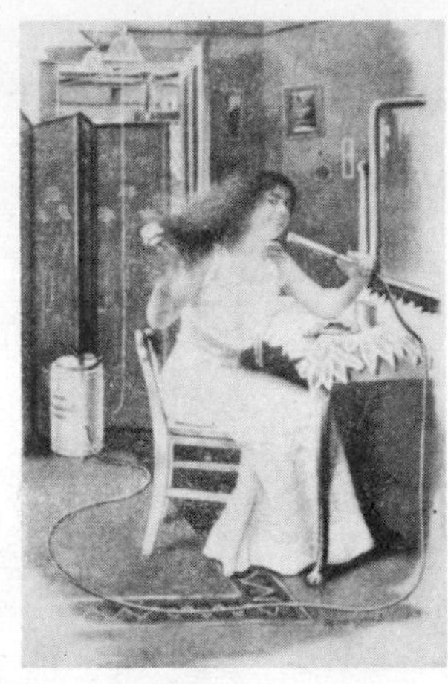

419. 'Pneumatic Cleaner' Used as Hair Drier, 1909. *'Using the current of pure, fresh air from the exhaust.' The electric cleaner here is the tank type, then rapidly reaching standard form.* (*Collection Tom J. Smith, Jr.*)

The specialists were skeptical throughout. Around 1912 they thoroughly disbelieved that a smaller and more dependable type was possible. One of them makes the point particularly clear by refusing to show or to demonstrate portable machines.[146] Another, who thoroughly treats the vacuum cleaner question in his time,[147] is somewhat less emphatic (1913): 'It will be the survival of the fittest.' The vacuum cleaner, he believed, 'is at the height of its career like the automobile.'

The skepticism of the experts was not wholly unfounded. This is evidenced by the diversity of attempts to find an adequate motor and satisfactory portable form. In 1910 the stationary installations, with suction pump and dust separator in the cellar, were mainly used in residences. Numerous catalogues of their time have been preserved.[148] The master of the house is shown in the parlor having the butler give his coat a few strokes of the vacuum; on the floor above

[146] Arthur Summerton, *A Treatise on Vacuum Cleaning*, London, 1912: 'We shall confine this treatise to the stationary system as we believe satisfactory results in cleaning cannot be expected from portable machines.'

[147] Cooley, op.cit. p.20.

[148] Mr. Tom J. Smith, Jr. of Cleveland, Ohio, Vice President of the Pressed Metal Institute and a veteran of the vacuum-cleaner business, instead of buying his prospective customer drinks at the bar, would get him interested in the history of the product. Later he gathered the material in more permanent form. He and Mr. C. G. Frantz, secretary since its beginning of the Vacuum Cleaner Manufacturers' Assn., and collector of comprehensive archives, have most obligingly and helpfully answered our enquiries.

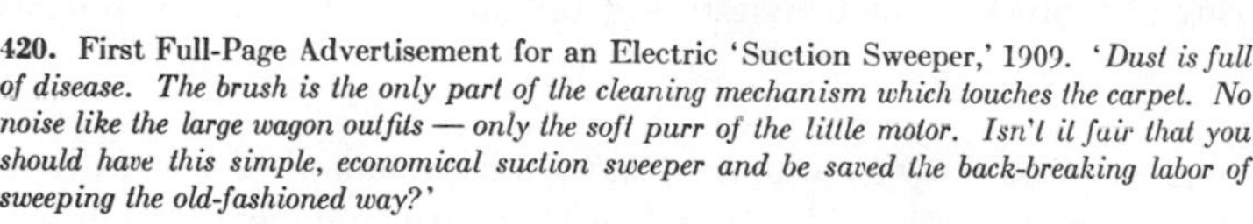

420. First Full-Page Advertisement for an Electric 'Suction Sweeper,' 1909. *'Dust is full of disease. The brush is the only part of the cleaning mechanism which touches the carpet. No noise like the large wagon outfits — only the soft purr of the little motor. Isn't it fair that you should have this simple, economical suction sweeper and be saved the back-breaking labor of sweeping the old-fashioned way?'*

the maid is doing the same to the lady's hat; while other domestics are cleaning the furniture and carpets. The vacuum cleaner and prosperity were soon identified (fig. 417).

Water motors or other prime movers were also used, as in the washing machines around 1910. They were always stationary installations, working by suction alone. 'All you have to do is to push a very light tool over the floor,' and it is assured, with a dig at the portable electric types, 'it never wears out, will last as long as your building . . . better results without any machinery . . . no dirty

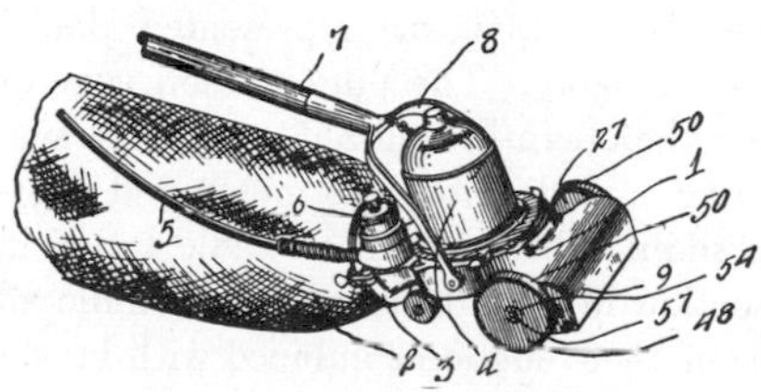

421. Electric 'Suction Carpet Sweeper,' 1915. *The electrical cleaner had reached a convenient household form by 1908 (fig. 372). The same inventor now develops it further. From now on the motto will be: simplify. This model seems to have formed the basis of the Hoover type.* (*U.S. Patent* 1,151,731, 31 *August* 1915)

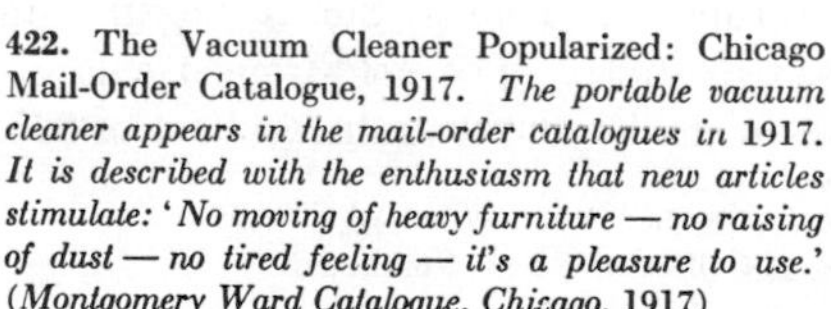

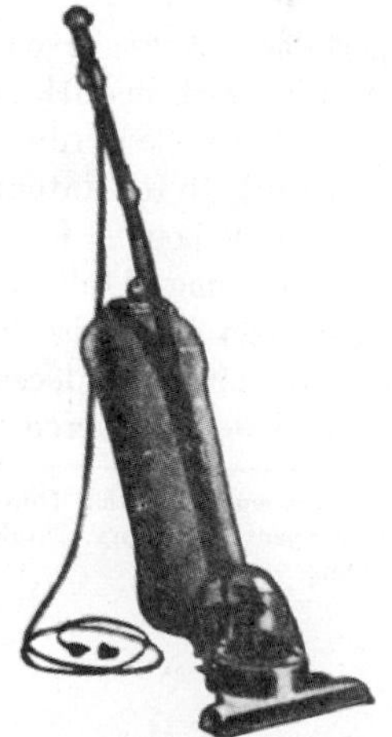

422. The Vacuum Cleaner Popularized: Chicago Mail-Order Catalogue, 1917. *The portable vacuum cleaner appears in the mail-order catalogues in* 1917. *It is described with the enthusiasm that new articles stimulate: 'No moving of heavy furniture — no raising of dust — no tired feeling — it's a pleasure to use.'* (*Montgomery Ward Catalogue, Chicago,* 1917)

bags with germs to empty. . . .'[149] Another appliance, the Water Witch, having light, 'almost entirely aluminum built suction pumps by means of a water wheel' can 'be set temporarily in the kitchen sink or bath tub' (fig. 418). The sucked-up dust is drawn through the tube and directly carried away by the water.[150] Enticing accessories are delivered with it: a massage vibrator outfit, or hair-drying apparatus. 'The heaviest head of hair is quickly and thoroughly dried after washing.'

All this suggests that the way was not clear. But promoters of water-driven cleaners held the wrong cards. Only one way held the true promise of the future: the use of the fraction horsepower electric motor. When in 1909, only a year after granting of the basic patent, the Hoover Company countered with a full-page advertisement in the *Saturday Evening Post* (fig. 420), it seemed to be deliberately trumping the Water Witch's claims; 'The motor will outlast the house you live in.' But the distinctive motto was: 'Sweep with electricity for 3 cents a week.' In spite of the haughty boast, 'We are now turning out hundreds of machines a week, the demand is enormous,' the number of rival attempts, a few of which we have mentioned, shows that the success was not unmitigated. But the path was the right one — electric drive.

The two basic types, that of 1859 and that of 1860, are represented almost equally in the electrified portable models of today. The pure suction type of 1859 survives in the 'tank' type,[151] where the operator still holds only the suction nozzle, as in the earlier, fixed vacuum installations; the motor and dust-containing unit are drawn behind on a sliding chassis. The 'handle type,' in which the rotary brushes, the motor, suction intake, dust bag, and handle all form a light trolley-unit, follows the type of 1860: suction combined with brushing action.

These easily portable vacuums give extraordinary opportunity to high-pressure salesmanship. Visiting with his machine from door to door, the salesman sold mainly on the pay-as-you-go terms by which American mass production — from the vacuum cleaner to the automobile and the house — became financially possible. The mail-order houses, founded in the 'seventies, also owe their tremendous growth in the time of full mechanization to this credit system.

Modern pay-as-you-go enterprise, according to Tom J. Smith, began with the photographic portraiture of deceased relatives. The gold-framed enlargements of the departed were delivered on an easel and, for an investment of $25,

[149] 'The Hydraulic' Catalogue, Collection Tom J. Smith, Jr.
[150] Vacuum Hydro Company, New York, Catalogue, Collection Tom J. Smith, Jr.
[151] As in the Electrolux.

honored with a sumptuous bow. So successful was this house-to-house and pay-as-you-go enterprise that it is supposed to have led the makers of household articles to adopt similar tactics.

A dealer organization spread across the whole country. As with agricultural machines long before, and later with washing machines, refrigerators, and ranges, the upkeep and repair service was a strong sales incentive.

Four years after the specialists pronounced themselves skeptical, the light models had already become American institutions: they appear in the mail-order catalogues of 1917 at the low price of $19.45 (fig. 422).

Earlier and more conspicuously successful than all other mechanized household appliances, the vacuum, which can be put away in any broom-closet, made its way through the world. By 1929 the conservative *Encyclopædia Britannica* was able to state: 'The light portable type is by far the most popular and represents 95% of all vacuum cleaners in use.' Except in America, its spread far exceeds that of the mechanized washing machine.

REFRIGERATION MECHANIZED

NATURAL ICE

The warm damp American climate, settled by northern peoples, stimulated from the first a desire for ice and cool drinks. It was no accident that ice cream later became a national dish. The effects of this climate caused astonishment to early travelers in the United States. An English visitor observed in 1800 that during the summer, meat became tainted in a day, poultry should not be killed until about four hours before it was wanted, and milk 'turned' one or two hours after it was taken from the cow.[152] This climatic peculiarity amply explains why the question was raised from the eighteenth century on, how can ice be stored through the summer months or artificially produced?

423. Cutting Ice on the Schuylkill in the 1860's. *Harvesting and storing ice grew into an industry in the U. S. A. during the nineteenth century; ice became an export commodity like cotton. The picture shows: (right) marking the field with the ice plane and ice plow; (left) the blocks being transported by inclined plane to an above-ground icehouse.* (*Courtesy the Historical Society of Pennsylvania*)

The houses for storing ice through the summer, as still found in Pennsylvania or other rural parts of the thirteen original states, are not native to America, although it is here that their development was vastly expanded. The tradition

[152] Isaac Weld, *Travels through the United States*, London, 1800, quoted after R. O. Cummings, *The American and His Food*, Chicago, 1940. Cummings deals briefly but excellently to the point with the advent of refrigeration.

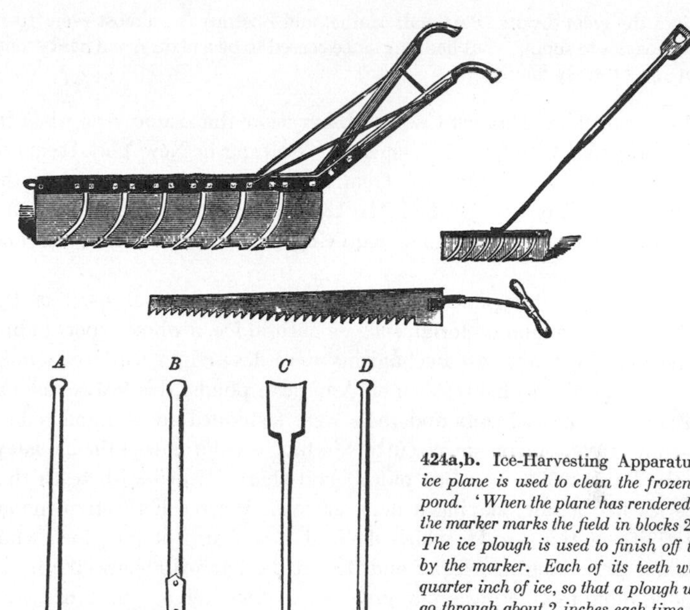

424a,b. Ice-Harvesting Apparatus, 1883. *The ice plane is used to clean the frozen surface of the pond. 'When the plane has rendered the ice smooth, the marker marks the field in blocks 22 by 32 inches. The ice plough is used to finish off the work begun by the marker. Each of its teeth will cut about a quarter inch of ice, so that a plough with 8 teeth will go through about 2 inches each time it passes along the grooves.' The blocks are broken up and manipulated with ice-hook (A); fork-splitting bar (B); grooving bar (C); channel hook bar (D).* (Appleton's Cyclopaedia of Applied Mechanics, *vol.* II, *New York*, 1883)

has its continuation in quite unexpected form today. George Washington had a large icehouse on his Mount Vernon estate. At first icehouses were dug into the ground, as in Europe, the excavation being covered by a roof. The above-ground icehouse, as Cummings notes, was introduced in the early nineteenth century; it was constructed with double walls and doors on the principle of the ice stores of the ships that exported ice to the West Indies. Wastage was thus reduced from 60 per cent to less than 8 per cent.[153]

Export of natural ice to the tropics began with shipments to Martinique in 1805, to Cuba ten years later, and in 1833 on the famous clipper ships to Calcutta, where a triple-walled ice store held 30,000 tons of ice.

Cutting and storing ice in large quantities for export and for domestic supply is [1872] a strictly American enterprise, which began nearly seventy years ago, and from a small beginning has grown to a great business employing thousands of men and millions of

[153] Cummings, op.cit. p.83.

capital. Besides the great depots (Portland, Maine, and Boston) . . . almost every town has its local companies to supply what has long since ceased to be a luxury, and has become a necessity in almost every family.[154]

This is well confirmed by Thomas Cook's observation that same year when he made a first world tour with his travel-agency. Nothing in New York seems to have more strongly impressed him, the Quaker and temperance man, than the jugs of iced water found on every table. 'In 1876 the amount required for home consumption was over 2,000,000 tons, requiring a force of 4,000 horses and 10,000 men.' [155]

As well as anything, it typifies the American entrepreneurial spirit of the times; that around a common material, such as natural ice, a whole export industry should be built up. Just as mechanisms were devised to tear tree trunks from the soil, so in order to harvest ice on American ponds, this heavy manual task was broken into its elements and tools were fashioned to ease and reduce it to a minimum. Invention of the ice cutters, which revolutionized the industry, dates from the late 1820's. The 'ice plows' had shares armed with teeth that cut into the ice like a saw, leaving a deep groove. We recall the tremendous inventive activity of this period, which devised new forms of the plow, while McCormick was perfecting his reaper and its cutting-bar with shark-like teeth. Scraping and planing tools, crowbars in great variety, as well as conveyor bands to transport the ice from the quarrying place to the icehouse, completed the ice-harvesting equipment. Even spiral conveyors were patented.

Such remained the normal method of obtaining ice throughout the century, as may be seen from the detailed illustrations given in a technical encyclopedia of the 1880's [156] (fig. 424).

Icehouses are directly linked with the time of full mechanization. Once more we find small houses scattered across the land, preserving supplies over long periods. This time, however, they are not for storing ice — obtainable by simpler, mechanized means — but for preserving perishable foods, which a new quick-freezing process allows to be kept for many months in unaltered freshness. The first installations of this kind are said to have been converted from unremunerative artificial ice factories.

---

[154] *The Great Industries of the United States*, Hartford, 1872, p.156.

[155] *Appleton's Cyclopedia of Applied Mechanics*, New York, 1883, vol. II, p.127.

[156] Ibid.

425. Ice-Delivery Trade Card, *c.*1830. *Refrigeration was first used to take dairy products to market in* 1803, *says Cummings, the historian of American food habits. The trade increased greatly after the invention of the ice plow, and especially when the above-ground icehouse was introduced in the* 1820's.

The universally minded eighteenth century was interested in the overall view, in cyclic processes. Giambattista Vico, in his *Scienza Nuova* (1730) looks for cyclical processes in history: who knows the history of one people knows the history of all peoples. Parallel with this, there is a turning of awareness to cyclic processes in physics and to their utilization in practical life. Contemporaries found a most strong stimulus to their inventive fantasy in the gas-to-liquid, liquid-to-solid cycle and its reverse.

The cyclic passage from water to steam and from steam back to water led the practical mind of James Watt, with a minimum of technical knowledge, to the invention of the condenser (1769), the function of which is to recondense water vapor after expansion to sub-atmospheric pressure. This supplied the missing link in the cycle, and the modern steam engine was made possible.

Mechanical refrigeration relies upon a similar method. A liquid of low boiling point is in turn evaporated and reliquefied. Through evaporation it absorbs heat from its environment, in other words produces cold. Michael Faraday is known as the first successful experimenter in mechanical refrigeration. He observed in 1823, during his study of gases, that ammonia heated in a U-tube would recondense in the other limb. Left to itself the ammonia would evaporate anew, producing intense cold. No more than he thought of utilizing for practical purposes the electric motor, whose principle he was to discover nine years later, did Faraday think of a utilitarian exploitation of the discovery upon which mechanical refrigeration is based.[157]

The first precise scientific vision of how cold might be mechanically produced and utilized is found in an apparently overlooked passage of Oliver Evans's *Abortion of the Young Steam Engineer's Guide*, Philadelphia, 1805. Oliver Evans, who introduced the earliest production line in the milling process, is, in conception at least, the father of modern cold-making. He starts from the observation: 'If an open glass be filled with ether and set in water under vacuo, the ether will boil rapidly and rob the water of its latent heat till it freezes. . . .'[158] Evans now sets himself a problem similar to the earlier one in which he transformed the endless belt and the Archimedean screw into the assembly line: how and for what purposes can physical laws be utilized? Evans imagines refrigeration of the drinking water reservoirs of American cities, and proposes a powerful vacuum pump driven by a steam engine to volatilize ether, thus taking heat

[157] Jacob Perkins, an American living in England, used ether in the first compression machines in 1834. Ferdinand Carré, who in 1857 patented the first commercially exploitable ice-making machine, later (1859) used like Faraday a solution of ammonia and water.

[158] Evans, op.cit. p.136.

from the water around it; a second pump recompresses the ether within a barrel immersed in water, and the ether is changed to vapor again. The Englishman Leslie succeeded in vaporizing ether under the vacuum pump in 1811.[159]

Oliver Evans was an embittered inventor. Embittered because he came too early for his environment, and was continually frustrated. After his short description, he cannot help likening himself 'lest I be thought extravagant,' to James Watt's unfortunate forerunner, the Marquess of Worcester, whose words also fell on closed ears.

HOME REFRIGERATION MECHANIZED

The prerequisites were the same as those for the other mechanized household tools: reduction to compact size, and the built-in electric motor. As with the washing-machine, motcr and equipment had to be merged into a unit not requir-

[159] A good account of the early efforts and of the development of ice-making machines down to the mid-'sixties is given in the contemporary Louis Figuier's *Les Merveilles de l'industrie ou description des principales industries modernes*, Paris, n.d., vol. III, pp.591–632.

426. Skating on Artificial Ice, Manchester, 1877. *This scene from a French catalogue of* **1877** *marks the period when the manufacture of ice by artificial means became commercially possible on a larger scale.* (*Raoul Pictet Cat*⁻*logue, Paris,* 1877)

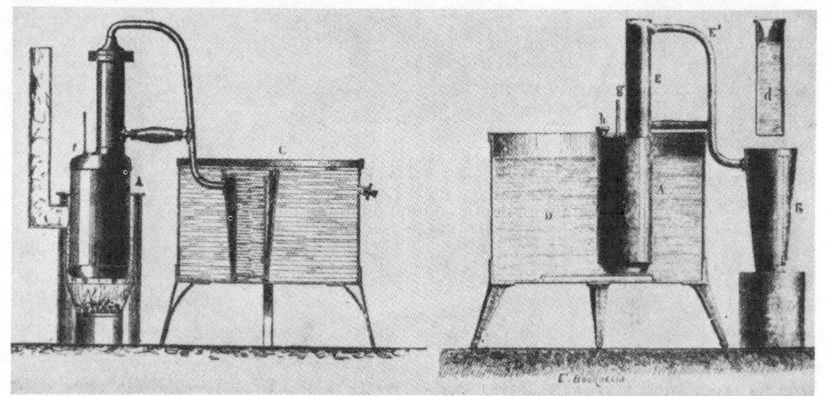

427. Forerunner of the Domestic Refrigerator: Ferdinand Carré's Artificial Ice Machine, 1860. *Ferdinand Carré invented the first practical ice machine, and later introduced the first household refrigerator. This is essentially a boiler three-quarters filled with ammonia, standing in a portable stove, and a small conic vessel with double walls immersed in cold water. When the ammonia gas liquefied by the surrounding water is volatilized, the heat thus absorbed causes the water in the smaller vessel to freeze. One kilogram of ice is produced in two hours.* (*Louis Figuier,* Les merveilles de l'industrie, *Paris, n.d.*)

ing supervision or maintenance. This calls for thermostatic control and the sealed motor housing. We need not go into the stages of this development.[160]

The ice machine of Ferdinand Carré, capable of producing thousands of pounds at a time, was a great attraction to visitors at the London Exhibition of 1862, who saw enormous blocks of ice manufactured almost continuously before their eyes. Ferdinand Carré not only built the first successful commercial freezing machine; he introduced in 1860 a forerunner of the household refrigerator (fig. 427). This 'appareil refrigérant pour la production de la glace' used ammonia as its refrigerant. It consisted of a small portable stove acting as the heat-source, a boiler three-quarters filled with ammonia, a freezing vessel, and a reservoir. Despite its small scale, this appliance was rather complicated for the housewife — one hour of heating and one hour of freezing to produce a kilogram of ice — and no truly automatic solution using a heat source was found before the time of full mechanization, when the Swedes refined upon Carré's principle and replaced the stove by a gas flame.

---

[160] Various technical works are informative on this point; especially so is H. B. Hull, *Household Refrigeration*, Chicago, 1924, 1927, 1933 — the three editions giving precise insight into the main period of development and vulgarization of the mechanical refrigerator.

428. Ice Box for Commerical Use, 1882. '*Refrigerator for butter, fish or fruit dealers, dining saloons, hotels, etc.' The chest form, which prevents the entrance of warm air more effectively than the upright type, is the forerunner of ice-cream cabinets refrigerated at* 0° *Fahrenheit. As mechanical ice-cream cabinets came onto the market, increasing numbers filtered into the hands of sportsmen who wished to preserve fish and game for out-of-season consumption. The earliest chest-type lockers other than ice-cream cabinets were made by Frigidaire in* 1930. *However, as with the automatic washers in the* 1920's, *it was not until a decade later were they able to command a market.* (*L. H. Mace and Co., Courtesy Bella C. Landauer Collection*)

The problem of mechanical cooling was in the air.[161] In the second decade of this century almost every country of Western civilization brought forth patents attempting to reduce the large machinery to the scale of the kitchen. Sweden, as we have mentioned, contributed the scheme in which a gas flame ensures the cycle. A large American corporation improved the patent of a French monk. The first French hand-built refrigerators driven by an electric motor are said to be still running today. Around 1916–17 the large corporations started production.

The price was still rather high, the refrigerator costing about $900. Not until the mid-'twenties did the mechanical refrigerator become popularized. 'It is only between the last five years that machines have been produced in quantities,' it was stated in 1924.[162] In 1923 there were 20,000 refrigerators in the United States; in 1933, 850,000. How the curve rises sharply: 1936, two million; 1941, three and a half million. With the automobile the mechanical refrigerator had become an indispensable element of the American household. Curves comparing the average retail price with annual production show a relation between price

[161] According to information communicated to us by George F. Taubeneck, editor and publisher, Business News Publishing Co., Detroit, Mich., Kelvinator got started in 1916; Frigidaire, then called 'Guardian,' in 1917, and Servel shortly afterwards. Back in 1911–12 E. T. Williams and Fred Wolfe were exhibiting hand-made home refrigerators.

[162] Hull, op.cit. 1924 ed., p.98.

429. Trend after World War II: Chest-Type Frozen-Food Locker, 1946. *Automatism immediately prevails in cold-storage equipment. The storage space, maintained at zero, is guarded by a double alarm system that gives sight and sound warning against rise of the temperature beyond a fixed safety point, and is convertible into quick-freezing space at* 10 *to* 20 *degrees below zero. Shining metal and streamlining seem to be inevitable adjuncts of mechanical progress in the* 1940's. (*Courtesy Refrigeration Corp. of America*)

and the democratizing of comfort. The mechanical refrigerator becomes popular as soon as its price is standardized and maintained at a minimum.

Observing the time dimension, we see that a half-century elapsed before the principle was taken up by industry (in 1873–5), and another half-century before the home refrigerator was made in considerable quantity. Despite external changes the standard form toward which it was moving at this time is patterned on the old icebox. The early American refrigerators around 1919 had the same dark wood exterior as the old iceboxes. Later they were exposed, like the automobile, to the streamlining fashion, and their bulk was deliberately inflated for selling purposes. The refrigerator stood out in the American kitchen of the 1930's as the sole element not yet incorporated with the unified working surfaces. Needless to say, it was improved year by year. The housewife learned to master its advantages and its pranks. She knows what will and what will not keep, and how to protect foodstuffs from drying out. All in all, however, the standard form achieved after a hundred years was of strikingly short duration. When it emerged on the market a new refrigerating method was being patented, and when finally in 1932 the mail-order houses entered it in their catalogues, quick-freezing equipment, destined to alter the very way of living, had already come on the market.

The time of full mechanization brings yet another penetration of organic substance: we recognize that it is one thing to keep an organic substance lingering in the neighborhood of freezing point and another to freeze it swiftly by use of low temperatures. A slow descent to freezing point — 32° Fahrenheit — bursts the cells of plants and animals. In quick freezing these cells remain intact and hold their flavor like wine corked in bottles.

While wintering in Labrador, Clarence Birdseye, as is well known, observed that the flesh of fish and reindeer congealed rapidly in the Arctic air. When the Eskimos returned months later, it was as fresh as the day when killed. Birdseye translated this into mechanical terms by bringing food to freezing point between metal plates. Soon after this process was patented in 1925, its commercial application began. In 1928 the first foodstuffs processed by this method reached the market. Their consumption grew by leaps — from 39 million pound-cartons in 1934 to 600 million in 1944.[163]

The sculptor Brancusi heard the dictum in the far East that fruit should not be eaten over thirty miles from the place where it grew. Quick freezing will perhaps help to supersede this wisdom, for it enables fruit to be plucked when fully ripe. 'Quick freezing starts at the moment of maximum palatability.'

Similarly with sea food. The catch is frozen as soon as it is lifted aboard the trawlers. Not even the entrails need be removed. In New York we have eaten crab from the Pacific Ocean tasting as if it had just been taken from the sea — far fresher, certainly, than when it has passed through the local markets in the traditional way, or has been extracted from the can.

The economic necessity of shipping livestock from the Great Plains to the Chicago or Kansas City slaughterhouses can in principle be dispensed with. Cattle can be processed on the farm.

What implications are in store?

The economic advantages are evident. Quick freezing affords protection against waste. 'Through refrigeration the farmer can preserve his entire crop and can now obtain full realization of his investment.[164]

Even more important seem to us the latent social potentialities. Quick freezing may be a way to attain better equilibrium in the matter of mass production and monopoly. Rightly used, it should help decentralization. It gives the small farmer a new chance to have his produce compete with the giant farms. He may install a freezer on the farm, as described in Boyden Sparks's small book, based on the first ventures in this direction, *Zero Storage in Your Home* (New

[163] George F. Taubeneck, *Great Day Coming!*, Detroit, 1944, p.185.
[164] Ibid.

York, 1944), or else a locker plant[165] may be operated by the community and made available to all on a co-operative basis — as has already been done in recently developed places. At an early date, in 1936, the farmers of the Tennessee Valley Authority region set up a co-operative freezing plant. Perhaps it will prove the means for an awakening of community interest. The locker plant may be part of the small civic center that must be planned today for every community of a few thousand people. Whether this is the course to be followed or whether the locker plants will become part of a gigantic concern extending from the Atlantic to the Pacific depends finally upon the will of the citizens.

What will be the influence of quick freezing upon city dwellers? Here, too, various outcomes are possible. We shall do no more than touch upon the two extremes.

In an American kitchen, fully pictured in *Life Magazine* (fig. 440), stands a heavy table, a cutting block as in the butcher's store. A butcher's block amid full mechanization? The architect, Fordyce, has indicated a white enameled receptacle, the quick-freezing chest, intended to preserve large sections of meat bought whole and requiring a block in order to be cut correctly.

The time of full mechanization brings back the possible laying-in of a store of meat or other foodstuffs, even by city dwellers. In 1945 fashionable New York apartment houses were to install basement locker plants with at least one locker for each tenant.

Provisions set aside almost on the medieval pattern; contact with natural materials, not cans; craftsmen-like pleasure in spontaneous culinary preparation. These things are possible too.

At the other extreme:

> Meats will be cooked in ton-size batches under the direction of world-famous chefs and packaged in containers. Then, one minute before dinner time, the housewife will place the pre-cooked frozen meal into a special electronic oven. This oven will employ high frequency radio waves which penetrate all foods equally . . . in a few seconds a bell will ring and the whole dinner will pop up like a piece of toast.

---

[165] 'A frozen-food locker plant,' as officially defined, is 'a term applied to a modern low temperature food storage. The services of such a plant include processing, preparation, and freezing. The principal components of a frozen-food locker plant are:

1. A chilling and aging room at 36–8° F., where fresh killed meat is chilled and aged and other products are chilled, prior to processing and preparation for freezing.
2. A processing room where meats are cut to order. Meats, fruits, and vegetables are packaged prior to freezing.
3. A quick-freezing cabinet is used to produce a completely frozen product.
4. A locker room containing several hundred separate lockers for rental to individuals. Temperature 0° F.'

Report of the Task Committee, War Production Board, July 1944, reprinted in Taubeneck, op.cit. p.375.

Such is the picture that some writers have painted at the end of World War II to tempt the palate of the American public.[166]

Is not the infra-red oven progress? The housewife need not waste a moment opening cans and waiting for the food to warm. All is done instantaneously. She does not even wash dishes, for the plastic container is thrown away.

In 1945 a number of frozen-food centers designed for 'self-service,' where the cartons are stacked in white enamel chests, were seen in New York and its suburbs. Will the frozen-food centers contain the fresh raw materials of cooking, or will the dominion of the tin can be further extended in the guise of ready-cooked, ready-made frozen foods? Will the assembly-line steak triumph (fig. 67), or will there be a return to spontaneous cooking in the home? As with the fate of rural locker plants, everything depends on the attitude of the consumer.

---

[166] S. S. Block, 'New Foods to Tempt Your Palate,' in *Science Digest*, New York, Oct. 1944.

STREAMLINING AND FULL MECHANIZATION

Full mechanization and the 'streamlining' habit entered hand in hand to a striking degree. In the American mid-'thirties attention converged on re-designing the objects of mass production. How far this was a result of the depression and of the need to stimulate sales by playing on emotional responses, and how far it may be ascribed to European purifications of form in prior decades, it is hard to say. All these factors and others seem to have joined in calling forth 'streamline style.'

The streamline, in hydrodynamics, is a curve whose tangent at any point gives the direction of the flow of a particle of the fluid at a given point. Streamline is thus the graphical representation of a movement, of problems such as have been mentioned time and again in the course of this book.

Streamline form is the shape given to a body (a ship, an airplane) to the end that its passage through a material (water, air) may meet with the least possible resistance.

Since mid-'thirties the word 'streamlined' has considerably broadened in connotation, being used in reference to widely dissimilar fields. One speaks of streamlining a business, or, even in the political sphere, an administration or government. Here, no doubt, the word unconsciously retains a part of its original connotation, i.e., a shape offering least resistance. In the popular sense, 'streamline' is used interchangeably with the word 'modern.'

From the start, it was understood that the phrase was not to be taken literally. Today the layman, unfamiliar with aerodynamics, calls almost everything streamlined' when he really means 'graceful lines.' We have 'streamline' radio cabinets, toasters, cigarette lighters, and even gasoline with 'streamline' action. The development of the science of aerodynamics and its application to airships and airplanes has created in the public a sense for fleeting lines, and these lines, being recognized by designers as a decorative element, have been emphasized to give the impression of speed. The automobile manufacturer, to give the sales appeal of a visual impression of the speed that the engineer has built into his machine, has used and is using 'streamlining' extensively.[167]

Streamlining began on trains. A tubular form was given to railroad cars in 1887.[168] But not until 1934 was the streamlined train, Diesel driven, with steel skeleton and corrugated aluminum skin,[169] put into service, whose cars were

[167] O. Kuhler, 'Streamlining the Railroads,' *Product Engineering*, New York, vol. VI, 1934, p.224.

[168] By the Meigs Elevated Railroad Construction Co., East Cambridge, Mass. O. Kuhler, op.cit. Illustrated. According to Kuhler the first attempts to streamline locomotives took place in Kassel (1904) and Munich (1912).

[169] The 'Burlington Zephyr' constructed by G. Budd Mfg. Co., Philadelphia. (Ibid.)

joined in a continuous line. Around that time the streamline automobile also gradually took shape.[170] A special bodywork (1932), which soon became popular, marked the beginning of the trend. At first one spoke not of streamline design but simply of redesign, whether of washing machines or of small mechanical parts. Serious attempts were made to improve the product in itself; thus we hear instances of pressed metal parts becoming 30 per cent cheaper to make, 37 per cent lighter, and at the same time improved in strength and performance.[171] This was called 'product engineering,' which phrase a trade journal, published in New York from 1930 on, adopted for its title long before 'Appearance Counts' became the motto.[172]

It was explicitly stressed that 'appearance does count' — for reasons of salesmanship — 'even in machinery that seldom appears in show-windows or in modern kitchens.'

There was soon considerable activity in redesigning with streamline form various elements of the mechanized household, the range, the kitchen, the refrigerator, and the washing machine. These should be transformed 'from a household machine to a piece of home equipment.' [173] Machinery gained in compactness in this time of full mechanization. The washing machines of 1914 left their loosely gathered components visible. The motor seemed isolated, the dangerous moving parts often lay exposed. Now the industrial designer takes over. He shapes the casing, sees to it that the visible mechanism disappears from sight, in short, streamlines its appearance. Like the train and the automobile, and at the same time, household appliances underwent redesign.[174] This sometimes led to the invention of new types, such as the table-top range, which compactly unites concentrated heat sources, working surfaces, and storage space with built-in appliances. It also favored the kitchen. These streamlined kitchens are so named because they were designed as integrated units around the work process. The styling of refrigerators began in 1933. Products thus catch the eye more readily in the department store. 'It was also reasoned that women can be sold much more easily on appearance than on mechanical superiority.' [175]

---

[170] W. D. Teague, *Design This Day, The Technique of Order in the Machine Age*, New York, 1940, p.31. Earlier automobiles (such as the 1924 Voisin model) were based on another principle: compactness.

[171] *Product Engineering*, vol. 1, New York, 1930, p.230.

[172] Ibid. p.284.

[173] T. J. Maloney, 'Case Histories in Product Design,' *Product Engineering* (1934), vol. 5, p.219.

[174] For specific examples, see ibid.

[175] George F. Taubeneck, 'The Development of the American Household Electric Refrigeration Industry,' in *Proceedings of the VIIth International Congress of Refrigeration*, 1936.

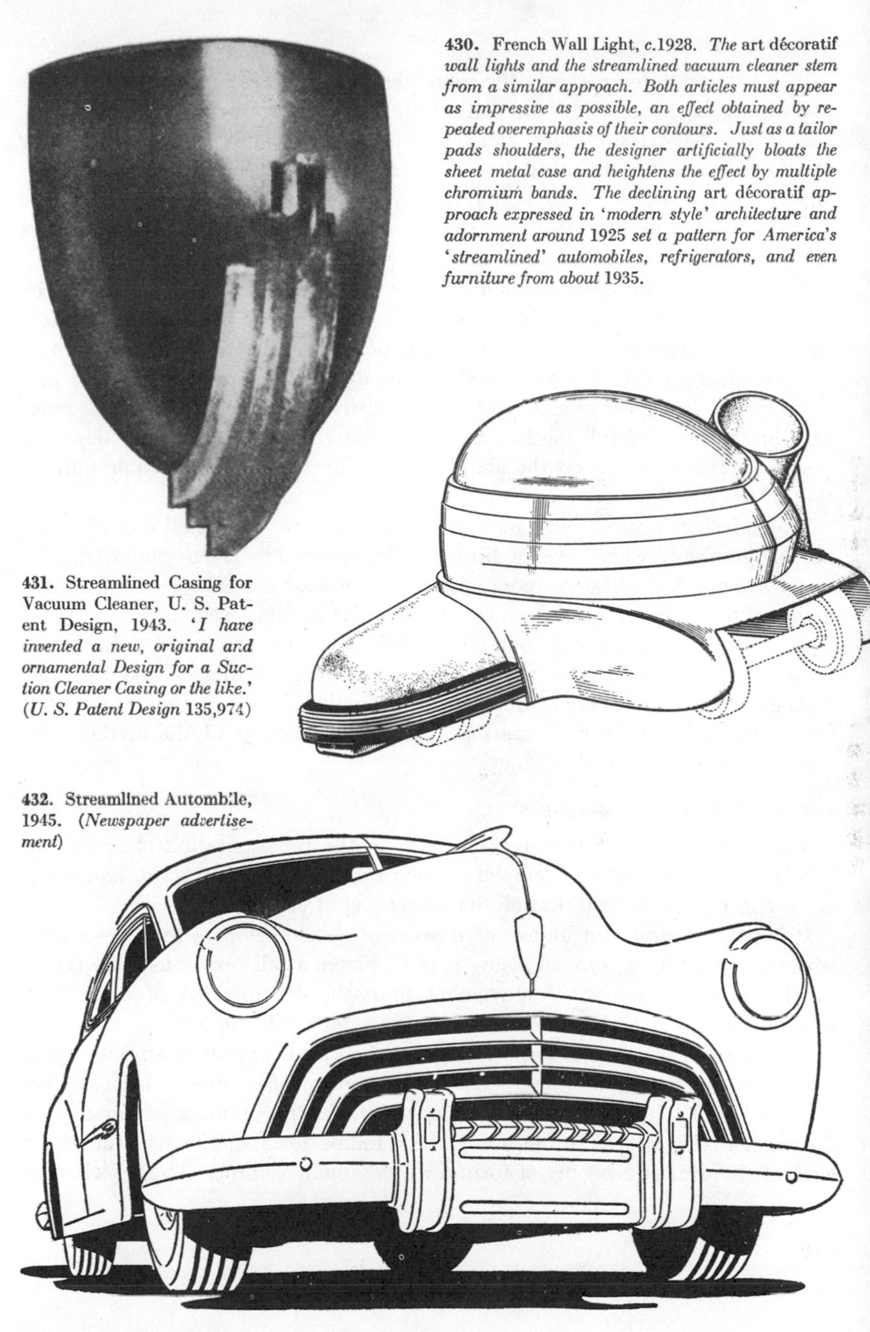

430. French Wall Light, *c.*1928. *The* art décoratif *wall lights and the streamlined vacuum cleaner stem from a similar approach. Both articles must appear as impressive as possible, an effect obtained by repeated overemphasis of their contours. Just as a tailor pads shoulders, the designer artificially bloats the sheet metal case and heightens the effect by multiple chromium bands. The declining* art décoratif *approach expressed in 'modern style' architecture and adornment around* 1925 *set a pattern for America's 'streamlined' automobiles, refrigerators, and even furniture from about* 1935.

431. Streamlined Casing for Vacuum Cleaner, U. S. Patent Design, 1943. *'I have invented a new, original and ornamental Design for a Suction Cleaner Casing or the like.'* (*U. S. Patent Design* 135,974)

432. Streamlined Autombile, 1945. (*Newspaper advertisement*)

THE INDUSTRIAL DESIGNER

The industrial designer was the man who brought these things to pass. His success can be gauged from the statistics. His power grew with the depression. On the one hand the businessman trusts the engineer who knows how a thing should be built. On the other, he lends a willing ear to the industrial designer. America, even around 1945, still largely regarded the architect as one whose business was to decorate the house, as a confectioner the cake. In the time of full mechanization, he had yet to reconquer his place.

The industrial designer as such is not a new phenomenon. We have seen how around 1850 Henry Cole exercised direct influence on English industry by the encouragement of artists and by criticism. The activity of the German Werkbund around 1910 also moved in this direction. But now we face new dimensions: The mass-produced objects, multiplied in such tremendous numbers in the time of full mechanization, all bear the stamp of the industrial designer. His influence on the shaping of public taste is comparable only to that of the cinema.

The industrial designer does more than trace curves. The studios of the leading design firms, where over a hundred draftsmen are often employed, also undertake market research, reorganizing of stores or factories, as well as the design of buildings. Thus they must be decorative artists, architects, and organizers in one. For them only one consideration counts: the merchandizer, dictator of taste in the United States. This is a source of danger and bondage. William Morris could argue from moral grounds. Now, in the time of full mechanization, the reform takes place under dictatorship of the market. All other considerations are secondary.

THE ORIGINS OF STREAMLINE STYLE

That streamline objects owe their form to the representation of speed can hardly be accepted as the complete explanation. Streamline style, like every artistic form, has its historical origins, deserving of enquiry.

It is only natural that an age of movement should adopt a form associated with movement as its symbol, using it in all places at all occasions. We recognized the representation of movement in itself, disembodied of everything corporeal, as a constituent element of contemporary painting too.

And in the Rococo does not the organic shell form appear again and again as a symbol of flexibility and comprehensiveness? Streamline form, unfortunately, unlike Rocaille or absolute movement in the painting of our day, is used inconsistently with its meaning. Streamline form in the scientific sense aims at the utmost economy of form, at a minimum volume. The exploitation of the streamline form in the objects of daily use aims to produce an artificial swelling of volumes.

One need only leaf through the design patents (the legal force of which was considerably strengthened in the time of streamline design[176]) to observe how year by year the casings, from automobile to vacuum cleaner, become increasingly bloated. If one compares such a casing with its manifold profiles to the idiom used at the French Exposition Internationale des Arts Décoratifs of 1925, the historical origins of 'streamline style' become obvious. A Parisian lighting fixture (fig. 430), with its swollen profile of sheet metal thrice repeated, and the 'streamline' casing for a vacuum cleaner (fig. 431) are, in their formal structure, one and the same.

French decorative art of 1925 was a sterile mixture of Art Nouveau and German arts and crafts. Like the furniture of the upholsterer in the Second Empire, its influence became world-wide. Its over-profiled furniture, ornaments, and lighting fixtures wielded a remarkable fascination. Even in the 'forties, the control board of automatic ranges, like the dashboards of automobiles, show that the public is still in the grip of the trend.

Streamline style, as we have seen, also brought forth improvements of form and new types. Its influence did more than inflate the sheet metal like the plush coverings of the *confortables* of the upholsterers. Reformistic tendencies cannot be overlooked when one compares a household appliance of 1940 with one of 1914. Nevertheless, both succumb to the temptation of lending the objects a heavier and more impressive aspect.

Thus, in a strange way the principles of nineteenth-century ruling taste linger on into the twentieth.

---

[176] Design patents authorized: Sec. 4929 R.S., U.S. Code, Title 35, sec. 73. As amended by act of 5 Aug. 1939.

Organization of the Work Process *c.* 1935

How the work process of the kitchen might be made to flow in rational sequence was a question that the feminine advocates of scientific housekeeping after 1910 had precisely analyzed and largely solved.

But in practice, as soon as they tried to bring together the various work surfaces and utensils, their assembly line behaved no more coherently than the contents of an attic. No element fitted any other, for each manufacturer shaped his utensils without any thought to what ranges, sideboards, sinks, or iceboxes the other manufacturers were making (fig. 345).

433. Standardized Range Units, 1847. *The tendency to standardize units and study the work-process is present at this early date. The small oven units are combined side by side in various ways according to the need. 'The ovens are all in front, avoiding the danger and inconvenience of reaching over the fire to use them and the main oven, being elevated, prevents the inconvenience of stooping.' (Boston advertisement. Courtesy Bella C. Landauer Collection, New-York Historical Society)*

Years before industry took up the idea, Christine Frederick had pointed to the hotel kitchens 'where the equipment is all related.' Hotels did not purchase 'a kitchen table here and a stove there. Similarly the home kitchen will have to be made efficient in the future with labor saving equipment, standardized and related by a definite system of work.' [177] We shall see a parallel link with the American hotel in the evolution of the compact bathroom.

At the time of these revindications, and as late as the 'thirties, American

[177] Christine Frederick, *Household Engineering*, op.cit. p.394.

industry had no financial incentive to treat the kitchen as a unit 'where the equipment is all related.'

The organized work-process kitchen around 1935, known as streamline kitchen, translated the thinking of some American women into terms of industrial production. Standardization of its components is the mark of the streamline kitchen. Its elements are sold, preferably in sets, by the large corporations or the mail-order houses (fig. 435). These sections are variously combinable and readily fit with all other sections of the unit. The range, the sink, and cabinets may be placed along one wall, two walls (*L*-shape), or three walls

434. Pantry, 1891. *The pantry with built-in base cabinets below and wall cabinets above the working surface is a stepping stone to the 'streamline' kitchen ensemble of the 'thirties. Note the movable shelves and sliding glass doors.* (Decorator and Furnisher, *New York*, 1891, *vol.* XVIII)

435. Standardized Units in the Mail-Order Streamline Kitchen, 1942. *The mail-order houses of the* 1940's *have applied the principles elaborated in the eighty years since Catherine Beecher. They make appealing sales talk: 'Everything within reach — cabinets arranged in logical order — no crowding.* Add cabinets as your budget permits. *Sears will help you plan your modern, efficient kitchen . . .* where work flows from storage to preparation, from cooking to serving. *Stainless steel bands and recessed drawer pulls add contrasting beauty and streamlining.*' (*Catalogue, Sears Roebuck and Co.*, 1942)

(*U*-shape). A trend toward standardization and combinability can be observed in American range-making at a surprisingly early season. One 'air-tight cooking range' of 1847, especially intended for hotels, ships, or hospitals, was built, as its advertisement shows (fig. 433), of standardized range sections, which could be added end to end, up to the desired length. Its parts were easily interchangeable: 'The iron work can be taken apart without disturbing the brick work.' Yet this trend toward standardization in the kitchen remained latent, as we have seen, for almost a century.

The rational arrangement of working surfaces and the use of wall cabinets owe their immediate inspiration to the serving pantry. Here — we are referring to a pantry of 1891 (fig. 434) — the continuous counter-top, built-in wall cabinets with sliding doors and the built-in sink were already long-familiar things.

Industry Enters the Field

Slowly American industry became interested in planning and selling the assembled kitchen. We can follow its progress step by step. By the mid-'forties three different industries had entered the field.

First came the mass producers of kitchen furniture. It was natural that they should envisage the kitchen as an accumulation of their individual pieces. The kitchen cabinet was their starting point. Normally detached, the cabinet was now built in, together with a narrow broom closet, china closets, or other storage units. The units were standardized and capable of yielding the most diverse combinations. They in turn gave rise to giant, ceiling-high closets, whose sole aim was compression, or what the makers called 'scientific use of space in the kitchen.'[178] So far as we could ascertain, the first closets of this type came on the market in 1922–3,[179] that is, at the same time as the Bauhaus at Weimar was building its kitchen organized around the work process in the Haus am Horn (fig. 340). The pioneer firm's catalogue, 'The Standardized Unit System for Kitchens,'[180] shows how the units were combined (fig. 339).

Catherine Beecher's classical proposals of 1869 and the suggestions advanced by Christine Frederick, under the inspirations of scientific management around 1912, had not yet had their effect on industry. But these combinable cupboards deserve our notice: They were sold as standardized units, to be assembled as one wished.

That was the first step. Next came standardized units that took the work-process into account. American industry first ventured into the use of continuous working surfaces around 1930 (fig. 344). A continuous top connected

[178] 'Standardized Unit System for Kitchens,' Catalogue of the Kitchen Maid Corporation, Andrews, Indiana, 1923.

[179] In answer to our enquiry concerning the origin of their 'built-in unit' the Kitchen Maid Corporation, Andrews, Indiana, wrote (24 Nov. 1943): 'These units were studied and put together between 1919 and 1921. They were offered for sale in 1922 and at about that time were put on display at the Architect's Samples, at 101 Park Avenue, New York. Mr. E. M. Wasmuth, the Chairman of our Board of Directors, was the man that started this built-in unit idea, probably little thinking that it would grow to such an extent and be entered into by so many.'

[180] Kitchen Maid Corporation, Catalogue.

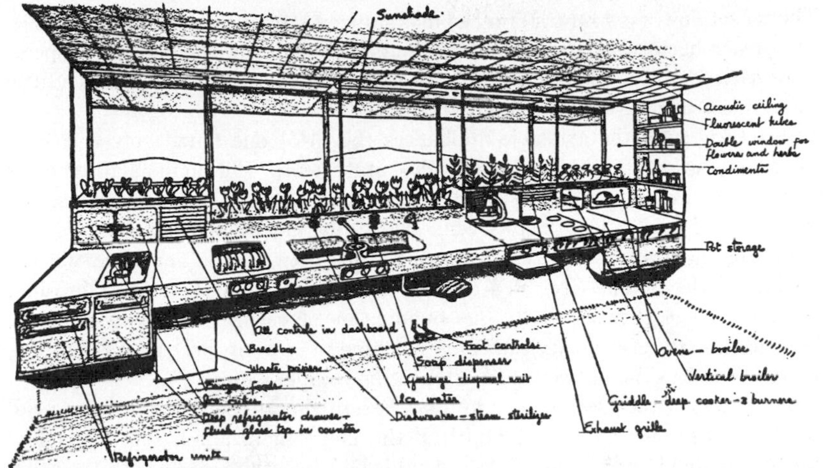

436a. Kitchen Work Center by George Nelson, 1944. Food Preparation Counter. *The architect's problem was to break down the functions of the large units — refrigerator, stove, etc. — as conventionally used, and reintegrate them in a way suited to assembly-line production.* (*Courtesy* Fortune Magazine, 1944)

436b. Kitchen Work Center by George Nelson, 1944. Floor Plan. *The food preparation center shown above is in close contact with the dining area, separated from it by light storage space.* (*Courtesy* Fortune Magazine, 1944)

the base cabinets and kitchen sink, above which were built in separate wall cabinets such as had long been customary in the serving pantries between kitchen and dining room. The connection with the most important tool of all, the range, remained unsolved.

Meanwhile the problem of kitchen organization was receiving the attention of another industry. The initiative came from a gas company that commissioned Lillian M. Gilbreth to study the kitchen as an industrial-production problem.[181] With the precision that distinguished the motion studies on which she had collaborated with her husband, Lillian Gilbreth investigated another work process.

[181] This was on the initiative of Miss Mary Dillon, President of the Brooklyn Gas Company, the research being based on a 10′ × 12′ kitchen. Cf. 'Efficiency Methods Applied to Kitchen Design,' *Architectural Record*, March 1930, p.291.

The object now was to transform the unorganized kitchen into an organized one. 'The rearrangement of the equipment resulted in reducing the number of operations from 50 to 24.' This can clearly be seen in a process chart, which is a little masterpiece of analysis.[182]

But turning to the available appliances (fig. 345) one found only a chaotic miscellany warranting Lillian Gilbreth's statement, 'The manufacturer must realize that at present [1930] he has little knowledge of what the housewife needs. She herself seldom knows what she wants, much less what she needs.' [183]

Full mechanization was to bring about unity between the appliance and the working surface. The electrified appliances that came on the market in rapid succession lent themselves to the building-in of refrigerator, water supply, electric motors, electric dishwashing machine [184] — even electric garbage disposers — and to the marketing of kitchens as complete units.

In 1932 General Electric and in 1934 Westinghouse Electric opened special cooking institutes. In the aftermath of the Depression, purchasing power had to be attracted in new ways. No doubt this had something to do with the opening of such institutes. But the main reason must be sought elsewhere; the time of full mechanization was at hand. Integration of all the equipment with the work process had become inevitable.

Instantly the tremendous resources of industry were made available; the work process in the kitchen was scientifically investigated down to the last detail of food preparation. Expert staffs of engineers, chemists, architects, nutritionists, and practicing cooks studied everything connected with the kitchen. The principles of scientific housekeeping could at last be put into practice; in little time the 'streamline kitchen' was complete.[185]

Soon the large corporations went even further. They understood that the reorganization of the kitchen had affected the whole house. Early in 1935 General Electric sponsored a competition for a 'House of Modern Living,' to stimulate an interest in the design and production of small homes that would take advantage of new methods of construction, the most up-to-date of equipment, and the new-found Government support of small home finance.[186]

---

[182] Cf. 'Efficiency Methods Applied to Kitchen Design,' *Architectural Record*, March 1930, pp.291–2.

[183] Ibid. p.294.

[184] It is said that one of the large corporations began to plan unit kitchens in order to foster a market for its expensive dishwashing machines.

[185] In 1945 standardization was agreed upon by twenty-five manufacturers of gas appliances and eight members of the kitchen-cabinet industry. 'Depth of counter top 25¼″ to accommodate automatic washer. . . . Height of base cabinets 36″, considered standard for woman of average stature. . . . Widths of base and top cabinets will be in units of three. . . .' *N. Y. Times*, 13 July 1945.

[186] 'The House for Modern Living,' *Architectural Forum*, Apr. 1935, p.275.

The *Architectural Forum* devoted generous space to the contest. The over 2000 entries produced nothing memorable from the architectural standpoint. The new architectural idiom as used by the Dutch in their housing settlements was handled with unfamiliarity. But the competition was otherwise significant: here the mechanized kitchen pierces through, with its unified working surfaces, cabinets, and appliances. The mechanical installations, such as heating, plumbing, electric lines, were to be shown, and the competitors were free to sketch one of the rooms in a perspective rendering.[187] Now in 1935, the architects' choice fell, with striking unanimity, upon the kitchen.

After the kitchen-furniture manufacturers (in the 'twenties), the gas (1930) and electrical corporations (1935), the third group of industries to enter the field were the mass producers of building materials (*c.* 1940): glass, plastics, and plywood.[188] Their development took place during the Second World War. The industries that now came to the fore were not tied to the construction of closets, ranges or refrigerators. They were in a position to offer the public new and exciting things, and sought to incorporate their materials on every possible occasion.

Now, over two decades after its uphill struggle on the Continent, architecture found belated allies in support of its preference for light materials and for the wide window space.

Typical of what the housewife wanted in the 1940's was her demand for a large 'picture window' above the kitchen sink. According to statistics these windows called forth more enthusiasm than any other suggested change.[189] Second in order of preference was the idea of placing a mirror in the kitchen.[190]

Outward-opening cabinet doors, which through some tyranny of standardization had persisted in the 'streamline kitchen,' disappear. The closet between the kitchen and the dining room becomes transparent. The connection of kitchen and dining room is stressed. The refrigerator will have glass walls (fig. 351). The housewives expressed satisfaction at the idea of watching the roast through the oven's tunnel-shaped glass cover, while others feared that the material might become discolored. We are referring here to the Libbey-Owens-Ford Company's 'Day after Tomorrow's Kitchen' which was exhibited for fifteen

[187] Ibid. p.276, Basement Playroom, Kitchen, or Laundry.

[188] A group of 23 manufacturers of building materials sponsored the 'Design for Post War Living' competition published in *California Arts and Architecture*, Los Angeles, Sept. 1943.

[189] Mary Davis Gillies, 'What Women Want in Their Kitchens of Tomorrow,' A Report of the 'Kitchen of Tomorrow' Contest Conducted by *McCall's Magazine*, New York, 1944.

[190] The 'Composite Tabulation of 1944 Consumer Ballots resulting from Exhibition of the Libbey-Owens-Ford Kitchen of Tomorrow' gave the following percentages. For the large picture window, yes: 96.6%. For a mirror in the kitchen, yes: 95.1% (1944).

months during 1944–5 in the department stores of the United States. This kitchen was a public sensation and the exhibition had to be circulated in three copies. Its range, kitchen sink, and refrigerator were for the time being wooden dummies. Over 1.6 million spectators beheld what the future had in store, but which could not be produced or tried out in wartime. When we went to visit this 'dream kitchen' in one of the large New York department stores, we heard the young ladies' explanations amid spectators five and six rows deep.

It is astonishing how rapidly — within a decade — the American woman came to appreciate and understand every detail of mechanical or organizational inter-

437. FRANK LLOYD WRIGHT: Dining Area of Affleck House, Bloomfield Hills, Mich., 1940. *In 1934 Frank Lloyd Wright circumvented the whole problem of the streamline kitchen by opening the entire length of the 'work space,' as he called it, into the dining room. In the Affleck house he carried this approach even further.* (Photo Joe Munroe)

est. No longer can it be said of her that 'She seldom knows what she wants and much less what she needs.' A comprehensive survey conducted by *McCall's Magazine*, offering excellent insight into the attitudes of the American woman of 1944, was based on a comparison of the Libbey-Owens-Ford exhibition model with the kitchen that had become a standard after 1935.

It shows that now the housewife knows exactly what she wants. She wishes fluorescent lighting in her kitchen, supplementary lighting above the sink, over the range, over the counter, and so on from detail to detail, down to the question whether a sink parallel to the window attracts her more than one at right angles to it. Of those answering McCall's survey, 46.6 per cent wish it at an angle and 53.6 per cent do not.

The isolated kitchen is abandoned in this third phase of the development. Just as the second phase is connected with scientific management, so the third is closely bound up with the servantless household. The servantless household affects the position of the kitchen in the house and is closely connected with the creation of a concentrated mechanical core. In what manner the glass or

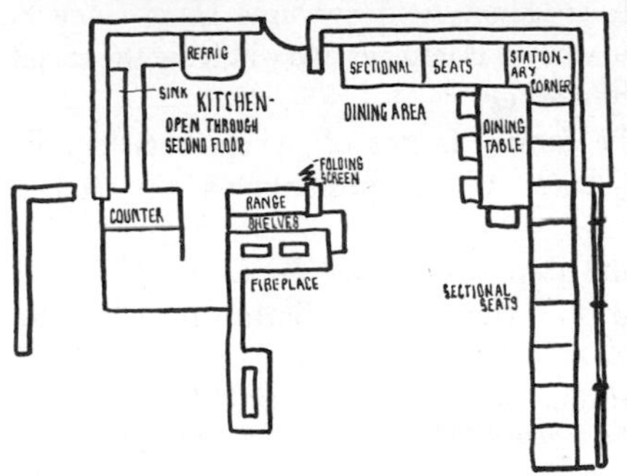

438a. FRANK LLOYD WRIGHT: Kitchen of Affleck House. Seen from Dining Area. *The kitchen is two stories high, so that cooking odors may rise directly upwards.* (*Photo Joe Munroe*)

438b. FRANK LLOYD WRIGHT: Kitchen of Affleck House. Ground plan.

plywood industries stimulated young American architects to a clearing of the way, we shall presently see.

The Kitchen in the Servantless Household

One problem could no longer be overlooked toward the end of the 'thirties, a problem that had passed down from decade to decade without solution: the servantless household. Now it was felt even by those who were heretofore accustomed to have servants in the house. The trend runs deeply within our time. Although not confined to America, it appears more clearly in the United States, where it had always been latent.

We have seen how, in 1841, Catherine Beecher faced the contradiction existing between the institution of 'domestic servants' and a democratic society. Her plan of the small kitchen in a town house (1869) (fig. 337) is actually an outline of the servantless household. Four decades later the advocates of the 'new housekeeping' clearly stated the problem and quite precisely pointed out the course of things.

Christine Frederick voices this awareness in 1912:

> I feel that when the present mistress-slave relation is changed to business-like one of employer-employee with schedule hours and extra pay for extra work done, the service will be put, as it should be, on the same plane as in other employments. . . . A girl in this class is isolated from her companionship, looked down on by them as inferior to typists and clerks. . . . I believe that we are practically coming to the abolishment of a permanent serving class. . . . I can see no practical reasons why we shall not have servants . . . who work for us . . . who come to us daily . . . as workers go to office and factory. . . . I believe we will come to it in all our homes.[191]

Three decades later, during the Second World War, the matter could no longer be put off. Now periodicals like the *Reader's Digest* bombard their millions of readers with headings such as 'Household Servants Have Gone Forever,' subtitle 'Your maid — after the war — if you get one will have the social or economic status of an office or factory worker.'[192]

The new situation of the family is not of merely sociological interest. It affects the house to its very core. What will become of the kitchen in the servantless household?

That important space-and-step saver, the *I*-, *L*- or *U*-shaped kitchen, is compact and self-contained, like the compact bathroom, which developed two

---

[191] *Ladies Home Journal* (Philadelphia), Dec. 1912, p.16.

[192] *Reader's Digest*, Apr. 1945, article condensed from the *American Magazine*.

439. Kitchen and Dining Area, by H. Creston Dohner, for Libbey-Owens-Ford Glass Co., 1943. *This dummy, which millions saw on display (for another view, see fig.* 351), *shows one of the trends of kitchen development. The kitchen is conceived as a work space, but its modern equipment can fold away to convert the area into a living room. Its dining area is not rigidly restricted to eating, for the table folds to the wall when not in use. Only a raised cabinet with sliding glass doors divides the dining area from the kitchen. The practice of lightly separating areas by cabinets on tubular steel legs is widely adopted two decades after LeCorbusier's Pavillon de l'Esprit Nouveau,* 1925 (*fig.* 318).

decades earlier. But in conception it is suited to the household with servants. At all events it segregates the housewife from the household. So one will hardly be surprised when (in 1945) newspapers such as *The New York Times*, under the heading 'Today's Compressed Efficiency Kitchen' admits that cooking in itself is not so laborious a duty. 'It's the isolation that hurts; why must this be done in solitary confinement?' [193]

[193] *The New York Times Magazine*, 10 June 1945, 'Designs for Living,' by Mary Roche.

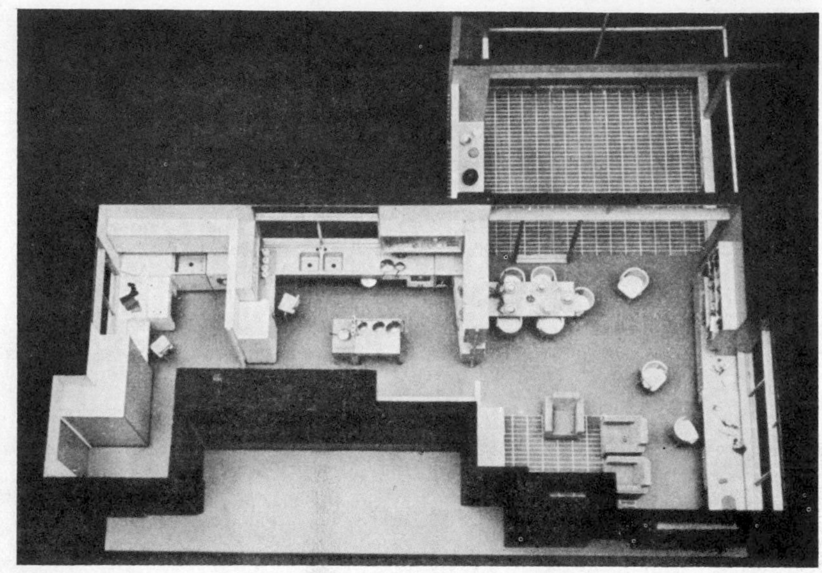

440a. Living Kitchen with Dining Area and Laundry, Raymond Fordyce, 1945. *In the 'forties the kitchen is restored to its functional value, and a trend toward larger area is noticeable. Fordyce terms this the 'living kitchen,' and wishes to make it an active center of household life, where the family can work, play, eat. We mentioned the butcher's block in the center, used to cut up large pieces of meat, in connection with quick freezing. Will the sociological trend to the servantless household bring a return to some medieval ways, and regard cooking as an interesting process that may be performed openly, not behind closed doors?* (*Courtesy* Life Magazine)

The problem is clear. The solution seems less evident. Is the family to take its meals in the kitchen, as in the burgher household down to the eighteenth century? Or should the kitchen be more closely drawn together with the dining room or living area? Should it remain a working tool exclusively? Or, when its function is fulfilled, should it turn into a parlor or play room?

Here we can but sketch the problem in the broadest strokes. The servantless household forms the framework. The actual solutions will depend on the mode of life aimed at.

The process here running its course is not limited to the kitchen. It is bound up with a changed conception of the house and with the development of the open ground plan. From mid-'twenties on, there grew a demand for, in place of the rigid room, an area in which one can freely move about. Even in modest interiors, the wish is ever more clearly voiced for a large room which may be flexibly used.

440b. Living Kitchen, Raymond Fordyce, 1945. View from Dining Area into Kitchen. *Here again the cupboard is glass-walled, and is raised from the ground like LeCorbusier's cabinet in* 1925. (*Courtesy* Life Magazine)

The Abandoning of the Isolated Kitchen and Isolated Dining Room

The giving up of the isolated kitchen is closely connected with the giving up of the isolated dining room. At the beginning of the movement, in the 'twenties, this trend was by no means clear. Thus, for instance, the kitchens of the Weissenhof settlement (1927) were still designed as isolated cells, whereas in many early examples the dining room had already disappeared in favor of a larger living room.

At the same time, instead of the large table, central in the dining room as nineteenth-century ruling taste prescribed in every dwelling of the middle class, we often find a more modest type, with its narrow end to the wall. The oversized central table stems from the same mode of feeling as the circular sofa or borne (fig. 212). Both result from fear of the void. The table is made less wide and is brought as close as convenient to the serving hatch; it almost returns to the rustic simplicity of its medieval ancestors (fig. 163). Often it folds to the wall so as to increase the free space of the room. At first these hints were cautiously employed in bachelor dwellings, as in an early Swiss example of 1927).[194] They appear in the luxurious dream kitchens of the 'forties (figs. 351, 439).

The opening of the ground plan made deep inroads into the isolation of the kitchen. With the force of one attacking single-handed, Frank Lloyd Wright leapt over the whole problem of the streamline kitchen. In 1934, just as American industry was growing receptive to his ideas, he tackled the problem more radically than any of the younger Americans a decade later. In one of his houses [195] he opened the kitchen along its whole length into the large living room. Wright points out to his biographer with his usual directness, 'Here for the first time the space of the kitchen, now called by Wright the "work space," is joined to that of the living room.' [196] He took up the problem again in 1940 in the Gregor Affleck House, Bloomfield Hills (Michigan). Now he builds his kitchen two stories high, so that the cooking odors may pass straight upwards (figs. 437, 438). Objections are possible. These individual solutions could hardly expect the same popularity as Wright's 'car port,' the doorless garage; but from the first the direction of the whole development is clearly and unambiguously announced.

Frank Lloyd Wright's solution implies that cooking need no longer be done behind closed doors, hidden from the eyes of the family or from guests. The detailed treatment of the kitchen, whether it shall be entirely opened or screened from the living room by transparent glass closets (figs. 439, 440), or marked off by panes of glass with view into the main room [197] lies in the hands of the architect and depends on his ability to find the living form demanded by new needs.

The Kitchen-Dining Room?

The minimal-sized kitchen and bedroom, which the architectural movement of the 'twenties brought to the fore, was a necessity. Only thus could the unorganized rooms reconquer their functional values. The trend toward larger bedrooms and larger kitchens — in short, toward space in which to move — asserts itself everywhere. The *L*- and *U*-shaped kitchens are now made larger, in order to serve as a dining room also, as stressed by J. J. P. Oud in his Weissenhof kitchen (1927). In 1945 the trend had gone so far that mechanized kitchen and laundry unit, also to be used as a sewing room as in Raymond Fordyce's pro-

---

[194] Illustrated in S. Giedion, *Befreites Wohnen*, Zurich, 1929.

[195] Malcolm Willey House, 225 Bedford Street, Minneapolis, Minn., 1934. Cf. Henry Russel Hitchcock, *In the Nature of Materials*, The Buildings of Frank Lloyd Wright, 1887–1941, New York, 1942.

[196] Hitchcock, ibid., p.318.

[197] I. M. Pei and E. H. Duhart, Competition entry for Post War Housing, 1943, *California Arts and Architecture*, Los Angeles, Jan. 1944, p.33.

posal[198] (figs. 440a and b) dominates the ground plan. The 'living kitchen,' he explains, 'seeks to make the kitchen an active center of household life, where a family can work, play, eat, and spend 90% of its working time and where, most important, a housewife can watch children and entertain without leaving her work. The living kitchen does this by combining four rooms which are usually kept separate: the laundry, the kitchen, the dining room and the living room.' Here the house has almost become a dependency of the kitchen.

Is the kitchen to become again the dining room and parlor it was to the petty nobleman of seventeenth-century France? In Latin countries there still survives, and not in hostelries alone, the vaulted kitchen at one end of which the cooking is performed while at the other the feasting company gathers.

One thing is certain: We are continuing to cast off the show values of the last century, which sharply isolated the kitchen, even that of a two-room apartment. In America the small eating section in the family kitchen never quite died out. This breakfast alcove (fig. 339) with collapsible seats is not a satisfactory solution. Informal dining facilities within the kitchen seem desirable in every servantless household. The most diverse ways of turning the kitchen into a living room are suggested, such as closing the sink and range as one might a piano, or the use of folding screens to hide the soiled dishes.[199] In the mechanized house there is no reason why the kitchen and the dining room should not be one and inseparable.

The House and the Mechanical Core

Mechanization brought with it difficulties of its own. There was on one hand the wish to use rooms as flexibly as possible and to enjoy the utmost freedom of ground plan; on the other hand, mechanization conflicted with this by seeking the utmost concentration of all installations. The costs of mechanization amounted to some 40 per cent of the building costs. If the market is to be broadened, these costs will have to be cut comparably with the lowering of automobile prices three decades ago.

The mechanical core of the house, embracing the kitchen, bath, laundry, heating, wiring, and plumbing, will therefore be factory-made and assembled before being brought to the building site. From 1927 on, Buckminster Fuller has been busy with the idea of the mechanical core. He incorporated the core within a mast, which carries the weight of his house. Circular or polygonal

---

[198] *Life Magazine*, 28 May 1945.

[199] Charles D. Wiley, First Prize in the Competition for the Design of Small Houses by the United Plywood Corporation, in *California Arts and Architecture*, Feb. 1945.

441. The Mechanical Core: H-shaped House by J. and N. Fletcher, 1945. *In a contest for a small house for the average family, a scheme that built around a mechanical core won the first prize. The mechanical core forms the cross-tie between living room and bedrooms — a symptom of its dominating influence.* (Courtesy Pencil Points)

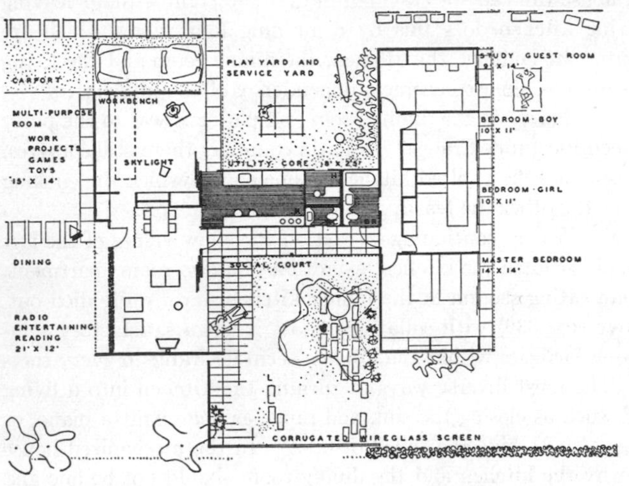

houses resulted, whose closed ground plan is in contradiction with the inherent trend of contemporary architecture.

How is the problem of the mechanical core to be solved without limiting freedom of ground plan? This question was in the air around 1940.[200] Rather

[200] Cf. special issue of the *Architectural Forum*, September 1942, 'The New House 194X,' American architects' proposals for the post-war development. Here the question of the mechanical core arises time and again. As, for instance, in Ralph Rapson and David Runnel's proposal for a standardized 'mechanical panel,' p.89.

typical were the results of a contest 'for the average small family house' sponsored by the Pittsburgh Plate Glass Company and the architectural journal, *Pencil Points* (May 1945): it was won by an architect who took the mechanical core as his point of departure.[201] On one side of the 'mechanicore,' which is to be picked up from the factory, he attaches living quarters, and on the other side sleeping quarters. This produces an *H*-shaped plan, in which the mechanical core forms the cross-tie; but this mechanized connecting element tends rather to draw the sleeping and living quarters apart, as if lodged in two distinct houses (fig. 441).

The industry-sponsored contests encourage the younger generation to develop their ideas, if only on paper. The question we are dealing with here is crucial to the future organization of the house and indeed to the very manner of living. Whether the mechanical core will be dissected into its components or gathered into a single unit has not yet become clear. And it is not certain whether the mechanical core will find its use in one-family houses or in large apartment buildings, the design of which, in America, is still in the hands of routineers.

Industry, produce as it will, is not suited to solve the problem of the mechanical core. The question is far to deeply interwoven with the organism of the house. It is a task for the American architects. Comparing the helplessness with which the architectonic idiom was used in the 1935 General Electric Competition, to the familiarity with which it was handled and taken for granted in 1945, one sees that the younger generation has caught up. The American architects seem called upon to provide the next step in the development. They have the longest experience with mechanical installations and have at hand the most highly developed industry, even if their influence upon production is extremely limited. Yet things can change rapidly in this respect, as the gaining influence of the industrial designer has shown. What matters is to domesticate mechanization, rather than to let the mechanical core tyrannize the house.

---

[201] J. B. and N. Fletcher, Birmingham (Mich.). Their house is intended for a returning soldier of World War II: 'First he goes to the factory to get the "mechanicore" which has all the latest conveniences, and then to the mill for lumber. . . .' *Pencil Points*, May 1945, pp.56–7.

PART VII THE MECHANIZATION OF THE BATH

THE MECHANIZATION OF THE BATH

Types of Regeneration

External Ablution or Total Regeneration?

THE BATH and its purposes have held different meanings for different ages. The manner in which a civilization integrates bathing within its life, as well as the type of bathing it prefers, yields searching insight into the inner nature of the period.

Bathing, in whatever fashion performed, is concerned with care of the body. To maintain the balance of this delicate instrument, to dwell in harmony with our organism, is a prime necessity of life. Some periods have viewed bathing as part of a broad ideal: total regeneration. Other periods have seen it as a mere ablution to be performed in swiftest routine. One age may weave bathing into the well-being of the whole man. Another age may see it as an isolated act, or neglect it almost altogether.[1]

The role that bathing plays within a culture reveals the culture's attitude toward human relaxation. It is a measure of how far individual well-being is regarded as an indispensible part of community life.

This is a social problem. Should society assume responsibility for guarding health and promoting well-being, or is this a private matter? Is it a duty of the state to provide the agencies of relaxation regardless of cost? Or should it regard its people as mere components of the production line, leaving them to their own devices as soon as they have finished their work?

The ancient world, like Islam, and to some extent the Middle Ages, too, regarded human regeneration as a basic social responsibility. This concept decayed during the Renaissance, while bodily care in the seventeenth and eighteenth centuries sank to the point of almost total neglect. But during the eighteenth century the culture of earlier ages slowly came back to remembrance.

The nineteenth, that century which looked so much to other cultures, awakened to the idea of regeneration. Bathing appeared around 1830, in the guise of a back-to-nature movement laying much stress upon cold-water treatments

---

[1] This chapter is partly based upon the author's earlier enquiries into the matter of regeneration, interrupted by other work in 1933. Extracts appeared at the time of *Das Bad im Kulturganzen* exhibition held at the Kunstgewerbe Museum, Zürich, in 1935. Cf. *Wegleitung des Kunstgewerbe Museums der Stadt Zuerich*, no. 125, Zürich, 1935, and 'Das Bad als Kulturmass,' in *Schweizerische Bauzeitung*, Zürich, July 1935.

(hydropathy). Around 1850 the Islamic concept gained recognition. And the home vapor bath had many advocates from around 1830 down to the end of the century. These types, together with the shower and the sun bath, appeared successively and existed side by side. Long and uncertain was the battle, but finally the tub bath remained the type unchallenged in popular choice.

The present-day type of bath, the tub, is actually a mechanization of the most primitive type. It belongs in the category of external ablution. The tub is understood as an enlarged washbowl. No period before ours has so unquestioningly accepted the bath as an adjunct to the bedroom. Each of its components was the outcome of a slow, tedious mechanization; hence the bathroom with running water emerged only toward the end of the last century, while not until the time of full mechanization between the two World Wars was it taken for granted. The fact nevertheless remains that the tub is a primitive bath type, found in Crete, for instance, from around 1800 to 1450 B.C., before the Greek gymnasium was conceived.

The brilliant Minoan age, the last matriarchy, possessed not only bathtubs, but sewer systems and water closets. Sir Arthur Evans' tireless excavating has given us better insight into this early period than we have, for instance, into the Greek gymnasium. The painted terra-cotta tub that Evans pieced together from the queen's apartment in the Palace of Knossos in Crete [2] informs us that this type of bath, like many other Minoan habits, was taken over by the Greeks of the Mycenean period, around 1250 B.C. The Cretan tub, modest in dimensions, fits the description of the Mycenean bath in which the Homeric heroes bathed. When Homer, looking back from around 800 B.C., tells of the bath ceremony, he refers to it as the restorative following 'soul-exhausting toil.' The stress here falls not upon cleanliness but upon relaxation.[3]

Sea-bathing was practiced in the same spirit. This goal, relaxation, is basic to the attitude of the ancients. The early Roman house — like that of the older Scipio — had its bathtub on the ground floor where drainage and heating facilities were combined. In his *Epistles* of Nero's time, Seneca somewhat wistfully and moralizingly recalls Scipio's simple habits and fortress-like house with window slits so narrow that the tub lay in near darkness.

As the thermae developed into public institutions in the first century B.C., the isolated bathtub lost its importance. Immense marble tubs and built-in basins, containing warm water and cold, stood in the hot-air rooms of the Roman baths. Islamic culture never accepted the tub. The Oriental held it unappetizing to bathe in his own dirt.

---

[2] Arthur Evans, *The Palace of Minos at Knossos*, London, 1921–35, 4 vols. vol. III, p.385, fig. 256.

[3] *Odyssey*, X, 358ff.

442. Winter Sun Bath of the Forum Thermae, Ostia. *The broad openings were filled with glass panes, behind which the sun bath was taken as part of the elaborate Roman bath procedure.* (*Photo S. Giedion*)

Regeneration in Antiquity

The Greek bath is indivisible from the institution that gave it meaning. It cannot be divorced from the gymnasium, the educational center of the Hellenes.[4] The Greek bath was most simply performed. It consisted mainly of cold showers and ablutions. The marble trough with running water, and the simple hollows for foot baths — as found in the Hellenistic gymnasium of Priene — reveal how simple was the process, and how it was woven into a wider purpose. The bath forms but one link within the gymnasium; its place is between strenuous gymnastic sport or pentathlon in the palestra, and philosophical discussion in the semi-circular exedra. It lies on the divide between the hours of strong physical effort and of contemplative discourse. No other period more organically fused the bath into human regeneration (fig. 445a).

The Roman thermae are technified gymnasia. They comprise almost the same elements as the Greek institutions; the stress, however, has shifted, and they grow to enormous dimensions. This occurs in the first century B.C. Herodotus' often-quoted remark [5] that the Greeks of his time, the fifth century B.C., generated steam by red-hot irons or heated stones, as the Middle Ages were to do later, points at best to a beginning. But how the development proceeded from the fifth century to the first century B.C. on Greek soil, in Asia Minor, or in Egypt, is still veiled in uncertainty.

---

[4] Tub baths were used in private houses at the time of the gymnasia. But the private bath was of minor importance in Greece.

[5] C. Daremberg and E. Saglio, *Dictionnaire des antiquités grecques et romaines*, 5 vols., Paris, 1877–1919, vol. I, 1881, p.649: Balneum.

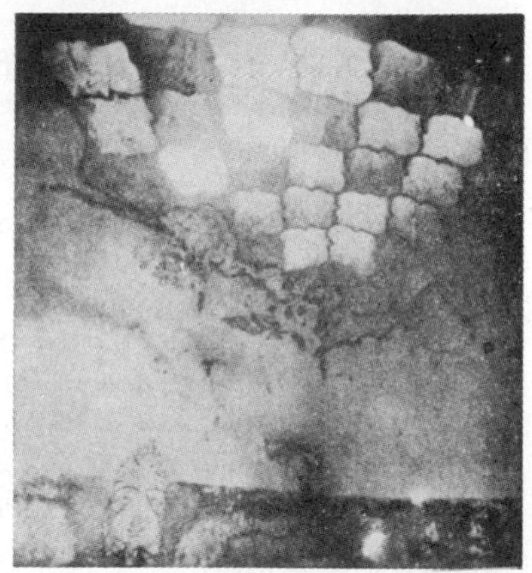

443. Steam Room (Maghtas) of an Islamic Bath. Hammam of Kalaour, Cairo. *The Islamic bather prefers quiescence, seclusion, and the dim light that is here obtained by means of honeycomb vaults.* (*E. Pauty,* Les Hammams du Caire, *Cairo,* 1933)

Near Alexandria in the Nile delta, the archaeologist Breccia [6] uncovered the remains of a bath — two circular buildings, which he assumed to have been heated to different temperatures. These circular halls appear in the Roman thermae as the Laconicum, the hottest of their rooms. We should not be surprised if the archaeologist were ultimately justified in his ascription of these baths to Ptolemaic times.[7] Alexandria of the third century B.C. was the direct heir of the Greek spirit, with its stress on technical invention. Here Euclid taught. In this focus, astronomy, experimental physics, surgery, and gynecology met — an atmosphere favorable to the rise of thermae. In what state of perfectedness the Romans found the Hellenistic thermae seems still an unanswered question.

Only with the Roman Empire did the thermae take on a sovereign significance, such as they attained neither before nor later. Their thermae became the monuments of a nation that controlled the material wealth of the world. Within their walls, the best in Roman technical, architectural, and sociological thought was united.

What the Roman engineering talent so thoroughly exploited for human regeneration was a scheme of appealing simplicity: this floor and wall-heating system, which Vitruvius has described in detail, is taken to have emerged in the first century B.C. The floor stood on low brick pillars (*hypocausts*) beneath which the fire gases passed. A system of square earthenware pipes (*tubulae*)

[6] E. Breccia, 'Di Alcuni bagni nei dinterni d'Alessandria,' *Bulletin de la Société Archéologique d'Alexandrie,* no. 18, Nouvelle Serie, vol. v, premier fascicule, pp.142–9.

[7] There is also palpable evidence that public baths were the common practice in Egypt of the third century B.C. Cf. A. Calderini, 'Bagni pubblici nell'Egitto greco-romano,' *Rendiconti del Reale Instituto Lombardo di Scienze e Lettere,* vol. 52 (1919), fasc. 9–11, pp.297–331.

carried the heat through the hollow walls. Wall and floor heating is not unusual in Roman settlements beyond the Alps. The technical scheme of the thermae is entirely based on this combined heating system, which distributed the heat throughout the room with greater evenness than could later be attained by any other method.

This heating system was used on the broad Roman scale in halls of dimensions hitherto unknown. Linked with its fires was another element: water. The aqueducts through which water came from the Alban hills were already a century-old institution by the time the thermae arose. Now they were multiplied. The enormous swimming pools of the Roman frigidaria and their lavish consumption of water were nova in civilization. Abundance of water and heat give the Roman thermae their unique stamp. What makes them impressive are not the quantities of water and amounts of heat they consumed, but the way they served total regeneration.

With the advent of the technified hot-air bath and its variously heated rooms (*tepidarium*, warm; *caldarium*, hot; *laconicum*, very hot), the function of the fifth-century Greek bath was definitively altered. The bath proper now becomes paramount. The individual parts of the gymnasium are retained, and likewise the palestra for sports and wrestling. The space of the open palestra in the Roman Imperial thermae, such as the baths of Caracalla, could have held more than one gymnasium like that of Priene. The form of the exedra also reappears, but its hemicircle is now a place for repose. It is no longer culture for the few, as in Athens. No Plato or Socrates could have developed amid the noise and crowds of the Roman palestra. The function of the exedra, instruction and discussion, is now shifted to the outer zone of the thermae, where it is more peaceful and where there is room for assembly and for a library.

The end to which a period solves its vaulting problems, or spreads out its designs, points almost invariably to its dominant interest. In the Gothic period it is for the nave of the cathedral, in the nineteenth century it is for industry, railway stations, and international exhibition halls. In Rome the cupola and barrel vaults, of a boldness unknown, appeared for the spanning of the vast areas of the tepidarium. Neither the fora, nor the amphitheatre, nor the circus buildings can rival the architectural originality of the thermae and their vast spatial problems. From the baths of Pompeii, or the Pantheon of Agrippa, to the thermae of Constantine's epoch [8] is as great a leap in architectural finesse as from the Romanesque to the late Gothic.

Light flooded the high-vaulted bath halls, above all, that of the tepidarium. Daylight poured through the great half-circle windows, with their two jambs.

[8] The thermae of Constantine are known only by vestiges today underlying the Quirinal.

The tepidaria of the thermae are, so far as we know, the first monumental interiors into which full daylight could enter through extensive window apertures. In the thermae of the forum at Ostia, Rome's port at the mouth of the Tiber and a bathing resort of Roman society under Augustus and Claudius, a room at ground level was uncovered. The function of this room was for a time not quite clear. Its southern wall opens into a single span supported only by two marble pillars (fig. 442). What this opening formed was a wall of glass, the room, with its southern exposure, serving as a winter sun bath.

The sociological invention lies in having made the place set aside for regeneration into a social center. The Romans spent a great part of their leisure in the thermae, and the baths arose wherever the Romans settled — on farms, on estates, in cities large or small, and in the military camps of Africa and Britain.

The Roman work day began at dawn, and normally ended at one or two o'clock. The thermae opened at noon.[9] One visited them at the close of work before the main meal. Their purpose was daily regeneration. As in the gymnasium, exercise in the palestra loosened up the body and stimulated circulation. This took time, as did a sojourn in the largest and most splendid of the rooms, the tepidarium, where perspiration was induced in about half an hour. Then the greater heat of the caldarium, culminating in a brief stay in the laconicum, whose hot, dry air, approaching 210° F., neared the limits of endurance. After that a soaping, a massage, and a plunge into the swimming pool of the frigidarium. Thus daily regeneration was inseparably bound up with Roman life. This does not mean that every Roman spent five hours in the thermae each day. But the baths were there; they were open to whoever wished to use them. Numerous foundations took care of that; Agrippa's baths were free as long as they operated.[10] The normal entrance fee was ridiculously low, and quite out of proportion to the expense and upkeep of the establishment. City thermae provided for the civilian public; those of military camps, for the legions. The Roman generals knew that tired soldiers fight badly. The wealthy stratum, who had mastered the art of otiose living, likewise used the thermae of their villas for social purposes. In the late Pompeiian Villa of Diomedes, the baths do not lie near the sleeping quarters, which are on a higher level, but to the left, directly opposite the entrance.

One first hears of the thermae that they were places of erotic abuse. Yet the institution can no more be blamed for this than the automobile if it is occasionally used for purposes other than transportation. Rostovtzeff has made it

[9] The opening time varied with the seasons of the year and from period to period.

[10] Hugo Bluemner, *Die roemischen Privataltertümer*, München, 1911, pp.420–35. Handbuch der Klassischen Altertums-Wissenschaft, Bd. 4, Abt. 2, Teil 2.

sufficiently clear that the decay of the Roman Empire was primarily the result of weaknesses in the social and economic structures of the provinces. Behind the thermae lay the insight that an institution is needed in public life to help restore the body's equilibrium once within its twenty-four-hour cycle.

The obstinacy with which Rome and Byzantium, until their decline, and Islam, until the onset of mechanized life, clung to their total regeneration shows how deep-seated in human nature is the need for such institutions.

With the growth of the thermae a new social factor entered history: Each individual was recognized as endowed with the same right to regeneration — moreover, to regeneration within the twenty-four-hour cycle.

The cutting off of the Roman water-supply when the nomads destroyed the Campagna aqueduct at the wane of the Empire has told upon our cultural life down to the present day.

Itinerary of the Regeneration Types

Where did the archetype originate? All signs point to the East, to the interior of the Asiatic Continent. The primitive type of total regeneration has maintained itself longest in Russia. It spreads to European Russia, to Siberia, and, around the twelfth century, into middle Europe and England. It reaches its fullest Western expansion in the late Gothic period. We find it mentioned in the earliest chronicles of the Russians and of the Finns. We shall deal more closely with this early type in our section on the vapor bath as a social institution.

The principle of the present-day Russian type was familiar to the Greek Herodotus, who describes a steam bath of the simplest kind. Whether it traveled to Greece through Asia Minor or over the Balkans, or along both paths, is not ascertainable. A well-developed version left its traces in the Nile Delta during the third century B.C., under the Ptolemies. From highly technified, Hellenistic Egypt, it passes to the Roman Empire — Pompeii, Rome — in the first century B.C. In this period a clear-cut form branches out, the Roman thermae, having a graduated series of hot rooms and incorporating the gymnasium of the Greeks (fig. 445).

If the archetype spread centrifugally from the interior of Asia, a similar process now takes place with Rome as its center. In the time of Rome's expansion the thermae will be carried to the frontiers of the civilized world.

A remarkable phenomenon is then observed. In Syria, during the third century A.D., the Roman type (thermae) comes up against the original Asiatic type, having no athletic culture, no palestra, no cold swimming pool (frigidarium). Striking similarities of plan and scale show that these small Syrian

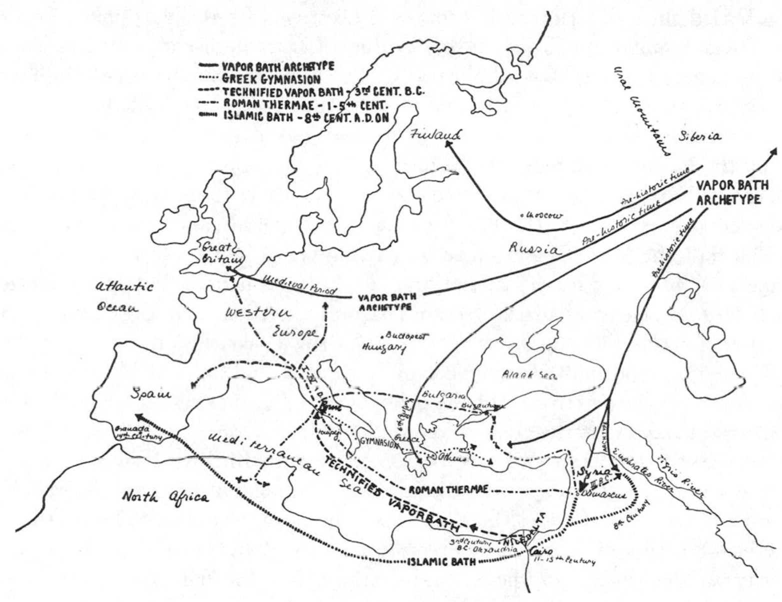

444. Itinerary of the Regeneration Types. *In this map we have tentatively traced the path of the different types of regeneration. From Central Asia the archetype — vapor or hot-air bath — spread in ancient times to Russia, Syria, the Greek world. This type was probably first elaborated technically in the Nile Delta during the Ptolemaic Period. In the first century* B.C. *the Roman Thermae, a crossing of archetype with the Greek gymnasium, spread with the expanding Empire. It was in Syria, in the third century* A.D., *that the Roman Thermae — marching east — met the archetype and were transformed into what later became the Islamic bath, a type that persisted until the influx of mechanization.* (*M. Ecochard and S. Giedion*)

baths (fig. 446) were not provincial simplifications, but descendants of the original type, absorbed and adapted to Greco-Roman living habits. The archetype will prove the stronger. Detail by detail the early Arabian conquerors of the eighth century will take them over, as comparison of a third-century Syrian bath with the caliph's bath at Kusair' Amra and other eighth-century Syrian installations graphically shows.

The bath F 3 of Dura Europos (third century A.D.),[11] which the caliph's bath at Kusair' Amra, for instance, will so resemble in scale and overall plan, had lain buried since this Roman outpost was destroyed by the Parthians. One of the things brought to light by the excavators of Dura in recent years transcends the archaeological report in implication. The large pool of the frigidarium was found to have been filled up with sand at some time before the city fell (A.D. *c.*256) and converted into a rest hall (*apodyterium*) — a pattern invariably adhered to by the Islamic bath in all its variations. Its direct prototype is not known. The Dura Europos bath cannot have served as a pattern to the Omayyad caliphs. The similarities suggest that it represents not a special case, but a type. This means that the West Roman type was relinquished in the Near East when it came face to face with its archetype. F. E. Brown immediately recognized bath F 3 as belonging to the Syrian-Oriental tradition, and Ecochard's comparison of scales [12] has further strengthened Brown's conclusion.

The Syrian type, built of stone, normally vaulted, and technified in the Roman manner, represents a crossing of the original type (which lives on in the log huts of Russia today) with the civilization of the West.

From Syria and Transjordania, this type spread with the Moslem expansion just as the thermae had spread with Rome's. Baghdad at first, and later Cairo, new-built by the Fatimides, become new centers of radiation. The north and northwest coasts of Africa and Spain up to the Pyrennean wall abundantly testify to the passage of the Islamic bath. After the fall of Constantinople (1453), the Osmans, using Byzantine modes of plan and vaulting, will carry it through the Balkans and Hungary to the frontiers of Austria.

Thus the archetype of total regeneration extends continuously in its many forms from prehistoric times down to present-day Russia, Finland, and the Near East.

Only Western culture, since the Counter-Reformation, has struck this thorough-going restorative of the human organism from the roster of its institutions.

Regeneration in Islam

The development took a fresh turn when Islam first encountered the Roman thermae in Asia Minor. Islam adopted and assimilated the thermae, reshaping

[11] F. E. Brown in Yale University, *The Excavations of Dura Europos, 6th Season*, edited by M. I. Rostovtzeff and others, Yale, 1936, pp.49–63. Excellent bibliography on Kusair' Amra, p.58. 'The great frigidarium pool was filled in with sand' (p.68). Brown thus describes Bath F 3 at Dura: 'Thoroughly unclassical in the absence of organic symmetry in plan, and in the way in which its separate units are allowed to define themselves externally. . . . Dissimilar to the great standard symmetrical bath type, it suggests itself as of oriental, Syrian origin . . . restricted to the far corner of the Eastern provinces until adapted to his purposes by the Arab conqueror.'

[12] Michel Ecochard and Claude LeCœur, *Les Bains de Damas*, Institut Français de Damas, I partie, 1941; II partie, 1943; II, pp.127–8.

to its own needs the Roman pattern it had found in Syria. The wise caliphs could thus compensate their subjects for the alcoholic joys forbidden by their faith.

What differentiates the *hammam* [13] or bath of Islam from the Roman bath? [14]

The palestra and its gymnastic games, together with the swimming pool in the frigidarium, disappear. So do the facilities for intellectual exercise, the Greek exedra, or Roman library. As Islam finds its own architectural expression, the high-windowed, light-flooded tepidarium gives way to cupolas sparsely pierced by the glow of colored bullions, or to stalactite cupolas in the smaller rooms. Half light, quiescence, seclusion from the outside world are preferred. In the cupolas' neardarkness the spirits, *djinns*, are said to meet. Here the active bather of the classical world yields to the passive repose of the oriental. A refined technique for loosening, cracking the joints, and a shampoo massage with special penetrative power supplant athletic sports. Rest beds enter in the place of the Greek exedra. Musicians play in the galleries of the rest hall. The buildings become smaller and less conspicuous. The technical equipment is simplified. There is a warm and a cold wing. Hypocausts are restricted to wall flues, and hot-air pipes run under the floor of the warm wing.

The nucleus of the Roman thermae, a graduated series of hot-air rooms, remains. Yet the balance of the whole organism has been modified.

In classical times, the apodyterium, or divesting hall, was used for that one purpose; the Orient enlarges its functions to those of a combined dressing-room and rest hall, the *maslak*. The bather sojourns in it at the beginning and at the conclusion of the regeneration cycle.

The focus of the Roman bath was the tepidarium, or luke-warm hall. The Romans lavished the greatest luxury and the largest share of space upon it. Time and again the tepidarium — as in the baths of Caracalla or Diocletian (fig. 445b) — tempted nineteenth-century architectural fantasy to essay reconstructions. The Roman tepidarium seems at least partly explicable on natural grounds. The bather entered it when exercise in the palestra had already stimulated his circulation. The tepid atmosphere encouraged the naturally ensuing relaxation, and sweating did not need to be artificially provoked. In the *hammam* the tepidarium dwindles to a mere passageway. The decline of the tepidarium

[13] *Hammam* or 'Dispenser of warmth.' The word derives from the Arabic *hamma*, to heat, and the Hebrew *Hamam*, to be warm. Cf. Edmond Pauty, *Les Hammams du Caire*, Le Caire, 1933, p.1 (Institut Français d'Archéologie Orientale du Caire; *Mémoires*, vol. 64).

[14] The various phases of the Islamic bath, especially its beginnings in Syria, are treated in monographs. For Damascus, see Ecochard and LeCœur, op.cit., indispensable for its precise architectural plates. For Constantinople, Heinrich Glueck, *Die Bäder Konstantinopels und ihre Stellung in der Geschichte des Morgen und Abendlands*, Wien, 1921; Karl Klinghardt, *Türkische Bäder*, Stuttgart, 1927. A general survey of the bath's development is not available. Without such a work true insight will hardly be possible.

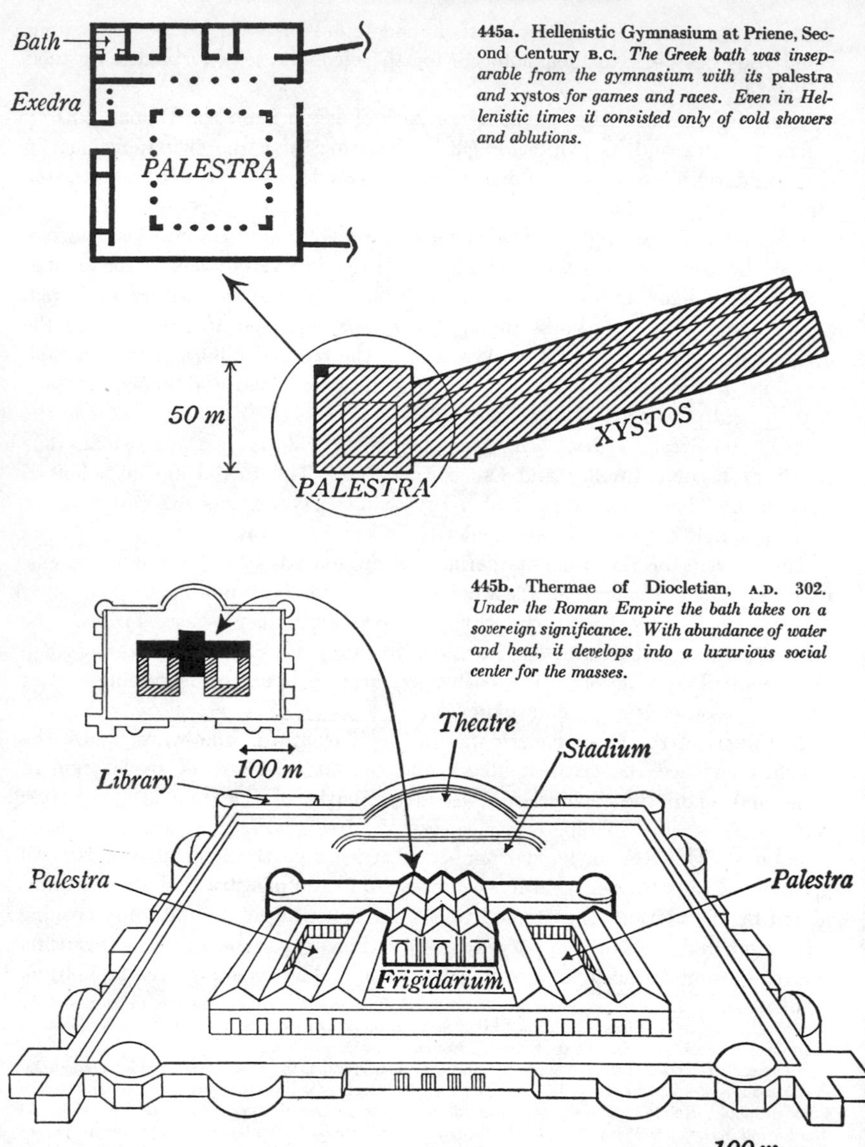

445a. Hellenistic Gymnasium at Priene, Second Century B.C. *The Greek bath was inseparable from the gymnasium with its palestra and xystos for games and races. Even in Hellenistic times it consisted only of cold showers and ablutions.*

445b. Thermae of Diocletian, A.D. 302. *Under the Roman Empire the bath takes on a sovereign significance. With abundance of water and heat, it develops into a luxurious social center for the masses.*

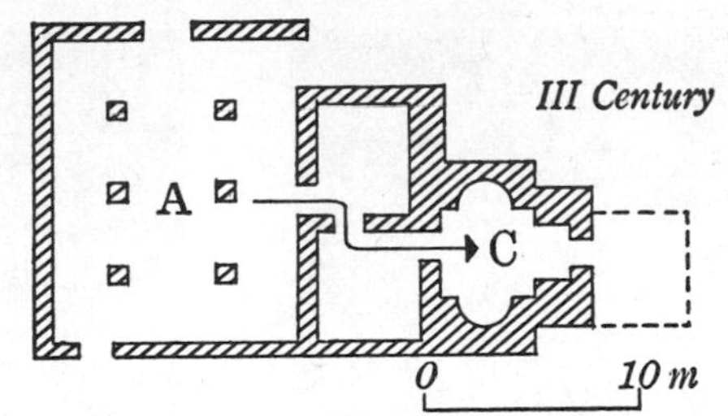

446a. Bath of Dura Europos. *The Roman thermae encountered its archetype in Syria and along the Eastern Roman frontiers. In the third century* A.D. *bath* F3 *at Dura was deliberately filled with sand and turned into a large Oriental rest hall* (A) (maslak).

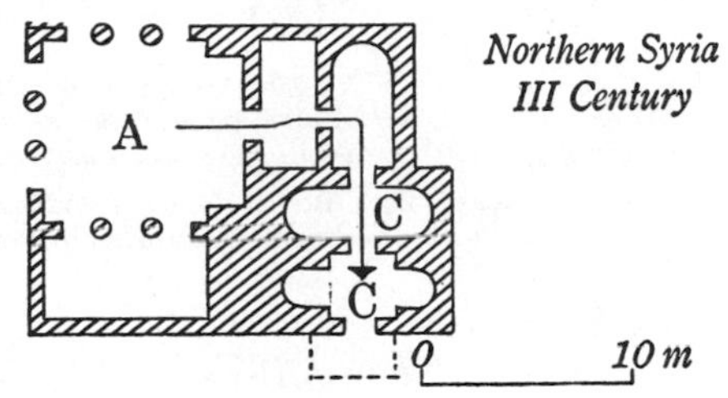

446b. Bath of Brad. *Growing emphasis on the rest hall* (maslak) *and hot chamber. The* frigidarium *and* palestra *have disappeared.*

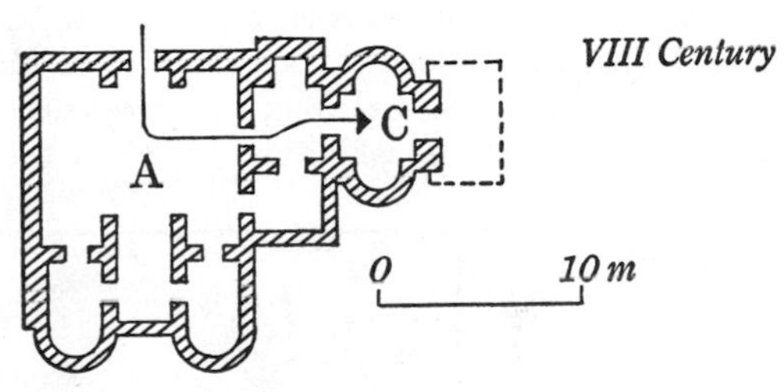

446c. Bath of Kusair' Amra. *The Omayyad caliphs took up the Syrian type and began to develop it into an Islamic institution. Same elements, same scale.*

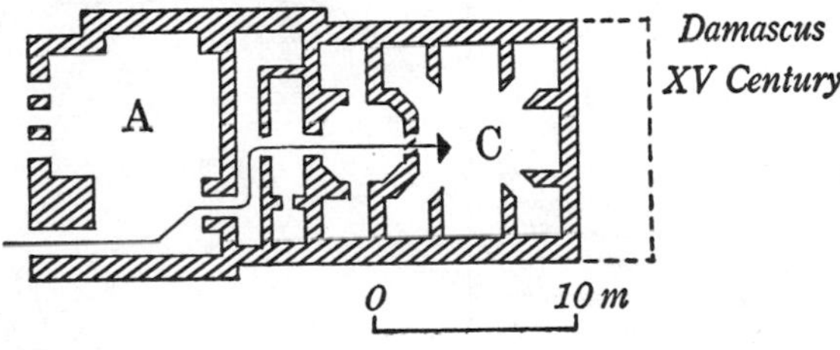

446d. Bath El Hajib. *Under Byzantine influence the installation becomes further differentiated: the hottest room* (C) *grows to conspicuous size, a trend that, as Ecochard has shown, continued down to the present. Each room is given a cupola and radial vapor chambers are grouped around the hot-air room.*

447a. Rest Hall of the Islamic Bath (Maslak, Apodyterium). *Here Islamic regeneration begins and ends. In contrast to the twilight of the bathing chambers, a brighter room is favored. The bather dozes, smokes, sips coffee. In the time of the caliphs, musicians played in the galleries.* (*Pauty,* Les hammams du Caire)

447b. Hot-Air Room of the Islamic Bath (Beit-al-Harara, Caldarium). *The hot-air room is a dim vaulted chamber. On a polygonal divan in the center massages are administered.* (*Pauty,* Les hammams du Caire)

is generally attributed to the warmer climate; yet this explanation hardly seems sufficient, for throughout North Africa, the Roman baths retained their tepid hall.

Now the hot-air room becomes central, the *beit-al-harara,* the caldarium, which in Rome never rivaled the tepidarium in importance. Later on, other chambers will radiate crosswise from it. Large marble troughs of hot and cold water stood in the Roman caldarium. Now, in the *beit-al-harara,* a polygonal

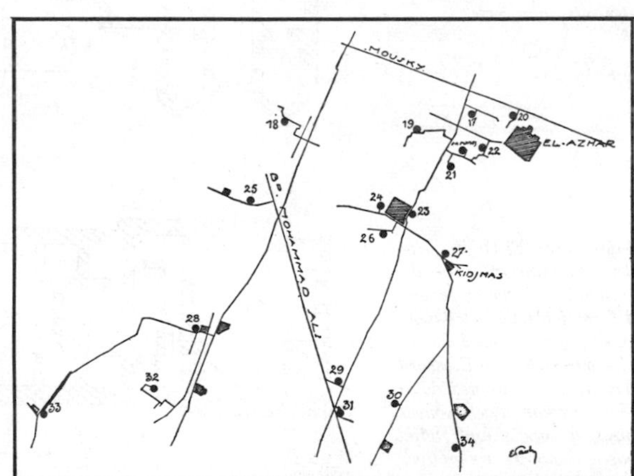

448. Distribution of Baths in a Quarter of Cairo. *In the* 1930's *some fifty hammams of the* 11*th to* 15*th centuries were still counted in Cairo, all of them small and serving their immediate neighborhood.* (*Pauty,* Les hammams du Caire)

449. Vapor Room and Pool in a Persian Bath, 16th Century. 'Caliph Al-Ma'mun and the Barber,' Persian miniature, 1548. *The caliph sits on the edge of the pool having his hair trimmed. Servants draw water to pour over the bathers. A massage is taking place in the foreground.* (*Courtesy of the Freer Gallery, Washington*)

couch occupies the center, where limbering and massage, a substituting for the Roman palestra, are performed by an attendant.[15]

In Rome the hottest chamber, the laconicum, had a hot, dry atmosphere, for the fire gases passed beneath its floor. In the *hammam* this becomes a steam bath, *maghtas*, the one room having a deep pool in its center (fig. 449). In tune

[15] A short but still classical description of this process is given by E. W. Lane, *Manners of the Modern Egyptians*, London, 1836; p.346 in Everyman edition, London, 1923. Edward Lane (1801–76) lived in Egypt during the years 1825–8 and 1833.

with the Oriental preference for steam bathing, two such *maghtas*, steamed to different temperatures, usually radiated from the *beit-al-harara.*

The ministration of the bath, as outlined by the ground plan (fig. 446) proceeds thus: from the divesting room (*apodyterium, maslak*) — the tepidarium has become a mere passageway — to the domed hot-air room (*caldarium, beit-al-harara*), where limbering and special massages are administered; hence to the steam bath (*maghtas*); finally a soap massage, and return to the *maslak* for a rest.

Islam found its basic scheme in the thermae of third- to sixth-century Syria.[16] Here the balance has already shifted. Disappearance of the palestra and frigidarium; dominance of the apodyterium (divesting and resting hall); dwarfing of the tepidarium; and increased importance of the caldarium. Hypocausts and double walls are already lacking. In comparison with the Roman buildings, everything is on an extremely reduced scale. The baths of early Christian times in Syria are to the thermae of imperial Rome what a primitive Romanesque mountain chapel is to the finesse of a Romanesque cathedral. Everything is provincially simplified, but at the same time adjusted to new surroundings. Here the provincialized version gave rise to a fresh development, as so often in history when foreign influences renew an older pattern.

When the Mohammedans shaped their own baths in the eighth century,[17] they instilled new life into the Syrian institutions. The builders of the earliest Islamic baths were Omayyad caliphs, who still preserved a half-bedouin way of life. They despised the shut-in and ordered life of cities. This trait was common to the Arabic conquerors everywhere: in Mesopotamia, in Egypt, and likewise in Syria. The bath of Kusair' Amra, near the Dead Sea, stands isolated in the desert wastes like a hotel among the glaciers. The initial chamber (*apodyterium, maslak*), for all its modesty of size, becomes a social hall with a gallery and delicate murals. The actual bath chambers, on the other hand, lose some of their importance. The dominant mood is undeniably one of intimacy, an atmosphere that was not lost even when, as time went on, the Islamic bath grew in scale. As in the Syrian prototypes the rooms form a continuous sequence. The caliph's bath in the Alhambra at Granada (fourteenth century), still follows this pattern. Alongside these, cruciform ground plans develop, as in the *hammams* of Cairo, which a French archeologist has so precisely revealed to us.[18] Here the domed caldarium (fig. 447) (*beit-al-harara*) becomes the architectural center.

---

[16] De Vogue, *Syrie Centrale, Edifices chrétiens et architecture civile du IVme au VIIme siècle*, pp.55–7. Pauty, op.cit. pp.14ff.

[17] Cf. Pauty, op.cit. p.17. Ruins of Kusair' Amra, built by an Omayyad caliph before 715. Also As-Sakarh, discovered in 1905.

[18] Pauty, op.cit.

Setting aside the athletic and intellectual framework, Islam makes regeneration a religious matter. Thus the *hammam* is regarded as complementary to the Mosque. Here the great ablutions are performed.[19] The endowment of *hammams* was regarded as an act of piety. The baths were open to the poor, payment being left to the bather's discretion. 'I leave it to the bather,' says a caliph in the *Thousand and One Nights*, 'to pay according to his rank.'[20] This custom was conscientiously observed to the end of the nineteenth century, for the gratuity given to bath attendants was considered a religious deed. And to promote the *hammams*, Islam made bath attendants tax-exempt subjects.

As in Antiquity, the bath was a place of social intercourse. To women, it meant the one opportunity to visit outside their home.

As late as 1933, Pauty could count in Cairo some fifty *hammams* of the twelfth, thirteenth, fourteenth, and fifteenth centuries, and a few of later date. Several of those built in the twelfth century — contemporaries of the north portals at Chartres — were still in use. Since everything athletic had been eliminated, a small area and narrow frontage, like that of any other house on the street, sufficed. Only the doorway was more richly treated, drawing the eye like an eighteenth-century innkeeper's sign. A glance at the map of a quarter of Cairo shows that the *hammams*, each serving its immediate neighborhood, were as numerous as are taverns in a European city (fig. 448). In view of the warmer climate, this was probably more convenient than the gigantic Roman installations with their crowds drawn from afar.

Like the thermae of the Roman Empire, *hammams* developed in all cities and city quarters, in villages and on highways, wherever Mohammedan influence reached. Lands in which fuel was very scarce burnt straw or cow and camel dung, and, to the present day, refuse from the native quarters — a rather neat mode of garbage disposal.

Hammams were to be found in the Balkans, in Persia, in Asia Minor, in Africa, from Egypt to Morocco, and in the Spain of the Moors. Cordova is said to have had about 900 baths at the peak of its development, around the year 1000.[21] In Budapest several hot-sulphur baths still stand today, their springs spanned by vaults dating back to Turkish times.

The most flourishing period of the Islamic bath coincides with the Romanesque and Gothic in the West. The *hammam* attained the height of its refinement in the fifteenth century. In other words: the Arabs had carried its organization to full maturity just as the Turks came upon it.

---

[19] Ibid. p.7.

[20] Quoted ibid. p.7.

[21] Such indications are not confirmable; in some cases they seem to have been exaggerated.

With the awakening of interest in things Oriental around 1830, the 'Turkish' bath impressed itself upon the notice of European travelers. An English diplomat, David Urquhart, was foremost in recognizing its human significance. He dreamed of bringing such baths to the industrial towns of mid-nineteenth-century England, as regeneration for all classes. When Urquhart first encountered the *hammam*, in Greece in 1830, it still flourished under the patronage of the well-to-do. Around 1850, its decline under Western influence could be foreseen, although there were as yet no bathrooms in the apartments. It seems to have been finally doomed when the mechanized bath began to penetrate the Oriental world. The *hammams* lost their wealthy patrons. Only the poorer classes, Pauty reports, now use the baths. Stripped of their ornaments, their carpets, their mosaics, the *hammams* have lapsed into dirtiness. The upper classes have adopted our habits and are now content with bathrooms in their own living quarters.

The Steam Bath as a Social Institution

Bathing in steam-saturated air is at once the simplest and the cheapest type of bath that will cleanse the body with desirable thoroughness. The moist heat stimulates the skin and sweat glands, promoting the elimination of waste products. A pile of heated stones and a pail of water is all the equipment needed. Such bathing is on record from the time of Herodotus on; it existed in the classical world, much as in any village of Russia or Finland today. The vapor bath's popularity begins with the twelfth century and perhaps even earlier. Like the wooden tumbler lock, it is found everywhere. But, in keeping with its trend, the nineteenth century produced no inventor who, with an eye to human needs, might have shaped the medieval vapor bath into an institution adequate to our period as successfully as Linus Yale transformed the wooden tumbler lock into a marvel of mechanization.

THE LATE GOTHIC VAPOR BATH

From Russia and Finland the archetype of the steam and hot-air bath continued its march toward Western Europe. Its full development occurs in the late Middle Ages.

In the West no less than in Russia, the medieval vapor bath was thought of as a social institution. Few differences exist between a Finnish *sauna*, a Siberian bath hut, and the late Gothic vapor bath, 'sweat-house,' 'stew,' or 'stove,' which we see depicted in Albrecht Dürer's 'Woman's Bath' (1496) (fig. 450). Dürer had just returned from his first journey to Italy. In this drawing, he wished to portray various postures of the female nude. He sought his models

450. Late Gothic Steam Bath. 'The Women's Bath,' Drawing by Albrecht Dürer, Nuremberg, 1496.

where they were most naturally to be found, in one of the thirteen vapor baths of fifteenth-century Nüremberg. Like Ingres for his 'Turkish Bath' (1859), Dürer used the bath moment as his pretext. Ingres drew upon the famous Letters of Lady Montague, and her description of a Turkish bath in Adrianapolis. Albrecht Dürer, like the onlooker in the background of his drawing, could witness the event. He recorded it with all the precision that was his: the pitilessly rendered nakedness of the old woman in the foreground, the various gestures and actions of the hands, the erect maiden striking her skin with the bath wisp, the low wainscoted room, the open hearth built up to ceiling height, the vats from which one sprinkled one's body with water, the pile of heated stones, the round or chest-shaped cauldrons, and the various levels within the bath chamber.

Medieval bath customs varied but little throughout Europe. When David Urquhart campaigned to introduce the Turkish bath among the English, he learned, in 1856, that the Isle of Rathlin, on the Irish coast, still possessed medieval sweating houses, and that 'especially at the Fair of the neighbourhood the people get themselves bathed.' [22] In Switzerland, in the Zürcher Oberland for instance, communal vapor baths remained in use even later. The abundant steam generated in breadmaking was often used for this purpose. Having introduced a tube into the oven, the company might bathe in the vapor so generously given off in the baking process. Conflicts arose from time to time between the bakers' guild and that of the bathmen, who resisted this injury to their trade.

THE RUSSIAN VAPOR BATH

The Russian vapor bath is the most simple of regeneration types and has proved the most enduring. The pattern apparently goes back to eras and regions for which we have no historical evidence. It was connected with the myths of pre-Christian times, with the worship of the dead, with the cult of springs and rivers. On holy days, on Maundy Thursday, before Easter, one left an offering of meat, eggs, and milk, heated the bathhouse, scattered ashes on the floor, bidding 'Wash-ye, spirits' to the beings that inhabited the place. For the furtherance of good health, herbs endowed with magical virtues were tied into the bath wisp.[23]

The origins of the vapor bath as practiced by the Russians and the Finns are so remote as to have left none but the most meager clues. Simple analysis of the type seems to give more reliable guidance than the written sources. Like the baths of Antiquity and of Islam, the Russian vapor bath is a social institution. But its type suggests an earlier social structure, a milieu that did not depend on slave labor. One bather serves the other. No provincial simplification, it is a type that, unlike the urban gymnasia and thermae, attained its common form in peasant surroundings and in wooded regions.

We side with one of the few precise investigators of the question, who discards the easy assumption of Greco-Roman origin. 'I would rather suppose,' he says, 'that the idea of this type was derived from the Orient or from the Scythians, who possessed such vapour baths [24] . . . or perhaps from the Sar-

[22] *Descriptive Notice of the Rise and Progress of the Irish Graefenberg, St. Ann's Hill, Blarney, to Which is Added a Lecture . . . by the Proprietor, Dr. Barter, on the Improved Turkish Bath*, London, 1858, p.15.

[23] Felix Haase, *Volksglaube und Brauchtum der Ostslaven*, Breslau, 1939, pp.137, 194, and 158.

[24] Cf. Herodotus, IV, 73–5.

451. The Russian Bath through 18th-Century Eyes. *Illustration to Abbé d'Auteroche's* Voyage en Sibérie en 1761.

matians or Khazans'[25] — that is, from the East. It never developed into a luxury institution. An eighteenth-century French visitor, whom we shall presently consult, stresses the fact that only greater cleanliness distinguished the baths of the well-to-do from the bath huts of the peasants.

The Russian bath remained what it was to start with: a log hut having an open hearth and a pile of red-hot stones. To provoke intensive perspiration in the steam-saturated atmosphere, a tub of cold water, a wisp of twigs for

[25] Lubor Niederle, *Institut des Etudes Slaves*, no. 4, *Manuel de l'antiquité Slave*, Paris, 1926, p.24. This author also refers to a tenth-century Arabian historian, Mas' ûdî, who calls these baths *al-itbâ*, a word apparently derived from the Slavic *istûba*. *Istûba* is associated with the Frankish word *stuba* — an oven within a room — and thus with the Franks in the West (cf. the later French *étuve;* English *stew, stove*). From the tenth century on, the Russian bath has been called *banya* (from L. *balneum*), and thus it appears in the earliest Russian chronicle, the so-called Chronicle of Nestor. Cf. *Chronique, dite de Nestor, traduite du Slavon-Russe par Louis Léger, pubs. de l'École des Langues Orientales Vivantes*, Paris, 1881, p.141. The article *banya* in the Great Soviet Encyclopedia, Moscow, 1930, vol. 4, includes a short historical notice likewise stating the obscurity of its origins and the uncertainty whether it was invented by the Russians themselves or borrowed from peoples with whom they had political or cultural relations.

stimulating the skin, a handful of leaves and onions for massage, are almost all that was needed. It was never raised into a sumptuous succession of halls at staggered temperatures. A few tiers of benches, at various distances from the ceiling where the heat is greatest, provided for this. In winter, the outside atmosphere and rolling in the snow supplied the necessary contrast; in summer the near-by river, or a dousing of cold water. This type is a nature bath in the fullest sense of the word. Simplest in means and simplest in pattern, it is one of the most thoroughgoing in regenerative effect.

POPULAR REGENERATION THROUGH WESTERN EYES

The Russian bath is the one type of total regeneration that has remained intact to this day. How does an educated mid-eighteenth-century Frenchman react on first encountering this age-old type of regeneration? Since this is not so much a personal reaction as one typifying the epoch, let us look more closely into his report. In 1761, the astronomer Abbé Chappe d'Auteroche, being sent by the French Academy, journeyed to Tobolsk in Siberia there to observe the eclipse of Venus. He later traveled with a similar aim to California, where he met his death in 1769. True to eighteenth-century universalism, his interest embraced the most diverse fields. He treats of geographical, geological, physical, religious, and ethnological matters. His three folio volumes [26] are the unembellished record of customs he observed, which struck or shocked him: executions by two adroit blows of the Knut, the tearing out of tongues, or his experiences in bathing as the Russians.

The Abbé had heard much talk of this bath on his eastward journey, and, thermometer in hand, he wished to test its effect on his own body. Deep in Russia on a winter's morning, he resolved to let himself be sledded from the house where he was staying to the bath hut by the river. He opened the door but such 'clouds of smoke' swirled around him that he quickly shut it again. 'I thought that a conflagration had broken out in the bathhouse. . . .' But one of the Russians would not cease his persuasion until the Abbé gave in. 'The abnormal heat was far from what I was prepared to meet with, for I had supposed that these baths were intended for cleansing.' They eventually gave him to understand that he was expected to perspire. But, he adds, 'As I was quite satisfied with my state of health I resolved to leave straightaway.' Not wishing, however, to offend the good people who had heated the bath overnight for his benefit, he made a third attempt. 'I undressed quickly and instantly fell to sweating.' The heat goes to his head; he imagines he is sitting on red-hot iron,

[26] *Voyage en Siberie fait par ordre du roi en 1761 . . . par M. l'Abbé Chappe d'Auteroche de l'Académie Royale des Sciences*, Paris, 1768, vol. 1.

452. The Russian Bath as It Appeared to the Early 19th Century, 1812. (*Rechenberg and Rothenloewen,* Les peuples de la Russie, *Paris,* 1812)

falls from his bench, shatters his thermometer, and is unable to dress again, for while he cannot force clothes on his damp body within the bathhouse, it is too cold to do so outside. In despair he slips on his nightgown and asks to be sledded back to his room. 'This first venture left me so displeased with the Russian baths that I remained in Tobolsk five months without trying them again, in spite of all the representations that were made to me.'

Later trials of the Russian bath failed to win the astronomer's affection, but did not prejudice his position as an impartial observer. He clearly sees its social function, its efficacy against maladies (scurvy and gout), and recommends it to Western Europe.

These baths are used throughout Russia; . . . everyone from the Tzar to the last of his subjects uses them twice weekly, and in identical manner [fig. 451]. Whoever possesses the most modest fortune adds such a bath to his home, the father, mother and children using it, often all of them together.

The lower classes of the people use public baths. These are shared by men and women alike. Planks partition the sexes but since both sexes leave the bath naked they see one another in this condition and stand conversing upon the most indifferent matters. In the poorer villages the sexes use the baths promiscuously.[27]

[27] Ibid., pp. 53–4.

The seventeenth century has also left us descriptions of the Russian bath.[28] More fortunate than the French Abbé was the Earl of Carlisle, ambassador of the crown to the court of the 'Great Duke of Muscovie,' who found the Russian baths a source of refreshment and delight. His account contains little that is new. He notes that 'their Bodies be well washed with Warm water, or some other liquor, and rubbed all over with hand-fuls of Hearbs . . . they commonly take a Dram of the bottle to re-inforce their Spirits.'[29] The bath, it is always stressed, is regarded as a means of regeneration for the masses, no less to maintain bodily sweetness than for the guarding of health.

Most interesting, perhaps, is the Earl of Carlisle's observation that the baths were believed very necessary for new married people . . . especially after their first congress, they always make use of this kind of purification'[30] — a custom of great tenacity, which, like the cult of spirits, points to a ritual significance. Carlisle's observation to the effect that the baths were more numerous in the countrysides than in the cities — 'they were as rare at *Mosco* as hunting'[31] — agrees with what the Great Soviet Encyclopedia has to say on the matter: the government of seventeenth-century Russia set up baths in the cities, and encouraged their operators by granting them freedom from taxes.

The fact that Russia was not permeated by mechanization in the nineteenth century may partly explain why the bath was able to maintain itself to the present day. After the Revolution of October 1917, this popular institution was promoted as an important instrument of national hygiene, and detailed specifications were promulgated.

When the first quarter of the nineteenth century sought to bring back vapor bathing, it transformed this social institution into a private steam cubicle or vapor-bed bath.

---

[28] Augustin, Baron de Mayerberg, *Relation d'un Voyage en Moscovie*, Paris, 1858 (a translation of his *Iter in Moscoviam*, 1661–2.

[29] *A Relation of Three Embassies from His Sacred Majesty, Charles II to the Great Duke of Muscovie, the King of Sweden and the King of Denmark, performed by the Rt. Hon. the Earl of Carlisle in the Years 1663 and 1664*, London 1669, p.53.

[30] Ibid.

[31] Ibid. p.142.

453. Interior of a Late Gothic Steam Bath, Fifteenth Century. Illuminated manuscript. (*Courtesy* Verve, *Paris, Bibliothèque Nationale, Paris, MS. Frçs.* 289)

The Decay of Regeneration

Regeneration in the Middle Ages

Twice, first at the beginning of the Middle Ages and again at their close, the peoples of Western Europe came in contact with other customs of regeneration: In the decline of the Ancient World, when the land-hungry nomads plundered Rome; and again some nine centuries later, when the Moors were finally driven from Spain around A.D. 1500. Many traits of the Moorish civilization were absorbed in the process, from irrigation to the treatment and ornamentation of leather seats.

But the Islamic bath, which, without any artificial stimulant, causes a feeling of well-being to arise from within the body proper, was rejected. This high culture of the bath was too much a symbol of Moorish ways to be accepted. A Queen of Aragon is said to have boasted that, exempt by birth and marriage, she had never bathed. The land that was educating an Ignatius Loyola (1491–

1556) was in no mood to take over the Islamic cult of bodily joy. The Escorial still re-echoes the gloom into which Spain increasingly sank.

Soon, under the influence of the Reformation and the Counter-Reformation, medieval regeneration habits began to decay. The Middle Ages had by no means been hostile to the idea of regeneration. Swimming was a common sport. And tub baths also were widely used. A well-known illumination of the Manesse manuscript (Heidelberg) shows a knight being attended in the bath by young women and showered with rose petals like Telemachus by the daughter of Nestor. There were also large-walled vats in which one might eat and listen to music, seen, for instance, in Albrecht Dürer's 'Men's Bath.' Medieval accounts bear witness to the important role of the bath in social life. Sometimes the stress falls on its erotic aspect (fig. 453), as in the late fifteenth-century miniature, where the naked guests are gathered around a table in an enormous wooden tub.

The picture of medieval streets as pest-ridden alleys, without any form of sanitation, is being given up. It has long been known that medieval castles were far better off in the matter of drains and privies than Versailles, whose builders paid little heed to such facilities. Fourteenth-century London, more recent research has shown, possessed ground sewers, cesspools, and public latrines.[32] The cleanliness of their streets was a point of especial pride with the Florentines of the fifteenth century.[33]

Hygienic precautions were habitual and included free hospitalization as well as measures for the checking of contagious diseases, concerning which the Middle Ages were better informed than Antiquity.[34] Among these institutions were numerous public baths under the supervision of barber-surgeons.

The Saturday bath of apprentices was provided for by a regular allowance. These baths, of which no example remains, were as frugally furnished as Gothic living quarters. Albrecht Dürer, in 'The Woman's Bath,' shows what a public bathhouse looked like. Exceedingly primitive, it is true, but the whole room with its fireplace, hot-water vessels, and various levels, immediately suggests how far these installations were everyday things.

A common trend links the medieval bath with the ancient and the Islamic: It was a place of social intercourse. In the bath, the men talked politics as in the taverns. The baths are also said to have been places where conspiracies were knotted during the Reformation. Instead of the Islamic massage expert

[32] Ernest L. Sabine, 'Latrines and Cesspools in Medieval London,' *Speculum*, vol. IX (Cambridge, Mass. 1934), pp.306–9.

[33] Lynn Thorndike, 'Baths and Street Cleaning in the Middle Ages and the Renaissance,' *Speculum*, vol. III (1926), p.201.

[34] Ibid.

454. The Rediscovery of Swimming and Physical Exercise. J. B. Basedow, 1774. *The pedagogist Basedow sought to balance training of the mind with training of the body. He was among the first to incorporate swimming, fencing, riding, and outdoor life in education. (Engraving by Chodowiecki for Basedow's* Elementarwerk, *Dessau,* 1774)

came a remarkable combination, the barber-surgeon. After the bath he would cut hair, shave beards, perform cupping, blood-letting, and minor operations. Thus the late-medieval bath was also connected with the practice of medicine. In the wane of the Middle Ages, the habit of regarding the bath as a social institution died out.

The Seventeenth and Eighteenth Centuries

Every period has its contradictions. The seventeenth and eighteenth centuries manifested a sublime feeling for space, music of the greatest distinction, acute and systematic thinking. They were acquainted with the refinements of living. But they stopped short in the matter of caring for the vessel that holds all these: the body. Our accounts may exaggerate in detail, but there is no doubt that the most elementary sense for cleanliness was lacking.

How can we explain this contradiction?

Among other causes the effects of the Counter-Reformation and Reformation are responsible. Both regarded nakedness as a sin. Whenever a bath appears in eighteenth-century French engravings, it is disguised as a chaise longue, a *baignoire*. The *baignoire* in such cases opens up, and a curved, shallow tub is placed in its frame. Cleanliness of the body could hardly have been its purpose. It forms the background for a scene between a gallant, a young woman, and a procuress. Bath and sin were one.

The stunting of the sense for cleanliness and, in the broader sense, for regeneration in the seventeenth and eighteenth centuries is so far as we know a phenomenon without parallel in any other highly civilized period. In many ways we are still suffering the effects today. When such an attitude has eaten its way into society it easily becomes an almost unshakable prejudice, a part of life that resists removal even when its causes have withered away.

The seventeenth century, which laid the spiritual foundations for the following period, carried neglect of the body to its lowest state. Slowly, the eighteenth century began the change. A start was made along two directions: through medicine, and through the rediscovery of nature; that is, by therapeutics and by a new orientation of feeling. The two will become intertwined in the course of the nineteenth century.

Medicine Paves the Way

The English doctor, John Floyer (1649–1734), tells us that 'baptismal immersion continued till the beginning of the last [seventeenth] century'[35] and connects its decline to the decay of bathing. John Floyer, said to have been the first to measure the pulse-beat, won considerable fame for his use of cold baths in disease, particularly in the cure of rickets. He strongly defended the reintroduction and the therapeutic effect of the cold bath. Floyer lists other factors that helped to inhibit the bathing tradition in his century. One of these was the rise of 'chymical doctors,' who introduced new medicines and imputed all diseases to crudity and acid salts. Finally he imputes a share of the blame to the newly imported narcotics and spices. 'I shall add one more reason of the disuse of cold baths, which was the increase of foreign trade last century, which then introduced all the *hot regimen* from the hot climates such as tobacco, coffee, tea, wine, brandy, spirits and *spices*, and these are unnatural to English bodies.

Soon in Germany too, around 1730, voices were heard defending the bath, the shower, and their beneficence. Boerhaave, a great Dutch physician of the eighteenth century, attributed so important a role to water in the cure of maladies that he later became the patron of hydropathy. Around mid-eighteenth century in England, attention turned to the curative virtues of sea bathing. But all these are exceptions and did not run within the broad stream of custom.

Use of the bath for any but medical purposes was regarded as unsound, and

---

[35] John Floyer, *Psychrolusia, or the History of Cold Bathing, Both Ancient and Modern*, 5th ed., London, 1722. Cf. Dedication. Originally published with the title: *Enquiry into the Right Use of Baths*, London, 1697.

Poitevin, who dared to open a public bath in Paris, was well advised in seeking the medical endorsement of the 'Doyens et Docteurs Regens' of the faculty. In a specially constructed ship anchored in the Seine, Poitevin placed cabins with warm baths and showers, to be used only upon a doctor's orders.

How far this was from being an everyday practice is measurable by the fact that even Europe's most enlightened minds, the editors of the Great Encyclopedia (1755), defined the word *douche* (shower) as 'terme de chirurgie.'[36]

Nevertheless such things were not beyond all discussion, for a few years after Poitevin's successful bath-boat in Paris, a medicinal bath on the Thames, 'adapted to the cures of many diseases, not to be remedied by other known means'[37] was proposed in one of the few English patents of the time.

Natural Education

Fear of contact with water, fear of nakedness and of the natural, began to break down before new attitudes. The influence of Rousseau, proclaiming 'back to nature,' was penetrating this sphere too. One rejected Rococo refinement and sought to make a fresh start.

The primary instincts of mankind would be recaptured. For it was at this time that primitive man, the noble savage, was discovered and romanticized, while even the classical world was approached with a fresh vision — 'noble simplicity, calm grandeur' [Winckelmann]. It was a period that aimed at the perfectibility of man. Through study of the child's mind, education according to nature, a new humanity would be formed, guided by tolerance and understanding: citizens of the world.

Not only was intercourse between men to be harmoniously equilibrated; but in the individual, too, the balance of mind and body was to be maintained. The earliest practical pedagogical efforts in this direction appeared during the last decades of the eighteenth century. Gymnastics, running, jumping, swimming, become necessary elements of education.

At Anhalt-Dessau, a small eighteenth-century German principality, Johann Bernhard Basedow (1723–90), moral philosopher and pedagogue, founded the educational institution which he named Philanthropin — school of human friendship for the teachers and the taught alike. On the fame of this philosopher's *Book of Methods for Fathers and Mothers of Families and Peoples* (1770), Leopold Friedrich Franz, Prince of Anhalt Dessau, had called Basedow to his small capital, there to put his ideas into practice. By modern standards Philanthropin had a ridiculously small student body; its tribulations were unending, and it

[36] *L'Encyclopédie ou dictionnaire raisonné des sciences, des arts et des métiers*, vol. 5, Paris, 1755.
[37] British Patent, 7 Feb. 1765.

455. Acrobats. J. B. Basedow, 1774. *In the 1770's there were no specifically gymnastic exercises. The educator went to the circus to find examples of bodily control.* (*Basedow,* Elementarwerk, *Dessau,* 1774)

closed down shortly after Basedow's death. Yet it had proved faithful to its aims. The dignity of man, independent judgment, intellectual freedom, these attitudes of the Age of Enlightenment were here introduced for the first time into education. By a historical hazard it was at this same place, Dessau, that the Bauhaus made the first attempts to fuse the artistic thought of our own time into pedagogical form.

Philanthropin had the enlightened classes on its side and the clergy against it. It dared to advocate the separation of church and state, banned denominational religious instruction, and taught only what all faiths held in common. Lessons in morality took the place of doctrinal teachings. Basedow's four-volume *Elements of Education,*[38] with its album which Chodowiecki charmingly illustrated with copper plates (fig. 454), sums up the attitudes of the school and its training. Typical of the late-eighteenth-century Enlightenment is Basedow's dedication of his work to the Prince of Anhalt-Dessau, to Joseph II of Austria, to Catherine, Empress of Russia, and to other enlightened rulers, 'at whose feet,' it was, in the phrase of the time, 'most humbly laid."

What interests us here is the stress that Basedow put on balancing education of the mind with education of the body. For six hours of class instruction, there were three hours of physical activity, and two of manual training. It is not yet systematic exercise of the muscles; it is rather control of bodily movement, in which dancing, fencing, riding, swimming, and music are included. Rousseau's 'return to nature' appears in the hardening cold washing, cool sleeping, early rising, and, in summer, 'living under canvas.' All this is carried out according to Basedow's principle that things shall not be learned by military compulsion, but in freedom and informality, just as, anticipating later methods, he taught the children languages without recourse to grammar.

---

[38] J. B. Basedow, *Elementarwerk,* Dessau, 1774, 4 vols. and atlas.

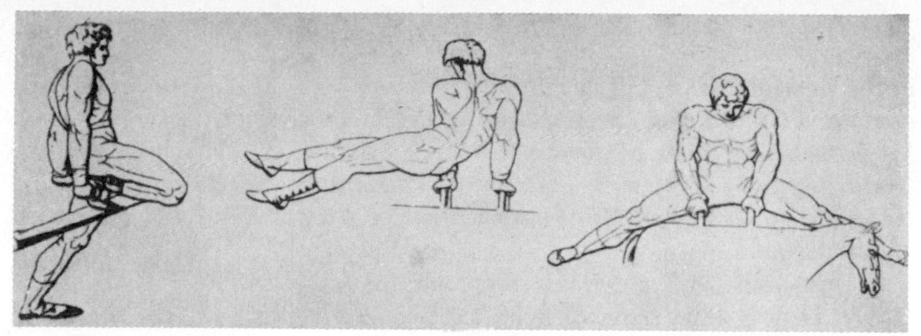

456. Beginnings of Gymnastic Apparatus in the Early Nineteenth Century. (*P. H. Clias*, Anfangsgruende der Gymnastik oder Turnkunst, *Bern*, 1886)

The next generation took a bolder step. Philanthropin had grown up within the hot-house atmosphere of princely patronage. Its exercises preserved the charm and also the luxury of courtly accomplishments. Johann Heinrich Pestalozzi (1746–1827), who belonged to this next generation, worked in more austere surroundings. The Swiss patricians who ruled his country were less open to innovation than the prince of Anhalt-Dessau. They would lend no ear to his proposals. Pestalozzi labored alone. He too was influenced by Rousseau's *Emile*, stimulator of pedagogical ideas in this period. Pestalozzi, the city dweller, a citizen of Zurich, having studied jurisprudence and theology, apprenticed himself to a farmer to learn the art of tilling the soil. For in the peasant, as against the townsman, he saw the 'power of nature more vital and alive' (*noch belebtere Naturkraft*). But his own ventures as a farmer ended in misfortune. He lost his own money and his friends' too. He gathered abandoned, homeless, or ill-treated children on his farm. Thus 'Neuhof' was no sojourn for the education of nobles or patricians; it became a poor-house that had to support itself by work in the fields in summertime, by spinning and weaving in winter. The year 1780 saw its bankruptcy and disbanding. But from this disappointing venture Pestalozzi had gained the experience from which nineteenth-century pedagogics were to emerge. His best years remained workless until patrician rule was overthrown (1798) and an opportunity to realize his pedagogical ideas at last came into sight. 'I could have spat in the face of the whole world.' Thus Pestalozzi summarizes the experience of his manhood years. In his new locale, Burgdorf, he introduced his free exercises, that is, exercises requiring no equipment (fig. 455).[39] Care of the body was for him, as for Basedow, the counterpart to spiritual activity. It was a coming into agreement with 'nature,' not

[39] Pestalozzi's article 'Ueber Koerperbildung als Einleitung auf den Versuch einer Elementar Gymnastik,' in *Wochenschrift fuer Menschenbildung*, Aarau, 1807, affords insight into his guiding principles.

in the Romantic sense, but in Pestalozzi's sense, with the nature of man. His exercises were to follow the articulation and functioning of the human body. In Germany his views on gymnastics were regarded as unmanly.[40] But the North, especially Sweden and Denmark, went firmly through with the more humanitarian eighteenth-century conception of gymnastics as the cultivation of litheness.

As Pestalozzi made public his proposals for an 'Elementary Gymnastics' (1807), Ludwig Jahn, the apostle of 'German Turnkunst,' was already giving gymnastics another meaning and direction. He too aimed to harden the body, but his were exercises of discipline. 'Military exercises, even without guns, build a manly character, awaken and stimulate the sense of order, and inculcate obedience to leadership.[41] Jahn therefore introduced military commands, drilling in squads, gray twill uniforms, at the first *Turnplatz* in the Berlin Hasenheide (1811). The equipment that Jahn and others used has remained almost unchanged to this day. Hardening and swimming also played a part. But all in all, specialized preparation for national and militaristic ends held the foreground. The nineteenth century was beginning.

---

[40] Even in 1850 criticism is made of Pestalozzi's methods that he would be better advised to take model upon the wrestlers of Emmenthal, and by 1817 Ludwig Jahn, founder of German *Turnkunst* was energetically attacking 'free exercises': 'Every exercise must have an object. Let us take fencing as an example: cutting and lunging at the air can amount to nothing more than mirror-play.' (Quoted in Carl Euler, *Encyclopaedisches Handbuch des Turnwesens*, Wien, 1894, vol. 1, p.340.

[41] Friedrich Ludwig Jahn, *Die deutsche Turnkunst*, Berlin, 1816, p.xvii.

The Bath in the Nineteenth Century

The type of bath prevailing in our day is, as we have said, but a mechanized version of the primitive type, which superficially cleanses the body from the outside by ablution or immersion in water of a given temperature. This mode of bathing has as its symbol the bathtub.

The bathroom with running water, and its standard fixtures — tub, wash-basin, and toilet — are the outcome of a long wavering. Which type was to prevail in our period hung in the balance through the nineteenth century as late as the 'nineties. This vacillation between the types — hot-air bath, steam bath, tub, or simple shower — will form our subject here. To which type shall preference be given? This question arises time and again. The *Encyclopædia Britannica's* view in 1854 may be indicative: 'The vapour bath is infinitely superior to the warm bath for all the purposes for which a warm bath can be given. An effective vapour bath may easily be had in any house at little cost and trouble.' [42] The solution offered seems reminiscent of what was practiced through the centuries. A brick, having been heated in the oven, is placed in a basin, water is poured over it to produce steam, while the bather, wrapped in a towel, sits on a chair.

From 1850 to the early 'nineties, strong endeavors were made to introduce communal baths affording fuller regeneration — hot-air or steam baths aided by massage and gymnastics — rather than the primitive bath within the dwelling. Again, in the early 'eighties, the shower was advocated in preference to the bathtub for private houses as well as for the public baths of the working class.

It may not be superfluous to recall that even in America, which was later to surpass all countries in this sphere, the tub remained a luxury until the twentieth century. American tenements around 1895 had no bathing facilities. Such amenities were held desirable, but usually in the shape of showers rather than tubs:

> A great step forward in the improvement of tenement houses would be made if they were provided with bathing facilities. As at present constructed, even the best of them have absolutely no bathing facilities. The reason therefore is . . . that tubs without hot water would rarely be used. . . . I am firmly convinced that the shower bath offers many advantages for the tenement houses. . . . It is not necessary to provide each tenement with a bath.[43]

Five out of six dwellers in American cities, a survey revealed in the 'eighties, had 'no facilities for bathing other than such as are provided by pail and sponge.'[44]

---

[42] *Encyclopædia Britannica*, Boston, 1854, vol. 4, p.507.

[43] William P. Gerhard, *On Bathing and Different Forms of Baths*, New York, 1895, p.23.

[44] Ibid. p.16.

The quest for total regeneration, which, in earlier cultures, gave rise to refined bath methods, was doomed to failure in our period. The mechanized, mass-produced tub triumphed. It is a product of the industrial era. England and America, the two countries most closely bound up with industrialization, took the lead in formulating the present-day type of bathing. England held the fore during the nineteenth century and America in the twentieth, in the time of full mechanization. Although there are no sharp boundaries, differences clearly mark off the English type from the American.

Before investigating these, however, we shall attempt to show how, here too, the universal approach was destined to bow before the specialistic.

Hydropathy and the Return to Nature

The nineteenth century, we must never fail to stress, has more than one side. In many of its manifestations, particularly in its first half, a parcel of universalism lives on. Consideration of man's nature as a totality — the late eighteenth-century aim — gave rise, around 1830, to a method uniting therapy with the return to nature. Central in the discussion stands a Silesian peasant, Vincenz Priessnitz, who shunned medicaments and healed by water.

Around 1770 Pestalozzi had turned farmer to discover for himself in this calling 'the power of nature more vital and alive.' But now, by 1830, a peasant lad, such as Vincenz Priessnitz (1799–1851), who had never studied, who never bothered with academic medicine, and who often did not even know how his prescriptions cured, could win world-wide fame at Graefenberg, amid the woods of his native Silesia. In America at this time a Presbyterian minister, Sylvester Graham, sought, as we recall, to bring man into agreement with his nature through unadulterated nutrition.

In full post-Metternichian period, one might have come upon the following sight in the pine forests, a half-hour's walk beyond Graefenberg: In the open air and in all weathers, ladies of the Austrian aristocracy, 'their bodies completely naked,' [45] expose themselves beneath a stream of water, thick as one's arm, cascading from the height of ten or twenty feet. It is spring water spurting from wooden pipes, which channel it straight out of the mountain side. Six

[45] R. J. Scoutetten, *De l'eau, ou de l'hydrothérapie*, Paris, 1843. Scoutetten was a learned French army doctor whom the French Government sent to Graefenberg.

457. Back to Nature: Priessnitz's Shower in the Silesian Woods. *A source is captured and channeled through pipes open to the sun. The shower is taken on a wooden platform built out over the stream. Half a century after Rousseau's 'Back to Nature,' the romantic outlook helped to win acceptance for the water therapy of Priessnitz and others.* (*Philo vom Walde,* Vincenz Priessnitz, *Prague,* 1884)

showers of this kind, fenced with planks, were set up here and there in the pine woods (fig. 457).

The fear of nakedness overcome; exposure of the body to the untempered climate; mountain springs and movement: all this indicates a return to more natural living.

Priessnitz' therapy consisted simply in strengthening the organism. He attacked maladies by restoring a healthy circulation, and almost ignored local affections. He used spring water for drinking, bathing, ablution; but the kernel of his teaching was 'to heed nature's beckoning and, setting actual medicaments aside, use plain water in various forms.' [46]

In the last decades of the eighteenth century, the literature favoring reintroduction of the bath constantly increased.[47] Some physicians, such as the Scotsman James Currie, advised cold-water ablutions and baths, obtaining undoubted success in the cold-water treatment of fevers and contagious disease. But none achieved this synthesis of movement, water, and air, which, in combined effect, gradually roused the body from its sluggishness and lethargy. Priessnitz found

[46] E. M. Seliger, *Vincenz Priessnitz*, Wien, 1852, p.24.

[47] Scoutetten, op.cit. gives an excellent chronologically arranged bibliography of the hydropathic literature from ancient times down to 1843.

the elements of his cure in a primitive setting, from which his period was totally estranged, which in itself was bound to make a stir. Equally uncustomary was the life of rustic rigor: rising at four in the morning; using damp towels and woolen blankets for several hours until sweat breaks out; then, a plunge in cold spring water, and a rub-down, followed by an hour's walk and water drinking; at eight o'clock, breakfast, bread and cold milk; more movement; repeated cold massage until the body becomes red; at one o'clock, a simple lunch. A cosmopolitan society is here assembled, speaking French 'as if by agreement.' After lunch, more exercise is prescribed, and finally a trip to the shower in the woods overlooking Graefenberg; rest; for supper, bread and milk, as in the morning.

Priessnitz began in 1829 with 45 patients. In 1843 he had over 1500 guests and a fortune of £50,000. Cold-water-cure establishments using Priessnitz' methods spread to all countries around 1840, from Russia to America. So suggestive was his example that the physician Barter named his institution the Irish Graefenberg (fig. 464).

In part, Priessnitz owed his success to almost magical powers of diagnosis and suggestion. The ground had been prepared by his medical forerunners in France, England, and Germany. Yet why did not the forces of established medecine, who cut open his sponges to see what drugs they concealed, crush him from the start? Behind him, as an invisible protector, stood the figure of Jean-Jacques Rousseau, a living force throughout the Romantic period. Priessnitz too seemed to his patients a part of nature, one in close touch with nature itself. With Priessnitz a new type of physician makes his appearance: the nature healer.

Priessnitz' approach — hardening of the body and living in contact with nature — was soon taken over by healthy people to offset the wear and tear of city life, thus passing from the realm of therapy into that of regeneration.

The Vapor Bath as a Private Cubicle c. 1830

In medicine, the vapor bath was never quite forgotten. An early English patent (1678) [48] gives directions for building sweat baths useful in the cure of gout and other ills. Nor were proposals lacking in the eighteenth century,[49] when medicinal baths in London and Brighton often furnished the pretext for amorous gatherings.

The early nineteenth century is ever bringing back accounts of the bathing

[48] British Patent No. 200, 25 Mar. 1678.

[49] British Patent No. 882, 11 Feb. 1767, 'The patient has an oil cloth covering let down on him.' British Patent, 20 Nov. 1798.

458. The Water Cure. America, 1840's. (*Joel Shew,* Hydropathy, or the Water Cure, *New York,* 1844)

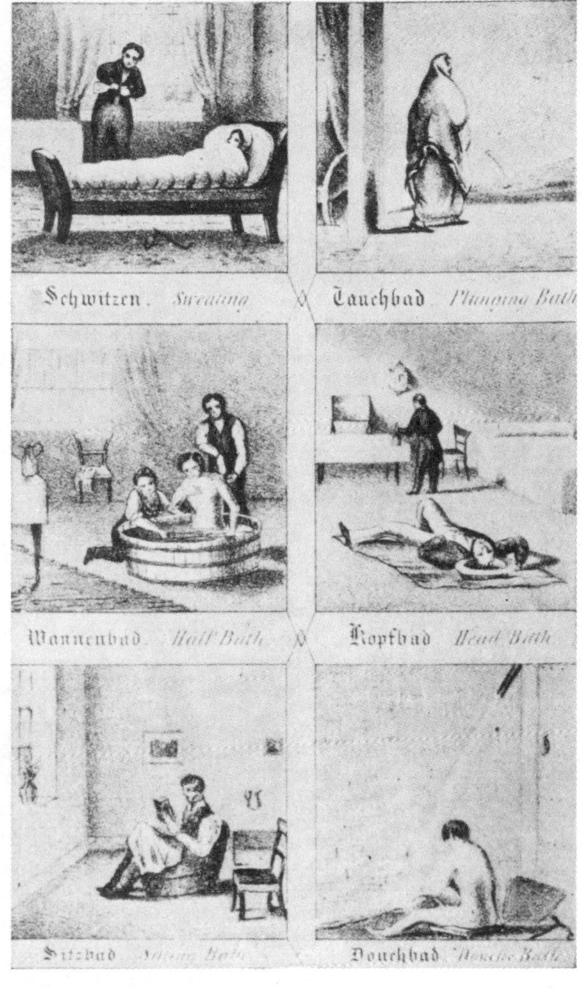

practiced by the Russians and the Tartars.[50] Russian baths, according to a contemporary French source, were first opened in Germany in 1824,[51] and their

[50] Rechenberg and Rothenloewen, *Les peuples de la Russie* (1812), vol. 1, 'Le bain russe'; Mary Holderness, *Notes relating to the Manners of the Crim Tartars* (1821).

[51] C. Lambert, *Traité sur l'hygiène et la médecine des bains russes et orientaux à l'usage des médecins et gens du monde,* Paris, 1842. 'Ces bains se sont en effet multipliés dans toutes les villes de l'Allemagne,' p. viii.

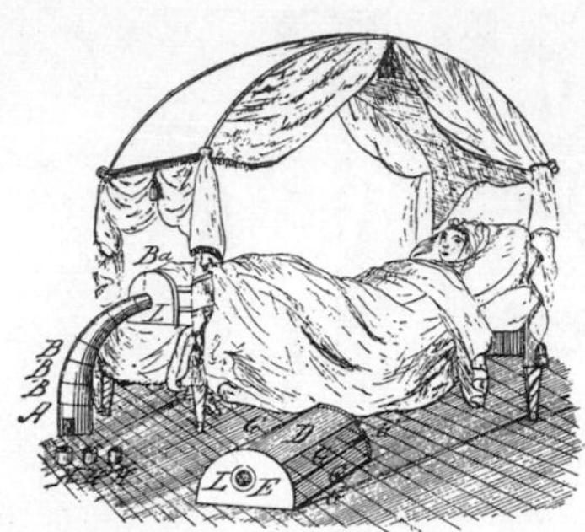

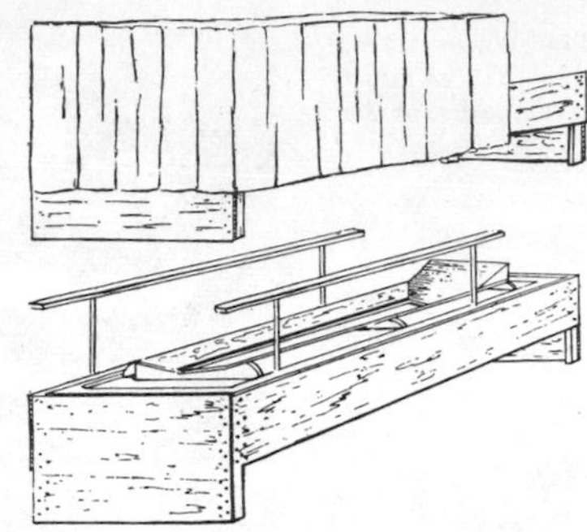

459. American Steam-Bed Bath, 1814. *The steam bath was regarded primarily as a medical treatment in the early nineteenth century — hence its frequent association with beds. Everywhere, from the beginning to the end of the century, apparatus generating steam in more or less complicated ways were invented.* (*U. S. Patent* 2049x, 21 *January* 1814)

460. Recumbent Steam Bath, 1832. *Portable steam baths were in use from the* 1830*'s on. The user sat on a chair, lay in a bed, a tent, a bag. Such collapsible apparatus could easily be ordered by mail.* (*E. L. Meissner,* Abhandlung ueber die Baeder, *Leipzig*, 1832)

introduction to England is also mentioned at this time. They were called 'Russian' and 'Oriental' rather indiscriminately. Properly speaking, they were neither the one nor the other, for, significantly enough, everything took place in small private cubicles.[52] Economy of steam was quite secondary in these baths intended for leisured society or for invalids. Rather was it fear of nakedness that inspired this segregation. The bath becomes a private matter.

Home steam baths of primitive design were proposed in all countries then issuing patents during the early part of the century. In America (fig. 459) [53] is found a steam bed bath of the type that was to be built throughout the period. Similar ones appeared in France.[54] There is no doubt that various portable and collapsible home steam baths were constructed in Germany during the 'thirties. It was the time when the fame of Vincenz Priessnitz's water cure was so rapidly spreading, and when Sylvester Graham in America was preaching a return to nature through the agency of nutrition.

Such apparatus for home vapor baths were on the market by 1832,[55] designed for various purposes, apparently along medical lines. There were vapor baths

[52] C. Lambert, op.cit., p.28.

[53] Vapor bath, U.S. Patent 2049x, 21 Jan. 1814.

[54] Boîte fumigatoire, French Patent 1816, 29 Nov. 1815.

[55] A pamphlet containing numerous illustrations and quoting prices for variously executed apparatus is F. L. Meissner, *Abhandlung ueber die Baeder im Allgemeinen und ueber die neuen Apparate, Sprudel und Dampfbaeder insbesondere*, Leipzig, 1832. Around this time vapor baths similar to those in Meissner's catalogue were patented in France also: 'Bain en forme de pluie,' M. Walz, French Patent No. 4230, 23 Oct. 1829.

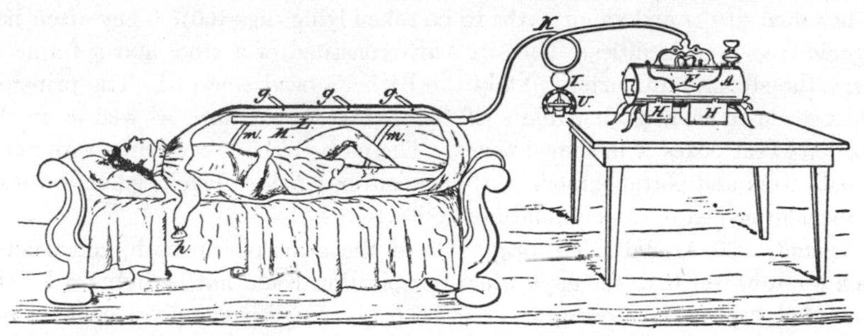

461. Steam-Bath Apparatus, 1855. *A bag channels the steam around the bather's body. 'The open end may be closed around the neck of the patient by means of tightening a cord strung in its edge.'* (*U. S. Patent* 13,467, 21 *August* 1855)

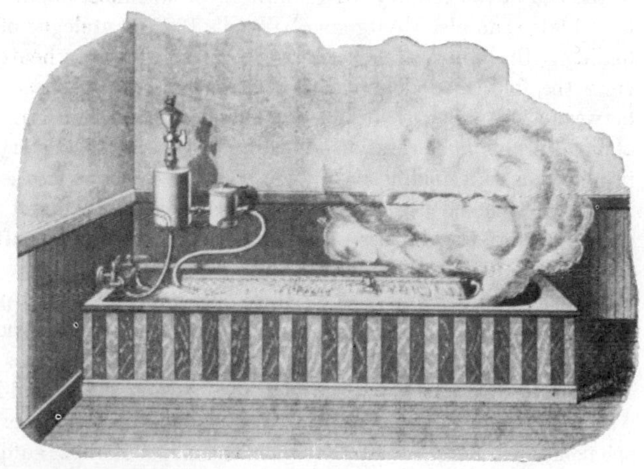

462. Apparatus for Vapor Bath, 1882. *Rarely does the nineteenth century divert its mechanical skill from production to maintain equilibrium of the human organism. Here a young inventor exploits the fact that hot water turns to steam when divided into a fine spray.* (New and Valuable Apparatus for Vapor Bath, *pamphlet in New York Academy of Medicine*)

to be taken sitting and vapor baths to be taken lying (fig. 460). They often had ingenious shower facilities. The sitz bath consisted of a stool and a frame to carry the steam-tight curtain. Only the bather's head emerged. The principle had been used in English patents of the eighteenth century, as well as in the wooden sweat boxes of medieval times. The baths to be taken lying were made in both fixed and portable models. The steam-bed baths, developed at the start of the century, enjoyed perennial favor.[56]

Around 1880 Arnold Rikli, originator of the atmospheric bath, constructed such a steam-bed bath for days when perspiration could not be induced by the heat of the sun. 'This portable steambath,' its English pamphlet claims, 'has the great advantage over the Russian or the Turkish bath that it can be taken in any room, that it leaves the head free and allows the lungs fresh air to breathe . . . and has the advantage of Priessnitz's dry packing in so far as it takes much less time.'[57] The folding types were constructed on the principle of the folding bed. The tub swings down from an upright container. Various showers were generally used in connection with it. In the United States, from the 'seventies to the end of the century, this folding type was most popular as a bathtub. To take a late example, Montgomery Ward's 1894–5 catalogue offers a wide range of folding baths, which often tuck the tub, as well as the heater, into a wardrobe. Here the folding models outnumber the non-folding ones. Their prices range between $20 and $60, according to quality and workmanship. 'A handsome piece of furniture of modern style (Antique or Sixteenth Century) and is as perfect in operation as a folding bed.' The gasoline heater is housed within the wardrobe, and when in use acts as a counterweight to prevent the container from capsizing onto the bather. The tub being folded back after use, the heater nestles in its hollow (fig. 474). How to dispose of the used water is a problem that each must solve as best he may. At any rate, the apparatus turns into a mirrored wardrobe 'in modern style.' The whole contrivance, with its mixture of technical lameness and false front, falls within the perilous regions of mimicry.

Domestic vapor baths were much used during the second half of the century. And understandably so, for they called for no running-water supply. An inconspicuous spirit lamp, as supplied with the model of 1832, sufficed to generate the steam. From time to time, down to the end of the century, the popular magazines advertise further, and often grotesque, proposals. Normally these home vapor baths, like that of 1830, consist of a rudimentary steam unit and a shell to channel the steam around the bather's body. The inventors show dismaying

---

[56] U.S. Patent 13,467, 21 Aug. 1855 (fig. 461).

[57] *Dr. Arnold Rikli's Physico-Hydriatic Establishment for the cure of chronic diseases at Veldes, Oberkrain, Austria*, Trieste, 1881, p.41.

helplessness as soon as their skill is applied to men instead of to machines. These devices have nothing of the century's technological refinement.

Finally we may cite the invention of a sixteen-year-old Cooper Union student, who, at least dexterously, exploited the observation that hot water, divided into a fine spray, turns almost instantly to steam. The young American's device consists of a 'portable, nickel-plated, perforated tube, running almost the length of the bathtub.' [58] As soon as the hot water 'in infinite division,' spurts from the tiny holes, the bathroom (if a rubber cover is used, the tub) fills with steam so that a satisfactory Russian bath may be enjoyed in one's own home without effort [59] (fig. 462). A hose connects the perforated tube to the water supply. That is all.

The idea, assuredly, was not new. In the *maghtas* or steam room of the Islamic bath, a thin jet of hot water issuing from a pipe in the ceiling saturated the air. And the creation of spray by means of a perforated tube is the principle of the lawn sprinkler. The only originality lay in applying the devices to domestic use. Such rudimentary apparatus may be regarded as symptomatic. It represents the vast areas in which the inventor seems to be dead. Why? Because a human orientation was lacking, and fantasy took flight in other directions.

Attempts at Total Regeneration, c. 1850

Priessnitz was one of the first to embrace the total organism. Yet his efforts were still a matter of medical recourse. Now, in mid-century, the passage is made from medicine to regeneration. This regeneration should be total in scope, cleansing the body from within as well as without. Such a tradition has been lost in Western culture. It was still found in the East, in Morocco and Turkey, where the Islamic bath continued to play its role in the pattern of life.

'We must have a standard of cleanliness as well as of truth; such a rule we can owe neither to freak nor fashion. We must look for one tested by long experience and fixed from ancient days; — this standard is THE BATH.' [60] Thus spoke around mid-century the English diplomat who became the most ardent propagandist for the reviving of regeneration in a total form.

David Urquhart (1805–77) had been attached for a time to the British embassy at Constantinople. He had intimate knowledge of East European politics and possessed considerable literary skill. Urquhart was in love with the Orient and pledged to its cause. No one waged so obstinate a campaign for the reintro-

[58] A special company, the Portable Vapor bath and Disinfector Company, New York, was founded for this patent. Their pamphlet, *New and Valuable Apparatus for Vapor Bath* (New York, 1882) is preserved in the Library of the New York Academy of Medicine.

[59] Ibid. p.11.

[60] Urquhart, *The Turkish Bath*, quoted in the *Free Press*, no. 13, 8 Nov. 1856, p.100.

duction of the hot-air bath as a means of regeneration. Urquhart was one of those critical and aggressive figures who spring forth when a country is essentially alive — figures who do not need to be geniuses or extraordinarily gifted men. We have seen how in England around 1850 the first reform movement against industrial production run wild issued from a group of Victorian civil servants.[61] Urquhart too belonged to this type of conservative fanatic. He sided with the oppressed, regardless of his government's attitude. In 1855, when he threw himself wholeheartedly into the task of building up a means of regeneration, he founded a political sheet, the *Free Press*, which numbered Karl Marx[62] among its contributors. He observed how wars came about in his time. He was interested in the intercourse of nations, and, toward the end of his life, in its codification, international law, which he saw the great powers ceaselessly violating.

Thus he was interested in interrelations. This may have helped to bring him to the Islamic bath, with its concern for the body as a totality. It was he who gave it the name it has retained: *Turkish bath.*[63] He recognized it as a survival of civilizations that did not disregard bodily regeneration. His stay in the Orient had whetted his sensibility, and he realized how barbaric was the condition in which Europe unsuspectingly lived. He regarded the smoke-blackened towns of industrial England and the life people led in them. What was being done for the regeneration of the working masses? The rare baths endowed by a few philanthropists were almost as nothing. What else remained? Gin and the pub. Why, he argued, was the heat and steam pouring from factory chimneys wasted on the air?[64] Could it not be used to better advantage? Around 1830, when wounded in the war of Greek liberation, he found the Turkish bath still thriving in Greece. He observed its slow dying out on Mediterranean shores as the Turks were pushed back. He wished to save this means of regeneration for England.[65] In his work *The Pillars of Hercules*, an account of a journey through southern Spain and Morocco in 1848, he was struck with the

[61] In our chapter 'The Mechanization of Adornment.'

[62] 'Revelations of the Political History of the Eighteenth Century,' by Dr. Karl Marx, *Free Press*, vol. I, 16 Aug. 1856. Urquhart's periodical later changed its name to *The Diplomatic Review*.

[63] Turkish Bath: In the light of subsequent archeological findings it is all too easy to correct Urquhart's scholarship, and point out that he might more accurately have called it the 'Islamic bath,' since the Turks never basically changed the specific form created by the Arabs. However as the 'Turkish bath' had lived for half a millennium under Osmanic protection, Urquhart was quite justified in naming it after them. The Islamic bath is a hot-air bath followed by a series of steam chambers at staggered temperatures. The 'Russo-Turkish' or 'Romano-Turkish' baths that arose after Urquhart's and other reformers' efforts are rudimentary hybrid forms without creative impulse.

[64] Urquhart, *The Pillars of Hercules*, London, 1850, vol. II, p.80.

[65] In contrast to Urquhart, E. W. Lane, in his still classical *Customs of the Modern Egyptians*, reported on the Islamic bath with the detachment of an anthropologist rather than the concern of a reformer.

463. A 'Moorish Bath' seen by an Englishman at the Time of the Islamic Bath Movement, 1858. *The rest hall* (maslak) *is portrayed. The author thus describes his experience in the* Illustrated London News (24 *April* 1858): '*The day was hot, the narrow streets were burning in the glare of noon. The prospect of the hot bath was not very inviting. I opened the door of the first apartment . . . All around it was a raised platform covered with mats on which lay several bathers in the state of profound repose. I was mounted on a pair of wooden clogs. The bath attendant rubbed and pinched and pulled every limb and joint of my body. He knelt upon my stomach so that I could hardly breathe, wrenched my arms and legs . . . Having been pinched and poked and pressed sufficiently, this genius of the bath lathered me from head to foot and took in hand a huge glove, with which he proceeded to thrub me with the most lively animation. The amount of matter he managed to peel off the crust of the body is certainly surprising. Having been well soused in cool water, I was softly wiped and dried by another attendant. This done, he wrapped me up from head to feet in soft towels and led me to the outer apartment* [maslak], *the air of which seemed very much like that of an ice-house. I sank exhausted on a divan. And now it was ecstatic enjoyment, it was elysium, nothing seemed wanting to perfect bliss.*'

failure of our time to use naturally available means to awaken man's joy in living. One chapter deals with his visit to the bath of a Moroccan Caïd, to which Urquhart gained access by ruse. This chapter, later reprinted by itself, effectively relates the various stages of the procedure: the loosening of the joints; the hot-air rooms, the refined shampoo-massage, followed by relaxation in dim halls. He would use all his eloquence, every means in his power, to convince the West of its need to assimilate such regeneration.

Urquhart recalls the nine hundred baths the Spaniards found on capturing

Cordova. He calls Byzantium to mind and points out that Constantinople with its half-million inhabitants still had over three hundred baths in operation. He reckons that London would need a thousand.

But how might they be financed? This problem always arises when human needs come into question in our period. How are they to be financed? As reformers do in every other period, Urquhart replies: by endowments by the city, or by the state.

For decades, together with his campaigns for justice and righteousness, Urquhart obstinately pressed the introduction of the Turkish bath, but in vain. He built a simple Turkish bath in his own house in London, and another which he opened to the public. He always wished to have the hot air at his side, and did not give up his custom when in later years he built a house on a spur of Mont-Blanc.[66]

He was able to carry out his idea on a broader scale in 1856, when Dr. Richard Barter, owner of the 'Irish Graefenberg,' the St. Ann's Hill water-cure establishment (fig. 464), placed 'land, workmen, materials, besides a number of patients,' at Urquhart's disposal.[67] Here Priessnitz's procedure was used in connection with the hot-air bath.

Urquhart spoke everywhere: in English country towns and bathing resorts he engaged with the doctors in debates, which he later published. He lectured in 1862 before the celebrated *Society of Arts*,[68] which had so often assisted new ideas. It was at this time that the first public Turkish bath, the 'Hammam,' still standing in Jermyn Street, London, was built under his supervision. It was a faithful reflection of his Eastern memories: 'The bathrooms have quite an oriental effect with the stars of stained glass sparkling in the sombre domed tepidarium.' [69] This installation became the prototype of hot-air baths both in Europe and in America. Exclusive bath clubs were formed in London during the 'seventies. In addition to their club rooms they possessed a complete gymnasium with hot-air baths and swimming pool excellently arranged.

Hot-air baths, also having a series of steam rooms (Turkish-Russian baths), played no small role during the latter half of the century, when it was still uncertain which type of bath would prevail and when private bathrooms were still a luxury. Unlike the Oriental baths, they never served the people as a

---

[66] Gertrude Robinson, *David Urquhart*, Oxford, 1920.

[67] Dr. Richard Barter, *On the Rise and Progress of the Irish Graefenberg*, London,1856, p. 15.

[68] *Lecture on the Art of Constructing a Turkish Bath*, London, 1862. On the Society of Arts and its role in the London Exhibition of 1851, cf. our chapter on the 'Mechanization of Adornment.'

[69] Robert Owen Allsop, *The Turkish Bath, its Design and Construction*, London, 1890, pp.18–19. According to more recent research it would be better to call it the 'caldarium,' for the Orientals, as we have seen, allowed the tepidarium to dwindle to minor dimensions.

464. First 'Turkish' Bath in Ireland: St. Ann's Hill Hydropathy Establishment, Cork Co., 1850's.
a. Sudatorium, or Hot Room (Beit-al-harara) **b.** Divan, or Cooling Room (Maslak)

In the 'Irish Graefenberg,' as its owner named it, the influence of the water doctor Priessnitz combines with that of the Turkish bath. Left: *the hot-air room with massage table in its center.* Right: *the rest hall. Both are in restrained Gothic revival style. Note the rest bed molding the shape of the body. Unfortunately the century's orientation did not allow fulfillment of these interesting beginnings.* (*Dr. Richard Barter,* On the Rise and Progress of the Irish Graefenberg, London, 1856)

whole, and were only accessible to the well-to-do. 'So little,' it was complained in England around 1890, 'has been done in connection with the Turkish-bath building for the people.' [70]

At this time one still discussed the idea of incorporating hot-air baths in the house; from David Urquhart's simple scheme of a tiled room, with insulated floor and ceiling, a stove, sofa, bench, and water vessels, to 'elaborate suites of apartments.' [71] But the times were not favorable.

The idea of total regeneration could not penetrate our period. These Turkish-Russian baths were for cultures having a dignified rhythm of life. In an age of mechanization, they were like exotic plants confined to forcing houses for lack of a natural soil in which to grow.

As the tub bath and the dwelling tended to become indivisibly associated, interest in these differentiated types progressively faded away.

The Atmospheric Bath, c. 1870

The most direct and accessible means of achieving the circuitous return to nature, through the radiation of air and sunlight, was rediscovered in 1869 by Arnold Rikli (1823–1906). Evolving it for curative purposes, he named it 'atmospheric cure.' Sun bathing, practiced in Antiquity, had long been for-

[70] Ibid. p.7. [71] Ibid. p.118.

gotten, just as the habit of sitting on chairs had fallen into oblivion in the early Middle Ages. Nineteenth-century medicine with its specialization knew less about the organism's reaction to sun bathing than Hippocrates, whose confident heliotherapeutic prescriptions suggest an experience gathered in the course of earlier ages. The Romans particularly enjoyed the sun bath. Everyone knew how to take it without ill effects. They like to avail themselves of it daily, summer and winter (fig. 442). When Seneca, looking back to the exemplary mode of life in Scipio the African's time, cites Scipio's fortress-like house with its bath, half lit by occasional window slits, adjoining the kitchen on the ground floor, he follows this description with a satirical comment on the softness of his own time, Nero's. 'We reckon a bath fit only for moth and vermin,' he writes in Epistle LXXXV, 'whose windows are not disposed so as to receive the rays of the sun during the whole course, unless we are washed and sunbathed at the same time.'

Like Priessnitz, the Swiss Arnold Rikli had to begin from scratch when he attempted to exploit systematically the effects of radiation. This was a quarter-century after Priessnitz began his work at Graefenberg. In 1855, at the height of hydrotherapy's vogue, Rikli too opened a nature-therapy establishment [72] in which the main stress fell on the atmospheric cure. Light and sun bathing, he discovered, favored more gradual and more organic healing than water used alone. Rikli proceeded with utmost prudence and circumspection until fourteen years of experience 'deeply convinced' him that air baths, that is, movement of the unclothed body in the open air 'formed the basic element of atmospheric cure and sun-bathing its necessary complement.' Later research bore him out in his insistence on bodily motion with the fewest possible coverings. Only thus can the easily weakened ultra-violet rays take effect. The sun bath, as Rikli continually emphasized, was but the last stage of the atmospheric bath. He did not senselessly leave the body to roast in the sun until burns appeared; he exposed the acclimatized organism to direct rays for about twenty or thirty minutes, keeping the head shaded. The patient lay on wool blankets on an inclined plane of boards.

Thus Rikli's basic idea consisted in utilizing rays to which, beginning with the Middle Ages, our bodies had become unaccustomed. How far our clothes with their insulating effect derive from the fear of nakedness lies beyond our present discussion. We are concerned only with the results, and with tracing the uphill path that Rousseau, Priessnitz, Rikli, and many others had to tread toward a more organic way of life that was taken for granted in the Ancient World.

---

[72] At Veldes, Upper Carniola, Austria. It outlived its founder, remaining in operation down to the first world war. The tradition was continued in Switzerland.

In Rikli's treatment the air bath was the foundation, the sun bath an intensification, and the sweat bath the conclusion. Even in his sweat bath he used the rays of the sun, the patient wrapping himself in the blankets on which he had been lying. Here too, Rikli instinctively decided against linen covers long before it was known that the sun's infra-red rays pass more readily through loose-woven materials. If the sun fails to shine, one is to sweat in a bed steam bath, which, as we have seen, was a widely used type in the nineteenth century. Some Swiss establishments, carrying on Rikli's tradition, offered sweat baths in the winter sun as well. This takes place in a sun lounge, a solarium having a southern wall of glass (1912), somewhat like the winter solarium (fig. 442) of the Forum thermae in Ostia. The winter sunlight and its intense refraction from the snow penetrate the transparent wall, warming the bathers within, who lie wrapped in their porous woolen blankets.

The skeptic must perhaps discover from experience how rapidly perspiration sets in even under the oblique winter rays, and how much greater is the psychological tonic of looking out upon snow and blue sky, rather than sitting imprisoned within an electric sweat box.

Contemporaries of Arnold Rikli's, such as Browns and Blunt (1877), pointed out the germ-killing power of sunlight. We are in the time of Pasteur's discoveries. There were also occasional advocates of sunlight for curative purposes earlier, in the eighteenth and nineteenth centuries.[73] But they had little to do with the subtle appraisal of the body as a whole. Rikli tried his idea out on himself, when still a boy. Not without opposition, he progressively laid off his clothing until he dared to stroll naked through the woods in his native canton of Berne. Like Priessnitz and Urquhart, he was an outsider to medicine.[74] He drew his direct inspiration from the prolific hydropathic literature of the mid-century and, as he himself points out, from the Renaissance advocate of moderate living, the Venetian Luigi Cornaro (1467–1566).

Of the bath types aiming at total regeneration that sought a place in the century, Rikli's air bath and sun bath came last: the cubicle vapor bath around 1825, the Turkish bath around 1855, and the sun bath around 1870.

Arnold Rikli's contribution was to have concentrated the effects of air and sun into an 'atmospheric bath.' He showed how sunlight — that intangible and dangerous medium — might be used with safety. In a time of light-excluding interiors and of flight from the sun, he could not hope for a popular following.

---

[73] Scott, *Story of Baths and Bathing*, London, 1939.

[74] He was of the class of small Swiss industrialists — his father had owned a dyeing-plant before him — who emigrated around the mid-century to sparsely industrialized regions, such as Italy or Austria. Rikli's 300-worker factory in outlying Carniola was quite successful, but he left it to his brothers, to found his sanatorium at Veldes castle.

465. Garment of the Ruling Taste, London Hygienic Exhibition, 1883. Venus de Milo Corset. (*Exhibition Catalogue*)

'For more than thirty years,' he writes, 'I stood alone with the cult of "atmospheric bathing."'

Later developments, both scientific and popular, show that Rikli's orientation stemmed from the innermost springs of the period. It was Dr. Auguste Rollier, discoverer of the curative effects of sunlight at high altitudes in the treatment of tuberculosis, who most directly elaborated Rikli's beginnings into a scientific therapy. In 1903, at Leysin, Waadt Canton, Switzerland, high above the Rhone valley, Rollier began his treatment of tuberculosis by well-gauged doses of mountain sunlight aided by favorable psychological conditions. Ray therapy was here coupled with occupational therapy, classes in the sun, workshops, university courses.

Medicine did not accept heliotherapy as a scientific curative agent until after Rikli's death, when, stimulated by Roentgen's discoveries, it was forced to acknowledge interrelation of the body with ray phenomena. Ray therapy, which embraces the ever-widening range of emanations, electrical and other, is unexplored in many of its areas. But even more shallowly explored is the type of daily regeneration in which radiation might find its place.

As a method, Rikli's treatment never made headway among the broad public. But a rougher and less satisfactory form of air and sun bath has become the common property of our time. In a radical form, the air bath has appealed to the partisans of nudism, which spread out from Germany after 1900 and established its colonies in many countries.

The sun bath as taken weekends by city dwellers, seeking to make up in a few hours, weeks or months of starvation for sun and air, has little in com-

Arnold Rikli,

hygienischer Arzt in Veldes (Krain) und in Triest.

Bekleidung für den Ausmarsch zum Lichtluftbad in Veldes.

466. Garments for the Atmospheric Cure. Dr. Rikli, *c.*1870. *In the 'sixties, the Swiss Arnold Rikli* (1823–1906) *attempted to exploit systematically the beneficial effects of radiation. Sun bathing and open-air exercise were the basic elements of his cure. Rikli made his patients wear shorts, sandals, and open-necked and short-sleeved shirts. In the time of parasols these garments were worn by a few eccentrics walking behind the high fences that surrounded his sanatorium.* (*Dr. Arnold Rikli,* Let There Be Light, or The Atmospheric Cure, 5*th ed.*, 1895)

mon with Rikli's prudent dosage of the rays. Altogether unskilled in its use, the people dazedly leave their bodies to roast in the sun. Civic authorities pride themselves when, after many struggles, they have succeeded in wresting a stretch of beach for the recreation of the masses. Establishments of this sort record all the ineptitude and helplessness of our period when faced with the problem of regeneration. The people are ignorant about what is permissible in dealing with the body and what is not. Everything is left to the dilettante fancy of the individual. There are books and rules, with do's and don't's, but the complete lack of a tradition in which, from childhood up, harmonious treatment of one's body might be so learned as to become second nature. The rules of sun bathing are often given as beauty hints in women's magazines.[75]

Around 1859 the pre-Raphaelite painter Burne-Jones commissioned the architect Philip Webb to design some drinking glasses for his personal use.

[75] *Glorify your Figure*, New York, Summer 1944.

They were plain, unornamented glasses conceived entirely according to function. One of them has a small bulge to provide a better hold. In form and execution, they are identical with the American drinking glasses turned out in mass production a half-century later, and found in every bar and ten-cent store. This does not mean that the glasses designed by the painter served as models for the later ones.[76] It means that these glasses, in their functional simplicity already embodied the inherent trend of the period.

Something similar occurs in the case of Rikli and the clothing he prescribed for the use of his patients. The frontispiece of Rikli's *Atmospheric Cure* (fig. 466) shows the enterprising lone walker, alpenstock in hand, breathing deeply, and wearing his 'clothing for the walk to the air bath' — a loose, open-necked, porous, and short-sleeved shirt, shorts that leave the thighs exposed, sandals carried around the waist; he is hatless, barefoot, and bareheaded. These things were quite out of question in the time of parasols, high-collared and corset-like clothes. Shelved inventions of the 'eighties, they were the insignia of a few eccentrics walking behind the palisades of the Veldes nature park. A half-century later replicas of the lone walker's outfit await the man in the street at every clothing store.

The People's Bath in the 'Eighties: The Shower

The nineteenth century gradually acquired hygiene.

It learned to control diseases that had formerly run unchecked. Even the year 1850 in England and Wales brought its 50,000 deaths from the cholera. Disease-bearing matter was to be eliminated at its source by disinfection and cleanliness.

But how were the masses to be won over to cleanliness? The public baths that appeared in England from the 'forties on, and in France under Napoleon III, were appendages to the public laundries, using whatever hot water was left after the clothes had been washed. But these never made much headway. The size of the populace was out of all proportion to the number of baths.

What, then, could be done?

The axiom that sound finance should have the last word when it came to public regeneration left but a single choice: 'cleansing stations' with shower baths. The belatedness with which the first acceptable scheme was proposed

---

[76] They were preserved in a rather inconspicuous place in the South Kensington Museum, London. Even photographs were not available until the Museum was kind enough to make them so to us.

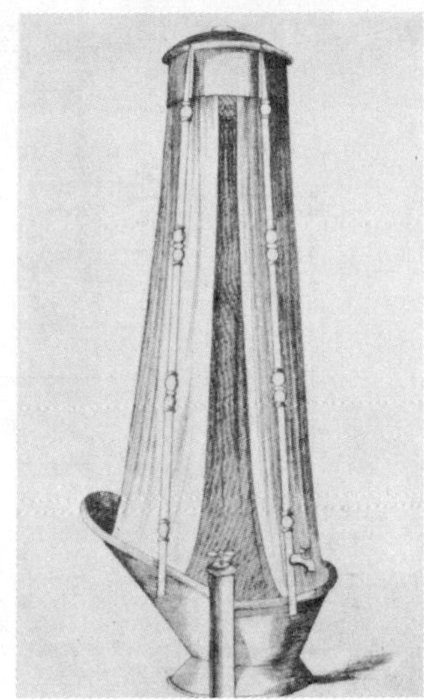

467. Symbolical Representation of the Shower, 1738. *The shower bath reappears in the eighteenth century in somewhat allegorical form. In the center of a baroque fountain, Atlas pouring water over a bather's head.* (*Sigmund Hahn,* Psychroluposia Vetus, *Schweidnitz,* 1738. *Detail of the frontispiece*)

468. Hip Bath with Shower, Birmingham, England, 1847. *With the demand for hygiene growing in an industrial civilization, solutions were attempted before plumbing was available. The water is raised by means of a hand pump, much as in Catherine Beecher's kitchen of* 1869. (*Catalogue, Victoria and Albert Museum, London*)

and carried out is indicative.[77] At the Berlin Hygiene Exhibition, in 1883, a Dr. Lassar set up his model bathing establishment, the People's Bath, of which he was the energetic propounder. The People's Bath was a corrugated-iron shelter partitioned into ten cubicles each containing a shower, five for men, five for women. At 10 pfennigs a head, soap and towel included, tens of thousands of visitors enjoyed a hot-water shower. At that time, Dr. Lassar's enquiries showed, the proportion in Germany was one public bath per 30,000 inhabitants. These showers, or 'cleansing stations' (fig. 472) as Dr. Lassar called them,

[77] A French doctor is said to have installed the first institutional showers in military barracks at Marseille (1857). Later they were systematically introduced into German barracks. Like the school baths, showers were found only in institutions, inaccessible to the masses. The specifically popular type, or 'People's Shower,' originated with Dr. Lassar.

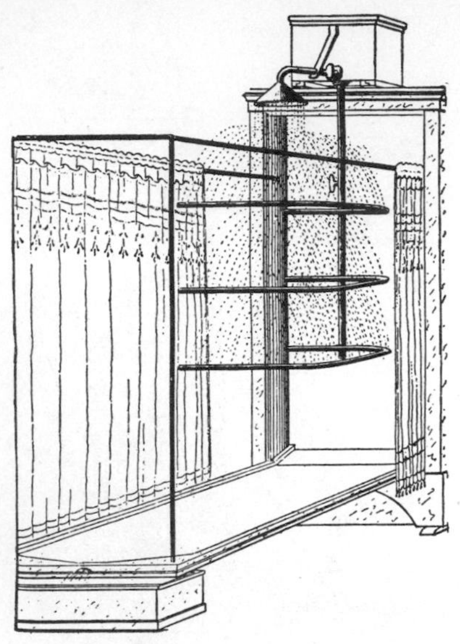

469. Collapsible Shower with Tank, 1832. *In this collapsible German 'rain bath,' water under pressure is supplied from a small tank, falling from above as well as spurting through perforated horizontal tubes.* (*Meissner*, Abhandlung ueber die Baeder, *Leipzig*, 1832)

470. Rain Bath for Medical Purposes. France, *c.*1860. *The doctor, watching from his observation platform, controls the treatment. 'It is no rare thing to see a subject who at this first shower betrays actual terror, shouts, struggles, runs away, experiences frightening suffocation and palpitation; and it is not rare to hear him say after a few moments "So that's all it is."'* (*L. Fleury*, Traité thérapeutique)

'were to be situated on the street to the end that passers-by might repeatedly be encouraged to make use of them.' [78]

Beneath water cascading from rocks, as the early Greeks loved to bathe, in forest clearings, as Priessnitz chose, or within a full regeneration system, the shower is an admirable thing. But to people lured in from the street, 'cleansed,' and dismissed five minutes later, it appears in a different light. Dr. Lassar was not wrong. Given the outlook of his time, the point of view that still prevails today, the shower alone was cheap enough for public use.

A few words concerning the typological development of the shower. The shower, jet bath, rain bath, or douche, as it was called at various times, rises

---

[78] Oscar Lassar, *Ueber Volksbaeder*, 2d ed., Braunschweig, 1888, pp. 18–19. *Die Douche als Volksbad* 'The rain bath is the people's bath' became the motto that soon spread to all countries. As we have noted, in the United States the shower rather than the tub was strongly recommended for tenement houses in 1895, when hot water was not yet laid on. No need was seen for a bath in each tenement.

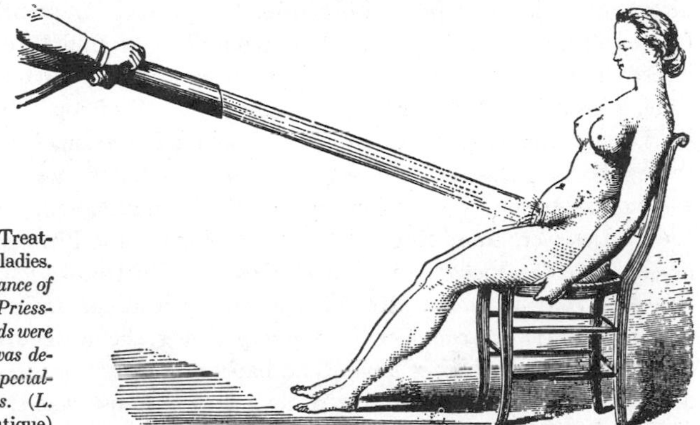

471. Shower for the Treatment of Abdominal Maladies. France, *c.*1860. *In France of the 'fifties and 'sixties Priessnitz's hydropathic methods were refined and apparatus was developed for increasingly specialized medical purposes.* (*L. Fleury*, Traité thérapeutique)

with roughly the same curve of popularity as the tub. In the nineteenth century it may seem at times to enjoy an independent vogue, but even then it would often form a unit in symbiosis with the bath.

On the copper-plate title page to a book much read during the eighteenth century, by one of Dr. Floyer's German disciples,[79] the shower appears in allegorical form. Atlas, balancing the earthly sphere on his shoulders, causes a stream of water to gush out of its depths, whereby he irrigates the head of a bathing man (fig. 467) — an allusion to the primeval force of water and a reminiscence of what must have been an everyday sight around the fountains of medieval cities.

The back-to-nature movement furthered the introduction of the shower just as it encouraged bathing of almost every type. Nevertheless even Priessnitz was more interested in its therapeutic value. As the century advances, the shower will rapidly outdistance the tub for two reasons: economy in use, and the influence of hydropathy.

Originally the shower used a stream of water flowing down from rocks or poured from vessels overhead. Priessnitz employs both of these modes in their most primitive form (fig. 457). Such solid streams are used for clinical purposes by water healers of the 'fifties. The French in particular, not generally the leaders in this sphere, devised various technical methods (figs. 470, 471).

---

[79] Hahn, *Psychroluposia Vetus*, Schweidnitz, 1738.

Usually the stream is broken by means of a perforated disk or other device. The Americans, when they sought to popularize it for working-class use around 1895, called it the 'rain-bath.' Its finely divided stream allows more imaginative directing of the jets: from either side, from above, from below, through perforated tubes arranged spirally or horizontally. Around 1830 the rain bath, as already mentioned, often merges in symbiosis with the vapor bath for home use. Even a head irrigator, whose shape suggests a coil of rope, then appears on the market. Water under pressure was supplied by a small elevated tank. All these models (and so it remained for decades to follow) were portable, for there was no water supply to which they might be permanently attached. Usually the devices were more simple. A rare catalogue of a Birmingham firm (1847), preserved in the Victoria and Albert Museum, illustrates such a standard model (fig. 468) that was to be used for decades, with minor variations, on each side of the Atlantic. A compact hand pump drives the water from a hip bath or other vessel into a higher tank. The bather draws a curtain around him. Not until plumbing brought running water into the house was this pump type displaced. In mid-century, the London Great Exhibition, where in so many respects the century's future was written, displayed a wide range of showers. The bathtubs, on the other hand, were quite primitive. As time went on this contrast became even more marked.

The catalogues of the 'eighties give less space to the bathtubs than to an astonishing selection of showers. Economy did not dictate the shower's triumph (they were destined for large houses) so much as the persuasion of hydropathy. Showers were introduced in American schools in the early 'nineties on the recommendation of a hydropathic physician.[80]

Whether we consult the sources of 1850 or those of 1890, we find popularization of the shower advocated for identical reasons: showers consume less water, less space, less time, require fewer repairs. In use, moreover, they are more hygienic than the tub bath.[81] Dr. Lassar, propounder of the People's Bath, is right again, for in large establishments the outlay and upkeep increase in geo-

[80] Cf. Wm. P. Gerhard, *The Modern Rain Bath*, New York, 1894: 'Quite recently Rainbaths have been introduced in the United States largely at the suggestion of the hydropathic physician Dr. S. Baruch, of New York City.'

[81] 'The baths most serviceable to the public generally are those . . . which do not require a large supply of water. . . . On looking over the different kinds, the shower bath appears to possess those qualities in an eminent degree. For apart from the medical qualities ascribed to it, a complete ablution may be obtained with a very small expenditure of water.' 'New Shower Bath,' *The Illustrated London News*, 17 Aug. 1850, p.154.

metrical proportion. 'One mark,' he points out in 1883, 'provides enough water for 666 showers but only for 33 tub baths. And for the whole of Germany,' he argues in his plea for the shower as a People's Bath, 'this means an approximate saving of over 66 millions a year. . . .'

Only by economic proof could Dr. Lassar hope to make the shower bath attractive to the authorities. Dr. Lassar's efforts were doubtless prompted by an ethical purpose, yet the spectacle also has its pitiful side: a century of mechanization able to offer nothing better than iron huts for the regeneration of the masses. No small gap lies between the outlook that produced the thermae of Rome and that for which iron huts seemed a solution. And the inspiration for these was apparently owed to the public urinals that sprang up on the street corners of Haussman's Paris as soon as the city obtained a more adequate sewer system.

472a. Thermae of the Nineteenth Century: Showers in Corrugated-Iron Shelters, Germany, 1883. *'The baths most serviceable to the public generally are those which do not require a large supply of water.' This English opinion of* 1850 *was that held throughout the century. Even in the 'eighties, showers were contemplated as the only economically possible form of 'people's bath.'* (*Lassar*, Ueber Volksbaeder, *2nd ed., Braunschweig*, 1888)

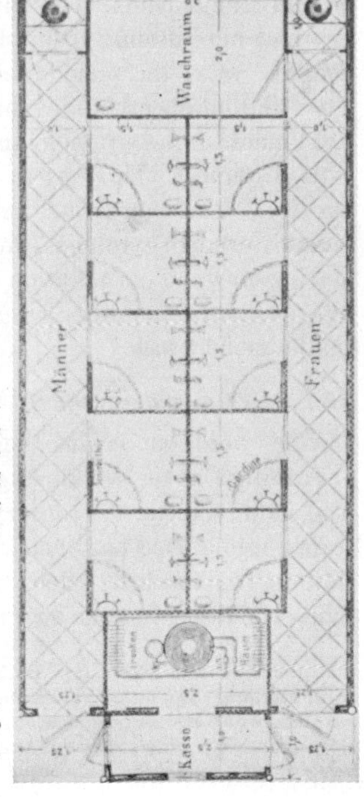

472b. Thermae of the Nineteenth Century: Groundplan. *These corrugated-iron huts were to be erected on the streets so as to encourage passers-by to use them.* (*Lassar*, Ueber Volksbaeder, *2nd ed., Braunschweig*, 1888)

The Bathroom Becomes Mechanized

Around 1900 it became clear that the bath cell with hot and cold running water was the type upon which our period had set its mind. Bathroom and bedroom eventually formed a unit, just as the apartments of the Baroque palaces were fused in inseparable unity of plan with their dependencies, wardrobes, toilets, or pantries.

But even in 1900, after the long period of indecision, the bathroom was still an amenity of the privileged classes. The essential elements of its popular diffusion were lacking. No bathtub comparable in serviceability and appearance to the luxury porcelain tub had yet reached standard form. Nor was the hot-water system satisfactory. Well thought-out accessories were likewise lacking.

It is not difficult to trace the clear-cut trends of such complex mechanisms as the automobile or the locomotive. But in tracing the development of the present-day bath, one wanders through a maze of quaint stories and anecdotes. The reason for this is invariably the same: Inspiration failed when it was needed for human requirements. The outcome was a technical lameness depressing to survey and unrewarding to dwell upon. We shall turn our attention to the last decades, when the period was beginning to see more clearly what it wished. Then the indispensable inventions were made. The bath cell rapidly attained its standard form, especially in the country that was the most eager for a democratized comfort. This was in the time of full mechanization. Straightway the two foci of mechanization, the bathroom and the kitchen, come to dominate, perhaps even to tyrannize, the plan of the house. Reasons of economy — the cutting down of installation costs through closest possible concentration of kitchen, bath and water closets — often curtail the architect's freedom more than he might wish.

From the Nomadic to the Stable

A few words concerning the type's morphological evolution.

Furniture in the Middle Ages passed from a nomadic to a stable condition. And in the nineteenth century this happened to the bath. The portable bath turned into a fixed bath anchored within a complex network of piping and ventilation. In medieval times, nomadicism was the result of the instability of living conditions; in our own period, of the instability of our orientation.

→

475. Bathroom with Heater, for a Barber Shop. Chicago, 1888. '*It is usual in our large cities to provide bathing facilities in all hotels as well as in the larger barber shops,' writes W. P. Gerhard* (1895). *This equipment made by a barber-chair manufacturer could be set up without a plumber's aid. The medieval combination of bathing and hair cutting reappears here, but with a very different emphasis: the bathroom has become a mere accessory to the barber shop.* (*Catalogue Th. Kochs, Chicago,* 1888)

473. Bathtub with Connected Boiler. England, 1850. *This combination of portable tub and heating unit was about all the technically minded mid-century could offer to the private bather. The principle itself was known to the late Middle Ages.* (*Henry Cole*, Journal of Design, 1850)

Warm Bath Apparatus, manufactured by Tylor and Son, London.

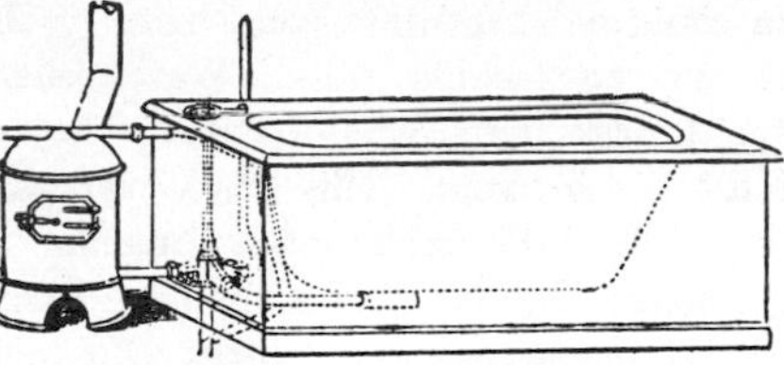

(At Deane, Dray, and Deane's, King William Street.)

A warm bath by means of circulation may be obtained in about half an hour. The apparatus is portable, and can be used in any room where there is a flue.

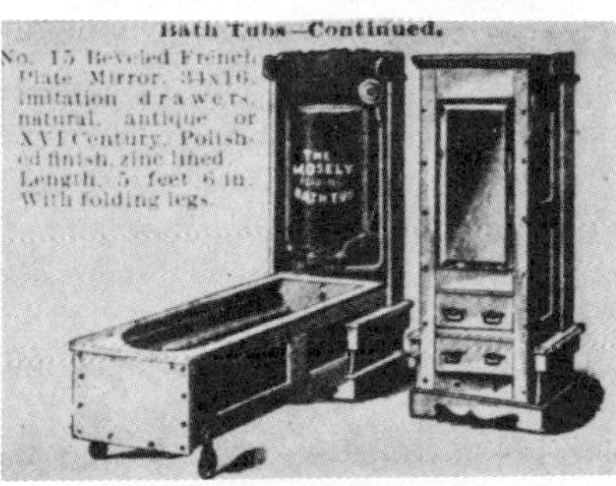

Gasoline Burner.

43695 A. Enameled galvanized iron heaters, with bracket $15.00

474a, b. Wardrobe Bathtub with Gasoline Heater. Mail-Order Catalogue, 1895. *The folding tubs without plumbing outnumber the normal type in this catalogue of the 'nineties.* (*Montgomery Ward Co., Chicago,* 1895)

The bathroom could not become a component of the middle-class dwelling so long as one element was lacking: water. Water sellers drove their carts with tubs of hot water through the streets of Paris. They carried the tub and the water up to the user's apartment. This was known as the *baignoire à domicile* as against the fixed tub of the public establishments. In 1838, Paris had 1013 of these *baignoires à domicile*, and 2224 of the fixed baths.

The Englishman of the 'sixties would carry a folding gutta-percha tub with him when he traveled on the Continent. At home (fig. 468), he would be likely to use a small hip bath, the shower in this case being more important than the tub.

The combination of tub and heater was often portable too. In 1850 Henry Cole recommends a tub and heater that might be used in any room having a stove pipe (fig. 473). A pair of tubes allowed the water to circulate directly between the tub and the heating unit. Rarely does Henry Cole show interest in technical inventions. But the apparatus apparently caught his fancy. Its principle was not a new one, being known to the late Middle Ages. Now, in 1850, the time so expert in using fire gases to heat industrial boilers, this was about all the inventors could devise.

This type, like the American folding bath already mentioned, starts from the assumption that no running water is available. It was to be found in American city houses during the last quarter of the century. Like the folding bed, it assumed the façade of a wardrobe when not in use. Later it gained considerable favor among the farmers. It is a most persistent type, appearing in the mail-order catalogues until well into our century. In the mid-'nineties its price and execution gave it an advantage over the fixed types (fig. 474).

Running Water

The seventeenth and eighteenth centuries cast a shadow behind them. In 1800 the large cities still had no regular water supply.

In Paris Napoleon sought to remedy this situation. A plan, dated 1812, upon which we chanced in the Bibliothèque Nationale, shows what was the state of canalization after Napoleon's enterprise: only the well-to-do districts such as the Faubourg St. Honoré had water laid on. The popular quarters still had to rely upon occasional street fountains, water sellers, and particularly upon water from the Seine.

During the second half of the century, cities everywhere were to be supplied with water throughout. Running water entered first the basement, then the storeys, and finally each apartment. Words are too static. Only a moving picture could portray water's advance through the organism of the city, its leap to the higher levels, its distribution to the kitchen and ultimately to the bath.

The same applies to the hot water supply. The nineteenth century — like Homeric times — drew its hot water from the kitchen in buckets. From the 'forties on, America began to use copper or iron boilers connected with the range. Various plans were put forward. The tall, upright, uninsulated boiler, adjacent to the range but distinct from it, became standard. Yet the development did not move forward directly.

Running hot water is another prerequisite of the mechanized bathroom. We may roughly trace the following phases: tub and heater forming a portable set; tub and heater permanently affixed to the bathroom plumbing; hot water supplied from a single point in the house [82] or, in our century, supplied to the apartment house from a central plant.[83] Running water was brought to the various fixtures in this general order: the kitchen sink, the washbasin, and, lastly, the bathtub. Piping water to the washbasin was an important labor-saving device. This may explain why America was foremost with this innovation. An English witness of the 'nineties reports: 'In America these fixtures are used in every mansion and in every dressing room. Domestic labor-saving appliances are more thoroughly appreciated on the other side of the Atlantic than with us. Patented appliances are more numerous in America for the same reason.' [84]

Washbasins fitted with faucets are to be found, it is true, in the catalogues of the 'fifties, but they drew their water by hand pump, like the sink in Catherine Beecher's kitchen of 1869. Here too, the sleeping car produced a technically adequate solution at an early date. In the 'seventies, as we shall see, a sensation was created when a Boston hotel provided running water in every room. Around 1890 the now forgotten face showers, which rose like a fountain from the bottom of the basin, were used for ablutionary purposes.[85]

With full mechanization, in the early 'twenties, almost lavish consumption of hot water became an everyday thing in America. One can almost exactly date this change. It corresponds to the sudden expansion of enameled sanitary fixtures, which almost doubled in number between 1921 and 1923.[86]

---

[82] Coke-fired iron boilers were used in the 'eighties. Cf. Catalogue of the L. Wolff Mfg. Co., Chicago, Ill., 1885, p.219. For 'Instantaneous Gas Water Heaters,' cf. Catalogue of the Crane Co., Chicago, Ill., 1898.

[83] The heating of city blocks by steam was operating in New York in the 'seventies.

[84] W. R. Maguire, *Domestic Sanitary Drainage and Plumbing*, London, 1890, p.293.

[85] Cf. Maguire, op.cit. p.287.

[86] In 1921 the production of enameled sanitary fixtures (washbasins, bathtubs, etc.) was 2.4 million pieces, almost the numbers of the prewar year 1915. It then rose to about 4.8 million a year, reaching a temporary maximum of 5.1 million in 1925.

476. George Vanderbilt's Bathroom, Fifth Avenue, New York, 1885. *In contrast to the principles of the ruling taste, the nickel-plated pipes and even the lead plumbing are left unconcealed in the Vanderbilt bathroom. Its compact arrangement seems to announce the future American bath cell.* (The Sanitary Engineer, *New York,* 1887)

The bath's transition from a nomadic to a stable condition took place instantaneously, as soon as running water and sewers became available. Before then it would have been useless to devote a room exclusively to the bath.

Now the problems begin, for the bathroom forms a new element in the organism of the house. Fresh questions thrust themselves to the fore.

What shall be the bathroom's importance in the household? How related to the other rooms?

What do we wish with regard to size, plan, disposition? Do we wish to bathe in a spacious room, or shall we tuck the bath into the smallest possible space?

The choice between the bath as a room among other rooms or the bath as a cell just large enough to hold the fixtures does not depend only on economic means. It corresponds to two stages of development, the first of which we may call the English, the second the American.

The English Bathroom around 1900

England fashioned the luxury bathroom of the world. No other country equaled the quality and distinction of English sanitary articles between 1880

477. English Bathroom, 1901. *Emerging from its nomadic and semi-nomadic phases, the bathroom has become a permanent part of the well-to-do English household. It is a large, windowed room, on which luxury is not spared. One such bathroom usually served the entire household. It is conceived as a room with furniture, not as a mere annex to the bedroom.* (*W. E. Mason, Catalogue*)

and 1910. The climax of the room was its heavy, double-shelled porcelain tub. It was to be found wherever means permitted: in St. Petersburg, in the palaces of Indian Rajahs, no less than in George Vanderbilt's Fifth Avenue house (fig. 476). In English middle-class homes or lodgings, of course, there were also plain zinc tubs, standing in small cubicles partitioned off within a room.

The heavy double-shelled porcelain tub, individually built like a Rolls Royce, is as typical for this phase as the American double-shell enamel tub built on the production line was to become for a later one. Luxury did not end here. Complex shower facilities, combined with the tub or independently of it, hip baths, bidets, toilets, washbasins, marble-topped and painted to order, completed the setting. This was luxury such as could not be compressed into a cubicle.

The bath of 1900 calls for a spacious room possessing a number of windows. The expensive fixtures were placed at dignified distances from one another (fig. 477). The central space was ample enough for moving freely about, even for exercising. It was this English bathroom, no less than its porcelain tub,

478. Individuality in the Bathroom: Hooded Bath, England, 1888. *'May be had in various woods to accord with the surroundings. Price £60.' Such products result from the nineteenth-century's idea that period furniture is equivalent to individual expression. The price asked for enclosure of bath and shower without fixtures — £60 — is some measure of the importance that was attached to them.* (*Doulton Co. Catalogue*, 1888)

which supplied the stimulus for an equally comfortable, yet less expensive model. Even the larger houses had but one such room, serving all the members of the family.

479. PERCIER AND FONTAINE: Washstand, 1801. *Late nineteenth-century mass production only magnified what the early years of the century had started. (Percier and Fontaine,* Recueil des Décorations Intérieurs, *Paris,* 1801)

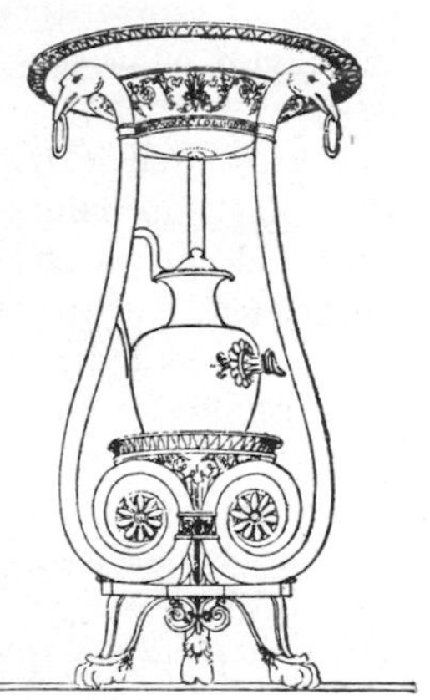

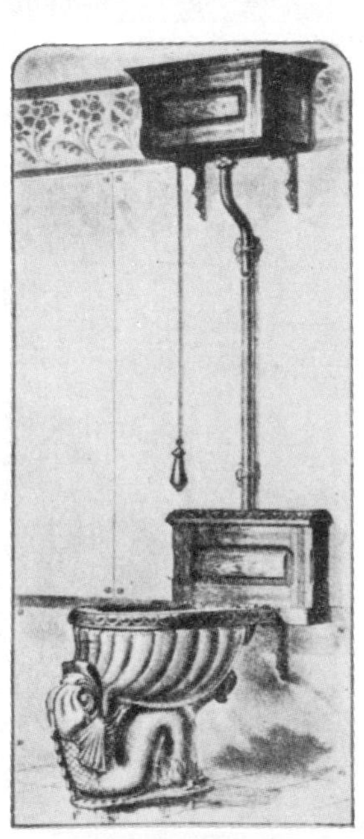

480. 'Art' in the Bathroom. 'The Dolphin,' Ivory-Tinted Toilet Fixture. America, 1880's. (*Advertisement*)

During the first two decades of this century the well-to-do European middle class adopted the English bathroom. Each might simplify its equipment according to his means. Normally one bathroom served all the occupants.

How were the individual fixtures to be arranged? There was space enough for variety, which explains the lack of a fixed ground plan for the English bathroom. Where the bathroom was to be located and how it was to be arranged fell to chance or to taste. Even in the most modern European buildings today, there is some uncertainty in the ground plan. The bathroom became smaller, but the question still remained: Is the bathroom a room in itself, or is it, even if walled off, a unit with the bedroom?

Bathroom Equipment and Ruling Taste

The mighty penetration of ruling taste into every sphere also reached the bathroom, sometimes with rather grotesque results. The tub, washbasin, and toilet were regarded as pieces of furniture, which should therefore express the personal taste of the owner.

The flight from pure forms, seen in furniture, architecture and adornment, left its mark on the bathroom fixtures too. As ruling taste reached its peak in the 'eighties the house of means would surround its tub and shower with massive 'enclosures' hiding both (fig. 478). In the bathroom the same process takes place that we observed among the *confortables*, those easy chairs whose structure

481. Plumber's Cabinet Woodwork. Encased Washstand, 1875. *Hitherto washtubs, bathtubs, and toilets were simply encased. But the cabinetmaker intervened, introducing ornate casings to conceal the fixtures. 'As generally fitted by carpenters these articles are plain and by no means an ornament to the room,' writes the* Manufacturer and Builder.

482. American Non-Encased Washbasin with Exposed Plumbing, 1888. *The unencased washbasin was thought fit only for more menial uses. (Catalogue, Standard Manufacturing Co., Pittsburgh)*

483. Standardization and Trimmings: One Hat, Many Effects. *By different trimmings, a standard model is adapted to various tastes and ages. Hats, houses, or bathrooms, all had to be pseudo-expressions of individuality.* (*Courtesy the Old Print Shop, New York*)

dissolved into cushions. Again and again the catalogues and handbooks of the 'eighties and 'nineties advise that the plumber's duty is to carry out the architect's wishes, both in the matter of form and of ornamentation. Thus the 'hooded baths,' showers, and enclosures for the English bathroom of 1888 (fig. 478) can be made 'in various woods to accord with the surroundings or the design' as well as 'modified to suit architect's requirements.' [88] The prices of these trappings attest the value that was attached to them: the enclosure alone, without bath, shower, or plumbing, cost some £60. In the absence of an enclosure, one had to be satisfied with many-colored painting. The standard models were covered with a diversity of ornaments in variegated styles, which in the 'eighties and 'nineties must have had a hypnotic effect on the consumer, similar to the streamlining of everyday objects at a later time. Hence the makers were unstinting of polychrome reproductions. Even in 1900, Twyford's *Twentieth Century Catalogue* carries tubs and washbasins in identical models adorned in alternative ways (fig. 484). One treated the bathtub in the same spirit as those hats (fig. 483) manufactured in a standard model, which by variegation of the trimmings can be made becoming to various ages and various tastes.

[88] Catalogue of the Doulton Co., London, 1888.

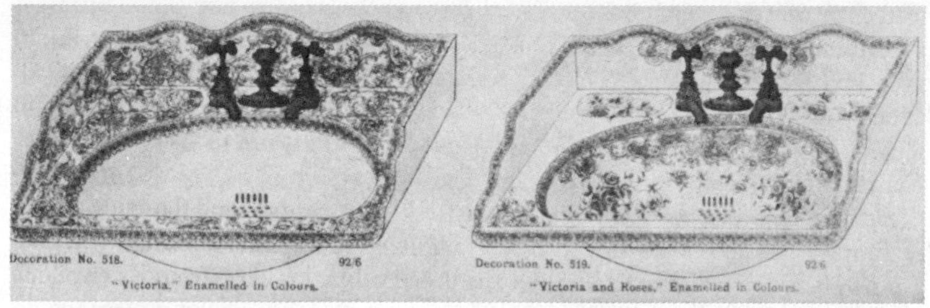

484. Standardization and Trimmings: One Basin, Many Effects. English Decorated Lavatory, 1900. *'Victoria' and 'Victoria and Roses' (in colors) are identical models adorned in different ways. (Twyford's* Twentieth Century Catalogue, 1900)

Soon the ornamentation of the washbasin was carried from the top and splash-back into the bowl itself, or over both. The urge for the seemingly new and aimlessly novel was running its irresistible course. Yet the grotesque outlook of the 'eighties, which could suffer no object without its share of 'art,' was already on the wane. The 'Dolphin,' a toilet glazed to an ivory tint, which for years had paraded itself in the magazines (fig. 480) is now set up as an object of ridicule.

As in all spheres, there was a struggle for natural form. What occurred on a large scale in architecture occurs here on a more intimate one. Whenever the

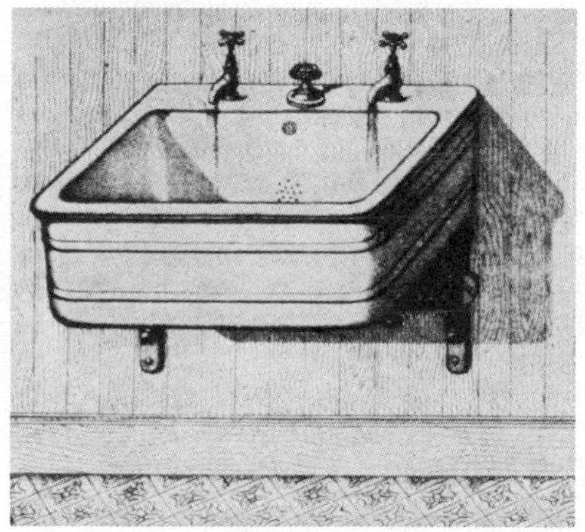

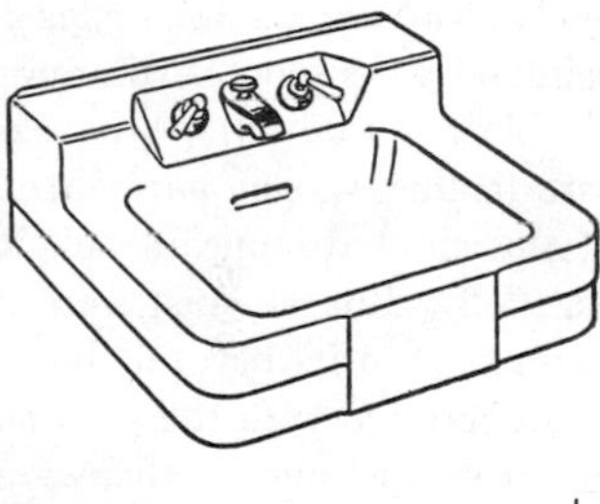

486. Washbasin, 1940. *Purified forms proceeded slowly from the kitchen to the more personal sphere of the bathroom. A half century separates the carefully designed kitchen sink of* 1888 *and the washbasin of* 1940. (*Catalogue, Crane and Co., Chicago*)

485. Pure Form in the Kitchen: American Sink, 1888. *The ruling taste at this date could not allow such simplified forms in the bathroom. Careful treatment given to every detail. Outlet and overflow are designed for perfected cleanliness.* (*Standard Manufacturing Co., Catalogue*)

nineteenth century feels unobserved, it becomes bold: from the broad spans of its exhibition halls to its laboratory utensils or a kitchen sink. When it came to the intimate setting, courage to choose intelligent form failed it. An American kitchen sink of 1888 (fig. 485) bears witness to this.[89] Each detail is given careful thought. Outlet and overflow, the catalogue brings out, are devised for perfect cleanliness in upkeep.

This weakness for adornment, expressed in the drapes and hangings from the Empire on, shows up in sanitary equipment too. Like a kernel emerging from its shell, the washbasin through the decades breaks loose from its envelope of furniture. The water-fearing centuries had caused all toilet apparatus to disappear from the dwelling rooms. The need for them, although still feeble, returns in the late eighteenth century, as one may judge from the new attention paid to toilet furniture by the English cabinetmakers. Shearer's 'dressing stand for lady,' 1788 (fig. 185),[90] conceals a small washbasin and four cups with 'a cistern behind to receive the water.' True, the facilities are tucked into a drawer, but at least they are available.

In the nineteenth century, the bowl and jugs gradually grow in size. Around 1820 the medieval tripod lavatorium developed into a cabinet of the circular form so highly favored at that time.[91] In England, in the 'thirties, broader washstands in the form of commodes or tables (fig. 187) made their appearance.

In the mid-century, the form that was to become typical came into fashion: one or two basins with jugs placed on the marble-topped eighteenth-century commode. As soon as running water becomes available, the basin is let into the marble top (fig. 481), but the commode remains. The 'seventies pay especial care to this wooden garment. In the 'eighties, especially in America, the front of the chest disappears, leaving only the marble top with its sunk-in basins (fig. 482). But we must wait until well into the twentieth century for the washbasin to gain its natural shape under the influence of mass production and for its integration with the plumbing (fig. 486). Only with the advent of mass-produced enamel and earthenware could natural forms truly pierce through. Yet the late 1930's brought backsliding trends, seeking to treat the bathroom and kitchen as furniture-containing rooms.

The standard reached around 1915 rests on the same awareness as the equipment of the Roman and Islamic baths: There can be no daintification of objects exposed to the daily action of steam and water.

---

[89] Catalogue of the Standard Mfg. Co., Pittsburgh, Pa., 1888.

[90] Shearer, *London Book of Prices*, London, 1788, p.159.

[91] La Mesangere, *Meubles et Objets de Goût*, Paris, 1820, pl. 504, Lavabo. Also in similar form a *toilette d'homme* (1817), ibid. pl.442.

THE INFLUENCE OF THE HOTEL

487. Mount Vernon Hotel, Cape May, New Jersey, 1853. *A bath with running water was installed in every bedroom, according to the* Illustrated London News (1853). *'Each room is complete in itself and contains all the conveniences for the comfort of the inhabitant.' This was half a century before the bathroom became an appendage of each hotel room.*

America piloted the development from the moment the bath became democratized; that is, from the middle of the second decade and in the time of full mechanization. Standard layouts now make their first appearance, for a clear stand has been taken: the bath shall be an appendage to the bedroom. This was not a matter of chance.

The American type had its origins outside the home: in the hotel. The hotel, it has been recognized, 'gave the Americans an opportunity to scrape their first acquaintance with the bath tubs, cold and hot running water, water closet and steam . . . Among the many things that entered American life through the hotels, of all the many ways in which American domestic life has been influenced by hotels, the influence of the hotel bathroom stands preeminent.' [92]

In his comprehensive *Greek Revival Architecture in America*, Talbot Hamlin

[92] Jefferson Williamson, *The American Hotel*, New York, 1930, p.55.

mentions a Boston hotel, the Tremont House, 1827–9, which had 'an elaborate battery of water closets and bathrooms with running water in the basement. In this building, for the first time in America, if not in the world, mechanical equipment became an important element in architectural design.'[93] The location, underground like Scipio's bathroom, is typical for this phase of the development, when running water was not yet piped to the floors.

We have but an exterior view (fig. 487) and a half ironical, half-admiring description of an American hotel that had equipped all its rooms with a bath and running water within the room. This was the Mount Vernon Hotel at Cape May, New Jersey, a sea-bathing resort (1853). 'Jonathan is as great in hotels as he is in everything else — sea-serpents and boiler explosions included,' we read in the *Illustrated London News*, 17 September 1853. 'The hotel contains 125 miles of gas- and water-pipes. Every guest has his bath in his bedroom, and there are hot and cold water taps for his use when he pleases . . .' The informant may have exaggerated details, but even at this date the basic American tendency to think of the bath as the appurtenance of every bedroom is discernible. The trend found in the Mount Vernon Hotel also appears, combined with a small built-in kitchen or kitchenette, in Catherine Beecher's flat of the late 'sixties (fig. 489). The tendency to combine plumbing units into the smallest space is continued in the later American development, as illustrated by our typical New York one-room apartment (fig. 490).

The goal, a bath to every bedroom, stood little chance of rapid achievement. Indeed the process took over half a century to complete.

Our knowledge of the development is fragmentary.[94] In 1877 a Boston hotel had running hot and cold water in all rooms, but only for washbasins.[95] A family hotel in Kansas City (1888) and another in Boston (1894) added bathrooms to their suites but not to their individual rooms.[96] At a time when Pullman was running his private sleeping cars, these bathrooms must have represented a similar luxury.

Democratization of the hotel bath cannot truly be spoken of before a bath became available at slight cost with every room. In 1908 Ellsworth M. Statler

---

[93] Talbot Hamlin, *Greek Revival Architecture in America*, New York, 1944, p.129, with illustration of the ground plan. The next step was 'the private bath as a fixed part of hotel service,' which, says Jefferson Williamson (op.cit. p.55), 'first appeared in 1844, when the aristocratic New York Hotel was opening.' This, incidentally, was the year London founded its 'Society for promoting the cleanliness of the poor.'

[94] No systematic researches are available. American hotels and American sanitary fixture manufacturers should show pride enough to produce a thorough and systematic study of the coming about of their present-day standards.

[95] Jefferson Williamson, op.cit. p.54.

[96] Ibid. p.62.

488. Plumber's Advertisement, Boston, 1850. *It was necessary to stress that 'the custom of frequent bathing finds strenuous advocates among the medical professors.' Normally there was no running water in the mid-century; the supply was generally raised by means of a hand pump, illustrated at the left.* (*Boston Directory*, 1850–51)

built a new hotel in Buffalo on the motto 'A Room and a Bath for a Dollar and a Half,' with immediate success.[97]

---

[97] The president of the Hotel Statler Company reports that the archives of his firm, which dates from 1908, contain no advertisements or pamphlets of that time. We quote from Mr. F. A. McKowne's letter (13 Oct. 1944): 'The first hotel to have a bath in every room was planned by the late Ellsworth M. Statler (founder of our company), and was completed and opened in Buffalo in 1908. It was the first of the Statler Hotels. The original portion of the hotel contained 300 rooms. Of these about two-thirds had tub baths and showers over each tub. The remaining rooms — small rooms on the court side — each had its bathroom but only with a shower bath stall. The hotel was immediately successful and the following year Mr. Statler added 150 additional rooms.'

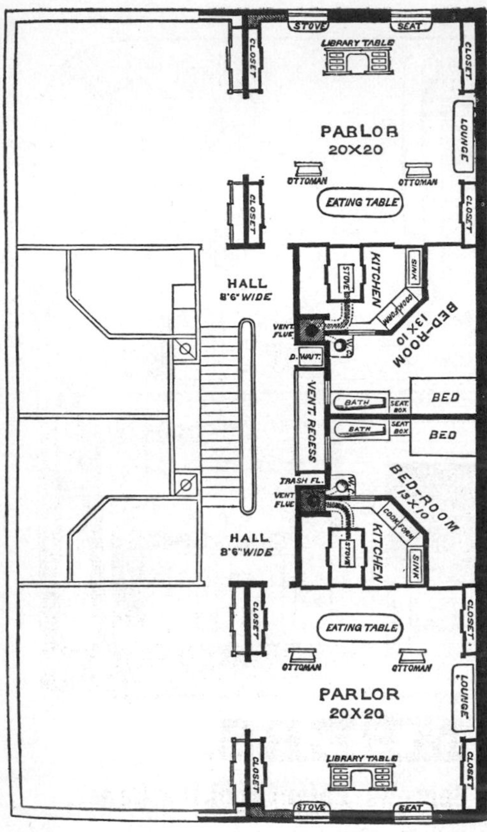

489. CATHERINE BEECHER: Plan of a City Flat, with Built-in Bedroom, Kitchenette, and Bath, 1869. *Just as Catherine Beecher's kitchen anticipates the present-day kitchen in its arrangement (fig.* 338), *her layout of a city flat realizes, in primitive form, the unit of bathroom, bedroom, and enclosed kitchenette.* (The American Woman's Home, 1869)

490. One-Room Apartment with Kitchenette and Bath Back to Back, 1930's. *Left of the entrance, a closet; to its right, an open kitchenette, which a wall separates from the bathroom. This wall carries the fixtures for both.* (850 *Seventh Avenue, New York. Sketch by Florence Schust)*

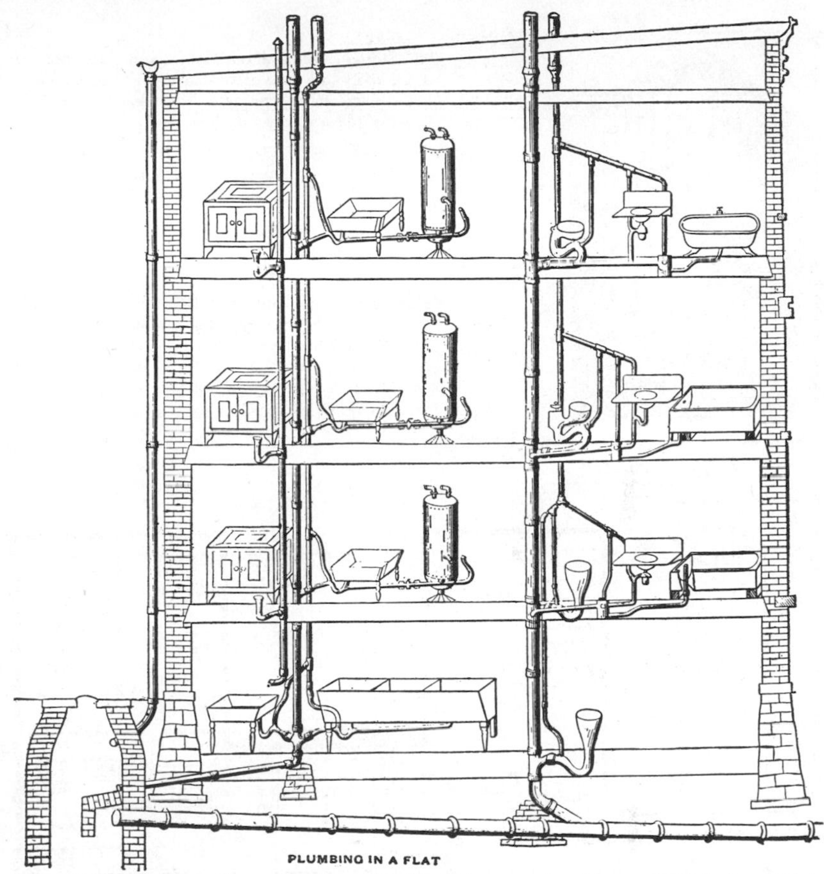

491. Chicago Apartment-House Plumbing, 1891. *The Chicago apartment houses of the 'nineties, which incorporated the most advanced standards, already show the fixtures aligned along one wall, but not in the most compact way. The bathtub is still set against the long wall. Later it will be turned 90°, as will the toilet.* (*Industrial Chicago*, 1891)

Like Pullman's sleeping car *The Pioneer* (1865), this marked an important step toward the democratization of comfort, when a middle-class hotel was built around a standard living unit of bedroom, bath, and closet. In Europe, even today, the combination of a room with private bath borders on luxury. Putting into practice the maxim 'a bath to every bedroom' immediately influenced the whole plan (figs. 492–4), and was as decisive for the hotel as the organization of the bath and kitchen for the plan of the private house. At once the standard American layout had appeared: The bath is a cell and an appendage to the bedroom.

492. Statler Hotel, Buffalo, 1908. (Now Hotel Buffalo) *'A bed and a bath for a dollar and a half' was the slogan for the cheap-renting unit of bedroom and bath in 1908. (Courtesy Hotels Statler Co., New York)*

493. Statler Hotel, Buffalo, 1908. Typical Floor Plan. *Providing a bath for every bedroom strongly affected the plan. The solution has become universal in the United States, spreading from the hotel to the apartment and the home: the bath is a cell and appendage to the bedroom. (Courtesy Hotels Statler Co., New York)*

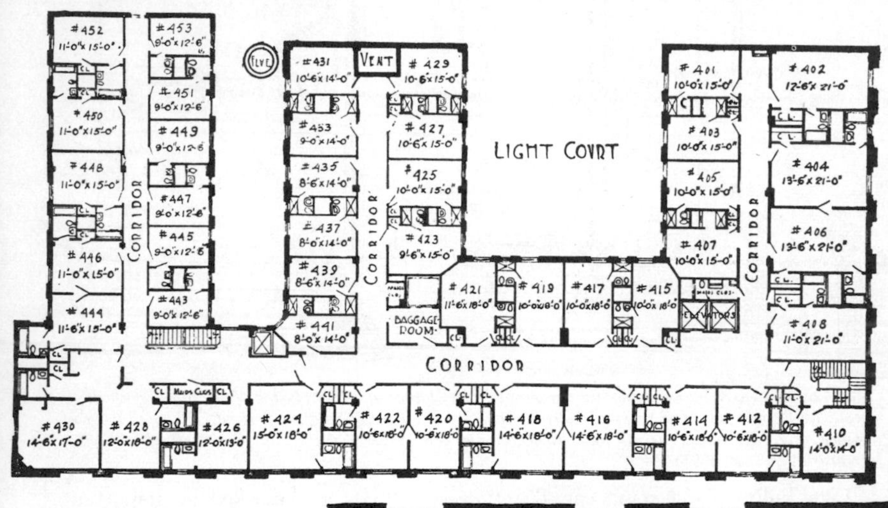

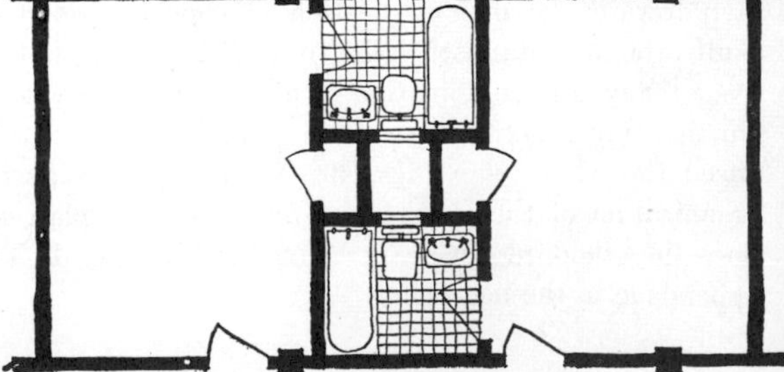

494. Statler Hotel, Buffalo, 1908. *Two rooms, each with bath and closet, form a unit with common ventilation and plumbing shaft. The compact bathroom is fully developed at an early stage. (Courtesy Hotels Statler Co., New York)*

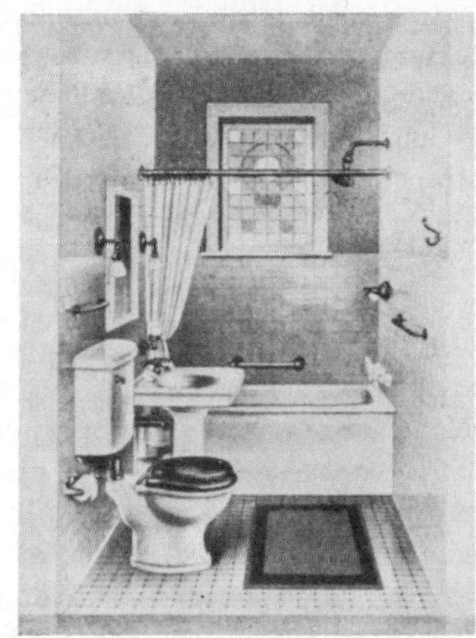

495. American Compact Bathroom, 1908. *Around* 1908 *catalogues show the compact bathroom as the new hotels were beginning to install it. Fixtures are still supplied from different walls; the tub is still raised on feet. Its position along the short wall contrasts with what was hitherto normal.* (*Catalogue*, *L. Wolff Co., Chicago*)

496. American Compact Bathroom, 1915. *Before the one-piece double-shelled tub could be mass produced leading American firms were already propagating the compact bathroom with recessed tub.* (*Catalogue, Crane and Co., Chicago*)

THE COMPACT BATHROOM

The rigid layout of the bath, basin, and toilet, and their compression within a minimum space, was what America called the compact bathroom. The prerequisite for this, the aligning of all fixtures along one wall, had long been anticipated in the United States. The bathroom of George Vanderbilt's Fifth Avenue house, 1885 (fig. 476), with its proudly displayed pipes and small intervals between the fixtures, already seems to announce the compact bathroom.

Chicago, in so many ways America's boldest testing ground of the late 'eighties, was also at the forefront in the comfort of the dwelling. Its apartment houses — a still unexplored development — with their triple 'Chicago windows,' no way betrayed the fear of light that darkened European houses at that time. Here the immediate forerunners of the compact bathroom are also to be found. *Industrial Chicago*, that indispensable source for the period, devotes one of its chapters to recent advances in plumbing. The page 'plumbing in a flat' (fig. 491) [98] records the most progressive standards of the day. As one might expect,

[98] *Industrial Chicago*, Chicago, 1891, vol. 2, pp.31–97.

the skyscrapers and their sanitary equipment grew up together. The arrangement of toilet, basin, and tub along one wall is already achieved. To complete the compact bathroom, there remained only to turn the tub 90° into a transversal position. All the fixtures are now concentrated on one wall.

What was the layout of the bathroom in the private house? The English bathroom, as we have mentioned, was scaled down to suit more modest circumstances, its fixtures being reduced in number, but the English layout being retained in its principle: loose arrangement of the fixtures.

Consider as many houses as one will, they exhibit one regularly recurrent feature: the tub is free standing and runs parallel to the long wall. Around 1908 the catalogues of the leading firms already show plans for the compact bathroom such as the new hotels were installing. Yet the fixtures are still distributed on different walls (fig. 495).[99] The cast iron, enameled tub is still raised on feet.

Around 1915 the domestic bathtub appears in its now familiar recessed form (fig. 496).[100] But only around 1920 could the double-shelled, enameled tub be made in one piece and put out in mass production. Its price was thus cut by some 20 per cent. Soon the five-foot tub established itself as the standard; it amounts to 75 per cent of the present output. The tub became a module determining the breadth of the cell, while the basin and toilet at minimal distances determine the long wall. The five-foot bathroom unit became standard. Private dwellings preserved these dimensions set by the hotels. The larger houses prefer to own six or seven standard-size bathrooms rather than one or two bathrooms of the 1900 English type. The bathroom now serves one person, or, as is still most commonly the case today, interconnects two bedrooms. American architects criticize nothing in the European ground plans so sharply as the separation by a passage of the bathroom from the bedroom. The compact bathroom attained its standard form around 1920. There have since been attempts to fill it with all manner of furniture and to give it the flavor of a living room, leading it back to the luxury standard. But these excursions need not be taken very seriously. Truer to the times were the attempts, beginning around 1931, to build the standard bathroom in larger units at the factory, thus reducing the installation costs. 'Studies showed that the bathroom-kitchen section of a dwelling — including foundations, floor and roof — cost 90 cents per cu. ft., with utilities included, as opposed to 25 cents per cu. ft. for a similar section without these provisions.' [101]

---

[99] Catalogue of the L. Wolff Mfg. Co., Chicago, Ill., 1908, p.391.

[100] Catalogue of the Crane & Co., Chicago, Ill., 1915.

[101] Alfred Bruce and Harold Sandbank, *A History of Prefabrication*, John B. Pierce Foundation, Research Study #3, New York, 1944, p.27.

The American bath unit takes its standard from the glossy enameled tub. A special form of this type, the one-piece, double-shelled, built-in tub, was developed in America around 1920 by mass production. It can be built with a minimum of time and expense. This type forms not only the standard of the American bathroom but its backbone and module.

The concise lines of this white bathtub will perhaps bear witness to later periods for the outlook of ours as much as the amphora for the outlook of fifth-century Greece. It is a luxury article, which the combination of refined metallurgical and technical skills transformed into a democratic utensil. In its own way, this double-shell tub, which on the other side of the Atlantic still smacks of luxury, numbers among the symbols of our time.

All seems so simple in this plain, undecorated type. Yet the emergence of the standard form from the chaos of inadequate solutions was long delayed. The awareness that the mechanized bathtub cannot be a plaything for the ornamentalist was driven home only when the method of its manufacture — cast iron, enamel — raised a natural veto.

***The Chaos around* 1900**

To give insight into the desolate confusion that still prevailed around 1900, we must let the expert [102] speak his pros and cons:

'What kind of a bathtub to use?

'This is not an easy matter when we are told of the many different kinds and finishes of bathtubs in the market. . . . One of the first we had was a wooden box, lined with sheet lead.' Characteristics: 'Lasting but could never be thoroughly cleaned.'

'The next bathtub we find making its way into the market was the wooden box lined with zinc.' Characteristics: 'Looked better and bright when new, but its lasting qualities were not good.' 'It almost disappeared.'

'Then came the wooden box lined with sheet copper.' Advantage: 'Could be kept looking clean for a long time.' Drawback: 'Copper . . . soft and easily penetrated.' 'Almost lost sight of today [1896].'

The cast-iron tub, which was later to triumph over all others, was available in many finishes: 'Plain cast iron painted,' usually marble-veined on the inside. Characteristics: 'Strong enough to last for ever, but when the paint is worn off it becomes rusty and unsanitary.'

'Cast iron tubs galvanized.' Characteristics: 'This coating soon wears off.'

'*Cast iron enameled bathtub* . . . a good sanitary article . . . but hard to get

[102] J. J. Lawler, *American Sanitary Plumbing*, New York, 1896, pp.227–33.

and this finish will not stand hard usage, as the enamel coating cracks easily and peels off.'

The popular tub, 'having quite a large sale, is the tub formed out of sheet steel' with 'an inner lining of sheet copper (no casing necessary) provided with cast-iron legs.'

Next come the three luxury versions. First 'the all-copper bathtub, a bathtub made from one piece of sheet copper, having no outside shell . . . neat iron support and a hard wooden cap. The all-copper bathtub is also meeting with great success.'

'The porcelain crockery enameled bathtub.' Characteristics: 'No chance for dirt . . . no wood work in or about it, made of one piece . . . this tub will last a life.' Drawback: 'Requires greatest care in handling to deliver it safely. . . . Very cold to the touch until it has become entirely warm from the hot water.'

And a final trump card: the new aluminum bathtub. Advantage: 'Very light, makes a beautiful finish, a perfectly sanitary article, but . . . very high in price and can only be bought by the rich.'

To the exceptionally discriminating client a sunken bath with richly ornamented tiles is recommended.

What, then, was the average man to choose if, of the dozen models, one alone, the aluminum tub, was allegedly without drawbacks — but at an inaccessibly high price?

The Shaping of the Standard Type, c. 1920

Such was the situation around 1900. From this chaos, the present-day standard type finally emerged around 1920. This was the durable cast-iron enameled tub. Its technical development had required close to half a century.

It made its appearance in America around 1870: Output of the leading manufacturer, one tub per day.[103] The mid-'seventies saw a slow rise in production. Yet in 1890, this tub was still being advised against: 'White-glass enamel looks well at first but it is certain to chip where hot water is used, as the iron expands and contracts much more freely than the enamel.'[104] Thus in the mid-'nineties, a pioneer Chicago firm could adduce long manufacturing experience as a strong point in favor of its wares.[105] Down to 1900, all sanitary fixtures were hand-

[103] Information concerning the early development will be found in John C. Reed, 'The Manufacture of Porcelain Enamelled Cast Iron Sanitary Ware,' an address delivered at the annual meeting of the Eastern Supply Assn., New York, 14 Oct. 1914. Manuscript in possession of the American Standard and Radiator Co., Pittsburgh, Pa.

[104] W. R. Maguire, op.cit., p.271.

[105] 'A quality of unsurpassed perfect workmanship and thorough experience, enable us to place on the market enamelled iron bathtubs of every size and description.' L. Wolff Mfg. Co., Chicago, Ill., Catalogue for 1895–6.

modeled.[106] Then partial mechanization set in, raising productivity to ten baths per worker per day, or five times the rate of the 'nineties.

No satisfactory picture can be given of the rise of the double-shell enameled bathtub, for the pioneer firms are often at variance in their accounts. The enameled bathtub came to the fore around 1910. The first patents for built-in tubs were granted in 1913. These types were enameled on the inside only. The outside surface was painted over or tiled in (as is still the European practice) or concealed by a separate one-piece enameled apron.[107]

Not until 1916 did it become possible to manufacture the one-piece, double-shell, cast-iron, enameled bathtub in mass production. Made-to-order examples of this type are said to have first been used in private Pullmans before 1900 — being as elegant as the porcelain tubs, and much lighter.[108] Mass production (aided, an official of a Chicago mail-order house informs us, through billboard advertising) brought the recessed tub to a far broader class of consumers. In 1940 the mail-order houses were selling the full set of fixtures — tub, basin, toilet — for around $70, as against the $200 price of the porcelain bathtub alone in the Crane (Chicago) catalogue for 1910.[109]

Due to the sparse and often completely lacking historical data, we sent out questionnaires in order to obtain an approximate picture of the development. A sample questionnaire and reply are here reproduced in full. The thoroughness of this answer, returned by Crane and Co., Chicago, was, however, not paralleled in every case.

Questionnaire

QUESTION 1. When did mass production of the one-shell enameled built-in bathtub begin?

ANSWER. Roll-rim tubs on feet in enameled iron, according to our records, started about 1893. Enameled tubs on legs with wood roll rim began about 1892 to 1895. Copper-lined wood bathtubs started about 1883 and continued in popularity until about 1898. Single shell or one-shell tubs began about 1910 and some manufacturers are making them at the present time.

Q. 2. When did mass production of the double-shell enameled built-in bathtub begin?

A. Double-shell enameled iron tubs were introduced in about 1915 and manufacturers are continuing to produce them up to the present time.

106 Reed, op.cit.

107 Separate enameled apron or front plates were made by the Standard Radiator Co. in 1909, by others in 1912.

108 According to oral information from the L. Wolff Mfg. Co., Chicago, Ill., these tubs were supplied by their firm to the Pullman Standard Car Co. The Pullman Co., Worcester, Mass., was unable to find photographs of these tubs, but blueprints of the early private cars are available.

109 Crane and Co. catalogue, Chicago, Ill., 1910, p.112.

Q. 3. To what extent did the mass production reduce the price of the built-in bathtub?

A. So far as we can determine from our past price schedules on built-in bath tubs, the price from 1918 to 1944 has been reduced about 20%.

Q. 4. What is the proportion of the production of the recess-type to the production of the corner-style type and of the leg type?

A. The 5′ 0″ recess double shell tub is by far the largest seller. It is approximately 75% of the market. The corner-style double shell tub has only a small sale and is used in unusual bathrooms which are larger than the conventional bathroom in homes, thus requiring a corner pattern tub instead of the recess type. At the present time, the leg-type tub popularity has dwindled until now it is about 25% of the overall bathtub sale.

Q. 5. Among the more expensive types, has the recess-bathtub or the corner bathtub been preferred?

A. The 5′ 0″ recess double shell tub is by far the most popular and preferred bathtub; possibly for two reasons — one, lower cost, and two, it permits a smaller-sized bathroom. As I have indicated above, the corner-type tub is only used in larger-sized bathrooms.

Q. 6. Did you reduce bathtubs to a few standard sizes? Which size is the preferred one?

A. The recess type double shell tub has four standard sizes; namely,

4′ 6″ 5′ 0″ 5′ 6″ 6′ 0″

By far the greatest sale and popularity is the 5′ 0″ size, in fact the 4′ 6″ and the 6′ 0″ size are used very occasionally, while possibly 10% of the business is 5′ 6″ size.

Q. 7. Do you think that the size of the built-in bathtub is largely responsible for the size of the present-day bathroom?

A. Without question, the universal acceptance of the 5′ 0″ recess double-shell tub has largely been responsible for the size and shape of present-day bathrooms. Over a period of years of experience with builders and architects, as well as home owners, we have found that the 5′ 0″ tub is averagely an adequate size bathtub for the average size person. The 4′ 6″ tub is used in extremely small rooms, while the 5′ 6″ and 6′ 0″ tubs are used by home owners that are of exceptional size and desire a larger size bathtub than the conventional 5′ 0″.

Q. 8. Which types of bathrooms are most prevalent in apartment houses and hotels? The type shown in my sketch or others?

Q. 9. Which types of bathrooms are most prevalent in private homes?

A. The most typical bathroom layout used in homes, apartment houses, and hotels at the present time is the regular 5′ 0″ recess tub with the lavatory and water closet and tub fittings all along one wall, thereby simplifying the roughing-in or the supply and waste piping in the wall. We attach a sheet indicating various types of bathroom layouts that have been used by architects and builders rather freely over the period of the last 15 or 20 years.

You will note that all of these lay-outs embody the conventional shape and design of fixtures.

Q. 10. What are the trends concerning future types of bathtubs and bathrooms? Will the present-day trend for small bathrooms with built-in bathtubs be continued?

A. At the present time, there are no trends that indicate a change in the shape or size of bathrooms for postwar use. The only other type bathroom layout that was used just prior to the war embodied the square-type tub, and I am enclosing a circular showing bathroom arrangements embodying this type of tub. We intend to continue this type of square tub after the war.

Q. 11. Will the trend, every bedroom with adjoining bathroom, be further developed?

A. As regards the trend of a bathroom for every bedroom, this has become rather accepted general practice amongst leading architects and builders throughout the country; in fact, the real requirements for good homes at the present time are a bathroom for each bedroom and a powder room or a small washroom on the main floor adjoining the living-room and the dining-room for guest use. At the present time, we do not see any trend indicating a change from this overall specification of requirements for homes.

Chicago, Ill., May 1944.

The double-shell tub is a product of full mechanization. The highly skilled workers, formerly essential in every phase of its production, are no longer needed. No hand touches the mold. A mechanism automatically distributes the sand. The castings are serially poured, cooled, and scoured. Automatic sifting devices lay on an even coating of powdered enamel prior to fusion in the kiln.[110]

If the bath and its equipment passed from a nomadic to a stable condition in the course of the nineteenth century, the growing popularity of the built-in tub meant its passing from the status of furniture to incorporation in the organism of the house.

Its incubation period at an end, the bath merged into this organism with

---

[110] In 1916. At this time earthenware tubs were first put into mass production. It was the enameled cast-iron tub that prevailed, but the mass manufacture of earthenware served to popularize the wash-basin and water-closet fixtures.

Previously the clay was 'placed on the mold and shaped by hand to get the impression. The making of the thickness was left entirely to the skill of the operator with the result that thicknesses varied' (Standard Potteries, Technical Article, n.d., p.3). This complex handicraft was eliminated when china-ware came to be cast in molds. Europe had succeeded in liquefying the clay by addition of water and chemical salts (1906). The Americans took over this method, and after some ten years of experiment built factories in which the liquid clay was distributed through tubes. This fluid was poured into plaster molds, which absorbed the water content. The result was a product of perfectly uniform thickness. The tubs were then baked in tunnel kilns, just like bread at the same period, their passage through the kiln being as accurately controllable as that of the loaves.

surprising speed. Around 1900 the triumph of the present-day bathroom became clear. Around 1920 it established itself as an appendage to the bedroom in the private house.

It may be said without exaggeration that this standard, the double-shell enameled tub attains a degree of comfort that had been pursued for thousands of years. By long technical training our age acquired the facility to solve almost any problem it cared to tackle. When the present-day standard type was called for, it too sprang into being.

The Bathroom and the Mechanical Core

What might be done to reduce that ever-growing part of the building outlay, the cost of mechanical utilities? The bathroom had at last acquired a standardized layout. Was it not time for mass production to step in? Could not the laborious mode of installation be simplified?

By 1945 the leading fixture companies were at work on assembled plumbing units that should satisfy a variety of requirements. Systematization should help abbreviate the labor of building, without curtailing the freedom of the architect.

Prior to this, in the early 'thirties, a movement to cut down sharply the cost of plumbing, still fitted laboriously by hand methods, had got under way among the engineers. Yet in 1945, satisfactory solutions were not at hand. The reason lay in the complexity of the task, for the bathroom, it soon became clear, is but part of a larger entity, the mechanical core. Kitchen, laundry, heating, atmospheric regulation, were claiming more and more space. In the basement of a luxurious American house having all the technical aids to comfort on the modern market, there was plant enough to run a small factory. To scale this down to the size of the normal household was no simple task. Another reason why the bath unit progressed so little toward a true solution lay in the isolated way technicians envisioned and handled the problem. For it could only be solved by submitting all parts of the house to thoroughgoing reconstruction.

The course chosen by the engineers — for it was they, and not the fixture manufacturers who made the first move — may be indicated by a few proposals which reached beyond the experimental stage. The aim is to mass-produce the entire bath unit — floor, ceiling, walls, from the plumbing down to the built-in soap holder, for shipment direct from the factory to the building site.

It is to be transported either as a structural unit or in a number of sections. If sectioned, the choice lies between horizontal slices or vertical ones. An early patent (1931) (fig. 497)[111] would deliver the sections of the bathroom in panel form to be assembled by 'a mason, a carpenter, and a plasterer,' the plumber being almost altogether done away with. The bath unit in horizontal sections is also deliverable 'in packaged form.' Its 'non-separable,' rounded corners were claimed as an especial advantage[112] (fig. 499).

Other early proposals (1931) make the bath cell a structural unit installable 'in sealed condition,' no workman having to set foot in it while the house is under construction. All the connections are on the outside, ready to be screwed through extensible joints to the units above and below. A crane swings the unit bodily from the truck to the exact spot in the building where it is needed[113] (fig. 498). It was mainly intended for the skeleton construction of apartment houses or hotels. Raymond Hood, inspirer of Rockefeller Center, planned (1932) to incorporate the plumbing and fixtures of an apartment house (unfortunately never executed) within a mechanical core.

In type, R. Buckminster Fuller's 'prefabricated bathroom'[114] (1938) (fig. 500) is a structural unit. His sectioning of the shell into two parts for easier indoor and outdoor transport is of minor importance. The solution is original, comprehensive, extreme. A model made of copper sheeting was shown in prominent places and aroused lively discussion.

Its every component, from the soap holder to the tub, forms an integral part of the wall or floor. The washbasin and toilet are placed opposite one another, with the somewhat raised bathtub behind them — a 4′6″ × 5′ layout such as is normal only in cramped circumstances. All the components are pressed simultaneously with the metal skin, their hollows sometimes helping to give the system additional rigidity. The exhaustive patent specification, a model of precision, is evidence of the care with which every square inch was worked out, so that the dies would have the highest industrial efficiency, and the bathrooms could be stamped out by the million at minimal cost. Why not seize this opportunity?

As so often in the eagerness of full mechanization, the construction ran away with the constructor and the human problem became lost in the stamping. From clean, hygienic enamel, the material is changed to thin metal sheeting, so that the machine may complete its work at one blow. In terms of comfort, this means

---

[111] U.S. Patent, 1,978,842, 30 Oct. 1934. The patent specification thoroughly describes the patchwork of hand-installed plumbing.

[112] Applied for in 1934. U.S. Patent, 2,087,121, 13 July 1937. This 'consolidated room unit' as it is called in the specification directly combines the pipe-elements and the walls — which suggests a difficult task of replacement should freezing cause a pipe to burst.

[113] Applied for 1931, Patent 2,037,895, 21 April 1936.

[114] Illustrated in A. Bruce and H. Sandbank, *A History of Prefabrication*, New York, 1944, p.26.

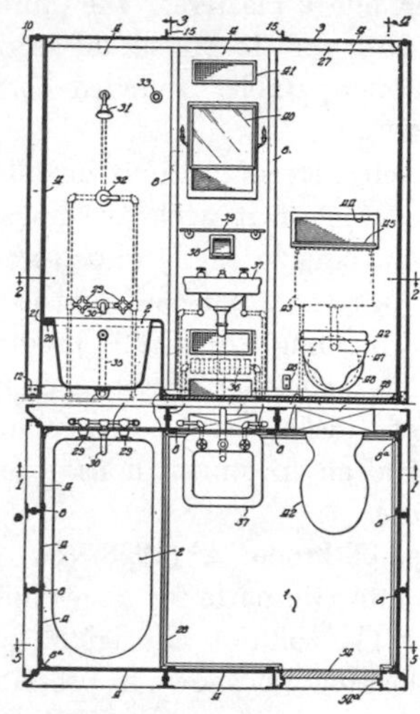

497. Prefabricated Bathroom, Vertical Panels, 1931. *The bathroom prefabricated to reduce plumbing costs was patented from the early 1930's on. Here the bathroom is divided into panels.* (*U. S. Patent* 1,978,842, 30 *October* 1934; *filed* 1931)

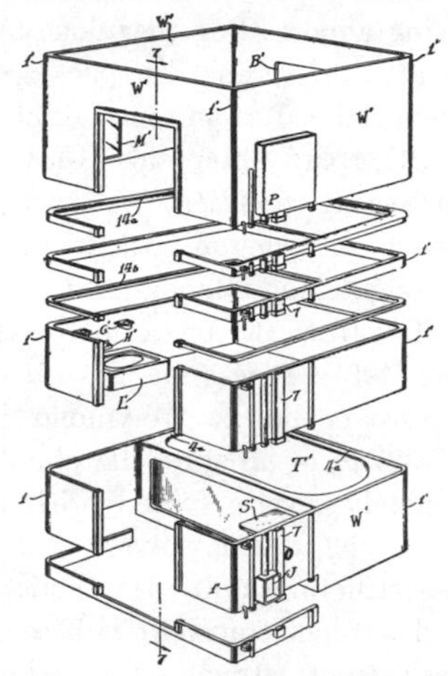

499a. Prefabricated Bathroom in Horizontal Sections, 1934. *The cell is divided into horizontal slices to be screwed together. Pipe elements and walls are combined.* (*U. S. Patent* 2,087,121, 13 *July* 1937; *filed* 1934)

499b. Prefabricated Bathroom in Horizontal Sections, 1934. *The bathroom assembled.* (*U. S. Patent* 2,087,121, 13 *July* 1937)

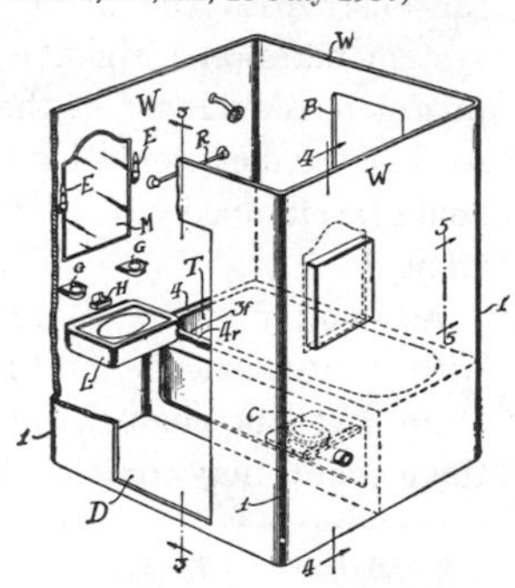

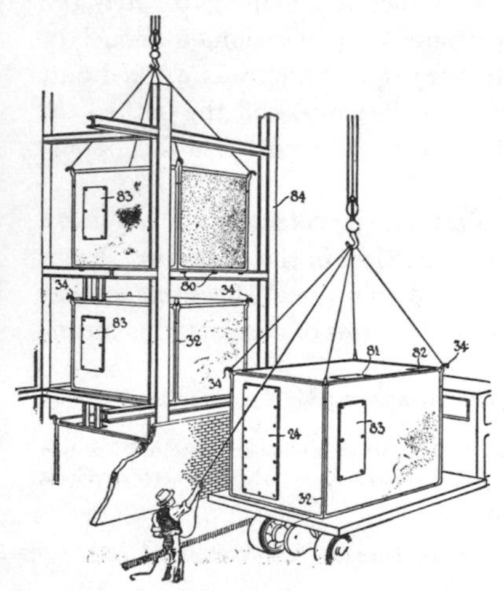

←

498. Prefabricated Bathroom Installable as a Sealed Unit, 1931. *The bathroom is shipped directly to the building plot, where a crane swings the unit to its exact location.* (*U. S. Patent* 2,037,895, 21 *April* 1936; *filed* 1931)

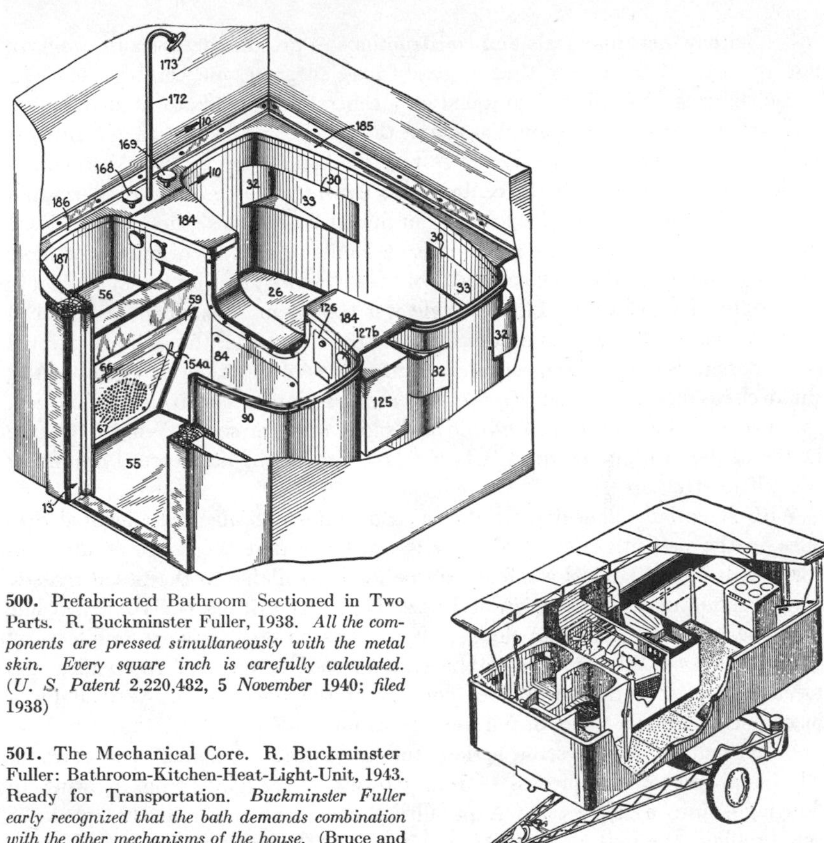

500. Prefabricated Bathroom Sectioned in Two Parts. R. Buckminster Fuller, 1938. *All the components are pressed simultaneously with the metal skin. Every square inch is carefully calculated.* (*U. S. Patent* 2,220,482, 5 *November* 1940; *filed* 1938)

501. The Mechanical Core. R. Buckminster Fuller: Bathroom-Kitchen-Heat-Light-Unit, 1943. Ready for Transportation. *Buckminster Fuller early recognized that the bath demands combination with the other mechanisms of the house.* (Bruce and Sandbank, A History of Prefabrication, *New York*, 1944)

the jettison of half a century's effort. To the crew of a submarine, or to men without a roof over their heads, a metal box in which one can barely turn around may come as a welcome solution. But this constructional element is too large and too rigid to be easily assimilated in the house having any flexibility of ground plan.

Buckminster Fuller was among the first to recognize that the bath is no isolated unit, but demands combination with the various other mechanisms of the house. In his first mast-house (1927) he gave shape to this idea. He placed the mechanical core within the 'mast' on which the dwelling hangs. Here too it is seen how new materials and constructions — presumably because we have not yet learned to master them — easily lead to grotesque throwbacks. The house, hanging like a merry-go-round on a central pole, tends to circular, polygonal shapes, or the half-pumpkin shape that Fuller developed in an airplane factory around 1945.[115] The idea of resting the house upon a central prop dates back well into the nineteenth century and can in some cases have charm and meaning.[116] But as a standard form, multiplied by millions, these self-enclosed huts become a city planner's nightmare. A similar surrender of human comfort is to be noted from the dweller's point of view. Slowly, adaptation of the house to the site, of which Frank Lloyd Wright was the foremost exponent, established itself beyond challenge. Communication with outer space, through a protected zone (porch), is one of the most attractive features of the American house. And the decisive factor: freedom to alter the ground plan or add to it is abolished, the dweller being imprisoned within the rigid, uniform shell. Why? Because in the center, within the mast, sits a robot, the mechanical core, tyrannizing the whole structure.

With attention-compelling fanaticism, Buckminster Fuller has devoted decades to the perfecting of his idea. His insistence that the house of this century, with its mechanical comfort, can be made available to the broad masses, by the simultaneous production and assembly of its utilities is certainly in line with the inevitable course of things. We have seen how the new architectural generation took this problem to heart, and sought ways of reconciling the mechanical core with the broader concept of the house. The demand for a mechanical core is a token of full mechanization.

In agriculture, at the same period, the harvesting 'combines' concentrated all the phases of the process — from mowing to bagging, from plowing to dunging — into a single one. A parallel phenomenon arises in the sphere of the dwelling: the unit that combines kitchen, bath, laundry, heating, climatic control, and plumbing in one mechanical nucleus; but here we speak not of a 'combine,' but of the mechanical core. In agriculture, after a century of mechanization, the problem became relatively easy to solve. In the house, our mechanical experience begins with the time of full mechanization. A quarter of a century is not much in a development. And again, the roots of the problem grow into the human sphere. It is too late for us still to be cheated by purely engineering solutions won at the expense of human comfort.

The mechanical core must share in the general direction to be followed by

[115] *Architectural Forum*, Mar. 1945.

[116] In a project for a glass-walled apartment house, Mies van der Rohe (1921) also rested his construction upon central pillars.

the coming development as a whole: co-ordination and freedom of treatment — no rigid, ever-repeated mold, adequate to everything and to nothing. The solution of the bath unit, of the mechanical core assembled from standardized elements, lies in this direction. A house is neither an automobile nor a trailer. Houses do not move. Houses stand on a specific site and must adapt themselves to this environment. Houses rolling ready-made off the assembly line will but rarely satisfy on this score. Hence, the solution of the mechanical core, like that of the prefabricated house, depends on one condition: freedom allied with co-ordination. For neither he who dwells in the house nor he who designs it should suffer himself to be tied. That is, the task of mechanization is not to deliver ready-made, stamped-out houses or mechanical cores, but flexible, standardized elements admitting of various constellations, so as to create better and more comfortable dwellings.

Regeneration a Gauge of Culture

Our aim throughout has been to trace the two basic types of bathing: the bath as an ablution and the bath as total regeneration. Both types are often found together, one usually dominating the other. Closely connected with the type of bath is its social significance. The ablution bath, by its very type, easily leads to the position that bathing is a private matter. Of this view, the tub bath, especially in its present-day mechanized form, is the chief exponent.

The regeneration bath, by its very type, favors social intercourse and almost automatically becomes a focus of communal life.

Periods have developed various types of regeneration just as they developed various types of comfort. The Greeks, in their regenerative type, were able to interweave invigoration of the body and invigoration of the mind to a degree unequaled by any other culture. Operating within a universal framework, their bath type did not have to be a complicated one. The Greeks of the fifth century B.C. were little inclined to technical refinement.

Not until post-Alexandrian times did the scientific thought of the Greeks move closer to practical ends. The basis which Alexandria had laid in the third and second centuries B.C., Roman engineering fully elaborated in the first. The thermae of the Roman masses have their center in the now-dominant hot-air bath and its accessories, the universal Greek framework, however, not being altogether discarded.

But in the Islamic type of regeneration, the games and athletics — self-invigoration — fall away. Instead, the organism is penetratingly worked upon by various massages, especially cracking of the joints, perhaps brought from India.

The Roman bath and the Islamic bath must rely upon numerous attendants. Both drew upon a plentiful labor supply. The Russian bath is the simplest of regeneration types, and perhaps the most natural. It calls for no massive buildings, no technified apparatus, and no slaves. The whole pattern suggests an origin in remote times, now lost in historical darkness. The austerity of the Russian bath corresponds to a humble standard of living. It is at the same time the most democratic and the most long-lived type of regeneration.

After late Gothic times, the bath ceased to be a social institution. We tried to show the chaos and helplessness in which the nineteenth century lingered before making a small part of its technical genius available to human requirements. Finally, this century, in the time of full mechanization, created the bath-cell, which, with its complex plumbing, enameled tub, and chromium taps, it appended to the bedroom. Yet the fact cannot be lost from sight that this convenience is no substitute for a social type of regeneration. It is tied to the plane of simple ablution.

A culture that rejects life in stunted form voices a natural demand for the restoring of the bodily equilibrium of its members through institutions open to all. Whether as Roman marble halls or as Siberian log-cabin is unimportant. Neither, as so often claimed, is finance the decisive factor. Financial considerations are often no more than pretexts.

A period like ours, which has allowed itself to become dominated by production, finds no time in its rhythms for institutions of this kind. That is why the nineteenth century failed in its efforts to revive the regeneration of former ages or to devise new types shaped to our specific needs. Such institutions stood in contradiction to the period.

Regeneration is something that cannot arise in isolation. It is part of a broader concept: leisure. Jacob Burckhardt found in the word ἀρετή the key to Greek conduct. Leisure, in this sense, means a concern with things beyond the merely useful. Leisure means to have time. Time to live. Life can be tasted to the full only when activity and contemplation, doing and not doing, form complementary poles, like those of a magnet. None of the great cultures has failed to support this concept.

IN CONCLUSION

MAN IN EQUIPOISE

We have tried to assemble fragments of the anonymous history of our period. The searchlight has fallen on scattered facts and facets, leaving vast stretches of darkness between. The complexes of meaning thus arising have not been explicitly linked. In the mind of the active reader new interrelations and new complexes of meaning will be found. This does not relieve us from answering the question: Does our present day accept mechanization?

The problem is so intricately related to social, economic, and emotional realities that mere affirmation or mere negation leads nowhere. Everything depends on how, and for what purposes, mechanization is used.

What does mechanization mean to man?

Mechanization is an agent, like water, fire, light. It is blind and without direction of its own. It must be canalized. Like the powers of nature, mechanization depends on man's capacity to make use of it and to protect himself against its inherent perils. Because mechanization sprang entirely from the mind of man, it is the more dangerous to him. Being less easily controlled than natural forces, mechanization reacts on the senses and on the mind of its creator.

To control mechanization demands an unprecedented superiority over the instruments of production. It requires that everything be subordinated to human needs.

From the very first it was clear that mechanization involved a division of labor. The worker cannot manufacture a product from start to finish; from the standpoint of the consumer the product becomes increasingly difficult to master. When the motor of his car fails, the owner often does not know which part is causing the trouble; an elevator strike can paralyze the whole life of New York. As a result, the individual becomes increasingly dependent on production and on society as a whole, and relations are far more complex and interlocked than in any earlier society. This is one reason why today man is overpowered by means.

No doubt mechanization can help eliminate slave labor and achieve better standards of living. Nevertheless, in the future it may have to be checked in some way so as to allow a more independent way of living.

On the Illusion of Progress

We are confronted with a great scrap heap of words and misused symbols and next to it an immense storehouse bursting with new discoveries, inventions, and potentialities, all promising a better life.

Never has mankind possessed so many instruments for abolishing slavery. But the promises of a better life have not been kept. All we have to show so far is a rather disquieting inability to organize the world, or even to organize ourselves. Future generations will perhaps designate this period as one of mechanized barbarism, the most repulsive barbarism of all.

At the beginning of this century an isolated and erratic thinker, Georges Sorel, castigated bourgeois society as synonymous with 'les illusions du progrès' (Paris, 1908). By 'illusions of progress' Sorel, who began as an engineer, meant those illusions of social life and habits of thought. He still spoke of technology and production methods as 'real progress.' Critics were even harder on the American scene, where mechanization had penetrated more deeply into everyone's life. Science was accused of having 'changed its base to an inputation of brute activity only' (Thorstein Veblen, 1906). This was too hasty and merciless a generalization, for simultaneously with these attacks the vanguard of science and art arrived at a new perception of the world, announcing the end of the age of rationalism.

Thereafter the skeptical attitude toward the consequences of progress spread rapidly. Now, after the Second World War, it may well be that there are no people left, however remote, who have not lost their faith in progress. Men have become frightened by progress, changed from a hope to a menace. Faith in progress lies on the scrap heap, along with many other devaluated symbols.

And it began so marvelously.

In 1750, in his essay on universal history, long before he became the reform minister of Louis XVI, the young Turgot proclaimed a noble belief in man's perfectibility: 'The human species remains the same through all its upheavals, like the waters of the sea through its tempests, and constantly advances toward perfection.' This belief in man's perfectibility became basic to any creed of progress.

The conception expressed by Turgot at the age of twenty-three became one of the incentives of the nineteenth-century urge to expand. Turgot was first to give physics a high priority over all other human knowledge. Art — being concerned only with human feelings — seemed to him limited in contrast to the limitlessness of science: 'Les sciences sont immenses comme la nature. Les arts, qui ne sont que des rapports à nous-mêmes, sont bornés comme nous.'

In the late eighteenth century, Condorcet in his last book pictured the long succession of epochs ascending toward the 'infinite perfectibility of mankind.' In the nineteenth century, revolutionaries and capitalists alike based their motives of action on the creed of progress. Comte's sociology is imbued with eighteenth-century thinking. Just a century after Turgot, Proudhon pathetically proclaims in his *Philosophie du progrès*, 1851: 'That which dominates all my efforts, their principle and their end, their base and their crown . . . that which I affirm, resolutely and irrevocably, in all ways and all places [is] progress.' Proudhon emphasizes that he understands by progress — in contrast to the abuse of the word in a purely materialistic sense — 'la marche de la société dans l'histoire.' The same belief stands invisibly behind Karl Marx's scientific solution of the social problem: the infinite perfectibility of man.

How was it possible for the foundation and very core of nineteenth-century thought and action to collapse so hopelessly?

Without a doubt, it was that mechanization was misused to exploit both earth and man with complete irresponsibility. Often it penetrated domains that were by nature unsuited to it. We have tried, here and there, to show the effects and limits of mechanization. No need to repeat this anew. The way in which this period handled mechanization is no isolated phenomenon. It has occurred practically everywhere. Means have outgrown man.

A century ago Thomas Carlyle stated that the 'fine arts' had got into 'an insane condition and walk abroad without keepers, nobody suspecting their bad state, and do phantastic tricks.' Art no longer plays 'phantastic tricks.' It tells the truth, and often the whole truth. But in nearly every other sphere the means have outgrown man and 'walk abroad without keepers.'

Before our eyes our cities have swollen into amorphous agglomerations. Their traffic has become chaotic, and so has production. The time mechanization took to penetrate so many spheres of life was comparatively long. But mechanization is a slow-working process. Today the situation has changed. With unbelievable speed atomic energy sprang from the worksheets and the laboratories into reality, playing 'phantastic tricks' and threatening human culture with annihilation.

The idea of progress faded because it stepped down from Turgot's visions to the lowest reaches of materialistic interpretation. It no longer corresponded to the modern conception of the world. It would have faded anyway.

The idea of progress supposes a final state of perfection. In the systems of Comte, Hegel, and even Marx, the final state was either already reached or was soon to come. Finality implies an approaching state of static equilibrium. This contradicts what the scientists have shown to be the essence of the universe, motion and unending change.

Today we do not agree with the moralists of the early Roman Empire, who identified progress in material comfort with luxury and corruption. But neither can we follow the thinkers of the last two centuries when they assert mankind's continuous march toward perfectibility. We can accept only the first part of Turgot's sentence: 'Le genre humain [est] toujours le même dans ses bouleversements comme l'eau de la mer dans les tempêtes. . . .'

The Ending of Mechanistic Conceptions

Mechanization is the outcome of a mechanistic conception of the world, just as technique is the outcome of science.

Since the beginning of the century we have been in a state of continuous revolution. During this period political upheavals have moved mainly along lines already traced a century before. In every sphere a revolution, arising from the depths of our mind, has shattered the mechanistic conception of the world.

In the hands of the physicists, with the revelation of the structure and functions of atomic forces, the conception of the essence of matter has changed and has lost its transcendental other-worldly nature. The resulting methodological change that has occurred in modern physics has affected many fields of human knowledge and has become the starting-point for new, more abstract conceptions.

The physicists penetrated to the interior of matter, as did the artists. Objects became transparent and their essence was revealed by methods other than rational perspective. In another place (*Space, Time and Architecture*, Cambridge, 1941) we have discussed these problems and the unconscious parallelism of the methods used in different spheres. Here we can merely touch on the disappearance of mechanistic conceptions in domains having to do with the human organism.

In *psychology* the *Gestalt* theory, dealing with apprehension of the whole, was first stressed by the Austrian professor Christian von Ehrenfels in 1890. *Gestalt* psychology ended the pseudo-mathematical mechanistic laws that nineteenth-century psychology had established for the human mind. It sees the whole as more than the sum of the parts, just as a melody is more than the sum of separate tones.

Similarly, in *biology* the animate being was considered simply as the sum of its separate parts, assembled like those of a machine. Organic processes were regarded as purely physico-chemical in nature, as if an organism were a kind of chemical plant.

As mechanization moved towards its peak, biologists recognized the deadlock into which this mechanical attitude toward research was leading them. Experiment had already proved that an organism was not entirely resolvable into its components, that it consisted of more than a simple sum of its parts. In the whole hierarchy of biological pattern, from the single cell to the complex human organism, there exist always centers directing the genesis of the various parts. The nature of wholes as a fundamental feature of the world was expounded by J. C. Smuts in his *Holism and Evolution*, 1926, in which he applied his method on a universal scale.

In *physiology* the concept of the human organism as a system of organized functions and not a mere assemblage of parts goes back to Claude Bernard, 1813–78.

The great French physiologist is still master of the universal outlook often found in the first part of the last century. In his *Introduction à la médecine expérimentale*, 1865, he expressed his views in more concentrated form.

The mechanistic outlook of the late nineteenth century, involving interest in every detail, lost the power to integrate. Our century is gradually rebuilding new universal conceptions as the basis of scientific research.

In 1921 the Englishman J. N. Langley (*The Autonomic Nervous System*, Cambridge, 1921) discussed that part of the nervous system that acts within the human organism independently of will (parasympathetic).

In 1929 the American W. B. Cannon (*Bodily Changes in Pain, Hunger, Fear, and Rage*, New York, 1929) explained the functioning of another and equally unconscious part of the nervous system (sympathetic).

In 1925 the Swiss W. R. Hess ('Ueber die Wechselbeziehungen zwischen psychischen und vegetativen Funktionen,' in *Schweiz. Archiv f. Neurologie und Psychiatrie*, 1925) elucidated the relation between the two systems that had previously been described independently, and co-ordinated them in an encompassing whole (the vegetative system). The discovery of the means by which a poised equilibrium is established between the different functions of these nervous systems may help us to discern the direction in which man himself is moving.

Through centuries our minds have been trained to start with objects, with matter, and with experimental research. Just as steel bridges are built springing from the ground and with one end freely poised in mid-air, renewed intellectual conceptions will arise piece by piece without the scaffolding of philosophical systems. The evolution away from merely materialistic and mechanistic conceptions must start from the new insight into the nature of matter and organisms.

Dynamic Equilibrium

Two apparently contradictory phenomena run through human history.

The human organism can be regarded as a constant. It is by nature confined within narrow limits of tolerance. It can adapt itself to a variety of conditions and it is physically in a perpetual state of change; but the physical pattern has changed very little, as far as science can record.

In order to function, man's organism requires a specific temperature, a specific quality of climate, air, light, humidity, and food. To function, in this context, means to preserve one's bodily equilibrium. Our organism means contact with the earth and things that grow. Thus far man's body is subject to the laws of his animal life.

On the other hand, the relations between man and his environment are subject to continual and restless change; from generation to generation, from year to year, from instant to instant, they are in danger of losing their equilibrium. There is no static equilibrium between man and his environment, between inner and outer reality. We cannot prove in a direct way how action and reaction operate here. We cannot tangibly grasp these processes any more than we can the nucleus of an atom. We can only experience them through the several ways in which they crystallize. The differing creations of the Romans, of medieval man, and of the Baroque evince the relentlessly changing relation between man and the external world.

No closed circles and no repetitive pattern exist to define the adjustments of inner and outer reality. They evolve in curves, never repeating themselves.

The feeling of delight that is produced when the human organism is in perfect health, functioning at its best, does not last for long. To restore this bodily equilibrium and thus impart physical happiness is, as we have said, the basic purpose of true regeneration.

As soon as inner and outer reality agree, corresponding developments occur in the psyche of man. There is never a standstill. All is in a state of flux.

Our period demands a type of man who can restore the lost equilibrium between inner and outer reality. This equilibrium, never static but, like reality itself, involved in continuous change, is like that of a tightrope dancer who, by small adjustments, keeps a continuous balance between his being and empty space. We need a type of man who can control his own existence by the process of balancing forces often regarded as irreconcilable: man in equipoise.

We have refrained from taking a positive stand for or against mechanization. We cannot simply approve or disapprove. One must discriminate between those spheres that are fit for mechanization and those that are not; similar problems arise today in whatever sphere we touch.

We must establish a new balance

between the individual and collective spheres.

We must discriminate between those domains reserved for individual life and those in which a collective life may be formed. We want neither extreme individualism nor overpowering collectivism: we must distinguish between the rights of the individual and the rights of the community. Today, both the life of the individual and the life of the community are frustrated and lack real shape and structure.

We must organize the world considered as a whole, and at the same time allow for the right of each region to develop its particular language, habits, customs.

We must establish a new balance

between the psychic spheres within the individual.

The relation between methods of thinking and of feeling is seriously impaired and even disrupted. The result is a split personality. Equipoise is lacking between the rational and the irrational; between the past — tradition — and the future — exploration of the unknown; between the temporal and the eternal.

We must establish a new balance

between the spheres of knowledge.

The specialized approach has to be integrated with a universal outlook. Inventions and discoveries must be integrated with their social implications.

We must establish a new balance

between the human body and cosmic forces.

The human organism requires equipoise between its organic environment and its artificial surroundings. Separated from earth and growth, it will never attain the equilibrium necessary for life.

These are only a few of the prerequisites of the new man. Some may regard them as futile and no more certain than sky writing. But we should not have dared to suggest the type of man our period calls for if physiology had not discovered astonishingly parallel trends.

The function of the vegetative system, which acts within our organism free of the interference of our will, is to maintain the 'normal atmosphere' that the cell requires by regulating and interrelating blood circulation, respiration, digestion, secretions, and body temperature.

Its functional structure was investigated recently by the physiologist W. R. Hess ('Das vegetative Funktionssystem,' in *Schweiz. Medizin. Jahrbuch*, Basel, 1942). It dominates the two other nervous systems, the sympathetic and the parasympathetic. The sympathetic adjusts the body to the conditions of the outer world. It controls the external activity of the body: its physical exertions. It carries the blood to the muscles in action, increases the activity of the heart, and checks the flow of blood to organs that are not being used.

The counterpart of this system (the parasympathetic) regulates the inner processes. It controls the complicated adjustments going on without our consciousness and continuously restores the inner equilibrium of the organs. The parasympathetic nervous system builds up the reserves. For instance, it carries the blood to the intestines, to absorb nutritive juices during the period of digestion.

These two systems interact and are always, as Hess calls it, in 'nervous dynamic equilibrium.' In a wider sense they are not antagonistic, but work together to secure the bodily equipoise of the individual, just as in the psychic sphere we try to restore the equipoise between inner and outer reality by reconciling trends often regarded as incompatible.

History does not produce repetitive patterns. The life of a culture is limited in time just as is the life of an individual. Since this is true of all organic existence, everything depends on what is accomplished within the allotted span.

Neither are there fixed rules for the dominance of rational or irrational, individual or collective, specialistic or universal conceptions. Manifold and often inexplicable reasons are responsible for the dominance of the one or the other of these tendencies in a given period. The prevalence of the one or the other is not necessarily bad in itself. It too is bound up with the incalculable diversity of human existence.

It is time that we become human again and let the human scale rule over all our ventures. The man in equipoise we must achieve is new only in contrast to a distorted period. He revives age-old demands which must be fulfilled in our own way if our civilization is not to collapse.

Every generation must carry both the burden of the past and the responsibility for the future. The present is coming to be seen more and more as a mere link between yesterday and tomorrow.

We are little concerned with the question whether man will ever attain a state of infinite perfection. We are closer to the ancient wisdom that saw in a possible moral evolution the course the world would take.

This does not mean that we must resign ourselves to cruelty, hopelessness, or despair. Every generation has to find a different solution to the same problem: to bridge the abyss between inner and outer reality by re-establishing the dynamic equilibrium that governs their relationships.

ILLUSTRATIONS

INDEX

IN THE NORTON LIBRARY

Aron, Raymond. *On War.* N107

Aron, Raymond. *The Opium of the Intellectuals.* N106

Bemis, Samuel Flagg. *The Latin American Policy of the United States.* N412

Billington, Ray Allen (editor) *The Reinterpretation of Early American History.* N446

Blair, Peter Hunter. *Roman Britain and Early England 55 B.C.–A.D. 871* N361

Bloch, Marc. *Strange Defeat: A Statement of Evidence Written in 1940.* N371

Bober, M. M. *Karl Marx's Interpretation of History.* N270

Brandt, Conrad. *Stalin's Failure in China.* N352

Brinton, Crane. *The Lives of Talleyrand.* N188

Brodie, Fawn. *Thaddeus Stevens.* N331

Brooke, Christopher. *From Alfred to Henry III, 871–1272* N362

Brown, Robert E. *Charles Beard and the Constitution.* N296

Burn, W. L. *The Age of Equipoise.* N319

Burnett, Edmund Cody. *The Continental Congress.* N278

Bury, J. B. *The Invasion of Europe by the Barbarians.* N388

Butterfield, Herbert. *The Whig Interpretation of History.* N318

Calleo, David P. *Europe's Future.* N406

Collis, Maurice. *Foreign Mud: The Opium Imbroglio at Canton in the 1830's and the Anglo-Chinese War.* N462

Cornish, Dudley Taylor. *The Sable Arm: Negro Troops in the Union Army, 1861-1865.* N334

Davies, John Paton, Jr. *Foreign and Other Affairs.* N330

Dehio, Ludwig. *Germany and World Politics in the Twentieth Century.* N391

De Roover, Raymond. *The Rise and Decline of The Medici Bank.* N350

Duckett, Eleanor. *The Wandering Saints of the Early Middle Ages.* N266

Dumond, Dwight Lowell. *Antislavery.* N370

East, W. Gordon. *The Geography Behind History.* N419

Erikson, Erik H. *Young Man Luther.* N170

Eyck, Erich. *Bismarck and the German Empire.* N235

Feis, Herbert. *Contest Over Japan.* N466

Feis, Herbert. *The Diplomacy of the Dollar.* N333

Feis, Herbert. *Europe: The World's Banker* 1870-1914. N327

Feis, Herbert. *Three International Episodes: Seen from E. A.* N351

Feis, Herbert. *The Spanish Story.* N339

Ferrero, Guglielmo. *The Reconstruction of Europe.* N208

Ford Franklin L. *Strasbourg in Transition, 1648-1789.* N321

Glueck, Nelson. *Rivers in the Desert: A History of the Negev.* N431

Gordon, Cyrus H. *The Ancient Near East.* N275

Grantham, Dewey W. *The Democratic South.* N299

Graves, Robert and Alan Hodge. *The Long Week-end: A Social History of Great Britain, 1918-1939.* N217

Green, Fletcher. *Constitutional Development in the South Atlantic States, 1776-1860.* N348

Gulick, Edward Vose. *Europe's Classical Balance of Power.* N413

Halperin, S. William. *Germany Tried Democracy.* N280

Hamilton, Holman. *Prologue to Conflict.* N345

Haring, C. H. *Empire in Brazil.* N386

Harrod, Roy. *The Dollar.* N191

Haskins, Charles Homer. *The Normans in European History.* N342

Herring, Pendleton. *The Politics of Democracy.* N306

Hill, Christopher. *The Century of Revolution 1603-1714.* N365

Himmelfarb, Gertrude. *Darwin and the Darwinian Revolution.* N455

Holmes, George. *The Later Middle Ages, 1272-1485.* N363

Hughes, H. Stuart. *The United States and Italy.* N396

Jolliffe, J. E. A. *The Constitutional History of Medieval England.* N417

Jones, Rufus *The Quakers in the American Colonies.* N356

Keir, David Lindsay. *The Constitutional History of Modern Britain Since 1485.* N405

Kendall, Paul Murray (editor). *Richard III: The Great Debate.* N310

Kennan, George. *Realities of American Foreign Policy.* N320

Kouwenhoven, John A. *The Arts in Modern American Civilization.* N404

Langer, William L. *Our Vichy Gamble.* N379

Leach, Douglass E. *Flintlock and Tomahawk: New England in King Philip's War.* N340

Maddison, Angus. *Economic Growth in the West.* N423

Magrath, C. Peter. *Yazoo: The Case of Fletcher v. Peck.* N418

Maitland, Frederic William. *Domesday Book and Beyond.* N338

Mason, Alpheus Thomas. *The Supreme Court from Taft to Warren.* N257

Mattingly, Harold. *The Man in the Roman Street.* N337

May, Arthur J. *The Hapsburg Monarchy: 1867-1914.* N460.

Morgenthau, Hans J. (editor). *The Crossroad Papers.* N284

Neale, J. E. *Elizabeth I and Her Parliaments,* 2 vols. N359a & N359b

Nef, John U. *War and Human Progress.* N468

Nichols, J. Alden. *Germany After Bismarck.* N463

Noggle, Burl. *Teapot Dome: Oil and Politics in the 1920's.* N297

North, Douglass C. *The Economic Growth of the United States 1790-1860.* N346

Ortega y Gasset, José. *Concord and Liberty.* N124

Ortega y Gasset, José. *History as a System.* N122

Ortega y Gasset, José. *Man and Crisis.* N121

Ortega y Gasset, José. *Man and People.* N123

Ortega y Gasset, José. *Meditations on Quixote.* N125

Ortega y Gasset, José. *Mission of the University.* N127

Ortega y Gasset, José. *The Origin of Philosophy.* N128

Ortega y Gasset, José. *What Is Philosophy?* N126

Pelling, Henry. *Modern Britain, 1885-1955.* N368

Pidal, Ramón Menéndez. *The Spaniards in Their History.* N353

Pocock, J. G. A. *The Ancient Constitution and the Feudal Law.* N387

Pollack, Norman. *The Populist Response to Industrial America.* N295

Pomper, Gerald. *Nominating the President.* N341

Robson, Eric. *The American Revolution, 1763-1783.* N382

Rostow, W. W. *The Process of Economic Growth.* N176

Roth, Cecil. *The Spanish Inquisition.* N255

Rowse, A. L. *Appeasement.* N139

Salvemini, Gaetano. *The French Revolution: 1788-1792.* N179

Silver, James W. *Confederate Morale and Church Propaganda.* N422

Spanier, John W. *The Truman-MacArthur Controversy and the Korean War.* N279

Sykes, Norman. *The Crisis of the Reformation.* N380

Thompson, J. M. *Louis Napoleon and the Second Empire.* N403

Tolles, Frederick B. *Meeting House and Counting House.* N211

Tourtellot, Arthur Bernon. *Lexington and Concord.* N194

Turner, Frederick Jackson. *The United States 1830-1850.* N308

Ward, Barbara. *India and the West.* N246

Ward, Barbara. *The Interplay of East and West.* N162

Warren, Harris Gaylord. *Herbert Hoover and the Great Depression.* N394

Wedgwood, C. V. *William the Silent.* N185

Whitaker, Arthur P. *The United States and the Independence of Latin America.* N271

Whyte, A. J. *The Evolution of Modern Italy.* N298

Wolfers, Arnold. *Britain and France between Two Wars.* N343

Wolff, Robert Lee. *The Balkans in Our Time.* N395

Woodward, C. Vann. *The Battle for Leyte Gulf.* N312

Wright, Benjamin Fletcher. *Consensus and Continuity, 1776-1787.* N402

Norton Library titles in
Art, Architecture and the Philosophy of Art

HENRY S. CHURCHILL
The City is the People N174

KENNETH CLARK
Rembrandt and the Italian Renaissance N424

IRWIN EDMAN
Arts and the Man N104

SIEGFRIED GIEDION
Mechanization Takes Command N489

HENRY-RUSSELL HITCHCOCK AND PHILIP JOHNSON
The International Style N311

ADOLF KATZENELLENBOGEN
Allegories of the Virtues and Vices in Mediaeval Art N243
The Sculptural Programs of Chartres Cathedral N233

FISKE KIMBALL
The Creation of the Rococo N268

JOHN A. KOUWENHOVEN
The Arts in Modern American Civilization N404

RENSSELAER W. LEE
Ut Pictura Poesis: The Humanistic Theory of Painting N399

MILLARD MEISS
Giotto and Assisi N384

C. R. MOREY
Christian Art N103

HUGH MORRISON
Louis Sullivan N116

CHARLES SEYMOUR, JR.
Notre-Dame of Noyon in the Twelfth Century N464

JOHN SUMMERSON
Heavenly Mansions N210

LEONETTO TINTORI AND MILLARD MEISS
The Painting of the Life of St. Francis in Assisi N393

EDGAR WIND
Pagan Mysteries in the Renaissance N475

RUDOLF AND MARGOT WITTKOWER
Born Under Saturn:
The Character and Conduct of Artists N474